Global Marketing Management

Global Marketing Management

A European Perspective

Warren J. Keegan

Lubin School of Business
Pace University, New York City and Westchester, US

Bodo B. Schlegelmilch

Vienna University of Economics and Business Administration
Wirtschaftsuniversität Wien, Vienna, Austria

FINANCIAL TIMES
Prentice Hall

An imprint of **Pearson Education**

Harlow, England · London · New York · Reading, Massachusetts · San Francisco · Toronto · Don Mills, Ontario · Sydney
Tokyo · Singapore · Hong Kong · Seoul · Taipei · Cape Town · Madrid · Mexico City · Amsterdam · Munich · Paris · Milan

Pearson Education Limited
Edinburgh Gate
Harlow
Essex CM20 2JE
England

and Associated Companies throughout the world

Visit us on the World Wide Web at:
www.pearsoneduc.com

———————————

Original sixth edition entitled *Global Marketing Management*
published by Prentice-Hall, Inc.
A Pearson Education company
© Prentice-Hall, Inc. 1999

This edition published by Pearson Education Limited 2001
© Pearson Education Limited 2001
Authorised for sale only in Europe, the Middle East and Africa.

ISBN 0-138-41826-8

British Library Cataloguing-in-Publication Data
A catalogue record for this book is available from the British Library

Library of Congress Cataloging-in-Publication Data
Keegan, Warren J.
    Global marketing management: a European perspective/Warren J. Keegan, Bodo B. Schlegelmilch.
        p. cm.
    Includes bibliographical references and index.
    ISBN 0–13–841826–8 (pbk.)
        1. Export marketing--Europe--Management. 2. Export
    marketing--Europe--Management--Case studies. I, Schlegelmilch, Bodo B. II. Title.

    HF1416.6.E85 K44 2001
    658.8′48′094--dc21

10 9 8 7 6 5 4 3 2 1
05 04 03 02 01

Set by 3 in 9/12 Stone Serif
Printed by Ashford Colour Press Ltd., Gosport

To Donald, Mark, and Tracy
(W.J.K.)

To Irene and Roger
(B.B.S.)

Contents

Preface

Global Marketing Management – A European Perspective, traces its ancestry to *Multinational Marketing Management*, a book that broke new ground in the field of international marketing when it was published in 1974. The first edition departed from the traditional export trade focus in the field of international marketing and adopted a strategic approach that reflected the growing importance of multinational corporations. The book combined the latest research findings, the most advanced experience of practitioners and classroom-tested case studies and was an immediate success. Since then, each revision has reflected the changes in current practice and attempted to anticipate the direction of development of the field. The objective: to maintain the book's authoritative position as the leading student and reference text for practitioners in international marketing.

This edition not only continues the path-breaking tradition of this book but also represents a completely new approach to the discussion of global marketing issues. Much of the discussion on global marketing and strategy is characterised by the tension between the desire for global standardisation and the need for local adaptation. This fruitful dialectic tension is carried into this text by an attempt to lend a distinctly European perspective to global marketing. In practice, this has been achieved by writing, for the first time, as a Euro–US author tandem. As a result, the radical overhaul of the text now offers the reader a number of new benefits:

- In each chapter, the discussion of global marketing topics is enriched further by relevant excerpts from newspapers, journals, EU documents, etc. These excerpts are presented in two forms:
  - Global Perspective
  - European Focus.
- For both, the Global Perspective and the European Focus sections, appropriate discussion questions (Food for thought) have been developed. The advantage for the reader: these sections double as up-to-date
  - *short cases* with *food for thought* questions.

- Of course, there is always the need for more in-depth cases that bring together different aspects of the global marketing issues discussed. To this end, this text offers
  - a variety of more detailed *different length cases* from *different countries and industries*.
- Learning is further supported by a whole range of pedagogical tools. In particular, these include:
  - introductory *practice links* illustrating the key topic covered in each chapter;
  - a list of important *concepts and definitions* at the end of each chapter;
  - mid-chapter highlights of important issues called *key points*;
  - end-of-chapter *summaries* and *discussion questions*;
  - *suggested readings* for further individual pursuit of discussed topics.
- In today's world of electronic media, no book would be complete without references to information technology. We have developed an entirely new chapter on the information technology environment and, for each chapter, have chosen some interesting and sometimes entertaining websites to entice further independent studies. And since the Web has long ceased to be the domain of Web-masters, these sites are presented as
  - *Webmistress's hotspots*.

The book is organised into six parts: Part I, Introduction and Overview, provides a big-picture approach and introduces the field of global marketing. Part II, The Global Marketing Environment, covers the major dimensions of the environment of global marketing: economic, social and cultural, political, legal and regulatory and, in particular in this day and age, the information technology environment. Part III, Analysing and Targeting Global Market Opportunities, is devoted to assessing marketing opportunities, as well as segmenting, targeting and positioning. Part IV focuses on Global Marketing Strategy and discusses issues like market selection and market entry alternatives as well as global competition and strategy. Part V, Creating

Global Marketing Programmes, covers the global marketing mix. It focuses on product and service decisions, global pricing, global logistics and channel decisions and global marketing communication. Part VI, Managing the Global Marketing Pro- gramme, concludes the book with a focus on implementation. It addresses the task of organising and controlling the global strategy and also attempts to provide a glimpse into the future of global marketing.

Companion Web Site

A Companion Web Site accompanies *Global Marketing Management*, by Keegan and Schlegelmilch

Visit the *Global Marketing Management* Companion Web Site at <u>www.booksites.net/globalmm</u> to find valuable teaching and learning material including:

For Students:
* Study material designed to help you improve your results

For Lecturers:
* A secure, password protected site with teaching material
* A syllabus manager that will build and host your very own course web page

Also: This regularly maintained site also has search functions.

Acknowledgements

Global Marketing Management – A European Perspective reflects the contributions, insights and labour of many persons. Our colleagues and associates and students at the Lubin School of Business, Pace University and the Vienna University of Economics and Business Administration (Wirtschaftsuniversität Wien); fellows and members of the Academy of International Business; our corporate clients, past and present, have all contributed.

On the US side special thanks go to Dorothy Minkus-McKenna, research associate. Hermawan Kartajaya, President of the Asia Pacific Marketing Federation and Chief Service Officer of MarkPlus, Jakarta, has been a knowledgeable and perceptive guide to marketing in South East Asia and a great source of insight and creative thinking about the marketing concept and discipline.

Mark Green, Professor, Simpson College, the co-author of *Principles of Global Marketing*, has generously shared his thoughts and suggestions for this edition.

Pace University has a unique doctoral programme that attracts an impressive group of students who have established themselves as leaders in their various fields and organisations, and who work toward their doctorate on a part-time basis while continuing their full-time careers. Special acknowledgement goes to the many contributions of the doctoral students in the doctoral seminar on Global Strategic Marketing. In particular, acknowledgement also goes to Michael Friedman, Chief Operating Officer, The Purdue Pharma L.P. Company, and Lubin School of Business, Pace University Adjunct Professor and doctoral student, for his many contributions to the strategy chapters in the book. Thanks also go to James L. Bauer, Vice President, Chase Bank; and James W. Gabberty, Director of Information Systems, Computer Horizons Corporation, New York.

Others who have made special contributions to this edition include Stephen Blank, Martin Topol, James Gould, Dennis Sandler, Larry Bridwell and Robert Vambery of the Lubin School of Business, Pace University; Howard Perlmutter, The Wharton School, Inc.; James A.F. Stoner, Fordham University; Robert M. Fulmer, W. Brooks George Professor, The College of William & Mary; Malcolm McDonald, Professor of Marketing Strategy, Cranfield School of Management;

Professor Dominique Xardel, Director MSGM, ESSEC (France); Dr Steven M. Burgess, PhD, Association of Marketers Professor, University of the Witwatersrand (South Africa); Donald Gibson, Professor, Macquarere, University (Australia); Raj Komaran, Professor, National University of Singapore; and Hermann Kopp, Professor, Norwegian School of Management.

Moreover, special thanks to my advisory board which includes Eli Seggev, President, Marketing Strategy and Planning, Inc. Terry Vavra, Marketing Metrics, John L. Neuman, Vice President, The Michael Allen Co., Leonard Vickers, Vickers Associates, and William J. Crerend, Chairman Evaluation Associates Capital Markets, David A. Heenan, Trustee, The Estate of James Campbell, and David Zenoff, Zenoff Associates.

In Europe, special thanks goes to Barbara Stöttinger of the Wirtschaftsuniversität Wien, who provided valuable insights and expertise to the current text and will, in fact, co-author a forthcoming German edition with us. Other Viennese colleagues of the Department of International Marketing and Management also contributed in various ways. Our thanks go to Elfriede Penz, Birgit Bacher, Veronika Moser and Peter Kreuz. As the only native Brit in sight, Irene Schlegelmilch spent hours proof-reading and showed tolerance whenever the writing took priority over family life.

The talented and creative people of Pearson Education, of course, also played a major role in the development of this book. After Julia Helmsley initiated the project, she was immediately promoted to a different job within the Pearson Group (she still asserts that there is no causal relationship). Subsequently, Liz Sproat took over and coaxed us, with a wonderful mix of encouragement, understanding and occasional treats, to the completion of the book. It has been a pleasure to work with Pearson.

Finally, our greatest debt is to our customers: the lecturers who adopt this book and the students and executives who purchase the book to study and learn about how to be a successful player in the exciting world of global marketing. To all of you a big thankyou for your support and inspiration and best wishes for your success in global marketing programmes.

Bodo B. Schlegelmilch
Warren J. Keegan

Publisher's acknowledgements

We are grateful to the following for permission to reproduce copyright material:

Figure 2.4 from the article 'Like herrings in a barrel' *The Economist* 31.12.99, © The Economist Newspaper Limited, London 1999; Figure 3.1 from Maslow, A. (1954) *Motivation and Personality*, reproduced with permission from HarperCollins Publishers; Figure 5.3 from http://www.nua.ie.surveys/graphs_charts/1998 graphs/location.html, 30.8.99, reproduced with permission from Nua Internet Surveys; Figure 5.4 from Morgan Stanley *The Internet Advertising Report*, reproduced with permission from Morgan Stanley Dean Witter; Figure 5.5 from Roland Berger & Partner (1999) *Erfolgsfaktoren im Electronic Commerce, Auszug aus den Ergebaissen der Studie*, reproduced with permission from Roland Berger & Partner GmbH; Figure 5.7 from Wilson, D.D. and Nunes, P.F. (1998) 'eEconomy: Ein Spiel mit neuen Relgeln' Sonderteil eCommerce: Wege zum Erfolg in der elektronischen Wirtschaft' *Outlook* Heft 1, reproduced with permission from Andersen Consulting; Figure 6.2 from Salzberger, T., Sinkovics, R. and Schlegelmilch, B.B. (1999) 'Data equivalence in cross-cultural research: A comparison of classical test theory and latent trait theory based approaches' *Australasian Marketing Journal*, Vol. 7, No. 2, reproduced with permission from the co-editor, Frank Alpert; Figure 7.1 from *Hidden Champions: Lessons from 500 of the World's Best Unknown Companies* by H. Simon, Boston, MA 1996, p. 4, Copyright © by the President and Fellows of Harvard College, all rights reserved, reprinted by permission of Harvard Business School Press; Figures 10.1, 10.2, 10.3, 10.4 and 10.7 from Porter, M.E. (1990) *The Competitive Advantage of Nations* copyright © 1980, 1998 by Michael E. Porter, and Figure 10.5 from Porter, M.E. (1980) *Competitive Strategy: Techniques for Analyzing Industries and Competitors* copyright © 1990, 1998 by Michael E. Porter, reproduced with permission from Macmillan Press Ltd and The Free Press, a Division of Simon & Schuster, Inc; Figure 10.8 from Douglas, S.P. and Craig, C.S. (1995) *Global Marketing Strategy* and Figure 14.1 from Cateora, P.C. (1993) *International Marketing* reproduced with permission from the McGraw-Hill Companies; Figures 12.2 and 12.3 from Simon, H. and Dolan, R. J. (1997) *Profit Durch Power Pricing* reproduced with permission from Campus Verlag; Figure 16.2 from 'The balanced scorecard – measures that drive performance' by R.S. Kaplan and D.P. Norton from *Harvard Business Review* (January–February, 1992), Copyright © 1992 by the President and Fellows of Harvard College, all rights reserved, reprinted by permission of Harvard Business Review; Figure 1, Part II Cases, reproduced with permission from Primark; Figure 2, Part III Cases, Gliss Kur/Poly Kur Figure, reproduced with permission from Henkel KgaA; Figure 1, Part V Cases, from BASF (1998) *BASF Facts and Figures-Charts 1998*, reproduced with permission from BASF; Figure 3, Part V Cases, from *Nokia Annual Report 1993*, reproduced with permission from Nokia.

Figure 14.2 'Breast Feeding', a photo by Oliviero Toscani, © Benetton Group SpA.

Business Link International for an extract adapted from 'Should Kurdistan be a nation' by Stephen Baker, published in '21 Ideas for the 21st Century', *Business Week* 30th August 1999; Chartered Institute of Management Accounting for an extract adapted from 'KPMG Peat Marwick's business measurement process – implementing change' by Kristine Mayer Brands in *Management Accounting*, January 1998; The Economist Newspaper Limited for an extract from 'Wretchedly oil-rich Azeris' © The Economist Newspaper Limited, London, 11.7.1998; The Financial Times for an extract by Peter Marsh from 'Changing the Pattern', 12.7.1999, an extract from 'PENOP: Signing up for E-Commerce' by Marcus Gibson, 7.7.1999 and for an extract from 'US gets go-ahead for trade sanctions', 27.7.1999, © Financial Times; Harvard Business School Publishing for an extract from 'Value innovation: The strategic logic of high growth' by W. Chan Kim and Renee Mauborgne in *Harvard Business Review* January/February 1997; Sage Publications and the author for the case study 'Norsk Hydro Fertilisers in the United States entering a highly competitive market' from *Cases in Marketing* by H.H. Larson; Washington Post Company for an extract adapted from 'US airlines "Handoffs" raise safety concerns: foreign partners come under scrutiny' in *The Washington Post* 7.3.1999, © 2000, The Washington Post and John Wiley & Sons for the case studies on Czech beer, MTV and Schwarzkopf from *Understanding Marketing: A European Casebook* by Phillips et al.

Whilst every effort has been made to trace the owners of copyright material, in a few cases this has proved impossible and we take this opportunity to offer our apologies to any copyright holders whose rights we may have unwittingly infringed.

About the authors

Dr Warren J. Keegan

Warren J. Keegan is a Fellow of the Academy of International Business, Professor of International Business, Marketing and Director of the Institute for Global Business Strategy at the Lubin School of Business, Pace University, New York City and Westchester, and Visiting Professor of Marketing and International Business at ESSEC (France). He is the founder of Warren Keegan Associates, Inc., a consulting consortium of experts in global strategic management and marketing. The firm is affiliated with MarkPlus, the leading marketing consulting firm of Indonesia.

Dr Keegan is the author or co-author of many books, including *Marketing Plans That Work: Targeting Growth and Profitability* (Butterworth Heinemann, 1997); *Principles of Global Marketing* (Prentice Hall, 1997); *Marketing* (2nd edn, Prentice Hall, 1996); *Marketing Sans Frontiers* (InterEditions, 1994); *Advertising Worldwide* (Prentice Hall, 1991); and *Judgments, Choices, and Decisions: Effective Management Through Self-Knowledge* (John Wiley & Sons). He has published numerous articles in leading journals including *Harvard Business Review*, *Administrative Science Quarterly*, *Journal of Marketing*, *Journal of International Business Studies*, and *The Columbia Journal of World Business*.

Dr Keegan is a former MIT Fellow in Africa where he served as Assistant Secretary, Ministry of Development Planning and Secretary of the Economic Development Commission for the Government of Tanzania. He was a consultant with Boston Consulting Group and Authur D. Little, and Chairman of Douglas A. Edwards, a New York corporate real estate firm.

Dr Keegan holds an MBA and a DBA from the Harvard Business School. He has been a visiting professor at New York University, INSEAD (France), IMD (Switzerland), The Stockholm School of Economics, Emmanuel College of Cambridge University, and at the University of Hawaii. He is a former faculty member of Columbia Business School, Baruch College, and the School of Government and Business Administration of The George Washington University.

He is a Lifetime Fellow of the Academy of International Business and is a current or former director of the S.M. Stoller Company, Inc., the Cooper Companies, Inc. (NYSE), Inter-Ad, Inc., Halfway Houses of Westchester, Inc., Wainwright House, and the Rye Arts Center.

Dr Bodo B. Schlegelmilch

Dr Schlegelmilch is Professor and Chair of International Marketing & Management at the Wirtschaftsuniversität Wien (Vienna University of Economics and Business Administration). He is also Academic Director of the Vienna Executive MBA and International MBA Programs, Fellow of the Chartered Institute of Marketing and Adjunct Professor of International Business Studies at the University of Minnesota, Carlson School of Management and at Kingston University, London, UK. Currently, he serves as the first ever European Editor-in-Chief of the *Journal of International Marketing*.

Previously he held tenured posts at Thunderbird, the American Graduate School of International Management in Arizona, the University of Wales in Swansea, and the University of Edinburgh in Scotland. At Thunderbird, he worked as Professor of Marketing and founding Director of the US Government-supported CIBER Institute for International Business Ethics. At the University of Wales, he held the British Rail Chair of Marketing, and at the University of Edinburgh, he was a Lecturer of Marketing and International Business. During his career, he also held visiting positions at the University of California at Berkeley and the University of Miami, and held commercial posts at Deutsche Bank and Procter & Gamble in Germany.

Dr Schlegelmilch has taught in international marketing programmes in Austria, Britain, China, Egypt, France, Germany, New Zealand, Russia, Thailand and the United States. He is the president of Canyon Consulting Corp. and has consulted and/or conducted executive education work in strategic marketing for major multinationals, including Allied Signals, Anheuser Busch, AT&T, Baxter, BellSouth, Black & Decker, Cable & Wireless, Citibank, Degussa-Hüls, Dow Chemical, Eastman Kodak, EDS, Eli Lilly, Estée Lauder, Goldman Sachs, Goodyear, Johnson & Johnson, MCI, Merck Sharp & Dohme, Stinnes, KPMG, Philip Morris, Pharmacia & Upjohn, Samsung, Schlumberger, Sunkyong and Universal Flavors.

Dr Schlegelmilch studied Business Administration at the Fachhochschule Köln and holds an MSc and PhD from the University of Manchester Institute of Science and Technology. In terms of research, Dr Schlegelmilch has been recognised as one of the world's top 15 authors publishing in leading international marketing journals and has been listed in "Who's Who in International Business Education and Research." His work focuses on a variety of topics in global marketing management and strategy. He has published over 100 academic papers and has presented his research at numerous international conferences and universities. Dr Schlegelmilch has served or is currently serving on the editorial boards of several leading academic journals, including the *Journal of International Business Studies, Journal of World Business, International Journal of Research in Marketing, Journal of Strategic Marketing, International Marketing Review, Journal of Marketing Management, Journal of Business Research and Marketing – Zeitschrift für Forschung und Praxis.*

PART I

Introduction and overview

CHAPTER 1

Introduction to global marketing

The real change agents in this world always swam against the tide.
WALTER JENS, GERMAN AUTHOR

In the environment of the 1990s, globalisation must be taken for granted. There will be only one standard for corporate success: international market share. The winning corporations will win by finding markets all over the world.
JACK WELCH, CEO GENERAL ELECTRIC

Overview

After reading this chapter, you will know:

- How the world economy developed over the past decades.
- The impact of globalisation on the marketing discipline.
- The interdependencies between management orientation and marketing performance in the global market.
- The difference between ethnocentric, polycentric, regiocentric and geocentric management orientation and their impact on a company's marketing activities.
- The factors supporting or inhibiting international marketing activities.

Why is this important? Here are three situations in which you would need an understanding of the above issues:

- You need to apply a new strategic marketing approach focusing on creating value for your company's stakeholders.
- You need to assess the opportunities for creating superior customer value in order to compete internationally.
- You need to evaluate whether your firm's management is ready for the global arena.

Practice link

We live in a global marketplace. As you read this book, you may be sitting in a chair imported from Brazil or at a desk imported from Denmark. You may have purchased these items from IKEA, the Swedish global furniture retailer. The computer on your desk could be either a low-priced personal computer (PC) clone from Taiwan or perhaps a Macintosh designed in the United States and manufactured in Ireland. Your shoes are likely to be from Italy, and the coffee you are sipping is from Latin America or Africa. Your hi-fi-system plays the latest CD of the Vienna Philharmonic Orchestra playing at the New York Met. The Italian director selected a piece by a Russian composer. The technology that drives your CD-changer stems from a Dutch-Japanese joint venture. Your sweater could be the latest fashion from Italy's Benetton. What time is it now? When you check your watch, can you tell where it was made? It may be from Japan, Hong Kong, Singapore, the Philippines, or Switzerland. Welcome to the new millennium. Yesterday's marketing fantasy has become today's reality: the world has turned into a global village!

In the past 150 years, a sweeping transformation has profoundly affected the people and industries of many nations. Prior to 1840, students sitting at their desks would not usually have had any item in their possession that was manufactured more than a few miles from where they lived – with the possible exception of the books they were reading. Some countries – most notably Great Britain – were actively involved in international trade in the mid-19th century. However, since the Second World War there has been an unparalleled expansion into global markets by companies that previously served only customers located in the home country.

Two decades ago, the phrase global marketing did not even exist. Today, businesses look to global marketing for the realisation of their full commercial potential. That is why you may own some of the products described in the preceding paragraph, no matter whether you live in Asia, Europe, or North or South America. However, there is another even more critical reason why companies need to take global marketing seriously: survival. A company that fails to become global in outlook risks losing its domestic business to competitors having lower costs, greater experience and better products.

MARKETING: A UNIVERSAL DISCIPLINE

The foundation for a successful global marketing programme is a sound understanding of the marketing discipline. Marketing is the process of focusing the resources and objectives of an organisation on environmental opportunities and needs. The first and most fundamental fact about marketing is that it is a universal discipline. It is applicable in the United States, or in Japan as well as in South Africa. Marketing is a set of concepts, tools, theories, practices, procedures and experience. Together, these elements constitute a teachable and learnable body of knowledge.

Although marketing is universal, marketing practice of course varies from country to country. Each person is unique, and each country is unique. This reality of differences means that we cannot always directly apply experience from one country to another. If the customers, competitors, channels of distribution, and available media are different, it may be necessary to change our marketing plan.

The concept of marketing

During the past three decades, the concept of marketing has changed dramatically. It has evolved from a focus on the product and on making a 'better' product where better was based on internal standards and values. The objective was profit, and the means to achieving the objective was selling, or persuading the potential customer to exchange his or her money for the company's product.

The new concept of marketing and the four Ps

The 'new' concept of marketing, which evolved in the 1960s, shifted its emphasis from product towards customer orientation. While profit still remained the primary goal, the means to achieve it were extended. The entire marketing mix consisting of four distinct instruments evolved. The four Ps, as they are also called, are product, price, promotion and place.

The strategic concept of marketing

By the 1990s, it was clear that the new concept of marketing was outdated and that the times demanded a strategic concept. The strategic concept of marketing, a major evolution in the history of marketing thought, shifted the focus of marketing from the customer or the product to the customer in the context of the broader external environment. Knowing everything there is to know about the customer is not enough. To succeed, marketers must know the customer in a context including the competition, government policy and regulation, and the broader economic, social and political macro forces that shape the evolution of markets.

Another revolutionary change in the shift to the strategic concept of marketing is in the marketing objective – from profit to *stakeholder value*. *Stakeholders* are individuals or groups who have an interest in a firm's internal and external activities. They include the employees and management, customers and shareholders, banks, society and government, to mention only the most important. There is a growing recognition that profits are a reward for performance (defined as satisfying customers in a socially responsible or acceptable way).

In order to compete successfully in today's markets, it is necessary to have an employee team which is committed to continuous improvement and to manufacturing high quality products. In other words, marketing must concentrate on two key tasks: (i) it needs to focus on the customer and his/her environment and (ii) it has to create value to consumers and other *stakeholders*.

A recent study asked US, Japanese and European top managers which constituency would provide the most significant contribution to stakeholder value. More than half of the respondents hold the opinion that *shareholders* provide the most significant contribution. Similarly many think that employees have a significant impact; 22 per cent see the contribution of suppliers and 10 per cent the impact of society on stakeholder value. Undisputedly however, the participants in the survey judge the customer as most influential on stakeholder value.[1]

EUROPEAN FOCUS

Stakeholder value – new to Europe?

Stakeholder value is the 'hottest' managerial concept in town. Customers, suppliers, employees and shareholders want to see their interests in a firm satisfied. For many European and Japanese firms this approach, however, may seem more like 'new wine in old bottles'.

As the German professor and consultant Hermann Simon outlined in his book *The Hidden Champions*, German companies have relied on these ideas, which now have reached a sudden popularity in the US under the title of stakeholder value, for years.

German *Mittelstand* companies such as Steiner Optik, with an 80 per cent world market share in military binoculars, or Krones, manufacturer of 70 per cent of all bottle labelling machines sold worldwide, founded their success on the ideas of stakeholder value. For years, they have balanced the varying demands of different stakeholders very well.

For example, long-term co-operation with suppliers provided stable product and service quality at an outstanding level for the firm and its customers and, consequently, economic stability for the supplier. Instead of hiring and firing employees, these companies have understood how to create attractive employment opportunities for their staff. This job security created an additional incentive for employees to acquire knowledge and skills, which due to its level of specialisation is of high value to the company, yet in little demand by other employers. As employees see their interests taken into consideration, they reciprocate with above average loyalty and commitment. This leads to excellence in all areas and finally to indisputable customer benefits.

In Germany, corporate law provides that employees' interests are taken care of by requiring employees' delegates on the board of directors. As such, employees gain access to management decisions and may use this forum to advocate their interests.

The modern name for it – stakeholder value!

Source: 'Valuing companies: a star to sail by?', *The Economist*, 344 (8028), 2 August 1997; 'Survey of business in Europe (6): taking the pledge – so much to do, so little time, *The Economist*, 341 (7993), 23 November 1996; 'Management focus: German lessons', *The Economist*, 340 (7974), 13 July 1996; 'Stakeholder capitalism: unhappy families', *The Economist*, 338 (7952), 10 February 1996; Hermann Simon, *Die heimlichen Gewinner* (Frankfurt: Campus Verlag, 1996); Peter Gomez, 'Stakeholder Value schlägt Shareholder Value ... nach Punkten!' *Thexis*, 2 (1998): pp. 62–63.

Profitability is not forgotten in the strategic concept. Indeed, it is a critical means to the end of creating stakeholder value. The means of the strategic marketing concept is strategic management, which integrates marketing with the other management functions. One of the tasks of strategic management is to make a profit, which can be a source of funds for investing in the business and for rewarding shareholders and management. Thus, profit is still a critical objective and measure of marketing success, but it is not an end in itself. The aim of marketing is to create value for stakeholders, and the key stakeholder is the customer. If your customer can get greater value from your competitor because your competitor is willing to accept a lower level of profit reward for investors and management, the customer will choose your competitor, and you will be out of business. The spectacular inroads of the clones into IBM's PC market illustrate that even the largest and most powerful companies can be challenged by competitors who are more efficient or who are willing to accept lower profit returns.

A third substantial change in the notion of marketing has taken place. The strategic concept of marketing has shifted the focus of marketing from a microeconomics maximisation paradigm to a focus on managing strategic partnerships and positioning the firm between vendors and customers in the value chain with the aim and purpose of creating value for customers. This expanded concept of marketing was termed boundaryless marketing by Jack Welch, chairperson and chief executive officer (CEO) of General Electric.

Key points	
	• **In the last 30 years, the notion of marketing has changed from a product and customer orientation to a strategic orientation. The strategic goal of marketing shifted from maximisation of profits as core goal to creating value for a company's *stakeholders*.**
	• **Stakeholders may be described as individuals or groups, who have a considerable interest in a firm's activities.**
	• **A firm's most important stakeholders are employees, the management, customers, shareholders, banks and the society as a whole.**

Marketing, in addition to being a concept and a philosophy, is a set of activities and a business process. The marketing activities are called the four Ps: product, price, place (distribution), and promotion (or communications). These four Ps can be expanded to five Ps by adding probe (research). Only recently, the concept was enriched by an additional three Ps in order to take the special characteristics of services marketing into account. The new dimensions are *physical evidence*, i.e. the environment in which the service is provided, *participants*, i.e. the people who take part in the provision of services, and the *process*, which covers how the process of service creation is designed.[2] The marketing management process is the task of focusing the resources and objectives of the organisation on opportunities in the environment.

MARKETING'S THREE CORNERSTONES

Marketing is based on three fundamental principles. The first one, the *value equation*, identifies the purpose and task of marketing, namely creating value for customers.

The second principle, *differentiation as competitive advantage*, deals with a firm's environment, in which marketing tasks are carried out. The third principle, *focusing*, offers an approach on how to achieve the first two cornerstones.

The value equation

The task of marketing is to create customer value that is greater than the value created by competitors. The value equation, shown in Figure 1.1, is a guide to this task. As suggested in the equation, value for the customer can be increased by expanding or improving product and/or service benefits, by reducing the price, or by a combination of these elements. Companies with a cost advantage can use price as a competitive weapon. Knowledge of the customer combined with innovation and creativity can lead to a total offering that provides superior customer value. If the benefits are strong enough and valued enough by customers, a company does not need to be the low-price competitor to win customers.

Differentiation

The second fundamental principle of marketing is obtaining competitive advantages through differentiation. A competitive advantage is a total offer, vis-à-vis relevant competition, that is more attractive to customers. The advantage can exist in any element of the company's offer: the product, the price, the advertising and point-of-sale promotion, and the distribution of the product. These advantages become manifest when they are applied within a specific industry to attract customers in specific market segments. Otherwise, these competitive advantages will not be sustainable over an extended period of time.

In creating a competitive advantage, it is of key importance that a company employs the strengths it already has, rather than aspire to those it does not have. Achieving high quality without possessing design and production skills for high-quality products is bound to fail. The German car manufacturer BMW has achieved its outstanding market position by applying two key competencies: superior production skills and marketing competencies, particularly in developing brand strategies that directly relate to consumer needs and desires. This superiority compared to competitors results in a superior product or service quality, in technical excellence, in the product variety or a more efficient distribution network.[3] In most cases, competitive advantages are not limited to a specific geographic market. Moreover, they are suitable for internationalisation. Honda conquered the US motorcycle market applying

Figure 1.1 The value equation

$$V = B/P$$

V = Value
B = Perceived benefits – perceived costs*
P = Price

*e.g. switching costs

the same competitive edge that led to its dominance of the Japanese market – its capability to produce an innovative, yet simple product at low cost.[4]

One of the most powerful strategies for penetrating a new national market is to offer a superior product at a lower price. The price advantage will get immediate customer attention and, for those customers who purchase the product, the superior quality will make an impression.

Focus

The third marketing principle is focus, or the concentration of attention. Focus is required to succeed in the task of creating customer value at a competitive advantage. All successful companies have understood and applied this principle. IBM succeeded and became a great company because it was more clearly focused on customer needs and wants than any other company in the emerging data processing industry. One of the reasons IBM found itself in crisis in the early 1990s was that its competitors had become much more clearly focused on customer needs and wants. Dell and Compaq, for example, focused on giving customers computing power at low prices; IBM was offering the same computing power with higher prices.

It is not only large firms that have internalised this strategy. As the following examples show, focusing is a very viable way for small and medium-sized industries to achieve a dominant position in the world market. Clean Concept, the German producer of contact-free lavatory systems, built its strength on clearly focusing on all capabilities and skills related to hygiene. As one company representative put it: 'We want to perform one job really well. Therefore, we do nothing else, but provide pure hygiene.'[5] A clear focus on core competencies has made the Austrian high-tech firm Frequentis a world-wide leader in the technology of digital air traffic control systems. Reaching an export share of over 90 per cent, Frequentis's air traffic control systems are installed from Mexico to China.[6] For over 100 years synthetic gem stones and crystal figures from Swarovski have been brightening our day. By focusing on its core strengths, Swarovski's products are found in art galleries as well on evening robes by Versace or shoes designed by Gian Franco Ferré.[7]

A clear focus on customer needs and wants and on the competitive offer is required to mobilise the effort needed to maintain a differential advantage. This can be accomplished only by focusing or concentrating resources and efforts on customer needs and wants and on how to deliver a product that will meet those needs and wants.

SCOPE AND BOUNDARIES OF GLOBAL MARKETING

Although the marketing discipline is universal, markets and customers are quite differentiated. This means that marketing practice must vary from country to country. Each person is unique, and each country is unique. This reality of differences means that we cannot always directly apply experience from one country to another. If the customers, competitors, channels of distribution, and available media are different, it may be necessary to change our marketing plan. This fact is also reflected in the body of knowledge that an international marketer should have. In this context, S. Tamer Cavusgil distinguishes three domains of knowledge relevant to international managers (see Figure 1.2).

Companies that don't appreciate the fact that marketing plans might need to be

GLOBAL PERSPECTIVE

McDonald's – a fast-food legend continues its triumph around the globe!

In more than 115 countries and over 24,500 restaurants, the Golden Arches are a symbol for quality and service in fast food. More than 14 billion customer visits per year provide an impressive evidence for this fact. But why go abroad, when the company already has more than 12,000 restaurants in the United States and serves up nearly one third of the hamburgers that Americans consume? The reason lies in a decline in the annual growth rates for the American fast-food industry as a whole, from an average of 7.1 per cent in the 1970s to less than 5 per cent in the 1990s, while sales outside the US increased by 16 per cent.

McDonald's has responded by stepping up its rate of new unit openings. In 1991, the company had 3,355 units in 53 countries; in 1994 more than 5,400 and by 1997 more than 12,000 overseas restaurants were in operation. While these overseas restaurants comprised only about 40 per cent of all outlets, they account for about half of the total sales and over 60 per cent of the operating profit. On 31 January 1990, after 14 years of negotiation and preparation, the first 'Bolshoi Mac' went on sale in the then Soviet Union. The Moscow McDonald's, located on Pushkin Square, is just four blocks from the Kremlin. It has 700 indoor seats and another 200 outside. It boasts 800 employees and features a 70-foot counter with 27 cash registers equivalent to 20 ordinary McDonald's restaurants rolled into one. The restaurant serves up 18,000 orders of fries, 12,000 Big Macs, and 11,000 apple pies every day. To ensure a steady supply of raw materials, the company built a huge processing facility on the outskirts of Moscow and worked closely with local farmers. Despite the turmoil stemming from the dissolution of the Soviet Union and the political upheaval in the fall of 1993, to date more than 140 million customers have been served since its market entry to Russia. McDonald's has also set its sights on Central and Eastern Europe. More than 350 new restaurants are scheduled to open in Croatia, Slovakia, Rumania and other countries in the region.

The menu in Moscow, where 'meat and potatoes' are staples, has the same basic offerings as in the United States. In other countries, however, McDonald's has adapted its fare in response to local tastes. The varied offerings include teriyaki burgers in Japan, banana fruit pies in Latin America, kiwi burgers (served with beetroot sauce) in New Zealand, beer in Germany, McSpaghetti noodles in the Philippines, and chilli sauce to go with fries in Singapore. In India, Hinduism as a prominent religious orientation prohibits in its principles the consumption of beef and thus called for a substitute. A so-called 'Maharaja Mac' was created, using a patty made from lamb. In some countries, McDonald's has been forced to change its food preparation methods as well; in Singapore and Malaysia, for example, the beef that goes into burgers must be slaughtered according to Muslim law. Having successfully begun to develop the Russian market, McDonald's has set its sights on China. The first Chinese restaurant opened in mid-1992 in central Beijing, a few blocks from the infamous Tiananmen Square. Meanwhile more than 180 restaurants operate successfully in China.

Despite McDonald's international success, the company has occasionally stumbled in its efforts to promote fast food around the world. A poster that was displayed in 66 Dutch restaurants in October 1991 caused a furore in France, where the first McDonald's opened in 1979. The poster featured a photo of five chefs examining a batch of dressed chickens; the caption indicated the chefs were actually dreaming of Big Macs. The poster caused an uproar for two reasons. One of the people in the photo was Paul Bocuse, a legendary three-star French chef. Also, the chickens were identified as being from a French region renowned for its poultry. All in all, the posters were taken as an insult to French haute cuisine. In a letter of apology to Bocuse, McDonald's only made matters worse by attributing the error in part to the fact that Bocuse is not well known in the Netherlands.

Despite such international incidents, McDonald's is moving forward with its expansion plans. As one of the most well-known brands worldwide, McDonald's is similar to Coca-Cola ten years ago. It is on the verge of becoming an international giant, with the United States as a major market, but overseas as the driving force.

Food for thought
- Why do you think McDonald's is so successful? What do they have to be particularly good at to sustain this success internationally?
- How much adaptation to local taste is necessary when McDonald's expands internationally? When would adaptation be taken too far?

Source: Robert Johnson, 'Fast food leader: McDonald's combines a dead man's advice with lively strategy', *The Wall Street Journal*, 18 December 1987, p. A1; Steven Greenhouse, 'McDonald's tries Paris, again', *New York Times*, 12 June 1988, p. 1; Barbara Dietrich, 'Cohon launches "Big Mac attack" on USSR', *Drake University Update*, Summer 1990, p. 13; Eben Shapiro, 'Overseas sizzle for McDonald's', *The New York Times*, 17 April 1992, p. C1; 'Broad, deep, long and heavy: assessing brands. The world's best brands', *The Economist*, 341 (792), 1996, pp. 72–75; 'Johannesburgers and fries', *The Economist*, 344 (8036), 27 September 1997, p. 75–76.

Figure 1.2 **Domains of knowledge for international managers**

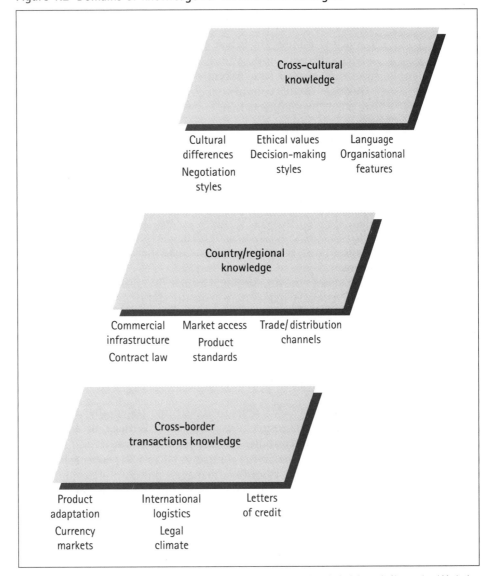

Source: Adapted from S. Tamer Cavusgil, 'Knowledge development in international marketing', *Journal of International Marketing*, 6, 2 (1998): p. 105.

adapted will soon learn, if they transfer irrelevant experience from one country or region to another. Nestlé, for example, sought to transfer its great success with a four-flavour coffee line from Europe to the United States. Their US competitors were delighted: the transfer led to a decline of one per cent in US market share![8] An important task in global marketing is learning to recognise the extent to which marketing plans and programmes can be extended world-wide, as well as the extent to which they must be adapted.

Much of the controversy about global marketing dates from Theodore Levitt's seminal article in the *Harvard Business Review*, 'The globalisation of markets'.[9] He argued that marketers were confronted with a 'homogenous global village'. Levitt advised organisations to develop standardised, high-quality world products and market them around the globe using standardised advertising, pricing and distribution. Some well-publicised failures by Parker Pen and other companies seeking to follow Levitt's advice called his proposals into question. Carl Spielvogel, chairman and CEO of the Backer Spielvogel Bates Worldwide advertising agency, told *The Wall Street Journal*, 'Theodore Levitt's comment about the world becoming homogenised is bunk. There are about two products that lend themselves to global marketing – and one of them is Coca-Cola.'[10]

Indeed, it was global marketing that made Coke a world-wide success. However, that success was not based on a total standardisation of marketing mix elements. In his book *The Borderless World*, Kenichi Ohmae explains that Coke's success in Japan could be achieved only by spending a great deal of time and money becoming an insider. That is, the company built a complete local infrastructure with its salesforce and vending machine operations. Coke's success in Japan, according to Ohmae, was a function of its ability to achieve 'global localisation', the ability to be as much of an insider as a local company but still reap the benefits that result from world-scale operations.

What does the phrase global localisation really mean? In a nutshell, it means a successful global marketer must have the ability to 'think globally and act locally'. As we will see many times in this book, 'global' marketing may include a combination of standard (e.g. the actual product itself) and non-standard (e.g., distribution or packaging) approaches. A 'global product' may be 'the same' product everywhere and yet 'different'. Global marketing requires marketers to behave in a way that is global and local at the same time by responding to similarities and differences in world markets.

As the Coca-Cola Company has demonstrated, the ability to think globally and act locally can be a source of competitive advantage. By adapting sales promotion, distribution, and customer service efforts to local needs, Coke established such strong brand preference that the company claims a 70 per cent share of the soft drink market in Japan. At first, Coca-Cola managers did not understand the Japanese distribution system. However, with considerable investment of time and money, they succeeded in establishing a salesforce that was as effective in Japan as it was in the United States. Today, Coca-Cola Japan generates higher profits than the US operation. To complement cola sales, the Japanese unit has created new products such as Georgia brand canned coffee expressly for the Japanese market.[11]

Coke is a product embodying marketing mix elements that are both global and local in nature. In this book, we do not propose that global marketing is a 'knee jerk' attempt to impose a totally standardised approach to marketing around the world. A central issue in global marketing is how to tailor the global marketing concept to fit a particular product or business.[12]

Finally, it is necessary to understand that global marketing does *not* mean entering every country in the world. Global marketing does mean widening business horizons to encompass the world when scanning for opportunity and threat. The decision to enter markets outside the home country depends on a company's resources, managerial mindset, and the nature of opportunity and threat. The Coca-Cola Company's soft drink products are distributed in more than 195 countries; in fact, the theme of a recent annual report was 'A Global Business System Dedicated to Customer Service'. Coke is the best-known, strongest brand in the world; its enviable global position has resulted in part from the Coca-Cola Company's willingness and ability to back its flag-ship product with a strong local marketing effort.

A number of other companies have successfully pursued global marketing by creat-ing strong global brands (see Table 1.1). Philip Morris, for example, has made Marlboro the number one cigarette brand in the world. In automobiles, Daimler-Benz has gained global recognition for its Mercedes nameplate. However, global marketing strategies can also be based on product or system design, product positioning, pack-aging, distribution, customer service, and sourcing considerations. For example, McDonald's has designed a restaurant system that can be set up virtually anywhere in the world. Like Coca-Cola, McDonald's also customises its menu offerings in accord-ance with local eating customs. Cisco Systems, which makes local area network routers that allow computers to communicate with each other, designs new products that can be programmed to operate under virtually any conditions in the world.[13]

Key points	<ul><li>Generally speaking, marketing is based on three fundamental principles: the value equation, differentiation and focus.</li><li>The marketing task is to create higher value to customers than the compe-tition in order to achieve a competitive advantage. The value for the cus-tomer can be increased by improving the product, reducing the price or a combination of both aspects.</li><li>Differentiation is the unique position a company holds vis-à-vis its com-petitors, seen from a customer's point of view. It is based on a firm's unique capabilities and skills to create superior value to consumers.</li><li>Focus means concentrating on customer needs and wants and thus creating opportunities for competitive advantages.</li><li>As international markets differ in many aspects, these fundamental prin-ciples can only be accomplished by *'global localisation'*. This implies that *global* marketing strategies are adjusted to *local requirements*.</li></ul>

Unilever uses a teddy bear in various world markets to communicate the benefits of the company's fabric softener. Volkswagen has brought back its world-wide marketing success – the Beetle – to international markets. As sales figures show, 'Beetle aficiona-dos' are still fondly attached to its unique design and product features. Gillette uses the same packaging for its flagship Sensor razor everywhere in the world. Benetton utilises a sophisticated distribution system to quickly deliver the latest fashions to its world-wide network of stores. The backbone of Caterpillar's global success is a net-work of dealers who support a promise of '24 hour parts and service' anywhere in the world. The Swedish furniture company IKEA thrills its customers with chic design at affordable prices to allow even less endowed wallets tasteful living. The key to success is global sourcing in low-wage countries, where furniture is manufactured based on Swedish design.

The particular approach to global marketing that a company adopts will depend on industry conditions and its source or sources of competitive advantage. Should Harley-Davidson start manufacturing motorcycles in a low-wage country such as Mexico? Will American consumers continue to snap up American-built Toyotas? Should GAP open stores in Japan? The answer to these questions is, 'It all depends'.

Table 1.1 **Examples of global marketing**

Global marketing strategies	*Company/home market*
Brand name	Daimler Chrysler (Germany/US), Philip Morris (US), Coca-Cola (US)
Product design	McDonald's (US), Volkswagen (Germany), Hennes & Mauritz (Sweden)
Product positioning	Nestlé (Switzerland), Unilever (UK/Netherlands), Harley-Davidson (US)
Packaging	Gillette (US)
Distribution	Benetton (Italy)
Customer service	Caterpillar (US)
Sourcing	IKEA (Sweden)

Because Harley's competitive advantage is based in part on its 'Made in the USA' positioning, shifting production outside the United States is not advisable. Toyota's success in the United States is partly attributable to its ability to transfer world-class manufacturing skills to America while using advertising to stress that its Camry is built by Americans, with many components purchased in the United States.

THE IMPORTANCE OF GLOBAL MARKETING

Activities in the international arena are of eminent importance to companies in achieving their maximum growth potential. Taking the US for example, the area represents about 25 per cent of the total world market volume for products and services. If, however, US firms want to take advantage of maximum sales potential, they are bound to seek these opportunities outside their home market. Even though the dollar value of the home market for Japanese companies is the second largest in the free world (after the United States), the market outside Japan is 85 per cent of the world potential for Japanese companies. For European countries, the picture is even more dramatic. Even though Germany is the largest single-country market in Europe, 94 per cent of the world market potential for German companies is outside of Germany.

Many companies have recognised the importance of conducting business activities outside the home country. Industries that were strictly national in scope only a few years ago are today dominated by a handful of global companies. The rise of the global corporation closely parallels the rise of the national corporation, which emerged from the local and regional corporation in the 1880s and the 1890s in the United States. The auto industry provides a dramatic and sobering example. In the first quarter of the 20th century, there were thousands of auto companies in the world, and more than 500 in the United States alone. Today, fewer than 20 companies remain world-wide (see Figure 1.3). In most industries, the companies that will survive and prosper in the next century will be global enterprises. Some companies that do not respond to the challenges and opportunities of globalisation will be absorbed by more dynamic enterprises; others will simply disappear.

This fact is illustrated by the stunning announcement of a merger between Daimler-Benz and Chrysler in 1998. This €30 billion deal, one of the largest industrial

EUROPEAN FOCUS

Hennes & Mauritz – on the highway to global success

In 1997 Hennes & Mauritz celebrated its 50th anniversary. And rightfully, its success is something to be proud of! Founded in Sweden in 1947, Hennes & Mauritz today operates more than 500 sales outlets in more than 12 countries. Sales figures have doubled about every five years, while the operating profit has increased by approximately 22 per cent over the last ten years. The cornerstone to success lies in a global product concept and its consistent implementation. At H&M, decision makers are convinced that the textile business is dominated by one trend: 'global fashion!' Satellite TV, the international film and the music industry as well as the Internet have moved the MTV-generation's world from Japan to the UK closer together. This development manifests itself in a decreasing importance of national boundaries as far as fashion tastes are concerned. H&M's design department develops fashion collections for the entire European market at competitive prices, which are changed and adapted constantly. Nothing remains on the shelf for longer than one month. This strategy aims to entice customers to enter the shops more often and buy clothes whenever they see something interesting.

A perfect marketing package supports the products' success. In this respect, the sales outlets play an important role. H&M's own outlet design department has developed a uniform shop design, which is implemented in every country market. After all, customers should be able to quickly find their way around. To immediately check out products, sizes and prices, the shop design provides detailed suggestions on how to present products within the store. In the end, a lambswool sweater will find itself in the same shelf area, regardless of whether you enter a shop in Gothenburg or Zurich!

H&M's international success is quite remarkable. Over 500 sales outlets operate throughout Europe and new ones are already scheduled. And since 1994, German sales have surpassed those in the home market Sweden, rendering it H&M's largest market! In France, H&M has impressively proven that its product concept has been successfully transferred beyond the Scandinavian and German markets.

H&M has put Spain, Italy, Japan and the US on the agenda of international expansion in the near future. In the US, a hard battle is waiting for H&M where it is facing The Gap, its major competitor, in its home market.

Food for thought
● Compare the international expansion of Hennes & Mauritz with that of 'The Gap'. Where are the differences and similarities?
● Do you think national boundaries are still important in the fashion industry? If so, why? If not, which segments are replacing country market segments?

Source: Mary Krienke, 'Hennes & Mauritz', *Stores*, 75, 2 (1993): pp. 34–37; 'Der Schwede mit den goldenen Hosen', *Süddeutsche Zeitung*, 9 November 1996, p. 37; 'Jeden Tag etwas Neues', *Die Welt*, 11 June 1997, p. 18; http://www.hm.com/ (31 July 1998); 'Knickers to the market: Hennes & Mauritz', *The Economist*, 346 (8057), 28 February 1998, pp. 68–69; 'H&M to expand after 32% lift', *Financial Times*, 5 February 1998, p. 21; Greg McIvor, 'Companies & finance: Hennes & Mauritz', *Financial Times*, 23 September 1998; Tim Burt, 'Buoyant H&M to expand into US', *Financial Times*, 17 April 1999.

take-overs in history, underlined the importance of economies of scale and scope in the global auto industry. The combined companies moved from 6th and 15th in the world to a combined 5th place ranking after GM, Ford, Toyota, and Volkswagen. Looking at the list of companies in Table 1.2, it is apparent that the pressure will build for further mergers in this industry. As Thomas Middelhoff, the newly appointed chairman of Bertelsmann AG said recently, 'There are no German and American companies. There are only successful and unsuccessful companies.'[14]

Table 1.3 shows 25 of *The Wall Street Journal*'s Top 100 company ranking in terms

Figure 1.3 Consolidating tendencies in the automotive industry

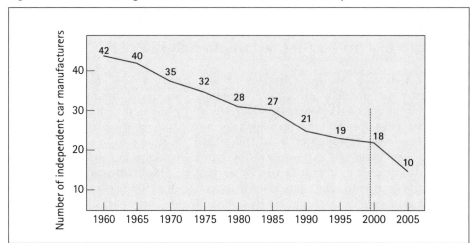

Table 1.2 Total vehicle sales world-wide

Company (country)	Sales (in million cars)	Market share (in %)
General Motors	6.8	16.2
Ford	6.9	12.9
Toyota	4.8	9.0
Volkswagen	4.6	7.9
Daimler/Chrysler	4.0	7.4
Fiat	2.9	5.3
Chrysler	2.9	5.3
Nissan	2.8	5.2
Peugeot Citroen	2.1	3.9
Honda	2.0	3.8
Mitsubishi	1.9	3.6
Renault	1.9	3.5
Suzuki	1.8	3.4
Hyundai	1.2	2.3
BMW	1.2	2.2
Daimler-Benz	1.1	2.1

Source: 'Automotive news', *New York Times*, 7 May 1998, p. D-5.

of market capitalisation, that is, the market value of all shares of stock outstanding. Table 1.4 provides a different perspective: the top 25 of *Fortune* magazine's ranking of the 500 largest service and manufacturing companies by revenues. Comparing the two tables, it is striking to note that, although General Electric has the highest market value, it ranked 12th in revenues and second in profits. One company that makes a strong showing in both rankings is Nippon Telegraph & Telephone (NTT): it is fourth in market capitalisation and 14th in revenues, but 100th in profits.

Table 1.4 also provides some interesting insights into Japanese companies, which underwent considerable turmoil in the mid 1990s. The Japanese companies Mitsui and Mitsubishi rank third and fourth in sales terms. As to their profitability however,

Table 1.3 The 25 largest corporations by market value (in € millions)

Rank 1997	Rank 1996	Company (country)	Market value (in € millions)
1	1	General Electric (US)	251,159
2	6	Microsoft (US)	226,533
3	3	Coca-Cola (US)	179,101
4	2	Royal Dutch/Shell (Netherlands/UK)	159,279
5	5	Exxon (US)	148,147
6	7	Merck (US)	135,614
7	18	Pfizer (US)	120,379
8	19	Wal-Mart Stores (US)	115,427
9	4	Nippon Telegraph & Telephone (Japan)	111,859
10	8	Intel (US)	106,645
11	12	Procter & Gamble (US)	103,589
12	17	Bristol-Myers Squibb (US)	97,043
13	49	Lucent Technologies (US)	92,583
14	27	Berkshire Hathaway (US)	92,180
15	14	International Business Machines (US)	91,834
16	20	Glaxo Wellcome (UK)	91,569
17	11	Novartis (Switzerland)	87,119
18	23	American International Group (US)	86,651
19	15	Johnson & Johnson (US)	84,410
20	9	Toyota Motor (Japan)	83,753
21	10	Philip Morris (US)	81,145
22	56	Cisco Systems (US)	80,951
23	30	AT&T (US)	78,707
24	29	Unilever Group (Netherlands/UK)	72,531
25	22	British Petroleum (UK)	72,017

Source: 'The world's 100 largest public companies', *Wall Street Journal*, 28 September 1998, p. R-18.

they find themselves only in positions 336 and 287, respectively. This discrepancy is in part due to the exchange rate situation towards the Yen in key markets.

MANAGEMENT ORIENTATION AND GLOBAL MARKETING

The form and substance of a company's response to global market opportunities depend greatly on management's assumptions or beliefs, both conscious and unconscious, about the nature of the world. The worldview of a company's personnel can be described as ethnocentric, polycentric, regiocentric and geocentric.[15] Management at a company with a prevailing ethnocentric orientation may consciously make a decision to move in the direction of geocentrism. The orientations – collectively known as the EPRG framework – are summarised in Figure 1.4.

Ethnocentrism

A person who assumes his or her home country is superior compared to the rest of the world is said to have an ethnocentric orientation. The ethnocentric orientation means company personnel see only similarities in markets and assume the products

Table 1.4 The *Fortune* Global 500: largest corporations by revenues (in € millions)

Rank 1997	Rank 1996	Company	Country	Revenues (in € millions)	Profits (in € millions)	Profitability ranking
1	1	General Motors	US	151,145	5,682	6
2	2	Ford Motor	US	130,322	5,870	5
3	3	Mitsui	Japan	121,042	227	336
4	4	Mitsubishi	Japan	109,365	329	287
5	6	Royal Dutch/Shell Group	UK/NL	108,702	6,581	3
6	5	Itochu	Japan	107,421	656	484
7	8	Exxon	US	103,814	7,177	1
8	11	Wal-Mart Stores	US	101,201	2,991	25
9	7	Marubeni	Japan	94,264	119	288
10	9	Sumitomo	Japan	86,862	177	360
11	10	Toyota Motor	Japan	80,705	3,140	21
12	12	General Electric	US	77,060	6,959	2
13	13	Nissho Iwai	Japan	69,470	20	443
14	15	Intl. Business Machines	US	66,598	5,169	8
15	14	Nippon Telegraph & Telephone	Japan	65,305	2,003	56
16	78	AXA	France	65,212	1,151	109
17	20	Daimler-Benz	Germany	60,705	3,935	12
18	24	Daewoo	South Korea	60,675	446	253
19	18	Nippon Life Insurance	Japan	60,558	1,797	62
20	21	British Petroleum	UK	60,393	3,432	16
21	16	Hitachi	Japan	58,165	24	441
22	23	Volkswagen	Germany	55,418	655	198
23	22	Matsushita Electric Industrial	Japan	54,529	646	202
24	25	Siemens	Germany	54,083	1,211	101
25	26	Chrysler	US	51,871	2,379	45

Source: 'Global 500', *Fortune*, 3 August 1998, p. F-1.

and practices that succeed in the home country will, due to their demonstrated superiority, be successful anywhere. At some companies, the ethnocentric orientation means that opportunities outside the home country are ignored. Such companies are sometimes called *domestic companies*. Ethnocentric companies that do conduct business outside the home country can be described as *international companies*; they adhere to the notion that the products succeeding in the home country are superior and, therefore, can be sold everywhere without adaptation.

In the ethnocentric, international company, foreign operations are viewed as being secondary or subordinate to domestic ones. An ethnocentric company operates under the assumption that 'tried and true' headquarters' knowledge and organisational capabilities can be applied in other parts of the world. Although this can sometimes work to a company's advantage, valuable managerial knowledge and experience in local markets may go unnoticed. For a manufacturing firm, ethnocentrism means foreign markets are viewed as a means of disposing of surplus domestic production. Plans for overseas markets are developed, utilising policies and procedures identical to those employed at home. No systematic marketing research is conducted outside the home country, and no major modifications are made to products. Even if consumer needs or wants in international markets differ from those in the home country, those differences are ignored at headquarters.

Nissan's ethnocentric orientation was quite apparent during its first few years of

Figure 1.4 **Different management orientations in the global arena – the EPRG framework**

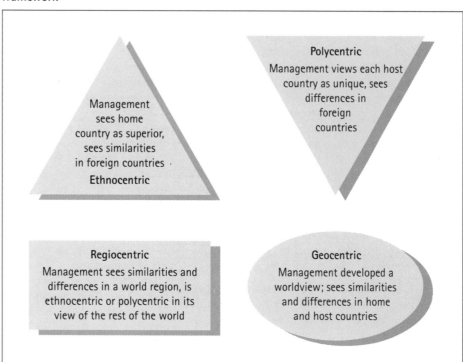

exporting cars and trucks to world markets. Designed for mild Japanese winters, the vehicles were difficult to start in many parts of the world during the cold winter months. In northern Japan, many car owners would put blankets over the hoods of their cars. Tokyo's assumption was that consumers in other countries would do the same. Until the 1980s, Eli Lilly also operated as an ethnocentric company in which activities outside the United States were tightly controlled by headquarters and focused on selling products originally developed for the US market.[16]

Fifty years ago, most business enterprises could operate quite successfully with an ethnocentric orientation. Today, however, ethnocentrism is one of the biggest internal threats a company faces.

Polycentrism

The polycentric orientation is the opposite of ethnocentrism. The term polycentric describes management's often unconscious belief or assumption that each country in which a company does business is unique. This assumption lays the groundwork for each subsidiary to develop its own unique business and marketing strategies in order to succeed; the term multinational company is often used to describe such a structure. Based on this philosophy, companies like Henkel, Unilever or international advertising agencies have served their customers world-wide extremely well. Until recently, Citicorp's financial services around the world operated on a polycentric basis. James Bailey, a Citicorp executive, offered this description of the company: 'We were like a

GLOBAL PERSPECTIVE

The global marketplace: the rest of the story

As indicated in the opening paragraph of this chapter, global marketing is practised by companies in many different countries. It was not so long ago, however, that some observers of the global scene predicted that American companies would dominate world trade. In his best-selling 1967 book, *The American Challenge*, J.J. Servan-Schreiber warned that within 15 years, American-owned companies operating in Europe, IBM and GM for example, would become the world's third greatest industrial power after the United States and the Soviet Union. He predicted dire consequences for Europe, resulting from market domination by global corporations. He wrote:

> The Americans have been reorganising their European operations. Everywhere they are setting up European-scale headquarters responsible for the firm's Continental business, with sweeping powers of decision and instructions not to pay any attention to national boundaries.

He cautioned that European industry could eventually play a secondary role to America, while Europe itself might become a mere satellite to the United States. How accurate was Servan-Schreiber's vision? For one thing, the Soviet Union has ceased to exist. Also, many companies mentioned in his book – Union Carbide, CPC International, Celanese, and American Express, as well as IBM and GM – have indeed evolved considerably since the mid-1960s. At the time Servan-Schreiber's book was written, it was characteristic of many international companies for headquarters to keep tight control over every aspect of business strategy. Today, the

way these same companies practise global marketing makes them distinctly different entities from the ones Servan-Schreiber was describing three decades ago. They have a different focus, vision, orientation, strategy, structure, operating style and communications pattern; also, their policies relating to research and development, human resources, finance, sourcing, new product development and investment have changed.

Moreover, today's global corporation, unlike the entities described by Servan-Schreiber, is not an exclusively American creation. Many industry sectors in Europe are alive and thriving. Numerous global corporations, including Nestlé, Philips, Volkswagen and Unilever, are headquartered in Europe. They have not fallen into secondary roles, as Servan-Schreiber feared. Indeed, American companies have passed the baton to the Europeans as well as the Japanese in a number of key industries. For example, Thomson, a consumer electronics company headquartered in France, now owns the GE and RCA television businesses. Today, some of the biggest competitive challenges facing both Europe and the United States come from companies located in Japan, South Korea and other Asian countries.

Food for thought

- Do companies' headquartered in Europe suffer a location disadvantage compared to US companies?
- Does location still matter in a world of e-commerce? Why are so many e-commerce companies clustered around Seattle?

Source: J.J. Servan-Schreiber, *The American Challenge* (New York: Atheneum, 1968): p. 4.

medieval state. There was the king and his court and they were in charge, right? No. It was the land barons who were in charge. The king and his court might declare this or that, but the land barons went and did their thing.'[17] Realising that the financial services industry is globalising, CEO John Reed is attempting to achieve a higher degree of integration between Citicorp's operating units. Like Jack Welch at GE, Reed is moving to instil a geocentric orientation throughout his company.

Regiocentrism and geocentrism

In a company with a regiocentric orientation, management views regions as unique and seeks to develop an integrated regional strategy. A European company, which focuses on the German speaking or Scandinavian countries and develops its marketing programmes for these regions, has a regiocentric orientation. Firms like Procter & Gamble, Volkswagen or Japanese car manufacturers pursue this regiocentric orientation. In contrast, companies with a geocentric orientation view the entire world as a potential market and strive to develop integrated world market strategies. A company whose management has a regiocentric or geocentric orientation is sometimes known as a global or transnational company.[18]

The geocentric orientation represents a synthesis of ethnocentrism and polycentrism; it is a 'worldview' that sees similarities and differences in markets and countries, and seeks to create a global strategy that is fully responsive to local needs and wants. A regiocentric manager might be said to have a worldview on a regional scale; the world outside the region of interest will be viewed with an ethnocentric or a polycentric orientation, or a combination of the two. Jack Welch's quote at the beginning of this chapter that 'globalisation must be taken for granted' implies that at least some company managers must have a geocentric orientation. However, recent research suggests that many companies are seeking to strengthen their regional competitiveness rather than moving directly to develop global responses to changes in the competitive environment.[19]

Key points	
	• Management's explicit and implicit assumptions and attitudes influence a firm's international activities and thus its success in the global arena.
	• The EPRG framework outlines the different management orientations.
	• Depending on the managerial orientation, international activities differ considerably. When a firm displays an ethnocentric orientation, it considers the home market as core business area and international markets are of less importance. On the other end of the continuum, geocentric organisations are globally active firms which perceive their home market as one among many.

The ethnocentric company is centralised in its marketing management, the polycentric company is decentralised, and the regiocentric and geocentric companies are integrated on a regional and global scale, respectively. A crucial difference between the orientations is the underlying assumption for each. The ethnocentric orientation is based on a belief in home-country superiority. The underlying assumption of the polycentric approach is that there are so many differences in cultural, economic and marketing conditions in the world that it is impossible and futile to attempt to transfer experience across national boundaries.

DRIVING AND RESTRAINING FACTORS ON GLOBAL MARKETING

The remarkable growth of the global economy over the past 50 years has been shaped by the dynamic interplay of various driving and restraining forces. During most of those decades, companies from different parts of the world in different industries achieved great success by pursuing international, multinational, or global strategies. During the 1990s, changes in the business environment have presented a number of challenges to established ways of doing business. Today, the growing importance of global marketing stems from the fact that driving forces have more momentum than the restraining forces. The forces affecting global integration are shown in Figure 1.5.

Figure 1.5 **Driving and restraining forces on global integration**

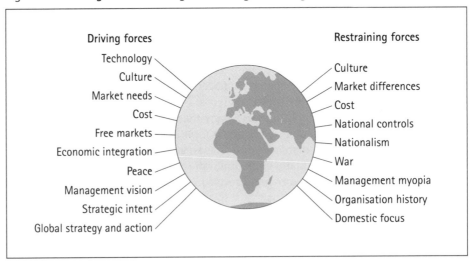

Driving forces
Technology
Culture
Market needs
Cost
Free markets
Economic integration
Peace
Management vision
Strategic intent
Global strategy and action

Restraining forces
Culture
Market differences
Cost
National controls
Nationalism
War
Management myopia
Organisation history
Domestic focus

EUROPEAN FOCUS

A change in pattern

Quick reactions were needed at Stoll, Europe's largest manufacturer of machinery and equipment to produce knitwear. The German company was facing increasing competition from Asian competitors. The Japanese firm Shima Seiki was targeting the European market to sell its products to the fashion industry.

In contrast to Stoll, which is a well-established, traditional and family-owned business, Shima was founded only in 1962 and produced its first machine to manufacture knitwear in 1978. Its sophisticated electronic control allowed Shima a rapid entrance in European markets. Stoll was hit particularly hard, as 90 per cent of its total sales was based on exporting and here mainly within Europe.

At Stoll, the management reacted quickly: all company areas were scrutinised for potential improvement. The results were remarkable: productivity doubled, R&D investments were significantly increased. In the meantime, the company employs ten times more software engineers than previously in order to optimise the electronic control of its machinery.

The markets responded extremely positively. To provide the capital necessary for expansion, Stoll now considers a listing at the stock exchange.

Source: Peter Marsh, 'Changing the pattern', *Financial Times*, 12 July 1999, p. 8.

FT

Driving factors

Converging market needs and wants, technology advances, pressure to cut costs, pressure to improve quality, improvements in communication and transportation technology, global economic growth, and opportunities for leverage all represent important driving forces; any industry subject to these forces is a candidate for globalisation.

Technology

Technology is a universal factor that crosses national and cultural boundaries. Technology is truly 'stateless'; there are no cultural boundaries limiting its application. Once a technology is developed, it soon becomes available everywhere in the world. This phenomenon supports Levitt's prediction concerning the emergence of global markets for standardised products. In his landmark *Harvard Business Review* article, Levitt anticipated the communication revolution that has, in fact, become a driving force behind global marketing.[20] Satellite dishes, globe-spanning TV networks such as CNN and MTV, and the Internet are just a few of the technological factors underlying the emergence of a true global village. In regional markets such as Europe, the increasing overlap of advertising across national boundaries and the mobility of consumers have created opportunities for marketers to pursue pan-European product positioning.

Regional economic agreements

A number of multilateral trade agreements have accelerated the pace of global integration. The *North American Free Trade Agreement* (NAFTA) as well as the treaties uniting European countries to the *European Union* (EU) have intensified trade relations in these regions. The *World Trade Organization* (WTO) aims to promote and protect free trade. The rules and regulations created by the WTO, which was ratified by more than 120 nations, is largely based on the *General Agreement on Tariffs and Trade* (GATT). Its rules govern the international exchange of products and services.[21]

Market needs and wants

A person studying markets around the world will discover cultural universals as well as cultural differences. The common elements in human nature provide an underlying basis for the opportunity to create and serve global markets. The word *create* is deliberate. Most global markets do not exist in nature. They must be created by marketing effort. For example, no one needs soft drinks, and yet today, in some countries, per capita soft drink consumption exceeds the consumption of water. Marketing has driven this change in behaviour, and today the soft drink industry is a truly global one. Evidence is mounting that consumer needs and wants around the world are converging today as never before. This creates an opportunity for global marketing. Multinational companies pursuing strategies of product adaptation run the risk of falling victim to global competitors that have recognised opportunities to serve global customers.

Marlboro is an example of an enormously successful global brand. Targeted at urban smokers around the world, the brand appeals to the spirit of freedom, independence, and open space symbolised by the image of the cowboy in beautiful, open western settings. The need addressed by Marlboro is universal, and the basic appeal and execution of its advertising and positioning are global. Philip Morris, which markets Marlboro, is a global company that discovered years ago how the same basic market need can be met with a global approach.

Transportation and communication improvements

The time and cost barriers associated with distance have fallen tremendously over the past 100 years. The jet airplane revolutionised communication by making it possible for people to travel around the world in less than 48 hours. Tourism enables people from many countries to see and experience the newest products being sold abroad. One essential characteristic of the effective global business is face-to-face communication, among employees and between the company and its customers. Without modern jet travel, such communication would be difficult to sustain. Modern communication technologies such as e-mail, fax and video teleconferencing allow managers, executives and customers to link up electronically from virtually any part of the world for a fraction of the cost of air travel.

A similar revolution has occurred in transportation technology. Physical distribution has declined in terms of cost; the time required for shipment has been greatly reduced as well. A letter from China to New York is now delivered in eight days – faster than domestic mail is delivered within many countries. The per-unit cost of shipping automobiles from Japan and Korea to the United States by specially designed auto-transport ships is less than the cost of overland shipping from Detroit to either US coast.

Product development costs

The pressure for globalisation is intense when new products require major investments and long periods of development time. The pharmaceutical industry provides a striking illustration of this driving force. While the cost of developing a new drug in 1976 was €46 million; by 1982, the cost had increased to €74 million. By 1993, the cost of developing a new drug had reached €305 million.[22] Such costs must be recovered in the global marketplace, as no single national market is likely to be large enough to support investments of this size. In the pharmaceutical industry, 75 per cent of sales are generated in seven countries.

Quality

Global marketing strategies can generate greater revenue and greater operating margins which, in turn, support design and manufacturing quality. A global and a domestic company may each spend 5 per cent of sales on research and development, but the global company may have many times the total revenue of the domestic because it serves the world market. It is easy to understand how Nissan, Matsushita, Caterpillar and other global companies can achieve world-class quality. Global companies 'raise the bar' for all competitors in an industry. When a global company establishes a benchmark in quality, competitors must quickly make their own improvements and come up to par. Global competition has forced all companies to improve quality. For truly global products, uniformity can drive down research, engineering, design and production costs across business functions. Quality, uniformity, and cost reduction were all driving forces behind Ford's development of its 'World Car', which is sold in the United States as the Ford Contour and Mercury Mystique and in Europe as the Mondeo.

Morocutti goes global

Since 1928, the Viennese family-owned business Morocutti has earned its money from a broad product range of cutlery and scissors. Its showroom in the 23rd district of Vienna offers a wide variety of products which may be bought on the spot. What's special about it? Basically not much; Morocutti's business is based on traditional and rare craftsmanship, employing four people – all family.

But since the last three years, things have never been the same! With its homepage on the Web, Morocutti's range of cutlery and scissors is available by mouseclick not only in Vienna, but around the world. And customers take advantage of it!

US customers in particular order heavily, to a large extent buying quality knives from Germany and Switzerland. European consumers are more interested in imitations of historic sabres and swords, such as those carried by Robin Hood, in *Excalibur* or by Samurai fighters – well-known from numerous Hollywood productions.

Meanwhile, the homepage contains everything related to cutting. The only item that customers will search for in vain are knives from the time of the Third Reich. And new things are coming up: plans to quote prices on the Web not only in

Euro, but in the home currency of the customer are well advanced. It goes without saying that these prices contain respective taxes and transportation costs.

Potential business partners are lured with a special incentive: if they set a link on their homepage to Morocutti's website, they are rewarded with a sales commission for every deal arising from this arrangement. This idea contributed significantly to Amazon.com's world-wide success.

The result: sales have increased by 400 per cent within three years – with a dramatically increasing trend!

P.S. In case you have always wanted a real Highlander sword (72 cm in length, with a grip of artificial ivory), this is the place to shop: http://www.knifeshop.com/!

Food for thought
- What problems might be caused by Morocutti's rapid international expansion?
- What risks and opportunities does the Internet offer for small firms like Morocutti that want to use e-commerce on a basis for their international expansion?

Source: Monika Bachhofer, 'Alle reden vom Internet, aber nur wenig tun es wirklich', *Der Standard*, 17/18 July 1999, p. 28.

World economic trends

There are three reasons why economic growth has been a driving force in the expansion of the international economy and the growth of global marketing. First, growth has created market opportunities that provide a major incentive for companies to expand globally. At the same time, slow growth in a company's domestic market can signal the need to look abroad for opportunities in nations or regions with high rates of growth.

Second, economic growth has reduced resistance that might otherwise have developed in response to the entry of foreign firms into domestic economies. When a country is growing rapidly, policy makers are likely to look favourably on outsiders. A growing country means growing markets; there is often plenty of opportunity for everyone. It is possible for a 'foreign' company to enter a domestic economy and to establish itself without taking business away from local firms. Without economic growth, global enterprises may take business away from domestic ones. Domestic businesses are more likely to seek governmental intervention to protect their local position if markets are not growing. Predictably, the world-wide recession of the early

1990s created pressure in most countries to limit access by foreigners to domestic markets.

The world-wide movement toward deregulation and privatisation is another driving force. The trend toward privatisation is opening up formerly closed markets; tremendous opportunities are being created as a result. For example, when a nation's telephone company is a state monopoly, it is much easier to require it to buy only from national companies. An independent, private company will be more inclined to look for the best offer, regardless of the nationality of the supplier. Privatisation of telephone systems around the world is creating opportunities and threats for every company in the industry.

Leverage

A global company possesses the unique opportunity to develop leverage. Leverage is simply some type of advantage that a company enjoys by virtue of the fact that it conducts business in more than one country. Four important types of leverage are experience transfers, scale economies, resource utilisation and global strategy.

Experience transfers. A global company can leverage its experience in any market in the world. It can draw on management practices, strategies, products, advertising appeals, or sales or promotional ideas that have been tested in actual markets and apply them in other comparable markets.

For example, Sweden's Asea Brown Boveri (ABB), a company with 1,300 operating subsidiaries in 140 countries, has considerable experience with a well-tested management model that it transfers across national boundaries. The Zurich-based company knows that a company's headquarters can be run with a lean staff. When ABB acquired a Finnish company, it reduced the headquarters staff from 880 to 25 between 1986 and 1989. Headquarters staff at a German unit was reduced from 1,600 to 100 between 1988 and 1989. After acquiring Combustion Engineering (an American company producing power plant boilers), ABB knew from experience that the headquarters staff of 800 could be drastically reduced, in spite of the fact that CE had a justification for every one of the headquarters staff positions.

Scale economies. The global company can take advantage of its greater manufacturing volume to obtain traditional scale advantages within a single factory. Also, finished products can be produced by combining components manufactured in scale-efficient plants in different countries. Matsushita Electric Company is a classic example of global marketing; it achieved scale economies by exporting video cassette recorders (VCRs), televisions, and other consumer electronics products throughout the world from world-scale factories in Japan. The importance of manufacturing scale has diminished somewhat as companies implement flexible manufacturing techniques and invest in factories outside the home country. However, scale economies were a cornerstone of Japanese success in the 1970s and 1980s.

Leverage from scale economies is not limited to manufacturing. Just as a domestic company can achieve economies in staffing by eliminating duplicate positions after an acquisition, a global company can achieve the same economies on a global scale by centralising functional activities. The larger scale of the global company also creates opportunities to improve corporate staff competence and quality.

Resource utilisation. A major strength of the global company is its ability to scan the entire world to identify people, money, and raw materials that will enable it to compete most effectively in world markets. This is equally true for established companies and start-ups. For example, the British Biotechnology Group, founded in 1986, raised €42.4 million from investors in the United States, Japan and Great Britain. For a global company, it is not problematic if the value of the 'home' currency rises or falls dramatically, because for this company there really is no such thing as a home currency. The world is full of currencies, and a global company seeks financial resources on the best available terms. In turn, it uses them where there is the greatest opportunity to serve a need at a profit.

Global strategy. The global company's greatest single advantage can be its global strategy. A global strategy is built on an information system that scans the world business environment to identify opportunities, trends, threats, and resources. When opportunities are identified, the global company adheres to the principles identified above: it leverages its skills and focuses its resources to create superior perceived value for customers and achieve competitive advantage. The global strategy also offers opportunities to proactively defend markets from competitors' aggressive market entry strategies or activities. Financial resources generated in one part of the world may be used to subsidise other markets. In the early 1970s, the French tyre manufacturer Michelin used profits generated in the European markets to attack Good Year in its home market, the US. This cross-subsidisation may not be confused with dumping, as products in this case are not sold below the price level on the home market. Cross-subsidisation rather allows a company to support markets financially, where competition is particularly fierce.[23]

The global/transnational corporation

The global/transnational corporation, or any business enterprise that pursues global business objectives by relating world resources to world market opportunities, is the organisation that has responded to the driving, restraining and underlying forces in the world. In its activities, the globally active firm has to take into account the extensive regulatory framework developed by international organisations and associations. Moreover, these global corporations have learned to operate within international financial frameworks and to take advantage of the expanding communication technologies in pursuing market opportunities and serving needs and wants on a global scale. The global enterprise has both responded to market opportunity and competitive threat by going global and at the same time has been one of the forces driving the world toward greater globalisation.

Restraining forces

Despite the impact of the driving forces identified above, several restraining forces may slow a company's efforts to engage in global marketing. Three important restraining forces are management myopia, an ethnocentric organisational culture, and national controls. As we have noted, however, in today's world the driving forces predominate over the restraining forces. That is why the importance of global marketing is steadily growing.

Management myopia and ethnocentric organisational culture

In many cases, management simply ignores opportunities to pursue global marketing. A company that is 'nearsighted' and ethnocentric will not expand geographically.

Myopia is also a recipe for market disaster if headquarters attempts to dictate when it should listen. Global marketing does not work without a strong local team that can provide information about local market conditions. Executives at Parker Pen once attempted to implement a top-down marketing strategy that ignored experience gained by local market representatives. Costly market failures resulted in Parker's buyout by managers of the former UK subsidiary. Eventually, the Gillette Company acquired Parker.

In companies in which subsidiary management 'knows it all', there is no room for vision from the top. In companies in which headquarters management is all-knowing, there is no room for local initiative or an in-depth knowledge of local needs and conditions. Executives and managers at successful global companies have learned how to integrate global vision and perspective with local market initiative and input. A striking theme emerged during interviews conducted by one of the authors with executives of successful global companies. Global success can be positively reinforced by a respect for local initiative and input by headquarters executives, and the corresponding respect for headquarters' vision by local executives.

National controls and barriers

Every country protects local enterprise and interests by maintaining control over market access and entry in both low and high-tech industries. Such control ranges from a monopoly controlling access to tobacco markets to national government control of broadcast, equipment, and data transmission markets. Today, tariff barriers have been largely removed in the high-income countries, thanks to the World Trade Organization (WTO), NAFTA, and other economic agreements. However, non-tariff barriers (NTBs) still make it more difficult for outside companies to succeed in foreign markets. The only way global companies can overcome these barriers is to become 'insiders' in every country in which they do business. For example, utility companies in France are notorious for accepting bids from foreign equipment suppliers but, in the end, favouring national suppliers when awarding contracts. Thorough preparation and continuous relationships with official authorities may help to circumvent these trade barriers.

Key points	
	• Activities in the global market arena are shaped by driving and restraining forces.
	• Among the forces driving globalisation are technology, such as globe-spanning TV networks or the Internet, regional economic integration, e.g. within NAFTA or the European Union, and globally converging consumption patterns. Transportation and communication improvements, increasing product development costs, world quality standards and global integration also foster the emerging of transnational/global companies.
	• On the other hand, there are factors which inhibit global economic activities. A management's nearsighted, ethnocentric vision of how business should be conducted, limits its expansion towards global markets. The focus on the home market neglects business opportunities abroad. National controls and barriers, which are imposed to protect local and national industries, are external restraining forces.

Summary

Global marketing is the process of focusing the resources and objectives of a company on global marketing opportunities. Companies engage in global marketing for two reasons: to take advantage of opportunities for growth and expansion, and to survive. Companies that fail to pursue global opportunities are likely to eventually lose their domestic markets because they will be pushed aside by stronger and more competitive global firms. This book presents the theory and practice of applying the universal discipline of marketing to the global opportunities found in world markets.

The basic goals of marketing are to create customer value and competitive advantage by maintaining focus. Company management can be classified in terms of its orientation toward the world: ethnocentric, polycentric, regiocentric and geocentric. An ethnocentric orientation characterises domestic and international companies; international companies pursue marketing opportunities outside the home market by extending various elements of the marketing mix. A polycentric worldview predominates at a multinational company, where the marketing mix is adapted by country managers operating autonomously. Managers at global and transnational companies are regiocentric or geocentric in their orientation and pursue both extension and adaptation strategies in global markets.

Global marketing's importance today is shaped by the dynamic interplay of several driving and restraining forces. The former include market needs and wants, technology, transportation improvements, costs, quality, global peace, world economic growth and a recognition of opportunities to develop leverage by operating globally. Restraining forces include market differences, management myopia, ethnocentric organisational culture, and national controls.

Concepts and definitions

Global marketing Deals with the development of the marketing programme for the global market. The co-ordination and integration of these marketing activities is carried out simultaneously in multiple international markets.

The EPRG framework The management orientation influences the way in which companies approach international markets. The EPRG framework outlines different patterns of management orientation and their impact on global marketing activities.

- *Ethnocentrism*: international business relations are of low priority. Marketing approaches which have proven successful in the home market are transferred unchanged to other countries.
- *Polycentrism*: every country market is unique and this needs to be taken into account. Marketing activities are conceptualised and implemented autonomously in different country markets.
- *Regiocentrism*: regions are considered as entity. Consequently, an integrated regional strategy is developed and implemented.
- *Geocentrism*: the world is considered an entire market. Companies aim at developing a global strategy which fulfils local needs and wants at the same time.

Factors supporting or inhibiting global marketing *Positive influences*
- Technology
- Regional economic agreements
- Market needs and wants

29

- Transportation and communication improvements
- Costs of product development
- Quality
- Global economic trends
- Leverage
- The global/transnational company

Negative influences

- Management myopia and home market-oriented organisational culture
- Country-specific regulations and barriers

Discussion questions

1 What are the basic goals of marketing? Are these goals relevant to global marketing?

2 What is meant by global localisation? Is Coca-Cola a global product? Explain.

3 Describe some of the global marketing strategies available to companies. Give examples of companies using the different strategies.

4 How do the global marketing strategies of Harley-Davidson and Toyota differ?

5 Describe the difference between ethnocentric, polycentric, regiocentric, and geocentric management orientations.

6 Identify and briefly describe some of the forces that have resulted in increased global integration and the growing importance of global marketing.

7 Define leverage, and explain the different types of leverage utilised by companies with global operations.

Webmistress's hotspots

Homepage of McDonald's
Ready for the latest news from 'Mac-Country'? Here you will find an update!
http://www.mcdonalds.com

Homepage of Hennes & Mauritz
Summer is here – so get dressed in swimwear from Hennes & Mauritz.
http://www.hm.com/

Homepage of Coca-Cola
... looking for some place cool!   http://www.coca-cola.com/

Homepage of Morocutti
The Highlander-sword – check it out!   http://www.knifeshop.com/

Exchange rate of EU currencies to the €
Here you will find the fixed exchange rates between the € and all currencies in the EU.   http://www.europa.eu.int/eurobirth/rates.html

The Fortune 'Global 500'
If you want to check which company is leading the 'Global 500'.
http://cgi.pathfinder.com/fortune/fortune500/

Suggested readings

Bannister, Geoffrey, C.A. Primo Braga and Joe Petry, 'Transnational corporations, the neo-liberal agenda and regional integration: Establishing a policy framework', *Quarterly Review of Economics & Finance*, 34, Summer (1994): pp. 77–99.

Barnet, Richard J. and John Cavanagh, *Global Dreams: Imperial Corporations and the New World Order*. New York: Simon & Schuster, 1994.

Bassiry, G.R. and R.H. Dekmejian, 'America's global companies: A leadership profile', *Business Horizons*, 36, 1 (January–February) (1993): pp. 47–53.

Collins, Robert S. and William A. Fischer, 'American manufacturing competitiveness: the view from Europe', *Business Horizons*, 35, July–August (1992): pp. 15–23.

Doz, Yves L. and K. Asakawa, *The Metanational Corporation*. Fontainebleau: INSEAD, 1997.

Franko, Lawrence G., 'Global corporate competition II: Is the large American firm an endangered species?', *Business Horizons*, 34, November–December (1991): pp. 14–22.

Halal, William E., 'Global strategic management in a new world order', *Business Horizons*, 36, November–December (1993): pp. 5–10.

Hu, Tao-Su, 'Global or stateless corporations are national firms with international operations', *California Management Review*, 34, 2 (1992): pp. 107–126.

Johansson, J.K. and I. Nonaka, *Relentless, The Japanese Way of Marketing*. New York: Harper Business, 1997.

Khanna, T. and K. Palepu, 'Why focused strategies may be wrong for emerging markets', *Harvard Business Review*, 75, 4 (1997): pp. 41–51.

Kogut, Bruce and Udo Zander, 'Knowledge of the firm and the evolution of the multinational corporation', *Journal of International Business Studies*, 26, 2 (1993): pp. 625–646.

Li, Jiatao and Stephen Guisinger, 'How well do foreign firms compete in the United States', *Business Horizons*, 34 (1991): pp. 49–53.

Malnight, T.W., 'Globalization of an ethnocentric firm: an evolutionary perspective', *Strategic Management Journal*, 16, 2 (1995): p. 125.

McHardy Reid, David, 'Perspectives for international marketers on the Japanese market', *Journal of International Marketing*, 3, 1 (1995): p. 74.

Miles, Gregory L., 'Tailoring a global product', *International Business*, March (1995): p. 50.

Miller, L.K., *Transnational Corporations: A Selective Bibliography*. New York: United Nations, 1992.

Morrison, Allen, David A. Ricks and Kendall Roth, 'Globalization versus regionalization: which way for the multinational?', *Organizational Dynamics*, 13, 3 (1991): pp. 17–29.

Ohmae, Kenichi, *The End of the Nation State: The Rise of Regional Economies*. New York: Free Press, 1995.

Rao, T.R., and G.M. Naidu, 'Are the stages of internationalization empirically supportable', *Journal of Global Marketing*, 1, 2 (1992): pp. 147–170.

Reich, Robert, B., *The Work of Nations*. New York: Vintage Books, 1992.

Smith, Paul M. and Cynthia D. West, 'The globalization of furniture industries/markets', *Journal of Global Marketing*, 7, 3 (1994): pp. 103–132.

Stahl, M.J. and Bounds, G.M., *Competing Globally Through Customer Value: The Management of Strategic Suprasystems*. Westport: Quorum Books, 1991.

Tahija, Julius, 'Swapping business skills for oil', *Harvard Business Review*, 71, 5 (1993): pp. 64–77.

Tiglao, Rigoberto, 'Is this the next Nestlé', *Far Eastern Economic Review*, 30 December 1993, pp. 54–55.

Wendt, Henry, *Global Embrace: Corporate Challenges in a Transnational World*. New York: Harper Business, 1993.

Yip, George S., 'Global strategy as a factor in Japanese success', *The International Executive*, 38, 1 (1996): pp. 145–167.

Notes

1. Peter Stippel, 'Stakeholder value: Kunde schlägt Shareholder', *Absatzwirtschaft*, 4 (1998): pp. 14–17.
2. David A. Collier, 'New marketing mix stresses service,' *Journal of Business Strategy*, 12, 2 (1991): pp. 42–45. Mohammed Rafiq and Pervaiz K. Ahmed, 'Using the 7Ps as a generic marketing mix: an exploratory survey of UK and European marketing academics', *Marketing Intelligence & Planning*, 13, 9 (1995): pp. 4–15. Valarie A. Zeithaml and Mary Jo Bitner, *Services Marketing* (New York: McGraw-Hill, 1996).
3. David Aaker, *Strategic Market Management* (New York: Wiley & Sons, 1995).
4. John Kay, *Foundations of Corporate Success* (New York: Oxford University Press, 1993).
5. Hermann Simon, *Die heimlichen Gewinner* (Frankfurt: Campus Verlag, 1996), p. 62.
6. Hermann Herunter, 'Frequentis: Spitzenleistungen aus Wien', *Trend*, 1999, pp. 74-75. 'Frequentis peilt US-Markt an', *Der Standard*, 19 February 1999.
7. 'Alloy formation', *Footwear News*, 8 March 1999, pp. 14ff. 'Donatella de Paris', *Women's Wear Daily*, 16 July 1998, pp. 4ff.
8. Interview with Raymond Viault, Vice Chairman of General Mills, Inc.

9. Theodore Levitt, 'The globalization of markets', *Harvard Business Review*, May–June (1983): p. 92.

10. Joanne Lipman, 'Ad fad: Marketers turn sour on global sales pitch Harvard guru makes', *The Wall Street Journal*, 12 May 1988, p. 1.

11. David McHardy Reid, 'Perspectives for international marketers on the Japanese Market', *Journal of International Marketing*, 3, 1 (1995): p. 74.

12. John A. Quelch and Edward J. Hoff, 'Customizing global marketing,' *Harvard Business Review*, May–June (1986): p. 59.

13. Gregory L. Miles, 'Tailoring a global product', *International Business*, March (1995): p. 50.

14. As quoted in 'Global Mall', *The Wall Street Journal*, 7 May 1998, p. 1.

15. Adapted from Howard Perlmutter, 'The torturous evolution of the multinational corporation', *Columbia Journal of World Business*, January–February (1969): pp. 9–18.

16. T.W. Malnight, 'Globalization of an ethnocentric firm: an evolutionary perspective', *Strategic Management Journal*, 16, 2 (1995): p. 125.

17. Saul Hansell, 'Uniting the feudal lords at Citicorp', *The New York Times*, 16 January 1994, p. 3-1.

18. Although the definitions provided here are important, to avoid confusion we will use the term *global marketing* when describing the general activities of global companies. Another note of caution is in order. Usage of the terms *international*, *multinational* and *global* varies widely. Alert readers of the business press are likely to recognise inconsistencies: usage does not always reflect the definitions provided here. In particular, companies that are (in the view of the authors as well as numerous other academics) *global* are often described as *multinational enterprises* (abbreviated MNE) or *multinational corporations* (abbreviated MNC). The United Nations prefers the term *transnational* company rather than *global* company. When we refer to an *international* company or a *multinational*, we will do so in a way that maintains the distinctions described in the text.

19. Allen Morrison, David A. Ricks, and Kendall Roth, 'Globalization versus regionalization: which way for the multinational?', *Organizational Dynamics*, 13, 3 (1991): pp. 17–29.

20. Theodore Levitt, 'The globalization of markets', *Harvard Business Review*, May–June (1983): p. 92.

21. http://www.wto.org/wto/inbrief/ (cited 14 July 1999).

22. T.W. Malnight, 'Globalization of an ethnocentric firm: an evolutionary perspective', *Strategic Management Journal*, 16, 2 (1995): p. 125.

23. Gary Hamel and C.K. Prahalad, 'Do you really have a global strategy', *Harvard Business Review*, July–August (1985): pp. 139–148. David Aaker, *Strategic Market Management* (New York: Wiley & Sons, 1995).

Which company is transnational?

Four senior executives of companies operating in many countries speak:

COMPANY A

We are a transnational company. We sell our products in over 80 countries, and we manufacture in 14 countries. Our overseas subsidiaries manage our business in their respective countries. They have complete responsibility for their country operations including strategy formulation. Most of the key executives in our subsidiaries are host-country nationals, although we still rely on home-country persons for the CEO and often the CFO (chief financial officer) slots. Recently, we have divided the world into world regions and the United States. Each of the world regions reports to our world trade organisation, which is responsible for all of our business outside the United States.

The overseas companies are responsible for adapting to the unique market preferences that exist in their country or region and are quite autonomous. We are proud of our international reach: we manufacture not only in the United States but also in Europe and the United Kingdom, Latin America and Australia.

We have done very well in overseas markets, especially in the high-income countries with the exception of Japan. We would like to enter the Japanese market, but let's face it, Japan is a protected country. There is no level playing field, and as you no doubt know, the Japanese have taken advantage of the protection they enjoy in their home country to launch an export drive that has been a curse for us. Our industry and our home country (the United States) has been a principal target of the Japanese, who have taken a real bite out of our market share here in the United States. We are currently lobbying for more protection from Japanese competition.

COMPANY B

We are a unique transnational media company. We do not dominate any particular area, but we have an important presence on three continents in magazines, newspapers and television. We have a global strategy. We are a global communications and entertainment company. We're in the business of informing people around the world on the widest possible basis. We know how to serve the needs of our customers who are readers, viewers and advertisers. We transfer people and money across national boundaries, and we know how to acquire and integrate properties as well as how to start up a new business. We started out as Australian, and then the weight of our effort shifted to the United Kingdom and today our main effort is in the United States. We go where the opportunity is because we are market driven.

Sure, there are lots of Australians in the top management of this company, but we started in Australia, and those Aussies know our business and the company from the ground up. Look around and you'll see more and more Americans and Brits taking the top jobs. We stick to English because I don't believe that we could really succeed in foreign print or broadcast. We know English, and so far the English-speaking world is big enough for us. The world is shrinking faster than we all realise, and to be in communications is to be at the centre of all change. That's the excitement of what we're doing and also the importance.

COMPANY C

We are a transnational company. We are committed to being the number-one company in our industry world-wide. Currently we still do all of our manufacturing in our home country because we have been able to achieve the lowest cost and the highest quality in the world by keeping all engineering and manufacturing in one location. However, the constantly rising value of our home currency is forcing us to invest in overseas manufacturing in order to maintain our cost advantage. We are doing this reluctantly but we believe that the essence of being global is dominating markets and we plan to do whatever we must do in order to maintain our position of leadership.

It is true that all of our senior managers at home and in most of our foreign markets are home-country nationals. We feel more comfortable with our own nationals in key jobs because they speak our language and they understand the history and the culture of our company and our country. It would be difficult for an outsider to have this knowledge, which is so important to smooth-working relationships.

COMPANY D

We are a transnational company. We have 24 nationalities represented on our headquarters staff, we manufacture in 28 countries, we market in 92 countries, and we are committed to leadership in our industry. It is true that we are backing off on our commitment to develop business in the Third World. We have found it extremely difficult to increase sales and earnings in the Third World, and we have been criticised for our aggressive marketing in these countries. It is also true that only home-country nationals may own voting shares in our company. So, even though we are global, we do have a home and a history and we respect the traditions and sensibilities of our home country.

We want to maintain our number-one position in Europe, and over time achieve the same position of leadership in our target markets in North America and Japan. We are also keeping a close eye on the developing countries of the world, and whenever we see a country making the move from low income to lower middle, or from lower middle to upper middle, or from upper middle to high income we commit our best effort to expand our positions, or, if we don't have a position, to establish a position. Since our objective is to achieve an undisputed leadership position in our industry, we simply cannot afford not to be in every growing market in the world.

We have always had a European CEO, and this will probably not change. The executives in this company from Europe tend to serve all over the world, whereas the executives from the United States and Japan serve only in their home countries. They are very able and valuable executives, but they lack the necessary perspective of the world required for the top jobs here at headquarters.

Discussion questions

1 Which company is transnational?

2 What are the attributes of a transnational company?

3 What is the difference between a domestic, international, multinational, global and transnational company?

4 What stage of development is your company and your line of business at today? Where should you be?

PART II

The global marketing environment

2 Economic environment

3 Social and cultural environments

4 The political, legal and regulatory environments of global marketing

5 Information technology environment

Part II Cases

CHAPTER 2

Economic environment

Economic co-operation works best, if one knows how the partner lives, thinks and talks.
RICHARD VON WEIZSÄCKER

After reading this chapter, you will know:

- The main differences between economic systems found around the globe.
- Ways of classifying countries by their market development.
- How to gain an understanding of consumption patterns in different countries.
- The most important elements of a country's balance of payments.
- The development and structure of world trade patterns.
- The impact of regional political and economic systems on trade and investment.
- The main regional economic co-operation agreements.

Why is this important? Here are three situations in which you would need an understanding of the above issues:

- You need to analyse countries or regions to find out whether they represent promising markets for your products or services.
- You need to assess the pros and cons of establishing a sales subsidiary in a country with a different economic system.
- You need to decide whether the balance of payment situation of a country might make it difficult to transfer profits from manufacturing in this country back to your home country.

Practice link

For many of us, life in countries suffering under severe economic difficulties is hard to imagine. Reporting on some lucrative oil deals the Azerbaijanien government made with companies planning to drill in the Caspian Sea, *The Economist* provides the following account of the conditions in the country:[1]

> About half the country's 7m people life below the poverty line. Some 850,000 of them are refugees, most as a result of a war over disputed, Armenian-populated mountain territory of Nagorno-Karabakh, which belongs to Azerbaijan in international law but was conquered three years ago by neighbouring Armenia. State salaries and pensions are pitifully low. Around a quarter of Azeris have no job. Farmers barely scratch a living.
>
> The economy all but collapsed after the Soviet Union broke up in 1991. Roads and railways are rotten. Outside Baku, electricity and gas supplies are patchy at best. Baku itself frequently runs out of water, despite the snow-capped Caucasus mountains a couple of hours drive to the north-west. Most of last winter the country's second city, Ganje, had to make do with only two hours electricity a day. Hundreds of factories across the land have ground to a halt.
>
> Local businessmen trying to get going in the post-communist era are hamstrung by corruption and red tape. Despite its boomtown tag, Baku still has only two passable hotels. It boasts just one foreign bank. Large foreign firms, including accountants such as Arthur Andersen and KPMG, wait months to get licences.

This chapter will identify the most salient characteristics of the economic environment to provide the framework for further considerations of the elements of a global marketing programme. Following a discussion of different economic systems, stages of market development, trade patterns, and other important issues of the economic environment, the chapter closes with a look at regionalisation of markets.

THE WORLD ECONOMY – AN OVERVIEW

Although most of us would not relish the idea of living in conditions similar to ones described in the above excerpt of *The Economist*, it is often precisely these countries that offer the most promising business opportunities. Indeed, the fastest growing markets, as we shall see, are in countries at the early stages of their economic development. Today, in contrast to any previous time in the history of the world, economic growth is not confined to high income countries. For the first time in the history of global marketing, markets in every region of the world are potential targets for almost every company from high tech to low tech, across the spectrum of products from basic to luxury. The economic dimensions of this world market environment are therefore of vital importance when considering the elements of a global marketing programme.

During the last 50 years, the world economy has changed profoundly.[2] Perhaps the most fundamental change is the emergence of global markets; responding to new opportunities, global competitors have steadily displaced local ones. Concurrently, the integration of the world economy has increased significantly. Economic integration stood at 10 per cent at the beginning of the 20th century; today, it is approximately 50 per cent. Integration is particularly striking in two regions, the European Union and the North American Free Trade Area. Below, this chapter focuses on the regionalisation of markets in depth.

Just 25 years ago, the world was far less integrated than it is today.[3] Take the car industry as an example: European cars, such as Renault, Citroen, Peugeot, Morris, Volvo and others were radically different from the American Chevrolet, Ford or Plymouth, or Japanese models from Toyota or Nissan. These were local cars built by local companies, mostly destined for local or regional markets. Today, the world car is a reality for Toyota, Nissan, Honda and Ford. Product changes reflect organisational changes as well: the world's largest car producers have, for the most part, evolved into global companies. And transatlantic megamergers such as that between Daimler Benz and Chrysler suggest that the globalisation of the industry is still ongoing.

Within the past decade, further remarkable changes in the world economy took place that hold important implications for business. A lot of these changes are dramatic and paradigmatic in nature and are closely linked to advances in information and communication technology. These developments are discussed in a separate chapter. Here, four of the new realities of the world economy are highlighted:

- Capital movements rather than trade have become the driving force of the world economy.
- Production has become 'uncoupled' from employment.
- The world economy dominates the scene. The macroeconomics of individual countries no longer control economic outcomes.
- The 75-year struggle between capitalism and socialism is over.

Focusing on the first point, a comparison of the volume of capital movements with the dollar value of world trade provides an interesting perspective. Trade in goods and services is running at roughly €3.4 trillion per year, a value greater than ever before in history. In comparison, the London Eurodollar market alone turns over €340 billion each working day.[4] That totals €85 trillion per year – 25 times the monetary value of world trade. In addition, foreign exchange transactions are running at approximately €0.85 trillion per day world-wide, which is €212 trillion per year – 40 times the volume of world trade in goods and services.[5] There is an inescapable conclusion in these data: global capital movements far exceed the volume of global merchandise and services trade. This explains, for example, the bizarre combination of US trade deficits and a continually rising dollar. Previously, when a country ran a deficit on its trade accounts, its currency would depreciate in value. Today, it is capital movements and trade that determine currency value.

The second change concerns the relationship between productivity and employment. Although total employment in Europe has remained more or less steady, productivity has grown substantially stronger than in the US over the last 35 years. A comparison with the US (Figures 2.1 and 2.2) is striking. In Europe, most productivity gains have been achieved by substituting labour through capital; the US in contrast, achieved a substantial increase in total employment. Looking at the long-term development of European employment by the major sectors (Figure 2.3) shows decreasing employment trends in agricultural and manufacturing, but increases for employment in the services sector. This pattern holds for all the other major industrial economies as well. Thus, manufacturing is not in decline – it is *employment* in manufacturing that is in decline.[6]

The third major change is the emergence of the world economy as the dominant economic unit. Company executives and national leaders who recognise this have the greatest chance of success. Those who do not recognise this fact will suffer decline and bankruptcy (in business) or overthrow (in politics). No company or government is powerful enough to determine the economic faith of its corporation or country independently of economic developments in the rest of the world. In Europe, the introduction of the Euro has further limited the scope of individual governments to determine domestic economic policy. Being no longer able to control money supply, exchange rates or interest rates has reduced the policy options Euro-countries can take to influence their domestic economies.

The last change is the end of the Cold War. The success of the capitalist market system caused the overthrow of communism as an economic and political system.

Figure 2.1 **Factor productivity: EU versus US**

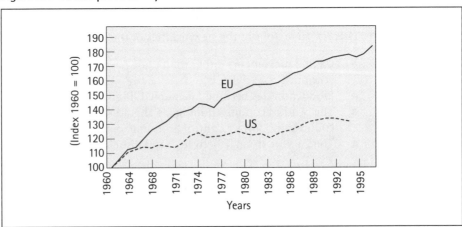

Source: Adapted from *Europäische Wirtschaft*, Generaldirektion Wirtschaft und Finanzen Nr. 63, Bruxelles, European Commission 1997, p. 65.

Figure 2.2 Employment: EU versus US

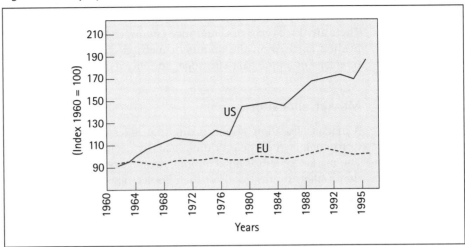

Source: Adapted from *Europäische Wirtschaft*, Generaldirektion Wirtschaft und Finanzen Nr. 63, Bruxelles, European Commission 1997, p. 65.

Figure 2.3 European employment by key industrial sectors

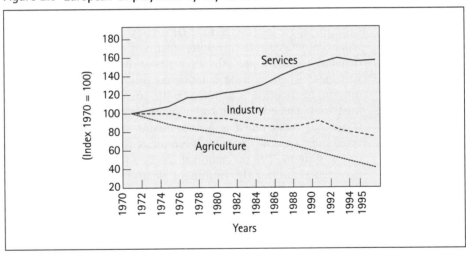

Source: Adapted from *Europäische Wirtschaft*, Generaldirektion Wirtschaft und Finanzen Nr. 63, Bruxelles, European Commission 1997, p. 49.

The overwhelmingly superior performance of the world's market economies has led socialist countries to renounce their ideology. A key policy change in such countries has been to abandon futile attempts to manage national economies with a single central plan. The different types of economic systems are contrasted in the next section.

ECONOMIC SYSTEMS

There are three types of economic systems: capitalist, socialist and mixed. This classification is based on the dominant method of resource allocation: *market allocation, command* or *central plan allocation*, and *mixed allocation*, respectively.

Market allocation

A market allocation system is one that relies upon consumers to allocate resources. Consumers 'write' the economic plan by deciding what will be produced by whom. The market system is an economic democracy – citizens have the right to vote with their wallets for the goods of their choice. The role of the state in a market economy is to promote competition and ensure consumer protection. Western European countries, the United States and Japan (the triad countries that account for three-quarters of gross world product) are examples of predominantly market economies. The clear superiority of the market allocation system in delivering the goods and services that people need and want has led to its adoption in many formerly socialist countries.

Command allocation

In a command allocation system, the state has broad powers to serve the public interest. These include deciding which products to make and how to make them. Consumers are free to spend their money on what is available, but decisions about what is produced and, therefore, what is available are made by state planners. Because demand exceeds supply, the elements of the marketing mix are not used as strategic variables.[7] There is little reliance on product differentiation, advertising and promotion; distribution is handled by the government to cut out 'exploitation' by intermediaries. Three of the most populous countries in the world, China, the former USSR and India relied upon command allocation systems for decades. All three economies are now engaged in economic reforms directed at shifting to market allocation systems. The prediction made by India's Jawaharlal Nehru nearly a half century ago regarding the imminent demise of capitalism has been refuted. Market reforms and nascent capitalism in many parts of the world are creating opportunities for large-scale investments by global companies. Indeed, Coca-Cola returned to India in 1994, two decades after being forced out by the government. A new law allowing 100 per cent foreign ownership of firms helped pave the way.

Mixed systems

There are, in reality, no pure market or command allocation systems among the world's economies. All market systems have a command sector, and all command systems have a market sector; in other words, they are 'mixed'. In a market economy, the command allocation sector is the proportion of GDP that is taxed and spent by government. For the 24 member countries of the Organisation for Economic Co-operation and Development (OECD), this proportion ranges from 32 per cent of GDP in the United States to 64 per cent in Sweden.[8] In Sweden, therefore, where 64 per cent of all expenditures are controlled by government, the economic system is more 'command' than 'market'. Conversely, farmers in most socialist countries were

Measuring the Russian economy

In today's Russia, average citizens aren't the only ones struggling to keep pace with rapid and revolutionary economic change; government statisticians can't even keep up. The result is that economic information and statistics coming from Russia are inaccurate, inadequate, distorted and biased.

Russia's main source of economic statistics is an agency called 'Goskomstat' or the Russian State Statistical Committee. The inherent problem with the statistics generated by Goskomstat is one of original intent: historically, Goskomstat measured the state economy of the Soviet Union; the purpose of the statistics that are still used for economic measurement today doesn't exist anymore because of the change from a planned economy to a market economy.

Goskomstat continues to collect data and measure production in the least productive sectors, namely industries that have not been privatised and farms still owned by the state. If those statistics were somewhat balanced by equivalent numbers from the private sector, Russian GNP might not be so severely underestimated. However, Goskomstat is not at all aggressive about counting the growing private sector in the Russian economy. The growth in Russian joint ventures, retail and service trade, and private banking has been well documented in the press, but not by Goskomstat.

The problem of gathering data from start-up businesses in the emerging private sector is compounded by the fact that those enterprises are reluctant to be included because of potential tax implications. Also, because of inadequate survey techniques, thousands of sole proprietorships, entrepreneurial and barter trade enterprises, as well as informal, black and grey markets are all outside the reach of Goskomstat's reckoning.

Even the data generated from the fading state sector is inadequate because organisations on the government dole are not motivated to report any increased production. Those enterprises could stand to lose government subsidies if production is up. Ironically, in the Soviet era, managers of state-owned businesses were inclined to inflate production numbers in order to reach goals set by state planners.

So what is the impact of the skewed numbers put forth by Goskomstat? The faulty numbers create a ripple effect world-wide. Other agencies that rely on this imperfect source for economic data include the World Bank, International Monetary Fund, US Department of Commerce, the CIA, plus countless banks, industrial and investment analysts. At the very least, statistics severely understate production, especially in the growing private economy. The estimated amount of underreported production ranges from 25 per cent to 60 per cent, with most experts estimating a 45 per cent undercount to be closest to reality. One consequence for the Russian economy is slowed growth, because nervous investors may be reluctant to enter a market depicted by such bleak numbers.

Food for thought

- Businesses often complain about governments' appetite for data and the associated administrative costs. On the other hand, companies need such data when planning their international market entry and expansion. Do you think too much data or too little data are collected by governments? What should/should not be collected?
- What impact does the lack of statistical data or incorrect statistical data have on a UK company planning to sell power drills to Russia?

Source: S. Frederick Starr, 'The "glass is half full" case for Russia', *The International Economy*, March/April (1995):, pp. 46ff; Judy Shelton, *The Coming Soviet Crash: Gorbachev's Desperate Pursuit of Credit in Western Financial Markets* (New York: Free Press, 1989).

traditionally permitted to offer part of their production in a free market. China has given considerable freedom to businesses and individuals in the Guangdong Providence to operate within a market system. Still, China's private sector only constitutes 1–2 per cent of national output.[9]

A recent report by the Washington DC-based Heritage Foundation ranked more than 100 countries by degree of economic freedom. Ten key economic variables were considered: trade policy, taxation policy, government consumption of economic output, monetary policy, capital flows and foreign investment, banking policy, wage and price controls, property rights, regulation, and the black market. The rankings ranged from 'Free' to 'Repressed', with 'Mostly Free' and 'Mostly Unfree' in between. Hong Kong is ranked no. 1 in terms of economic freedom; Cuba and North Korea are ranked lowest.[10] However, it appears doubtful that Hong Kong can hold this position now that the UK has handed it back to China. The report's findings are summarised in Table 2.1.

STAGES OF MARKET DEVELOPMENT

Global country markets are at different stages of development. GNP per capita provides a very useful way of grouping these countries. Using GNP as a base, we have divided global markets into five categories. Although the income definition for each of the stages is arbitrary, countries in the five categories have similar characteristics.

Table 2.1 Index of economic freedom

Free	25. Sweden	50. Kenya	77. Madagascar
1. Hong Kong	26. Belize	51. Mexico	78. Mali
2. Singapore	27. Colombia	52. Zambia	79. Tanzania
3. Bahrain	28. Panama	53. Israel	80. Zimbabwe
4. US	29. Paraguay	54. Algeria	81. Albania
5. Japan	30. Slovak Rep.	55. Honduras	82. Romania
6. Taiwan	31. Greece	56. Nigeria	83. Belarus
7. UK	32. Hungary	57. Pakistan	84. Yemen
	33. Jamaica	58. Bolivia	85. Guyana
Mostly free	34. Portugal	59. Ecuador	86. India
8. Canada	35. Sri Lanka	60. Ivory Coast	87. China
9. Germany	36. Argentina	61. Malta	88. Ethiopia
10. Austria	37. Tunisia	62. Poland	89. Bangladesh
11. Bahamas	38. Costa Rica	63. Brazil	90. Congo
12. Czech Rep.	39. Jordan	64. Fiji	91. Nicaragua
13. S. Korea	40. Morocco	65. Ghana	92. Ukraine
14. Malaysia	41. Swaziland	66. Philippines	93. Sierra Leone
15. Australia	42. Uruguay	67. Mongolia	
16. Ireland	43. Uganda	68. Guinea	**Repressed**
17. Estonia		69. Indonesia	94. Moldova
18. France	**Mostly unfree**	70. Dominican R.	95. Haiti
19. Thailand	44. S. Africa	71. Malawi	96. Sudan
20. Chile	45. Turkey	72. Peru	97. Angola
21. Italy	46. Venezuela	73. Russia	98. Mozambique
22. Spain	47. Botswana	74. Bulgaria	99. Vietnam
23. El Salvador	48. Gabon	75. Cameroon	100. Cuba
24. Oman	49. Guatemala	76. Egypt	101. N. Korea

Thus, the stages provide a useful basis for global market segmentation and target marketing. The categories are shown in Table 2.2.

High income countries

High income countries, also known as advanced, industrialised, post-industrial or First World countries, are currently defined as those with a GNP per capita above €7,960. With the exception of a few oil-rich nations, the countries in this category reached their present income level through a process of sustained economic growth.

The phrase 'post-industrial countries' was first used by Daniel Bell of Harvard to describe the United States, Sweden and Japan and other advanced, high-income societies. Bell suggests that there is a difference between the industrial and the post-industrial societies that goes beyond mere measures of income. Bell's thesis is that the sources of innovation in post-industrial societies are derived increasingly from the codification of theoretical knowledge rather than from 'random' inventions. Other characteristics are the importance of the service sector (more than 50 per cent of GNP); the crucial importance of information processing and exchange; and the ascendancy of knowledge over capital as the key strategic resource, of intellectual technology over machine technology, of scientists and professionals over engineers and semiskilled workers. Other aspects of the post-industrial society are an orientation toward the future and the importance of interpersonal relationships in the functioning of society.

Product and market opportunities in a post-industrial society are more heavily dependent upon new products and innovations than in industrial societies. Ownership levels for basic products are extremely high in most households. Organisations seeking to grow often face a difficult task if they attempt to expand share of existing markets. Alternatively, they can endeavour to create new markets. For example, in the 1990s, global companies in a range of communication-related industries were seeking to create new markets for interactive forms of electronic communication.

Upper middle income countries

Upper middle income countries, also known as industrialising countries, are those with GNP per capita between €2,575 and €7,960. In these countries, the percentage

Table 2.2 Stages of market development

Income group by per capita GNP	1997 GNP (€ millions)	1997 GNP per capita (€)	% of world GNP	1997 Population (million)
High income countries GNP per capita > 7,960	19,196.5	20,998.8	81.39	914
Upper middle income countries GNP per capita > 2,575 but < 7,960	1,807.3	3,347.4	7.66	540
Lower middle income countries GNP per capita > 650 but < 2,575	1,278.2	1,174.9	5.42	1,088
Low income countries GNP per capita < 650 (**Basket cases**)	1,303.9	393	5.53	3,317.7

of population engaged in agriculture drops sharply as people move to the industrial sector and the degree of urbanisation increases. Many of the countries in this stage, Malaysia, for example, are rapidly industrialising. They have rising wages and high rates of literacy and advanced education, but they still have significantly lower wage costs than the advanced countries. Countries in this stage of development frequently become formidable competitors and experience rapid, export-driven economic growth.

Lower middle income countries

Lower middle income countries (also known as less developed countries or LDCs) are those with a GNP per capita of more than €650 and less than €2,575. These countries are at the early stages of industrialisation. Factories supply a growing domestic market with such items as clothing, batteries, tires, building materials, and packaged foods. These countries are also locations for the production of standardised or mature products such as clothing for export markets.

Consumer markets in these countries are expanding. LDCs represent an increasing competitive threat as they mobilise their relatively cheap, and often highly motivated, labour to serve target markets in the rest of the world. LDCs have a major competitive advantage in mature, standardised, labour-intensive products such as athletic shoes. Indonesia, the largest non-communist country in Southeast Asia, is a good example of an LDC on the move: per capita income has risen from €212 in 1985 to more than €933 in 1997. Several factories there produce athletic shoes under contract for Nike.

Low income countries

Low income countries, also known as pre-industrial countries, are those with incomes of less than €650 per capita. The characteristics shared by countries at this income level are:

1 Limited industrialisation and a high percentage of the population engaged in agriculture and subsistence farming.
2 High birth rates.
3 Low literacy rates.
4 Heavy reliance on foreign aid.
5 Political instability and unrest.
6 Concentration in Africa south of the Sahara.

In general, these countries represent limited markets for all products, and are not significant locations for competitive threats. Still, there are exceptions; for example, in Bangladesh, where per capita income is about €212, a growing garment industry has enjoyed burgeoning exports. The dollar value of finished clothing exports surpasses that of jute, tea and other agricultural exports.[11]

Basket cases or special cases

A basket case is a country with economic, social, and political problems that are so serious they make the country unattractive for investment and operations. Some basket cases are low income, no-growth countries such as Ethiopia and Mozambique that lurch from one disaster to the next. Others are one-time growing and successful countries that have become divided by political struggles. The result is civil strife, declining income, and, often, considerable danger to residents. In the mid 1990s, the former Yugoslavia is a case in point. Basket cases embroiled in civil wars are dangerous areas; most companies find it prudent to avoid these countries during active conflict.

The newly independent countries of the former USSR present an interesting situation: in many of these countries, reported income is declining and there is considerable economic hardship. Are these nations basket cases or are they attractive opportunities with good potential for moving into the high-income category? Life expectancy, for example, has been declining in Russia, while it is rising in the rest of the world. Between 1990 and 1994, life expectancy for Russian men and women declined dramatically from 63.8 and 74.4 years to 57.7 and 71.2 years, respectively.[12] On the other hand, there is a growing private economy in Russia and in the other CIS countries which is 95 per cent 'underground' or unreported.

The reality in Russia is a growing wealthy class who have profited from the privatisation of economic activity and growing poverty and a growing number of people who are living in poverty. The real issue is whether or not Russia and the other CIS countries are an opportunity or a trap. These countries present an interesting risk/reward trade-off; while many companies have 'taken the plunge', many others are still assessing whether or not to take the risk. The potential returns are great, but so are the risks. Timing is important, and risk is unavoidable.

INCOME AND PURCHASING POWER PARITY AROUND THE GLOBE

When a company charts a plan for global market expansion, it often finds that, for most products, income is the single most valuable economic variable. After all, a market can be defined as a group of people willing and able to buy a particular product. For some products, particularly those that have a very low unit cost – cigarettes, for example – population is a more valuable predictor of market potential than income. Nevertheless, for the vast range of industrial and consumer products in international markets today, the single most valuable and important indicator of potential is income.

Ideally, gross national product and other measures of national income should be converted to Euro (or your own national currency) on the basis of purchasing power parities (i.e. what the currency will buy in the country of issue) or through direct comparisons of actual prices for a given product. This would provide an actual comparison of the standards of living in the countries of the world. Unfortunately, these data are not available in regular statistical reports. Throughout this book we use, instead, conversion of local currency measured at the year-end Euro foreign exchange rate or US$, since many international statistics are reported in this way. The reader must remember that exchange rates equate, at best, the prices of internationally traded goods and services. They often bear little relationship to the prices of those goods and services not traded internationally, which form the bulk of the national product in most countries. Agricultural output and services, in particular, are often priced lower in relation to industrial output in developing countries than in industrial countries. Furthermore, agriculture typically accounts for the largest share of output in developing countries. Thus the use of exchange rates tends to exaggerate differences in real income between countries at different stages of economic development. Table 2.3 ranks the top 10 countries in terms of 1997 GNP per capita; the last two columns show the rankings adjusted for purchasing power parity.

Beyond the exchange distortion illustrated in Table 2.3, there is the distortion of money itself as an indicator of a nation's welfare and standard of living. A visit to a mud house in Tanzania will reveal many of the things that money can buy: Radios, an iron bed frame, a corrugated metal roof, beer and soft drinks, bicycles, shoes, photographs, and razor blades. What Tanzania's per capita income of €212 does not reflect is the fact that instead of utility bills, Tanzanians have the local well and the sun. Instead of nursing homes, tradition and custom ensure families will take care of the elderly at home. Instead of expensive doctors and hospitals, villagers might turn to witch doctors and healers. In industrialised countries, a significant portion of national income is generated by taking goods and services that would be free in a poor country and putting a price on them. Thus, the standard of living in many countries is often higher than income data might suggest.

A striking fact is the concentration of income in the 'Triad' (North America, Western Europe and Japan). The Triad accounted for 74 per cent of global income but only 14 per cent of global population in 1997. With the exception of China and Brazil, the top ten countries in 1997 are all located in the Triad (see Table 2.4).

No one knows what the future will bring, but an extrapolation of the growth to the year 2010 produces an interesting result, shown in Table 2.5. The United States, Japan and Germany remain in the top three positions. China overtakes France, the United Kingdom and Italy. South Korea appears on the list for the first time, and surpasses Brazil and Canada. These extrapolation results suggest that China, with its combination of high real income growth and relatively low population growth, is a strong candidate to become a leading world economic power.

An examination of the distribution of wealth within countries also reveals patterns of income concentration, particularly in the less developed countries outside the former communist bloc. Adelman and Morris[13] found that, in less developed countries, the average share of GNP accruing to the poorest 20 per cent of the population was 5.6 per cent as compared with 56.0 per cent going to the top 20 per cent. The income of the bottom 20 per cent was about one-fourth of what it would have been

Table 2.3 **Top 10 nations ranked by GNP per capita and purchasing power parity**

1997 GNP per capita		*1997 GNP adjusted for purchasing power (PPP)*	
1. Luxembourg	$35,611	1. Luxembourg	$32,182
2. Switzerland	$34,605	2. United States	$23,530
3. Japan	$28,988	3. Switzerland	$21,937
4. Norway	$27,362	4. Kuwait	$20,184
5. Denmark	$26,120	5. Hong Kong	$19,487
6. Singapore	$25,517	6. Singapore	$19,339
7. Germany	$23,945	7. Japan	$18,766
8. Austria	$23,677	8. Norway	$18,617
9. United States	$23,530	9. Belgium	$18,382
10. Belgium	$21,891	10. Canada	$18,285

Source: Warren J. Keegan, *Global Income and Population: 1997 and Projections to 2000 and 2010* in *Global Marketing Management*, 6e, Prentice Hall, 1999, pp. 587–625.

Table 2.4 World GNP Top 10, 1997

Country	GNP (in € millions)
US	6,303,177
Japan	3,665,674
Germany	1,980,065
France	1,280,656
UK	960,505
Italy	956,551
China	754,887
Canada	513,881
Brazil	500,726
Spain	477,233

Source: Warren J. Keegan, *Global Income and Population: 1997 and Projections to 2000 and 2010* in *Global Marketing Management*, 6e, Prentice Hall, 1999, pp. 587–625.

Table 2.5 World GNP top 10, 2010

Country	GNP (in € millions)
US	10,464,772
Japan	5,899,056
Germany	3,186,407
China	2,487,995
France	2,060,887
UK	1,590,023
Italy	1,444,444
South Korea	1,042,144
Canada	984,709
Brazil	897,401

Source: Warren J. Keegan, *Global Income and Population: 1997 and Projections to 2000 and 2010.*

had income been distributed uniformly throughout the population. This study suggests that the relationship between the share of income at the lowest 20 per cent and economic development varies with the level of development. Economic development is associated with increases in the share of the bottom 20 per cent only after relatively high levels of socio-economic development have been attained. At the early stages of the development process, economic development works to the *relative* disadvantage of the lowest income groups. Brazil, for example, has become one of the world's most unequal societies, with the top fifth of the country's population earning some 65 per cent of national income; the bottom fifth earns less than 3 per cent. This is the most extreme income inequality that the World Bank has measured and is worse than Bangladesh's.[14] China is experiencing the same type of inequality. As one politician noted, 'Economic reform not only changes economic systems but is also a revolution in ideas.'[15]

Although the problem of poverty has not been eliminated in all the industrialised countries, those countries with homogeneous populations and an advanced collective social conscience have indeed greatly reduced poverty within their borders. However, there is a growing gap between the richest and the poorest countries. In 1960, the income difference between the top and bottom fifth of the world population was 30:1, today, it is about 75:1. In 1998, Bill Gates, CEO of Microsoft, the Sultan of Brunei and the Walton-Family, owner of Wal-Mart, had accumulated assets equivalent to the GDP of the 43 poorest countries taken together.[16]

Between 1850 and 1992, the industrial countries' share of world income increased from 39 to 75 per cent. During this period, annual compound rates of growth of 2.7 per cent in total output and 1.8 per cent in per capita output profoundly altered the world's distribution of income. The magnitude of change, as compared with the previous 6,000 years of our civilised existence, is enormous; over one-third of the real income and about two-thirds of the industrial output produced by people throughout recorded history were generated in the industrialised countries in the last century. Note that *relatively small average annual rates of growth have transformed the economic geography of the world.* What the industrial countries have done is to systematise economic growth. Put another way, they have established a process of continuous, gradual change.

One researcher has calculated that India, one of the poorest countries in the world, could reach US income levels by growing at an average rate of 5 to 6 per cent in real terms for 40 to 50 years. This is no more than the lifetime of an average Indian. Japan was the first country with a non-European heritage to achieve high-income status. This was the result of sustained high growth, the ability to achieve high-income status. This was the result of sustained high growth, the ability to acquire knowledge and know-how, first by making copies of products and then by making improvements. As Japan has dramatically demonstrated, this is a potent formula for catching up and achieving economic leadership.

Today, much more than was true 2,000 years ago, wealth and income are concentrated regionally, nationally, and within nations. The implications of this reality are crucial for the global marketer. A company that decides to diversify geographically can accomplish this objective by establishing operations in a handful of national markets.

Key points

- There are three basic types of economic systems: market allocation, command allocation and mixed systems.

- Different stages of market developments are usually captured by a comparison of GNP per capita.

- A more accurate measure of differences in the standard of living between countries is the purchasing power parity.

- A common classification of country markets is: high income countries, upper middle income countries, lower middle income countries, low income countries and basket cases.

THE LOCATION OF POPULATION

We have already noted the concentration of 74 per cent of world income in the Triad (North America, Western Europe and Japan). In 1997, the 10 most populous countries in the world accounted for 51 per cent of world income, and the 5 largest account for 34 per cent (see Table 2.6). The concentration of income in the high income and large population countries means that a company can be global – that is, derive a significant proportion of its income from countries at different stages of development – while operating in ten or fewer countries.

For products whose price is low enough, population is a more important variable than income in determining market potential. Although population is not as concentrated as income, there is, in terms of size of nations, a pattern of considerable concentration. The 10 most populous countries in the world account for roughly 60 per cent of the world's population today.

People have inhabited the earth for over 2.5 million years. The number of human beings has been small during most of this period. In Christ's lifetime there were approximately 300 million people on earth, or roughly one-quarter of the number of people on mainland China today. World population increased tremendously during the eighteenth and nineteenth centuries, reaching one billion by 1850. Between 1850 and 1925 global population had doubled, to 2 billion, and from 1925 to 1960 it had increased to 3 billion. World population is now approximately 6 billion. At the present rate of growth it will reach 10 billion by the middle of the next century. Simply put, global population will probably double during the lifetime of many students using this textbook (see Figure 2.4).

There is a negative correlation between population growth rate and income per capita. The lower the income per capita, the higher the rate of population growth. According to a United Nations report, 97 per cent of the world's population growth is likely to come from developing and undeveloped countries.[17]

Table 2.6 The ten most populous countries: 1997 with projection to 2010

Global income and population	1997 Population (thousands)	% of world population	Projected population 2010	1997 GNP (€ million)	Per capita GNP (€)	% of world GNP
WORLD TOTAL	5,859,548	100.0	7,192,935	23,585,880	–	100.0
1. China	1,231,650	21.0	1,438,249	754,887	613,321	3.2
2. India	965,009	16.5	1,220,483	298,962	309,630	1.27
3. United States	267,876	4.6	297,998	6,303,177	23,530,145	26.7
4. Indonesia	199,904	3.4	246,446	187,057	935,675	0.79
5. Brazil	164,358	2.8	200,047	500,726	3,046,245	2.12
6. Russian Federation	149,086	2.5	156,558	255,208	1,711,869	1.08
7. Pakistan	137,816	2.4	197,914	55,255	401,246	0.23
8. Japan	126,455	2.2	133,190	3,665,733	28,988,108	15.5
9. Bangladesh	124,607	2.1	159,619	26,291	211,227	0.11
10. Nigeria	117,820	2.0	169,199	26,117	221,406	0.11

Source: Warren J. Keegan, *Global Income and Population: 1997 and Projections to 2000 and 2010.*

Figure 2.4 World population growth

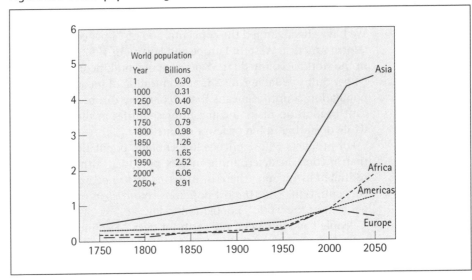

World population	
Year	Billions
1	0.30
1000	0.31
1250	0.40
1500	0.50
1750	0.79
1800	0.98
1850	1.26
1900	1.65
1950	2.52
2000*	6.06
2050+	8.91

Source: 'Like herrings in a barrel', *The Economist*, 31 December 1999, p. 13.

MARKETING AND ECONOMIC DEVELOPMENT

An important concern in marketing is whether or not it has any relevance to the process of economic development. Some people believe the field of marketing is relevant only to the conditions that apply in affluent, industrialised countries where the major problem is one of directing society's resources into ever-changing output or production to satisfy a dynamic marketplace. In the less developed countries, the argument goes, the major problem is the allocation of scarce resources toward obvious production needs. Efforts should focus on production and how to increase output, not on customer needs and wants.

Conversely, it can be argued that the marketing process of focusing an organisation's resources on environmental opportunities is a process of universal relevance. The role of marketing, to identify people's needs and wants, and to focus individual and organisation efforts to respond to these needs and wants, is the same in both low and high income countries. For example, pursuing alternative sources of energy such as wind and solar power is important for two reasons: the lack of coal reserves in many countries, and concerns that over-reliance on fossil fuels will contribute to global warming. These concerns have led to the development of solar-powered lanterns that are used in villages in India. Similarly, solar water heaters have been installed in Gaborone, the capital of Botswana, eliminating as much as 40 per cent of the energy requirement for thousands of families.

The economics literature places a great deal of emphasis on 'the role of marketing in economic development' when marketing is defined as distribution. In his book *West African Trade*, P.T. Bauer considered the question concerning the number of traders and their productivity.[18] The number and variety of traders in West Africa had been much criticised by both official and unofficial observers. Traders were condemned as wasteful and said to be responsible for wide margins both in the sale of merchandise and in the purchase of produce. Bauer examined these criticisms and concluded that they stemmed from a misunderstanding. In his view, the West African system economised in capital and used a redundant resource, labour. Therefore, Bauer argued, it was a productive system by rational economic criteria.

A simple example illustrates Bauer's point. A trader buys a packet of cigarettes for one shilling and resells them one at a time for two cents each, or for a total of two shillings. Has this person exploited society to the tune of one shilling, or has he provided a useful service? In a society where consumers can afford to smoke only one cigarette at a time, the trader has provided a useful service in substituting labour for capital. In this case, capital would be the accumulation of an inventory of cigarettes by a consumer. The possession of a shilling is the critical first obstacle to this accumulation. However, even if a consumer were able to accumulate a shilling, his standard of living would not allow him to smoke the 20 cigarettes fast enough to prevent them from going stale. Thus, even if he were able to save and accumulate a shilling, he would end up with a packet of spoiled cigarettes. The trader in this case, by breaking bulk, serves the useful function of making available a product in a quantity that a consumer can afford and in a condition that is attractive. As income levels rise, the purchaser will smoke more frequently and will be able to buy an entire packet of cigarettes. In the process the amount of local resources consumed by distribution will decline and the standard of living will have risen. Meanwhile, in less developed countries where labour is redundant and cheap and where capital is scarce, the availability of this distribution function represents a useful, rational application of society's resources. Moreover, experience in the distributive sector is valuable because it generates a pool of entrepreneurial talent in a society where alternatives for such training are scarce.

Key points	
	• About three-quarters of world income is concentrated in the triad countries (North America, Western Europe and Japan).
	• Marketing plays an important role in the economic development of a country.
	• World population has doubled since 1960 and is currently about 6 billion. At the present rate of growth, it is projected to reach 10 billion in the sixth or seventh decade of the 21st century.

BALANCE OF PAYMENTS

The balance of payments is a record of all of the economic transactions between residents of a country and the rest of the world. As an illustration, excerpts from the German and British balance of payments statistics for the period 1989 to 1996 are shown in Tables 2.7 and 2.8. Note that the degree of detail reported by various countries differs. Britain, for example, does not provide any figures for the capital account and the International Monetary Fund merely notes 'No estimates are currently available'.[19] The format here closely mirrors that used by the International Monetary Fund in its *Balance of Payments Yearbook,* which summarises economic activity for all the countries of the world.[20]

Table 2.7 German balance of payments, 1989–1996 (US$ billions)

Balance of payments	1989	1990	1991	1992	1993	1994	1995	1996
A. Current account	56.73	48.11	−17.88	−19.39	−14.12	−21.23	−23.53	−13.07
1. Goods: exports f.o.b.	340.01	410.92	403.37	430.48	382.68	430.58	523.60	519.44
2. Goods: imports f.o.b.	−264.73	−341.88	−383.45	−402.28	−341.49	−379.65	−458.52	−448.22
Balance on goods	*75.28*	*69.04*	*19.92*	*28.20*	*41.19*	*50.93*	*65.08*	*71.21*
3. Services: credit	51.83	66.57	68.56	68.96	64.64	66.00	81.50	84.64
4. Services: debit	−64.34	−83.78	−89.66	−99.70	−97.76	−105.89	−127.29	−128.06
Balance on goods + services	*62.77*	*51.84*	*−1.18*	*−2.53*	*8.07*	*11.04*	*19.29*	*27.79*
B. Capital account	0.08	−1.33	−0.65	0.60	0.49	0.15	−0.65	−0.02
5. Capital account: credit	0.39	0.41	0.77	1.12	1.38	1.56	1.68	2.71
6. Capital account: debit	−0.32	−1.73	−1.41	−0.52	−0.89	−1.42	−2.33	−2.74
Total, Groups A plus B	*56.81*	*46.78*	*−18.53*	*−18.79*	*−13.63*	*−21.08*	*−24.19*	*−13.09*
C. Financial account	−59.08	−54.78	5.22	51.80	16.21	29.32	46.12	14.18
7. Direct investment abroad	−15.26	−24.20	−23.72	−19.67	−15.26	−17.18	−38.53	−27.79
8. Direct investment in Germany	7.15	2.53	4.11	2.64	1.95	1.68	11.96	−3.18
9. Portfolio investment assets	−26.63	−15.17	−17.96	−48.06	−32.66	−53.99	−22.08	−38.15
10. Portfolio investment liabilities	24.40	13.44	42.25	80.00	152.39	23.06	59.10	90.68
Total, Groups A through C	*−2.27*	*−8.00*	*−13.31*	*33.01*	*2.58*	*8.24*	*21.93*	*1.08*
D. Net errors and omissions	5.12	15.26	7.12	4.17	−16.78	−10.27	−14.71	−2.28
Total, Groups A through D	*2.86*	*7.25*	*−6.18*	*37.18*	*−14.20*	*−2.04*	*7.22*	*−1.20*
E. Reserves and related items	−2.86	−7.25	6.18	−37.18	14.20	2.04	−7.22	1.20
Conversion rates: DM per US $	1.8800	1.6157	1.6595	1.5617	1.6533	1.6228	1.4331	1.5048

Source: Adapted from *Balance of Payments Statistics Yearbook, Part 1: Country Tables*, 1997, Washington, DC: International Monetary Fund, p. 296.

The balance of payments is divided into a so-called 'current' and 'capital' account. The current account is a record of all of the recurring trade in merchandise and service, private gifts and public aid transactions between countries. The capital account is a record of all long-term direct investment, portfolio investment, and other short- and long-term capital flows. The minus signs signify outflows of cash. The changes in reserves and net errors and omissions are the entries that make the balance of payments balance. In general, a country accumulates reserves when the net of its current and capital account transactions shows a surplus; it gives up reserves when the net shows a deficit. The important fact to recognise about the overall balance of payments is that it is always in balance. Imbalances occur in subsets of the overall balance. For example, a commonly reported balance is the 'current account' balance. Table 2.9 shows these balances for selected countries for the period 1990 to 1996. In this context, it is interesting to note the persistently large deficits in the US compared to the surpluses in Japan.

TRADE PATTERNS

Since the end of the Second World War, world merchandise trade has grown faster than world production. In other words, import and export growth has outpaced the rate of increase in GNP. Moreover, since 1983, foreign direct investment has grown

Table 2.8 British balance of payments, 1989–96 (US$ billions)

Balance of payments	1989	1990	1991	1992	1993	1994	1995	1996
A. Current account	−36.66	−32.50	−14.26	−18.35	−15.51	−2.34	−5.86	−0.45
1. Goods: exports f.o.b.	150.70	181.73	182.58	188.45	182.06	206.45	241.53	259.91
2. Goods: imports f.o.b.	−191.24	−214.47	−200.85	−211.88	−202.30	−223.41	−259.84	−279.38
Balance on goods	*−40.54*	*−32.74*	*−18.27*	*−23.43*	*−20.24*	*−16.95*	*−18.31*	*−19.47*
3. Services: credit	47.93	56.23	54.32	62.17	58.61	64.30	73.52	79.39
4. Services: debit	−42.40	−49.67	−47.99	−53.53	−50.38	−56.99	−62.68	−68.15
Balance on goods + services	*−35.02*	*−26.18*	*−11.94*	*−14.79*	*−12.00*	*−9.64*	*−7.47*	*−8.23*
B. Capital account	...	...	...	...	...	...	...	...
5. Capital account: credit	...	...	...	...	...	...	...	...
6. Capital account: debit	...	....	....	...	...	...	...	...
Total, Groups A plus B	*−36.66*	*−32.50*	*−14.26*	*−18.35*	*−15.51*	*−2.34*	*−5.86*	*−0.45*
C. Financial Account	22.47	29.20	18.51	1.12	23.39	−3.60	2.30	−3.53
7. Direct investment abroad	−35.48	−19.32	−16.31	−18.99	−26.58	−33.80	−44.09	−44.59
8. Direct investment in UK	30.55	32.43	16.21	16.14	15.54	9.18	22.50	32.35
9. Portfolio investment assets	−63.12	−32.43	−55.56	−51.09	−132.45	34.85	−64.16	−91.92
10. Portfolio investment liabilities	28.71	24.82	14.78	25.92	43.06	55.00	61.37	64.75
Total, Groups A through C	*−14.19*	*−3.30*	*4.25*	*−17.23*	*7.88*	*−5.94*	*−3.56*	*−3.98*
D. Net errors and omissions	6.16	3.34	0.46	10.56	−2.44	7.42	2.70	3.53
Total, Groups A through D	*−8.03*	*0.04*	*4.70*	*−6.67*	*5.44*	*1.48*	*−0.85*	*−0.45*
E. Reserves and related items	8.03	−0.04	−4.70	6.67	−5.44	−1.48	0.85	0.45
Conversion Rates: £ per US $	0.61117	0.56318	0.56702	0.56977	0.66676	0.65343	0.63367	0.64096

Source: Adapted from *Balance of Payments Statistics Yearbook, Part 1: Country Tables*, 1997, Washington, DC: International Monetary Fund, p. 840.

Table 2.9 Current account balances for selected countries (€ millions)

Current account balances	1990	1991	1992	1993	1994	1995	1996
USA	−77,907.02	−4,942.96	−48,057.04	−76,833.08	−112,764.52	−109,593.57	−126,164.27
Japan	37,391.37	57,856.61	95,496.52	111,667.67	110,495.32	94,198.63	55,889.40
Austria	989.12	51.75	67.02	−515.77	−1,873.89	−4,106.62	−3,564.56
France	−8,435.50	−5,529.22	3,302.43	7,626.22	5,966.09	13,948.60	17,399.48
Germany	40,809.17	−15,169.30	−16,448.54	−11,978.84	−18,010.26	−19,963.89	−11,088.98
Italy	−14,414.31	−20,994.58	−25,526.20	7,022.22	11,206.89	21,321.17	34,814.23
UK	−27,569.75	−12,096.76	−15,566.31	13,157.13	−1,985.02	−4,971.04	−381.74
Netherlands	7,821.33	6,648.13	6,291.84	11,474.11	15,374.59	20,099.62	17,371.20
China, People's Rep. of	10,177.06	11,258.64	5,429.97	−9,847.91	5,860.06	1,375.55	6,144.24
Russia	...	...	...	...	9,096.32	8,464.34	9,669.77

Source: Adapted from *Balance of Payments Statistics Yearbook*, 1997, Washington, DC: International Monetary Fund, p. 10.

five times faster than world trade and 10 times faster than GNP.[21] The structure of world trade is summarised in Figure 2.5. The importance of the triad countries is quite pronounced: North America, Western Europe and Japan accounted for two-thirds of world exports and imports. Industrialised nations have increased their share of world trade by trading more among themselves, and less with the rest of the world.

According to the Organisation for Economic Co-operation and Development (OECD), the US share of the world's export trade has slightly increased over the last

Figure 2.5 World trade in 1997 (€ billions)

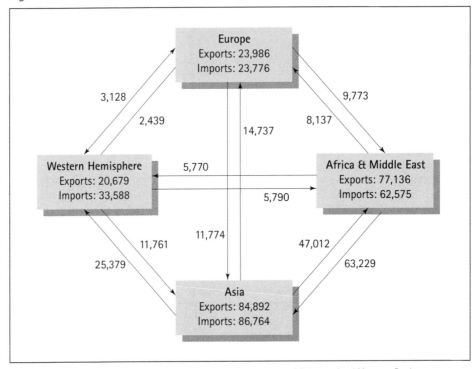

Source: Adapted from *Direction of Trade Statistics Yearbook*, 1998, Washington, DC: International Monetary Fund.

decade. US shipments amounted to approximately 11 per cent of total export trade between 1985 and 1987, and to more than 12 per cent between 1993 and 1995. Over this same period, the export share of other OECD countries (relatively developed nations) fell from 62 per cent to under 60 per cent, and the export share of non-OECD countries (developing nations) expanded from 27 per cent to 28 per cent.

Despite the growing US trade deficit, her share of world imports actually declined over the past 10 years, falling from 18 per cent to 16 per cent between 1985 and 1995. Similarly, the share of other OECD countries dropped from 57 per cent to 54 per cent. Thus, developing countries' share rose from 25 per cent to nearly 30 per cent over this period.

As the US has captured a larger share of the world markets, exports have become more important to her economic performance. In 1995, exports accounted for 13.2 per cent of US GDP, up from 7.2 per cent in 1985. This puts the US roughly on a par with Japan, where exports account for 12.5 per cent of total output, but below Germany, where exports make up 25 per cent of GDP.[22]

Merchandise trade

Table 2.10 shows trade patterns for the world. In 1997, the value of world trade was approximately €5.5 trillion; 65 per cent of world export was generated by industrialized countries, and 35 per cent by developing countries. In 1998, Western Europe accounted for 44 per cent. Demand growth in Western Europe contrasted with a

Figure 2.6 Exports as share of gross domestic product

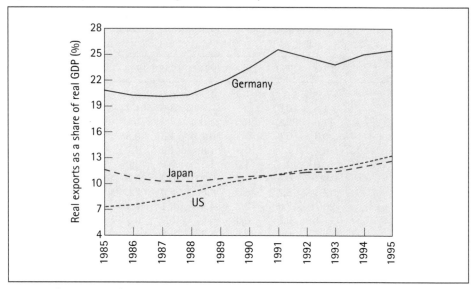

Source: http://www.clev.frb.org/research/feb96et/wortrd.htm#1c, 26 July 1999.

weaker global economy in 1998. This led to an import expansion which, for the first time since 1992, exceeded the region's growth rate. Western Europe represents the only major region which recorded an increase in export value in 1998.[23]

Looking at the exports of EU countries in detail shows that between 1958 and 1994, intra-European trade increased from 37.2 to 58.4 per cent of total exports. In contrast, over the same period, the proportion of exports directed to developing countries decreased from 27.4 to 14.2 per cent, while the proportion of exports flowing into the US remained more or less stable (Table 2.11).

The top 10 exporting and importing countries of the world (as reported by the International Monetary Fund) are shown in Table 2.12. The United States, Germany and Japan are occupying the top three positions, both in terms of being the world's largest exporters and importers. China shows a spectacular export growth in exports (293 per cent) and imports (311 per cent) compared to 1990.

Table 2.10 **1997 World merchandise exports and imports to and from areas and groups listed (in billions €)**

Areas	Exports to 1997	Imports from 1997
DOT world total	5,528	5,626
Industrial countries	3,616	3,620
Developing countries	1,909	2,001
Africa	109	128
Asia	1,043	1,072
Europe	264	272
Middle East	202	175
Western hemisphere	291	354

Source: *Direction of Trade Statistics Yearbook*, 1998, Washington, DC: International Monetary Fund.

Table 2.11 **Structure of EU exports – Part I**

	B/L		DK		GER		EL		E		F	
Exports to	*1958*	*1994*	*1958*	*1994*	*1958*	*1994*	*1958*	*1994*	*1958*	*1994*	*1958*	*1994*
B/L	–	–	1.2	1.9	6.6	6.7	1.0	1.6	2.1	2.8	6.3	8.5
DK	1.6	0.9	–	–	3.0	1.8	0.2	0.8	1.7	0.6	0.7	0.9
GER	11.6	20.8	20.0	23.0	–	–	20.5	21.1	10.2	13.4	10.4	17.7
EL	0.8	0.6	0.3	0.7	1.3	0.8	–	–	0.1	0.9	0.6	0.7
E	0.7	2.9	0.8	1.8	1.2	3.2	0.2	2.2	–	–	1.6	6.9
F	10.6	19.3	3.0	5.6	7.6	12.0	12.8	5.4	10.1	19.0	–	–
IR	0.3	0.4	0.3	0.5	0.3	0.5	0.4	0.3	0.3	0.4	0.2	0.6
I	2.3	5.2	5.3	4.0	5.0	7.6	6.0	13.9	2.7	8.7	3.4	9.8
NL	20.7	13.0	2.2	4.3	8.1	7.5	2.0	2.5	3.2	3.6	2.0	4.5
P	1.1	0.8	0.3	0.5	0.9	0.9	0.3	0.4	0.4	7.4	0.8	1.4
UK	5.7	8.3	25.9	8.8	3.9	8.0	7.6	5.9	15.9	7.6	4.9	9.8
Exports into												
Other EU countries	55.4	72.1	59.3	51.2	37.9	48.9	50.9	54.2	46.8	64.5	30.9	60.7
Other European OECD countries	8.7	5.8	16.6	22.2	22.7	16.9	10.3	8.1	12.4	5.8	9.0	7.8
USA	9.4	4.9	9.3	5.5	7.3	7.9	13.6	4.8	10.1	4.6	5.9	7.0
Canada	1.1	0.4	0.7	0.5	1.2	0.6	0.3	0.5	1.3	0.5	0.8	0.7
Japan	0.6	1.3	0.2	4.0	0.9	2.6	1.4	1.0	1.7	1.1	0.3	1.9
Australia	0.5	0.3	0.3	0.6	1.0	0.7	0.1	0.4	0.3	0.4	0.5	0.4
LDC countries total	18.0	11.3	9.3	10.9	20.9	12.7	7.2	17.2	18.4	20.7	46.9	18.0
thereof												
– OPEC	3.3	1.7	2.3	1.8	4.8	2.6	0.9	4.0	2.6	3.0	21.3	3.7
– other LDC countries	14.7	9.6	7.0	9.1	16.1	10.1	6.3	13.2	15.8	17.7	25.6	14.3
Rest of the world and others	6.3	3.9	4.3	5.1	8.1	9.7	16.2	13.8	9.0	2.4	5.7	3.5
World (excl. EC)	44.6	27.9	40.7	48.8	62.1	51.1	49.1	45.8	53.2	35.5	69.1	39.3
World (incl. EC)	100	100	100	100	100	100	100	100	100	100	100	100

Services trade

Probably the fastest-growing sector of world trade is trade in services. Services include travel and entertainment, education, business services such as engineering, accounting, and legal services, and payments of royalties and licence fees. Unfortunately, the statistics and data on trade in services are not as comprehensive as those for merchandise trade. There are, for example, thousands of different statistical categories which are used to report exports or imports of physical goods. In contrast, there are fewer than 50 categories to report trade of services.

Many countries (especially low income countries) are also lax in enforcing international copyrights protecting intellectual property and patent laws. As a result, countries that export service products like software and video entertainment suffer major losses in income. According to the Software Publishers Association, annual world-wide losses due to software piracy amount to $6.8 billion. In China and the countries of the former Soviet Union, more than 95 per cent of the personal computer software in use is believed to be pirated.

Table 2.11 Structure of EU exports – Part II

| | Exports from | | | | | | | | | | | |
| | IR | | I | | NL | | P | | UK | | EUR | |
Exports to	1958	1994	1958	1994	1958	1994	1958	1994	1958	1994	1958	1994
B/L	0.8	3.9	2.2	3.0	15.0	13.9	3.7	3.7	1.9	5.5	4.8	6.0
DK	0.1	1.1	0.8	0.8	2.6	1.6	1.2	2.3	2.4	1.4	2.0	1.3
GER	2.2	14.1	14.1	19.0	19.0	28.6	7.7	18.7	4.2	12.9	7.6	13.6
EL	0.1	0.5	1.9	1.8	0.6	1.0	0.5	0.5	0.7	0.7	0.8	0.9
E	0.8	2.3	0.7	4.6	0.8	2.5	0.7	14.3	0.8	3.8	1.0	3.8
F	0.8	9.2	5.3	13.1	4.9	10.6	6.6	14.7	2.4	10.2	4.7	10.5
IR	–	–	0.1	0.3	0.4	0.6	0.3	0.5	3.5	5.4	1.1	1.1
I	0.4	3.9	–	–	2.7	5.5	4.3	3.3	2.1	5.1	3.1	6.1
NL	0.5	5.5	2.0	2.9	–	–	2.5	5.2	3.2	7.1	5.3	5.7
P	0.1	0.4	0.7	1.3	0.4	0.8	–	–	0.4	1.0	0.8	1.3
UK	76.8	27.5	6.8	6.5	11.9	9.6	11.3	11.7	–	–	5.9	7.7
Exports into												
Other EU countries	82.4	70.0	34.5	53.4	58.3	74.7	38.9	75.1	21.7	54.1	37.2	58.4
Other European OECD countries	0.9	6.9	18.9	11.3	11.9	6.7	5.1	8.1	9.1	8.2	13.7	10.7
USA	5.7	8.1	9.9	7.8	5.6	4.0	8.3	5.3	8.8	12.0	7.9	7.3
Canada	0.7	0.9	1.2	0.9	0.8	0.4	1.1	0.7	5.8	1.4	2.3	0.7
Japan	0.0	3.1	0.3	2.1	0.4	1.0	0.5	0.8	0.6	2.3	0.6	2.1
Australia	0.1	0.6	0.8	0.7	0.7	0.4	0.6	0.3	7.2	1.4	2.4	0.7
LDC countries total	1.6	6.7	26.2	17.1	17.6	8.3	42.3	7.9	33.6	16.4	27.4	14.2
thereof												
– OPEC	0.2	1.4	7.5	3.8	4.5	1.8	2.0	0.8	7.0	3.6	7.6	2.9
– other LDC countries	1.4	5.3	18.7	13.3	13.1	6.5	40.3	7.1	26.6	12.8	19.8	11.3
Rest of the world and others	8.6	3.7	8.2	6.7	4.7	4.5	3.2	1.8	13.2	4.2	8.5	5.9
World (excl. EC)	17.6	30.0	65.5	46.6	41.7	25.3	61.1	24.9	78.3	45.9	62.8	41.6
World (incl. EC)	100	100	100	100	100	100	100	100	100	100	100	100

Source: Adapted from *Europäische Wirtschaft*, Generaldirektion Wirtschaft und Finanzen, Nr. 67, Bruxelles, European Commission, 1997, p. 166.

Table 2.12 Leading export and import countries in 1996 (€ billions)

Leading exporters	1996	Percentage change 1990/96	Leading importers	1996	Percentage change 1990/96
1. United States	520.84	158	1. United States	681.38	161
2. Germany	440.64	126	2. Germany	380.23	131
3. Japan	339.56	142	3. Japan	268.67	149
4. France	232.49	131	4. United Kingdom	236.99	130
5. United Kingdom	220.48	143	5. France	219.67	117
6. Italy	212.79	147	6. Italy	161.19	112
7. Canada	174.58	158	7. Canada	149.08	145
8. Netherlands	148.92	135	8. Netherlands	131.98	132
9. Belgium-Luxembourg	130.99	140	9. Korea	121.82	221
10. China	128.16	293	10. China, P.R.	111.59	311

Source: Adapted from *Balance of Payments Statistics Yearbook Part 2: World and Regional Tables*, Washington, DC: International Monetary Fund, 1997, p 20.

Table 2.13 shows the services exports and imports of selected industrial countries in 1990 and 1996. Note that the United States and, to a lesser degree, the UK, France and Switzerland produce a surplus in their services trade, whereas Japan and Germany suffer substantial deficits.

Table 2.13 **Exports and imports of services: selected countries (€ million)**

	Exports		Imports	
Country	1990	1996	1990	1996
United States	125.00	199.09	99.79	129.59
Canada	16.29	24.19	24.01	30.34
Japan	35.10	57.45	71.49	110.25
Austria	19.74	20.62	12.05	19.04
Belgium-Luxembourg	24.11	30.82	22.55	28.68
France	64.86	75.41	51.79	61.15
Germany	56.47	71.80	71.07	108.63
Italy	42.25	59.30	42.46	57.21
Netherlands	26.23	41.73	25.62	38.80
Switzerland	16.03	22.25	9.50	13.06
United Kingdom	47.70	67.35	42.14	57.81
China, People's Rep. of	4.97	17.47	3.69	19.16
Korea	9.51	22.74	9.56	27.27

Source: Adapted from *Balance of Payments Statistics Yearbook Part 2: World and Regional Tables*, Washington, DC: International Monetary Fund, 1997, p. 22.

Key points

- The balance of payments is a record of all economic transactions between residents of a country and the rest of the world.
- The capital account records all long-term direct investment, portfolio investment, and other short- and long-term capital flows.
- The current account captures all trade in merchandise and service, private gifts and public aid transactions between countries.
- Since the end of the Second World War, world merchandise trade has grown faster than world production, i.e. it has outpaced the rate of increase in GNP.
- The fastest-growing sector of world trade is trade in services.

THE REGIONALISATION OF MARKETS

Since the Second World War, there has been a tremendous interest among nations in economic co-operation. This interest has been stimulated by the success of the European Community. There are many degrees of economic co-operation, ranging from agreements between two or more nations to reduce trade barriers, to the full-scale economic integration of two or more national economies. The best-known preferential arrangement of the 20th century was the British Commonwealth preference system. This system provided a foundation for trade between the United Kingdom, Canada, Australia, New Zealand, India, and certain other former British colonies in Africa, Asia and the Middle East. The decision by the United Kingdom to join the European Economic Community resulted in the demise of this system and illustrates the constantly evolving nature of international economic co-operation. Table 2.14 illustrates that there are four degrees of economic co-operation and integration.

Economic co-operation and integration

Free trade area

A free trade area (FTA) is a group of countries that have agreed to abolish all internal barriers to trade among themselves. Countries that belong to a free trade area can and do maintain independent trade policies with third countries. A system of certificates of origin is used to avoid trade diversion in favour of low-tariff members. The system discourages importing goods in the member country with the lowest tariff for shipment to countries within the area with higher external tariffs; Customs inspectors police the borders between members. The European Economic Area is an FTA that includes the 15-nation European Union and Norway, Liechtenstein and Iceland. The Canada–US Free Trade Area formally came into existence in 1989. In 1992, representatives from the United States, Canada, and Mexico concluded negotiations for the North American Free Trade Agreement (NAFTA).

Customs union

A customs union represents the logical evolution of an FTA. In addition to eliminating the internal barriers to trade, members of a customs union agree to the establishment of common external barriers. The Central American Common Market, Southern Cone Common Market (Mercosur), and the Andean Group are all examples of customs unions.

Common market

A common market goes beyond the removal of internal barriers to trade and the establishment of common external barriers to the important next stage of eliminating the barriers to the flow of factors (labour and capital) within the market. A common market builds on the elimination of the internal tariff barriers and the establishment of common external barriers. It seeks to co-ordinate economic and social policy within the market to allow free flow of capital and labour from country to country. Thus, a common market creates an open market not only for goods but also for services and capital.

Table 2.14 Degrees of international economic integration

Stage of integration	Abolition of tariffs and quotas	Common tariff and quota system	Removal of restrictions on factor movements	Harmonisation of economic, social, and regulatory policies
Free trade area	Yes	No	No	No
Customs union	Yes	Yes	No	No
Common market	Yes	Yes	Yes	No
Economic union	Yes	Yes	Yes	Yes

Economic union

The full evolution of an economic union would involve the creation of a unified central bank; the use of a single currency; and common policies on agriculture, social services and welfare, regional development, transport, taxation, competition and mergers, construction and building, and so on. A fully developed economic union requires extensive political unity, which makes it similar to a nation. The further integration of member nations of fully developed economic unions would be the formation of a central government that would bring together independent political states into a single political framework.

The European Union (EU) is approaching its target of completing most of the steps required to create a full economic union but major hurdles remain. One of the greatest is a single currency. Member countries recognise that the use of multiple currencies in the EU is a source of economic 'drag' on their economy, but they also realise that the adoption of a single currency would expose the member countries to economic risks that the countries do not face when operating with separate currencies. There is also the realisation that having a currency is a key element of national control and in the end is what distinguishes a nation from a sub-national unit of political organisation. Countries have currencies, and 'states' or 'provinces' do not. Those EU member states that adopt a single currency are no longer in control of inflation and interest rates, the two key levers of monetary policy which are crucial to any sovereign country for controlling economic destiny.

The World Trade Organization and General Agreement on Tariffs and Trade

The process towards stronger international economic integration is closely linked with two initiatives: the General Agreement on Tariffs and Trade (GATT) and the World Trade Organization (WTO). GATT was a treaty between 125 nations whose governments agreed, at least in principle, to promote trade among members. GATT was intended to be a multilateral, global initiative, and GATT negotiators did indeed succeed in liberalising world merchandise trade. GATT was also an organisation that handled 300 trade disputes, many involving food, during its half century of existence. GATT itself had no enforcement power (the losing party in a dispute was entitled to ignore the ruling), and the process of dealing with disputes sometimes stretched on for years.

The successor to GATT, the World Trade Organization (WTO), came into existence on 1 January 1995. From its base in Geneva, the WTO provides a forum for trade-related negotiations. One of the WTO's first major tasks was hosting negotiations on the General Agreement on Trade in Services, in which 76 signatories made binding market access commitments in banking, securities and insurance. The WTO's staff of neutral trade experts will also serve as mediators in global trade disputes. The WTO faced its first real test when representatives from the United States and Japan met to try and resolve a dispute over US claims that the Japanese engaged in unfair trade practices that limited imports of US car parts.

Since 1947, the member countries of GATT completed eight rounds of multilateral trade negotiations. Tariffs have been reduced from an average of 40 per cent in 1945 to 5 per cent today. The result has been a tremendous growth in trade: Between 1945 and 1975, the volume of world trade expanded by roughly 500 per cent.[24] The seventh round of negotiations was launched in Tokyo and ran from 1973 to 1979. These talks succeeded in cutting duties on industrial products value at $127 billion by another 30 per cent so that the remaining tariffs averaged about 6 per cent. In terms of agricultural trade, there was a major clash between the United States and protectionist European and Japanese markets. The clash pitted American farmers, the world's most efficient producers, against the high-cost, but politically powerful, farmers of Europe and Japan. These deep-rooted differences resulted in little change in the agricultural area during the Tokyo round. The most notable feature of the Tokyo round was not the duty cuts, but rather a series of nine new agreements on non-tariff trade barriers.

GATT officials also devoted considerable attention to the services industry, addressing market-entry barriers in banking, insurance, telecommunications and other sectors. The services issue was so volatile that the opening of the Uruguay round was delayed from 1982 until 1986. In addition to trade in services, these negotiations focused on the above-mentioned non-tariff measures that restrict or distort trade, including agricultural trade policy, intellectual property protection, and restrictions on foreign investment.[25]

Agricultural subsidies and quotas that have developed outside the multilateral framework also proved to be another divisive issue. Affluent countries protect and subsidise farm production. While home-market consumers pay high prices, surplus output is sold abroad at artificially low prices. France, for example, is intent on preserving its agricultural subsidies. According to the OECD, the total cost of these subsidies to rich-country taxpayers and consumers is more than $170 billion a year. Poor countries (including those in Eastern Europe) are denied their natural path out of poverty, namely food exports.[26] The Uruguay negotiations were suspended in December 1990 after 30,000 French farmers took to the streets of Brussels to protest a proposed 30 per cent cut in agricultural export subsidies. Negotiations resumed a few months later and finally succeeded in reaching agreement by December 1993. A stalemate over agricultural subsidies was broken, with France and the EU agreeing to reductions. However, agricultural policy offers plenty of new battle-grounds, as evidenced by the dispute over hormone-treated beef between the US and the EU (see Global Perspective).

Competitive companies will benefit as tariffs are cut or eliminated entirely. The Triad nations agreed to end tariffs in pharmaceuticals, construction, agricultural equipment, Scotch whisky, furniture, paper, steel and medical equipment. Major issues remain unresolved in the entertainment industry; France has insisted on preferences and subsidies for French producers of television programming and motion pictures in order to limit what they feel is 'cultural imperialism'. Efforts to reduce European broadcast restrictions on US produced movies and television programming were unsuccessful.[27]

In addition to the multilateral initiative of GATT and the WTO, countries in each of the world's regions are seeking to lower barriers to trade within their regions. The following section briefly describes the major regional agreements.

MAJOR REGIONAL AGREEMENTS

The European Union (EU)

The European Union (formerly known as the European Community [EC]) was established by the Treaty of Rome in January 1958. The six original members were Belgium, France, Holland, Italy, Luxembourg, and West Germany. In 1973, Britain, Denmark,

GLOBAL PERSPECTIVE

US gets go-ahead for trade sanctions

The World Trade Organization yesterday authorised the US to impose trade sanctions on European Union goods in retaliation for the EU's ban on hormone-treated beef.

From 29 July, the US will impose punitive 100 per cent duties on imports from the EU, including delicacies such as foie gras, truffels and Roquefort cheese as well as beef, pork, canned tomatoes and mustard. US officials said last week the sanctions, worth a total of €99 m, would target goods from France, Germany, Italy and Denmark as these were the countries most influential in preserving the 10-year-old beef hormone ban.

The ruling is the second this year in which the WTO has approved US trade sanctions against the EU. In April, the US was given permission to impose sanctions on nearly €170 m of European imports in retaliation for the EU's failure to comply with a WTO judgement against its banana import regime.

Rita Hayes, US ambassador to the WTO, hailed yesterday's decision as a victory. 'We now have a combination of more than €255 m in beef and bananas retaliation against the European Union.'

The WTO's dispute settlement body yesterday also granted Canada authorisation to impose trade sanctions worth C$11.3m (€6.4 m) annually in the dispute over beef hormones. Canada said it would announce the products on which it would impose punitive tariffs by the end of the month, although it was still open to talks on compensation.

The WTO ruled against the beef ban because it said the EU had not provided adequate scientific evidence that hormone-treated beef posed a danger to health, as trade rules require.

Brussels was told to comply with the WTO judgement by mid-May but chose to keep the ban while it conducted new scientific studies on the health risks.

A final report on these studies is due by the end of the year, although a disputed interim report argued that one of the six hormones used by US farmers could cause cancer.

Food for thought
- Should the EU have the right to decide, on their own, which products not to import on safety or health grounds? Why does the World Trade Organisation get involved?
- Should individual EU countries have the right to impose trade sanctions against other member countries (for example in the context of the well-publicised British beef ban)?

Source: *Financial Times*, 27 July 1999, p. 1.

and Ireland were admitted, followed by Greece in 1981 and Spain and Portugal in 1986. Effective 1 January 1995, the three newest members are Finland, Sweden, and Austria. (In November 1994, voters in Norway rejected a membership proposal.) Today, the 15 nations of the EU represent 379 million people, a combined GNP of €7.5 trillion, and a 39 per cent share of world exports. The map in Figure 2.7 shows the EU membership; the darker shaded countries are the three newest members.

Beginning in 1987, the 12 countries that were EC members at that time set about the difficult task of creating a genuine single market in goods, services, and capital. Completing the single-market programme by year-end 1992 was a major EC achievement; the Council of Ministers adopted 282 pieces of legislation and regulations to make the single market a reality. Now, citizens of the 15 countries are able to freely cross borders within the Union. Further EU enlargement has become a major issue. In December 1991, Czechoslovakia, Hungary and Poland became associate members through the so-called 'European Agreements'. The Baltic countries – Latvia, Lithuania and Estonia – are also hoping to join and thus lower their dependence on Russia.

Figure 2.7 **EU countries**

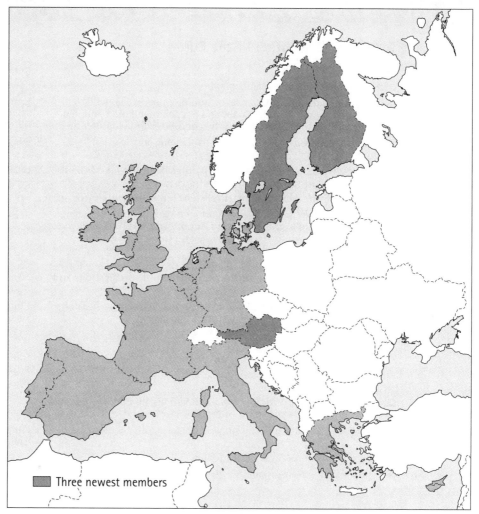

Three newest members

Under provisions of the Maastricht Treaty, the EU is working to create an economic and monetary union (EMU) that includes a European Central Bank and a single European currency, the Euro. Implementation of the Euro will require working out the extent to which countries sharing the currency need to co-ordinate taxes and budgets. As of January 1999, Belgium, Germany, Spain, France, Ireland, Italy, Luxembourg, The Netherlands, Austria, Portugal and Finland are participating in the Euro, but it is widely expected that Britain will join the Euro in the not too distant future. The single currency will eliminate costs associated with currency conversion and exchange rate uncertainty. However, until the completion of the changeover to a single currency, many obstacles must still be overcome. The European Focus illustrates the comprehensive timetable for the conversion of the different currencies to the Euro, which has been developed by the EU.

During its history, the European Union has grown greatly in terms of the area it covers, its political significance and its institutions. The founding Treaties have been revised three times: in 1987 (the Single Act), in 1992 (the Treaty on European Union)

EUROPEAN FOCUS

Timetable for the final adoption of the Euro

Timing	Action	Responsibility
Spring 1998	Decision on participating Member State.	European Council
	Decision adopted on the existence, or not, of an excessive public deficit in each of the Member States and a recommendation adopted identifying those that have fulfilled the conditions for adopting the Euro.	Economic and Finance Ministers Council (ECOFIN)
	Extraordinary session of the European Parliament on the ECOFIN recommendation.	European Parliament
	Decision on which Member States will participate in the Euro from the start.	Heads of State and Government
	Adoption of all the remaining practical steps for introducing the Euro.	
	Bilateral rates between participating currencies announced; President and Executive Board of the European Central Bank (ECB) recommended. Nominated in late May by Heads of State and Government after consultations with Parliament and EMI.	
	Legal texts adopted; establishing the Euro as the single currency for participating Member States; for the coins' technical specifications and for ECB legislation.	Economic and Finance Ministers Council (ECOFIN)
During 1998	European Central Bank created and its executive board appointed.	Council (Member States participating in EMU only)
	Start production of Euro banknotes and coins.	Council and Member States
	Adoption of necessary secondary legislation.	Commission proposes, Council decides
1 January 1999	Conversion rates are irrevocably fixed and various legislation come into force, notably on the legal status of the Euro.	
	Definition and execution of the single monetary policy in Euro.	European System of Central Banks (ESCB)
	Foreign exchange operations start in Euro.	
	New public debt issued in Euro.	Member States, European Investment Bank, Commission
1 January 1999 to 1 January 2002	Changeover to the Euro by the banking and finance industry.	
	Assist the whole economy in an orderly changeover.	Commission and Member States
1 January 2002	Start circulation of Euro banknotes.	European System of Central Banks (ESCB)
	Start circulation of Euro coins.	Member States
	Complete changeover to the Euro in public administration.	Member States
1 July 2002	Cancel the legal tender status of national banknotes and coins.	Member States, European System of Central Banks (ESCB)

Food for thought

- What do you think about the replacement of many national European currencies by the Euro? Which EU countries have/have not adopted the Euro? Will the split between those countries that did/did not adopt the Euro endanger the cohesion of the European Union?
- What impact does the Euro have for a marketing manager based inside the Euro-zone?

Source: Adapted from http://europa.eu.int/euro/html/calendrier5.html?lang=5, 26 July 1999.

and in 1997 (the draft Treaty of Amsterdam). The ultimate goal of the European Union is an ever closer union among the peoples of Europe, in which decisions are taken as closely as possible to the citizen; the objective is to promote economic and social progress which is balanced and sustainable, assert the European identity on the international scene and introduce a European citizenship for the nationals of the Member States.

The Union's main objectives for the coming years are: the implementation of the Treaty of Amsterdam (which contains new rights for citizens, freedom of movement, employment, strengthening the institutions) enlargement of the EU, to take in the applicant countries from central and eastern Europe (Agenda 2000) and, of course, the launching of the Euro.

North American Free Trade Agreement (NAFTA)

In 1988, the United States signed a free trade agreement with Canada (US–Canada Free Trade Agreement, or CFTA), the scope of which was enlarged in 1993 to include Mexico. The resulting free trade area had a 1995 population of 381 million and a gross national product of $6.4 trillion.

All three governments will promote economic growth through expanded trade and investment. The benefits of continental free trade will enable all three countries to meet the economic challenges of the decades to come. The gradual elimination of barriers to the flow of goods, services, and investment, coupled with strong intellectual property rights protection (patents, trademarks, and copyrights), will benefit businesses, workers, farmers and consumers. Canada and Mexico rank first and third as the United States' most important trading partners (Japan ranks second). The NAFTA countries are shown in Figure 2.8.

Asia–Pacific Economic Co-operation – APEC

Each November, representatives of 18 countries that border on the Pacific Ocean meet formally to discuss prospects for liberalising trade. Collectively, the countries that make up the Asia–Pacific Economic Co-operation (APEC) forum account for about 40 per cent of world trade, 38 per cent of world population, and 52 per cent of world economic output. APEC provides a chance for annual discussions by people at various levels: academics and business executives, ministers, and heads of state. Some small Asian countries view APEC as a welcome means of using the United States to counterbalance the dominance of Japan and China in the region. As noted in *The Economist*, 'Not so long ago, the thought of South Korea or Indonesia, let alone China, having anything to do with even a "vision" of free trade would have been fantastic.'

In 1993, at the fifth APEC forum in Seattle, the United States hoped to boost trade with fast-growing Asian Pacific Rim nations by cutting tariffs, reaching agreement on competition policies, and eliminating subsidies. In fact, after the heads of government met, an announcement was made regarding commitment to a 'vision' of free trade.

Much debate among APEC members has centred on whether all trade barriers in Asia can be eliminated, without exception, by the year 2000. It has become apparent that policymakers and farmers in South Korea, China and Japan still support agricultural subsidies. Agricultural producers in the United States, Canada and Australia want to sell more food products in Asia. Although the Japanese government took

Figure 2.8 NAFTA countries

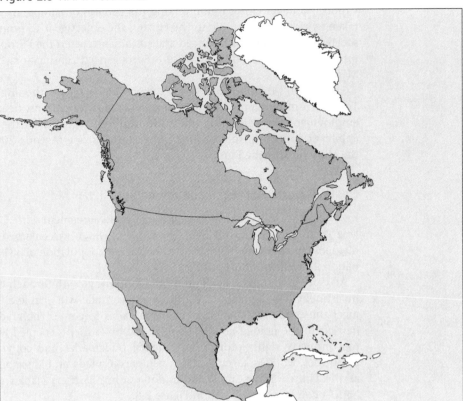

action in 1993 to end an outright ban on imports of foreign rice, market access is still restricted. Australian farmers have worked particularly hard to develop varieties of rice that will appeal to finicky Japanese consumers. Notes a member of an Australian rice growers' co-operative, 'Japanese are connoisseurs of rice. If we can sell our product in Japan, we can sell it anywhere. All we need is the market to open up.'

In 1997, the APEC meeting in Vancouver, British Columbia, faced a surprising challenge: the so-called 'Asian Flu' financial crisis that began in Thailand and quickly spread to Malaysia, Indonesia, Korea and even Japan. This crisis, caused by careless lending and borrowing practices in the private sectors of these countries, led to a crisis in investor confidence in security values, which led to a collapse in prices in equity markets, a major decline in currency values, and a massive increase in exports from countries in the region to the United States. The entire world was caught off guard by this crisis, which underlined the fact that lending and banking practices in the region had become quite 'loose' and sloppy. The world realised that the Asian 'miracle' had some major deficiencies that needed to be repaired. These repairs presented a challenge to the world economy: how to fix the problems in Asia without spreading the 'flu' to the rest of the world. It was clear to economists that as long as the economic leaders of the high-income countries of the world did not allow aggregate demand in their markets to collapse or trade barriers to be imposed, it would be possible for the countries in the Asian region to clean house. This would require ending the traditional close relationship that had existed in many countries between business and government and the establishment of a more rigorous system of private sector responsibility for investment decisions.

Association of Southeast Asian Nations – ASEAN

The Association of Southeast Asian Nations (ASEAN) is an organisation for economic, political, social, and cultural co-operation among its ten member countries: Brunei, Cambodia, Indonesia, Laos, Malaysia, Myanmar, the Philippines, Singapore, Thailand and Vietnam. ASEAN was established in 1967 with the signing of the Bangkok Declaration (see Figure 2.9).

There is a growing realisation among ASEAN officials that broad common goals and perceptions are not enough to keep the association alive. A constant problem is the strict need for consensus among all members before proceeding with any form of co-operative effort. Although the countries of ASEAN are geographically close, they have historically been divided in many respects. One of the reasons the association remained in existence is that it did almost nothing. The situation is changing today, however; in 1994, economic ministers from the member nations agreed to implement an ASEAN Free Trade Area (AFTA) by 2003, five years earlier than previously discussed. Under the agreement, tariffs of 20 per cent or more will be reduced to 0 to 5 per cent.[28]

Other regional co-operations

Beyond the co-operations discussed above, there are a number of other initiatives which aim to reduce trade barriers in various regions of the world. The most important of those will briefly be discussed below.

Figure 2.9 **ASEAN countries**

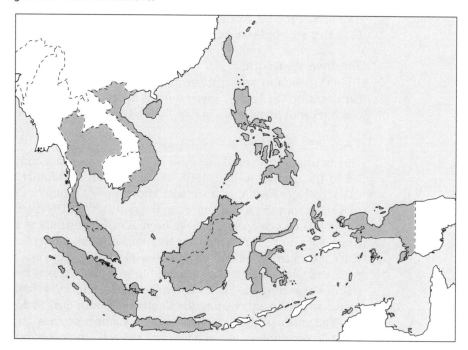

Central American Common Market

Central America is trying to revive its common market, which was set up in the 1960s. It collapsed in 1969 when war broke out between Honduras and El Salvador. The five members, El Salvador, Honduras, Guatemala, Nicaragua, and Costa Rica, decided in July 1991 to re-establish the common market.

Andean Group

The Andean Group was formed in 1969 to accelerate development of its member states, Bolivia, Colombia, Ecuador, Peru and Venezuela, through economic and social integration.

Southern Cone Common Market

Argentina, Brazil, Paraguay and Uruguay, with a combined population of 200 million people, agreed in March 1991 to form a customs union known as the Southern Cone Common Market (in Spanish, Mercado del Sur, or Mercosur).

Caribbean Community and Common Market – CARICOM

The Caribbean Community and Common Market (CARICOM) was formed in 1973 as a movement toward unity in the Caribbean. Members are Antigua and Barbuda, the Bahamas, Barbados, Belize, Dominica, Grenada, Guyana, Jamaica, Montserrat, Saint Christopher and Nevis, Saint Lucia, Saint Vincent and the Grenadines, and Trinidad and Tobago.

European Economic Area

After 14 months of negotiations, the then-EC and the seven-nation European Free Trade Association (EFTA) reached agreement on the creation of the European Economic Area (EEA) beginning January 1993. The EEA is a free trade area, not a customs union with common external tariffs. With Austria, Finland and Sweden now members of the EU, Norway, Iceland and Liechtenstein are the sole remnants of the EFTA that are not EU members (Switzerland voted not to be part of the EEA).

The Lomé Convention

The EU maintains an accord with 70 countries in Africa, the Caribbean, and the Pacific (ACP). The Lomé Convention was designed to promote trade and provide poor countries with financial assistance from a European Development Fund.

Central European Free Trade Association

The transition in Central and Eastern Europe from command to market economies led to the demise, in June 1991, of the Council for Mutual Economic Assistance. COMECON (or CMEA, as it was also known) was a group of Communist bloc countries allied with the Soviet Union. In the post-COMECON era, a number of proposals for multilateral co-operation have been advanced, including the creation of a successor body to be called the Organisation for International Economic Co-operation (OIEC). Ultimately, most proposals were blocked by potential member states whose representatives feared that a membership in a new regional bloc would hinder their chances of joining the EU. In December 1992, Hungary, Poland and Czechoslovakia signed an agreement creating the Central European Free Trade Association (CEFTA). The signatories pledged co-operation in a number of areas, including infrastructure and telecommunications, sub-regional projects, inter-enterprise co-operation, and tourism and retail trade.[29] Romania, Slovenia and the two countries created by the division of Czechoslovakia, Czech Republic and Slovakia, are also CEFTA members. Meanwhile, within the Commonwealth of Independent States, formal economic integration between the former Soviet republics is proceeding slowly. In May 1995 the governments of Russia and Belarus agreed to form a customs union and remove border posts between their two countries.

Co-operation Council for the Arab States of the Gulf

The organisation generally known as the Gulf Co-operation Council (GCC) was established in 1981 by six Arab states: Bahrain, Kuwait, Oman, Qatar, Saudi Arabia and United Arab Emirates. In 1989, two other organisations were established. Morocco, Algeria, Mauritania, Tunisia and Libya banded together in the Arab Maghreb Union (AMU); Egypt, Iraq, Jordan and North Yemen created the Arab Co-operation Council (ACC).

Economic Community of West African States

The Treaty of Lagos establishing the Economic Community of West African States (ECOWAS) was signed in May 1975 by 16 states, with the object of promoting trade, co-operation, and self-reliance in West Africa. The members are: Benin, Burkina Faso, Cape Verde, the Gambia, Ghana, Guinea, Guinea-Bissau, the Ivory Coast, Liberia, Mali, Mauritania, Niger, Nigeria, Senegal, Sierra Leone and Togo.

South African Development Co-ordination Conference

The South African Development Co-ordination Conference (SADCC) was set up in 1980 by the region's black-ruled states to promote trade and co-operation. The members are Angola, Botswana, Lesotho, Malawi, Mozambique, Namibia, Swaziland, Tanzania, Zambia and Zimbabwe.

Key points

- There are many different forms of economic co-operation between countries. The most important are free trade areas, customs unions, common markets and economic unions.

- Among the most important regional co-operation agreements are the EU, NAFTA and ASEAN.

- The World Trade Organisation (WTO) was established in 1995 as the successor of GATT. It serves as mediator in global trade disputes and ensures that trade flows as smoothly, predictably and freely as possible.

Summary

The economic environment is a major determinant of global market potential and opportunity. The world's economies can be categorised as market allocation systems, command allocation systems, and mixed systems. A major trend in recent years has been the transition toward market economies in many countries that had been centrally controlled. Countries can be categorised in terms of their stage of economic development: Low income, lower middle income, upper middle income, high income, and basket cases. It is possible to identify distinct stages and formulate general estimates about the type of demand associated with a particular stage of development. Since, for many products, the single most important indicator of market potential is income, the first step in determining the potential of a country or region is to identify the total and per capita income.

Market potential for a product can be evaluated by determining product saturation levels in the light of income levels. In general, it is appropriate to compare the saturation levels of countries or of consumer segments with similar income levels. Balance of payments issues are also important economic considerations. An analysis of a country's balance of payments provides insights into the flow of goods, services and capital into and out of the country.

There has been a strong interest among nations in forming economic co-operations. A distinction can be made between free trade areas, custom unions, common markets and economic unions. This chapter briefly describes the most important co-operations, including the EU, NAFTA, APEC and ASEAN.

Concepts and definitions

Common Market	In addition to having the properties of a free trade area and a customs union (see below), a common market strives to eliminate the barriers to the flow of labour and capital within the market.
Customs Union	In addition to eliminating the internal barriers to trade – as in a free trade area (see below) – members of a customs union agree to establish common external barriers.
Economic Union	The most advanced form of a regional co-operation. It includes the creation of a central bank, the use of a common currency and the adoption of common policies. The European Union is completing the steps required to create such a union.
Free Trade Area	A group of countries that have agreed to abolish internal barriers to trade among themselves.
General Agreement on Tariffs and Trade (GATT)	A treaty between 125 nations whose governments agreed to promote trade among members.
Gross Domestic Product	Gross Domestic Product (GDP) refers to the value of all goods and services produced by residents of a country during a year. GDP differs from Gross National Product (GNP) by excluding net factor income received from abroad, such as dividends, interest and royalties.
Gross National Product	Gross National Product (GNP) refers to the sum of the money values of all final goods and services produced during a year. Expressed differently, it is the sum of (1) personal consumption expenditures, (2) gross private domestic investment, (3) government purchases of goods and services and (4) net exports, i.e. exports minus imports.
Purchasing Power Parities	A comparison of the goods and services which can be bought with local currency in different countries.
Triad countries	North America, Western Europe and Japan.

1 Explain the differences between a market allocation economic system, a command allocation system, and a mixed system.

2 What are the stages of national market development, and what percentage of world income is found in each of the stages?

3 What is the pattern of income distribution in the world today? How do developing country markets compare with high income country markets in the proportion of income going to the bottom and the top 20 per cent of the population?

4 Are income and standard of living the same thing? What is meant by the term 'standard of living'?

5 Describe the similarities and differences of a free trade area, a customs union, a common market, and an economic union. Give an example of each.

6 What are the major characteristics of the world's regional markets? Which region is the fastest growing? Why?

Webmistress's hotspots

Homepage of the World Trade Organization
Provides an overview of trade topics, various resources (incl. trade statistics) and recent press clippings. Great source for up-to-date trade information.
http://www.wto.org/wto/

Homepage of NAFTA
Gives an introduction to the mandate of NAFTA and describes the NAFTA dispute resolution processes.
http://www.nafta-sec-alena.org/english/index.htm

Official homepage of the European Union
This site offers more information about the European Union than you are likely to need. It even allows you to listen to the European anthem! Good cross-links to the home pages of European institutions, such as the parliament, council, commission, court of justice and the European Central Bank.
http://www.europa.eu.int/index.htm

Eurostat: European statistics
It is Eurostat's job to provide official statistics on EU institutions, trade and industry, private and public institutions, universities, the news media, etc. Thus, if you ever need good statistics on Europe, this is *the* place to look.
http://www.europa.eu.int/en/comm/eurostat/serven/part1/1som.htm

Official site of the US State Department
Includes a great deal of information on US policy, regions and countries. It also tells you how you can become a US diplomat if you happen to be a US citizen.
http://www.state.gov/www/regions.html

Graph: Development of world population
A graph on the development of the world population, some appropriate comments

(in German) and a counter which provides an up-to-the-minute estimate of the world population. What more does one need to plan a family?
http://neuro.biologie.uni-freiburg.de/Skriptum/Gentechnik/Bevoelkexpl.html

Graph: Development of world population by region
Another graph and some figures showing the development of the world population by regions.
http://people.delphi.com/rd100/worldpop.html

Homepage of the United Nations
A great site for all UN-related information. It allows you to access a vast variety of UN documents and, very handy, includes a search facility.
http://www.un.org

Suggested readings

Ardrey, William J., Anthony Pecotich and Clifford J. Schultz, 'American involvement in Vietnam, Part 11: Prospects for US business in a new era', *Business Horizons*, 38 (March/April 1995): pp. 21–27.

Drucker, Peter, 'Marketing and economic development', *Journal of Marketing* (January 1958): pp. 252–259.

Enghold, Christopher, *Doing Business in Asia's Booming 'China Triangle'*. Upper Saddle River, NJ: Prentice Hall, 1994.

'The European Community – Survey', *The Economist*, 11 July 1992, pp. 5–30.

Galbraith, John Kenneth, *The Nature of Mass Poverty*. Cambridge, MA: Harvard University Press, 1979.

Gilder, George F., *Microcosm: the Quantum Revolution in Economics and Technology*. New York: Simon & Schuster, 1989.

Golden, Peggy A., Patricia M. Doney, Denise M. Johnson and Jerald R. Smith. 'The dynamics of a marketing orientation in transition economies: a study of Russian firms', *Journal of International Marketing*, 3, 2 (1995): pp. 29–49.

Isaak, Robert A., *International Political Economy*. Upper Saddle River, NJ: Prentice Hall, 1991.

Johansson, J.K. and M. Hirano, 'Japanese marketing in the post-bubble era', *The International Executive*, 38 (January/February 1996): pp. 33–51.

Kennedy, Paul, *The Rise and Fall of Great Powers*. New York: Random House, 1987.

Porter, Michael E., *The Competitive Advantage of Nations*. New York: The Free Press, 1990.

Prowse, Michael, 'Is America in decline?' *Harvard Business Review* (July–August 1992): pp. 36–37.

Shapiro, Alan C., *Multinational Finance Management*. 3rd edn. Boston: Allyn & Bacon, 1989.

Thurow, Lester, *Head to Head: The Coming Economic Battle Among Japan, Europe and America*. New York: William Morrow and Company, 1992.

Yan, Rick, 'To reach China's consumers, adapt to Guo Qing', *Harvard Business Review* (September–October 1994): pp. 66–74.

Notes

1. 'Wretchedly oil-rich Azeris', *The Economist*, 11 July 1998, p. 34.
2. See Peter F. Drucker's excellent article 'The changed world economy', *Foreign Affairs* (Spring 1986), and various issues of *The Economist*. For example, 'The European Community – survey', *The Economist*, 11 July 1992, or 'When China wakes', *The Economist*, 28 November 1992.
3. As economist Paul Krugman points out, the trend toward global integration that began in the 1970s is actually the second of the century; the first ended with the outbreak of the First World War. Krugman has written extensively expressing a contrarian view of the extent of global integration. See, for example, 'A global economy is not the wave of the future', *Financial Executive* (March–April 1992): pp. 10–13.
4. A Eurodollar is a US dollar held outside the United States. US dollars are subject to US banking regulations; Eurodollars are not.
5. Alan C. Shapiro, *Multinational Finance Management*, 3rd edn (Boston: Allyn and Bacon, 1989): p. 116.
6. Some companies have cut employment by outsourcing or subcontracting non-manufacturing activities such as data processing, housekeeping and food service.
7. Peggy A. Golden, Patricia M. Doney, Denise M.

Johnson and Jerald R. Smith, 'The dynamics of a marketing orientation in transition economies: a study of Russian firms', *Journal of International Marketing,* 3, 2 (1995): pp. 29–49.

8. *OECD Economic Outlook,* no. 50, December 1991 (Paris: OECD, 1991): 206.

9. Jack Goldstone, 'The coming Chinese collapse,' *Foreign Policy* (Summer 1995): 35–52.

10. Kim R. Holmes, 'In search of free markets', *The Wall Street Journal,* 12 December 1994, p. A17.

11. Marcus W. Brauchli, 'Garment industry booms in Bangladesh', *The Wall Street Journal,* 6 August 1991, p. A9.

12. Francis C. Notzon, Yuri M. Komarov, Sergei P. Ermakov, Christopher T. Sempos, James S. Marks and Elena V. Sempos, 'Causes of declining life expectancy in Russia', *Journal of the American Medical Association,* (March 1998): pp. 279, 793–800.

13. Irma Adelman and Cynthia Taft Morris, *Comparative Patterns of Economic Development, 1850–1914* (Baltimore: Johns Hopkins University Press, 1988); Irma Adelman and Cynthia Taft Morris, *Economic Growth and Social Equity in Developing Countries* (Stanford, CA: Stanford University Press, 1973).

14. Jim Rohwer, 'Empurrar com a barriga', *The Economist,* 7 December 1991, pp. S6–S7.

15. Marcus W. Brauchli, 'Great Wall: as the rich in China grow richer, the poor are growing resentful,' *The Wall Street Journal,* 4 January 1994, p. A1.

16. Georg Hoffmann-Ostenhof, 'Im Schatten des Fortschritts: Wie die Kluft zwischen Arm und Reich geschlossen werden kann', *Profil,* 19 July 1999, p. 71.

17. James Cook, 'The ghosts of Christmas yet to come', *Forbes,* 22 June 1992, pp. 92–95.

18. Peter T. Bauer, *West African Trade* (London: Routledge and K. Paul, 1963).

19. *Balance of Payments Statistics Yearbook, Part 3, Methodologies, Compilation Practices and Data Sources,* 1997, Washington DC: International Monetary Fund, p. 312.

20. Balance of payments data are available from a number of different sources, each of which may show slightly different figures for a given line item.

21. 'Who wants to be a giant?', *The Economist,* 24 June 1995, Survey, p. 1.

22. This section has been adapted from: http://www.clev.frb.org/research/feb96et/wortrd.htm#1c, 26 July 1999.

23. http://www.wto.org/statis/i06e.htm

24. 'GATT's last gasp', *The Economist,* 1 December 1990, p. 16.

25. Joseph A. McKinney, 'How multilateral trade talks affect the US', *Baylor Business Review* (Fall 1991): pp. 24–25.

26. 'Free trade's fading champion', *The Economist,* 11 April 1992, p. 65.

27. Bob Davis and Lawrence Ingrassia, 'Trade acceptance: after years of talks, gatt is at last ready to sign off on a pact', *The Wall Street Journal,* 15 December 1993, pp. A1, A7.

28. 'ASEAN economic ministers agree to accelerate AFTA', *ASEAN Business Report,* 5, 9 (September 1994): pp. 1, 6.

29. Bob Jessop, 'Regional economic blocs, cross-border cooperation, and local economic strategies in post-socialism', *American Behavioral Scientist,* 38 (March 1995): pp. 689–690.

CHAPTER 3

Social and cultural environments

Culture reflects the homogeneity of artistic expressions in all facets of a people's way of life.
FRIEDRICH WILHELM NIETZSCHE 1844–1900[1]

After reading this chapter, you will know:

- How important cultural and social differences are in global marketing.
- Which fundamental concepts provide an understanding of cultural differences.
- Where potential conflicts may arise in global business relations.
- How cultural differences impact on the marketing of products.
- The approaches used by international companies to deal with cultural diversity.

Why is this important? Here are three situations in which you would need an understanding of the above issues:

- It might be your task to decide whether an adaptation of the marketing mix is necessary, when marketing your product or service in foreign markets.
- Your overall conduct during negotiations can have a considerable impact on success or failure. Therefore, knowing a foreign language is not enough. Behaviour as well as communication styles are important in negotiations between foreign partners.
- Strategic alliances represent an important way of obtaining competitive position in today's business environment. Such co-operations often involve the alignment of different corporate as well as national cultures. Willingness to understand and learn from another culture constitutes an important prerequisite for success.

Practice link

The opening quote by the famous philosopher Friedrich Nietzsche is a reminder that culture has always been a source of disagreement and misunderstanding. What does Nietzsche mean when he refers to 'culture'? As you will soon see, the meaning of culture to a global marketer is quite different than it was to Nietzsche, who is probably referring to art, literature, and perhaps even music. All of these elements of 'high' and 'low' culture are important, but as global marketers know, culture is about much more than art. It is definitely a major influence on what happens in the marketplace.

Volkswagen represents a corporation well familiar with the impact culture might have on the marketing of products and services. Although the VW Golf is still quite popular in the European market, this model, known as the Rabbit, never managed to convince the American customer. The opposite holds for the New Beetle!

Most of us still remember the VW Beetle, which was marketed for the first time in the USA in 1949.[2] In 1973, this model was the world's most popular car. Although the launch of the Golf captured considerable attention, the Mexican production of the Beetle never stopped. Exhibiting the prototype of the New Beetle at the Detroit Motor Show represented a kind of rebirth of the once so famous and popular car.[3] Although the model was never meant for production, demand in North America more than justified the realisation of the concept. Of 1998's capacity of 120,000, only 50,000 Beetles were originally allocated to North America. However, after sales of 60,000 cars to the US and Canada, the model was totally sold out for the rest of the year.

Steve Wilhite, sales and marketing manager at Volkswagen of America, considered the American market to be the perfect place to launch the New Beetle, although this had never happened before throughout the history of VW. In his opinion, the American market tends to be more emotional than the rest of the world. With special ads targeting different age groups, the extraordinary shape of the car managed to really capture people's hearts:[4] in fact, a real Beetlemania has been triggered off.[5] Initially, the situation in Europe appeared to be just as promising, taking into consideration 200,000 advance orders.[6] However, predictions of the future demand across Europe proved to be inaccurate as the New Beetle did not conform to conventional market segment or buyer classifications. It did not even fit into existing lifestyle categories.[7] In addition, the car was priced at a premium in the European market. With the car being produced in Mexico, prestige could not justify a price of approximately €18,500.[8] Overall, the launch of the New Beetle in Europe is referred to as a disappointment for Volkswagen. After not even selling a minimum of 75,000 cars per year, plans to build the New Beetle in Wolfsburg have been put on hold.[9]

The wide acceptance of the New Beetle in North America illustrates how products can be especially successful in foreign markets. This chapter focuses on the important differences in world markets and the equally important similarities that express the fact of cultural universals. To help marketers better understand social and cultural dynamics in the global marketplace, several useful analytical approaches are explained. These include Maslow's hierarchy, Hofstede's cultural typology, the self-reference criterion, and diffusion theory. The chapter offers specific examples of the impact of culture and society on the marketing of both industrial and consumer products. The chapter ends with approaches designed to overcome cross-cultural difficulties and a review of cross-cultural training procedures currently being used in global companies.

BASIC ASPECTS OF SOCIETY AND CULTURE

Anthropologists and sociologists define culture as 'ways of living', by a group of human beings, that are passed on from one generation to another. A culture acts out its ways of living in the context of social institutions, including family, educational, religious, governmental and business institutions. Culture includes both conscious and unconscious values, ideas, attitudes and symbols that shape human behaviour and that are passed on from one generation to the next. In this sense, culture does not include one-time solutions to unique problems, or passing fads and styles. As defined by the Dutch organisational anthropologist Geert Hofstede, culture is 'the collective programming of the mind that distinguishes the members of one category of people from those of another'.[10]

In addition to agreeing that culture is learned, not innate, most anthropologists share two other views. First, all facets of culture are interrelated: influence or change one aspect of a culture and everything else is affected. Second, because it is shared by the members of a group, culture defines the boundaries between different groups.[11]

Culture consists of learned responses to recurring situations. The earlier these responses are learned, the more difficult they are to change. Taste and preferences for food and drink, for example, represent learned responses that are highly variable from culture to culture and can have a major impact on consumer behaviour. Preference for colour is culturally influenced as well. For example, although green is a highly regarded colour in Moslem countries, it is associated with disease in some Asian countries. White, usually associated with purity and cleanliness in the West, can signify death in Asian countries. Red is a popular colour in most parts of the world (often associated with full flavour, passion, or virility); it is poorly received in some African countries.[12] Of course, there is no inherent attribute to any colour of the spectrum; all associations and perceptions regarding colour arise from culture.

Attitudes toward whole classes of products can also be a function of culture. For example in Europe, customers are especially concerned about the seating features and comfort of their cars and they are willing to pay for it. In particular, safety, weight and comfort targets have to be met.[13] Differences in preference reflect cultural diversity.

As we noted in the last chapter, income levels also influence consumer behaviour and attitudes around the world. Indeed, a basic question that must be answered by marketers who want to understand or predict behaviour is, 'How much do social and cultural factors influence behaviour independent of income levels?' Sometimes, the influence is strong. Resistance of European customers against big, four-wheel-driven sport-utility vehicles has led to the development of smaller models. Car companies such as Renault with its 'Mégane minivan' and Ford Europe have not only realised varying preferences among cultures, but have also taken into account the problem of comparatively high fuel prices in Europe.[14]

Another example refers to the music industry. Although a marketer within this industry has to be very cautious referring to cultural differences, strategy is often determined by the income level of the respective country. The Czech market was worth approximately €73 million in 1996, whereas Slovakia (with about half the population of the Czech Republic) only accounted for €7.5 million. As per capita spending on recorded music is very low in Slovakia, signing and promoting local music appears to be very expensive for major label companies.[15]

Nevertheless, the demand for convenience foods, luxury consumer products, electronic products, disposable products, and soft drinks in the United States, Europe, Asia, Africa and the Middle East suggests that most consumer products have broad, almost universal, appeal. As communication continues to shrink the world, more and more products will be marketed and consumed globally. This implies that an important characteristic of culture i.e. that it defines boundaries between people, will not limit the global reach of companies that want to extend their operations globally. This does not suggest, however, that these companies can ignore cultural factors. The fact that there is a global market for a product does not mean that one can approach the market in different countries identically. Cultural sensitivity to differences spells the difference between global success and failure.

The search for cultural universals

An important quest for the global marketer is to discover cultural universals. A universal is a mode of behaviour existing in all cultures. Universal aspects of the cultural environment represent opportunities for global marketers to standardise some or all elements of a marketing program. A partial list of cultural universals, taken from cultural anthropologist George P. Murdock's classic study, includes the following: athletic sports, body adornment, cooking, courtship, dancing, decorative art, education, ethics, etiquette, family feasting, food taboos, language, marriage, mealtime, medicine, mourning, music, property rights, religious rituals, residence rules, status differentiation and trade.[16] The astute global marketer often discovers that much of the apparent cultural diversity in the world turns out to be different ways of accomplishing the same thing.

Music provides one example of how these universals apply to marketing. Music is part of all cultures, accepted as a form of artistic expression and a source of entertainment. However, music is also an art form characterised by widely varying styles. Therefore, although background music can be used effectively in broadcast commercials, the type of music appropriate for a commercial in one part of the world may not be acceptable or effective in another part. A jingle might use a bossa nova rhythm for Latin America, a rock rhythm for North America, and 'high life' for Africa. Music, then, is a cultural universal that global marketers can adapt to cultural preferences in different countries or regions.

Because music is a cultural universal, it should come as no surprise that the music business is going global. However, this does not mean that the world's music is uniform.

The German music channel VIVA has realised that further expansion can only be reached by adapting to local preferences when penetrating new markets. Therefore, VIVA has started to produce foreign-language programming for its broadcast to Poland. However, not only the language will be adapted. The programme will also focus on local acts, on the local music scene and will be hosted by local DJs. The same concept will be pursued in the Swiss market. In case those ventures prove to be successful, similar projects will be implemented in Hungary, Spain and Italy.[17] As can be seen from this example, the company employs the same fundamental concept for all markets, the same process of value creation for the customer, however adapted to local preferences.

Increasing travel and improving communications mean that many national attitudes toward style in clothing, colour, music, food and drink are converging. The globalisation of culture has been capitalised on, and even significantly accelerated, by companies that have seized opportunities to find customers around the world. Coca-Cola, Pepsi, Levi Strauss, McDonald's, IBM, Heineken, Benetton and Gilette are some of the companies breaking down cultural barriers as they expand into new markets with their products. Similarly, new laws and changing attitudes toward the use of credit are providing huge global opportunities. Smart cards have become an integral part of European life, used for everything from phone calls to betting on horse races. Now, plastic is invading health care. At present, about 200 million Europeans hold medical smart cards. The European Commission is currently working together with local governments to develop a coherent, interlinked system. For the vendors of this project, France's Gemplus, Groupe Bull, Schlumberger and Siemens, a continent-wide scheme could prove a huge win, especially, if a further launch takes place in the US enlarging the system to a global network.[18]

The anthropologist's standpoint

As Ruth Benedict points out in her classic text, *The Chrysanthemum and the Sword*, the way a person thinks, feels and acts has some relation to his or her experience of the world. It does not matter if (normal) actions and opinions are thought of as bizarre by outsiders. Successful global marketers must understand human experience from the local point of view, and become insiders with cultural empathy in the process, if they are to understand the dynamics of markets outside the home country.[19]

Any systematic study of a new geographic market requires a combination of tough-mindedness and generosity. The appreciation of another way of life cannot develop when one is defensive about one's own way of life; it is necessary to be secure in one's own convictions and traditions. In addition, generosity is required to appreciate the integrity and value of other ways of life and points of view to overcome the prejudices that are a natural result of the human tendency toward ethnocentricity. When people from other countries complain that the (Americans, Japanese, French, British, Chinese, and so on) are haughty, patronising, or arrogant, home-country ethnocentricity is probably contributing to the problem. Global marketers need to develop an objective standpoint that recognises diversity and seeks to understand its origins. There are many paths to the same end in life. The global marketer knows this and rejoices in life's rich diversity.

High- and low-context cultures

Edward T. Hall has suggested the concept of high and low context as a way of understanding different cultural orientations.[20] In a low-context culture, messages are explicit; words carry most of the information in communication. In a high-context culture, less information is contained in the verbal part of a message. Much more information resides in the context of communication, including the background, associations and basic values of the communicators. In general, high-context cultures function with much less legal paperwork than is deemed essential in low-context cultures. Japan, Saudi Arabia and other high-context cultures place a great deal of emphasis on a person's values and position or place in society. In such cultures, a business loan is more likely to be based on who you are than on formal analysis of pro forma financial documents. In a low-context culture such as the United States, Switzerland or Germany, deals are made with much less information about the character, background and values of the participants. Much more reliance is placed on the words and numbers in the loan application.

In a high-context culture, a person's word is his or her bond. There is less need to anticipate contingencies and provide for external legal sanctions because the culture emphasises obligations and trust as important values. In these cultures, shared feelings of obligation and honour take the place of impersonal legal sanctions. This helps explain the importance of long and protracted negotiations that never seem to 'get to the point'. Part of the purpose of negotiating for a person from a high-context culture is to get to know the potential partner.

For example, insisting on competitive bidding can cause complications in low-context cultures. In a high-context culture, the job is given to the person who will do the best work and whom you can trust and control. In a low-context culture, one tries to make the specifications so precise that a builder is forced by the threat of legal sanction to do a good job. According to Hall, a builder in Japan is likely to say, 'What has that piece of paper got to do with the situation? If we can't trust each other enough to go ahead without it, why bother?'

Although countries can be classified as high or low context in their overall tendency, there are exceptions to the general tendency. These exceptions are found in subcultures. Companies which are closely linked to those subcultures have to take this factor into account. This is what WEA Germany did. The company, which is positioned in the music business, works mainly with new successful artists, which arise from subcultures and underground structures. In order to be able to achieve optimal results and with respect to the high-context culture of their customers within a low context culture environment, the company has been restructured. By dividing up the company into four smaller 'mini companies', shorter communication, direct exchange of know-how and high motivation have been achieved. Furthermore, a capability of quick responses to new trends and retail structures has been developed. One major concern, which triggered the restructuring, has also been the high degree of specialisation and knowledge necessary when serving those 'niches'. The benefits arising from this new procedure have already been demonstrated by such labels as Frankfurt techno or the Berlin dub and jungle specialist Downbeat, all of which have been using the company's service department.[21] Table 3.1 summarises some of the ways in which high- and low-context cultures differ.

It would be easy to get paranoid about the hazards of doing business across cultures, but, in fact, the main obstacle is attitude. If you are sincere and truly want to learn about a culture, you will find that people respond to your sincerity and interest and will help you acquire the knowledge you need to be effective. If you are arrogant and insincere and believe that you are right and 'they' are wrong, you can expect a full measure of trouble and misunderstanding. The best antidote to the problem of mis-perceiving a situation is constant vigilance and an awareness that there are many opportunities to err. This should create an attitude of openness. Every global marketer should strive to suspend judgement and simply listen, observe, perceive, and take in the facts.

Communication and negotiation

The ability to communicate in our own language is, as most of us have learned, not an easy task. Whenever languages and culture change, additional communication challenges will present themselves. For example, 'yes' and 'no' are used in an entirely different way in Japanese than in Western languages. This has caused much confusion and misunderstanding. In English, the answer 'yes' or 'no' to a question is based on whether the answer is affirmative or negative. In Japanese, this is not so. The answer 'yes' or 'no' may indicate whether the answer affirms or negates the question. For example, in Japanese, the question, 'Don't you like meat?' would be answered 'yes' if the answer is negative, as in, 'Yes, I don't like meat'. The word *wakarimashita* means

Table 3.1 High- and low-context cultures

Factors/dimensions	High context	Low context
Lawyers	Less important	Very important
A person's word	Is his or her bond	Is not to be relied on; 'get it in writing'
Responsibility for organisational error	Taken by highest level	Pushed to lowest level
Space	People breathe on each other	People maintain a bubble of private space and resent intrusions
Time	Polychronic – everything in life must be dealt with in its own time	Monochronic – time is money Linear – one thing at a time
Negotiations	Are lengthy – a major purpose is to allow the parties to get to know each other	Proceed quickly
Competitive bidding	Infrequent	Common
Country/regional examples	Japan, Middle East	United States, Northern Europe

both 'I understand' and 'I agree.' To avoid misunderstandings, Westerners must learn to distinguish which interpretation is correct in terms of the entire context of the conversation. The Global Perspective shows other ways the verbal component of cross-cultural communication can get lost in translation.

The challenges presented by non-verbal communication are perhaps even more formidable. For example, Westerners doing business in the Middle East must be careful not to reveal the soles of their shoes to hosts or pass documents with the left hand. In Japan, bowing is an important form of non-verbal communication that has many nuances. People who grow up in the West tend to be verbal, whereas those from the East are more non-verbal. Not surprisingly, there is a greater expectation in the East that people will pick up non-verbal cues and understand intuitively without being told.[22] Westerners must pay close attention not only to what they hear, but also to what they see when conducting business in such cultures.

Knowledge and understanding of cross-cultural differences is crucial during negotiations. Negotiations put global marketers face to face with counterparts from diverse cultural backgrounds, challenging both sides to surmount verbal and non-verbal communication barriers. Table 3.2 lists some important aspects of the French and British way of doing business, including negotiation styles. In addition, some useful suggestions are given on how to adapt one's own behaviour and appearance when doing business with either the French or the British. However, managers doing business abroad always have to bear in mind that these lists can only function as guidelines, as they consist of typologies not taking into account the particular individual. Still, in every generalisation lies some truth.

Social behaviour[23]

There are a number of social behaviours and comments that have different meanings in other cultures. In Western companies it is taken for granted that members of the organisation from different departments and hierarchical levels show different points of view. In contrast, Japanese enterprises, which constitute a kind of family, assume that harmony prevails. Therefore, a Western manager will seek to support collective decision-making and improve communication within his organisation, whereas Japanese and Chinese firms pursue their goal of harmony.[24]

Other social behaviour, if not known, will place the international traveller at a disadvantage. For example, in Saudi Arabia, it is an insult to question a host about the health of his spouse, show the soles of one's shoes, or touch or deliver objects with the left hand. In Korea, both hands should be used when passing objects to another person, and it is considered impolite to discuss politics, communism, or Japan. Also in Korea, formal introductions are very important. In both Japan and Korea, ranks and titles are expected to be used in addressing hosts. In the United States, there is not a clear rule on this behaviour, except in select fields such as the armed forces or medicine. In Indonesia, it is considered rude to point at another person with a finger. However, one may point with the thumb or gesture with the chin.

When greeting someone, it is appropriate in most countries to shake hands. In some countries, the greeting includes a handshake and more. In Japan, a handshake may be followed by a bow, going as low and lasting as long as that of the senior person. In Brazil, Korea, Indonesia, China and Taiwan, a slight bow is also appropriate.

In some countries, the greeting involves more contact. For instance, in Venezuela,

Table 3.2 Cross-cultural business behaviour[25]

	French style	*British style*
The language of business	Despite the fact that so many French business people speak English well, French is the language of business. Written correspondence should be in French and the key parts of your product literature should be translated as well. Despite the local sensitivity to the language, do try to use your French even if you make mistakes or have a foreign accent. You will be given credit for trying.	Few British people today speak another language well enough to handle a serious business negotiation. Visitors whose English is not fluent should consider arranging for an interpreter.
Making the initial contact	Connections count heavily in this market. Trade shows and official trade promotion missions are good ways to make initial contact. The alternative is to arrange for a formal introduction to potential customers, distributors or partners. Ask your country's embassy to introduce you. France is definitely a country of personal networks. You get things done more quickly by working through inside contacts than by 'going through channels'. The French want to know a good deal about you before discussing business, but building rapport involves less small talk than in some other cultures. Showing a knowledge of French history, literature, art and philosophy is a good way to build rapport.	Famously a land of old school ties and the old boys' network, Britain is a market where referrals, recommendations and testimonials are extremely useful. Write in English with basic information about your company and your product, adding that you will contact them soon to set up an appointment. Follow this with a phone call requesting a meeting two or three weeks hence. Your British counterpart will suggest the time and place.
Orientation to time	Business behaviour tends toward the polychronic, though visitors are expected to be roughly on time for business meetings, particularly if they are selling. It is not unusual for your local counterpart to appear a few minutes late. Nor do meetings always follow a fixed agenda. Instead you may experience free-form discussion with everyone present having his or her say.	While visitors are expected to be on time, locals are often a few minutes late for meetings. Still, the British are definitely clock-obsessed compared with most Latins, Arabs and Africans as well as the majority of South and Southeast Asians.
Hierarchy and status	Level of education along with family background and wealth determine status in France. French bosses tend to run their companies in an authoritarian style. Managers are expected to be highly competent and to know the answer to virtually every question that arises. They are often reluctant to delegate authority.	Status in Britain is largely determined by one's regional origin, social class, family background and accent. Personal achievement is regarded as less important. The existence of relatively large status distinctions explains the formality in social interaction. The British usually prefer to stay with Mr or Mrs until at least the second or third meeting. Visitors, however, find that younger British business people are becoming less formal.
Verbal communication	While they relish conflict, the French dislike getting straight to the point. They tend to favour subtle, indirect language and like to present their point of view with Cartensian logic, elegant phrasing and verbal flourishes. This is one reason Gallic business people prefer to negotiate in French: their verbal pyrotechnics are lost when expressed in another language.	Upper-class Britons favour vague, oblique language while others speak more directly. Visiting negotiators should be mentally prepared to encounter either verbal style.

Table 3.2 continued

	French style	*British style*
Non-verbal communication	The French use many more hand and arm gestures than Asians and Anglo-Saxons. Always shake hands when meeting and when leaving someone.	The British use far less body language in comparison to the French. Eye contact tends to be less direct than in expressive cultures such as the Italians. Two Englishmen in conversation will often stand at a 90-degree angle to each other rather than facing each other directly. A very direct gaze may be interpreted as rude and intrusive.
Dress code	As might be expected in a hierarchical, status-conscious society, the French dress and behave formally in a business setting. And of course being French they dress with style, panache and elegance. Male business visitors should wear a dark suit; women should choose tasteful, somewhat conservative clothing and accessories.	Men wear dark suits, plain shirts, conservative ties and polished black shoes. Avoid striped ties, they can be seen as imitating prestigious British regimental ties. Women should likewise dress conservatively, avoiding garish colours and too much jewellery.
Meeting and greeting	Handshake with moderate pressure and steady eye contact. Among males the older or higher status person should initiate the handshake. Women of any rank can decide whether or not to offer their hand.	While men exchange light to moderate handshakes, some women choose not to offer their hand. Men should always wait for the woman to extend her hand.
Forms of address	Greet your local counterparts with monsieur, madame or mademoiselle without the person's name. Always use the *vous* (formal) pronoun rather than the informal *tu*.	Use Mr, Mrs, Miss or Ms until your counterpart suggests switching to given names.
Sales presentation	Avoid hard-sell tactics, hyperbole and flippant humour. Prepare a sober presentation with a logical sequence of arguments. If you encounter forceful disagreement on some points, be prepared to respond with factual counter-arguments. Vigorous disagreement with specific issues does not necessarily signal lack of interest in your overall proposal.	Accustomed to understatement, British buyers are turned off by hype and exaggerated claims. Presentations should be straightforward and factual. Humour is acceptable, but visitors from abroad should remember that it rarely translates well.
Bargaining style	Be prepared for long, relatively unstructured negotiating sessions punctuated frequently with verbal confrontation. Your counterpart may also attack the thought process behind your bargaining position. The French pride themselves on their logical thinking and often seem to relish faulting the logic of others. Expect decision-making to take longer than in Anglo-Saxon countries.	English negotiators have been doing business all over the world for hundreds of years. They may put a safety margin in their opening position so as to leave room for substantial concessions during the bargaining process. Time-is-money Americans may find the British process too time-consuming, but for the rest of the world's business cultures it is quite normal. Expect emphasis on the legal aspects and the fine points of the written agreement.

Source: Richard R. Gesteland, *Cross-Cultural Business Behaviour: Marketing, Negotiating and Managing across Cultures* (1999), Copenhagen, Copenhagen Business School Press.

close friends greet each other with a full embrace and a hearty pat on the back; in Indonesia, a social kiss is in vogue, and a touching of first the right then the left cheek as one shakes hands. In Austria, especially when coming to Vienna, a slight kiss on either cheek is used to greet friends. In Malaysia, close friends grasp with both hands; and in South Africa, blacks shake hands, followed by a clench of each other's thumbs, and another handshake.

In most countries, addressing someone as Mr, Mrs, Miss, or Ms is acceptable. It is sometimes the case that conversation occurs as greetings are exchanged. In Sweden, the greeting is 'goddag'; in the Netherlands, it is 'pleased to meet you'; in the United Kingdom, it is 'how do you do'; and in Israel, it is 'shalom'. Other greetings vary by country. In many countries, as mentioned in Table 3.2, men do not shake hands with a woman unless she extends her hand first. In India, women, or a man and a woman, greet each other by placing the palms of their hands together and bowing slightly; and in Mexico simply by a slight bow. In some countries, such as India, it is not advisable for men to touch or talk alone with a woman.

Although many of the social behaviours mentioned vary from the home-country norm, negative judgements should not be made about them. When trying to explain what took so long in closing a deal, home office executives need to understand that drinking tea, socialising, and relationship building are important components in accomplishing corporate international goals.

Intercultural socialisation

In addition to knowing specific courtesies, personal space, language and communication, and social behavioural differences, there are numerous intercultural socialisation behaviours that an international business traveller should learn. Knowing a culture means knowing the habits, actions and reasons behind the behaviours. It is a mistake to make assumptions about what is culturally proper or incorrect based on one's own experiences.

For example, in the United States, the bathtub and toilet are likely to be in the same room. Americans assume that this is the world norm. Some cultures, however, such as the Japanese, consider it unhygienic. Other cultures think it unhygienic even to sit on a toilet seat. In many cultures, toilet paper is not the norm. One of the authors remembers his first visit to the toilet of an Indonesian ministry. It was here that he discovered that the Indonesian government in Jakarta does not offer toilet paper to toilet users. This is something that you will not discover in the Intercontinental Hotel in Jakarta.

It is not always necessary for an international business traveller to understand the 'whys' of a culture, but it is important to accept them and to abide by them while on foreign soil. Becoming aware of the culture in which you will be visiting or working will pay excellent dividends.

However, it is not only essential to be aware of the foreign culture. People often encounter problems when having to describe their own culture. This experience was made by students with differing cultural backgrounds taking part in a global marketing course. One of their group assignments involved the collection and discussion of characteristics referring to each culture represented within the group. Table 3.3 shows some of the results. In particular, those students who had spent some time abroad found that they were more aware of the host-culture than their own culture back home.

The reason cultural factors are a challenge to global marketers is that they are hidden from view. Because culture is learned behaviour passed on from generation to

Table 3.3 Cultural differences expressed by students

Finland	• Transaction based – not personal • Great importance of privacy • Nationalistic • Environmentally concerned • Leisure time important
Spain	• Social importance • Food is extremely important • Fast-food not important • Low environmental awareness
China	• Strong cultural identity • Conservative • Lifestyle changes, especially in younger generation • Importance of image and status • Difference between young and old • Different languages/regulations
USA	• 'Fast-food' culture • Convenience lifestyle • Forward-thinking, less conservative • Service orientation, power of consumers • Work hard, play hard • Melting pot
Belgium	• Mixture of influences • Food is extremely important • Different languages (French/Dutch) • International orientation • Easy market access

generation, it is difficult for the inexperienced or untrained outsider to fathom. Becoming a global manager means learning how to let go of cultural assumptions. Failure to do so will hinder accurate understanding of the meaning and significance of the statements and behaviours of business associates from a different culture.

The following examples illustrated how misperceptions of a culture may result in considerable costs for the respective company. Fomabo, a Dutch building company, agreed to form a strategic alliance with two Malaysian enterprises to build prefabricated houses in Malaysia. Despite numerous bureaucratic barriers the first group of houses was finally built. However, sales appeared to be disappointing and soon the reason for this was revealed. As in the Netherlands, the walls of the Fomabo houses were made of reinforced concrete, whereas Malaysian houses consist of wood. This feature enables Malaysians to hang pictures and other objects on their walls, which traditionally is an important factor in making them feel comfortable and at home. In addition, given the abundance of cheap labour in this country, the cost advantage of prefabricated building technology did not provide any new perceived benefits. In the end, these factors resulted in Fomabo having to leave the Malaysian market.

Another example is given by a well-known North European brewer, who was involved in a special promotional campaign during the 1994 World Cup soccer tournament. Among other things, the flags of all countries qualifying for the World Cup Finals were imprinted under the bottle cap of their leading brand of beer. This, however, raised the anger of Muslims all around the world. As the Saudi Arabian flag shows a holy verse from the Koran, the association with an alcoholic beverage led to negative reactions within the Muslim congregation. As a result, the brewer had to recall all bottles and discontinue its campaign.

Finally, Knorr had to discover that its dry soups turned out to be a failure in the US market. Although considerable market research efforts revealed positive result concerning the taste, the company overlooked that American consumers were not prepared to spend 15 to 20 minutes in front of their stoves.[26]

To transcend ethnocentricity and cultural myopia, managers must make the effort to learn and internalise cultural differences. There are several guidelines that will improve the ability to learn about other cultures:

1 The beginning of wisdom is to accept that we will never fully understand ourselves or others. People are far too complex to be 'understood'. As Goethe said 'confusion and misunderstandings' are the 'source of activity and entertainment'.[27]

2 Our perceptual systems are extremely limited. We 'see' almost nothing. Our nervous systems are organised on the principle of negative feedback. That is, the only time our control system is brought into play is when input signals deviate from what we have learned to expect.

3 We spend most of our energy managing perceptual inputs.

4 When we do not understand the beliefs and values of a particular cultural system and society, things that we observe and experience may seem 'bizarre'.

5 If we want to be effective in another culture, we must attempt to understand that culture's beliefs, motives and values. This requires an open attitude that allows us to transcend perceptual limitations based on our own culture.

Key points

- The buying behaviour of consumers is heavily influenced by tastes and preferences of their own culture. This, in turn, has a considerable impact on the marketing of a company's products in foreign markets.

- Although consumer tastes and preferences vary considerably from market to market, an international marketer should seek to discover cultural universals such as music, religious rituals or language.

- Managers doing business abroad have to take account of the culture (high- or low-context) they are in, have to adapt to local negotiation and communication approaches as well as to social behaviour typical for the respective country. Business success or failure can be determined by proper conduct in a foreign culture.

- An international manager has to be aware of, and sensitive to, foreign cultures. There has to be a willingness to adapt his/her own behaviour and appearance to the local behaviour and attitudes.

GLOBAL PERSPECTIVE

A matter of culture: getting lost in translation

An American airline operating in the Brazilian market advertised the plush 'rendezvous lounges' on its jets only to discover that *rendezvous* in Portuguese has the meaning of hiring a room for lovemaking. Fresca, which is the name of a soft drink, is a slang word for 'lesbian' in Mexico. Pepsi's advert 'Come alive with Pepsi' was presented in Germany as 'Come alive out of the grave with Pepsi'.

These examples are hardly unique, but they underscore the importance of language and translation for persons and companies doing business across national boundaries. In Eastern Europe, translation problems often arise because the meanings of many Western business terms are not widely known or are difficult to translate.

Sometimes, translation errors result in bloopers that are harmless but funny. Consider this assortment of hotel signs from around the world translated into English:

Paris: 'Please leave your values at the front desk.'
Japan: 'You are invited to take advantage of the chambermaid.'
Zurich: 'Because of the impropriety of entertaining guests of the opposite sex in the bedroom, it is suggested that the lobby be used for this purpose.'
Romania: 'The lift is being fixed for the next day. During that time we regret that you will be unbearable.'

In Japan, many consumer packaged goods, including some that are not imported, have English, French or German on the labels to suggest a stylish image and Western look. A Westerner may wonder, however, what point the copywriters are actually trying to get across. For example, English on the label of City Original Coffee proclaims 'Ease Your Bosoms. This coffee has carefully selected high quality beans and roasted by our all the experience.'

The intended message: Drinking the coffee provides a relaxing break and takes a load off your chest. Other products, such as casual wear and sports apparel, are also emblazoned with fractured messages. These words appeared on the back of a jacket: 'Vigorous throw up. Go on a journey.' A sports bag bore the message, 'A drop of sweat is the precious gift for your guts.' Finally, consider the message printed on the cover of a notebook: 'Be a man I recommend it with confidence as like a most intelligent stationary of basic design.' One expert on 'Japanese English' believes messages like these highlight basic differences between Japanese and other languages. Many Western languages lack exact equivalents for the rich variety of Japanese words that convey feelings. This presents difficulties for copywriters trying to render feelings in a language other than Japanese. The message on the back of the notebook was supposed to convey manliness. As the English-speaking Japanese copywriter explained, 'I wanted to say I am proud to present the product to the customer because it has got a simple, masculine image.' While a Westerner might argue whether the copywriter succeeded, Japanese retailers do not seem at all concerned that the messages are gibberish. As one retailer explained, the point is that a message in English, French or German can convey hipness and help sell a product. 'I don't expect people to *read* it,' she said.

Food for thought
- Can you think about other examples where language or translation caused problems for international marketers?
- Given that English is nearly universally understood by educated Europeans, would you recommend the development of standardised advertising copy in English for PCs, mobile phones and hand-held scanners?

Source: Del I. Hawkins, Roger Best and Kenneth Coney, *Consumer Behaviour – Building Marketing Strategy* (Boston: McGraw-Hill 1998); Yumiko Ono, 'A little bad English goes a long way in Japan's boutiques', *The Wall Street Journal*, 20 May 1992, pp. A1, A6; Charles Goldsmith, 'Look see! Anyone do read this and it will make you laughable', *The Wall Street Journal*, 19 November 1992, p. B1.

ANALYTICAL APPROACHES TO CULTURAL FACTORS

Maslow's hierarchy of needs

The late A. H. Maslow developed an extremely useful theory of human motivation that helps explain cultural universals.[28] He hypothesised that people's desires can be arranged into a hierarchy of five needs. As an individual fulfils needs at each level, he or she progresses to higher levels (see Figure 3.1). Once physiological, safety and social needs have been satisfied, two higher needs become dominant. First is a need for esteem. This is the desire for self-respect, self-esteem, and the esteem of others and is a powerful drive creating demand for status-improving goods. The status symbol cuts across the stages of country development described in Chapter 2.

Today, this kind of behaviour can already be found by young people. The compilation 'Hits for Kids', signed by the record label Universal in Denmark, Sweden and Norway, features the same tracks as comparable records for grownups. By doing so, the need of kids and young people for esteem from the grownup world can be satisfied.[29] Another example for the need for esteem are women in East Africa, who wore their bras with straps exposed to show the world that they can afford them. In Asia today, young women are taking up smoking and showing a preference for Western brands as a symbol of their improved status and increased affluence.

The final stage in the need hierarchy is self-actualisation. This need, such as the desire for developing one's own skills as well as latent existing potentials, is also called deficit-motive.[30] When all the needs for food, safety, security, friendship, and the esteem of others are satisfied, discontent and restlessness will develop unless one is doing what one is fit for. A musician must make music, an artist must create, a poet must write, a builder must build, and so on.

Maslow's hierarchy of needs is, of course, a simplification of complex human behaviour. Other researchers have shown that a person's needs do not progress neatly from one stage of a hierarchy to another. For example, highly developed societies increasingly involved with the Internet show a growing need for safety. Protecting computer networks from unauthorised access and related financial losses capture remarkable attention all over the world today.[31] Nevertheless, the hierarchy does suggest a way for relating consumption patterns and levels to basic human need-fulfilling behaviour. The usefulness of Maslow's hierarchy is its universality.[32]

Figure 3.1 Maslow's hierarchy of needs

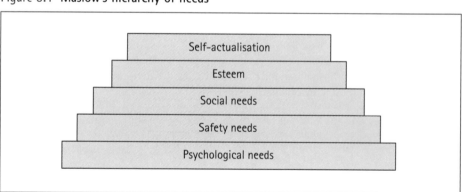

The model implies that, as countries progress through the stages of economic development, more and more members of society are operating at the esteem need level and higher, having satisfied physiological, safety and social needs. It appears that self-actualisation needs begin to affect consumer behaviour as well. For example, there is a growing tendency in high-income countries to reject material objects as 'status symbols'. The automobile is no longer the classic American status symbol it once was, and many younger consumers are turning away from material possessions. This trend toward rejection of materialism is not, of course, limited to high-income countries. In India, for example, there is a long tradition of the pursuit of consciousness or self-actualisation as a first rather than a last goal in life. However, each culture is different. For example, in Germany today, the automobile remains a supreme status symbol. Germans give their automobiles loving care, even going so far as to travel to distant locations on weekends to wash their cars in pure spring water.

Hofstede's cultural typology[33]

The organisational anthropologist Geert Hofstede has argued that the cultures of different nations can be compared in terms of four dimensions. The first, power distance, is the extent to which the less powerful members of a society accept or even expect that power should be distributed unequally. To paraphrase George Orwell: all societies are unequal, but some are more unequal than others. The second dimension is a reflection of the degree to which individuals in a society are integrated into groups. In individualist cultures, each member of society is primarily concerned with his or her own interest and those of the immediate family. In collectivist cultures, all of society's members are integrated into cohesive in-groups. Masculinity, the third dimension, describes a society in which men are expected to be assertive, competitive and concerned with material success, while women fulfil the role of nurturer and are concerned with issues such as the welfare of children. Femininity, on the other hand, describes a society in which the social roles of men and women overlap, with neither gender exhibiting overly ambitious or competitive behaviour. Hofstede notes that the first three dimensions refer to expected social behaviour; the fourth dimension is concerned with, in Hofstede's words, 'man's search for truth'. Uncertainty avoidance is the extent to which the members of a society are uncomfortable with unclear, ambiguous or unstructured situations. Some cultures express strong uncertainty avoidance with aggressive, emotional, intolerant behaviour; they are characterised by a belief in absolute truth. The manifestation of low uncertainty avoidance is behaviour that is more contemplative, relativistic and tolerant.

Hofstede's research convinced him that, although the four dimensions yielded interesting and useful interpretations, they did not provide any insight into possible cultural bases for economic growth. Hofstede was also disturbed by the fact that the surveys used in the research had been developed by Western social scientists. Because many economists failed to predict the explosive economic development of Japan and the 'tigers' (i.e. South Korea, Taiwan, Hong Kong and Singapore), Hofstede surmised that some cultural dimensions in Asia were eluding the researchers. The underlying assumption referred to the idea that not only managers and their behaviour are culturally influenced. Hofstede wondered whether the results of his studies were effected by a Western bias introduced by the common Western background of the researchers. Co-operating with the Canadian Michael Bond, he therefore conducted a further study on attitudes and values of students. In order to bypass the Western bias the questionnaire, the so-called Chinese Value Survey (CVS), had been developed by Chinese researchers and was subsequently translated from the Chinese into different languages. Analysing the CVS data, three dimensions significantly correlating with the IBM dimensions of power distance, individualism and masculinity were produced. The fourth dimension discovered, however, did not support uncertainty avoidance. Hofstede called this new dimension Long-term versus Short-term Orientation. It was composed of items rooted in the teachings of Confucius (therefore also called Confucian dynamism); items which were not included in the IBM questionnaire. On the long-term side, values oriented towards the future such as thrift (saving) and persistence can be found, whereas the short-term side is characterised by an orientation towards the past and present.[34]

In order to illustrate cultural influence on management and research behaviour, one of Hofstede's own examples is described in the following, including the dimensions of power distance and uncertainty avoidance. These two dimensions affect both the way in which people write about organising and the way in which people organise themselves. At INSEAD, the American professor Owen James Stevens used a case study describing a conflict between two department heads within a company as an examination assignment for his Organisational Behaviour class. The three largest national groups among the students were French, German and British. The diagnosis of the case resulted in widely differing interpretations, depending on the nationality of the group.

The majority of the French students saw the problem in the negligence of the General Manager to whom the two department heads reported. In their opinion the two opponents would have to take the conflict to their common boss, who would have to issue orders on how to settle such problems in future. Stevens saw the implicit model of the French organisation as a pyramid of people with the Chief Executive at the top and each successive level at its proper place below. This view coincides with large power distance and strong uncertainty avoidance.

The German majority diagnosed a lack of structure to be solved by the establishment of procedures. In their opinion, the fields of competence of each department head had never been laid down accurately. In order to solve the conflict, this national group suggested calling in a consultant to nominate a task force or ask the common boss for advice. These solutions are based on an organisation where management intervention is limited to exceptional cases because the rules should settle all daily problems. This corresponds with a strong uncertainty avoidance combined with limited power distance.

Finally, the British saw a human relations problem underlying this conflict. Poor negotiations skills on either side should be trained. This matches the idea of an organisation comparable to a village market where neither hierarchy nor rules, but the demands of the situation determine what will happen, illustrating a combination of small power distance and weak uncertainty avoidance.[35]

The self-reference criterion and perception

As we have shown, a person's perception of market needs is framed by his or her own cultural experience. A framework for systematically reducing perceptual blockage and distortion was developed by James Lee and published in the *Harvard Business Review* in 1966. Lee termed the unconscious reference to one's own cultural values the self-reference criterion, or SRC. To address this problem and eliminate or reduce cultural myopia, he proposed a systematic four-step framework.

1 Define the problem or goal in terms of home country cultural traits, habits and norms.
2 Define the problem or goal in terms of the host culture, traits, habits and norms. Make no value judgements.
3 Isolate the SRC influence and examine it carefully to see how it complicates the problem.
4 Redefine the problem without the SRC influence and solve for the host-country market situation.[36]

The Euro Disney cases (see Appendix) provide an excellent vehicle for understanding SRC. As they planned their entry into the French market, how might Disney executives have done things differently?

● *Step 1.* Disney executives believe there is virtually unlimited demand for American cultural exports around the world. Evidence includes the success of McDonald's, Coca-Cola, Hollywood movies, and American rock music. Disney has a stellar track record in exporting its American management system and business style. Tokyo Disneyland, a virtual carbon copy of the park in Anaheim, California, has been a runaway success. Disney policies prohibit sales or consumption of alcohol inside its theme parks.
● *Step 2.* Europeans in general, and the French in particular, are sensitive about American cultural imperialism. Consuming wine with the midday meal is a long-established custom. Europeans have their own real castles, and many popular Disney characters come from European folk tales.
● *Step 3.* The significant differences revealed by comparing the findings in steps 1 and 2 suggest strongly that the needs upon which the American and Japanese Disney theme parks were based did not exist in France. A modification of this design was needed for European success.
● *Step 4.* This would require the design of a theme park that is more in keeping with French and European cultural norms.

The lesson that SRC teaches is that a vital, critical skill of the global marketer is unbiased perception, the ability to see what is what in a culture. Although this skill is as valuable at home as it is abroad, it is critical to the global marketer because of the widespread tendency toward ethnocentrism and use of the self-reference criterion. The SRC can be a powerful negative force in global business, and forgetting to check for it can lead to misunderstanding and failure. While planning Euro Disney, chairman Michael Eisner and other company executives were blindsided by a lethal combination of their own prior success and ethnocentrism. Avoiding the SRC requires one to suspend assumptions based on prior experience and success and be prepared to acquire new knowledge about human behaviour and motivation.

Environmental sensitivity

Environmental sensitivity is the extent to which products must be adapted to the culture-specific needs of different national markets. A useful approach is to view products on a continuum of environmental sensitivity. On the one hand are environmentally insensitive products that do not require significant adaptation to the environments of various world markets. On the other hand are products that are highly sensitive to different environmental factors. A company with environmentally insensitive products will spend relatively less time determining the specific and unique conditions of local markets because the product is basically universal. The greater a product's environmental sensitivity, the greater the need for managers to address country-specific economic, regulatory, technological, social and cultural conditions.

The sensitivity of products can be represented on a two-dimensional scale, as shown in Figure 3.2. The horizontal axis shows environmental sensitivity, the vertical axis the degree of product adaptation needed. Any product exhibiting low levels of environmental sensitivity, integrated circuits for example, belongs in the lower left of the figure.

Intel has sold over 100 million microprocessors, because a chip is a chip anywhere around the world. Moving to the right on the horizontal axis, the level of sensitivity increases, as does the amount of adaptation. Computers are characterised by moderate levels of environmental sensitivity; variations of voltages in different countries require some adaptation. In addition, the computers' software documentation should be in the local language. At the upper right of Figure 3.2 are products with high environmental sensitivity. Food sometimes falls into this category, because it is sensitive to climate and culture.

Beer consumption per capita (Figure 3.3) illustrates how environmentally sensitive, or culture bound, this product is.

Group Danone, the French food and glass packaging group, is celebrating worldwide success. This is, amongst other things, due to the company's ability to respond quickly to international trends and tailoring its products to local tastes. Although in Asian countries milk is thought of as being indigestible and about 80 per cent of consumers experience difficulties in absorbing lactose, Group Danone did not hesitate to enter these markets with its drinking yoghurts. As yoghurt is fermented, it does not cause digestion problems. Danone saw this as a favourable opportunity, positioning its product as a dessert for happy digestion. Today, Danone Yoghurts are produced in Thailand, Singapore, Japan, South Korea and Australia as well as Shanghai.[37]

Figure 3.2 **Environmental sensitivity – product adaptation matrix**

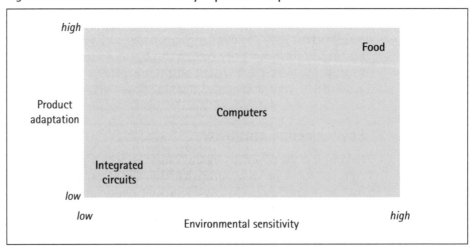

Figure 3.3 Beer consumption per capita 1996

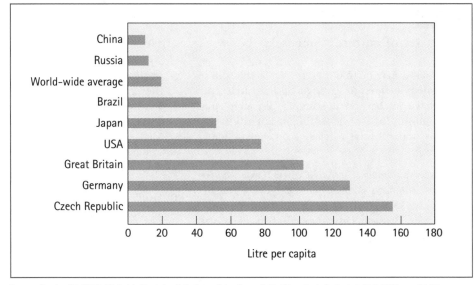

Source: Carolyn Pfaff, 'Die Welt drinkt wieder Heineken – Interview mit Karl Vuursten', *Outlook*, 1. Heft 1998, pp. 14–17.

Key points

- There are a number of theoretical frameworks which help in the under-standing of cultural diversity and universals.

- Maslow has developed his so-called 'hierarchy of needs', which is extremely useful in explaining cultural universals.

- Hofstede has discovered four, respectively five, cultural typologies, which constitute a useful tool in comparing different cultures. His cultural dimensions are: power distance, individualism vs. collectivism, masculinity vs. femininity, uncertainty avoidance and, the fifth dimension, Confucian dynamism.

- The self-reference criterion helps international managers understand and accept cultural diversity.

- Environmental sensitivity of a product or service determines the degree of necessary adaptation.

HANDLING CULTURAL DIVERSITY

The impact of social and cultural environments on marketing industrial products

The various cultural factors described earlier can exert important influences on industrial products marketed around the globe. They must be recognised in formulating a global marketing plan. Some industrial products may exhibit either low levels of environmental sensitivity, as in the case of computer chips, for example, or high

EUROPEAN FOCUS

A matter of culture: 'Sincerely'

Although it may be true that 'brevity is the soul of wit', when it comes to signing a business letter, the French go far beyond the simple 'Sincerely' that often suffices for anyone writing in English. Below are the 'top 10' ways to close a business letter in French.

1 *Nous vous prions d'agréer, Monsieur, l'expression de nos sentiments dévoués.* 'We beg you to receive, sir, the expression of our devoted sentiments.'

2 *Agréez, Monsieur, l'assurance de mes meilleurs sentiments.* 'Accept, sir, the assurance of my best sentiments.'

3 *Je vouz prie d'agréer, Monsieur le Directeur, mes meilleures saluations.* 'I beg you to accept, Mr Director, my best greetings.'

4 *Je vous prie d'agréer, Madame la Directrice, mes meilleures salutations.* 'I beg you to accept, Ms Director, my best greetings.'

5 *Veuillez, croire, Messieurs, à l'assurance de ma haute considération.* 'Please believe, Gentlemen, the assurance of my highest consideration.'

6 *Recevez, Messieurs, mes sincéres salutations.* 'Receive, Gentlemen, my sincere greetings.'

7 *Je vous prie d'agréer, Monsieur, l'expression de mes sentiments les meilleurs.* 'I beg you to accept, Sir, the expression of my best sentiments.'

8 *Je vous prie d'agréer, Mademoiselle, mes respectueurses salutations.* 'I beg you to accept, Miss, my respectful greetings.'

9 *Veuillez agréer, Monsieur, l'expression de mes sentiments distingués.* 'Please accept, Sir, the expression of my distinguished sentiments.'

10 *Veuillez agréer, Messieurs, avec mes remerciements anticipés, l'expression de mes sentiments distingués.* 'I beg you to accept, Gentlemen, with my anticipated thanks, the expression of my distinguished sentiments.'

Food for thought

● What do you think about the described French approaches to signing business letters? Are the French simply more courteous than, for example, the British, Germans or Americans?

● How important, in your view, is knowledge of foreign languages for an international marketing executive? Does it make a difference whether his/her mother tongue is English?

levels, as in the case of turbine generators when 'buy national' government policy puts foreign bidders at a disadvantage.

Economic turmoil in the Asian area have, amongst other things, led to a change in Japanese business ethos. This has to be taken into consideration by suppliers trying to enter this specific market. To support those companies wishing to take advantage of opportunities offered by the region, the Pacific Rim Electronics Business Association (Preba) was launched in 1996. In addition to a guide for doing business in Japan developed by the successor of Preba, the Japan Electronics Business Association, the British Industry Centre provides a base by offering reasonably priced office accommodation and a support staff.[38]

The impact of social and cultural environments on marketing consumer products

Research studies show that, independent of social class and income, culture is a significant influence on consumption behaviour and durable goods ownership.[39] Consumer products are probably more sensitive to cultural difference than are industrial products. Hunger is a basic physiological need in Maslow's hierarchy; everyone needs to eat, but what we want to eat can be strongly influenced by culture. Evidence from the front lines of the marketing wars suggest that food is probably the most sensitive category of consumer product. Throughout the European Union certain trends can be found. Scandinavian countries are generally assumed to mainly eat fish; however, these nations are the largest consumers of bread and cereals, particularly pasta. In the consumption of fish Portugal and Spain top the list. Greece turns out to have a special preference for animal products: 68 per cent of their daily consumption consists of milk, cheese and meat.[40]

Thirst also shows how needs differ from wants. Liquid intake is a universal physiological need. As is the case with food and cooking, however, the particular beverages people want to drink can be strongly influenced by culture. Coffee is a beverage category that illustrates the point. In the United Kingdom, instant coffee has 90 per cent of the total coffee market as compared with only 15 per cent in Sweden. The other European countries fall between these two extreme points. Instant coffee's large share of the British market can be traced to the fact that, in the hot beverage category, Britain has historically been a nation of tea drinkers. Only in recent times have the British been persuaded to take up coffee drinking. Instant coffee is more like tea than ground coffee in its preparation. Not surprisingly, when the British did begin to drink coffee, they opted for instant because its preparation was compatible with past experience. Another reason for the popularity of instant coffee in Britain is the practice of drinking coffee with a large quantity of milk, so that the coffee flavour is masked. Differences in the coffee flavour are thus hidden, so that a 'better cup' of coffee is not really important. In Sweden, however, coffee is the hot beverage of choice. Swedes consume coffee without large quantities of milk, and therefore the coffee flavour is not masked and brewed coffee is preferred.

As can be seen from Table 3.4, Switzerland took the lead in annual coffee consumption in 1997.

However, consumer behaviour not only varies in respect to hot beverages. Soft drink consumption also shows differing patterns world-wide. In France and Italy, for

Table 3.4 Annual coffee consumption per capita[41]

Country	Annual consumption per capita (kg)
Switzerland	8.72
Finland	8.21
Sweden	7.23
Luxembourg	7.00
Norway	6.85
Austria	6.22
Denmark	6.17
Germany	5.42
Singapore	5.31
The Netherlands	4.86
Canada	4.54
Belgium	4.42
USA	4.18
France	3.56
Greece	3.31

example, 30 to 40 times as much wine is consumed as in America on a per capita basis. The French also prefer mineral water to soft drinks; the converse is true in America, where soft drink consumption surpasses that of water. Germany far exceeds the United States in per capita consumption of beer. Does culture alone account for the difference between the popularity of soft drinks in Western Europe and the United States? No; in fact, several variables – including culture – are responsible for the differences, as portrayed in the following equation:

$$Y = f(A, B, C, D, E, F, G)$$

where

Y = consumption of soft drinks
f = function of
A = influences of other beverages' relative prices, quality, and taste
B = advertising expenditure and effectiveness, all beverage categories
C = availability of products in distribution channels
D = cultural elements, tradition, custom, habit
E = availability of raw materials (particularly of water)
F = climatic conditions, temperature, and relative humidity
G = income levels

To be sure, culture affects the demand for soft drinks. Note, however, that it is only one of several variables. Therefore, culture is an influencing, rather than a determining, factor. If a soft drink marketer in Western Europe launches an aggressive marketing programme (including lower prices, more intensive distribution and heavy advertising) consumption can be expected to increase. However, it is also clear that any effort to convert Europeans to soft drinks will run up against cultural tradition, custom and competition from widely available alternative beverages. Culture in this case is a restraining force, but, because culture is changing so rapidly, it is a restraint that can be overcome. Consumption of bottled water in different nations constitutes one good example for illustration. In 1994, only 9 litres per capita were consumed in Great Britain, whereas France showed an average of 110 and Germany of 94 litres per capita.[42] Today, British producers have realised the great potential of bottled water. Consumers are not only becoming more individualistic in their choice, but also want to express themselves in what they consume. When bottled water was introduced to the UK market, it had a premium image and was regarded as something to be used on special occasions. Today, bottled water is seen as an alternative to tap water.[43] Also, innovative products such as Lipton iced tea had to be adapted to British preferences. The refreshing soft drink had to be reformulated, repackaged and refocused at a younger audience.[44] The penetration of the US beverage market by bottled water producers is another excellent example of the impact of an effective creative strategy on a firmly entrenched cultural tradition. Prior to the 1980s, drinking bottled water was not an important part of US culture. The general attitude in the United States was, 'Why pay for something that is free?' Source Perrier SA, the French bottled water firm, decided to take aim at the US market. It hired Bruce Nevin, an experienced American marketing executive, and gave him a free hand to formulate a creative strategy.

Nevin decided to reposition Perrier from an expensive, imported bottled water (which no sane, red-blooded American would touch) to a competitively priced, low-calorie beverage in the soft drink market. To back up this positioning, Nevin launched a major consumer advertising campaign, lowered prices, and moved the product from the gourmet section of the supermarket to the soft drink section. The strategy boiled down to significant adjustment of three marketing mix elements: price, promotion and place. Only the product was left unchanged.

The campaign succeeded beyond even the most optimistic expectations, essentially creating an entirely new market. By the mid-1980s, the €1,9 billion bottled water category had become the fastest-growing segment of the US beverage industry. Perrier's annual US sales grew from about €34 million to €679 million, and Perrier commanded 80 per cent of the US bottled water market. The success of this strategy was rooted in two indisputable facts: Americans were ready for bottled water, and the tactics were brilliantly executed. The results illustrate how the restraining force of culture can be changed by a creative marketing strategy grounded in market possibilities.

Key points	
	● **The culture of a nation has a considerable impact on the marketing of both industrial and consumer products.**
	● **Consumer goods are usually more sensitive to cultural diversity than industrial products.**
	● **Culture is changing so rapidly that innovative marketing may be able to change established consumption patterns routed in cultural differences.**

CROSS–CULTURAL COMPLICATIONS AND SUGGESTED SOLUTIONS

Global marketing activities are conducted in an ever-changing environment that blends economic, cultural, and social forces. Stepping out of the global perspective for a moment, we should acknowledge one thing: even when the parties to a commercial transaction belong to the same low-context society – the United States, for example – and the terms of the deal are spelled out 'in black and white', different understandings of the respective obligations of the parties will often occur.

Business relationships between parties of different cultures and/or nationalities are subject to additional challenges. Parties from different countries may have trouble coming to contract terms because of differences in the laws governing their respective activities and problems of enforcement across international boundaries. No matter what is stated in a contract, taking another party to court for breach of contract will probably require a suit in the defendant's own home turf, which may be an insurmountable advantage for the home-country participant.

When a party from a high-context culture takes part in a business understanding, the proceedings are likely to be further complicated by very different beliefs about the significance of formal business understandings and the ongoing obligations of all parties. The business environment in many countries outside the Triad markets can be characterised by all manner of 'hostile' elements: natural and human-induced catastrophes, political problems, foreign exchange inconvertibility, widely fluctuating exchange rates, depressions, and changes in national economic priorities and tariff schedules. One cannot predict precisely how the most carefully laid plans will go awry, only that they will. Marketing executives and managers with dealings outside the home market must build mutual trust, rapport and empathy with business contacts; all are required to sustain enduring relationships. Appointing a host-country national to a position as sales representative will not automatically guarantee success. If a corporation constantly shuffles its international staff, it risks impeding the formation of what we might call 'high-context subcultures' between home office personnel and host nationals. This diminishes the company's chances of effectively dealing with the business crises that will inevitably occur.

Mexico's government imposed severe foreign exchange restrictions during a recent financial crisis. Companies that had sold products or services to Mexican parties on terms other than 'confirmed irrevocable international letter of credit' learned that they would have a lengthy wait before receiving payment in US dollars or other 'hard' currencies. Mexican companies dependent on essential ingredients, spare parts and other critical foreign supplies had to deal with a rationed supply of foreign exchange to pay for new orders. In this situation, personal relationships superseded contractual obligations. In some instances, government officials needed to be convinced that a certain transaction deserved a priority allocation of foreign exchange. Some foreign sellers had to accept payment in Mexican products or in pesos that had to be invested in Mexico. Such contingencies arise routinely as companies conduct business around the globe. Solutions often result from individual initiative; personal ties create opportunities for both sides to keep a business relationship alive.

India is an important supplier of crude and processed agricultural and forest product raw materials to world markets. Small family-owned enterprises collect, process and sell these materials. Typically, months before the crop is in, sellers are required to contract with foreign buyers for later delivery of these products. The buyers, in turn, make long-term contractual commitments to their own customers. It is not possible for the Indian firms to hedge reliably by making forward crop purchases; there are no regulated commodity exchanges for these products. The farmers and forest product collectors do not have the resources to cover their sales if the crop fails. There are major problems during most growing seasons: natural disasters or insufficient plantings result in short crops; strikes, protracted power shortages, or the lack of spare parts result in excessive shipment delays and reduced capacity. Business downturns or unexpected changes in required inventory levels may prompt buyers to request – or even insist – that shipments be held back or prices be reduced. Of course, such actions will cause the supplier severe financial hardship. Sometimes, the supplier is unable to comply precisely with the terms of the contract and therefore provides a substitute order (usually without advance notice). The hope is that the buyer will inadvertently pay before discovering the switch and then reluctantly accept the merchandise with only minor adjustment.

Ongoing business between India and its global customers is, of course, perpetuated by mutual interest, but personal relationships are what make it possible. False rumours, supplier defaults, and customer cancellations are prevalent. Therefore, the greatest importance is assigned to contacts and business associates who can be fully trusted and whose culture-influenced perceptions are understood and predictable. Indian society is at least as ethnically and culturally diverse as that in Europe, and business practices are probably even more varied than in Europe.

Caroline International Inc., a British record company, conducts business mainly in Asia. Korea, Taiwan, China and Indonesia represent just a few of their numerous markets. Regional rules and regulations constituted major barriers to the company since starting their activities years ago. In Korea, for example, the company had to overcome hard censors and high import duties. Jonathan Gillbride, managing director, identified fast and efficient service, good information flow, personal visits and especially personal relationships as the key aspects of their strategy. The company is faced with a €153,900 fax bill to Asia. However, the strategy is paying off: today, Asia represents one of the most important and still growing markets of Caroline International.[45]

Training in cross-cultural competency

Personal relationships are an essential ingredient for the international business-person. One third of a US Peace Corps volunteer's training is devoted to learning about the ways things are done in the host country (particularly personal relationships). The international businessperson should have comparable preparation and a willingness to at least consider the merits of accommodating to the host culture's ways of doing business. The stakes are high: experts estimate that between €1.7 and €2.1 billion worth of business is lost each year because of employee mistakes that occur in other cultures.[46]

Multinational companies such as BP, Thomson Corporation and Marks and Spencer agree that the tasks of international managers are becoming increasingly complex: today, their jobs involve greater sensitivity and cultural awareness. High profile examples of managers such as Lindsay Owen Jones, chairman of L'Oreal, Alex Trotman, chairman of Ford or Graham Morris, board member of Audi, who are able to transfer their skills across markets and nations, are rare. This is why the creation and training of cross-cultural employees is seen as an increasingly important aim for many companies operating in overseas markets.[47]

The goal of training managers is to improve their ability to deal effectively with customers, suppliers, bosses and employees from other countries and regions. Managers must learn to question their own beliefs, to overcome the SRC, and to adapt the way they communicate, solve problems, and even make decisions. Multicultural managers must learn to question and to re-evaluate their feelings concerning such rudimentary management issues as leadership, motivation, and teamwork; this means an examination of some extremely fundamental and personal systems of belief. Finally, managers must learn to overcome stereotypes they hold regarding individuals of various races and religions from other countries; managers must also diplomatically deal with stereotypes others may have about them.

There are a number of companies who offer cultural training to internationally expanding organisations: one example represents Waterbridge International in Great Britain. The company provides British companies expanding to Japan, and Japanese companies located in the UK, with training and consulting regarding the foreign culture. Waterbridge's clients include, among others, BT, Cable and Wireless, ICI, Unilever and Toshiba.[48]

Another widely used approach to accomplish sensitisation is the use of workshops, incorporating case studies, role playing and other exercises designed to permit participants to confront a relevant situation, contemplate what their own thoughts and actions would be in such a situation, and analyse and learn from the results. Participants must be able to understand and evaluate their motivations and approaches. Often, role playing will bring out thoughts and feelings that otherwise might go unexamined or even unacknowledged. A variety of other techniques have been used for cross-cultural training; the common goal is to teach members of one culture ways of interacting effectively in another culture. The Centre for International Briefing in Farnham Castle in Surrey offers two broad tracks on their training programme. One is concerned with business needs. The second track offers support on social etiquette of the respective culture. The company has spent the last 40 years training international managers on cultural diversity. It offers programmes for over 150 countries as well as intensive tuition in 25 languages. The Centre of International Briefing specialises in briefing sessions which vary in the number of participants. These take place either in the client's own business premises or a central location such as a hotel or conference centre. A briefing will generally include lectures and workshops covering the following issues: business and working environment, living conditions, languages and communication, cultural adaptation, ethics and religion, foods, women's issues, health and security as well as financial advice and negotiation skills.[49]

When planning to be active globally, international adaptability and cultural awareness should constitute an integral part of one's personality. Nigel Nicholson of the London Business School identified those individuals who are more likely to succeed in a foreign assignment: these people will be extroverted, autonomous, energetic and ambitious and show a great interest in and sensitivity to foreign cultures. In addition, these individuals will have good communication skills and are able to learn quickly.[50]

However, an adequate personality might not be enough. Training and support is essential, too. A&C Export, a small company in Spalding, Lincolnshire, has reacted to this need by providing its staff with courses on foreign languages. In addition, the company takes great care in responding to the cultural requirements of its customers. A&C's effort has resulted in its being the only firm dealing directly with Italian supermarkets. Among the organisation's customers are the two leading Italian chains, La Stranda and Pam. In Germany, the company doubled its exports in only one year.[51]

In Germany and the UK, however, the need for adequate preparation and support in advance of a foreign assignment is still rather neglected. In most cases, the individual's technical ability is the only criterion for selection. Only 16 per cent of German and 20 per cent of UK companies assess the potential of their managers for international assignments.[52]

If you cannot attend a formal training and orientation session or programme, at the minimum you should take advantage of the written, audio and visual material available on the country you will be visiting. Brigham Young University publishes a series called Culturgram on more than 140 areas of the world. A Culturgram is a product of native commentary and original, expert analysis. It is a general introduction to the culture of a world area or country.

Key points	
	• Culture always has been a major source of disagreement and misunderstandings. In the business world especially this can lead to costly failures.
	• Companies around the world realise the importance of training and supporting their staff in cultural awareness.
	• A number of organisations offer professional support and consultancy for companies planning to expand into foreign markets. By using workshops, case studies, role playing or language courses, the cultural awareness and sensitivity of international managers can be developed and enhanced and the rate of successful foreign assignments can be increased.

Summary

Culture, a society's 'programming of the mind', has both a pervasive and changing influence on each national market environment. Global marketers must recognise the influence of culture and must be prepared to either respond to it or change it. Human behaviour is a function both of a person's own unique personality and that person's interaction with the collective forces of the particular society and culture in which he or she has lived. A number of concepts can help guide anyone seeking insight into cultural issues. Nations can be classified as high- or low-context cultures; communication and negotiation styles can differ from country to country. Maslow's hierarchy, Hofstede's typology, and the self-reference criterion can provide clues about cultural differences and similarities.

Global marketing has played an important – even leading – role in influencing the rate of cultural change around the world. This is particularly true of food, but it includes virtually every industry, particularly in consumer products. Soap and detergent manufacturers have changed washing habits, the electronics industry has changed entertainment patterns, clothing marketers have changed styles, and so on. Although culture can also affect characteristics of industrial products, it is more important as an influence on the marketing process, particularly in the way business is conducted. Global marketers have learned to rely on people who know and understand local customs and attitudes for marketing expertise. Even so, many persons doing business in a new culture avail themselves of training opportunities to help avoid potential cross-cultural complications.

Concepts and definitions

Culture

'Culture is the complex whole that includes knowledge, belief, art, law, morals, customs and any other capabilities and habits acquired by humans as members of society.'[53]

Maslow's hierarchy of needs

According to Maslow, the various motives which influence human behaviour can be divided into five hierarchical levels. The sequence of these levels relates to the urgency with which each need has to be satisfied. The first four levels of the hierarchy constitute so-called growth motives. They consist of the psychological needs, safety needs, social needs and esteem needs. Self-actualisation, also referred to as deficit-motives, represents the pike of the hierarchy.[54]

Hofstede's cultural typologies

At the beginning of the 1980s Geert Hofstede conducted an empirical study with IBM staff from 50 different countries. Analyses have disclosed four different dimensions by which cultures can be compared on a national basis: Power Distance, Masculinity versus Femininity, Individualism versus Collectivism and Uncertainty Avoidance.[55] A fifth dimension, labelled Confucian Dynamism, has been discovered during a study based on the Chinese Value Survey (CVS).

The self-reference criterion

The unconscious reference to one's own cultural values. It represents an instrument which enables the individual to adapt to new situations. However, it may also be responsible for complications in international business relations, as one's own values are not always transferable to another culture.[56]

Diffusion theory   The diffusion process describes the way of spreading innovation throughout the market whereby the market can comprise the whole society or one particular target group. Independent of the kind of innovation the diffusion process always follows an S-shaped curve: slow growth is followed by a period of rapid growth which slows down again toward the end of the process.[57]

Discussion questions

1 What is culture? Is there such a thing as a cultural universal? If so, give an example. If not, explain why there is no such thing.

2 Can Hofstede's cultural typologies help marketers better understand cultures outside their home country? If so, explain how, and if not, explain why not.

3 Explain the self-reference criterion. Go to the library and find examples of product failures that might have been avoided through the application of the SRC.

4 What is the difference between a low-context culture and a high-context culture? Give an example of a country that is an example of each type, and provide evidence for your answer.

5 Consider the equation $Y = f(A, B, C, D, E, F, G)$, where Y stands for consumption of soft drinks and D is the variable for cultural elements. How would this equation help a soft drink marketer understand demand for soft drinks in global markets?

Webmistress's hotspots

The Maslow Library
See the future in Maslow's 'Politics 3'. This site contains the complete Politics 3 paper along with other Maslow materials and related literature.
http://www.nidus.org/

The Maslow book list
The site contains a list of books from Maslow, also details about ordering.
http://www.wynja.com/personality/bookstore/maslow/maslowbc.html

Hofstede's cultural dimensions
Hofstede's four cultural dimensions are introduced. In addition, scales and indexes referring to the respective dimensions are included.
http://omni.cc.purdue.edu/~stohl/Hofstede.html

Fun with and information on the Beetle (official VW homepage)
'Here I am'. Have a closer look at facts and figures as well as useful information on the new Beetle.
http://www.beetle.de/

Heineken homepage
The refreshed homepage of Heineken. Get to know the first world-wide chain of virtual bars, find out about the latest news, take part in the classic travel game and get introduced to music and sports with Heineken.
http://www.heineken.com/

Danone homepage
'Every day, we bring you better foods, more varied flavours, more healthy pleasures.' Get to know the Danone network as well as the company, its brands and possible career paths and learn about the latest news.
http://www.danonegroup.com/

Lipton homepage
'Life's A Little Better with Lipton Tea'. Make your life a little easier by visiting the Lipton kitchen site with thousands of recipes, demonstrations and articles.
http://www.lipton.com/

Perrier homepage
'The Art of Refreshment'. Enjoy sparkling entertainment, get some information on the Perrier Tennis Game and make use of Gayots Restaurant Guide.
http://www.perrier.com/

Suggested readings

Benedict, Ruth, *The Chrysanthemum and the Sword*. Rutland: Charles E. Tuttle, 1972.

Bonvillian, Gary and William A. Nowlin. 'Cultural awareness: an essential element of doing business abroad', *Business Horizons*, 37, 6 (1994): p. 44.

DiBenedetto, Anthony C., Miriko Tamate and Rajan Chandran, 'Developing strategy for the Japanese marketplace', *Journal of Advertising Research*, (January–February 1992): pp. 39–48.

Hall, Edward T., *Beyond Culture*. Garden City, New York: Anchor Books, 1977.

Hofstede, Geert and Michael Harris Bond, 'The Confucius connection: from cultural roots to economic growth', *Organizational Dynamics*, (Spring 1988): pp. 5–21.

Jung, C.G., *Critique of Psychoanalysis, Bollingen Series XX*. Princeton, NJ: Princeton University Press, 1975.

Lee, James A., 'Cultural analysis in overseas operations', *Harvard Business Review*, (March–April 1966): pp. 106–114.

Lublin, Joann S., 'Companies use cross-cultural training to help their employees adjust abroad', *The Wall Street Journal*, 4 August 1992: p. B1.

Maslow, A.H., 'A theory of human motivation'. In *Readings in Managerial Psychology*, ed. Harold J. Levitt and Louis R. Pondy. Chicago: University of Chicago Press, 1964.

Murdock, George P., 'The common denominator of culture'. In *The Science of Man in the World Crisis*, ed. Ralph Linton. New York: Columbia University Press, 1945.

Schaninger, Charles M., Jacques C. Bourgeois and Christian W. Buss, 'French-English Canadian subcultural consumption differences', *Journal of Marketing*, (Spring 1985): pp. 82–92.

Still, Richard R. and John S. Hill, 'Multinational product planning: a meta market analysis', *International Marketing Review* (Spring 1985): p. 60.

Notes

1. Bodo Harenberg, *Harenberg Lexikon der Sprichwörter & Zitate* (Dortmund: Harenberg Kommunikation, 1997).
2. 'Return of the Beetle', *The Economist*, 346, 10 January 1988: p. 54.
3. http://homepage.eurobell.co.uk/howardsw/bughist2.htm, (cited 7/8/1996).
4. Jean Halliday, 'Auburn, Michigan: Steve Wilhite, Volkswagen', *Advertising Age International Supplement*, 14 December 1998, p. 12.
5. Ralph Kisiel, 'Volkswagen stirs up Beetlemania with new equipment, models', *Automotive News*, 29 March 1999, p. 3.
6. Dagmar Mussey and Laurel Wentz, 'Der new Beetle storms into Europe; will it succeed?', *Advertising Age*, 69, 23 November 1998, p. 10.
7. Edmund Chew, 'New Beetle enters into the unknown', *Automotive News Europe*, 9 November 1998, p. 12.
8. Dagmar Mussey, and Laurel Wentz, 'Der new Beetle storms into Europe; will it succeed?,' *Advertising Age*, 69, 23 November 1998, p. 10.
9. Dorothee Ostle and Ralph Kisiel, 'VW rethinks Beetle strategy in Europe', *Automotive News Europe*, 8, 12 April 1999, p. 9.

10. Geert Hofstede and Michael Harris Bond, 'The Confucius connection: from cultural roots to economic growth', *Organizational Dynamics* (Spring 1988): pp. 5–21.

11. Edward T. Hall, *Beyond Culture* (Garden City, New York: Anchor Books, 1977).

12. Richard R. Still and John S. Hill, 'Multinational product planning: A meta market analysis', *International Marketing Review* (Spring 1985): p. 60.

13. Edmund Chew, 'Market leaders increase dominance', *Automotive News Europe,* 2, 21 (1997): p. 18.

14. Heidi Dawley, 'Autos: Do you have that in small? Carmakers hope little 4x4s will rev up Europe's market', *Business Week,* 29 December 1997, p. 21.

15. SOZA, 'Czech soundcarriers market rises 20%, Slovakian market doubles in 1996', *Music & Copyright,* 26 March 1997, p. 8.

16. George P. Murdock, 'The common denominator of culture'. In *The Science of Man in the World Crisis,* edited by Ralph Linton, New York: Columbia University Press, 1945.

17. Scott Roxborough, 'VIVA is speaking in tongues', *Hollywood Reporter,* 8 December 1998, p. 87.

18. Inka Resch, 'Medical care on a card', *Business Week,* 14 September 1998, p. 85.

19. Ruth Benedict, *The Chrysanthemum and the Sword* (Rutland: Charles E. Tuttle, 1972).

20. Edward T. Hall, *Beyond Culture* (Garden City, New York: Anchor Books, 1977).

21. Wolfgang Spahr, 'WEA Germany splits four ways', *Billboard,* 14 January 1995, p. 107.

22. Anthony C. DiBenedetto, Miriko Tamate and Rajan Chandran, 'Developing strategy for the Japanese marketplace', *Journal of Advertising Research* (January–February 1992): pp. 39–48.

23. Adapted from Gary Bonvillian and William A. Nowlin, 'Cultural awareness: an essential element of doing business abroad', *Business Horizons,* 37, 6 (1994): p. 44.

24. David J. Hickson and Derek S. Pugh, *Management Worldwide* (London: Penguin Books, 1995).

25. Richard R. Gesteland, *Cross-Cultural Business Behavior: Marketing, Negotiating and Managing across Cultures* (Copenhagen: Copenhagen Business School Press, 1999).

26. Tevfik Dalgic and Ruud Heijblom, 'Educator insights: International marketing blunders revisited – some lessons for managers', *Journal of International Marketing,* 4, 1 (1996): pp. 81–91.

27. Bodo Harenberg, *Harenberg Lexikon der Sprichwörter & Zitate* (Dortmund: Harenberg Kommunikation, 1997).

28. A. H. Maslow, 'A theory of human motivation'. In *Readings in Managerial Psychology,* ed. Harold J. Levitt and Louis R. Pondy (Chicago: University of Chicago Press, 1964).

29. Charles Ferro, 'Universal Denmark launched compilation album targeted at children', *Billboard,* 54, 7 November 1998.

30. Henner Dr Schierenbeck, *Grundzüge der Betriebswirtschaftslehre* (München: Oldenburg Verlag, 1993).

31. 'Smart cards fill a network safety need', *Newsletter* (March 1999): p. 1.

32. However, not all agree with the notion that Maslow's hierarchy is universal. Dr Rajah V. Komaran, lecturer in the Department for Marketing at the National University of Singapore, for example, argues that Malsow's hierarchy is 'not exactly a good model for understanding the Asian psyche'. Private communication to Warren Keegan, 25 June 1996.

33. Geert Hofstede and Michael Harris Bond, 'The confucius connection: from cultural roots to economic growth', *Organizational Dynamics* (Spring 1988): pp. 5–21.

34. Geert Hofstede, 'Cultural constraints in management theories', *Academy of Management Executive,* 7, 1 (1993): pp. 81–93.

35. Geert Hofstede, 'Management scientists are human', *Management Science,* 40, 1 (1994): pp. 4–13.

36. James A. Lee, 'Cultural analysis in overseas operations', *Harvard Business Review* (March–April 1966): pp. 106–114.

37. Miller-Freeman plc, 'Danone pushes East', *Food Manufacture International,* 12, 4 (1995): pp. 18ff.

38. Miller-Freeman plc, 'Eastern opportunity knocks', *Electronics Times,* 22 June 1998.

39. Charles M. Schaninger, Jacques C. Bourgeois, and Christian W. Buss, 'French-English Canadian subcultural consumption differences', *Journal of Marketing* (Spring 1985): pp. 82–92.

40. Eurostat Statistics, 'Household consumption in the EU', *European Economic Digest,* 1, 2 (1998).

41. 'Consumers go for more exotic teas and coffees', *Newsletter, Euromonitor* (October 1998).

42. Diane Summers, 'Heat dividend for the soft drink business', *Financial Times,* 24 August 1995.

43. Simone Cave, 'Soft drinks find a niche', *Food Manufacture,* 37, 3 (1995).

44. Diane Summers, 'Heat dividend for the soft drink business', *Financial Times,* 24 August 1995.

45. Miller Freemann plc, 'Caroline International', *Musik Week Midem Asia,* 12, 11 May 1996.

46. Joann S. Lublin, 'Companies use cross-cultural training to help their employees adjust abroad', *The Wall Street Journal,* 4 August 1992, p. B1.

47. Vanessa Houlder, 'Cultural exchange – roving executives with truly transportable skills are in short supply', *Financial Times,* 5 April 1995.

48. Joanna Pitman, 'When a nod can lead to a contract', *The Times,* 2 March 1995.

49. 'Learning to cope with corporate culture clashes', *Irish Independent,* 20 March 1998.

50. John W. Hunt, 'Go abroad, young manager: Learning how to do business in a foreign culture comes from first-hand experience, not training seminars', *Financial Times*, 8 October 1998.

51. Alison Thomas, 'Exporter enjoys the fruits of learning foreign languages', *The Sunday Times*, 3 November 1996.

52. Vanessa Houlder, 'Foreign culture shock', *Financial Times* (March 1996).

53. Del Hawkins, Roger Best and Kenneth Coney, *Consumer Behaviour: Building Marketing Strategy* (Boston, Massachusetts: McGraw Hill, 1998).

54. Henner Dr Schierenbeck, *Grundzüge der Betriebswirtschaftslehre* (München: Oldenburg Verlag, 1993).

55. Frank Brück, Claudia Feichtinger, Astrid Kainzbauer and Sylvia Schroll-Machl, 'Arbeitsunterlagen zum Interkulturellen Training', *Kultur & Management*, Arbeitspapier Nr. 3 (June 1996): pp. 1–18.

56. James A. Lee, 'Cultural analysis in overseas operations', *Harvard Business Review* (March–April 1966): pp. 106–114.

57. Del Hawkins, Roger Best and Kenneth Coney, *Consumer Behaviour: Building Marketing Strategy* (Boston, Massachusetts: McGraw Hill, 1998).

CHAPTER 4

The political, legal, and regulatory environments of global marketing

When in Rome, live as the Romans do: when elsewhere, live as they live elsewhere.
ST AMBROSE, AD 340–397

Nothing on earth is broken as much as the law – except for light maybe.
ALFRED POLGAR, AUSTRIAN AUTHOR AND CRITIC

There are political necessities which are so compelling that in the long run they simply have to succeed.
KONRAD ADENAUER, GERMAN POLITICIAN

Chapter objectives

After reading this chapter, you will know:

- The importance of the political environment for global marketing activities.
- The consequences of different legal systems (case vs. code law).
- The influence of the political and legal framework on global company activities such as the establishment of new firms, ownership, trademark protection etc.
- The opportunities of dispute settlement in international litigations.
- The main international organisations and their influence on the political environment of global marketing activities.

Why is this important? Here are three situations in which you would need an understanding of the above issues:

- In your international activities, you have contacts with different legal systems and want to assess the implications for your firm.
- You have a trade dispute with your Mexican business partner and need to find out the best means for settling this dispute.
- You want to find out how EU regulations affect your international business.

Practice link

While governments in many countries consider environmental issues, particularly recycling, Germany already has a packaging ordinance that has shifted the cost burden for waste material disposal onto industry. The German government hopes the law, known as *Verpackungsverordung*, will create a 'closed loop economy'. The goal is to force manufacturers to eliminate nonessential materials that cannot be recycled and adopt other innovative approaches to producing and packaging products. Despite the costs associated with compliance, industry appears to be making significant progress toward creating the closed loop economy. Companies are developing new packaging that uses less material and includes more recycled content.

The German packaging law is just one example of the impact that political, legal and regulatory environments can have on marketing activities. Each of the world's national governments regulates trade and commerce with other countries and attempts to control the access of outside enterprises to national resources. Every country has its own unique legal and regulatory system that impacts the operations and activities of the global enterprise, including the global marketer's ability to address market opportunities. Laws and regulations address the cross-border movement of products, services, people, money and know-how. The global marketer must attempt to comply with each set of national and in some instances, regional constraints. These efforts are hampered by the fact that laws and regulations are frequently ambiguous and continually changing.

In this chapter, we consider the basic elements of the political, legal and regulatory environments of global marketing, including the most pressing current issues and some suggested approaches for dealing with those issues. Some specific topics, such as rules for exporting and importing industrial and consumer products, standards for health and safety, and regulations regarding packaging, labelling, advertising and promotion are covered in later chapters devoted to individual marketing mix elements.

THE POLITICAL ENVIRONMENT

Global marketing activities take place within the political environment of governmental institutions, political parties and organisations through which a country's people and rulers exercise power. Any company doing business outside its home country should carefully study the government structure in the target country and analyse salient issues arising from the political environment. These include the governing party's attitude toward sovereignty, political risk, taxes, the threat of equity dilution, and expropriation.

Nation-states and sovereignty

Sovereignty can be defined as supreme and independent political authority. It implies that the nation-state is the decision-making authority of last resort in its territory and that it is independent from other nation-states. A nation-state executes undivided power over persons and property and regulates domestic affairs without external interference.[1]

Two key factors govern a nation-state's activities: its economic development and the political and economic system in the country. Many governments in developing countries exercise control over their nations' economic development by passing protectionist laws and regulations. Their objective is to encourage economic development by protecting emerging or strategic industries. Conversely, when many nations reach advanced stages of economic development, their governments declare that (in theory, at least) any practice or policy that restrains free trade is illegal. Antitrust laws and regulations are established to promote fair competition. Advanced country laws often define and preserve a nation's social order; laws may extend to political, cultural and even intellectual activities and social conduct. In France, for example, laws forbid the use of foreign words such as le weekend or le marketing in official documents. To counteract the exposure of its young citizens to American-style fast foods, the French National Council of Culinary Arts designed a course on French cuisine and 'good taste' for elementary school students.[2]

While most of the world's economies combine elements of command and market systems, the sovereign political power of a government in a predominantly command economy reaches quite far into the economic life of a country. A current global phenomenon in both command and market structures is the trend toward privatisation, that is, government actions designed to reduce direct governmental involvement in an economy as a supplier of goods and services. In Europe, one of the last industries to be privatised is the energy industry. The European Commission has urged its member countries to open 23 per cent of their energy markets to private suppliers by 1999. Until 2005, one third of the market is to be in private hands. While the British and most of the Scandinavian energy markets are successfully deregulated, other countries are only at the beginning of this process.[3] Also, in economically less developed countries like Mexico, where the government previously controlled over 1,000 companies, the trend towards deregulation is clearly observable. Most of these 1,000 firms such as two Mexican airlines, mining companies, banks and others have been privatised. Russia too has been caught by a wave of privatisation: between 1992 and 1995, 30 million Russians developed into shareholders of more than 75,000 small and 14,000 large companies.[4]

Some observers believe global market integration is eroding national economic sovereignty. Economic consultant Neal Soss notes, 'The ultimate resource of a government is power, and we've seen repeatedly that the willpower of governments can be overcome by persistent attacks from the marketplace.'[5] Some people perceive this as a disturbing trend. At the same time however, there are commentaries which downplay these – maybe purposefully fomented – concerns as 'globaloney'. The journalist David Selbourne sees the often deplored decrease of national governance as suitable legitimisation for a national government's incapability to resolve social and economic problems on its territory. Often politicians excuse these troubles as out of their span of control. Selbourne offers the following example: unanimously, global warming is qualified across the world as an urgent – global – problem. When it comes to counter-actions however, national viewpoints are far from being unanimous. Many national governments act slowly and reluctantly when it comes to regulations against emission and pollution. Pointing at the 'global nature' of the problem, solutions are outsourced under the motto 'may those responsible for global problems take care about it'.[6]

If the issue is framed in terms of marketing, the concept of the exchange comes to the fore: nations may be willing to give up sovereignty in return for something of value. If countries can increase their share of world trade and increase national income, perhaps they will be willing to cede some sovereignty. The European Union (EU) countries are giving up individual rights to set their own product standards, for example in exchange for improved market access.

Political risk

Political risk, the risk of a change in government policy that would adversely impact a company's ability to operate effectively and profitably, can deter a company from investing abroad. When the perceived level of political risk is lower, a country is more likely to attract investment. The level of political risk is inversely proportional to a country's stage of economic development: all other things being equal, the less developed a country, the greater the political risk. The political risk of the triad countries, for example, is quite limited as compared to a country in an earlier stage of development in Africa, Latin America or Asia.

The recent rapid changes in Central and Eastern Europe and the dissolution of the Soviet Union clearly demonstrate the risks and opportunities resulting from political upheavals. The current political climate of Eastern Europe is characterised by a high degree of uncertainty. Having thrown off the shackles of communism, this region is subject to substantial political risk; political forces could drastically change the business environment with little advance notice. Because of the potential for such volatility, businesspersons need to stay up to date on the formation and evolution of political parties in Russia, particularly those with an ultranationalist (i.e. anti-Western) orientation.[7]

Taxes

It is not uncommon for a company to be incorporated in one place, do business in another and maintain its corporate headquarters in a third. This type of diverse

GLOBAL PERSPECTIVE

National influences: a barrier to global marketing?

Many countries attempt to exercise control over the transfers of goods, services, money, people, technology and rights across their borders. Historically, an important control motive was economic: the goal was to generate revenue by levying tariffs and duties. Today, policymakers have additional motives for controlling cross-border flows, including protection of local industry and fostering the development of local enterprise. Such policies are known as protectionism, or economic nationalism.

Differing economic and political goals and different value systems are the primary reasons for protectionism. In the time of the Cold War, the barriers between Western European countries, the US and the communist countries of the former Eastern Bloc existed because of major differences between the values and objectives of these countries.

The world's farmers, be they Japanese, European or American, are committed to getting as much protection as possible from their respective governments. Because of the political influence of the farm lobby in every country, and in spite of the efforts of trade negotiators to open up agricultural markets, controls on trade in agricultural products continue to distort economic efficiency. Such controls work against the driving forces of economic integration.

The price of protection can be very high, for two basic reasons. The first is the cost to consumers: when foreign producers are presented with barriers rather than free access to a market, the result is higher prices for domestic consumers and a reduction in their standard of living. The second cost is the impact on the competitiveness of domestic companies. Companies that are protected from competition may lack the motivation to create and sustain world-class competitive advantage. One of the greatest stimuli to competitiveness is the open market. When a company faces world competition, it must figure out how to serve a niche market better than any company in the world, or it must figure out how to compete in face-to-face competition.

Food for thought
- Can you think about situations where protectionism is justified? Please answer this question from the perspective of your own country as well as from the perspective of a developing country.
- Can (temporary) protectionism lead to an increase in competitiveness of local industry? Why? Why not?

geographical activity requires special attention to tax laws. Many companies make efforts to minimise their tax liability by shifting the location of income. For example, it has been estimated that tax avoidance by foreign companies doing business in the United States costs the US government several billion dollars each year in lost revenue. In one approach, called earnings stripping, foreign companies reduce earnings by making loans to US affiliates rather than using direct investment to finance US activities. The US subsidiary can deduct the interest it pays on such loans, thereby reducing its tax burden.

There are no universal international laws governing the levy of taxes on companies that do business across national boundaries. To provide fair treatment, many governments have negotiated bilateral tax treaties to provide tax credits for taxes paid abroad. In 1977, the Organization for Economic Cooperation and Development (OECD) passed the Model Double Taxation Convention on Income and Capital to help guide countries in bilateral negotiations. Generally, foreign companies are taxed by the host nation up to the level imposed in the home country, an approach that does not increase the total tax burden to the company.

Dilution of equity control[8]

Political pressure for national control of foreign-owned companies is a part of the environment of global business in lower-income countries. The foremost goal of national governance is to protect the right of national sovereignty, especially in all aspects of domestic business activity. Host-nation governments sometimes attempt to control ownership of foreign-owned companies operating within their borders. In underdeveloped countries, political pressures frequently cause companies to take in local partners.

Legislation that requires companies to dilute their equity is never popular in the boardroom, yet the consequences of such legislation are often surprisingly favourable. Dennis J. Encarnation and Sushil Vachani examined corporate responses to India's 1973 Foreign Exchange Regulation Act (FERA), which restricted foreign equity participation in local projects to 40 per cent. The researchers identified four options available to companies faced with the threat of dilution:

1 *Follow the law to the letter.* Colgate Palmolive (India) took this course, became an Indian company, and maintained its dominant position in a growing market.
2 *Leave the country.* After some years of negotiating, IBM decided that the loss of control arising under the new conditions was higher than the profit which could be expected from the jointly continued company activities. Consequently, IBM decided to leave the market. In 1991, IBM returned to India and entered a joint venture with Tata Information Systems Limited (TISL), one of the largest Indian corporations. Today, the 50:50 joint venture is located in India's 'Silicon Plateau', Bangalore, and operates subsidiaries in all major cities.[9]
3 *Negotiate under the law.* Some companies used the equity dilution requirement to raise funds for growth and diversification. In most cases this was done by issuing fresh equity to local investors. Ciba-Geigy increased its equity base 27 per cent to €15 m, for example, and also negotiated an increase in production that doubled the sales of Hindustan Ciba-Geigy.
4 *Take pre-emptive action.* Some foreign firms initiated defensive strategies well before FERA's passage. These included proactive diversification to take advantage of investment incentives, gradual 'Indianisation' of the company, and continuously updating technology and maintaining export sales.

Encarnation and Vachani's study offers some important lessons.

1 *First, look at the range of possibilities.* There is no single best solution, and each company should look at itself and at the country situation to decide on strategy.
2 *Companies should use the law to achieve their own objectives.* The experiences of many companies demonstrate that by satisfying government demands, it is possible to take advantage of government concessions, subsidies, and market protection.
3 *Anticipate government policy changes.* Create a win–win situation. Companies that take initiatives are prepared to act when the opportunity arises. It takes time to implement changes; the sooner a company identifies possible government directions and initiatives, the sooner it will be in a position to propose its own plan to help the country achieve its objectives.
4 *Listen to country managers.* Country managers should be encouraged to anticipate government initiatives and to propose company strategy for taking advantage of opportunities created by government policy. Local managers often have the best

understanding of the political environment. Experience suggests that they are in the best position to know when issues are arising and how to turn potential adversity into opportunity through creative responses.

The threat of equity dilution has caused some companies to operate in host nations via joint ventures or strategic alliances. These alternatives create special legal problems; there should be clauses in the joint venture or alliance agreement regarding its subsequent dissolution, as well as for the ownership of patents, trademarks or technology realised from the joint effort, including cross-licensing after dissolution of intellectual property rights developed under joint operations.

Expropriation

The ultimate threat a government can pose toward a company is expropriation. Expropriation refers to governmental action to dispossess or significantly control a company's ownership to a large extent.[10] Compensation is generally provided to foreign investors, although not often in the 'prompt, effective and adequate' manner demanded by international standard. Nationalisation occurs if ownership of the property or assets in question is transferred to the host government. If no compensation is provided, the action is referred to as confiscation.[11]

Short of outright expropriation or nationalisation, the phrase *creeping expropriation* has been applied to severe limitations on economic activities of foreign firms in certain developing countries. These have included limitations on repatriation of profits, dividends, royalties, or technical assistance fees from local investments or technology arrangements. Other issues are increased local content requirements, quotas for hiring local nationals, price controls, and other restrictions affecting return on investment. Global companies have also suffered discriminatory tariffs and non-tariff barriers that limit market entry of certain industrial and consumer goods, as well as discriminatory laws on patents and trademarks.

For example, in the mid-1970s, Johnson & Johnson and other foreign investors had to submit to a host of regulations in India to retain majority equity positions in companies already established. Many of these rules were later copied in whole or in part by Malaysia, Indonesia, the Philippines, Nigeria, Brazil, and many other developing countries. By the late 1980s, after a 'lost decade' in Latin America characterised by debt crises and low gross national product (GNP) growth, lawmakers reversed many of these restrictive and discriminatory laws. The goal was to again attract foreign direct investment and badly needed Western technology. The end of the Cold War and restructuring of political allegiances contributed significantly to these changes.[12]

When governments expropriate foreign property, there are impediments to action to reclaim that property. Representatives of expropriated companies may seek recourse through arbitration at the World Bank Investment Dispute Settlement Center (International Centre for Settlement of Investment Disputes, or ICSID). It is also possible to buy expropriation insurance from a private insurance company.

INTERNATIONAL LAW

International law may be defined as the rules and principles that nation-states consider binding upon themselves. There are two categories of international law: public law, or the law of nations; and international commercial law.

The roots of modern international law can be traced back to the early Middle Ages in Europe and later the 17th-century Peace of Westphalia. Early international law was concerned with waging war, establishing peace, and other political issues such as diplomatic recognition of new national entities and governments. Elaborate international rules gradually emerged that covered, for example, the status of neutral nations. The creation of laws governing commerce developed on a state-by-state basis, evolving into what is termed the law of the merchant. International law still has the function of upholding order, although in a broader sense than dealing with problems arising from war. At first, international law was essentially an amalgam of treaties, covenants, codes and agreements. As trade grew among nations, order in commercial affairs assumed increasing importance. Whereas the law had originally dealt only with nations as entities, a growing body of law rejected the idea that only states can be subject to international law.

Paralleling the expanding body of international case law in the 20th century, new international judiciary organisations have contributed to the creation of an established rule of international law. These include the International Court of Justice (ICJ), which was established as the judicial arm of the United Nations by article 7 of the United Nations Charter. Disputes arising between nations are issues of public international law, and they may be taken before the ICJ located in the Hague. Article 38 of the ICJ Statute defines recognised sources of public international law:

> The Court, whose function is to decide in accordance with international law such disputes as are submitted to it, shall apply:
> a. international conventions, whether general or particular, establishing rules expressly recognised by the contesting states;
> b. international custom, as evidence of a general practice accepted as law;
> c. the general principles of law recognised by civilised nations;
> d. subject to the provisions of Article 59, judicial decisions and the teachings of the most highly qualified publicists of the various nations, as subsidiary means for the determination of rules of law.

In case a nation has allowed a case against it to be brought before the ICJ and then refuses to accept a judgement against it, the plaintiff nation can seek recourse through the UN's highest political arm, the United Nations Security Council. This council can use its full range of powers to enforce the judgement.

Case versus code law

Looking at legal systems in different countries, there are two fundamentally different approaches: legal systems based on case law, and those grounded on code law. Code law is based on written norms in the form of codices, which are supplemented by judicial decisions. Case law, on the other hand, rests on tradition and precedence stemming from past jurisdiction. Under code law, there is a distinction between civil, commercial and criminal law. Trade law possesses its own administrative structure, which takes over the execution of legal regulations. For example, property rights are established through formal registration of property at commercial courts. Under case law, commercial law does not constitute a separate body of law. Another difference lies in the definition of 'acts of God'. Under case law, this notion solely refers to floods, storms and other acts of nature unless expanded by contract. In code-law countries, 'acts of God' would also cover damages which are out of the control of the parties in the contract and which could not have been avoided with appropriate care.[13] In code-law countries, intellectual property rights must be registered, whereas in common-law countries, some, such as trademarks but not patents, are established by prior use.

Despite the differences in systems, three distinct forms of laws are common to all nations. Statutory law is codified at the national, federal or state level; administrative law originates in regulatory bodies and local communities; and case law is the product of the court system. As mentioned before, different legal systems developed historically in different geographical regions. The US, Canada, the UK and the former British colonies (Australia; New Zealand; India; Hong Kong; the English-speaking former African colonies) founded their systems on common law. Historically, much of continental Europe was influenced by Roman law and, later, the Napoleonic Code. Asian countries are split: India, Pakistan, Malaysia, Singapore and Hong Kong, all former British colonies, are common-law jurisdictions. Japan, Korea, Thailand, Indochina, Taiwan, Indonesia and China are civil-law jurisdictions. Today, the majority of countries have legal systems based on civil-code traditions, although an increasing number of countries are blending concepts, and hybrid systems are emerging.

As various countries in Eastern and Central Europe wrestle with establishing legal systems in the post-communist era, a struggle of sorts has broken out with consultants representing both common-law and civil-code countries trying to influence the process. In much of Central Europe, including Poland, Hungary and the Czech Republic, the German tradition prevails. As a result, banks not only take deposits and make loans, but also engage in the buying and selling of securities. In Eastern Europe – particularly Russia – the United States has had greater influence. Germany has accused the United States of promoting a system that is so complex it requires legions of lawyers. The United States has responded that the German system is outdated.[14] In any event, the constant stream of laws and decrees issued by President Boris Yeltsin created an unpredictable, evolving legal environment. Specialised publications, such as the Russian and Commonwealth Business Law Report, are important resources for anyone doing business in Russia or the CIS.

Key points

- A company's international activities are heavily influenced by the political and legal situations in the target markets. In particular, issues such as the tax situation, or the equity control of subsidiaries are affected by the political and legal climate abroad.

- The political and legal environment requires close monitoring, as situations can change quickly and necessitate a company's immediate reaction.

- To reduce legal uncertainties, international organisations, such as the United Nations, attempt to provide generally accepted guidelines.

- There are two fundamentally different approaches to legal systems in different countries: *code law*, which is based on written norms in form of codices, and *case law*, which rests on tradition and precedence.

WAYS TO AVOID LEGAL PROBLEMS

Clearly, the global legal environment is very dynamic and complex. Therefore, the best course to follow is to get expert legal help. However, the astute, proactive marketer can do a great deal to prevent conflicts from arising in the first place, especially concerning issues such as establishment, jurisdiction, patents and trademarks, antitrust, licensing, trade secrets, and bribery.

Scope of legal regulations

Under what conditions can trade be established? To transact business, citizens of one country must be assured that they will be treated fairly in another country. In Western Europe, for example, the creation of the European Union now assures that citizens from member nations get fair treatment with regard to business and economic activities carried out within the Common Market.

Most countries have signed treaties of friendship, commerce and navigation. These agreements provide their citizens the right to non-discriminatory treatment in trade, the reciprocal right to establish a business, and, particularly, to invest. Commercial treaties provide one with the privilege, not the right, to engage in business activities in countries other than one's own.[15] This can create problems for business managers who may still be under the jurisdiction of their own laws even when they are out of their native country. US citizens, for example, are forbidden by the Foreign Corrupt Practices Act to give bribes to an official of a foreign government or political party, even if bribes are customary for conducting business in that country.

Jurisdiction

Company personnel working abroad should understand the extent to which they are subject to the jurisdiction of host-country courts. Employees of foreign companies working in the United States must understand that courts have jurisdiction to the extent that the company can be demonstrated to be 'doing business' in the state in which the court sits. The court may examine whether the foreign company maintains an office, solicits business, maintains bank accounts or other property, or has agents or other employees in the state in question. Revlon Inc. sued United Overseas Ltd (UOL), in the US District Court for the Southern District of New York. Revlon charged the British company with breach of contract, contending that UOL had failed to purchase some speciality shampoos as agreed. UOL, claiming lack of jurisdiction, asked the court to dismiss the complaint. Revlon countered with the argument that UOL was, in fact, subject to the court's jurisdiction; Revlon cited the presence of a UOL sign above the entrance to the offices of a New York company in which UOL had a 50 per cent ownership interest. The court denied UOL's motion to dismiss.[16]

Normally, all economic activity within a nation is governed by that nation's laws. When a transaction crosses boundaries, it has to be established which nation's laws apply. If the national laws of country X pertaining to a simple export transaction differ from those of country Y, the question arises, which country's laws apply to the export contract? Which apply to the letter of credit opened to finance the export transaction? The parties involved must reach agreement on such issues, and the nation whose laws apply should be specified in a jurisdictional clause. There are several alternatives to choose from: the laws of the domicile or principal place of business of one of the parties, the place where the contract was entered, or the place of performance of the contract. If a dispute arises under such a contract, it must be heard and determined by a neutral party such as a court or an arbitration panel. If the parties fail to specify which nation's laws apply, a fairly complex set of rules governing the 'conflict of laws' will be applied by the court or arbitration tribunal.[17]

Intellectual property: patents and trademarks

Patents and trademarks that are protected in one country are not necessarily protected in another, so global marketers must ensure that patents and trademarks are registered in each country where business is conducted. In France, the fashion designer Yves Saint-Laurent was prevented from marketing his new luxury perfume under the name of 'Champagne', as under French law this name is exclusively reserved for sparkling wine from the region Champagne. Nevertheless, Saint-Laurent launched the product under the name of 'Champagne' in countries such as the US, the UK, Germany and Belgium, where geographic names are not protected by law.[18]

In 1991, Germany's Bayer AG received permission from Russia's patent office to register 'aspirin' as a trademark in that country. Rival pharmaceutical companies, such as France's Laboratoire UPSA, were infuriated because the ruling meant they would effectively be shut out of the Russian market of 150 million people. According to a spokesman for the French company, 'The word never should have been registered in the first place. It's a universally accepted generic name.' The issue, which is considered critical to Russia's evolving system of patent law, is under appeal.[19]

Trademark and copyright infringement is a critical problem in global marketing and one that can take a variety of forms. Counterfeiting is the unauthorised copying and production of a product. Such products are usually sold with a product name that differs slightly from a well-known brand, but are close enough that consumers will associate them with the genuine product. Another type of counterfeiting is piracy, the unauthorised publication or reproduction of copyrighted work. This form of piracy is particularly damaging to the entertainment and software industries; computer programs, videotapes, cassettes and compact discs are particularly easy to duplicate illegally. Counterfeit sales are hard to quantify, as their production and trade are illegal and thus escape official control. It is assumed that the US music industry loses sales at an estimated €255 million per year in its home market and €1.7 billion world-wide due to bootlegging. The software industry lists damages between €10 and 14 billion, accounting for about 40 per cent of all software sales world-wide. In some countries, up to 90 per cent of all software used stems from illegal copies. The Internet also opens up new possibilities for brand pirates: they get the name of a producer of well-known branded products as an Internet domain and take advantage of the high brand value and attractiveness to consumers for their own products. The original manufacturer then sees itself compelled to buy back its own name for amounts up to €5,000 and 12,000.[20]

Microsoft has reacted in an incredibly relaxed fashion given the damages of €850 million, which the company has encountered over the last 10 years from software piracy in China. While the US government continued intensive lobbying in the 1990s to curb illegal software copying, Microsoft remained calm in the light of doubling losses. Now it has become clear why: Microsoft won two lawsuits against Chinese companies which had used illegally copied software for their own company

GLOBAL PERSPECTIVE

The end of cybersquatting?

It shall no longer happen that brand pirates can use a well-known brand as an Internet domain and take advantage of its attraction to consumers for their own products. At least, this will be true, if Francis Gurry, the Vice President of the *World Intellectual Property Organization* (WIPO) gets his way. The organisation, affiliated with the United Nations, sees itself as an agency in charge of protecting intellectual property. To preserve consumers' faith in the Internet as a safe place to trade goods and services, WIPO deals with the problem of *cybersquatting* and how it could be prevented.

Cybersquatting describes the fact that someone uses someone else's identity wrongfully. To put it differently: clever people choose an Internet domain in a way that it may easily be confused with a 'prominent namesake'. For example, when the son of the former US president George Bush, George W. Bush Jr, announced his candidacy for president, 39 registrations for his name as an Internet domain already existed. So if George W. Bush Jr decided to put up a website for his campaign under his own name, he most likely would have had to pay a significant amount of money to buy his 'name' back. Similarly, the German car manufacturer Porsche identified 126 Internet addresses which could easily be confused with the sports car's brand – the majority of these webpages display clearly suggestive content.

The WIPO proposes several counteractions. First, it defines cybersquatting more clearly. According to the WIPO guidelines, malpractice occurs, if

- the domain name is identical or misleading with respect to an existing brand, or
- the owner of the domain has no rights or rightful interest in the name, or
- the domain name is registered and used for dubious purposes.

In this case, the Internet domain should be cut off and the registration cancelled immediately. A similar procedure will also take place if the holder of a domain cannot be identified due to incorrect or missing information. WIPO has also developed a clear procedure for cases to be litigated. It outlines ways how to assist people or companies affected by cybersquatting.

Food for thought
- Do the attempts of the World Intellectual Property Organization to free the web from cybersquatting lead to an own-regulated Internet?
- Does e-commerce increase or decrease the importance of brand names?

Source: Adapted from http://wipo2.wipo.int/process/eng/processhome.html (21 July 1999).

use. The Chinese government was not willing to support actions against illegal copying of software, as it perceived them as a means to achieve more widespread use of PCs throughout the country and to foster economic development. In the case of the two lawsuits, however, Microsoft saw its opportunity coming: although the use of illegally copied software by companies will continue to be hard to trace, the punishments fought out in court are, for the first time, quite substantial. Microsoft officials therefore hope that they serve as a deterrent and that the message has got through.[21]

Of the many separate international patent agreements, the most important is the *International Convention for the Protection of Industrial Property,* also known as the *Paris Convention.* In 1974, the convention was renamed the World Intellectual Property Organization (WIPO). In 1996, an agreement of co-operation was established with the World Trade Organization (WTO).[22] The convention, which was signed in 1883 by more than 100 countries, facilitates multi-country patent registrations by ensuring that, once a company files in a signatory country, it will be afforded a 'right of priority' in other countries for one year from the date of the original filing. In case the filing does not take place, companies run the risk of losing their patent rights abroad.[23]

Two other treaties deserve mention. *The Patent Cooperation Treaty* (PCT) has numerous signatories, including Australia, Brazil, France, Germany, Japan, North and South Korea, the Netherlands, Switzerland, Russia and the United States.[24] The members constitute a union that provides certain technical services and co-operates in the filing, searching and examination of patent applications in all member countries. On 1 January 1994, China became an official signatory of the PCT. The *European Patent Office* administers applications for the *European Patent Convention*, which is effective in the EU and Switzerland. An applicant can file a single patent application covering all of the convention states; the advantage is that the application will be subject to only one procedure of grant. Whereas national patent laws remain effective under this system, approved patents are effective in all member countries for a period of 20 years from the filing date. Table 4.1 provides an overview of patents filed with the European Patent Office.

In the United States, trademarks are covered by the Trademark Act of 1946, also known as the Lanham Act. President Reagan signed the Trademark Law Revision Act into law in November 1988. The law makes it easier for companies to register new trademarks; as a result, the number of filings has increased dramatically. After years of discussion on the patent environment in Japan, the United States and Japan have agreed to make changes in their respective systems; Japan has promised to speed up

Table 4.1 European Patent Office – registrations filed (by country of origin)

Country	1997	1998
Austria	643	762
Belgium	877	1,038
Denmark	531	579
Finland	746	854
France	5,091	5,644
Germany	13,846	16,117
Greece	23	47
Ireland	119	182
Italy	2,485	2,845
Liechtenstein	122	141
Luxembourg	82	121
Monaco	14	28
Netherlands	3,292	3,504
Portugal	21	18
Spain	386	432
Sweden	1,455	1,742
Switzerland	2,786	3,159
United Kingdom	3,991	3,972
Japan	12,856	13,813
US	20,497	23,502
Others	3,041	3,582
Total	**72,904**	**82,087**

Source: European Patent Office – Annual Reports 1997, 1998.

patent examinations, eliminate challenges to patent submissions, and allow patent applications to be filed in English. Effective 7 June 1995, in accordance with the General Agreement on Tariffs and Trade (GATT), new US patents are granted for a period of 20 years from the filing date. Previously, patents had been valid for a 17-year term effective after being granted. Thus, US patent laws now harmonise with those in the EU as well as Japan. Even with the changes, however, patents in Japan are narrower than those in the United States. As a result, companies such as Caterpillar have been unable to protect critical innovations in Japan because products very similar to those made by American companies can be patented without fear of infringement.[25]

Antitrust

Antitrust laws are designed to combat restrictive business practices and to encourage competition. The European Commission prohibits agreements and practices that prevent, restrict, and distort competition. The interstate trade clause of the Treaty of Rome applies to trade with third countries, so that a company must be aware of the conduct of its affiliates. The Commission also exempts certain cartels from articles 85 and 86 of the Treaty in an effort to encourage the growth of important businesses. The intention is to allow European companies to compete on an equal footing with Japan and the United States.

In many European countries, individual country laws apply to specific marketing mix elements. For example, some countries permit selective or exclusive product distribution. However, community law can take precedence. In one case, Consten, a French company, had exclusive French rights to import and distribute consumer electronics products from the German company Grundig. Consten sued another French firm, charging the latter with bringing 'parallel imports' into France illegally. That is, Consten charged that the competitor bought Grundig products from various foreign suppliers without Consten's knowledge and was selling them in France. Although Consten's complaint was upheld by two French courts, the Paris Court of Appeals suspended the judgement, pending a ruling by the European Commission on whether the Grundig–Consten arrangement violated articles 85 and 86. The Commission ruled against Consten on the grounds that 'territorial protection proved to be particularly damaging to the realisation of the Common Market'.[26] The principle being transgressed was that of the free flow of goods defined in articles 24 to 30 of the Rome Treaty.

A major antitrust case involving a US-based global company pitted the European Community against IBM during the 1970s and 1980s. IBM was the European market leader in mainframe computers with 55 per cent unit share in 1983. The company's operations were especially strong in Great Britain, France and West Germany. IBM was charged with four specific violations of article 86: failure to supply competitors with timely information about interfaces; selling computers without including memory capacity in the price; selling computers without software necessary to operate them; and refusing to supply IBM software to companies that used competing brands of computers. Coincidentally, the US Justice Department had also filed an antitrust case against IBM in the United States, with the aim of breaking up the company (the suit was dropped in 1982 after 14 years of litigation). The European Community action, however, was an attempt to force IBM to disclose proprietary designs and other trade secrets of benefit to European companies that were IBM suppliers.[27] More recently, Microsoft and Intel are objects of antitrust investigations in both the United States and Europe. Intel is accused of refusing to provide key customers with information on interfaces, which they would need for further product development. The plaintiffs put forward that in the case of legal actions, Intel might use its market power to harm its counterparts economically. Intel, however, argued that with a market share of 97 per cent in the premium microchip segment, it would not consider itself a monopolist. The same would apply to its competitors AMD and Cyrix, which hold a similarly dominant position in the low-price segments. In addition, a key characteristic of a monopolist is to be able to raise prices based on its dominant market position. The criterion was not true for Intel, as the company had routinely cut prices over the years. The last word will be up to the courts engaged in the legal battle.[28]

Licensing and trade secrets

Licensing is a contractual agreement in which a licensor allows a licensee to use patents, trademarks, trade secrets, technology or other intangible assets in return for royalty payments or other forms of compensation. These issues are treated differently in different regions of the world. In contrast to the EU, Australia and Japan, US laws do not regulate the licensing process per se. The duration of the licensing agreement and the amount of royalties a company can receive are considered a matter of commercial negotiation between licensor and licensee, and there are no government restrictions on remittances of royalties abroad. In many countries, these elements of licensing are regulated by government agencies.

Important considerations in licensing include analysis of what assets a firm may offer for license, how to price the assets, whether to grant only the right to 'make' the product or to grant the rights to 'use' and to 'sell' the product as well. The right to sublicense is another important issue. As with distribution agreements, decisions must also be made regarding exclusive or non-exclusive arrangements and the size of the licensee's territory.

To prevent the licensee from using the licensed technology to compete directly with the licensor, the latter may try to limit the licensee to selling only in its home country. The licensor may also seek to contractually bind the licensee to discontinue use of the technology after the contract has expired. In practice, host government laws may make such agreements impossible to obtain. Licensing is a potentially dangerous action: it may be instrumental in creating a competitor. Therefore, licensors should be careful to ensure that their own competitive position remains advantageous. This requires constant innovation. There is a simple rule: if you are licensing technology and know-how that is going to remain unchanged, it is only a matter of time before your licensee will become your competitor, not merely with your technology and know-how, but with his own improvements on that technology and know-how.

As noted, licensing agreements can come under antitrust scrutiny. In one recent case, Bayer AG granted an exclusive patent licence for a new household insecticide to S.C. Johnson & Sons. The German firm's decision to license was based in part on the time required for Environmental Protection Agency (EPA) approval, which had stretched to three years. Bayer decided it made better business sense to let the American firm deal with regulatory authorities in return for a 5 per cent royalty on sales. However, a class action suit was filed against the companies, alleging that the licensing deal would allow Johnson to monopolise the market. Then, the US Justice

Department stepped in, calling the licensing agreement anti-competitive. In a statement, Anne Bingaman, head of the Justice Department's antitrust unit, said, 'The cosy arrangement that Bayer and Johnson maintained is unacceptable in a highly concentrated market.' Bayer agreed to offer licences to any interested company on better terms than the original contract with Johnson. Johnson agreed to notify the US government of any future pending exclusive licensing agreements for household insecticides. If Bayer is party to any such agreements, the Justice Department has the right to veto them. Not surprisingly, the reaction from the legal community has been negative. One Washington lawyer who specialises in intellectual property law noted that the case 'really attacks traditional licensing practices'. As Melvin Jager, president of the Licensing Executives Society, explained, 'An exclusive license is a very valuable tool to promote intellectual property and get it out into the marketplace'.[29]

Another issue is the fact that a licensee gains knowledge of the licensor's trade secrets. Trade secrets are confidential information or knowledge that have commercial value, are not in the public domain, and for which steps have been taken to keep them secret. Trade secrets include manufacturing processes, formulas, designs and customer lists. To prevent disclosure, the licensing of unpatented trade secrets should be linked to confidentiality contracts with each employee who has access to the protected information.

The 1990s saw widespread improvements in laws pertaining to trade secrets. Several countries adopted trade secret statutes for the first time. Mexico's first statute protecting trade secrets became effective on 28 June 1991; China's first trade secret law took effect 1 December 1993. In both countries, the new laws were part of broader revisions of intellectual property laws. Japan and Korea have also recently amended their intellectual property laws to include trade secrets. Many countries in Central and Eastern Europe have also enacted laws to protect trade secrets. When the North American Free Trade Agreement (NAFTA) became effective on 1 January 1994, it marked the first international trade agreement with provisions for protecting trade secrets. The next evolutionary step was the Agreement on Trade-Related Aspects of Intellectual Property Rights (TRIPs) that resulted from the Uruguay Round of GATT negotiations. The TRIPs agreement requires signatory countries to protect against acquisition, disclosure, or use of trade secrets 'in a manner contrary to honest commercial practices'.[30] Despite these formal legal developments, in practice, enforcement is the key issue. Companies transferring trade secrets across borders should be aware not only of the existence of legal protection but also of the risks associated with lax enforcement.

Bribery and corruption: legal and ethical issues

History does not record a burst of international outrage when Charles M. Schwab presented a €170,000 diamond and pearl necklace to the mistress of Czar Alexander's nephew. In return for that consideration, Bethlehem Steel won the contract to supply the rails for the Trans-Siberian railroad.

Even today, opinions deviate on what are ethically correct business principles and what not. Where is the difference between a small gift for the host and bribery? Is it bribing, when you invite a business partner out to dinner? What if the dinner includes a trip to the coast and a weekend in a hotel? Does it make a difference who is the beneficiary – a government official or a private business partner?

As practices and habits differ from country to country, these and similar ethical questions are of growing importance in global business.[31] Laws and rules which try to tackle this touchy subject of international business ethics exist on a national level (e.g. the *Foreign Corrupt Practices Act* in the US), on the level of official international organisations (e.g. the OECD's *Anti-Bribery Resolution*), at the level of international private initiatives (e.g. *Transparency International*) and finally also at a corporate level in the form of codices on ethical business practices (*Corporate Codes of Ethics*). These different regulations are discussed below.

In 1977, the US introduced the *Foreign Corrupt Practices Act (FCPA)*. Its existence is related to the Watergate scandal, when more than 300 US companies were discovered to have been bribing high-ranking foreign government officials. The FCPA aims to provide a clear definition of ethical and legal business practices in order to curb bribery and gift giving. As bribery is part of common business practices in many countries, the FCPA *allows* payments to low ranking officials, as long as these payments are documented correctly. Interestingly, the regulations make a difference between *bribe* and *facilitating payment*. Facilitating payments comprise amounts of money transferred to low-ranking officials in order to facilitate routine procedures in cross-border transactions, whereas payments are considered a bribe if they provide a company preferential treatments compared to competitors. Punishments for bribery are severe: companies may pay up to €850,000, the responsible managers €8,500 and/or up to five years in prison.[32]

Due to the FCPA, US companies have to deal with the most stringent legal regulations world-wide with respect to bribery. To prevent disadvantages for US companies, the American government has tried to convince the *Organization for Economic Cooperation and Development* (OECD) to adapt similar regulations. In April 1996, the OECD finally issued a recommendation that bribes paid to foreign government officials may no longer be accepted to reduce tax burdens. Some observers were surprised that the OECD issued this recommendation, as the discussion upfront was rather controversial on these issues. Meanwhile there is hope that the OECD will agree on a further resolution which will criminalise bribery.[33]

Among the private international initiatives, one stands out in particular: *Transparency International* (TI). This organisation was founded in 1993 by Peter Eigen, former Director of the World Bank; it now has representatives in over 40 countries. With its headquarters in Berlin, TI aims to promote and support world-wide legal reforms which deal with the battle against corruption in business and administration.[34] Accordingly, TI's aim is not to unveil cases of bribery or corruption, but to increase political awareness and to support managers and politicians in their efforts against bribery and corruption.

In addition, most internationally active firms have undertaken steps to safeguard the ethically correct business behaviour of their managers. These efforts are reflected in ethics training, ethics committees and so-called ethics codes or credos.[35] These codices or credos give guidance to managers on what kind of behaviour their companies expect from them with regard to gifts, payment to customers and suppliers or conflicts of interest. In many companies, the legal department creates these documents and has them signed by employees. It has to be noted, however, that the majority of these codices are rather general; they also differ from country to country and from industry to industry.[36] While the large majority of US and Japanese companies have introduced ethics codes, European firms still lag behind.

If firms engage in international activities without the legal restrictions of their home countries, they face a broad variety of actions with respect to their ethical behaviour. On one end of the scale, they can maintain their national habits without adapting to local specifics. On the other end of the scale, they may completely give up their ethical behaviour practised in their home country and adapt entirely to the local habits. A third solution is to combine these two strategies and apply some of the ethical norms of their national background and adapt to the local habits.

Bribery as part of international business is not likely to disappear all of a sudden, just because governments do not approve. How should firms react to attempts of bribery by a competitor? The company's total offer must be as good or even better than the one of its competitor which includes the bribe. To offset the competitive disadvantage it may be possible to offer a better product at better conditions, through better sales channels and more effective communication. A superior product is the best weapon against these kinds of practices from competitors. In this case, the attempt to bribe will not influence the buying decision.

CONFLICT RESOLUTION, DISPUTE SETTLEMENT AND LITIGATION

Countries vary in their approach toward conflict resolution. Table 4.2 shows the number of practising lawyers per 100,000 population in selected countries. The United States has more lawyers than any other country in the world and is arguably the most litigious nation on earth. In part, this is a reflection of the low-context nature of American culture, a spirit of confrontational competitiveness, and the absence of one important principle of code law: the loser pays all court costs for all parties. The degree of legal co-operation and harmony in the EU is unique, and stems in part from the existence of code law as a common bond. Other regional organisations have made far less progress toward harmonisation.

Conflicts will inevitably arise in business anywhere, especially when different cultures come together to buy, sell, establish joint ventures, compete and co-operate in global markets. Many companies choose their home country jurisdiction for disputes with a foreign party. The issue can be litigated in the country where a company and its attorneys might be said to enjoy 'home court' advantage. Litigation in foreign courts, however, becomes vastly more complex. This is due in part to differences in language, legal systems, currencies, and traditional business customs and patterns. In addition, problems arise from differences in procedures relating to discovery. In essence, discovery is the process of obtaining evidence to prove claims and determining which

Table 4.2 Lawyers: an international comparison (1990)

Country	Lawyers per 100,000 people
US	227.0
Germany	199.4
Australia	157.2
UK	121.4
France	99.2
Hungary	73.9
Japan	11.4
Korea	4.7

Source: Ota Shoza and Kahei Rokumoto, 'Issues of the lawyer population: Japan', *Case Western Reserve Journal of International Law* (Spring 1993).

evidence may be admissible in which countries under which conditions. A further complication is the fact that judgements handed down in courts in another country may not be enforceable in the home country. For all these reasons, many companies prefer to pursue arbitration before proceeding to litigate.

Alternatives to litigation for dispute settlement[37]

Extrajudicial, alternative approaches often provide a faster, easier and less expensive way to resolve commercial disputes than litigation. Indeed, alternative approaches have a tradition that is centuries old. Chambers of trade and commerce first began to hear and resolve disputes as trade developed between different tribes or nations. Settlement of modern trade disputes takes various forms and occurs in many locations. Formal arbitration is one means of settling international business disputes outside the courtroom. Arbitration generally involves a hearing of all parties before a three-member panel. The result is usually a decision that the parties agree in advance to abide by. Courts of Arbitration have long existed in London and Zurich. For decades, business arbitration has also been promoted through the Paris-based International Chamber of Commerce (ICC). However, because it is the best-known international business organisation, it has the biggest backlog of cases. Thus, the ICC has gained a reputation for being slower, more expensive and more cumbersome than some alternatives. The United Nations Convention on the Recognition and Enforcement of Foreign Arbitral Awards (also known as the New York Convention) has more than 50 signatories. The New York Convention facilitates arbitration when disputes arise, and signatories agree to abide by decisions reached through arbitration.

Arbitration can be a minefield due to the number of the issues that must be addressed. For example, if the parties to a patent licensing agreement agree in the arbitration clause that the validity of the patent cannot be contested, such a provision may not be enforceable in some countries. Which country's laws will be used as the standard for invalidity?

Pursuing such an issue on a country-by-country basis would be inordinately time consuming. In addition, there is the issue of acceptance: by law, US courts must accept an arbitrator's decision in patent disputes; in other countries, however, there is no general rule of acceptance. To reduce delays relating to such issues, experts suggest drafting arbitration clauses with as much specificity as possible. To the extent possible, for example, patent policies in various countries should be addressed; persons drafting arbitration clauses may also include provision that all foreign patent issues will be judged according to the standard of home-country law. Another provision could forbid the parties from commencing separate legal actions in other countries. The goal is to help the arbitration tribunal zero in on the express intentions of the parties.[38]

Other agencies for settling disputes include the American Arbitration Association (AAA) or the Swedish Arbitration Institute of the Stockholm Chamber of Commerce. This agency frequently administered disputes between Western and Socialist countries, and has gained credibility for its even-handed administration. Other alternatives have proliferated in recent years. In addition to those mentioned, active centres for arbitration exist in Vancouver, Hong Kong, Cairo, Kuala Lumpur, Singapore, Buenos Aires, Bogotá and Mexico City. A World Arbitration Institute was established in New York; in the United Kingdom, the Advisory, Conciliation and Arbitration Service (ACAS) has achieved great success at handling industrial disputes. The International

Council for Commercial Arbitration (ICCA) was established to co-ordinate the far-flung activities of arbitration organisations. The ICCA meets in different locations around the world every four years.

The United Nations Conference on International Trade Law (UNCITRAL) has also been a significant force in the area of arbitration.[39] UNCITRAL rules have become more or less standard, as many of the organisations named above have adopted them with some modifications. Many developing countries, for example, long held prejudices against the ICC, AAA, and other developed-country organisations. Representatives of developing nations assumed that such organisations would be biased in favour of multinational corporations. Developing nations insisted on settlement in national courts, which was unacceptable to the multinational firms. This was especially true in Latin America, where the Calvo Doctrine required disputes arising with foreign investors to be resolved in national courts under national laws. The growing influence of the ICCA and UNCITRAL rules, coupled with the proliferation of regional arbitration centres, have contributed to changing attitudes in developing countries and have resulted in the increased use of arbitration around the world.

Key points

- A key issue in international trade is the question of jurisdiction. If trade relations work out as planned, this aspect will not be of great importance. However, companies can go through painful experiences, if they have neglected to establish which law will be applicable in case of litigation. Trials in court take on a whole new dimension if they have to be fought under foreign or even the international partner's home country law.

- Intellectual property has been a constant top priority issue for many international firms and organisations. While patents and trademarks are protected in one country, this need not necessarily be the case in other countries. Wrongful use is therefore a common issue of debate. The United Nations and its sub-organisation, the World Intellectual Property Organization, are seeking a common understanding of this controversial topic.

- Bribery and facilitating payments are a non-negligible problem in international trade, as they can distort the competitive situation considerably. Thus, governments (such as in the US), international organizations and private initiatives (such as Transparency International) have developed laws or international agreements to curb bribery.

- As international lawsuits can be very time- and cost-consuming, many international organisations provide alternative solutions for conflict settlement. Institutions such as the International Chamber of Commerce and others have established Courts of Arbitration which can be employed by internationally active firms.

INTERNATIONAL INSTITUTIONS AND THEIR POLITICAL ROLE

The regulatory environment of global marketing consists of a variety of agencies, both governmental and non-governmental, that enforce laws or set guidelines for conducting business. They address a wide range of marketing issues, including the following: price control, valuation of imports and exports, trade practices, labelling, food and drug regulations, employment conditions, collective bargaining, advertising content, competitive practices, and so on. Their decisions are binding and are carried out by the member states. Table 4.3 provides an overview of some of these institutions.[40]

The European Union's role in international trade

The Treaty of Rome established the European Economic Community (EEC), the precursor to the EU. The Treaty contains hundreds of articles, several of which are directly applicable to global companies and global marketers. Articles 30 to 36 estab-

Table 4.3 International organisations with a regulatory influence on global marketing

Abbreviation	Full name
APPA	African Petroleum Producers' Association
ATPC	Association of Tin Producing Countries
CAEU	Council of Arab Economic Unity
CARICOM	Caribbean Economic Community
CCASG	Cooperation Council for the Arab States of the Gulf
ECCAS	Economic Community of Central African States
EEA	European Economic Area
EFTA	European Free Trade Association
EU	European Union
FAO	Food and Agricultural Organization
GATT	General Agreement on Tariffs and Trade (now WTO)
IBRD	International Bank for Reconstruction and Development (World Bank)
ICAO	International Civil Aviation Organization
IDA	International Development Agency
IEA	International Energy Agency
IFC	International Finance Corporation
IMF	International Monetary Fund
ITPA	International Tea Promotion Association
MIGA	Multilateral Investment Guarantee Agency
OECD	Organization for Economic Cooperation and Development
OPEC	Organization of Petroleum Exporting Countries
UNCTAD	United Nations Conference on Trade and Development
UNIDO	United Nations Industrial Development Organization
UNITAR	United Nations Institute for Training and Research
WACU	West African Customs Union
WHO	World Health Organization
WMO	World Meteorological Organization
WTO	World Trade Organization (formerly GATT)

Source: Adapted from Sergi A. Voitovich, 'Normative acts of international economic organizations in international law making', *Journal of World Trade*, 24, 4 (August 1990): pp. 21–38.

Thinking green in Germany

One of the goals of Germany's packaging laws is to reduce packaging waste. Several types of material are covered by the regulations. Transport packaging, including pallets and crates that retailers accumulate, constitute one third of all packaging by weight. Most manufacturers pay a fee to retailers, who in turn arrange for the material to be collected and recycled. Paper, plastic, cardboard and other so-called primary packaging account for about two thirds of all German packaging. These materials – milk cartons, soup cans, and other packaging that consumers take home – fall under an ordinance known as Der Grüne Punkt (the Green Dot).

The Green Dot Ordinance originally specified two separate mechanisms for reclaiming primary packaging. First, retailers were required to take back boxes, cartons, and similar primary packaging materials. The success of the 'take back' effort depended on voluntary consumer co-operation. Second, the ordinance mandated that consumers pay charges on non-refillable beverage, detergent and paint containers. German legislators left the door open for alternative proposals. German businesses responded by establishing a non-profit organisation, Duales System Deutschland (DSD), that is responsible for collecting and recycling the materials. Retailers pay DSD a licensing fee in exchange for the right to display the green dot on packaging. This arrangement eliminates the need for consumers to pay charges. DSD provides designated drop-off areas as well as curbside pickup for Green Dot packaging.

Response to the programme was so enthusiastic that the amount of material collected exceeded Germany's recycling capacity. In its first two years alone, the Green Dot programme reduced the amount of packaging waste by 600 million tons. Many retailers refuse to stock products that do not display the green dot. Ironically, the success of the Green Dot programme has resulted in costs hundreds of millions of dollars more than DSD expected. As a result, fee structures have been adjusted to reflect the true costs of handling different types of packaging material. Horst-Henning Wolf, head of BMW's recycling project, notes, 'There is no such thing as "free of charge". Someone always pays.' Still, Clemens Stroetmann, Germany's Secretary of State for the environment, says, 'It is indisputable that this is a sensible idea. Germany has no more room for landfills and almost no natural resources left, so we need the increasingly precious resources we have.'

Food for thought

- What is the role of laws in reducing packaging waste? Could one expect the same results through industry self-regulation and appeals for voluntary constraints?

- Should companies emphasise their responsible environmental behaviour in advertising and PR messages? What are the potential advantages and dangers?

Source: Lester B. Lave, Chris Hendrickson and Francis C. McMichael, 'Recycling decisions and Green', *ES&T*, 28, 1, pp. 18A–24A; Ferdinand Protzman, 'Germany's push to expand the scope of recycling', *New York Times*, 4 July 1993, Sec. 3, p. 8; Bette Fishbein, *Germany, Garbage, and the Green Dot: Challenging the Throwaway Societey* (New York: INFORM, 1994); Ada S. Rousso and Shvetank P. Shaw, 'Packaging taxes and recycling incentives: the German Green Dot Program', *National Tax Journal*, XLVII, 3 (September 1994): pp. 689–701; Gene Bylinsky, 'Manufacturing for reuse', *Fortune* (6 February 1995): pp. 102–104 ff.

lish the general policy referred to as 'Free Flow of Goods, People, Capital and Technology' among the member states. Articles 85 and 86 contain competition rules, as amended by various directives of the EU Commission. These articles and directives constitute community law.

The European Court of Justice, based in Luxembourg, hears disputes that arise among the 15 EU member nations on trade issues such as mergers, monopolies and trade barriers. The Court is also empowered to resolve conflicts between national law and EU law. In most cases, the latter supersedes national laws of individual European countries. Marketers must be aware, however, that national laws should always be consulted. National laws may be more strict than community law, especially in such areas as competition and antitrust. Community law is intended to harmonise national laws as far as possible, thus promoting the purposes defined in articles 30 to 36. The goal is to bring the 'lax' laws of some member states up to designated minimum standards.

A case from Germany helps illustrate the point. A German court ruled that Pronuptia, a French wedding dress maker and retailer, could not require its German franchisees to buy all their goods from the parent company. Pronuptia took its case to the European Court of Appeals, the EU's main forum for arbitration that makes recommendations to the Court of Justice. Had the German court's ruling been upheld on antitrust grounds, all franchisers doing business in Europe including such well-known companies as McDonald's, Midas Muffler, and PepsiCo's Kentucky Fried Chicken and Pizza Hut would have been stripped of their ability to operate US-style franchises in Europe. Key policies, including the right to dictate corporate logos, store designs and outside suppliers, would have been nullified. After intense lobbying by the International Franchising Association, the Court issued a ruling that was generally favourable to franchisers. Still, the new regulations prohibit franchisers from requiring franchisees to sell specific branded products from outside suppliers. Thus, while McDonald's retains the right to designate suppliers for commodities such as meat and potatoes, it cannot force franchisees to conform to the US policy that calls for selling only Coca-Cola beverages at its restaurants.[41]

The World Trade Organization and its role in international trade

When in 1948 twenty-three countries underlined in the General Agreement on Tariffs and Trade their determination to reduce import tariffs, this was considered a milestone in international trade relations. GATT was based on three principles. The first concern non-discrimination: each member country must treat the trade of all other member countries equally. The second principle was open markets, which were encouraged by the GATT through a prohibition of all forms of protection except customs tariffs. Fair trade was the third principle, which prohibits export subsidies on manufactured products and limits the use of export subsidies on primary products. In reality, none of these principles has been fully realised as yet, although much progress was made during the Uruguay round on issues such as non-tariff barriers, protection of intellectual property rights, and government subsidies.

Another major breakthrough at the Uruguay round was the establishment of the World Trade Organization (WTO). In contrast to GATT which was more loosely organised, WTO as a permanent institution is endowed with much more decision-making power in undecided cases. These extended competencies have become manifest in visible consequences. While in the 50 years of its existence only 300 complaints in international trade disputes were filed with GATT, since its installation in 1995 the WTO has already dealt with 132 cases.

The World Trade Organization can look back at a very successful start. Since its beginning, the number of member countries has increased to more than 130. Over 30 countries, with China and Russia among them, have also shown interest in participating in the WTO.[42]

EUROPEAN FOCUS

'Europe going bananas' – the end of an endless story?

For years, the EU and the US have been fighting fierce battles about a seemingly unimportant issue: bananas. It all started some decades ago with the so-called Lomé treaty. In 1957, a group of nations from Africa, the Caribbean and the Pacific area (also called ACP countries) agreed with their former colonial masters on banana supply to Europe. The ACP countries were granted the status of preferential suppliers, which was supported by a number of measures such as import tariffs and import quotas.

With increasing European integration, agreements of this kind conflicted with the intention to reduce trade barriers. Additional pressure came from the US and its large multinational fruit processing and marketing companies such as Del Monte or Chiquita, as well as some Latin American banana growers, who saw their market access to Europe dramatically restrained.

Instead of fundamentally reforming the import regulations for bananas into the EU, the so-called 'EU Banana Regime' was introduced. This regime provides a total quota for the import of bananas into the EU amounting to 2.5 million tons per year. This quota should then be split among producing countries at different tariff rates. This resulted in the following situation: while the import tariff on bananas from ACP countries amounted to €75 per packaging or weight unit, bananas from other countries were levied with €850 in tariffs, which made the consumer price prohibitive for market success.

Officially, the EU justifies the preferential treatment as economic assistance to the economically less developed ACP countries and to protect them from the influence of US multinationals. A second look, however, shows that this treatment has nothing to do with 'Robin Hood' sentiments. In exchange for the favourable import conditions, the ACP countries granted European exporters a better access to their markets.

For this support, the European tax payer is charged €1.7 billion per year, which amounts to 42.4 cents per kilogram. Half of this amount remains with distributors, while the banana growers, who were to be supported, only receive €130 million per year.

As political pressure did not lead to considerable changes, the US, Ecuador, Guatemala, Honduras and Mexico sued the European Union in 1995 at the WTO's court of arbitration. In 1997, the complaint was judged justified.

However, the EU reacted only very slowly and with minor changes. EU officials argued that an immediate abolition would have fatal effects on the ACP countries. Therefore, they proposed changes by the end of 1998. As fundamental changes were not in sight, the US asked the WTO for an intervention. The American plan provided that a duty of 100 per cent be imposed on EU imports of 14 selected product categories to the US. Among the product categories affected were biscuits, candles, chandeliers, cashmere textiles, coffee products and handbags. As France and the UK were particularly reluctant in pursuing reforms, their industries were hurt the most by the sanctions imposed.

After the WTO had asked the EU three times since 1995 to change the banana regime, it finally agreed to implementing the US sanctions. This decision was of historical significance: it was the first time in its 50 years of existence that the WTO (or its predecessor GATT) had authorised retaliatory sanctions. In March 1999, the sanctions were put in place, import tariffs totalling €163 million were allowed to be imposed. In turn, the EU announced negotiations with the trading partners to bring the controversial issue to an end. A solution, however, would require a couple of months.

Still, an end to the trade disputes is not in sight. Even if the case on banana imports is settled, there are more battles ahead, such as meat treated with hormones or genetically manipulated vegetables and grain from the US. Overall, this controversy damaged most severely those exporters, who were not at all related to bananas. They now suffer the consequences to the same extent as US consumers, who have to make do without prosciutto from Italy or cashmere sweaters from Scotland.

Addendum: The banana growers in the ACP countries will also take action. The changes in import regulations for bananas into the EU are expected to significantly damage their economic development. However, these countries have found a solution to these problems: in 1997, President Clinton offered some ACP countries preferential trade treatments if they would team up with the US in its fight against drug trafficking. It is more than likely that the US government will be reminded of this promise in the next couple of months....

Food for thought

- Does the 'EU Banana Regime' neglect the interest of the consumer? Why? Why not?
- Can the WTO be a fair arbitrator? Which countries/interest groups wield most influence in the WTO?

Source: 'Expelled from Eden', *The Economist*, 345 (8048), 20 December 1997, pp. 35–38; Frances Williams, 'EU accepts ruling on the banana regime', *Financial Times*, 26 September 1997; Frances Williams, 'US wins formal authorisation for sanctions', *Financial Times*, 13 April 1999; Neil Buckley, Guy de Jonquieres, and Frances Williams, 'US unveils final hitlist in EU banana trade dispute', *Financial Times*, 22 December 1998; Richard Wolffe, 'EU plea for delay in banana sanctions', *Financial Times*, 19 December 1998; 'Schiedsgericht zwingt EU zur Änderung der Bananenordnung', *Der Standard* (8 April 1999): p. 21; 'Fruitless but not harmless: the banana trade row', *The Economist*, 10 April 1999; 'Stealing from the poor: the EU's Lomé Convention', *The Economist*, 24 April 1999; Daniel Birchmeier, 'Krumme Geschäfte ohne Bananen', *Der Standard* (8 April 1999): p. 9; Wolfgang Böhm, 'Der krumme Weg einer Marktordnung', *Die Presse* (8 April 1999): p. 11; Nancy Dunne, 'US lists sanctions over bananas', *Financial Times*, 10 April 1999; Frances Williams, 'The EU "needs 8 months" to end banana crisis', *Financial Times*, 20 April 1999.

Summary

The political environment of global marketing comprises governmental institutions, political parties, and organisations that are the expression of the people in the nations of the world. Anyone engaged in global marketing should have an understanding of the importance of sovereignty to national governments. The political environment varies from country to country, and risk assessment is crucial. It is also important to understand a particular government's actions with respect to taxes, dilution of equity control, and expropriation.

The legal environment consists of laws, courts, attorneys, and legal customs and practices. The countries of the world can be broadly categorised in terms of the common-law system or code (civil)-law system. While most European nations rely on code law, the United States, United Kingdom, and the British Commonwealth countries, which include Canada, Australia and New Zealand, the former British colonies in Africa, and India are common-law countries. Some of the most important legal issues pertain to establishment, jurisdiction, patents and trademarks, licensing, antitrust and bribery. When legal conflicts arise, companies can pursue the matter in court or use arbitration.

The regulatory environment consists of agencies, both governmental and non-governmental, that enforce laws or set guidelines for conducting business. Global marketing activities can be affected by a number of international or regional economic organisations; in Europe, for example, the EU makes laws governing member states. The WTO will have broad impact on global marketing activities in the years to come. Although the political and legal environment is complex, astute marketers plan ahead to avoid situations that might result in conflict, misunderstanding or outright violation of national laws.

Concepts and definitions

National sovereignty	It implies that a nation-state holds the decision power of last resort; it also includes the state's independence from others. National sovereignty enables undivided jurisdiction over all persons and property without external interference.
Political risk	Describes the risk of changes in government policy, which may negatively affect company activities. If the political risk is low, investors are more inclined to consider a country for investment. Countries with high political risk are in many cases economically less developed.
Case vs. code law	Case law is based on tradition and precedence from past jurisdiction. Code law is grounded on written norms in form of legal writings (codices), which are complemented by court decisions.
Cybersquatting	Describes the fact that someone uses an Internet domain in a way that it may easily be confused with a 'prominent namesake'. This malpractice occurs, if (i) the domain name is identical or misleading with respect to an existing brand, or (ii) the owner of the domain has no rights or rightful interest in the name, or (iii) the domain name is registered and used for dubious purposes.
Alternative settlement of litigations	Describes the possibilities to settle international litigations outside a legal court in a court of arbitration. Numerous international organisations offer arbitration services.

Discussion questions

1 What is sovereignty? Why is it an important consideration in the political environment of global marketing?

2 Briefly describe some of the differences between the legal environment of a country that embraces common law as opposed to a country that observes civil law.

3 Global marketers can avoid legal conflicts by understanding the reasons conflicts arise in the first place. Identify and describe several legal issues that relate to global commerce.

4 You are an Austrian citizen travelling on business in Africa. As you are leaving country X, the passport control officer at the airport tells you there will be a passport 'processing' delay of one hour. You explain that your plane leaves in 30 minutes, and that the next plane out of the country does not leave for three days. You also explain how valuable your time is (at least €250 an hour) and that it is urgent that you catch the flight you have reserved. The official listens carefully to your appeal, and then 'suggests' that a contribution of €850 would definitely assure your passport clearance priority treatment, and considering how valuable your time is, it is quite a bargain. Would you comply with the 'suggestion'? Why? Why not? If you would not comply, what would you do? If you comply with the suggestion, have you violated any laws? Explain. If the official requests €20, would that make a difference?

5 'See you in court' is one way to respond when legal issues arise. What other approaches are possible?

6 Should a company operating internationally adhere to a single standard of conduct, or should it adapt to local conditions? Why?

Webmistress's hotspots

Objectives and activities of the World Intellectual Property Organization
You are so enthusiastic about your latest invention of a cup for left-handers that you want to have it internationally protected. This website provides information on what is considered an invention and which possibilities there are to protect it.
http://www.wipo.org/

Homepage of the European Patent Office
If you want to know who holds the world-wide patent on a plaster through which the skin can absorb aspirin, visit this site (by the way, it is William Byrne and Dermot McCafferty, and the patent number is WO9704759).
http://www.european-patent-office.org/

Transparency International
Here you will find further information on the objectives and capabilities of Transparency International. This private initiative aims at curbing international corruption and bribery.
http://www.transparency.de/

Conflict resolution through the International Chamber of Commerce
Here you find interesting information on the services provided by the International Chamber of Commerce in the case of international trade disputes.
http://www.iccwbo.org/

UN trade laws
This page provides an overview of the UN agenda on international trade and humanitarian law.
http://www.un.org/law/

International Court of Justice
Here you will find historic verdicts as well as currently ongoing trials at the UN's International Court of Justice.
http://www.icj-cij.org/

Suggested readings

Akhter, Syed H. and Yusuf A. Choudhry 'Forced withdrawal from a country market: Managing political risk', *Business Horizons*, 36, 3 (1993): pp. 47–54.

Albright, Katherine and Grace Won, 'Foreign Corrupt Practices Act', *American Criminal Law Review*, Spring (1993): p. 787.

Bagley, Jennifer M., Stephanie S. Glickman and Elizabeth B. Wyatt, 'Intellectual property', *American Criminal Law Review*, 32, Winter (1995): pp. 457–479.

Basu, K. and A. Chattopadhyay, 'Marketing pharmaceuticals to developing nations: Research issues and a framework for public policy', *Canadian Journal of Administrative Sciences*, 12, December (1995): pp. 300–313.

Braithwaite, John, 'Transnational regulation of the pharmaceutical industry', *Annals of the American Academy of Political & Social Science*, 525, January (1993): pp. 12–30.

Chukwumerige, Okezie, *Choice of Law in International Commercial Arbitration*. Westport, CT: Quorum Books, 1994.

Epstein, M.J. and M.-J. Roy, *Strategic Learning through Corporate Environmental Management: Implementing the ISO 14001 Standard*. Fontainebleau: INSEAD's Center for the Management of Environmental Resources, 1997.

Fishbein, Bette K., *Germany, Garbage, and the Green Dot: Challenging the Throwaway Society*. New York: Inform, 1994.

Garg, R. and G. Kumra, 'Four opportunities in India's pharmaceutical market', *McKinsey Quarterly*, 4 (1996): pp. 132–145.

Gillespie, Kate, 'Middle East response to the US Foreign Corrupt Practices Act', *California Management Review*, 29 (1987).

Graham, John L., 'The Foreign Corrupt Practices Act: a new perspective', *Journal of International Business Studies*, 4 (1984): pp. 107–121.

Jacoby, Neil H., Peter Nehmenkis and Richard Eells, *Bribery and Extortion in World Business*. New York: McMillan, 1977.

Kaikati, Jack and Wayne A. Label, 'The Foreign Antibribery Law: friend or foe', *Columbia Journal of World Business*, Spring (1980): pp. 46–51.

Katsh, Salem M. and Michael P. Dierks, 'Globally, trade secrets laws are all over the map', *The National Law Journal*, 8 May 1995, pp. C12–C14.

Nash, Marian Leich, 'Contemporary practice of the United States relating to international law', *American Journal of International Law*, 88, October (1994): pp. 719–765.

Neimanis, G.J., 'Business ethics in the former Soviet Union: a report', *Journal of Business Ethics*, 16, 3 (1997): pp. 357–362.

Ohmae, Kenichi, *The Borderless World*. New York: Harper Perennial, 1991.

Ohmae, Kenichi, 'Putting global logic first', *Harvard Business Review*, 73, 1 (1995): pp. 119–125.

Ortego, Joseph and Josh Kardisch, 'Foreign companies can limit the risk of being subject to US courts', *National Law Journal*, 19 September 1994, pp. C2–C3.

Pines, D., 'Amending the Foreign Corrupt Practices Act to include a private right of action', *California Law Review*, January (1994): pp. 185–229.

Robock, S.H. and K. Simmonds, *International Business and Multinational Enterprises*. Homewood, IL: Irwin, 1989.

Rodgers, Frank A., 'The war is won, but peace is not', *Vital Speeches of the Day*, 14 May 1991, pp. 430–432.

Roessler, Frieder, 'The scope, limits and function of the GATT legal system', *World Economy*, September (1985): pp. 287–298.

Root, F.R., *Entry Strategies for International Markets*. New York: Lexington Books, 1994.

Samuels, Barbara C., *Managing Risk in Developing Countries: National Demands and Multinational Response*. Princeton, NJ: Princeton University Press, 1990.

Slomanson, William R., *Fundamental Perspectives on International Law*. St Paul, MN: West Publishing, 1990.

Sohn, Louis B., *Basic Documents of the United Nations*. Brooklyn: The Foundation Press, 1968.

Spero, Donald M., 'Patent protection or piracy: A CEO views Japan', *Harvard Business Review*, 68, 5 (1990): pp. 58–62.

Vagts, D., *Transnational Business Problems*. Mineola, NY: The Foundation Press, 1986.

Vernon, Raymond, 'The World Trade Organization: A new stage in international trade and development', *Harvard International Law Journal*, 36, Spring (1995): pp. 329–340.

Vogel, David, 'The globalization of business ethics: Why America remains distinctive', *California Management Review*, 35, Fall (1992): pp. 30–49.

Voitovich, S.A., 'Normative acts of international economic organizations in international law making', *Journal of World Trade*, August (1990): pp. 21–38.

Notes

1. C. Creifelds, *Creifelds Rechtswörterbuch* (München: Beck'sche Verlagsbuchhandlung, 1997).
2. J. Valente, 'The land of cuisine sees taste besieged by "Le Big Mac" ', *The Wall Street Journal*, 25 May 1994, p. A1.
3. T. Peterson, M. Larner, W. Echikson and A. Robinson, 'Energy: the walls come tumbling down', *Business Week*, 1 June 1998, pp. 36–37.
4. 'A decade of privatisation', *The Financial Times*, 27 December 1995.
5. K. Pennar, 'Is the nation-state obsolete in a global economy?', *Business Week*, 17 July 1995, p. 80.
6. David Selbourne, 'Tony, you're talking globaloney', *The Times*, 28 April 1999.
7. D. Yergin and T. Gustafson, *Russia 2010 and What It Means for the World* (New York: Vintage Books, 1995).
8. This section is based on D.J. Encarnation and S. Vachani, 'Foreign ownership: when hosts change the rules', *Harvard Business Review*, September–October (1985): pp. 152–160.
9. http://www.ibm.com/ibm/Emerging/linkind.html (cited 4 February 1999) .
10. C. Creifelds, *Creifelds Rechtswörterbuch* (München: Beck'sche Verlagsbuchhandlung, 1997).
11. F.R. Root, *Entry Strategies for International Markets* (New York: Lexington Books, 1994).
12. R. Radway, 'Legal dimensions of international business'. In *International Encyclopedia of Business and Management*, ed. M. Warner. Thomson: London, 1996.
13. *Law & Commercial Dictionary* (München: Beck'sche Verlagsbuchhandlung, 1985).
14. M.M. Nelson, 'Two styles of business vie in East Europe', *The Wall Street Journal*, 3 April 1995, p. A14.
15. S.H. Robock and K. Simmonds, *International Business and Multinational Enterprises* (Homewood, IL: Irwin, 1989).
16. Joseph Ortego and Josh Kardisch, 'Foreign companies can limit the risk of being subject to US courts', *National Law Journal*, 19 September 1994, pp. C2–C3.

17. R. Radway, 'Legal dimensions of international business'. In *International Encyclopedia of Business and Management*, ed. M. Warner (London: Thomson, 1996).

18. K. Vermeulen, 'Champagne perfume launched in United States but barred in France', *Wine Spectator*, 31 October 1994, p. 9.

19. M. Fogel, 'Bayer trademarks the word "aspirin" in Russia, leaving rivals apoplectic', *The Wall Street Journal*, 29 October 1993, p. A13. 'Bayer verliert Exklusivrechte in Russland', *Die Welt*, 10 June 1994, p. 15. 'Bayer and UPSA clash over aspirin in Russia', *Marketletter*, 24 February 1997.

20. 'US record industry loses $300 million annually to piracy', *Security*, 1996, p. 18. C. Baum, 'Counteracting piracy', *Security*, 1996, p. 14–18. 'Chaos abstellen: Gegen Markenpiraterie im weltweiten Datennetz Internet können sich Unternehmen wehren', *Wirtschaftswoche*, 46 (1996): pp. 154–155. Bodo B. Schlegelmilch, and Barbara Stöttinger, 'Der Kauf gefälschter Markenprodukte: die Lust auf das Verbotene', *Marketing ZfP*, 3 (1999): pp. 196–208.

21. 'The politics of piracy', *The Economist*, 20 February 1999, p. 74.

22. http://www.wipo.org/eng/main.htm (cited 1 September 1999).

23. F.R. Root, *Entry Strategies for International Markets* (New York: Lexington Books, 1994).

24. H. Collin, *Internationale Patentsysteme und -praxis* (Vienna: Orac, 1992).

25. J. Carey, 'Inching toward a borderless patent', *Business Week*, 5 September 1994, p. 35.

26. D. Vagts, *Transnational Business Problems* (Mineola, NY: The Foundation Press, 1986).

27. D. Sanger, 'IBM's European accord: Concessions end a decade of debate', *The New York Times*, 3 August 1984, p. 38.

28. S.B. Garland, A. Reinhardt and P. Burrows, 'Now, it's Intel in the dock', *Business Week*, 1 March 1999, pp. 28–29.

29. B. McMenamin, 'Eroding patent rights', *Forbes*, 24 October 1994, p. 92.

30. S.M. Katsh and M.P. Dierks, 'Globally, trade secrets laws are all over the map', *The National Law Journal*, 8 May 1995, p. C12.

31. Bodo B. Schlegelmilch, *Marketing Ethics: An International Perspective* (London: International Thomson Publishing, 1998).

32. G.A. Pitman and J.P. Sanford, 'The Foreign Corrupt Practices Act revisited: attempting to regulate "ethical bribes" in global business', *International Journal of Purchasing and Materials Management*, 30, 3 (1994): pp. 15–24.

33. C. Van Haste, 'Corruption, bribery, and US law: A deck stacked against US developers', *Electrical World*, 210, 5 (1996): pp. 37–39.

34. S. Kaltenhauser, 'When bribery is a budget item', *World Business*, 2, 2 (1996): p. 11.

35. D. Robertson and Bodo B. Schlegelmilch, 'Corporate institutionalization of ethics in the United States and Great Britain', *Journal of Business Ethics*, 12, 4 (1993): pp. 301–312.

36. Bodo B. Schlegelmilch and D. Robertson, 'The influence of country and industry on ethical perceptions of senior executives in the US and Europe', *Journal of International Business Studies*, 26, 4 (1995): pp. 859–881.

37. '29 nations agree to outlaw bribing foreign officials', *The New York Times*, 11 November 1997, pp. 1, D-2.

38. J.M. Allen, Jr and B.G. Merritt, 'Drafters of arbitration clauses face a variety of unforeseen perils', *National Law Journal*, 17 April 1995, pp. C6–C7. B. Londa, 'An agreement to arbitrate disputes isn't the same in every language', *Brandweek*, 26 September 1994, p. 18.

39. J. Schwappach, *EU-Rechtshandbuch für die Wirtschaft* (München: Beck'sche Verlagsbuchhandlung, 1996).

40. S.A. Voitovich, 'Normative acts of international economic organizations in international law making', *Journal of World Trade*, August (1990): pp. 21–38.

41. P. Revzin, 'European bureaucrats are writing the rules Americans will live by', *The Wall Street Journal*, 17 May 1989, pp. A1, A12.

42. 'GATT at 50: fifty years on', *The Economist*, 16 May 1998.

CHAPTER 5

Information technology environment

Understanding that technology can transform an entire industry requires a shift in the mindset at the CEO and boardroom level.
GEORGE SHAHEEN, MANAGING PARTNER & CEO, ANDERSEN CONSULTING

Technology is moving so fast that what was brand new this morning may be obsolete by tomorrow ... It changes everything about how we structure our business, how and where our employees work and how we serve our customers. One thing is certain, your business will be more, not less dependent on information technology. And you will depend on it not just for reducing costs, as in the past, but for fundamentally creating competitive advantage.
JAMES UNRUH, CHAIRMAN AND CEO, UNISYS

Chapter objectives

After reading this chapter, you will know:

- The main drivers of the information and communication technology.
- The role of the Internet in providing a platform for e-commerce.
- How the new technological environment impacts on global marketing activities.
- The components of the electronic value chain.

Why is this important? Here are three situations in which you would need an understanding of the above issues:

- You need to analyse the potential for a new Internet auction service your company is planning to implement.
- You need to assess the importance of middle men when selling your product via the Web.
- You need to devise an appropriate market penetration strategy for an innovative Web service.

Practice link

Technology and technological change have always been important issues. Imagine yourself as a weaver in late 18th-century England. You are working in a small hut weaving the wool your cousin span on her spinning-wheel. The loom you are using was built by your grandfather. You are a competent craftswoman, the work process has stood the test of time and the technology is reliable. You are weaving cloth for the provincial nobility, who owns most of the land in the surrounding countryside.

In a few years, the world as you know it will have ceased to exist. Machines will manufacture textiles with unimaginable speed and consistency. Your sons and daughters will look for work in rapidly growing towns, where entrepreneurs invest capital into huge factories. The impoverished nobility, committed to maintaining the old order, will wear shabby clothes and will try to rescue their wealth.

Today, we find ourselves in a similar situation: as the steam engine revolutionised the life of the English weavers, networked computers are changing our environment. And again, the changes are not evolving in comfortable incremental steps, but are turbulent, erratic and often rather uncomfortable. To illustrate the dramatic and paradigmatic nature of the changes brought about by information and communication technology (ICT), researchers resort to metaphors: parallels are drawn with the invention of electricity, the invention of the steam engine or even the invention of the wheel. Deighton[1] states that the 'technological shock' will completely reshape the way marketing is done. And as to global marketing, ICT is turning out to be the driving force for globalisation, promoting the frequently proclaimed transformation of the world into a global village.

In this chapter, we look at some of the basic elements of the new technological environment and discuss how the changes we are experiencing impact on the way global marketing is conducted. The chapter opens by considering some of the key drivers of the ICT revolution, most importantly the Internet. Subsequently, we discuss the influence of these fundamental changes on competitive strategies. Finally, the changes the technological environment brings for the configuration of the global value chain are considered.

LIVING IN AN AGE OF TECHNOLOGICAL DISCONTINUITIES

Price plunges indicate speed of technological progress

So what are the drivers of the technology revolution we are witnessing? Arguably, the changes with the most dramatic impact on globalisation occurred in two fields: transportation and communication. Dicken[2] refers to these two areas as 'enabling technologies'. In transportation, key advances have been made in air travel, container shipments and speedier loading and unloading. On the communication side, the reduced cost of long-distance telecommunication is most remarkable. Today, a three-minute telephone call between New York and London costs about $2; in 1930 it would have cost about $250 when expressed in today's prices. Market liberalisation is expected to bring down international rates by as much as 80 per cent over five years.[3] The Cambridge Strategic Management predicts that by 2005, a transatlantic video-phone call will cost only a 'a few cents an hour'.[4] Already, about two-thirds of the world's new telephone subscriptions are for mobile phones and in developed countries, this share is as high as 75 per cent.[5]

A second important cost reduction is the vertiginous decline in computer-processing power: it now costs only 1 per cent of what it did in the early 1970s. Expressed differently, 'If cars had developed at the same pace as microprocessors . . . a typical car would now cost less than $5 and do more than 250,000 miles to the gallon.'[6] These price reductions reflect the breathtaking speed of technological change; indeed, never before have such dramatic price falls been observed.

Technological convergence and ubiquity of technology

In information and communication technology, it is not only the improved speed and reliability of devices which have brought about rapid technological change, but the convergence between the transmission of information and the processing of information. Moreover, it is expected that the next few years will witness a convergence of different types of information and communication technologies into one common Internet standard. Figure 5.1 illustrates this development.

A second development has been labelled technological ubiquity. Andersen Consulting describes it as follows: 'A world in which information technology is an integral part of everything we see and do in the workplace and at home.'[7] Thus, every kitchen device, car, or exercise machine will be packed with easy-to-use electronics that will add value to the product, be it by tailoring it to personal preferences, enabling remote communication, etc.

Explosive growth of the Internet

Arguably, the Internet represents one of the most important drivers of the technological revolution, in that it led to the development of an entirely new form of doing business, so-called e-commerce (see below). The history of the Internet can be traced back to 1969, when a department of the US Ministry of Defence introduced the

Figure 5.1 **Convergence of information and communication technologies**

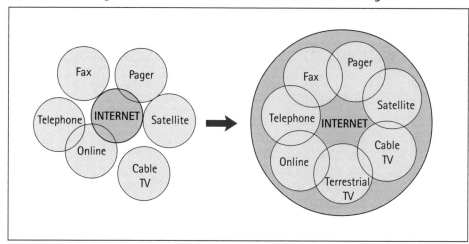

so-called ARPANET. Apart from enabling access to remote computers, the net already permitted the transfer of electronic messages (e-mail).[8] At this stage, the users were restricted to a few military researchers. Although subsequent years witnessed an extension of users and the development of similar nets springing up from a co-operation between, among others, NASA, IBM and MCI, the true breakthrough occurred only in 1992. In this year, Tim Berners-Lee at the Conseil Européen pour la Recherche Nucléaire (CERN), a European research institute in Switzerland, introduced the World Wide Web (WWW). For the first time, this protocol permitted the graphic representation of information in the Internet. In connection with Web browsers used to navigate the network of hyperlinks that make up the World Wide Web, this development is widely seen as the origin of the explosive growth of the Internet. Today, the World Wide Web is often used synonymously for the entire Internet, although the latter also hosts traditional Internet services like Telnet, Gopher and FTP.[9] Figure 5.2 shows the development of the Internet hosts over time and Figure 5.3 depicts the geographical distribution of users.

For a global marketer, it is of concern that Web access is still very much skewed towards developed countries. Moreover, a number of countries connected to the Internet merely offer only e-mail,[10] and are consequently cut off from the wealth of information available on the Web. Despite the fact that current developments and growth rates, in particular in China and South America, will contribute to an easing of the problem of geographically unequal access, there is still concern. Richard Jolly, author of the latest development report of the United Nations,[11] notes that technology is a double-edged sword, opening new ways for many but also cutting off access: in Bangladesh, for example, a computer costs eight times the average annual income.

Technological change as such, of course, is nothing new. What is remarkable today is the speed of change. While it took, for example, some 38 and 25 years respectively for the radio and telephone to reach 50 million US consumers, TV only needed 13 years and cable 10 years to reach the same threshold. The Internet with the World Wide Web achieved the same penetration level in less than five years (Figure 5.4). On a world-wide basis, the Internet has expanded by about 2000 per cent in the last decade and is doubling in size every 6 to 10 months.[12] By 2003, there are projected to

Figure 5.2 Development of Internet hosts

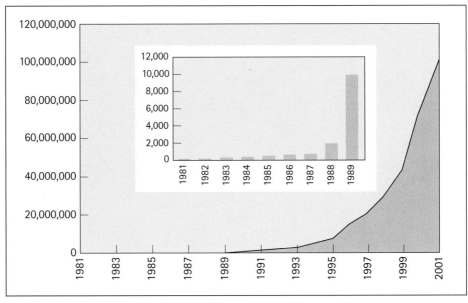

Source: Adapted from: http://www.mids.org/mapsale/data/trends/trends-199907/sld004.htm, 30 August 1999.

Figure 5.3 Geographical distribution of Internet users (1998)

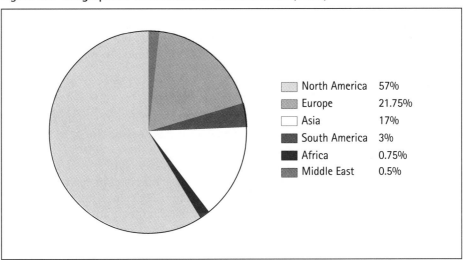

Source: http://www.nua.ie/surveys/graphs-charts/1998graphs/location.html, 30 August 1999.

be 350 million users, split between North America (35 per cent), Europe (30 per cent), Asia Pacific (21 per cent), South America (9 per cent) and the rest of the world (about 5 per cent). Other forecasts expect the Internet to reach the one billion user mark by 2008. To appreciate the magnitude of this growth, it took until 1999 for telephone users to reach the one billion mark.[13] Freeing the Internet access from the confines of computer keyboards and enabling access via mobile phones, pagers, etc. will fuel this growth.

Figure 5.4 Uptake of consumer technologies

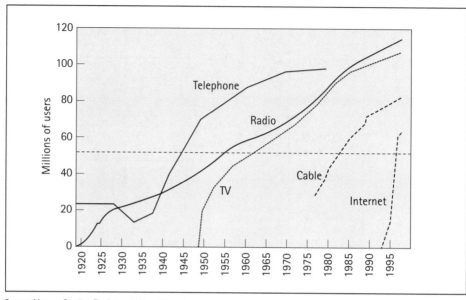

Source: Morgan Stanley, *The Internet Advertising Report.*

Another revolution, voice recognition technology, is just round the corner. Rendering keyboards largely superfluous and thus finally fulfilling the science fiction notion of commanding a machine through the human voice, this technology will dramatically accelerate the use of computers and drive ICT into completely new applications: objects we talk to, drive with, touch or wear.[14]

The development of e-commerce

Technology, and in particular information and communication technology (ICT), is more than merely an 'enabler'. It has become the basis for an entirely new business model. Starting with electronic data exchange (EDI), i.e. the transfer of standardised data between corporations, the Internet has undergone a metamorphosis from a medium primarily used to advertise a product or service, to an e-commerce platform combining information, transaction, dialogue and exchange. In short, the Internet has given birth to an entirely new business model and opened completely novel opportunities for global marketing. The German-based consulting firm Roland Berger & Partner illustrates this development as shown in Figure 5.5.

The scope for new developments arising from the new technologies is considerable. Consider the example of the well-known electronic bookseller Amazon.com. Using a virtual network which seamlessly connects suppliers and customers, the firm has changed the way in which books are traded. Over 30,000 'associated websites' are recommending the company for a commission and provide links to the Amazon site. Of course, Amazon not only offers books but also informs customers about new publications and encourages readers to post reviews of books they have read. Virtual chatrooms and meetings with authors also foster the formation of an Amazon community. Already, more than half the business Amazon conducts is with loyal customers.

Figure 5.5 The evolution of electronic commerce

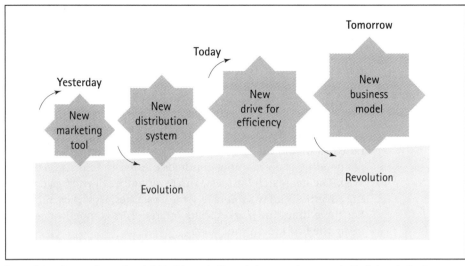

Source: Roland Berger & Partner (1999) *Erfolgsfaktoren im Electronic Commerce: Auszug aus den Ergebnissen der Studie*, Wien/Frankfurt am Main, p. 12.

Further examples of companies that developed their business around the possibilities offered through e-commerce are Dell Computers, which shows growth rates that exceed those of conventional computer manufacturers by a factor of four; E*Trade, an online brokerage with annual growth rates of 200 per cent and eBay, which offers online auctions and has an annual transaction volume of more than $300 million. At eBay, customers provide the entire content, starting from the goods on offer up to the chat-rooms in which they exchange background information on these goods.

But while most media attention has focused on consumer marketing on the Internet, the large majority of Internet activities are generated in the business-to-business field. Forester Research puts to relationship between business-to-business and business-to-consumer e-commerce at 5:1.[15]

However, rapid technological change not only affects high-tech companies that like to include an 'e' in their name. Michael Hruby[16] considers sport shoes. Thirty years ago, he argues, such shoes were inexpensive, made out of canvas and came in two designs and three colours. Today, their high-tech descendants boast inflatable air bladders and gel inserts. They come in dozens of styles, colours and materials and, of course, are different for each sport. They are not athletic shoes any longer, they are equipment. And they are not cheap. Moreover, some of the household names in the business, such as Nike, do not produce a single shoe. Instead they use outsourcing to get the shoes manufactured in low labour-cost countries and concentrate on what they can do best, i.e. global marketing.

For a global marketer, rapid technological advances in general, and the unprecedented speed of change in ICT in particular have resulted in numerous new challenges: virtual organisations, symbiotic relationships, electronic markets, new forms of co-option, blurring corporate boundaries and flatter organisational hierarchies are among the most important.[17] While these challenges open entirely new business opportunities, they also represent fundamental threats to established organisations. Companies have to learn how to live with a high degree of volatility. John Stopford of the London Business School eloquently pointed to the reduced value of incumbency.[18] Companies that were success stories only a few years ago are now fighting to survive; Westinghouse or DEC spring to mind. On the other hand, there are companies that have appeared virtually overnight. In this context, one of the authors coined the phrase mushroom companies.[19] A well-known characteristic of mushrooms is, of course, that they grow virtually overnight but then often disappear rather quickly. Consider Yahoo Inc., which provides the largest search engine on the Internet. Only a few years ago, Yahoo's co-founder David Filo, was a relatively poor ex-student. Today, his online service leads the field in both traffic and advertising revenues. But while Internet search companies like Yahoo, Infoseek, Lycos and Excite raised $170 million by going public in 1996, Internet search facilities have become a commodity. There are now hundreds of ways to find and retrieve information on the Web. The net search business, where a number of engines compete for a pool of willing advertisers, may soon take some casualties. However, Yahoo might well survive. It has three times the market share of any of its competitors and has the advantage of being the first kid on the block.

Another example is Netscape, which was founded in 1994 as Mosaic Communications. It offered the first version of its Internet Navigator one year later and, at its peak in the first quarter of 1997, generated revenues in excess of $150 million p.a. However, since October 1997, the company's stock has lost in value on fears that it will be the big loser in its browser war with Microsoft's Internet Explorer.

Given these dramatic business histories, it is not surprising that Microsoft's CEO Bill Gates supposedly said: 'We are always two years away from failure', and Intel's CEO Andy Grove coined the motto: 'Only the paranoid survive.'

Key points

- The speed of technological change has accelerated dramatically.
- Today, our environment is characterised by technological convergence and technological ubiquity.
- Arguably, the Internet represents the most important driver of technological change.
- For a global marketer, the changes in ICT in particular have resulted in numerous new challenges; virtual organisations, symbiotic relationships, electronic markets, new forms of co-option, blurring corporate boundaries and flatter organisational hierarchies are among the most important.

NEW TECHNOLOGIES CHANGE THE RULES OF COMPETITION

In addition to increasing volatility, the move from an industrial to a post-industrial e-economy also presents the global marketer with a new set of business rules. Long-established principles, such as the emphasis of retailers on 'location, location, location', are passé. Why should a busy executive spend her valuable time and fight traffic to buy some books or videos for her children in town? She can do the same in much greater comfort from home via the Web. Looking at the changing business principles forced by the new e-economy, Arvind Rangaswamy[20] of Penn State University summarised the situation as in Table 5.1.

Table 5.1 Evolution in business context and strategies

From	To
● Market share	● Strategic control
● Technology as an enabler	● Technology as a driver
● Seller-centric market	● Buyer-centric markets
● Physical assets	● Knowledge assets
● Vertical integration based on size	● Vertical integration based on speed
● Decreasing return to scale	● Increasing return to scale
● Firm-centric marketing strategies	● Network-centric marketing strategies

Source: Adapted from Arvind Rangaswamy, 'Toward a model of ebusiness performance', Presentation at the American Marketing Association Summer Educators' Conference, San Francisco, 7–10 August 1999.

In a similar vein, Andersen Consulting[21] stated that the new economy will force companies to adopt some new game plans. Among the most important are:

1 to secure a dominant market position as quickly as possible;
2 to form alliances based on their potential for market access and synergies;
3 to anticipate very high start-up investments;
4 to defend positions through an ongoing process of innovations.

Below, we will look at some of these issues in more depth.

Importance of dominant market positions

In the industrial environment, scale advantages have their limits. This is referred to as decreasing returns to scale. While a large factory might be more cost efficient than a small one, there is a point where adding capacity at the same location will be uneconomical. The cost of adding labour and material will exceed the added returns. This effect permits smaller competitors to compete against those with larger market shares, providing they can achieve production sizes that yield optimal efficiency. Under the new technological regime, the rule of decreasing returns to scale does not universally hold any more. In many cases, the optimal output is not determined by the factory size but based on the point where the market is saturated. This can be observed in markets where fixed costs are much higher than variable costs. Examples are computer software or pharmaceutical products, which demand a high degree of intellectual factor input. The same holds for products or services that become more valuable when used by more people, i.e. products that develop into a de facto standard and profit from the frequently mentioned *network effect*. Microsoft Office is an example that shows how useful it is to use the same product as many other people. In all these cases, the returns achieved through increasing market shares are not diminishing over time, but grow! – a reversal of the 'law' of decreasing returns. Figures 5.6 and 5.7 illustrate the argument.

Being placed in such a technological environment, it is important for companies to gain market share quickly and, as Rangaswamy states, to achieve strategic control. This explains why America Online (AOL) distributes its disks through all sorts of available media, for example glued into journals and handed out at supermarkets. New subscribers are lured with irresistible trial offers. Netscape pursued a different strategy. It gave its product away in the hope of earning money with follow-up deals. The new technological environment has increased the importance of achieving market share.

Figure 5.6 **Decreasing returns to scale**

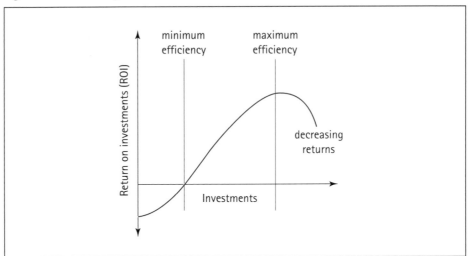

Figure 5.7 **Increasing returns to scale**

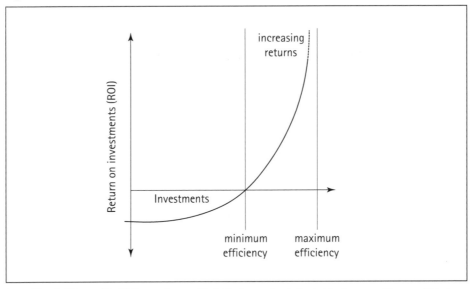

Source: Diane D. Wilson and Paul F. Nunes, *eEconomy: Ein Spiel mit neuen Regeln* (Sonderteil eCommerce: Wege zum Erfolg in der elektronischen Wirtschaft) *Outlook*, Andersen Consulting, Heft 1, 1998, p. 49.

Conversely, the global marketer can no longer afford to tolerate even small attacks from competitors, but has to be prepared for a vigorous defence of its market position.

Importance of strategic alliances

The post-industrial e-economy is more and more characterised by a dilution of traditional corporate structures and boundaries in favour of a move toward symbiotic alliances with external partners. Companies involve legally and economically inde-

Net pledge can get you a PC virtually free: buyers must sign contracts

The price of a personal computer is dropping as low as it can go: to zero. Taking a page from the book written by cellular telephone carriers, Internet service providers America Online, Prodigy and Microsoft's MSN Internet Access are subsidising personal computers for customers willing to sign long-term contracts. A $400 (€340) rebate makes a $399 (€338) eMachines PC free.

Among the deals:

- Electronics retailer Best Buy is offering $400 (€340) rebates on most desktop computers to customers who sign up with Prodigy Internet for three years of service at $19.95 (€16.90) per month. Rebates of $250 (€212) and $100 (€85) are available for two-year and one-year contracts, respectively

- Until July 31, buyers of any PC from Circuit City or a retailer that carries eMachines budget PCs can get a $400 (€340) rebate if they sign up for three years with CompuServe, an online service owned by AOL. Monthly service is $21.95 (€18.60). AOL may strike similar deals with other retailers.

- Microsoft is offering $400 (€340) coupons toward PC purchases to customers who sign up for three years' MSN Internet Access at $19.95 (€16.90) per month at Staples office supply stores. The one-week trial, which ends on Saturday, expands on a similar offer through the smaller computer chain Micro Center. That offer will remain in effect indefinitely.

Basic PCs usually cost about $399 (€338) to $799 (€678) for the central processing unit (CPU).

Monitors, printers and accessories add about $300 (€255) to the typical purchase price. 'We're seeing the next wave of mass-market consumers coming on line,' AOL spokeswoman Wendy Goldberg says. 'We want to keep coming up with innovative and attractive offers.'

These offers not only lure new customers on line but also lock buyers into an Internet service. 'When you have a customer turnover rate of 4 per cent to 6 per cent a month and can get a guarantee that someone will stick around for two or three years, that's valuable,' says Don LaVigne, CEO of Free-PC. His company offers PCs and Internet service free to consumers willing to accept targeted ads. AOL and other Internet companies are also looking at subsidising other low cost Internet access devices, such as a $199 (€169) Internet access device called the 'iToaster' by Microworkz.

Customers who end their contracts early face penalties, and existing customers must set up new accounts to qualify for rebates, Goldberg says. AOL also announced a minority investment in eMachines this week.

Food for thought

- Use a spread-sheet to draw-up three different numerical scenarios for the iToaster, each time assuming different contribution margins for the device and AOL as well as different customer retention rates. Run your example over a time frame of three years.

- How would you advise a new ISP to approach pricing, given the current competitive environment?

Source: Adapted from S. Booth, 'A free PC!' *Adweek*, Vol 40, 6 September 1999; S. Booth, 'A free PC!' *Mediaweek*, Vol 9, 6 September 1999; E. Foster, 'What's behind a free PC? A whole lot of trouble and a substandard warranty', *InfoWorld*, Vol 21, 15 November 1999, p. 155; L. Armstrong, 'The free PC game: Lure 'em in and lock 'em up', *Business Week*, 19 July 1999, p. 80.

pendent firms to fulfil various tasks. Technology is important in this context, since the use of ICT leads to a reduction of transaction costs and thus promotes the market- and alliances-orientation of companies.[22] Video-conferencing, electronic data exchange (EDS), extranets, etc. offer companies involved in symbiotic alliances cost-efficient means of communication.

Three types of alliances can be distinguished. Vertical co-operations describe partnerships between companies active in different stages of the value-chain, such as a collaboration between a manufacturer and a retailer in the marketing of an innovative product. Horizontal co-operations comprise companies in the same industry, such as research and development co-operations of two or more microelectronic companies. Diagonal co-operations, finally, refer to situations in which companies from different industries collaborate.

While co-operations and alliances as such are not a new phenomenon, the changes in the technological environment have not only made cross-country alliances easier to manage, but have also influenced the motivation behind the alliances. Besides the desire to increase efficiency, it is now primarily the desire to gain market access and market share which drives co-operations. The desire to utilise network effects and to achieve synergies in products and services, for example, was behind the co-operation between the American Broadcasting Company (ABC), the New York Times and America Online (AOL). Indeed, the benefit of gaining access to its customers allowed AOL to bill the other two companies $1 billion.[23] Airlines can serve as another example of strategic alliances. E-commerce permits airlines to utilise their brand names in online-reservations through so-called 'code-sharing'. This, in turn, eventually results in higher market shares for the globally networked partner airlines.

Importance of anticipating high start–up investments

Increasing returns to scale in many e-based industries necessitate high start-up costs in order to achieve the desired market share. A substantial part of the investment must be committed for years before the revenues eventually exceed the costs. AOL for example had to invest $500 million per year into marketing and sales before it reached its current position as market leader.[24] Toys 'R' Us Inc. recently announced that it planned to update its website organised as a separate company in order to fight increasing web competition in the toy industry. The anticipated costs for this website update are $80 million.[25] Many e-based companies need the backing of well-established financially strong corporations or are forced to turn to the stock exchange to raise the required capital. The high stock market valuation of the so-called Internet stocks in comparison to the stocks of traditional companies shows that the market, contrary to its reputation as being too short-term oriented, is willing to take a long-term view. Table 5.2 illustrates this argument.

Importance of ongoing innovations

In the traditional technical environment, innovations were primarily a means to gain a few points of market share. It was a rare event that consumers changed allegiances in droves. Information about goods and services diffused relatively slowly and there were significant gaps between lead and lag countries in the uptake of technology.

In today's technological environment, the situation is drastically different. Not only has the diffusion speed increased significantly (70 per cent of the computer industry's revenue, for example, comes from products that did not exist two years ago),[26] but the penalties for falling behind the latest world-class technological standard are quick and sharp. Consider Word-Perfect which for a long time, was the leading word processing package in the world. Its fall was drastic, when Microsoft Word offered a more up-to-date technological standard.

Increasing use of ICT is leading to greater efficiencies in all stages of the new

GLOBAL PERSPECTIVE

US airlines' 'handoffs' raise safety concerns

A burgeoning practice of sharing or combining flights, known as 'code-sharing,' allows airlines to create marketing alliances that give passengers almost seamless travel around the globe. But the scramble for partnerships into regions such as Asia and Africa – with some of the world's least-safe airlines, has begun to trouble some airline executives and federal officials.

China Airlines of Taiwan, for example, is an American Airlines and Continental Airlines code-share partner. Airclaims Ltd of London, which tracks airline accidents, lists three China Airlines crashes with 465 deaths in the past decade. And a 1996 Conde Nast survey listed China Airlines as having an accident rate throughout its existence of 11.43 fatal accidents per one million flights, compared with a 0.15 rate for American and a 0.29 rate for Continental.

A person flying from Dallas to Taipei tonight, for instance, would depart on American Flight 691 and transfer in San Francisco to American Flight 6123. At least that's what the ticket would say. But American Flight 6123, which leaves shortly after midnight, is really China Airlines Flight 3.

American has been quietly working with the Taiwanese airline on safety in the past few months, officials said.

Under code-sharing, one airline buys a block of tickets on another airline's flight and lists the flight in reservation systems under its name, or 'code'. The tickets will read as if the passengers are flying on a US carrier, even though they actually transfer to a plane flown by another airline. Passengers are supposed to be notified, but many pay little attention until they show up at the gate and find themselves boarding a plane of a different colour. Code-sharing is attractive for airlines, because it increases feeder traffic on domestic routes and makes an airline's international reach seem much greater.

Food for thought
- What are the factors driving the need for strategic alliances in the airline industry?
- Draw up a checklist of factors an airline could use to help evaluate the suitability of a potential strategic partner.

Source: Adapted from: Don Phillips, 'U.S. Airlines' "handoffs" raise safety concerns: foreign partners come under scrutiny', *The Washington Post*, 7 March 1999, p. A01.

Table 5.2 Market valuations

Digital economy valuations (1998)			*Traditional economy valuations (1998)*		
Company	Annual revenues ($m)	Market cap ($m)	Market cap ($m)	Annual revenues ($m)	Company
AOL	2,600.0	149,800	149,800	14,700	Pfizer
Yahoo	203.3	34,500	34,700	15,100	Allied Signal
ebay	47.4	24,000	24,300	18,400	J.P. Morgan
Amazon	610.0	23,000	23,000	15,500	Alcoa
Priceline	35.2	17,900	17,700	15,900	Fed Ex
@Home	48.0	16,800	16,900	26,300	Lockeed Martin
E*Trade	285.0	12,900	13.500	19,200	AMR
CMGI	91.5	11,200	11,400	8,300	Ingersoll Rand
RealNetworks	64.8	5,700	5,500	11,200	Toys 'R' Us

Source: *Fortune*, 26 April and 24 May 1999; Hoover.com; Arvind Rangaswamy, 'Toward a model of ebusiness performance'. Presentation at the American Marketing Association Summer Educators' Conference, San Francisco, 7–10 August 1999.

product development process. Many companies are encouraging their employees, customers and suppliers to submit ideas for new products or improvements through interactive websites or e-mail. Toyota, for example, generated over two million suggestions for improvements from its employees alone.[27] After new ideas are generated, expert systems can be used in the evaluation of these ideas. At the design stage, computer-aided design (CAD) and design teams that work in parallel in different time zones substantially speed up this stage. ICT applications such as virtual reality further aid the development process. To achieve a better fit between the product features and the customer needs, customers are increasingly involved in the design of the product. Smart, for example, permits customers to design their own version of the car on the Web.

Business and marketing analyses, running concurrently with the technical development of new product ideas, may use ICT in form of data mining to identify whether there is a likely demand for the new product from existing customers. Finally, simulated test markets again speed up the new product development process. Such approaches use mathematical modelling of marketing mix data to gauge the likelihood of the new product's success and may render real-life test marketing superfluous.

Key points	
	● Network effects and fixed costs which are dramatically higher than variable costs have further increased the importance of market share.
	● The post-industrial e-economy is more and more characterised by a dilution of traditional corporate structures and boundaries in favour of a move toward symbiotic alliances with external partners.
	● Many e-based industries require high start-up costs in order to achieve the desired market share.
	● The use of ICT is leading to greater efficiencies in all stages of the new product development process. Time as a competitive factor is fuelling the need to continuously focus on innovation.

COMPONENTS OF THE ELECTRONIC VALUE CHAIN

For global marketers, one of the most dramatic and relevant effects of the technological changes has been the 'death of distance'. As Frances Cairncross[28] of the *Economist* put it: 'The death of distance as a determinant of the cost of communications will probably be the single most important economic force shaping society in the first half of the next century. It will alter, in ways that are only barely imaginable, decisions about where people live and work, concepts of national borders, patterns of international trade. Its effects will be as pervasive as those of the discovery of electricity.' Some effects are already emerging in the shape of a re-configuration of the value chain.[29] Figure 5.8 illustrates that ICT permits an organisational structure where not all parts of the value chain need to be *physically* present in each country, although they may be viewed as *virtually* present from the perspective of suppliers and customers.

Figure 5.8 Location of value chain across countries

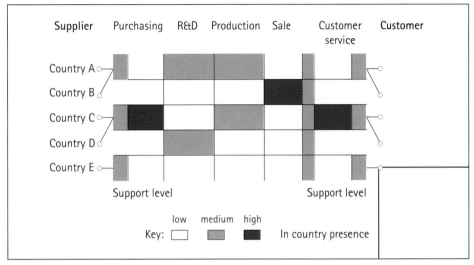

Source: Adapted from J. Griese, 'Auswirkungen globaler Informations- und Kommunikationssysteme auf die Organisation weltweit tätiger Unternehmen', in W.H. v. Staehle and P. Conrad (eds), *Managementforschung* 2 (Berlin/New York: de Gruyter, 1992), p. 423.

A major part of the attractiveness and dynamics of the new technological environment stems from the ability to 'modularise', 'segment' or 'fragment' the value chain into small and distinct customer-oriented processes. ICT facilitates the co-ordination between these modules in largely non-hierarchical systems and increases the scope for outsourcing specific modules.[30] Closely related to the modularisation within companies is the transformation of linear value chains into multidimensional networks. For the customer, it is often not transparent which part of a transaction is carried out by which particular member of the network. For example, the customer usually does not know which reservation system a travel agency uses to book a flight. Indeed, most often he does not care as long as the required goods or services are delivered as requested. What appears to emerge under the new technological regime is a network of specialists, which permits participants to focus on their respective core values. Figure 5.9 illustrates this point.

Context suppliers

Context suppliers, also called *portals*, support the use of the electronic channel both for customers and suppliers. Their key functions are to offer access to the channel and reduce the complexity of the electronic environment. Among the most important context providers are Internet online services like America Online, Web browsers like Netscape Communicator and Microsoft Explorer or search engines like Yahoo and Lycos. In 1998, the top nine portals generated approximately 15 per cent of all Internet traffic. However, their growth appears to slow down, and it has been estimated that by 2003, the net traffic flowing through the top nine portals will plateau at 20 per cent. [31]

Figure 5.9 The middlemen as networks of specialists

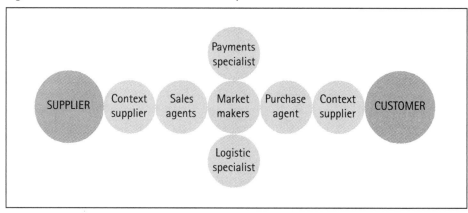

Source: Adapted from Paul F. Nunes and Brian S. Pappas, 'Der Vermittler auf der Suche nach Reichtum und Glück', *Outlook*, Andersen Consulting, Heft 1, 1998, p. 55.

Sales agents

These companies support suppliers primarily through offering high quality address banks of potential customers. Metromail provides an example. It offers suppliers carefully sifted address banks of potential customers that typically contain a wealth of information about customers' preferences, demographics, etc. One of the latest services is referred to as 'firefly technique'. It helps companies to target consumer groups and provide special product offerings based on profiles of musical/reading preferences.[32]

Purchase agents

On the customers' side, electronic purchase agents help the Internet shopper to find the desired goods or services. Auto-By-Tel, for example, is a service that helps customers find the right car for the right price. Similarly, search robots like PriceSCAN permit consumers to find the best price on thousands of computer hardware and software products. Such programs automatically travel the Web and gather data from magazine ads, vendor catalogues, etc. Web robots are also sometimes referred to as Web crawlers, or spiders. Companies like BizBots are developing a 'real time 24 by 7 (24 hours a day, 7 days a week) automated market of markets' that link multiple sites in various business sectors (such as chemicals) to provide complete transparency for buyers and sellers.[33]

Market makers

Market makers are mediators that bring together buyers and sellers and increase market efficiency. Typical examples are the numerous auction sites that have sprung up on the Web. According to its website, Onsale, for example, has more than 160,000 visitors per day and in excess of 1,100,000 registered users.[34] And the need to innovate can also be felt in this part of the supply chain. eBay,[35] with some 5.6 million registered users the world's leading person-to-person online trading community, recently announced the availability of pagers featuring 'eBay a-go-go', a new service that allows users to receive updates on their eBay auctions via pagers. PlasticNet.com for plastics, Metals.com for steel and various other sites bring together buyers and sellers in business-to-business markets.

Payment and logistic specialists

Currently, one of the main stumbling blocks for the use of electronic markets is still payment through the Internet. However, the development of efficient electronic payment systems is advancing rapidly. It is expected that by the year 2005, some 30 per cent of all consumer payments will be based on digital payment systems.[36] In the meantime, traditional credit card companies like VISA are managing the transfer of payments and the associated risks. The following European Focus provides some insights on how a British company helps to overcome one of the last hurdles facing a paperless business culture, namely the need for a signature on documents.

Physical distribution via the Internet is only possible for software products or information services (e.g. investor, stock-market, database information). All other products have to be shipped via traditional channels. Nevertheless, the Internet and the Web offer a complete new view for the traditional distribution function. While physical distribution was one of the core functions for the traditional retail/commerce systems, this aspect can be unbundled and outsourced using international distribution experts (e.g. UPS). Moreover, the logistic functions of warehouses get outsourced to logistic experts and software companies.

Key points

- Information and communication technology has a profound impact on the composition of the value chain across countries.

- The new e-commerce environment is transforming traditional value chains into a network of specialists that focus on their respective core values.

- Key components of the electronic value chain are context suppliers, sales agents, purchase agents, market makers and payment and logistic specialists.

Summary

The rapid advances in information technology are profoundly affecting the way global marketing is conducted. The global, instant reach of customers has not only opened up additional distribution and communication channels and enabled precise targeting (segment of one), customisation and interaction, but has given rise to fundamentally new business models. Technological changes have also empowered customers by proving more transparency, allowing them to propose their own prices,[37] and offering a platform for dealing directly with each other at auction sites. This chapter documented some of the paradigmatic changes in the technological environment and discussed the impact of these changes on established rules of competition. The need to reach a dominant market position in a very short time, the shift from firm-focused strategies to strategic alliances and networks, high start-up investments requirements and the heightened importance of ongoing innovations are among the issues raised in this context. Finally, we have taken a closer look at the components

PENOP: Signing up for e-commerce

One of the last hurdles facing the introduction of e-commerce and a paperless business culture is the need for a signature on documents such as contracts, loans and government-related forms. But PenOp, a British company, has achieved considerable success with its electronic signature technology which legally binds a handwritten digital signature to electronic documentation. PenOp now has 60,000 users world-wide, mostly in the US, ranging from the Food and Drugs Administration and judges in Georgia to insurance salesmen. PenOp's software is linked to the personal computer either as an integral software kit or used via an electronic signature pad now commonly found on laptops, dedicated PC peripherals and PalmPilots. When a manager writes his signature on the pad, PenOp notes 30 different physical aspects of the action, including pressure of the pen and its angle of elevation. The rhythm of the action is recorded 100 times per second, as well as the exact symmetry in the curves of the script. The signature's electronic profile is then automatically encrypted. To deter fraud, the date and time of the event is also logged. 'This element delivers evidential force to the signature,' says Christopher Smithies, who founded the company with Jeremy Newman, 'and can be used in future audit trails or forensic examinations.' The software also includes a 'ceremony box' to remind the writer that a legally binding act under common law is taking place. Even more important, PenOp's software prevents the content of that document from being altered after it has been signed. PenOp's chief financial officer, Robert Levin, says: 'Our technology's security is much stronger than paper ... With paper, a buyer can subsequently repudiate an order for whatever reason, but with secure, irrefutable electronic signatures this isn't so easy.'

In the US it is estimated that 2.8m signatures are written on paper every minute, and the total cost of printing and posting items of mail can cost $50 each. But using PenOp, the FDA has set up online drug trials forms that open the way to a completely electronic application process for pharmaceutical companies. In Gwinnett County, Georgia, where distances are large, judges who once had to be visited in person by police officers to sign out-of-hours arrest and home search warrants are now connected via PCs to local police stations. 'A video conference link enables the judge to discuss the warrant and, if they're satisfied, sign it using the PenOp system which no one at the police station can tamper with,' says Mr Levin. In Tennessee, the First American Bank offers insurance at its retail branches using PenOp software to verify signatures, and a local insurance company with a sales force of 7,000 uses it to collect signatures for policy application forms. American General Life and Accident, the insurer, has saved $2–3m in costs, cut its error rate to nil, and accelerated the despatch of policy certificates. With the cost of peripheral digitisers falling from $200 to as little as $30, PenOp believes the market is ready to explode. 'It's an end-solution that removes paper completely,' says Mr. Levin. 'We think it's the "last mile" in enabling e-commerce.' Recently, the software has been made compatible with Windows CE technology.

In the UK, PenOp has been used at DSS offices in Liverpool to combat fraud based on impersonation. 'When three dole claimants saw that they had to sign on a computer, they left quickly,' says Mr Smithies. PenOp also expects digitisers to become widespread for the checking of signatures on credit card transactions. 'Credit card companies charge retailers more when no signature is involved in the transaction,' says Mr Smithies. 'And, by contrast, identification via smart cards does not provide proof of intent. Ours does.' In the autumn, PenOp will launch a second patented product that combines its technology with that of IriScan, a US company. James Cambier, chief technology officer at IriScan, says his system will provide confirmation of the person's identity while PenOp will secure legal proof of intent by the author as well as the 'bonding' of the signature to the document. In streamlining the signatory process, whether across the Internet, intranets or extranets, PenOp believes it can remove an important and unnecessary bottleneck hindering the development of e-commerce.

Food for thought
- Assume you are the international marketing manager for PENOP, draw up a list of factors which can be used to prioritise market opportunities for this new technology?
- What are the potential barriers affecting the adoption of the new product? How would you seek to overcome them?

Source: Marcus Gibson, 'Signing up for e-commerce', *Financial Times*, 7 July 1999, p. XV.

FT

of the electronic value chain to demonstrate the different roles global marketers can play in e-commerce.

Concepts and definitions

E-commerce
Trading goods and services over the Internet, both business-to-consumer and business-to-business. The latter is sometimes also referred to as e-business.

Extranet
A computer network based on the technical standards of the Internet. It links two or more different companies but, in contrast to the Internet, is not open to the general public and, in contrast to the intranet, is not entirely private.

Internet
The largest computer network in the world, which links over 130 million people. By 2003, this number is projected to have grown to 350 million users, split between North America with 35 per cent, Europe with 30 per cent, Asia Pacific with 21 per cent, South America with 9 per cent and the rest of the world with about 5 per cent.[38]

Portals
Context suppliers that attract millions of Web users with a wide swath of information, search services, e-mail and chat-rooms. Among the most important context providers are Internet online services like America Online, Web browsers like Netscape Communicator and search engines such as Yahoo.

Web browser
Software used to navigate the hyperlinks that make up the World Wide Web.

World Wide Web
Makes the Internet more accessible and easier to use by non-experts. Technically a system of hypermedia linking text, graphics, sounds and video on computers spread across the globe.

Virtual reality
Imaginary 'worlds' created by cutting-edge computer technology. For example, wearing special headsets, consumers might get the impression of walking through a house and visualising and experiencing the rooms before the house is actually built.

Discussion questions

1 What are the key players in an electronic value chain and which functions do they serve?

2 What are the main characteristics of consumers buying on the Internet and how do these differ from the characteristics of 'ordinary' consumers?

3 Which strategic marketing implications arise from the so-called 'network effect'?

4 How can information and communication technology contribute to shorter new product development cycles? Please provide examples.

5 What are the implications of the described technological changes on (i) the organisational structure of corporate activities across countries and (ii) the importance of organisational boundaries?

6 It has been argued that the Internet gave rise to new business models. Do you agree with this proposition? Please provide reasons why you do or do not support this notion.

Internet trends

This site gives the latest figures on the trends and growth of the Internet. It also shows you how many .com, .edu, .org, etc. exist around the world.

http://www.mids.org/mapsale/data/trends/trends-199907/index.htm

Build a Smart

If you want to design your own frog-green and yellow Smart with exchangeable body-panels, this is the place to go.

http://mitglied.tripod.de/~smartinfo/new2.htm

Shopping agents

Want to buy a new computer and use a shopping agent to find out the lowest price? This is your site: eSmarts has done extensive testing on shopping agents for computers and rated them on a scale of one to five.

http://www.esmarts.com/computers/computers-shopping-agents.html

Onsale.Com

Onsale is one of the largest and oldest online auctions. They hold several large auctions each week with lots of merchandise, especially in computers, sports and fitness, home and office and travel.

http://www.onsale.com/

VirtualVineyard.com

In case you are dying to buy a 1997 Pinot Noir from the Martinborough Vineyard in New Zealand and save some travel money, this is the way to shop. Apparently, the Pinot Noir is absolutely stunning, and an indication of what can come out of New Zealand in a good vintage. Ripe, quite full-bodied and tasty.

http://www.virtualvin.com/

Suggested readings

'Going digital: how new technology is changing our lives', *The Economist*, 1998, p. 19.

'Special report: let's talk', *Business Week*, February 23 1998, pp. 44–56.

'This toy war is no game', *Business Week*, August 9 1999, p. 54.

Afemann, Uwe, 'Verschärfung bestehender Ungleichheiten', *Forum Wissenschaft*, Heft 1 (1996): pp. 21–26.

Browning, John, *Pocket Information Technology*. London: The Economist Books, 1997.

Cairncross, Frances, 'The death of distance', *Economist: Special Report on Telecommuniations*, 30 September 1995, p. SS5.

Deighton, John, 'Commentary on exploring the implications of the internet for consumer marketing', *Journal of the Academy of Marketing Science*, 24, 4 (1997): pp. 347–351.

Dicken, P., *Global Shift. The Internationalization of Economic Activity*. London: Paul Chapman Publishing, 1992.

Griese, J., 'Auswirkungen globaler Informations und Kommuniktionssysteme auf die Organisation weltweit tätiger Unternehmen'. In *Managementforschung 2*, ed. W.H.V. Staehle and P. Conrad, pp. 163–175. Berlin: de Gruyter, 1992.

Komenar, Margo, *Electronic Marketing*. New York: John Wiley & Sons, Inc., 1996.

Picot, Arnold, Ralf Reichwald and Rolf T. Wigand, *Die grenzenlose Unternehmung: Information, Organisation und Management*. 2nd edn. Wiesbaden: Gabler Verlag, 1996.

Picot, A., T. Ripperger and B. Wolff, 'The fading boundaries of the firm', *Journal of Institutional and Theoretical Economics* (1996): pp. 65–72.

Römer, Marc, *Strategisches IT-Management in internationalen Unternehmungen*. Wiesbaden: Gabler, 1997.

Schlegelmilch, Bodo B. and R. Sinkovics, 'Marketing in the Information Age – can we plan for an unpredictable future?', *International Marketing Review*, 14, 3 (1998): pp. 162–170.

Sivadas, E., R. Grewel and J. Kellaris, 'The Internet as a

micro marketing tool: targeting consumers through preferences revealed in music newsgroup usage', *Journal of Business Research*, 41, 3 (1998): pp. 179–186.
Wilson, Diane D. and Paul F. Nunes (eds), *eEconomy: Ein*

Spiel mit neuen Regeln. Sonderteil eCommerce: Wege zum Erfolg in der elektronischen Wirtschaft edn. Vol. 1, *Outlook*: Andersen Consulting, 1998.

Notes

1. John Deighton, 'Commentary on exploring the implications of the Internet for consumer marketing', *Journal of the Academy of Marketing Science*, 24, 4 (1997): pp. 347–351.

2. P. Dicken, *Global Shift. The Internationalization of Economic Activity* (London: Paul Chapman Publishing, 1992): p. 103.

3. 'The World in 1998', *The Economist* (London, 1997): p. 90.

4. 'Going digital: How new technology is changing our lives', *The Economist* (London, 1998): p. 19.

5. 'Economic indicators', *The Economist* (London, March 28): p. 112.

6. 'Going digital: How new technology is changing our lives', *The Economist* (London, 1998): p. 19.

7. 'Technology visioning workshop' (Andersen Consulting, Sophia Antipolis, July 1999).

8. Robert Zakon, http://info.isoc.org/guest/Internet/History/HIT.html#Growth, 29 August 1999.

9. John Browning, *Pocket Information Technology* (London: The Economist Books, 1997): pp. 97–99.

10. Uwe Afemann, 'Verschärfung bestehender Ungleichheiten', *Forum Wissenschaft*, Heft 1 (1996): pp. 21–26.

11. 'UN-Entwicklungsbericht: Technik vergrößert Not vieler Menschen', *Kölner Stadt-Anzeiger*, 13 July 1999, p. 7.

12. Donna L. Hoffmann and Thomas P. Novak, 'Marketing in hypermedia-computer-mediated environments: conceptual foundations', *Journal of Marketing*, 60 (July 1996): pp. 50–68.

13. Jerry Wind, and Vijay Mahajan, 'Digital marketing', unpublished Working Paper, Wharton School, University of Pennsylvania, 1999, p. 7.

14. 'Special report: Let's talk', *Business Week*, 23 February 1998, pp. 44–56 and 'Smitten with the written word', *Financial Times*, 12 February 1998, p. 21.

15. 'E-business: what every CEO needs to know', *Business Week*, 22 March 1999, p. 10.

16. Michael F. Hruby, *Technoleverage: Using the Power of Technology to Outperform the Competition* (New York: AMACOM, 1999).

17. For an excellent in depth analysis of these issues see: Arnold Picot, Ralf Reichwald and Rolf T. Wigand, *Die grenzenlose Unternehmung: Information, Organisation und Management* (Wiesbaden: Gabler Verlag, 1996).

18. John Stopford, 'Global strategies for the Information Age'. Presentation at the 23rd EIBA Conference on Global Business in the Information Age, Stuttgart, 14–16 December 1997.

19. Bodo B. Schlegelmilch, and R. Sinkovics, 'Marketing in the Information Age – can we plan for an unpredictable future?', *International Marketing Review*, 14, no. 3 (1998): pp. 162–170.

20. Arwind Rangaswamy, 'Toward a model of ebusiness performance'. Presentation at the American Marketing Association Summer Educators' Conference, San Francisco, 7–10 August 1999.

21. Diane D. Wilson and Paul F. Nunes (eds), *eEconomy: Ein Spiel mit neuen Regeln*. Sonderteil eCommerce: Wege zum Erfolg in der elektronischen Wirtschaft, *Outlook*: Andersen Consulting, Heft 1, 1998, pp. 45–50.

22. A. Picot, T. Ripperger, and B. Wolff, 'The fading boundaries of the firm', *Journal of Institutional and Theoretical Economics* (1996): pp. 65–72.

23. Diane D. Wilson, and Paul F. Nunes (eds), *eEconomy: Ein Spiel mit neuen Regeln*. Sonderteil eCommerce: Wege zum Erfolg in der elektronischen Wirtschaft, *Outlook*: Andersen Consulting, Heft 1, 1998, pp. 45–50.

24. Diane D. Wilson, and Paul F. Nunes (eds), *eEconomy: Ein Spiel mit neuen Regeln*. Sonderteil eCommerce: Wege zum Erfolg in der elektronischen Wirtschaft, *Outlook*: Andersen Consulting, Heft 1, 1998, pp. 45–50.

25. 'This toy war is no game', *Business Week*, 9 August 1999, p. 54.

26. 'Going digital: how new technology is changing our lives', *The Economist*, 1998, p. 19.

27. John O'Conner and Eamonn Galvin, *Marketing & Information Technology: The Strategy, Application and Implementation of IT in Marketing* (London: Pitman Publishing, 1997).

28. Frances Cairncross, 'The death of distance', *Economist: Special Report on Telecommuniations*, 30 September 1995, p. SS5.

29. J. Griese, 'Auswirkungen globaler Informations und Kommuniktionssysteme auf die Organisation weltweit tätiger Unternehmen.' In *Managementforschung 2*, edited by W.H.V. Staehle and P. Conrad (Berlin: de Gruyter, 1992), p. 163–175.

30. Arnold Picot, Ralf Reichwald and Rolf T. Wigand, *Die grenzenlose Unternehmung: Information, Organisation und Management* (Wiesbaden: Gabler Verlag, 1996).

31. 'Portals are mortal after all', *Business Week*, 21 June 1999, pp. 66–67.

32. E. Sivadas, R. Grewel and J. Kellaris, 'The Internet as a micro marketing tool: targeting consumers through preferences revealed in music newsgroup usage', *Journal of Business Research*, 41, 3 (1998): pp. 179–186.

33. Jerry Wind and Vijay Mahajan, 'Digital marketing', unpublished Working Paper, Wharton School, University of Pennsylvania, 1999, p. 6.

34. http://www.ebay.com/index.html (cited 30 August 1999).

35. http://www.ebay.com/index.html (cited 30 August 1999).

36. Georg Kristoferitsch, *Digital Money, Electronic Cash, Smart Cards: Chancen und Risiken des Zahlungsverkehrs via Internet* (Wien: Überreuter, 1998).

37. For example at Priceline.com.

38. Jerry Wind and Vijay Mahajan, 'Digital Marketing', unpublished Working Paper, Wharton School, University of Pennsylvania, 1999, p. 7.

Swatchmobil/Smart car*

Nicolas Hayek, one of the most famous businessmen in Switzerland, was the brilliant architect of the revival and recovery of the Swiss watch industry in the early 1980s. His plan for the Swiss Corporation for Microelectronics and Watchmaking Industries (SMH) included the design and positioning of the now famous Swatch (Swiss Watch).

The Swatchmobil concept was based on Nicolas Hayek's conviction that consumers become emotionally attached to cars just as they do to watches. His vision was of high safety, ecology, and a very consumer-friendly area to sit in. Like the Swatch, the Swatchmobil was to be affordable, durable and stylish. Hayek noted that safety would be a key selling point, declaring, 'This car will have the crash security of a Mercedes.' Further, the car was to emit almost no pollutants, thanks to its electric engine. The car would also be capable of gasoline-powered operation, using a highly efficient, miniaturised engine. Hayek predicted that world-wide sales would reach one million units, with the United States accounting for about half the market.

The first internal combustion version of the car, formally known as the Smart (Swatch, Mercedes Benz and art) was scheduled to go on sale in April 1998. Smarts were slated for sale only in Europe. The 2.5 metre-long, 1.5 metre-high and similarly wide, two-seater car (for two adults or one adult and two children) is supposed to consume 5 litres/100 km and cost between €7,700 and 10,000. 'It's so small that they're trying to get the parking regulations in Europe changed so that you can get three of them crosswise in a parking space,' said Fred Heiler, spokesman for Mercedes-Benz of North America.

Smart will have Swatch's wacky and trendy appeal, with interchangeable outside colour panels. They will be removed by a dealer in 1 to 2 hours for between €250 and €420 a change. They not only allow an individualised car suiting the consumer's mood, but also are of practical value. With regards to servicing needs, parts may be easily changed for new ones. In case you have always wanted to know what your dream Smart in aqua green or mad red with boomerang blue interior would look like, check it out virtually under http://www.smart.com/! According to Hayek, inside, the car will be 'a modern, new and young Mercedes. You never feel you are in a small car.'

Some observers attributed the hoopla surrounding the Swatchmobil concept to Mr Hayek's charismatic personality. Some believed his automotive vision was overly optimistic, noting that other attempts at extending the Swatch brand name to new categories, including a brightly coloured unisex clothing line, had flopped. Other products such as Swatch telephones, pagers, and sunglasses have also met with lukewarm consumer acceptance. Industry observers also warned that both the Swatch and Mercedes names could be hurt if the Swatchmobil was plagued by recall or safety problems.

Discussion questions

1 What do you think of the Swatchmobil/Smart car?

2 What does Mercedes stand to gain from the joint venture? Does this project make sense for Mercedes? Why? Why not?

3 What are the advantages to SMH? Does the project make sense for SMH? Why? Why not?

4 Is the Smart an international or a global product? Do you agree with the European-only launch plans? Why? Why not?

* In autumn 1999, the Swatch Group withdrew its commitment as a joint venture partner in the Smart project. Subsequently, DaimlerChrysler went into collaboration talks with other car manufacturers such as PSA Peugeot Citroen or Fiat.

Source: 'Crunch time: DaimlerChrysler's disappointments', *The Economist*, 25 September 1999; 'Not so Smart', *Marketing Week*, 23 September 1999; Daphne Angles, 'Swiss watchmaker joins the auto game', *The New York Times*, 7 July 1991, pp. 3/10; Mary Lu Carnevale, 'BellSouth Unit and Swatch to introduce wristwatch pager, joint marketing plan', *The Wall Street Journal*, 4 March 1992, p. B5; Andy Dworkin, 'San Marcos firm designing "Swatchmobil" battery hybrid European car aiming for efficiency', *The Dallas Morning News*, 22 April 1997, p. 4d; Kevin Helliker, 'Swiss movement: can wristwatch whiz switch Swatch cachet to an automobile?', *The Wall Street Journal*, 4 March 1994, p. A1, A3; Diana T. Kurylko, 'One wacky city car may rattle auto industry', *The San Diego Union-Tribune*, 21 December 1996, pp. 2–5; Tony Major, 'DaimlerChrysler in small-car hunt', *Financial Times*, 29 February 2000; Ferdinand Protzman, 'Off the wrist, onto the road: a Swatch of wheels', *The New York Times* 4 March 1994, p. C1; William Taylor, 'Message and muscle: an interview with Swatch titan Nicolas Hayek', *Harvard Business Review*, March–April 1993, pp. 99–110.

Coca-Cola: Just for the taste of it – assessing opportunities in China and India

On 15 April 1996, Douglas N. Daft, the President of the Middle and Far East Group for Coca-Cola Company, was in a quandary. He had just come back from a senior executive committee meeting where the main focus was on the concern over the additional investment in India and China, two countries that reported directly to him. He was baffled by the concern the committee was placing on funding these new investments. Coca-Cola's strategy had always been to take risks in emerging markets. It had always understood the need to be first in new markets to gain the competitive advantage. Even in tough markets, Coca-Cola ultimately wins market share. For instance, during apartheid in South Africa, the company stayed in the country by maintaining a presence through independent bottlers while Pepsi left the country. Coke now dominates the market.

Daft could not understand the committee's reluctance to go ahead with these investments. China's market potential was vast. With a population of 1.2 billion and per capita consumption of only four (meaning each person in China consumed only four units of 0.25l servings of a company beverage per year), the opportunities were infinite (see Table 1). The investment slated for China was to build five additional plants in 1996 and two more in 1997, which would bring the total number of plants to 23. A recent survey done by the company indicated that Coke and Sprite were the two leading soft drink brands in China. In addition, China's sales volume grew by 30 per cent last year.

India's market potential was similar to China's. Its population of 936 million and per capita consumption of two also made it a desirable market to be in. Although volume sales were up 21 per cent over 1995, there was a concern about anti-multinational sentiment. The company already had a large, visible presence there, and given the negative attitude toward large multinationals, the committee felt further investment might not be a financially prudent decision at that time.

Daft quickly got on the phone to John Farrell, head of the China Division, and Andrew Angle, head of the Southeast and West Asia Division, to discuss this new turn of events. Information needed to be gathered, and things need to be hammered out before going back to committee with his recommendations. What

Table 1 Per capita consumption and market populations

Per capita consumption*	Markets	Populations (in millions)
179	Argentina	35
292	Australia	18
169	Benelux/Denmark	31
122	Brazil	162
181	Canada	29
248	Chile	14
4	China	1,221
107	Colombia	35
30	Egypt	63
71	France	58
201	Germany	82
125	Hungary	10
2	India	936
8	Indonesia	198
232	Israel	6
87	Italy	58
136	Japan	125
71	Korea	45
45	Morocco	27
322	Mexico	94
256	Norway	4
105	Philippines	68
65	Romania	23
6	Russia	147
147	South Africa	41
179	Spain	40
60	Thailand	59
114	UK	56
343	United States	263
60	Zimbabwe	11

* 1 serving = units at 0.25l (excluding products distributed by Coca-Cola Foods)

were the political and economic risks of these two countries and how could it affect Coca-Cola? If Coca-Cola chose not to increase its investment in these countries, would it be missing out on an opportunity to further establish itself in these markets and to gain market share?

Coke articulated its vision in its annual report: 'We have become mindful of one undeniable fact – the average body requires about 2 litres of liquid every day just to survive, and our beverages currently account for not even 0.06 litres of this amount. For every person on this planet, consuming 2 litres is not an option; but choosing where those litres come from is.' Daft's concerns addressed this vision.

BOTTLING

During the 1980s, Coca-Cola aggressively acquired smaller family-owned bottlers in the United States. Between 1980 and 1984, bottlers representing 50 per cent of the company's volume underwent a change of ownership. Small, family-owned bottlers were purchased by either the company or large regional bottlers. This was done in order to control bottlers so that the company had the ability to do nation-wide advertising, knowing that their bottlers would do the complementary promotional activities, as well as aggressive discounting when needed.

During the 1990s, Coke began the implementation of a programme consolidation and company investment in bottling operations in the rest of the world. Currently, Coke is consolidating its bottlers in markets overseas.

Today, Coca-Cola is investing heavily in bottling operations in order to maximise the strength and efficiency of production, distribution and marketing. Their strategy is to get involved in the bottling business so that it fuels continued growth of their syrup business. The company has three criteria for making a bottling investment:

1 The company needs to move quickly in an emerging market.

2 When an existing bottler lacks the resources to meet the company's objectives.

3 To help ensure long-term strategic alignment with key bottling partners.

BRAND EQUITY

The Coca-Cola trademark is invaluable. If all of the company's assets burned to the ground today, it would have no trouble borrowing the money to rebuild, based on the strength of its trademark alone. Its brand is pervasive around the world. Table 2 indicates how strong the brand Coca-Cola is in specified markets.

The company's strategy for sustaining its brand image is the three Ps:

1 Pervasive *Penetration* in the marketplace.

2 Offering consumers the best *Price* relative to value.

3 Making Coca-Cola the *Preferred* beverage everywhere.

In addition, Coca-Cola is finding new ways of building relevant value into Coke and all its other brands by further differentiating them, making them unique and distinctive. Three years ago, the company abandoned the practice of entrusting all advertising and marketing to one single agency. Now, agencies are selected on the basis of their particular expertise in enhancing a particular brand; this year, agency compensation is being tied to the results their ads produce.

Table 2 **How strong is the brand Coca-Cola?**

	Market leader	*Leadership margin**	*Second place*
Australia	Coca-Cola	3.9:1	Diet Coke
Belgium	Coca-Cola	7.7:1	Coca-Cola Light
Brazil	Coca-Cola	3.3:1	Brazilian brand
Chile	Coca-Cola	4.6:1	Fanta
France	Coca-Cola	4.3:1	French brand
Germany	Coca-Cola	3.1:1	Fanta
Greece	Coca-Cola	3.8:1	Fanta
Italy	Coca-Cola	3.1:1	Fanta
Japan	Coca-Cola	2.3:1	Fanta
Korea	Coca-Cola	2.1:1	Korean brand
Norway	Coca-Cola	3.3:1	Coca-Cola Light
South Africa	Coca-Cola	4.1:1	Sparletta
Spain	Coca-Cola	3.0:1	Spanish brand
Sweden	Coca-Cola	3.8:1	Fanta
UK	Coca-Cola	1.9:1	Diet Coke

* Over second place brand
Source: Company data/store audit data

Moreover, Coca-Cola is rekindling the symbols that encapsulate the essence of their brand – the Dynamic Ribbon device, the contour bottle for Coke, the Coca-Cola script, the colour red, and the dimpled bottle for Sprite. The new contour bottle, which was launched in April 1994, is credited with increasing sales by 500 million cases globally in 1994. Up to June 1995, volume increases for Coke were approaching 45 per cent in the United States, 23 per cent in Japan, and 30 per cent in Spain. In addition, it is currently linking its brands with one-of-a-kind events and activities such as the Olympic Games in 1996 and doing more in-store promotions and displays, especially in the US market where growth is considered slow.

Coca-Cola's commitment to building and sustaining its brand image is indicated by the amount of money it spends on marketing. For instance, in 1995, the company spent €3.2 billion on marketing. Ad spending, which is still considered one of the best tools for building brand equity, was €1.1 billion. Their major rival, PepsiCo, spent more on advertising, at €1.5 billion, but had to allocate these funds to its restaurant and snack-food segments as well.

FINANCIALS

Coca-Cola is the largest and most profitable soft drink company in the world. Over a 10-year period, rev-enues have grown at a compound growth rate of 11.9 per cent. By 1995, world-wide revenues exceeded €15 billion, and net income was a little under €2.5 billion (see Table 3). Its operating income margin outpaced its major competitor, PepsiCo, significantly. While PepsiCo's beverage segment operating margin was 10 per cent for 1995, Coca-Cola's was 23 per cent. Its superior performance is further indicated by its return on equity, which was 56 per cent in 1995, and its market year-end price of €63 at the end of 1995, which showed an appreciation of 44 per cent.

Coca-Cola's strong financial performance over the last five years has been due primarily to increased expansion overseas, especially in the company's bottling and canning operations. In fact, international operations account for the majority of Coca-Cola's revenues and operating profits: in 1995, the company derived 71 per cent of its revenues and 82 per cent of its operating profit outside the United States (see Figures 1 and 2). Coke operates in 200 countries and employs 32,000 people world-wide.

CURRENT INDUSTRY OUTLOOK AND TRENDS

The US soft drink market is considered mature, growing at approximately 3–4 per cent annually. This is down considerably from the 1985 growth rate of 6.5 per cent.

Table 3 Consolidated statements of income (in € million)*

	1995	1994	1993
Net operating revenues	**15,283**	13,725	11,843
Cost of goods sold	5,887	5,232	4,377
Gross profit	**9,396**	8,493	7,467
Selling, administrative and general expenses	5,926	5,341	4,830
Operating income	**3,470**	3,152	2,636
Interest income	208	153,524	122,141
Interest expense	231	168,792	142,498
Equity income	143	113,659	77,186
Other income (deductions) – net	17	–88,213	–1,696
Gain on issuance of stock by Coca-Cola Amatil	63	–	10,178
Income before income taxes and change in accounting principle	**3,671**	3,162	2,702
Income taxes	1,138	996	846
Income before change in accounting principle	**2,533**	2,166	1,856
Transition effect of change in accounting for post-employment benefits	–	–	(10.2)
Net income	**2,533**	2,166	1,846
Income per share			
Before change in accounting principle	€2.01	€1.68	€1.43
Transition effect of change in accounting for post-employment benefits	–	–	(0.008)
Net Income per share	**€2.01**	**€1.68**	€1.42
Average shares outstanding	**1,262**	**1,290**	1,302

* Year Ended 31 December (in millions except per-share data)

Figure 1 **Net operating revenues by geographic area**

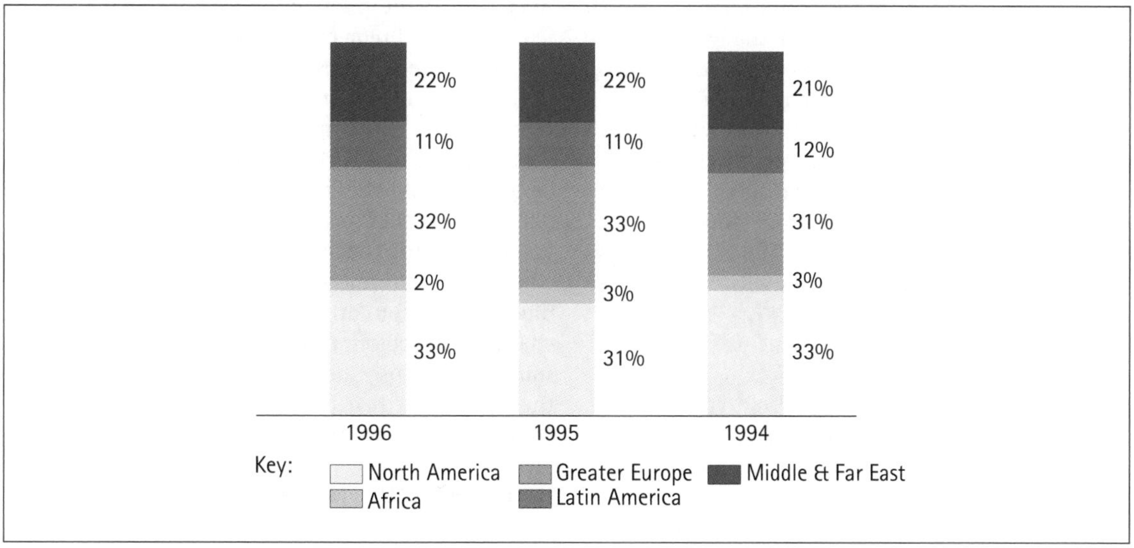

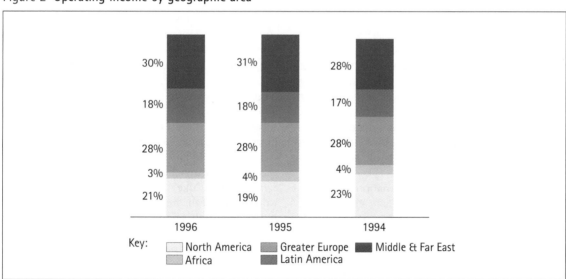

Note: Charts and percentages are calculated exclusive of corporate operations.

Figure 2 **Operating income by geographic area**

Note: Charts and percentages are calculated exclusive of corporate operations.

In 1994, domestic retail sales were €44 billion, up 2.6 per cent, year to year. Coca-Cola had 41 per cent of the retail market and Pepsi had 31 per cent. Coca-Cola's growth outpaced the industry at 7 per cent and accounted for 80 per cent of the US soft drink's industry growth last year.

Although there is increased competition from other beverage choices, soft drinks remain the beverage of choice among US consumers, accounting for more than one of every four drinks consumed. Colas continue to dominate the soft drink category but are slowly losing market share. They were 66 per cent of all soft drinks consumed in 1994, down from 70 per cent in 1990. International markets appear to mirror this trend.

The international market has been the high growth segment in the beverage industry, growing at 8–10 per cent annually.[1] In 1996, Coke sales grew at 8 per cent, and it had 47 per cent of the world market. Growth rates varied considerably around the world. Some emerging markets grew phenomenally. For example, last year China grew at 32 per cent and Brazil grew at 52 per cent. In 1997, world-wide growth was expected to be 6 per cent to 7 per cent for soft drinks. The highest growth was expected from developing Asian countries, including China, India, Korea and Indonesia. Moreover, continued growth from South America was expected. Internationally, Coke outsells Pepsi three to one.

COMPETITION

Coca-Cola's major competitor is PepsiCo (see Table 4). PepsiCo has three segments: beverage (35 per cent of total revenues), snack foods (28 per cent), and restaurants (37 per cent).

Over a 10-year period, revenues have grown at a compound rate of 15 per cent. In 1995, €1.35 billion was generated from €25.8 billion of revenues, representing a net income margin of 5 per cent (see Table 5). Its growth has been fuelled by the success of its beverage and snack-foods segments.

PepsiCo's beverage income was €8.9 billion for 1995, and it generated €1.1 billion in operating profit, representing a 10 per cent margin. Although overall beverage revenue and operating income were up 9 per cent and 8 per cent, respectively, its significant revenue growth came from overseas, at 13 per cent. Yet, international revenue and operating profit accounted for only 34 per cent of total beverage revenue and 12 per cent of total beverage operating profits (see Table 6).

To gain more market share internationally, Pepsi is unveiling a comeback plan called 'Project Blue,' which is expected to cost €424 million. It calls for revamping manufacturing and distribution to get a consistent-tasting drink around the globe, as well as

an overhaul of marketing and advertising. The most risky part of the programme calls for giving up the red, white, and blue can in favour of an electric blue one. In addition, Pepsi-Cola plans to establish new freshness standards and quality controls. Currently, Coke outsells Pepsi three to one overseas; however, Pepsi predicts that with its new marketing plan it will be able to close the gap to 2 to 1 by the year 2000. According to *The Economist*, this could be a risky strategy, considering the fact that Pepsi has spent decades convincing consumers that Pepsi in a red, white and blue can is cool to drink. Image is a delicate thing. By changing the colour of its can, it may appear to consumers that Pepsi-Cola is trying too hard to convince them to drink their brand, and thus, this plan may come off as just another blatantly obvious gimmick.[2]

INTERNATIONAL MARKETS

Coca-Cola's world-wide philosophy has been:

> We understand that as a practical matter our universe is infinite, and that we, ourselves, are the key variable in just how much of it we can capture.[3]

Coca-Cola always sees two litres of opportunity. It currently has 2 per cent of the world's daily consumption of two litres of liquid. In emerging markets, its potential remains high, as 60 per cent of the world's population live in markets where the average person consumes less than 10 servings of Coca-Cola products per year.

For decades, Coca-Cola has had an established position in foreign markets. The first foreign office was started in 1926, and by the 1940s and 1950s, Coke was already entrenched overseas. In 1950, *Time* magazine wrote, 'Coke's peaceful near conquest of the world is one of the remarkable phenomena of the age. It has put itself always within an arm's length of desire.'[4]

Today, the international segment has grown so

Table 4 US soft drink market share (in %)

	1989	1990	1991	1992	1993	1994
Coca-Cola	40.1	40.4	40.7	40.4	40.4	40.7
PepsiCo	31.8	31.8	31.5	31.3	30.9	30.9
Dr Pepper/7Up*	9.9	9.9	10.6	11.2	11.4	11.6
Cadbury Schweppes	5.0	5.0	5.0	5.0	4.9	4.8
National Beverage	2.2	2.1	2.1	2.0	1.9	2.0
Royal Crown	2.7	2.6	2.4	2.3	2.2	2.0

* Cadbury Schweppes acquired Dr Pepper/7Up on 2 March 1995.
Source: S&P Industry Surveys, 24 August 1995, p. F26.

Table 5 PepsiCo – consolidated statement of income (in € millions)*

	1995 (52 weeks)	1994 (53 weeks)	1993 (52 weeks)
Net sales	25,806	24,153	21,225
Costs and expenses, net			
Cost of sales	12,627	11,634	10,134
Selling, general and administrative expenses	9,935	9,538	8,368
Amortisation of intangible assets	268	265	258
Impairment of long-lived assets	441	–	–
Operating profit	2,534	2,715	2,466
Gain on stock offering by an unconsolidated affiliate	–	15,268	–
Interest expense	(579)	(547)	(486)
Interest income	108	76	76
Income before income taxes and cumulative effect of accounting changes	2,063	2,260	2,055
Provision for income taxes	701	745	708
Income before cumulative effect of accounting changes	1,362	1,513	1,347
Cumulative effect of accounting changes			
Post-employment benefits (net of income tax benefit of €25)	–	(47)	–
Pension assets (net of income tax expense of €13)	–	20	–
Net income	€1,362	€1,486	€1,347
Income (charge) per share			
Before cumulative effect of accounting changes	€1.69	€1.883	€1.662
Cumulative effect of accounting changes			
Post-employment benefits	–	(0.06)	–
Pension assets	–	0.03	–
Net income per share	€1.69	€1.88	€1.66
Average shares outstanding	804	804	810

* In millions except per-share amounts; financial year ended 30 December 1995, 31 December 1994 and 25 December 1993.

Table 6 PepsiCo revenue and operating income

(€ million)	1995	1994	1993	% growth rates 1995	% growth rates 1994
Net sales					
In the US	5,918	5,548	5,019	7	11
International	3,029	2,668	2,307	14	16
	8,947	8,216	7,326	9	12
Operating profit reported					
In the US	971	866	795	12	9
International	139	165	146	(16)	13
	1,110	1,031	940	8	10
Ongoing					
In the US	971	866	795	12	9
International	192	165	146	16	13
	1,163	1,031	940	13	10

much that it now contributes 71 per cent to total revenue. Because of the importance of international markets to Coca-Cola's future growth, it has eliminated its prior structure of two groups – international and domestic – and formed five operating groups: North America, Latin America, Greater Europe, the Middle and Far East, and Africa. The breakdown of unit case volume by group is found in Figure 3. As indicated by the pie chart, North America, which includes the United States and Canada, accounted for the largest, at 32 per cent, and Latin America accounted for 24 per cent of sales. Greater Europe and the Middle and Far East accounted for 21 per cent and 18 per cent, respectively. Africa trails at only 5 per cent.

The hottest battles between Coca-Cola and PepsiCo will be in international markets, especially emerging ones. First-mover advantages can be crucial in the international soft drink war. The strategic challenge is

Figure 3 **World-wide unit case volume by region (1995)**

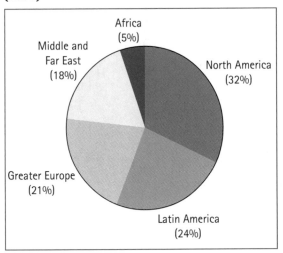

to establish greater brand awareness and preference through advertising on a scale similar to that of the domestic market. Another challenge is to make their brands as accessible and ubiquitous as they are in the United States. This is not often easy, and the effort often requires the direct intervention of the country managers (CMs) to secure improvements in the efficiency, co-operation, and competitive aggressiveness of overseas bottlers. For example, in 1995, Coca-Cola acquired bottling interests in Italy and Venezuela and took steps to consolidate its system in Germany. Although Coca-Cola controls the wealthy markets of Greater Europe, PepsiCo has been more successful in emerging markets such as India, the Arab nations of the Middle East, and Russia. Entry into new markets has often required creative manoeuvring and increasingly flexible accommodations by the CMs.

As the war heats up between Coca-Cola and PepsiCo, both CMs will be forced to take more risks. Pepsi is a company going global 50 years late and cannot afford to follow the leader, Coca-Cola, but must alter the market as indicated by its 'Project Blue' plan. Moreover, PepsiCo has rejuvenated the Pepsi Challenge for overseas markets. In 1994, PepsiCo launched its first challenge internationally in Mexico, one of Pepsi's largest markets. The result was that 55 per cent preferred Pepsi over Coke. In addition, PepsiCo plans to stage these challenges world-wide in such markets as Singapore, Malaysia, and Portugal. PepsiCo's international commitment is both long term and aggressive, as indicated by its approval of a €1.7 billion investment plan over five years for the international beverage segment, starting in 1994.

Of course, Coca-Cola does not take these aggressive moves sitting down. Coca-Cola will fight back, as it did with the Pepsi Challenge, by slashing prices, purchasing bottlers, and creating slick ads and promotions.

DAFT'S REPORT TO THE COMMITTEE

Douglas Daft recently met with John Farrell, who was responsible for China, and Andrew Angle, who was responsible for India. Both Farrell and Angle wished to go ahead with the investments in their respective countries. However, Douglas Daft was not sure he had enough information on the political and economic risks of each country to make an informed decision. Thus, he asked Farrell and Angle to update him on the political and economic status of their respective countries. After he read their reports, he would make his recommendations to the senior executive committee. Their reports are reproduced in Appendices I and II.

Discussion questions

1 What is Coca-Cola's international strategy?

2 What competitive advantages does Coca-Cola have over its major rival, PepsiCo?

3 What are the pros and cons of Coca-Cola's investing further in India's market?

4 What are the pros and cons of Coca-Cola's investing further in China's market?

5 What should Douglas Daft recommend to the senior executive committee concerning further investment in the emerging markets of China and India? Why?

APPENDIX I

The India Report by Andrew Angle, Southeast and West Asia Division

In 1994, India's economy grew at 6 per cent; 8 million new jobs were created, and there was €694 million of US direct investment. For all these positive signs, however, it appears that there has been a backlash against the economic reforms started five years ago. Why? First, for the 190 million Indians who live below the poverty line, five years of economic reforms have not improved their standard of living. Millions of poor believe that only the elite have benefited from economic liberalisation. Second, soaring short-term interest rates, coupled with competition from foreigners, have hurt local businesses and caused enthusiasm for further economic change to wane. Now that foreign companies can increase their investment to

51 per cent, up from 40 per cent, in most industries and even 100 per cent in others, some locals worry that foreigners will run roughshod over them.

Third, the Hindu right, led by the Bharatiya Janata Party (BJP), is divided over just what kind of foreign investment should be allowed. The BJP has adopted a much-used phrase – 'microchips, not potato chips' – to describe what sort of investment should be allowed.[5] Thus, it appears that the BJP is against big American consumer brands such as PepsiCo, McDonald's, Colgate, and even ourselves, and they are the ones protesting against the multinationals. Pepsi's KFC braved protests and saw one of its outlets briefly closed. Most of the anti-multinational sentiment has been against American companies, which bear the brunt of Indian worries about cultural imperialism. In contrast, Japanese and German companies encounter few such problems.

Last, these anti-multinational demonstrations are being allowed to continue due to the upcoming democratic elections, which will begin on 27 April and finish on 7 May. The existing Indian government, led by Prime Minister P.V. Narasimha Rao, dismisses these protests against foreign companies as grumblings of fringe groups. In truth, Rao and his government face stiff competition from the BJP and do not want to alienate voters by seeming to be pro foreign. Therefore, the existing government does little to defend these companies in the eyes of the public.

India's legal system, though it may be slow, provides some recourse against failure to perform in contracts. For instance, India backed away from a €2.4 billion power project with Enron, an American company. Negotiations are resuming primarily because Enron has a cast-iron case for compensation.

However, the most fundamental problem is that a backlash has set in before India has taken the most painful changes. The government has not touched sacrosanct labour laws that make it virtually impossible for any company employing more than 20 workers to lay anyone off. In addition, India must come up with a policy to deal with the state sector. About 200 of the country's 220 centrally owned companies are chronic money losers. Heavy borrowing by government companies – €51 billion from the central government alone – drives up interest rates.

Regardless of who wins the upcoming election – Rao's government, the BJP, or the Left–Front National Front, they will not turn back reforms already taken place. Some foreign investors have turned bullish on India, pouring €1 billion in the Bombay exchange for the first four months of 1996. Some companies such as McDonald's, Baskin–Robbins, and PepsiCo are moving ahead with investments despite the difficulties. The risk is that India's reforms will not be quick enough to appease the growing discontent among its large population. Moreover, there are many examples of foreign investors who have already had great success in China, but there are relatively few in India.

APPENDIX II
The China Report by John Farrell, China Division
According to a *Business Week* article entitled 'Rethinking China':

> In stunningly short order, a powerful China has emerged. As an economic force, it is entering and altering the global marketplace – and in some cases – writing its own rules. . . [6]

China had a €29.7 billion trade surplus with the United States last year, whereas its own markets remain closed in sectors where US businesses are competitive. Moreover, China is notorious as one of the world's greatest rip-off artists and bent on strong-arming US and European companies into transferring jobs and technology as the cost for entering its markets. Although China has cleaned up some intellectual property abuses, piracy remains rampant, and the toll on US businesses is growing. Trade officials estimate that bootlegging in China cost US business nearly €2.1 billion in lost sales last year, and the tendency is towards another steep increase.

Tax preferences for foreign investors have been scaled back, and there is currently a proposal to change the tax system in a way that puts foreign businesses at a disadvantage to local ones. In addition, foreign companies in China must grapple with changing central government rules, grasping local officials and capricious local business partners. The central government is cracking down on joint ventures that provincial officials used to wave through. In addition, contracts are not always enforceable in Chinese courts.

However, there is growing evidence that firms that are prepared to shrug off such obstacles and build a business presence in China will be rewarded. The playing field may be tilted against foreign companies, but domestic rivals are barely up and running. In the more open climate, domestic companies already competing are not able to rely so heavily on their connections, privileged information, and crony networks. Thus, the battle for China's markets has been and will continue to be played out by foreigners for the time being.

This is especially true in the fast-moving consumer-goods markets in which gross margins average 18 per cent to 25 per cent, partly due to the fact that the Chinese love a good brand. Just as in the United States, Procter & Gamble fights Unilever for Chinese consumers. Many multinationals contend that transferring technology is largely risk free. Many pioneers in China have reaped rewards without creating new competitors. Yet, China's effort to milk more out of foreigners means few secrets are really safe. The demands on multinationals to help make Chinese industry competitive are unrelenting. For example, Microsoft, under threat of having its software banned, co-developed a Chinese version of Windows 95 with a local partner and agreed to aid efforts to develop a Chinese software industry.

To keep control of China's economy, Communist leaders are retreating on many risky economic policies, which means no major reform of state enterprises or the banking system – both seen as crucial to completing the transformation of China's economic system. There are two reasons. First, to control economic growth and its resulting inflation, Vice Premier Zhu Rongji engineered an austerity programme in 1993 to curb inflation; it worked. Growth in 1995 slowed to about 10 per cent from 12.6 per cent, a year earlier, while retail price increases eased from 21.7 per cent in 1994 to 15 per cent in 1995. Second, the central government fears that the poor inland provinces are falling too far behind. Many of its 700 million peasants live in near-feudal conditions, and 100 million have flooded into cities looking for work. The government fears that high unemployment will only fuel crime and corruption, which is already on the rise.

This recentralisation is an attempt to enable the central government to set the pace of economic development rather than cede the power to the coastal provinces. The most needed reforms are in the state sector, which is one of the biggest drags on the economy. However, because state-owned factories employ 50 per cent of the urban population, the leadership will not let them go bust. Yet the state's companies churn out goods that nobody wants and then demand loans from the state banks, ultimately causing more inflation.

Nevertheless, other economic reforms are accelerating, such as a convertible currency tied to outside financial markets and regulations to protect intellectual property rights. The best hope for major reform is for China to enter into the World Trade Organization (WTO) because as a member, China would be forced over a designated period of time to liberalise its economy by dropping many trade barriers. However, chances of China's entering are slim. China would like to enter with developing-country status, which would allow it to protect domestic industries from foreign competition, but the United States would like China to enter on terms similar to those of other industrial nations.

The bottom line is that China's already large economy is set to double in the next eight years, making it the world's sixth-largest economy, and those companies anxious to get access to China's riches are willing to take the risks.

Notes

1. Timothy J. Muris, David T. Scheffman and Pablo T. Spiller, *Strategy, Structure, and Antitrust in the Carbonated Soft Drink Industry* (Westport, CT: Quorum Books, 1993).
2. 'Turning Pepsi Blue', *The Economist*, 13 April 1996, p. 15.
3. 'Annual Report', Coca-Cola, 1995.
4. Beverage World, *Coke's First 100 Years* (Kentucky: Keller International Publishing Company, 1986).
5. Sharon Moshavi, 'Get the "Foreign Devils" ', *Business Week*, 23 October 1995, pp. 48–50.
6. Joyce Barathan, Stan Crock and Bruce Einhom, 'Rethinking China', *Business Week*, 4 March 1996, pp. 57–58.

This case was prepared by Donna Cristo, doctoral candidate, Pace University, Lubin School of Business.

Euro Disney (A)

Michael Eisner, chairperson of Walt Disney Company, was sitting in his Los Angeles office. It was New Year's Eve 1993, and Eisner had one meeting left before he could go home to celebrate a quiet holiday. The meeting was with yet another group of high-powered consultants from one of the world's most prestigious general management and strategy consulting companies. The consultants had assembled a multidisciplinary team including financial, marketing and strategic planning experts from the New York and Paris offices. The meeting couldn't wait until after the holidays – the topic, what to do about Euro Disney, was that critical. The consultants were asked by the consortium of bank lenders to provide an additional perspective on the problems of Euro Disney and to make recommendations to Eisner and Disney management on what should be done.

In the 10 years since Eisner and his senior management team had arrived, they had turned Disney into a company with annual revenues of €7.2 billion, compared with €850 million in 1984. For Eisner, his track record was impeccable. 'From the time they came in, they had never made a single misstep, never a mistake, never a failure,' according to a former Disney executive. 'There was a tendency to believe that everything they touched would be perfect.' Eisner was particularly proud of the success of the immensely profitable Tokyo Disneyland, which had more visitors in 1993 than even the two parks in California and Florida. Based on the company's success in the United States and Japan, Eisner had vowed to make Euro Disney, located outside Paris, the most lavish project that Disney had ever built. Eisner was obsessed with maintaining Disney's reputation for quality and he listened carefully to the designers who convinced them that Euro Disney would have to brim with detail to compete with the great monuments and cathedrals of Europe. Eisner believed that Europeans, unlike the Japanese, would not accept carbon copies. Construction of the park alone (excluding the hotels) was approaching €2.4 billion. In developing Euro Disney, Eisner had learned from some of the mistakes made on other projects. For example, in Southern California, Disney let other companies build the hotels to house visitors and in Japan, Disney merely collected royalties from the park rather than having an equity ownership stake.

In preparing for the meeting with the consultants, Eisner was shuffling through some of the papers on his desk. An article in that week's French news magazine *Le Point* quoted Eisner as saying that Euro Disney might be shut down if Disney failed to reach an agreement with its creditor banks on a financial rescue plan by 31 March. The company's annual report for 1993 said that Euro Disney was the company's '... first real financial disappointment' since Eisner had taken over in 1984. Eisner's defence had been to publicly blame the performance on external factors including the severe European recession, high interest rates, and the strong French franc. Eisner picked up the financials from the comparable periods from the initial two years' operations of Euro Disney (Table 1) and then quickly, after reviewing the numbers, put them down. The situation was deteriorating quickly, he thought. Eisner then turned to the attendance figures, which were also trending downward (Table 2).

Table 1 Euro Disney profits and losses, six months ending 30 September, 1992 and 1993 (in € million)

	1993	1992
Revenues	274.5	472.8
Profit/(loss)	−167.8	106.7

Table 2 Annual attendance figures, years ending April (initial opening April 1991)

	1993	1992
Attendance	9.5 million	10.5 million

REVIEW OF PROJECTIONS/THE INITIAL PLAN

Eisner walked to his bookshelf from which he took down a bound copy of the initial 30-year business plan for Euro Disney. The plan was done in the typical detailed and methodical Disney fashion. The table of contents was exhaustive, appearing to cover virtually every detail. Over 200 locations in Europe were examined before selecting the site just outside Paris, with Paris being Europe's biggest magnet for tourism. A huge potential population could get to Euro Disney quickly (see Table 3).

European vacation habits were also studied. Whereas Americans average two to three weeks'

Table 3 European population proximity to Euro Disney

Population (millions)	Time to Euro Disney
17	2-hour drive
41	4-hour drive
109	6-hour drive
310	2-hour flight

vacation, French and Germans typically have five weeks' vacation. Longer vacations should translate into being able to spend more time at Euro Disney.

The French government was spending hundreds of millions of francs to provide rail access and other infrastructure improvements. Within 35 minutes, potential visitors could get to the park from downtown Paris. The opening of the Channel Tunnel in 1993 would make the trip from London 3 hours and 10 minutes.

While the weather in France was not as warm as that in California or Florida, waiting areas and moving sidewalks would be covered to protect visitors from wind, rain and cold. Tokyo Disney had been built in a climate similar to Euro Disney and the company had learned a lot about how to build and run a park in a climate that was colder and wetter than those of Florida and California.

The attractions themselves would be similar to those found in the American parks, with some modifications to increase their appeal to Europeans. Discoveryland, for example, would have attractions based on Frenchman Jules Verne's science fiction; a theatre with a 360-degree screen would feature a movie on European history. The park would have two official languages, English and French; a multilingual staff would be on hand to assist Dutch, German, Italian and Spanish visitors. Basically, however, Euro Disney's strategy was to transplant the American park. Robert Fitzpatrick, a US citizen with extensive ties to France and the chairperson of Euro Disney, felt 'it would have been silly to take Mickey Mouse and try to do surgery to create a transmogrified hybrid, half French and half American.'

Other aspects of the American parks would also be transferred to France. These include Main Street USA and Frontierland, as well as Michael Jackson's Captain EO 3-D movie. Like the American parks, wine and other alcoholic beverages would not be served.

Fitzpatrick's greatest fear was '... that we will be too

successful' and that too many people would come at peak times, forcing the park to shut its gates.

Eisner turned to the financing plan, which had been prepared by chief financial officer (CFO) Gary Wilson, a man known as a tough negotiator with a knack for creating complex, highly leveraged financing packages that placed the risk for many projects outside of Disney while keeping much of the upside potential for the company. Wilson had subsequently left Disney to become chief executive officer (CEO) of the parent company of Northwest Airlines.

The plan had set up a finance company to own the park and lease it back to an operating company. Under the plan, Disney held a 17 per cent stake in the company, which was to provide tax losses and borrow capital at relatively low rates. Disney was to manage the resort for large fees and royalties, while owning 49 per cent of the equity in the operating company, Euro Disney SCA. The remaining shares were sold to the public, largely to small individual European investors. A total of €3 billion in construction loans was raised from dozens of banks eager to finance the project.

Euro Disney was just the cornerstone of a huge real estate development planned by Disney in the area. Initially, the area was to have 5,200 hotel rooms, more than are available in the entire city of Cannes. The number of rooms was expected to triple after a second theme park opened in the area. Subsequent phases of the plan also included office space that would rival the size of France's largest office complex, La Defense, in Paris. Other plans showed shopping malls, golf courses, apartments and vacation homes. Key to the plan's financial success was that Euro Disney would tightly control the design and build almost everything itself and then sell off the completed properties at a large profit.

THE JAPANESE EXPERIENCE

Eisner put the book down and picked up another file that contained an assessment of the incredible success of Tokyo Disneyland. Seeking to determine if there were any parallels between the Japanese and European experiences, he had commissioned a study of why the Japanese venture was doing so well.

Tokyo Disneyland had been open about 11 years and had been drawing larger crowds than the US parks. Located less than 10 miles from Tokyo, the park drew over 16 million visitors from throughout Asia in 1993. Tokyo Disneyland is a near replica of the American original. Most of the signs are in English, with only occasional Japanese; the Japanese flag is never seen but variations on the Stars and Stripes appear throughout the park. In the file, Eisner found a study written by Masako Notoji, a Tokyo University professor, who studied the hold that Tokyo Disneyland has over Japanese people. Notoji wrote that the 'Japanese who visit Tokyo Disneyland are enjoying their own Japanese dream, not the American dream. In part, this is because the park is so sanitised and precise in how it depicts an unthreatening, fantasy America that it has become totally Japanese, just the way that Japanese want it to be.' It has been compared to the Japanese garden, which is a controlled and confined version of nature that becomes more satisfying and perfect than nature itself. The Japanese Disneyland, some say, outdoes the American parks because it is probably cleaner due to the Japanese obsession with cleanliness.

Notoji's report also noted that Tokyo Disneyland opened in 1983, a period in which the Japanese economy was especially strong. During that time period, the United States was perceived as a model of an affluent society. At the same time, as a result of its growing affluence, Japan was starting to feel part of world culture. Tokyo Disneyland became a symbol for many people of Japan's entry into world culture.

In commenting on the differences between Tokyo and France, Notoji's research hypothesised that '... the fakeness of (Tokyo) Disneyland is not evident because (the Japanese) only had fantasy images of these things before' while 'Europeans see the fakeness because they have their own real castles and many of the Disney characters come from European folk tales.'

Eisner's secretary announced that the consulting team had arrived and that the meeting would be held in his conference room. The meeting started with Eisner explaining the assignment and the short time frames in which solutions had to be developed.

EURO DISNEY PROBLEMS

In early February, a team of consultants returned to Eisner's office with the first phase of their study completed. Given the size and complexity of the problems that they expected to find, the study had been divided into three phases. The first phase was a top-level assessment of the problems that they had uncovered in the initial month of the study, without any recommendations as to what should be done. The second phase was to identify the most critical problems that needed to be addressed immediately and to develop action plans. The third phase was to identify the remaining, less critical problems, and develop recommended plans of action.

The consultants' report identified six critical major problem areas:

1 Management hubris
2 Cultural differences
3 Environmental and location factors
4 French labour issues
5 Financing and the initial business plan
6 Competition from US Disney parks

Management hubris

The first issue addressing the way in which Disney management had approached the development of the project and tactical errors made by members of the management team was the most sensitive. Because of the sensitivity of this subject, the consulting firm had brought in the head of their European practice, based in Paris, to analyse the problem and make the presentation. Extensive interviews had been conducted with members of the Disney management teams, both in the United States and in France; academicians who have studied French and American culture; and executives of the European banks that had made many of the construction loans as well as workers at the park.

'The initial premise of Euro Disney in the mid-1980s was that there was no limit to the European public's appetite for American imports given the success of Big Macs, Coke, and Hollywood movies,' the presentation started off. That initial assumption totally failed to take into consideration the fact that 'the French flatter themselves that they are more resistant to American cultural imperialism'. The 'hermetically sealed world of the theme park did not give the French an ability to put their own mark on the park. Disney was exporting the American management system, experience and values with a management style that was brash, frequently insensitive, and often overbearing'. The Americans were overly ambitious and always sure that it would work because they were Disney, and it had always worked in the past. By starting off on this premise, Euro Disney quickly became known as a 'cultural Chernobyl' and it created hostility from the French people. The initial arrogance of American management further demoralised the workforce, creating a spiralling effect that cut down on the number of French visitors.

Much of this arrogance, the report continued, created tension and hostility among the management team. The first general manager, Robert Fitzpatrick, an

American, spoke French and was married to a French woman; however, he was distrusted by some American as well as French executives. Management, unfamiliar with the French construction industry, had made a number of critical mistakes including selecting the wrong local contractors, some of whom went bankrupt. Fortunately, Fitzpatrick had already been replaced with a French native.

Cultural differences

The firm's senior marketing strategist presented the second part of the report, which focused on cultural and marketing differences between the US and European markets. The first phase of the analysis had uncovered a number of obvious problems, some of which had already been rectified. The purpose in identifying these problems, the consultants said, was to be able to be sensitive and to identify other, possibly more subtle cultural and marketing problems.

While attendance was initially strong at the park, the length of the average stay was considerably different than at the US parks. Europeans stayed in Euro Disney an average of two days and one night, arriving early in the morning of the first day and checking out early the next day. By comparison, the average length of the visit in the United States was four days. In large part, this was because the American parks in Florida and California had multiple parks in the immediate areas, while there was only one park at Euro Disney.

Attendance at the park was also highly seasonal, with peaks during the summer months when European children had school vacations and troughs during non-vacation periods. Unlike American parents who would take their children out of school for vacations, European parents were reluctant to do this. Europeans were also accustomed to taking one or more longer vacations, while Americans favoured short mini-vacations.

Revenues from food were also significantly lower at Euro Disney compared with the other parks, the report found. Three of the reasons that had been identified just after the park had opened were related to misunderstandings about European lifestyles. The initial thinking was that Europeans did not generally eat a big breakfast and, as a result, restaurants were planned to seat only a small number of breakfast guests. This proved incorrect, with large numbers of people showing up for fairly substantial breakfasts. This problem was corrected by changing the menus as well as providing expanded seating for breakfast through the expansion of cafeteria facilities. While

the park offered fast-food meals, they were priced too high, restraining the demand. This problem, too, had been taken care of by reducing the prices at the fast-food restaurants. At the US parks, alcohol was not served, in keeping with the family-oriented values. The decision not to serve alcohol at Euro Disney failed to account for the fact that alcohol is viewed as a normal part of daily life and a regular beverage with meals. This error, too, was rectified after it was discovered.

Revenues from souvenir shop sales were also considerably below those in the other parks, particularly Tokyo Disneyland. In Japan, great value was placed on purchasing a souvenir from the park and giving the souvenir as a gift to friends and family upon one's return home. Europeans were far less interested in purchasing souvenirs.

In the initial design of the project, it was assumed that Europeans would be like Americans in terms of transportation around the park and from the hotels to the park attractions. In the United States, a variety of trains, boats, and tramways carried visitors from the hotels to the park. Although it was possible to walk, most Americans chose to ride. Europeans, on the other hand, chose to walk rather than ride, leaving the vehicles significantly under-utilised. While not directly affecting revenue, the capital as well as ongoing costs for this transportation were considerable.

It was also assumed, given the automobile ownership statistics in Europe, that the majority of visitors would drive their own cars to Euro Disney and that a relatively small number of tourists would arrive by bus. Parking facilities were built accordingly, as were facilities for bus drivers who would transport passengers to the park. Once again, the initial planning vastly underestimated the proportion of visitors who would arrive by bus as part of school, community, or other groups. Facilities for bus drivers to park their buses and rest were also inadequate. This, too, was a problem that was initially solved.

The consultant concluded this portion of the presentation by saying that these were just a few examples of problems that resulted from a misunderstanding of the differences between the US and Japanese parks that had already been identified and fixed.

Environmental and location factors

Next to speak was a team that included experts from an environmental planning firm. This presentation would be brief, since the problems that they identified were virtually impossible to correct at this stage in the project.

They initially noted that given the location in middle to northern Europe and the fact that there were only about six months of temperate weather when it was truly pleasant to be outside, the park was clearly sited in a location that did not encourage visitors on a year-round basis. Although accommodations were made (including the covered sidewalks), the fact that off-season visits had to be heavily discounted and promoted to groups to get even reasonable attendance still represented a major problem that needed to be corrected. Whether through pricing changes or the development of other attractions or other marketing and promotional vehicles, attendance in the off-peak months had to be increased.

The second problem that they identified, the location east of Paris rather than to the west, was also something that could not be rectified. It was reported that this was again related to overconfidence on the part of the initial planning team, which thought that even though most Parisians who would visit the park currently live west of the city, the longer-term population growth would be in the east. Consequently, it was felt that the park should be built in the east. Again, they noted, Disney executives disregarded the initial advice of the French.

French labour issues

Next to speak was a European labour economist. This problem, which stemmed from differences in the United States and Europe, could potentially be solved. Disney did not understand the differences in US versus European labour laws, he said. In the United States, given the cyclicality and seasonality of the attendance at the parks, US workers were scheduled based on the day of the week and time of year. This provided US management with a high degree of flexibility and economy in staffing the park to meet peak visitor demand. French labour laws, however, did not provide this kind of flexibility and, as a result, management could not operate Euro Disney as efficiently and labour costs were significantly higher than the US parks.

Financing and the initial business plan

The consulting team had hired a major global investment banking concern to review the plan, identify the problems, and develop a restructuring plan.

The firm's senior managing director spoke: 'Financing and the assumptions of the initial business plan is the area that has created the greatest problems for the park; its restructuring is most critical to the ability of the venture to continue operating and become profitable and, as a result, is the most important problem that needed to be addressed short term.'

His presentation identified the following problem areas:

1 The initial plan was highly optimistic and extraordinarily complex. There was little room for error in this plan, which was based on overleveraged financial scenarios that depended on the office parks and hotels surrounding the park to pay off, rather than the park itself. In addition to the plan being highly leveraged, significant cost overruns in the construction of the park further increased the start-up costs, making the achievement of the promised returns even more unlikely. Disney itself had imposed an arbitrary deadline of 31 March to develop a refinancing package with the creditor banks, further putting pressure on developing a credible and viable restructuring plan. A separate team was already at work to develop such a restructuring plan.

2 The initial plan was presented as financially low risk; shares were largely sold to individual investors with little tolerance for risk. The plan was constructed in the mid-1980s, a period of high-flying free-market financing in the United States. European investors did not understand these kinds of deals and propositions.

3 A severe European recession, a drop in the French real estate market, and revaluation of European currencies against the French franc severely undercut all of the assumptions on which the plan was depending in order to succeed.

4 Euro Disney management, faced with the problem of trying to achieve an unrealistic plan, had made serious errors in pricing. Among the mistakes were charging €35.90/day for admission to the park compared with a €25 daily fee for the US and Tokyo parks. Hotel prices were set similarly, with a room costing €290, equivalent to a top hotel room in Paris. Inside the park, food prices were also too high.

Competition from US Disney parks

Finally, given the strengthening of the European currencies against the French franc and US dollar, it was often less expensive for Europeans to travel to the United States, especially Florida. Not only did their currencies buy more, but there were other attractions surrounding Orlando and the weather was warm and sunny year around. In addition, the US park provided the real experience compared with the European simulation.

WHAT TO DO?

The consultants' phase-one report was concluded. As these problems were identified, teams had already been formed to develop potential solutions to the problems that could be solved. The investment bankers were already examining restructuring options. While it was critical to enable the park to remain open beyond the 31 March deadline, the long-term issues appeared to be in the area of marketing. In particular, park attendance and revenues per visitor

needed to be increased while providing value and meeting Europeans' expectations about the Euro Disney experience.

The meeting adjourned after the group had agreed that phase two of the consultants' report, identifying action plans for the most critical issues, would be presented on 15 March.

Discussion questions

1 What did Disney do wrong in its planning for Euro Disney?

2 What recommendations would you make to Disney to deal with the problems of Euro Disney?

3 What lessons can we learn from Disney's problems with Euro Disney?

This case was prepared by James L. Bauer, Vice President, Consumer Market Management at Chemical Bank and doctoral candidate, Pace University Lubin School of Business under the direction of Dr Warren J. Keegan, Professor of International Business and Marketing and Director of the Institute for Global Business Strategy as a basis for class discussion rather than to illustrate either effective or ineffective business leadership and management. © 1998 by Dr. Warren J. Keegan.

Euro Disney (B)

THE FIRST BIENNIUM: 'MELTDOWN AT THE CULTURAL CHERNOBYL'

In the 24 months since it first opened in 1992, the Euro Disney theme park suffered from the confluence of a number of environmental and internal problems. On the one hand, Euro Disney was adversely affected by an untimely European recession and a strong French franc, which, when combined with the park's high admission prices, conspired to keep European tourists from visiting the park and from spending money once they got there. Also, the financial performance of the park was greatly restrained by a massive debt burden. This debt was largely due to the cost overruns incurred in building the park combined with a slump in the French property market, which had left Euro Disney with a number of hotels – each built with borrowed money – that it had originally hoped to sell once the park became operational. In all, the interest charges for fiscal year (FY) 1993 came to around €850,000 per day.

Although the parent company, Walt Disney Company, was quick to blame the poor performance of its French subsidiary on the adverse conditions in the European environment, in reality these uncontrollable problems were exacerbated by the arrogant

attitude and cultural naiveté of the American management. Inspired by their record financial performance during the 1980s, the Disney team had led itself to believe that it had perfected the recipe for success. In striving to apply this formula in the European market, however, Disney succeeded only in alienating its French stakeholders, namely the creditor banks, the minority shareholders, the labour unions, and, most importantly, the general public.

To its credit, Disney responded proactively and decisively once its mistakes had been recognised. To counter the perception of management hubris, Walt Disney actively promoted Europeans into the top management team. Robert Fitzpatrick, the French-speaking American chairman of Euro Disney SCA, was replaced by Philippe Bourguignon, a Frenchman who had spent 10 years working in the United States. The new chairman initiated a number of measures aimed at repositioning the theme park as a less expensive and more efficiently run resort. The admission price charged to locals was lowered and the park's stores had the number of lines of merchandise reduced from 30,000 to 17,000. In the Euro Disney hotels, labour-saving magnetic cards replaced meal vouchers, and the number of food items offered was slashed from

5,400 to 2,000. Moreover, a central purchasing department replaced the separate arrangements each hotel had had with its own suppliers. Finally, staff in 950 administrative posts, equivalent to 8.6 per cent of the total workforce, were laid off in late 1993.

At the same time, environmental conditions in the European market were improving. Not only was the European economy coming out of recession, but the opening of the Channel Tunnel, combined with the 50th anniversary of the Normandy Invasion, augured well for the tourist season of 1994.

Yet, despite these measures and environmental changes, Euro Disney's future was never darker. Attendance figures recorded for FY 1994 were only 8.8 million, the lowest since the park had opened, while total revenue from the park and the five hotels fell 21 per cent to €177 million. As one French analyst observed with perspicacity: 'They're getting fewer visitors at a lower price; that's definitely no good at all.'

Why had the number of visitors fallen? Largely because of circulating rumours that Euro Disney was about to be closed down. As far back as the end of 1993, Euro Disney's financial situation had deteriorated so much that the usually upbeat Michael Eisner, who had earlier labelled Euro Disney 'probably the best thing we ever built', distanced himself from the prodigal subsidiary by stating in his annual report to Walt Disney shareholders:

> We certainly are interested in aiding Euro Disney SCA, the public company that bears our name and reputation. We will deal in good faith .... But in doing so, I promise all shareholders of the Walt Disney company that we will take no action to endanger the health of Disney itself.

Statements such as these were no doubt intended to communicate Walt Disney's reluctance to bear the brunt of the growing financial burden of the theme park.[1] By distancing itself from its subsidiary, Disney hoped to counter the widespread perception among Euro Disney's other stakeholders that it had cut a 'sweet deal' in structuring its relationship with the theme park. Back in 1989, when Euro Disney SCA had been floated, Walt Disney had purchased 49 per cent of the new company's shares for €1.5 each. In contrast, public shareholders paid €11 and later, when the theme park had opened in 1992, share prices had soared to €25.

In all, Walt Disney had arranged €3.4 billion to finance the park, of which they had contributed only €144 million (for a 49 per cent equity stake) while

the public had paid €850 million (for the remaining 51 per cent). The rest of the start-up capital (nearly €2.5 billion) had been borrowed. Also included in the initial deal was a management fee of 3 per cent of gross revenues, an increasing 'incentive management fee' of 30 to 50 per cent of pre-tax cash flow, and royalties of 5 per cent and 10 per cent on food and admission, respectively. This meant that the parent company could make money even while Euro Disney was running at a loss. Indeed, analysts predicted that the profit per visitor to Euro Disney would actually decrease as attendance went up due to the proportion of fees that was to be repatriated to Walt Disney.

However, when Euro Disney's debt reached €3 billion, this no-lose deal for Walt Disney meant that banks would no longer lend money to the French subsidiary without a guarantee from the parent company. Thus, Euro Disney became an Achilles' heel to the parent company, giving Walt Disney its first quarterly net loss (in September 1993) since Michael Eisner had become chairman in 1984.

In the end, things had come to a head as Euro Disney simply ran out of cash. Walt Disney provided emergency funds, but it also imposed a deadline for a restructuring of the subsidiary's financial arrangements: Walt Disney had no intention of injecting further funds beyond the end of March 1994. Euro Disney's fate was sealed, and its stakeholders were compelled to come up with a rescue plan that either eliminated some of the crippling interest burden, converted debt into equity, or raised funds by some other means. The question was, who would pay how much and when?

THE RESCUE PLAN

A number of issues affected the restructuring activities and influenced the bargaining power of the major stakeholders. On one side of the equation, Euro Disney's 63 creditor banks and bondholders agreed that Walt Disney should carry much of the burden for the bail-out, reflecting its relationship with the French company. However, Walt Disney's legal relationship was with Euro Disney SCA, the operating company, and not with the beleaguered theme park itself, which was owned by a finance company that leased the park back to the operating company. (Disney had just a 17 per cent stake in the finance company.) Nevertheless, the banks argued that the park was Disney's 'creation and responsibility' – after all, Euro Disney's top management had been put in place by Walt Disney – and consequently called for 'an asymmetrical sharing of the pain'.

On the other side of the equation, Walt Disney wanted the banks to write down some of their debt or to convert the debt into equity. Although it appeared that Disney was not bargaining from a position of strength, the parent company did have the option of putting Euro Disney into bankruptcy, a position from which it could dictate the terms of the restructuring.

However, although Michael Eisner had hinted at closing the park, there were a number of good reasons why Disney probably would not exercise this option, not the least of which would be the impact on Disney's already tarnished corporate image in France. Conversely, some of the French banks, including the recently privatised Banque Nationale de Paris, were concerned about the risk of substantial losses and the consequent effect on their credit ratings. Similarly, other stakeholders (such as the French government) also stood to lose if the theme park closed and the 40,000 jobs that were indirectly related to the park were eliminated. Thus, there was some speculation that the state-owned Caisse de Depots and Consignations, which was Euro Disney's largest creditor with €671 million in loans, might be compelled to lower its interest rates. However, despite the common interest in keeping Euro Disney afloat (Table 1), drafting a rescue plan that would satisfy all the stakeholders seemed problematic.

Just prior to the 31 March deadline, Euro Disney was at its lowest point financially, with debts now approaching €3.7 billion. Curiously, a glimmer of hope was to be found across the Atlantic in the growing interest of US 'vulture' funds, which had begun

purchasing Euro Disney debt at around 60 per cent of face value. These secondary debt–market transactions reflected growing speculation that the debt would eventually be worth substantially more than what it was being purchased for.

Finally, two weeks ahead of schedule, a rescue plan was announced. In essence, the plan contained two elements. First, the plan comprised a deferment of interest and royalty payments. Specifically, the creditor banks forgave 18 months of interest payments and postponed principal payments for a period of three years. This reflected a saving to Euro Disney of €290 million. Conversely, Walt Disney said it would eliminate management fees (worth €68.6 million p.a.) and royalties on sales of tickets and merchandise for a period of five years. It would, however, still receive an incentive fee based on Euro Disney profits. Finally, Disney agreed to purchase some of the park's under-utilised assets for €213.5 million and lease them back on terms favourable to Euro Disney.

The second part of the plan called for a rights issue to raise funds, which would be used to eliminate debt. This issue worked by giving existing shareholders the right to purchase a number of shares at below-market prices (€1.5) in the same proportion as their present equity stake. In this case, shareholders were to be permitted to subscribe to seven new shares for every two shares held. This meant that Disney would end up paying just under €457.5 million for 49 per cent of the offering.

The rights issue was approved by a meeting of shareholders on 8 June 1994. (Getting shareholder approval was a mere formality given the size of Walt Disney's holdings.) Euro Disney's share price immediately fell, reflecting the dilutive nature of the issue. Nevertheless, the rights issue succeeded in raising a total of €907.4 million, which enabled Euro Disney to reduce its debt burden by 23 per cent to €2.5 billion.

In evaluating the efficacy of the rescue plan, it is worth noting how the major stakeholders fared in the exercise. First, who were the winners? Although the plan called for the parent company to substantially increase its financial stake in Euro Disney – an additional €640 million million on top of the €300 million already spent – Walt Disney benefited from the plan because the fees it deferred would have been lost if the park had closed down. Moreover, the concessions they made served to improve their tarnished corporate image in the French market. The banks were pleased with the deal because they did not end up owning or managing the park's assets, while Euro

Table 1 Euro Disney's stakeholders and their financial interests

Walt Disney Co.	Total outlay of €300 million: based on initial outlay of €144 million for 49% equity and the subsequent injection of emergency funds
Public shareholders	Initial outlay of €850 million for subscribed shares
63 creditor banks	€2.2 billion in loans
French government	Provided €640 million in low-interest loans, built road and rail links to the park, and sold Disney land at low prices
Bondholders	€610 million of convertible bonds

Disney's bondholders were happy just to be excluded from the plan. Finally, it is safe to assume that the labour unions and the French government also benefited from the bailout.

The only clear losers in the rescue plan were the minority shareholders. With 770 million shares now in the market – about four times the original number – Euro Disney's earnings per share inevitably fell, as did the company's share price. On the day the rights issue was announced, Euro Disney's market capitalisation dipped 8 per cent to €5.2 per share, and by the end of the month, shares were worth just €1.96. However, things were about to get worse before they got better, and within two months Euro Disney's share price had dropped to just €1.15 (Figure 1).

Despite the drop in its share price, the magnitude of the devaluation of Euro Disney's market capitalisation was minimised by the timely appearance of a new player in the market. In the spring of 1994, Prince Al-Waleed bin Talal bin Abdulaziz Al Saud, the 37-year-old nephew of Saudi Arabia's King Fahd, announced his intention to purchase a significant equity stake in the company. By mid-October, the prince had acquired 74.6 million shares, reflecting a 24.6 per cent equity stake (acquired for around €300 million). Some of these shares had been purchased from Walt Disney, whose stake in the company had consequently been reduced from 49 per cent to 39 per cent.

THE SECOND BIENNIUM: EURO DISNEY GETS A REPRIEVE

The rescue plan effectively gave Euro Disney a three- to five-year reprieve from its interest and royalty charges. However, implicit in this reprieve was the mandate to make Euro Disney a profitable company as soon as possible, and Philippe Bourguignon and his staff wasted little time in enacting a revamped marketing strategy geared to this objective.

Perhaps the most significant marketing change made was the renaming of the theme park itself. The name 'Euro Disney' had been chosen in a period of pre-1992 unification hype. However, events in the past few years had seen some commentators come to equate Euro Disney with Euro Disaster. Consequently, and to reflect the new lease on life that had been given to it by the rescue plan, Euro Disney renamed the theme park 'Disneyland Paris' to capitalise on its proximity to the French capital, the world's top tourist destination. (Euro Disney SCA would remain the name of the operating company.) By a fortuitous twist of fate, the newly renamed park received some timely publicity when Michael Jackson and Lisa Marie Presley visited Disneyland Paris on their honeymoon.

At the end of 1994 a 22 per cent reduction in admission prices for the 1995 peak season was announced (Table 2). Simultaneously, further efficiency measures were introduced. The park's total workforce had now been reduced to 12,000 from 17,000, of which 4,000 staff were employed on a seasonal basis. Moreover, new trainees were now required to undergo 6 to 12 months of training. Previously, new staff had received only one day of training. Also, negotiations with labour unions were under way to make staffing arrangements more flexible, in line with fluctuating attendance patterns. This meant that staff would now work longer hours on weekends and during the summer months when demand was greatest.

Other changes included the decentralisation of

Figure 1 **Euro Disney's share price**

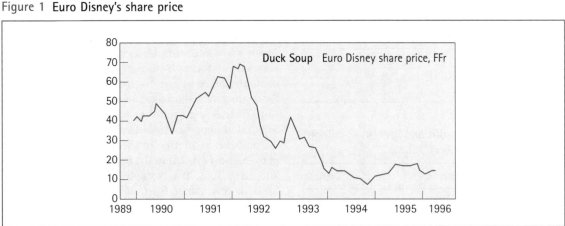

Source: Datastream

Table 2 Admission price changes (in €)

| | Adult price | |
	Peak (1 April–1 October)	Off-peak
Old price	38	27–34
1995 price	30	23

decision-making authority to 'small world' units consisting of 30 to 50 staff, with each unit given responsibility for achieving management targets and improving visitor satisfaction. Managers of these autonomous units would received performance-based bonuses whereas other staff, or 'cast members', would receive non-financial rewards, such as better promotion prospects.

At the end of FY 1995 the cumulative effect of these changes in strategy and the rescue plan were evident. Not only did the park receive a record attendance of 10.7 million visitors (Table 3), but Euro Disney SCA also recorded its first-ever profit (Table 4). However, it is sobering to note that the reported profit of €17.4 million is overstated because of the deferred royalty and interest payments and Euro Disney's buyback of 2.7 million convertible bonds. Profit before exceptional items was only €0.3 million.

Although the figures for 1995 indicated that Euro Disney SCA had turned the corner, much remained to be done in the next few years before the long-term viability of the venture could be established. Although Disneyland Paris has become Europe's number one paid tourist destination, there is a clear need to increase attendance even further. Philippe Bourguignon estimated that the park needs 12.5 million visitors per year to break even once royalty

Table 3 Annual attendance figures in millions (FY ending 30 September)

1993	9.8
1994	8.8
1995	10.7

Table 4 Euro Disney profit and loss (in € million) (FY ending 30 September)

	Revenue	Profit/loss
1993	747	– 808
1994	625	– 275
1995	732	17

demands and interest payments resume in 1998. This figure, which before 1995 seemed an impossible target, even now appears highly optimistic.

Such an attendance target seems even more unlikely when the rapidly rising level of competition within the European amusement park industry is taken into consideration. While US Disney parks posed a competitive threat in the early 1990s, the appearance of a number of new theme parks in Europe, such as Spain's Port Aventura, which opened in May 1995, and Germany's Warner Brothers Movie World, is likely to present a greater threat in the late 1990s. Despite high barriers to entry, many new parks are being built while established parks are investing in new attractions. Much of this demand-driven investment activity has been stimulated directly by the marketing appeals of Euro Disney. In 1993, an estimated 58 million people spent around €1.3 billion on Europe's theme parks. As the managing director of the United Kingdom's Thorpe Park observed, 'We enjoyed 1993 on the back of Disney's promotional budget, but it's a tough and competitive business.'

Indeed, with around 30 to 40 amusement parks, Western Europe is fast coming to resemble the North American market where Disney is the dominant player among a crowd of competitors (including Six Flags, Universal Studios, and Sea World). However, unlike North America, where there typically are clusters of parks in close proximity in places such as Orlando and Southern California (thus creating an incentive for visitors to stay a week or more in each locale), in Europe the amusement parks are scattered across the continent.

In addition to the direct competition from parks such as Alton Towers, the United Kingdom's largest theme park, Disneyland Paris also competes indirectly with other entertainment-based attractions such as roller-coaster parks, including Blackpool's Pleasure Beach and Goteborg's Liseberg. Furthermore, a new competitive threat is also emerging in the form of computer-based interactive entertainment, which has led to the establishment of a number of tourist attractions such as Sega's new Virtual World Center, located in London's popular Trocadero complex.

Competition in the amusement park industry is perhaps most evident in the introduction of new rides and attractions. For example, Euro Disney's record-breaking attendance figures for 1995 were positively influenced by the opening of Space Mountain, a roller coaster ride based on Jules Verne's book, *From the Earth to the Moon*. Across the Channel, Alton Towers also enjoyed record attendances in 1995 based largely on the crowd-pulling power of two newly opened rides, Nemesis and Energiser, while in Barcelona the Tussaud's-owned Port Aventura promotes its Dragon Khan roller coaster as being the first to turn thrill seekers upside down eight times.

THE THIRD BIENNIUM: WHAT TO DO?

In seeking to increase the attendance of Disneyland Paris and ensure the sustained profitability of the company beyond 1998, Philippe Bourguignon must deal with a number of issues.

1 How should the park differentiate itself from the competitive threat posed by the growing number of European amusement parks?

2 What target marketing strategy should be pursued in the face of the changing competitive environment?

3 What branding-strategy decisions are relevant?

4 What can be done to make better use of under-utilised resources (such as the hotels) while increasing the profitability of well-patronised facilities?

Note

1. The Economist suggested on 5 February 1994 that Michael Eisner was scaremongering in order to push down Euro Disney's share price to minimise the amount Walt Disney would have to pay out in the event of a rights issue. In hindsight, it appears that this may have indeed been the motivation for his comments.

Source: 'Big Stakes in a "Small World" ', *The Financial Times*, 13 January 1995, p. 12; 'Bourguignon, into the black and off for a break in Tahiti', *The Financial Times*, 31 July 1995, p. 7; 'Disney records loss on charge for Europe park', *The Wall Street Journal*, 11 November 1993, p. A3; 'Disney's Eisner gives "D" Grade to Euro Disney', *The Wall Street Journal*, 30 December 1993, p. A2; 'Euro Disney makes communication its theme', *The Financial Times*, 16 November 1995, p. 20; 'Euro Disney mulls renaming park to highlight Paris', *The Wall Street Journal*, 13 September 1994, p. A14; 'Euro Disney posts first annual profit, stock slides 14%', *The Wall Street Journal*, 16 November 1995, p. A15; 'A faint squeak from Euro Mickey', *The Economist*, 29 July 1995, p. 44; 'The future of the past', *New Statesman and Society*, 29 May 1992, p. 31; 'Introducing Walt d'Isigny', *The Economist*, 11 April 1992, p. 53; 'Investors sing the theme song: the park market is becoming increasingly crowded', *The Financial Times*, 16 August 1995, p. 15; 'The kingdom inside a republic', *The Economist*, 13 April 1996, pp. 68–69; 'Meltdown at the cultural Chernobyl', *The Economist*, 5 February 1994, pp. 65–66; 'Mickey goes to the bank', *The Economist*, 16 September 1989, pp. 78–79; 'The Not-So-Magic Kingdom', *The Economist*, 26 September 1992, pp. 87–88; 'Restructuring of Euro Disney hits bond snag', *The Wall Street Journal*, 1 February 1994, p. A11; 'Step right up, Monsieur', *The New York Times*, 23 August 1995, pp. C1/1; 'Theme parks expect thrills and spills', *The Financial Times*, 1 May 1995, p. 2; 'With a variety of markets, Europe holds great potential', *Amusement Business*, 17 August 1998, p. 16.

This case was prepared by Paul D. Ellis, Assistant Professor, The Hong Kong Polytechnic University. Used with permission.

PART III

Analysing and targeting global market opportunities

CHAPTER 6

Assessing global marketing opportunities

The real change agents in this world always swam against the tide.
WALTER JENS, GERMAN AUTHOR

In the environment of the 1990s, globalisation must be taken for granted. There will be only one standard for corporate success: international market share. The winning corporations will win by finding markets all over the world.
JACK WELCH, CEO GENERAL ELECTRIC

Chapter objectives

Chapter objectives

After reading this chapter, you will know:

- The key global information needs of a company.
- The impact of globalisation on the marketing research discipline.
- How environmental differences impinge on primary and secondary research.

Why is this important? Here are three situations in which you would need an understanding of the above issues:

- You need to organise the global marketing research process.
- You need to provide relevant information for market entries or expansions.
- You need to develop a global marketing information system.

Practice link

Information, or useful data, is the raw material of executive action. The global marketer is faced with a dual problem in acquiring the information needed for decision making. In high-income countries, the amount of information available far exceeds the absorptive capacity of an individual or an organisation. The information problem is superabundance, not scarcity. Although advanced countries all over the world are in the middle of an information explosion, there is less information available on the market characteristics of less developed countries.

Thus, the global marketer is faced with the problem of information abundance and information scarcity. The global marketer must know where to go to obtain information, the subject areas that should be covered, and the problems of global information gathering. Once acquired, information must be processed in an efficient and effective way.

Club Med, Inc., the French-based travel and leisure company that offers 'the antidote for civilisation', has attempted to reposition itself away from the sexy, swinging-singles image that was integral to its early success. In particular, the company has tried to increase its appeal to Americans, who make up about 20 per cent of the club's total guests. The most elusive prospect is a traveller who has never taken a Club Med vacation. Club Med's creative advertising generates a high volume of telephone inquiries to the company's telephone reservation centre in Scottsdale, Arizona. Names, addresses and telephone numbers of all the callers become part of the database. For years, however, unless a caller actually took a Club Med vacation, the information was not put to further use.

Club Med executives realised that the 150,000 'hot prospects' in its information system represented a potential gold mine. These prospects were people who had responded to ads and requested promotional material and information in the past five years but who had never actually tried Club Med. These prospects were regarded as having high potential to actually book a vacation. The company decided to hire an outside firm, Gannett TeleMarketing, Inc., to call these households and obtain several pieces of important information, including family profiles, a list of activities the family enjoyed, and an indication of what activities the family would like Club Med to offer.

Club Med's actions combine elements of a marketing information system with market research. In general, global marketers must know where to go to obtain information, what information and subject areas to look for, the different ways information can be acquired and the various means of analysing data.

This chapter opens with a discussion of global information needs and key idiosyncrasies of global marketing research. Subsequently, data compatibility and equivalence issues in global marketing research are examined. The role and use of secondary and primary marketing data is described next. The chapter concludes with a discussion of how to manage the marketing information system and marketing research effort.

GLOBAL INFORMATION NEEDS

In collecting information for global marketing decisions, management needs data relating to the general business environment in a country, for example political situation and regulatory environment. While this is information taken for granted in the domestic market, internationally it has to be acquired and it is of enormous importance in determining the most attractive market opportunities. Figure 6.1 illustrates the various dimensions which need to be examined in the global environment.

Economic and competitive environment

The macro dimensions of the environment are economic, social and cultural, political, regulatory and legal, and technological. Global marketing research must ensure that managerially relevant information is available for each of these dimensions. Each dimension is important, but arguably the single most important characteristic of the global market environment is the economic dimension. The existence and strength of competing firms in a given market are, of course, also of primary importance.

Figure 6.1 Dimensions to be examined in the marketing environment

Market potential for a product, for example, can be evaluated by determining product saturation levels in the light of income levels. In general, it is appropriate to compare the saturation levels of countries or of consumer segments with similar income levels. Balance-of-payments issues are also important economic considerations.

Technological environment

The importance of the technological environment depends on the specific product category. Market researchers working in companies that manufacture technologically sophisticated equipment are likely to be concerned with engineering skills, and with the level of education in a given country.[1]

Political environment

The political environment of global marketing is the set of governmental institutions, political parties and organisations that are the expressions of the people in the nations of the world. Anyone engaged in global marketing should have an overall understanding of the importance of sovereignty to national governments. The political environment varies from country to country, and for global marketing research, risk assessment is crucial. It is also necessary to understand a particular government's actions with respect to taxes, dilution of equity control and expropriation.

Regulatory environment

The regulatory environment consists of agencies, both governmental and non-governmental, that enforce laws or set guidelines for conducting business. Global marketing activities can be affected by a number of international or regional economic organisations. In Europe, for example, the EU makes laws governing member states; world-wide the WTO will have a broad impact on global marketing activities in the years to come. Although these environments are complex, marketing researchers need to provide information that enables marketers to plan ahead and to avoid situations that might result in conflict, misunderstanding or outright violation of national laws.

Legal environment

The legal environment consists of laws, courts, attorneys, and legal customs and practices. The countries of the world can be broadly categorised in terms of the common law system or civil law system. The United States, United Kingdom and the British Commonwealth countries, which include Canada, Australia and New Zealand, the former British colonies in Africa, and India are common law countries; other countries are based on civil law. Global marketing research is charged to provide information on some of the most important legal issues pertaining to establishment, jurisdiction, patents, trademarks, licensing, antitrust and bribery.

Social and cultural environments

Anthropologists and sociologists define culture as 'ways of living, built up by a group of human beings, that are transmitted from one generation to another'. Culture

Inadequate international marketing research can cause costly mistakes

Without adequate information, marketers cannot develop effective marketing strategies. Information is critical, whether a firm is just entering international markets, expanding its international operations, or attempting to rationalise its global activities. As the following examples illustrate, many mistakes occur because companies ignore the need for information.

After learning that ketchup was not available in Japan, a US company is reported to have shipped the Japanese a large quantity of its popular brand-name ketchup. Unfortunately, the firm did not first determine why ketchup was not already marketed in Japan. The large, affluent Japanese market was so tempting that the company feared that any delay would permit its competition to spot the 'opportunity' and capture the market. A market test would have revealed the reason behind the lack of availability of ketchup; soy sauce was the preferred condiment there. The company involved, however, was able to purchase Japanese soy sauce for profitable resale in the United States.

Kentucky Fried Chicken reportedly found itself in a similar situation when it attempted to enter the Brazilian market. Hoping to eventually open 100 stores, the company began with two operations in Sao Paolo. Sales, though, were unexpectedly low. Why? The firm had not thoroughly researched possible competition. A local variety of low-priced charcoal-broiled chicken was available on almost every corner of the city. Because the locals considered this chicken tastier than the Colonel's recipe, Kentucky Fried Chicken hastily revised its plans and began offering hamburgers, Mexican tacos and enchiladas. The company's troubles were not over, however, for these food products were practically unknown in Brazil and met with little customer interest.

A well-known US soft drink company predicted the existence of a large Indonesian market for its product, but the prediction was based on a faulty market research study. The study was conducted in large Indonesian cities and the results were projected to be representative of the entire population. Unfortunately, major differences existed between rural and urban areas of Indonesia. During the study, the cities housed many foreign visitors who purchased the soft drink. When the company concluded that a major market existed, it set up large bottling and distribution facilities but only realised limited sales to city tourists. In conducting market research tests, it is important to determine who is purchasing the product and how representative they are of the entire population.

CPC International met some resistance when it first tried to sell its dry Knorr soups in the United States. The company had test marketed the product by serving passersby a small portion of its already prepared warm soup. After the taste tests, the individuals were questioned about buying the product. The research revealed US interest, but sales were very low once the packages were placed on grocery store shelves. Further investigation uncovered that the market tests had not taken into account the American tendency to avoid dry soups. During the testing, the individuals interviewed were unaware that they were tasting a dried soup. Had the interviewees have been told that the soup was sold in a dry form and that the preparation required 15–20 minutes and occasional stirring, they would have shown less interest in the product. In this case, the soup's method of preparation was extremely important to the consumer, and the company's failure to test for this unique product difference resulted in an unpredicted sluggish market.

Marketing research can guide product development for a foreign market. Based on a research study conducted in the United States, one US firm introduced a new cake mix in England. Believing that homemakers wanted to feel that they participated in the preparation of the cake, the US marketers devised a mix that required homemakers to add an egg. Given the success in the US market, the marketers confidently introduced the product in England. The product failed, however, because the British did not like the fancy American cakes. They preferred cakes that were tough and spongy and could accompany afternoon tea. The fact that homemakers had to add an egg to the mix did not eliminate basic taste and differences.

GLOBAL PERSPECTIVE continued

Food for thought

● What are the potential sources of error in an international market research project that do not exist in a domestic project?

● Which criteria would you suggest for the selection of an international market research agency?

Source: David A. Ricks, Blunders in International Business (Cambridge, Mass.: Blackwell Publishers Inc., 1993); David A. Ricks, *Big Business Blunders* (Homewood, Ill.: Dow-Jones-Irwin, 1983); Tevfik Dalgic and Ruud Heijblom, 'Educator insights: International marketing blunders revisited – some lessons for managers', *Journal of International Marketing* 4, 1 (1996): pp. 81–91.

includes both conscious and unconscious values, ideas, attitudes and symbols that shape human behaviour.

Global marketing research must analyse the influence of culture for managers to either respond to cultural differences or to change them. Human behaviour is a function both of a person's own unique personality and that person's interaction with the collective forces of the particular society and culture in which he or she has lived.

IDIOSYNCRASIES OF GLOBAL MARKETING RESEARCH

Although the objectives may be the same, the techniques and tools of international research differ substantially from the process of domestic research. Below three major differences are illustrated:

Complexity of factors to be considered

In crossing national borders, a firm encounters factors not found in domestic marketing research. Marketers need to learn about the various aspects of foreign market environments mentioned above. A firm that has done business only domestically will have had little or no prior experience with these requirements and conditions. Information on each of them must be obtained in order for management to make appropriate business decisions.[2]

Competition

As more and more firms decide to enter into global markets, competition profilerates and results in new threats and dangers. In addition to facing competition from well-established multinationals and from domestic firms entrenched in their respective product or service markets, firms face growing competition from firms in newly industrialising countries and previously protected markets in the Third World.[3] As a result, a firm has to determine the breadth of competition and evaluate its impact on the planned operations.

Lack of research infrastructure

In developing countries, the research infrastructure is not as well organised as in industrial countries. If sound research organisations are not available, management may have to rely on sketchy or secondary data or may be forced to develop its own research capabilities. Unfortunately, underdeveloped communications infrastructure and limited availability of secondary data can also significantly influence the information collection and survey administration.

Consequently, in some countries management may have to take decisions based on less reliable information than is typically available in the domestic market.

Key points

- **The execution of global marketing research may differ substantially from the process of domestic research.**

- **Global market researchers are faced with broader competition, different variables to be considered, and a lack of infrastructure.**

- **Marketers need to learn about various aspects of foreign market environments.**

- **Underdeveloped communication infrastructure can hinder the information collection process.**

DATA COMPATIBILITY AND EQUIVALENCE IN GLOBAL MARKETING RESEARCH

Marketers engaged in global research face special problems and conditions that differentiate their task from that of the domestic market researcher. Instead of analysing a single national market, the global market researcher must analyse many national markets, each of which has unique characteristics. However, it is important that data have the same meaning or interpretation, and the same level of accuracy, precision of measurement, and reliability. The need of data compatibility in global marketing research gives rise to a number of issues. Figure 6.2 illustrates the various aspects of equivalence.

At the problem definition stage, the equivalence of research topics represents the minimum requirement for cross-cultural research. In examining equivalence of research topics, a first issue to consider is that concepts, objects or behaviours studied may not necessarily be functionally equivalent, that is, they may not have the same role or function in all countries studied.[4]

For example, while bicycles are predominantly used in the US for recreation, in The Netherlands or China they provide a basic mode of transportation. This implies that the relevant competing product set must be defined differently. In the US it will include other recreational products such as tennis rackets or golf equipment, while in The Netherlands or China it will include alternative modes of transportation such as public transportation.[5]

The conceptual equivalence is concerned with the concepts used to identify the 'activity-function relationships' in the markets under study. The assumption is that many concepts are culture-bound and may therefore not be appropriate for research in the countries in which research is being conducted. The definition of product quality, for example, is likely to be different for a European consumer to one in the emerging markets of Eastern Europe or China.[6] To take another familiar example, the Japanese and Western concepts of decision-making differ considerably. In the West, decision-making is seen much more as a discrete event than in Japan.[7]

Figure 6.2 **Equivalence in global marketing research**

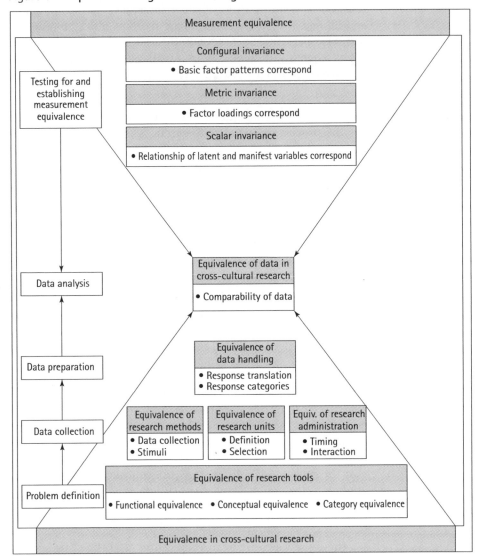

Source: T. Salzberger, R. Sinkovics and B.B. Schlegelmilch: 'Data equivalence in cross-cultural research: A comparison of classical test theory and latent trait theory based approaches', *Australasian Marketing Journal*, 7, 2 (1999): p. 3.

The third type of equivalence relates to the category in which objects or other stimuli are placed. Product class definitions may differ from one country to another. In the beverage market, for example, what is considered a soft drink as well as forms of soft drinks such as canned or bottled sodas, mineral waters, fruit juices, iced tea and powdered and liquid fruit concentrates vary significantly from one culture to another. In addition, the characteristics or attributes perceived by customers as relevant in evaluating a product a product class may differ from one country to another.[8]

Once the equivalence of research topics has been examined, the next step is to consider equivalence aspects of data collection. For instance, the reliability of different sampling and survey administration procedures may vary from one country to another. While in most industrialised countries telephone directories are readily available, in developing countries no such sampling frames exist, and different procedures such as block sampling may be needed.

At the stage of data preparation, care has to be taken that data are equally handled. A major aspect in this context concerns translation of the instruments so that it is understood by respondents in different countries and has equivalent meaning in each research context. The need for translation questionnaires where research is conducted in countries with different languages is readily apparent.

The ultimate goal of quantitative cross-cultural research lies in the equivalence of data. It is always an empirical issue whether data equivalence is achieved or not. To this end, statistical procedures suitable to test for measurement equivalence have to be carried out. The possible outcome of such an analysis, namely that the data does not support comparability, might cause a reluctance among researchers to engage in rigorous testing of data equivalence. This is unfortunate, as non-equivalence should in itself be a highly valued research result with far-reaching consequences for subsequent studies.

Cross-cultural marketing research may utilise two fundamentally different approaches for the investigation or measurement equivalence. The first approach is based on the multiple group confirmatory factor analysis (CFA) and the second approach rests on the paradigm of Latent Trait Theory (LTT) and is also referred to as Item-Response Theory (IRT) in general. The basic idea of the CFA Approach is a structural identity of the construct intended to be measured across cultures, which is necessary and sufficient for conducting mean comparisons. In this context, three increasingly stringent levels of cross-cultural invariance may be distinguished, each allowing different types of comparisons: configural invariance, metric invariance and scalar invariance. While more specialised literature (e.g. Salzberger, Sinkovics, Schlegelmilch) should be consulted for a detailed description of the various levels of measurement equivalence to be tested through CFA approaches and a discussion of latent trait theory based approaches, the most important thing a researcher can do, and should do, is to take care of those facets of equivalence which can only be assessed qualitatively, i.e. equivalence of research topics, data collection and data preparation.[9]

Key points

- **The global market researcher must analyse many national markets, each of which has unique characteristics. However, it is important that data have the same meaning or interpretation, and the same level of accuracy, precision of measurement, and reliability.**

- **The need of data compatibility in global marketing research gives rise to a number of issues, reaching from the problem defintion to the data analysis stage.**

USING SECONDARY DATA FOR GLOBAL MARKETING RESEARCH

A low-cost approach to marketing research and data collection begins with desk research. Governments, international organisations and trade associations are just a few of the data sources that can be used with minimal effort and cost. Data from these sources already exist and are known as secondary data because they were not gathered for the specific project at hand. Below, the major sources are briefly reviewed.

Governments

Government agencies and departments have the widest range of economic, demographic and social data available. These information sources are often available at embassies and consulates. Most industrialised countries also have National Statistical Offices, which publish country yearbooks and other statistical information on the country. Unfortunately, in some cases these yearbooks are published only in the native language.

Typically, the information provided by governments addresses macro and micro issues. Macro information includes, for example, population trends, general trade flows and agricultural production. Micro information include, for instance, material on specific industries in a country, their growth prospects and their foreign trade activities.

International organisations

International organisations provide significant amounts of data relevant to global marketing activities. The Statistical Yearbook of the United Nations, for example, contains international trade data on products and provides information on exports and imports by country. The World Bank is another important source of economic, social and natural resource indicators for over 200 countries and territories. The World Development Indicators include over 600 measures covering population, growth trends and GNP figures. The European Commission publishes an extensive range of statistics and reports relating to the European Union. These include basic statistics and comparisons with principal trading partners of the Union. Last but not least, the Organisation for Economic Cooperation and Development (OECD) publishes quarterly and annual trade data on its member countries.

Trade associations

Most associations, e.g. the International Chamber of Commerce, gather and publish detailed information on topics such as international trade flows and trends affecting international markets.[10] Useful information can also be obtained from industry associations. These groups, formed to represent industry segments, often collect a wide variety of data from their members that are then published in aggregate form. The information provided is often quite general in nature because of the wide variety of clientele served. Nevertheless it can provide valuable initial insights into international markets.[11]

Directories

Any careful marketing strategy requires an understanding of existing and potential competitors and customers. Directories are useful for locating firms or companies that could provide information. Trade directories supply a great variety of information on individual companies, including addresses, names of chief executive officers, product ranges and brand names. The quality of a directory depends, of course, on the quality of input and the frequency of updates.

Electronic databases

Even with the array of printed bibliographies, directories and indices, a search can be very time-consuming. Recent advances in computer technology have

Table 6.1 Examples of secondary data sources

Category	Source	Content	Homepage
Governments	International Trade Administration	The ITA helps businesses to select export markets by providing industry and country analyses	www.ita.doc.gov
	STAT-USA	National Trade Databank	www.stat-usa.gov
	FedWorld	135 Bulletin Boards	www.fedworld.gov
	US Agency for Int. Development (USAID)	International Development Information	www.info.usaid
International organisations	OECD	Main Economic Indicators National Accounts	www.oecd.org
	World Bank	World Tables Social Indicators of Development	www.worldbank.org
	UN	Statistical Yearbook	
	European Commision	Statistics relating to the European Union	www.europa.eu.int
	Electronic Embassy	Index of Embassies	www.embassy.org
Trade associations	Japan Export Trade Organisation (JETRO)	International Investment	www.jetro.go.jp
	Tradefair International	Over 500 Trade Shows	www.tradefair.com
Electronic databases	Euromonitor	European Marketing Data	www.euromonitor.com
	Economist Intelligence Unit	International Market Information	www.eui.com
	ESOMAR	European Society of Marketing Research	www.esomar.nl

resulted in more efficient methods of cataloguing, storing, and retrieving published data.

These data bases provide global marketing information ranging from the latest developments in international trade to new writings in the academic press and the latest updates in international statistics.

With continuing improvements and progress in the area of telecommunications and computerisation, the use of such data bases will increase greatly in the future. Table 6.1 provides some examples of data sources available on the World Wide Web.

Key points

- Secondary data sources can be used with minimal effort and cost. Data from these sources already exist because they were not gathered for the specific research project.

- The major secondary data sources are governments, international organisations, trade associations, directories and electronic databases.

- The criteria for using secondary data sources are accuracy, availability, timeliness, costs and comparability of data.

PRIMARY RESEARCH IN GLOBAL MARKETING

The process of collecting data and converting it into useful information can be divided into five basic steps: identifying the research problem, developing a research plan, collecting data, analysing data and presenting the research findings. Each step is discussed below.

Step I: Identify the research problem

The following story illustrates the first step in the formal marketing research process.

The vice presidents of finance and marketing of a shoe company were travelling around the world to estimate the market potential for their products. They arrived in a very poor country and both immediately noticed that none of the local citizens were wearing shoes. The finance vice president said, 'We might as well get back on the plane. There is no market for shoes in this country.' The vice president of marketing replied, 'What an opportunity! Everyone in this country is a potential customer!'

The potential market for shoes was enormous in the eyes of the marketing executive. To formally confirm his instinct, some research would be required. As this story shows, research is often undertaken after a problem or opportunity has presented itself. Perhaps a competitor is making inroads in one or more important markets around the world, or, as in the story recounted above, a company may wish to determine whether a particular country or regional market provides good growth potential. It is a truism of market research that 'a problem well defined is a problem half solved'. Thus, regardless of what situation sets the research effort in motion, the first two questions a marketer should ask are, 'What information do I need?' and 'Why do I need this information?'

The research problem often involves assessing the nature of the market opportunity. This, in turn, depends in part on whether the market that is the focus of the research effort can be classified as existing or potential. Existing markets are those in which customer needs are already being served by one or more companies. In many countries, data about the size of existing markets – in terms of dollar volume and unit sales – are readily available. Information Resources Inc. and Nielsen Marketing Research, the largest research organisation for example (see Table 6.2), compile exhaustive amounts of data about sales in various product categories world-wide. Data about the Asian markets is available from the Hong Kong-based Survey Research Group. In countries in which such data are not available, a company focusing on existing markets must first estimate the market size, the level of demand, or the rate of product purchase or consumption. A second research objective in existing markets may be assessment of the company's overall competitiveness in terms of product appeal, price, distribution, and promotional coverage and effectiveness. Researchers may be able to pinpoint a weakness in the competitor's product or identify an unserved market segment. Potential markets can be further subdivided into latent and incipient markets. A latent market is, in essence, an undiscovered segment. It is a market in which demand would materialise if an appropriate product were made available. In a latent market, demand is zero before the product is offered. In the case of existing markets, the main research challenge is to understand the extent to which competition fully meets customer needs. With latent markets, initial success is not based on a company's competitiveness. Rather, it depends on the prime mover advan-

Table 6.2 Honomichl Global 25: Largest research organisations by revenues (in € millions)

Rank 1998	Rank 1999	Organisation	Country	No. of countries with subsidiaries	Full-time employees	Research revenues € (millions)
1	1	ACNielsen Corp.	US	80	20,700	1,209.2
2	–	IMS Health Inc.	US	74	8,000	919.6
3	3	The Kantar Group Ltd.	UK	1	4,347	572.5
		Research International	UK	24	1,770	278.2
		Millward Brown	US	15	1,377	192.1
		Other Kantar	UK	14	1,200	102.1
4	4	Taylor Nelson Sofres plc.	UK	35	4,500	465.5
5	5	Information Resources Inc.	US	17	4,600	433.7
6	9	NFO Worldwide Inc.	US	32	3,100	359.9
		NFO Worldwide Inc.	US	21	2,180	212.4
		Infratest Burke AG	Germany	12	920	147.5
7	–	Nielsen Media Research	US	2	2,486	340.9
8	6	GfK Group AG	Germany	33	3,111	299.4
9	12	IPSOS Group SA	France	20	1,538	192.0
10	7	Westat Inc.	US	1	1,203	174.2
11	10	The Arbitron Co.	US	2	609	165.0
12	11	United Information Group Ltd.	UK	5	1,058	154.1
13	13	Maritz Marketing Research Inc.	US	3	720	143.4
14	15	The NPD Group Inc.	US	13	970	117.5
15	14	Video Research Ltd.	Japan	2	343	116.6
16	16	Market Facts Inc.	US	2	915	115.8
17	18	Marketing Intelligence Corp.	Japan	2	366	68.0
18	25	IBOPE Group	Brazil	7	1,400	61.5
19	25	J.D. Power and Associates	US	5	475	55.0
20	19	Audits & Surveys Worldwide Inc.	US	4	241	49.5
21	24	Opinion Research Corp. International	US	5	422	49.4
22	23	Dentsu Research Inc.	Japan	1	118	46.8
23	–	Burke inc.	US	3	239	44.5
24	–	Sample Institut GmbH & Co. KG	Germany	6	346	44.0
25	–	Roper Starch Worldwide Inc.	US	3	344	43.5

Source: 'Honomichl Global 25', *Marketing News*, 16 August 1999, p. H1.

tage – a company's ability to uncover the opportunity and launch a marketing programme that taps the latent demand. Sometimes, traditional marketing research is not an effective means for doing this. As Peter Drucker has pointed out, the failure of American companies to successfully commercialise fax machines – an American innovation – can be traced to research that indicated no potential demand for such a product. The problem, in Drucker's view, stems from the typical survey question for a product targeted at a latent market. Suppose a researcher asks, 'Would you buy a telephone accessory that costs upwards of $1,500 and enables you to send, for $1 a page, the same letter the post office delivers for 25 cents?' On the basis of economics alone, the respondent most likely will answer, 'No.'

Drucker explains that the reason Japanese companies are the leading sellers of fax machines today is that their understanding of the market was not based on survey research. Instead, they reviewed the early days of mainframe computers and other information and communications products. The Japanese realised that, judging only by the initial economics of buying and using these new products, the prospects of market acceptance were low. Yet, each of these products had become a huge success after people began to use them. This realisation prompted the Japanese to focus on the market for the benefits provided by fax machines, rather than the market for the machines themselves. By looking at the success of courier services such as Federal Express, the Japanese realised that, in essence, the fax machine market already existed.[12]

Incipient demand is demand that will emerge if a particular economic, technological, political or sociocultural trend continues. If a company offers a product to meet incipient demand before the trends have taken root, it will have little market response. After the trends have had a chance to unfold, the incipient demand will become latent, and later, existing demand.

Step 2: Developing a research plan

After defining the problem to be studied or the question to be answered, the marketer must address a new set of questions. What is this information worth to me in Euro (dollars or yen, etc.)? What will we gain by collecting this data? What would be the cost of not getting the data that could be converted into useful information? Research requires the investment of both money and managerial time, and it is necessary to perform a cost–benefit analysis before proceeding further.

In some instances, a company may pursue the same course of action no matter what the research reveals. Even when more information is needed to ensure a high-quality decision, a realistic estimate of a formal study may reveal that the cost to perform research is simply too high. As discussed earlier, a great deal of potentially useful data already exists; utilising such data instead of commissioning a major study can result in significant savings. In any event, during the planning step methodologies, budgets, and time parameters are all spelled out. Only when the plan is completed should the next step be undertaken.

Step 3: Collecting data

When data are not available through published statistics or studies, direct collection is necessary. Primary data pertains to the particular problem identified in step one. Survey research, interviews, and focus groups are some of the tools used to collect primary market data. Personal interviews – with individuals or groups – allow researchers to ask 'why' and then explore answers. A focus group is a group interview led by a trained moderator who facilitates discussion of a product concept, advertisement, social trend or other topic. For example, the Coca-Cola Company convened focus groups in Japan, England and the United States to explore potential consumer reaction to a prototype 12-ounce contoured aluminium soft drink can.

In some instances, product characteristics dictate a particular country location for primary data collection. For example, Case Corporation recently needed input from farmers about cab design on a new generation of tractors. Case markets tractors in North America, Europe and Australia, but the prototypes it had developed were too expensive and fragile to ship. Working in conjunction with an Iowa-based marketing research company, Case invited 40 farmers to an engineering facility near Chicago for interviews and reactions to instrument and control mock-ups.

The visiting farmers were also asked to examine tractors made by Case's competitors and evaluate them on more than 100 different design elements. Case personnel from France and Germany were on hand to assist as interpreters.[13]

Survey research often involves obtaining data from customers or some other designated group by means of a questionnaire. Surveys can be designed to generate quantitative data ('How often would you buy?'), qualitative data ('Why would you buy?'), or both. Survey research generally involves administering a questionnaire by mail, by telephone, by e-mail or in person. Many good marketing research textbooks provide details on questionnaire design and administration.

Sampling

Sampling is the selection of a subset or group from a population that is representative of the entire population. The two basic sampling methods in use today are probabilistic and nonprobabilistic sampling. In a probabilistic sample, each unit chosen has a known chance of being included in the sample. In a random sample, which is one type of probabilistic sample, each unit has an equal chance of being selected. The results of a probabilistic sample can be projected to the entire population with statistical reliability. The results of a nonprobabilistic sample, on the other hand, cannot be projected with statistical reliability.

The disadvantage of a probability sample is the difficulty of selecting elements from the universe on a random or probability basis. The quota sample, a nonprobability sample, does not require selection on a probability basis and is, therefore, much easier to implement. Its main disadvantage is the possible bias that may exist in the sample because of inaccurate prior assumptions concerning population or because of unknown bias in selection of cases by field workers.

One form of nonprobability sample is a convenience sample. As the name implies, researchers select people who are easy to reach. For example, in one study comparing consumer shopping attitudes in the United States, Jordan, Singapore and Turkey, data for the latter three countries were gathered from convenience samples recruited by an acquaintance of the researcher. While data gathered in this way are not subject to statistical inference, they may be adequate to address the problem defined in step one. In this study, for example, the researchers were able to identify a clear trend toward cultural convergence in shopping attitudes and customs that cut across modern industrial countries, emerging industrial countries, and developing countries.[14]

Step 4: Analysing research data

There are vast numbers of different approaches to data analysis. Which type of analysis is finally conducted not only depends on the objective of the study, but also on the sample size, the measurement of the variables (e.g. a metric measure such as the age of consumers or a non-metric measure such as a ranking of products as best, second best and third best) and other factors. Again, good marketing research books are available to guide one through the process of data analysis.[15] Below, some techniques are briefly described that are of particular relevance in an international context.

Demand pattern analysis

Industrial growth patterns provide an insight into market demand. Because they generally reveal consumption patterns, production patterns are helpful in assessing market opportunities. Additionally, trends in manufacturing indicate potential markets for companies that supply manufacturing inputs. At the early stages of growth in a country, when per capita incomes are low, manufacturing for low demand centres on such necessities as food and beverages, textiles, and other forms of light industry. As incomes grow, the relative importance of these industries declines as heavy industry begins to develop. As incomes continue to rise, service industries rise to overtake manufacturing in importance.

Income elasticity measurements

Income elasticity describes the relationship between demand for a good and changes in income. Income elasticity studies of consumer products show that necessities such as food and clothing are characterised by inelastic demand. Stated differently, expenditures on products in these categories increase but at a slower percentage rate than do increases in income. This is the corollary of Engel's law, which states that as incomes rise, smaller proportions of total income are spent on food. Demand for durable consumer goods such as furniture and appliances tends to be income elastic, increasing relatively faster than increases in income.

Market estimation by analogy

Estimating market size with available data presents challenging analytic tasks. When data are unavailable, as is frequently the case in both less developed and industrialised countries, resourceful techniques are required. One resourceful technique is estimation by analogy. There are two ways to use this technique. One way is to make cross-sectional comparisons, and the other is to displace a time series in time. The first method, cross-sectional comparisons, amounts simply to positing the assumption that there is an analogy between the relationship of a factor and demand for a particular product or commodity in two countries. This can best be explained as follows:

Let

X_A = demand for product X in country A
Y_A = factor that correlates with demand for product X in country A, data from country A
X_B = demand for product X in country B
Y_B = factor that correlates with demand for product X in country A, data from country B

If we assume that:

$$\frac{X_A}{Y_A} = \frac{X_B}{Y_B}$$

and if X_A, Y_A, and Y_B are known, we can solve for X_B as follows:

$$X_B = \frac{(X_A)\,(Y_B)}{Y_A}$$

Basically, estimation by analogy amounts to the use of a single-factor index with a correlation value obtained from one country applied to a target market. This is a very simple method of analysis, but in many cases it is an extremely useful, rough estimating device whenever data are available in at least one potentially analogous market.

Displacing time series is a useful method of market analysis when data are available for two markets at different levels of development. This method is based on the assumption that an analogy between markets exists in different time periods or, put another way, that the markets in question are going through the same stages of market development. The method amounts to assuming that the demand level for product X in country A in time period 1 was at the same stage as demand in time period 2 in country B. This can be illustrated as follows:

Let

X_{A1} = demand for product X in country A during time period 1
Y_{A1} = factor associated with demand for product X in country A during time period 1
X_{B2} = demand for product X in country B during time period 2
Y_{B2} = factor or factors correlating with demand for product X in country A and data from country B for time period 2

Assume that

$$\frac{X_{A1}}{Y_{A1}} = \frac{X_{B2}}{Y_{B2}}$$

If X_{A1}, Y_{A1}, and Y_{B2} are known, we can solve for X_{B2} as follows:

$$X_{B2} = \frac{(X_{A1})\,(Y_{B2})}{Y_{A1}}$$

The time displacement method requires a marketer to estimate when two markets are at similar stages of development. For example, the market for Polaroid instant cameras in Russia in the mid-1990s might be comparable to the instant camera market in the United States in the mid-1960s. By obtaining data on the factors associated with demand for instant cameras in the United States in 1964 and in Russia in 1994, as well as actual US demand in 1964, one could estimate potential in Russia at the present time. However, the example also illustrates the danger of this approach. Because video cassette recorders (VCRs) and digital cameras were not available in the United States in the mid-1960s, the analogy is seriously flawed. Indeed, for the Polaroid camera, there is no market today that is analogous to markets anywhere in the world in the 1960s and 1970s because the competing electronic imaging technologies of today were not available then.

Several issues should be kept in mind in using estimation by analogy:

1 Are the two countries for which the analogy is assumed really similar? To answer this question with regard to a consumer product, the analyst must understand the cultural similarities and differences of the two countries. If the market for an industrial product is under study, an understanding of the respective national technology bases is required.
2 Have technological and social developments resulted in a situation in which demand for a particular product or commodity will leapfrog previous patterns, skipping entire growth patterns that occurred in more developed countries? For example, washing machine sales in Europe leapfrogged the pattern of sales in the United States.
3 If there are differences in terms of the availability, price, quality, and other variables associated with the product in the two markets, potential demand in a target market will not develop into actual sales of a product because the market conditions are not comparable.

Comparative analysis

One of the unique opportunities in global marketing analysis is to conduct comparisons of market potential and marketing performance in different country markets at the same point in time. One form of comparative analysis is the intracompany cross-national comparison. For example, general market conditions in country X (as measured by income or stage of industrialisation) may be similar to those in country Y. If there is a significant discrepancy between per capita sales of a given product in the two countries, the marketer might reasonably explore whether any actions need to be taken. Soon after George Fisher became chief executive officer (CEO) of Kodak, he asked for a review of market share in colour film on a country-by-country basis. Fisher was shocked to learn that Kodak's market share in Japan was only 7 per cent, compared with 40 per cent in most other countries. The situation prompted Fisher to lodge a petition with the US Trade Representative, seeking removal of alleged anti-competitive barriers in Japan.[16]

A second form of comparative analysis looks at national and subnational markets. Table 6.3 is a comparison between France, a national market, and California, a subnational market. The two markets are substantially different in terms of total population and total income. France's population is nearly double that of California, although it was growing much more slowly. French gross national product is double that of California. Despite these differences, there are striking similarities in the consumption of many products. Indeed, for many products, such as microwave ovens and dishwashers, California is a bigger market than France.

Cluster analysis

The objective of cluster analysis is to group objects (e.g. people, households, companies) into clusters that maximize within-group similarities and between-group differences. Cluster analysis is well suited to global marketing research because similarities and differences can be established between local, national and regional markets of the world. For example, Claritas/NPDC uses geodemographic data to cluster neighbourhoods into types. Claritas has begun matching some US cities to 'twins' in Canada.[17]

Step 5: Presenting the findings

The report conducted on the marketing research must be useful to managers as input to the decision-making process. Whether the report is presented in written form,

Table 6.3 **National/subnational market comparisons, 1995**

	France	*California*	*California as percentage of France*
Gross National Product (GNP)	€ 1.1 trillion	€ 553.1 billion	48
GNP per capita	€ 19,510.9	€ 22,055.8	113
Population	58,344,000	31,589,000	54
Population growth (1990–1995)	0.6 %	6.27 %	1,045
Population density (1995; per sq. mile)	273	202.5	75
Principal city	Paris	Los Angeles	
Population of largest city	8,589,000	9,150,000	107
Motor vehicle registrations (1994)	28,500,000	22,339,000	78

Source: Data adapted from US Bureau of the Census, Statistical Abstract of the United States: 1996, 116th edn (Washington DC, 1996). Table prepared by Warren Keegan.

orally, or electronically via videotape, it must relate clearly to the problem or opportunity identified in step one. Many managers are uncomfortable with research jargon and complex quantitative analysis. Results should be clearly stated and provide a basis for managerial action. Otherwise, the report may end up on the shelf where it will

EUROPEAN FOCUS

When European consumers talk, Whirlpool listens

The Whirlpool Corporation, headquartered in Benton Harbor, Michigan is one of the largest appliance companies in the world. The company sells almost €7.6 billion worth of 'white goods' worldwide each year. Its success has been achieved in part by offering products in three different price ranges: top-of-the-range Kitchen Aid appliances, the medium-priced Whirlpool and Sears Kenmore lines, and Roper and Estate at the low end. Faced with a slow-growing domestic market, Whirlpool has been aggressively pursuing overseas plans.

In Europe, the presence of more than 100 competitors makes the appliance industry highly fragmented – and highly competitive. In Western Europe, Whirlpool takes second place to Electrolux. Whirlpool relies heavily on market research to maintain its market position. 'Research tells us that the trends, preferences, and biases of consumers, country by country, are reducing as opposed to increasing', Hank Bowman, president of Whirlpool Europe BV, said.

Each year the company mails its Standardised Appliance Measurement Satisfaction (SAMS) survey to 180,000 households, asking people to rate all their appliances on dozens of attributes. When a competitor's product ranks higher, Whirlpool engineers rip it apart to see why. The company pays hundreds of consumers to fiddle with computer-simulated products at the company's Usability Lab while engineers record the users' reactions on videotape.

What customers want isn't always obvious, says vice president of marketing John Hamann: 'The consumer speaks in code.' SAMS showed, for instance, that people wanted clean refrigerators. Did this mean fridges that were easy to clean? After analysing the data and asking more questions, Whirlpool decided most consumers want their refrigerators to look clean with minimum fuss. Its latest models have stucco-like fronts and sides that hide fingerprints.

CEO David Whitwham is betting that Whirlpool's consumer research methods will translate into big gains outside the US, where appliance sales have more room to grow. The company has already scored gains, for instance in selling Europeans microwave ovens. Until recently, fewer than one-third of European households had them, but research suggested that more people would buy if microwaves performed more like conventional ovens. In late 1991, Whirlpool introduced the VIP Crisp, a model that incorporates a broiler coil for top browning and a unique dish that sizzles the underside of the food. Result: an oven capable of frying bacon and eggs in Britain and crisping pizza crusts in Italy. The Crisp is now Europe's best-selling microwave.

Food for thought

- Which factors do you need to take into consideration when making a decision on whether to standardise or adapt white goods for different European country markets?
- Which potential problems exist in transferring scales, such as SAMS, between different countries and cultures?

Source: Sally Solo, 'How to listen to consumers', *Fortune*, 11 January 1993, pp. 77–79; Joe Jancsurak 'Big plans for Europe's Big Three', *Appliance Manufacturer*, April 1995, pp. 26–30; Tobi Elkin, 'Product pampering', *Brandweek*, 16 June 1997, pp. 28–40; http://www.whirlpoolcorp.com/ (30 November 1999); Gale Cutler, 'Asia challenges Whirlpool technology', *Research-Technology Management*, Sept/Oct 1998, pp. 4–6; Tim Triplett, 'Brand personality must be managed or it will assume a life of its own', *Marketing News*, 9 May 1994, p. 9; Robert L. Rose, 'Whirlpool is expanding in Europe despite the slump', *The Wall Street Journal*, 27 January 1997, p. B4.

gather dust and serve as a reminder of wasted time and money. As data provided by a corporate information system and marketing research become increasingly available on a world-wide basis, it is possible to analyse marketing expenditure effectiveness across national boundaries. Managers can then decide where they are achieving the greatest marginal effectiveness for their marketing expenditures and can adjust expenditures accordingly.

Key points

- When secondary data are inadequate, direct collection or primary research is necessary.

- The process of collecting data and converting it into useful information can be divided into five basic steps: identifying the research problem, developing a research plan, collecting data, analysing data, and presenting the research findings.

- The two basic sampling methods are probabilistic and nonprobabilistic sampling. The major advantage of a probabilistic sample is that it provides results of statistically measurable accuracy.

ORGANISING THE GLOBAL MARKETING RESEARCH PROCESS

Deciding on research responsibilities

An important issue for the global company is where to locate control of the organisation's research capability. The difference between a multinational, polycentric company and a global, geocentric company on this issue is significant. In the multinational, responsibility for research is delegated to the operating subsidiary. The global company delegates responsibility for research to operating subsidiaries but retains overall responsibility and control of research as a headquarters function. In practice, this means that the global company will ensure that research is designed and executed so as to yield comparable data.

Comparability requires that scales, questions and research methodology be standardised. To achieve this, the company must inject a level of control and review of marketing research at the global level. The director of world-wide marketing research must respond to local conditions as he or she searches for a research programme that can be implemented on a global basis. It is most likely that the marketing director will end up with a number of marketing programmes tailored to clusters of countries that exhibit within-group similarities.

The director of world-wide research should not simply direct the efforts of country research managers. His or her job is to ensure that the corporation achieves maximum results world-wide from the total allocation of its research resources. Achieving this requires that personnel in each country are aware of research being carried out in the rest of the world and involved in influencing the design of their own in-country research as well as the overall research programme. Ultimately, the director of world-wide research must be responsible for the overall research design and programme. It is his or her job to take inputs from the entire world and produce a coordinated research strategy that generates the information needed to achieve global sales and profit objectives.

Designing global marketing information systems

The purpose of a global marketing information system (MIS) is to provide managers and other decision makers with a continuous flow of information about markets, customers, competitors and company operations. An MIS should provide a means for gathering, analysing, classifying, storing, retrieving, and reporting relevant data about

GLOBAL PERSPECTIVE

Older women are the most loyal buyers of Procter & Gamble's Oil of Olaz

American consumers tend to buy new toothbrushes only when they see hundreds of them in special supermarket displays. Midwesterners prefer their shampoo in big bottles, but men and women on the East Coast consistently buy toiletries in smaller sizes.

A decade ago, it would have taken several weeks and hundreds of market researchers to pinpoint trends such as these. Today, buying patterns and consumer habits can be analysed in a matter of days, thanks to the huge amounts of data now available from marketing information systems used by a global marketing firm. In the €7.6 billion personal care industry, the ability to react swiftly to these patterns makes or breaks its bottom line. That's why many companies are automating the way they track and analyse retail data, which in turn is driving promotional programmes for everything from soap to shaving cream.

Cincinnati-based Procter & Gamble Co. (P&G) collects and analyses retail sales data, says Frank Caccamo, P&G's chief information officer. This information is then used by marketing to target specific groups of consumers.

For example, by analysing scanner-based consumer data, P&G was able to pinpoint older women as the most loyal customers of the company's Oil of Olaz product line. To attract new buyers, P&G launched an advertising campaign geared specifically at teenagers and young women. Thanks to daily reports sent to headquarters by laptop-using salespeople, P&G's marketing unit can also now see the effects of pricing and marketing activity in a

matter of days or weeks as opposed to months, he says.

During the winter of 1992, for example P&G analysed weekly retail data in conjunction with regional weather patterns to measure how weather effects sales of its Vick's Formula and Niquil cold products. 'By looking at the data weekly, we can see the effects the cough/cold and flu seasons have on our products,' Caccamo says. 'Seeing that, we can then put in place appropriate consumer response programmes.' These programmes, he says, might include special sales or coupon giveaways in cold regions.

Before P&G implemented marketing decision systems, it received sales data from A.C. Nielsen Corp. and Information Resources, Inc. every two months. Now, 'we get all of the data for any given week at the end of that week. The tracking system furnishes invaluable marketing intelligence. It helps us to better understand regional differences in buying habits,' Caccamo says.

Food for thought

- What kind of consumer market research information should be gathered through scanner data, consumer panels or consumer surveys? Give examples for each of these data collection methods in the context of Oil of Olaz.
- Does the widespread use of scanner data influence the relative power of retailers and manufactures in distribution channels?

Source: Robert L. Scheier, 'Procter & Gamble growth push may centralise It', *Computerworld*, 32, 7 September 1998, p. 4; Christopher Koch, 'Value judgements', *CIO*, 11, 1 February 1998, pp. 30–38; http://www.pg.com; Karen M. Carrillo, 'Document-management deals', *Informationweek*, 11 August 1997, pp. 103–105; Eldon Y. Li *et al.*, 'Marketing information systems in the Fortune 500 companies: past, present and future', *Journal of Management Information Systems*, 10 (Summer 1993): pp.165–192; Eldon Y. Li, 'Marketing information systems in small companies', *Information Resources Management Journal* (Winter 1997): pp. 27–35; Michael M. Masoner and Andreas I. Nicolaou, 'An empirical examination of information systems development strategies in organisational contexts', *The Mid-Atlantic Journal of Business*, 4 October 1996, pp. 206–219; Julia King, 'Coral lipstick? It sells big in Florida', *Computerworld*, 26, 11 May 1992, pp. 117–118.

customers, markets, channels, sales and competitors. A company's MIS should also cover important aspects of a company's external environment. For example, companies in any industry need to pay close attention to government regulations, mergers, acquisitions and alliances. The proposed acquisition of MCI by British Telecommunications (BT) in late 1996 is an example of a development that overnight changed AT&T from a perceived global leader to an underdog in the global telecommunications market share wars.

Poor operating results can often be traced to insufficient data and information about events both inside and outside the company. For example, when a new management team was installed at the American unit of Adidas AG, the German-headquartered athletic shoe marketer, data was not even available on normal inventory turnover rates. A new reporting system revealed that arch-rivals Reebok and Nike turned inventories five times per year, compared with twice a year at Adidas. This information was used to tighten the marketing focus on the best-selling Adidas products.

The task to organise, implement, and monitor global marketing information and research strategies and programmes must be coordinated in a coherent manner that contributes to the overall strategic direction of the organisation. The MIS and research function must provide relevant information in a timely, cost-efficient and actionable manner.

Increased global economic integration, the demise of communism, volatile currency exchange rates, and other factors are driving the demand for access to credible world-wide business and political information. Today's economic and political environments require world-wide news information on a daily basis. Geocentric, global companies generally have intelligence systems that meet these challenges. Typically, the strategic planning or market research departments staff these systems. They distribute information to senior management and to managers throughout the organisation.

A more detailed discussion of the workings of an intracompany MIS is beyond the scope of this book. The discussion that follows focuses on the actual collection of information. This can be accomplished using either surveillance or search.

Scanning modes: surveillance and search

In the surveillance mode, the marketer engages in informal information gathering. Globally oriented marketers are constantly on the lookout for information about potential opportunities and threats in various parts of the world. They want to know everything about the industry, the business, the marketplace and consumers. This passion shows up in the way they keep their ears and eyes tuned for clues, rumours, nuggets of information, and insights from other people's experiences. Browsing through newspapers and magazines and surfing the Internet is one way to ensure exposure to information on a regular basis. Global marketers may also develop a habit of watching news programmes from around the world via satellite. If a particular news story has special relevance for a company – such as the entry of a new player into a global industry, for example, Samsung into the car industry – marketers in that and related industries and all its competitors will pay special attention, tracking the story as it develops.

The search mode is characterised by more formal activity. Search can be described as the deliberate seeking out of specific information. Search often involves investigation, a relatively limited and informal type of search. Investigation often involves seeking out books or articles in trade publications or searching the Internet on a particular topic or issue. Search may also consist of research, a formally organised effort to acquire specific information for a specific purpose.

One study found that nearly 75 per cent of the information acquired by headquarters executives at US global companies comes from surveillance as opposed to search. To be effective, a scanning system must ensure that the organisation is viewing areas where developments that could be important to the company might occur. Innovations in information technology have increased the speed with which information is transmitted and simultaneously shortened the life of its usefulness to the company. Advances in technology have also placed new demands on the global firm in terms of shrinking reaction times to acquired information. In some instances, the creation of a full-time scanning unit with responsibility for guiding and stimulating the process of acquiring and disseminating strategic information may be advisable.

Key points

- A global company needs to develop an efficient and effective system that will scan and digest published sources and technical journals in the headquarters country as well as all countries in which the company has operations or customers.

- Most large companies engage in daily scanning, translating, digesting, abstracting, and electronic input of information into a market intelligence system. Despite the advances in global information, its translation and electronic input is mostly manual. This will continue for the next few years, particularly in developing countries.

- Global marketers need to expand information coverage from their home-base to other regions of the world.

Summary

Information is one of the most basic ingredients of a successful marketing strategy. For global marketing decisions, management needs data relating to the general business environment.

Global marketing research presents a number of challenges. First, research on a number of different markets may be required, some of which are so small that only modest research expenditures can be made. Further problems might be caused by the large numbers of factors involved and the lack of marketing research infrastructure. Data compatibility and equivalence issues may further complicate the global marketing research efforts.

Formal research is often required before decisions can be made regarding specific problems or opportunities. After developing a research plan, data are collected using either primary or secondary sources. A number of techniques are available for analysing data, including demand pattern analysis, income elasticity measurements, estimation by analogy, comparative analysis, and cluster analysis. Research findings must be presented clearly to facilitate decision making.

A final issue is how much control headquarters should have over research and the overall management of the organisation's information system. Marketing information systems should ensure that companies scan the environment to keep in touch with an area of interest via surveillance or by actively seeking out information.

Concepts and definitions

Challenges of global marketing research

Although the objectives of marketing research may be the same, the execution of international research may differ substantially from the process of domestic research. The three primary idiosyncrasies are the number of different variables to be considered, the broader competition and the lack of research infrastructure in some countries.

Global information needs

For global marketing decisions, management needs data relating to the general business environment in a country. The aspects to be examined include:
- Economic and competitive
- Technological
- Political
- Regulatory
- Legal
- Social and cultural

Global marketing information systems

The purpose of a global marketing information system (MIS) is to provide managers and other decision makers with a continuous flow of information about markets, customers, competitors, and company operations. A MIS should provide a means for gathering, analysing and reporting relevant data about customers, channels, sales and competitors.

Marketing research

Marketing research is the function which links the consumer, customer and public to the marketer through information – information is used to identify and define marketing opportunities and problems; generate, refine, and evaluate marketing actions; monitor marketing performance; and improve our understanding of marketing as a process.[18]

Primary research process

The process of collecting data and converting it into useful information can be divided into five basic steps:
- Step 1: Identifying the research problem
- Step 2: Developing a research plan
- Step 3: Collecting data
- Step 4: Analysing research data
- Step 5: Presenting the findings

Discussion questions

1 What are major global information needs?

2 What are major challenges of global marketing research?

3 Describe the different dimensions of equivalence and data compatibility, starting at the problem definition and ending at the data analysis stage.

4 Outline the basic steps of the marketing research process.

5 What is the difference between existing, latent and incipient demand? How might these differences affect the design of a marketing research project?

6 Assume that you have been asked by the president of your organisation to devise a systematic approach to scanning the business environment. The president does not want to be surprised by major market or competitive developments. What would you recommend?

Webmistress's hotspots

Homepage of AC Nielsen Corp.
The global leader in market research, information and analysis.
http://www.acnielsen.com

Homepage of International Monetary Fund
The IMF provides an variety of statistics on its 182 member countries.
http://www.imf.org

Institute for Agriculture and Trade Policy
The homepage contains diverse international data including trade news, strategies and fact sheets. http://www.iatp.org/

Virtual Africa homepage
This homepage provides business and international trade information regarding Africa. It also has an investors guide, contacts and research information for South Africa. http://www.africa.com

Whirlpool Corporation
Welcome to the Whirlpool Corporation on the World Wide Web.
http://www.whirlpoolcorp.com/

Suggested readings

Backhaus, K. and B. Erichson, *Multivariate Analyse-methoden*, 7. Auflage edn. Berlin: 1994.

Bauer, E., *Internationale Marktforschung*. München: Oldenbourg, 1995.

Berekoven, Ludwig, *Marktforschung*. Wiesbaden: Gabler, 1996.

Cavusgil, S. Tamer, 'Qualitative insights into company experiences in international marketing research', *Journal of Business and Industrial Marketing*, Summer (1987).

Craig, C. Samuel and Susan P. Douglas, *International Marketing Research*. Chichester: Wiley, 1999.

Crossen, Cynthia, *Tainted Truth: Manipulation of Fact in America*. Upper Saddle River, NJ: Simon & Schuster, 1994.

Czinkota, M.R. and I.A. Ronkainen, 'Market research for your export operations, Part I', *International Trade Forum*, 3 (1994): pp. 22–33.

Czinkota, M.R. and I.A. Ronkainen, 'Market research for your export operations, Part II', *International Trade Forum*, 31 (1995): pp. 16–21.

Davidson, Lawrence S., 'Knowing the unknowable', *Business Horizons*, 32 (1989): pp. 2–8.

Diamantopoulos, Adamantios and Bodo B. Schlegelmilch, *Taking the Fear out of Data Analysis*. London: The Dryden Press, 1997.

Glazer, Rashi, 'Marketing in an information-intensive environment: strategic implications of knowledge as an asset', *Journal of Marketing*, (1991): pp. 1–19.

Green, Robert, and Eric Langeard, 'A cross-national comparison of consumer habits and innovator characteristics', *Journal of Marketing*, July (1975): pp. 34–41.

Hüttner, Manfred, *Gründzüge der Marktforschung*. München: Oldenbourg, 1999.

Kelly, John M., *How to Check Out Your Competition: A Complete Plan for Investigating Your Market*. New York: Wiley, 1987.

King, W.R. and V. Sethi, 'Developing transnational information systems: A case study', *Omega*, January (1993): pp. 53–59.

Meffert, Heribert, *Internationales Marketing-Management*. Stuttgart: Kohlhammer, 1998.

Mullen, Michael R., 'Diagnosing measurement equivalence in cross-national research', *Journal of International Business Studies*, 26 (1995): pp. 573–596.

Naumann, Earl, Jr., Donald W. Jackson and William G. Wolfe, 'Examining the practices of US and Japanese market research firms', *California Management Review*, Summer (1994): pp. 49–69.

Stanat, Ruth, 'Tracking your global competition', *Competitive Intelligence Review*, Spring (1991): pp. 17–19.

Wasilewski, Nikolai, 'Dimensions of environmental scanning systems in multinational enterprises', Pace University, Working Papers no. 3, May (1993).

Weekly, James K. and Mark K. Cary, *Information for International Marketing: An Annotated Guide to Sources*. New York: Greenwood Press, 1986.

Notes

1. Susan P. Douglas and C. Samuel Craig, *Global Marketing Strategy* (McGraw-Hill, Inc., 1995).

2. Michael R. Czinkota and Ilkka A. Ronkainen, *Global Marketing* (Harcourt Brace College Publishers, 1996).

3. C. Samuel Craig and Susan P. Douglas, 'Responding to the challenges of global markets', *Columbia Journal of World Business*, Winter (1996): pp. 6–17.

4. J.W. Berry, 'On cross-cultural comparability', *International Journal of Psychology*, 4 (1969): p. 119.

5. C. Samuel Craig and Susan P. Douglas, *International Marketing Research* (Wiley 1999).

6. Harold Chee and Rod Harris, *Global Marketing Strategy* (Financial Times Pitman Publishing, 1998).

7. Brian Toyne and Peter G.P. Walters, *Global Marketing Management: A Strategic Perspective* (Boston: Allyn and Bacon, 1989).

8. C. Samuel Craig and Susan P. Douglas, *International Marketing Research* (1999).

9. Thomas Salzberger, Rudolf Sinkovics, and Bodo B. Schlegelmilch, "Data Equivalence in cross cultural research: A comparison of classic test theory and latent trait theory based approaches", *Australasian Marketing Journal*, Vol. 7, 2 (1999).

10. Gilbert A. Churchill Jr., *Marketing Research: Methodological Research* (Harcourt Brace College Publishers, 1995).

11. Michael R. Czinkota and Ilkka A. Ronkainen, *Global Marketing* (Harcourt Brace College Publishers, 1996).

12. Peter F. Drucker, 'Marketing 101 for a fast-changing decade', *The Wall Street Journal* (8 November 1990): p. A17.

13. Jonathan Reed, 'Unique approach to international research', *Agri Marketing* (1995): pp. 10–13.

14. Eugene H. Fram and Riad Ajami, 'Globalization of markets and shopping stress: Cross country comparisons', *Business Horizons* (1994): pp. 17–23.

15. Adamantios Diamantopoulos and Bodo B. Schlegelmilch. *Taking the Fear out of Data Analysis,* (London: The Dryden Press, 1997).

16. Wendy Bounds, 'George Fisher pushes Kodak into digital era', *The Wall Street Journal* (1995): p. B1.

17. Claudi Montague, 'Is Calgary Denver's long-lost twin', *American Demographics,* (1993): pp. 12–13.

18. Peter D. Bennet, *Dictionary of Marketing Terms*, 2nd edn (Chicago: American Marketing Association, 1995).

CHAPTER 7

Global segmentation, targeting and positioning

A spirit caught up in various businesses is not able to focus.
MARTIN LUTHER, TISCHREDEN

What is reasonable is real; that which is real is reasonable.
GEORG WILHELM FRIEDRICH HEGEL; GRUNDLINIEN DER PHILOSOPHIE DES RECHTS

Chapter objectives

After reading this chapter, you will know:

- The objectives and usefulness of global market segmentation.
- The approaches to global market segmentation using different segmentation criteria to define target groups.
- The variables which may be used to select target groups for global marketing strategies.
- Different ways of positioning products in global markets.

Why is this important? Here are three situations in which you would need an understanding of the above issues:

- You want to define your target segments in order to create effective marketing strategies.
- You have a number of potential target groups and need to make a selection.
- You review the design of your marketing mix in order to excel above your competitors.

Practice link

Every afternoon at 2 p.m. Mike Sullivan, Volkswagen car dealer in Santa Monica, California, pulls down the shades of his showroom: not to close the shop, but to keep curiosity seekers out. The object of desire – his latest product, the New Beetle. The huge number of curious passers-by keeps sales personnel away from talking to potential customers. Although Mike Sullivan is quite impressed by the customers' interest, he has also experienced some trouble. 'When I am driving on the highway, it is next to impossible to change lanes. Other drivers come up really close so as to get a better glimpse of the New Beetle.'

The success is impressive: compared to the 49,533 cars sold in 1997, Volkswagen reached a staggering 200,000 cars in 1998. To a large extent, this may be attributed to the overwhelming performance of the New Beetle. Even though the sales volume designated for the US was raised from 50,000 to 60,000 units in 1998, the demand could not be satisfied. The New Beetle was sold out!

Apart from the impressive product concept, the creators of success are found in the company's marketing departments. Since 1995, they have been working on defining key target groups and on how to position the New Beetle in the competitive environment. Liz Vanzura of Arnold Communications, the advertising agency in charge, describes the success story as follows: the experience with buyers of the 'classic' Beetle has taught marketers that conventional demographic segmentation falls short. Beetle fans were to be found across age, income and education groups. For the New Beetle, similar assumptions were formulated. As a result, differing creative strategies were developed which allowed media placement and spending to be specifically targeted. This approach is reflected, for example, in the new media mix which included magazines such as *Architectural Digest* or *GQ*.

While potential Beetle buyers may differ as to their demographic features, their purchasing motives appear very similar. Thus, the communication strategy was oriented towards psychographic and benefit-related aspects. In the competitive environment, the New Beetle was positioned as follows: while most ads would promote experiences of peace and quiet while driving, Volkswagen went completely in the opposite direction. A New Beetle was supposed to be a car in which the driver turns down the window, cherishes the breeze and the music coming from the sound system. Not seclusion, but connectedness to the world is the message. The key slogan *'On the road of life, there are passengers and drivers. Drivers Wanted.'* aims at creating a desire and an invitation at the same time to be a 'driver', i.e. an innovator and not a follower.

Whether the New Beetle will continue its victory outside of the US remains to be seen. Experts are somewhat sceptical: 'there is no mechanistic way of defining key target segments for this car', says VW marketing boss Berthold Krüger. 'A lot of emotions are attached to this car, which do not necessarily fit conventional lifestyle categories.' Positioning the New Beetle still remains a question mark. While in the US the New Beetle was positioned primarily as a car for the mass market, the price premium will make it more like a niche product in Europe.

Also, the communication campaign will focus less on nostalgia. However, with reference to the unique design, many people still believe that 'also in Europe the world will be round again!'[1]

GLOBAL MARKET SEGMENTATION

Market segmentation is

> the process of subdividing a market into distinct subsets of customers that behave in the same way or have similar needs. Each subset may conceivably be chosen as a market target to be reached with a distinctive marketing strategy. The process begins with a basis of segmentation – a product-specific factor that reflects differences in customers' requirements or responsiveness to marketing variables (possibilities are purchase behaviour, usage, benefits sought, intentions, preference, or loyalty).[2]

Global market segmentation is the process of dividing the world market into distinct subsets of customers that behave in the same way or have similar needs, or, as one author put it, it is 'the process of identifying specific segments – whether they be country groups or individual consumer groups – of potential customers with homogeneous attributes who are likely to exhibit similar buying behaviour'.[3] Interest in global market segmentation dates back several decades. In the late 1960s, one observer suggested that the European market could be divided into three broad categories – international sophisticate, semi-sophisticate, and provincial – solely on the basis of consumers' presumed receptivity to a common advertising approach.[4] Another writer suggested that some themes (e.g. the desire to be beautiful, the desire to be healthy and free of pain, the love of mother and child) were universal and could be used in advertising around the globe.[5]

In the 1980s, Professor Theodore Levitt advanced the thesis that consumers in different countries increasingly seek variety and that the same new segments are likely to show up in multiple national markets. Thus, ethnic or regional foods such as sushi, Greek salad or hamburgers might be in demand anywhere in the world. Levitt described this trend as the 'pluralisation of consumption' and 'segment simultaneity' that provides an opportunity for marketers to pursue a segment on a global scale.[6] In the following, approaches to international market segmentation are outlined and explained.

Geographic segmentation

Geographic segmentation is dividing the world into geographic subsets. The advantage of geography is proximity: markets in geographic segments are closer to each other and easier to visit on the same trip or to call during the same time window. Geographic segmentation also has major limitations: the mere fact that markets are in the same world geographic region does not mean that they are similar. Japan and Vietnam are both in Southeast Asia, but one is a high-income, post-industrial society and the other is an emerging, less developed, pre-industrial society. The differences in the markets in these two countries overwhelm their similarities. Simon found in his sample of 'hidden champions', that geography was ranked lowest as a basis for market segmentation (see Figure 7.1).

Demographic segmentation

Demographic segmentation is based on measurable characteristics of populations such as age, gender, income, education and occupation. A number of demographic trends such as fewer married couples, fewer children, changing roles of women, and higher incomes and living standards suggest the emergence of global segments.[7]

For most consumer and industrial products, national income is the single most important segmentation variable and indicator of market potential. Annual per capita income varies widely in world markets, from a low of €76 in Mozambique to a high of €36,000 in Luxembourg. A traditional approach to demographic segmentation involved clustering countries into segments of high, middle and low income; companies simply targeted those with the highest income levels.

The US market, with per capita income of €23,500, more than €6 trillion in 1997 national income, and a population of more than 267 million people, is enormous. Little wonder, then, that Americans are a favourite target market! Despite having comparable per capita incomes, other industrialised countries are nevertheless quite small in terms of total annual income. In Sweden, for example, per capita gross

Figure 7.1 Importance of market definition criteria

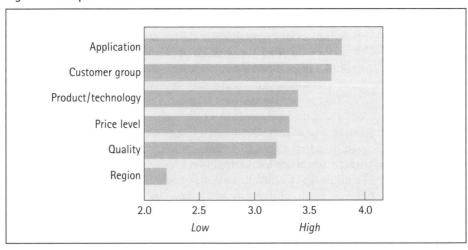

Source: Hermann Simon, *Hidden Champions: Lessons from 500 of the World's Best Unknown Companies* (Boston, MA: Harvard Business School Press, 1996), p. 4.

national product (GNP) is €20,000; however, Sweden's smaller population, 8.9 million, means that annual national income is only about €180 billion. About 75 per cent of world GNP is located in the Triad. Thus, by segmenting in terms of a single demographic variable – income – a company could reach the most affluent markets by targeting three regions: the European Union, North America and Japan.

Many global companies also realise that for products with a low enough price, for example cigarettes, soft drinks, and some packaged goods, population is a more important segmentation variable than income. Thus, China and India, with respective populations of 1.2 billion and 965 million, might represent attractive target markets. In a country like China, where per capita GNP is only €610, the marketing challenge is to successfully serve the existing mass market for inexpensive consumer products. Procter & Gamble, Unilever, Kao, Johnson & Johnson, and other packaged-goods companies are targeting and developing the China market, lured in part by the possibility that as many as 100 million Chinese customers are affluent enough to spend, say, €1 for a single-use pouch of shampoo.[8]

Segmenting decisions can be complicated by the fact that the national income figures such as those cited above for China and India are averages. There are also large, fast-growing, high-income segments in both of these countries. In India, for example, 100 million people can be classified as 'upper middle class', with average incomes of more than €1,200. Pinning down a demographic segment may require additional information; India's middle class has been estimated to be as low as a few million and as high as 250 million to 300 million people. If middle class is defined as 'persons who own a refrigerator', the figure would be 30 million people. If television ownership were used as a benchmark, the middle class would be 100 million to 125 million people.[9] The lesson is to guard from being blinded by averages.

Note also that the average income figures quoted above do not reflect the standard of living in these countries. In order to really understand the standard of living in a country, it is necessary to determine the purchasing power of the local currency. In low-income countries, the actual purchasing power of the local currency is much higher than that implied by exchange values. In India, for example, the authors' colleague recently returned from a trip during which he received a slight cut on his forehead from a taxi trunk lid. He decided to visit a doctor to get a tetanus shot and, because he knew that malaria was a hazard in India, a prescription and a one-month supply of malaria pills. He did this, and the bill from the doctor for the shot, the pills, and the prescription was 30 rupees or €1.

Age is another useful demographic variable. One global segment based on demographics is global teenagers – young people between the ages of 12 and 19.[10] Teens, by virtue of their interest in fashion, music and a youthful lifestyle, exhibit consumption behaviour that is remarkably consistent across borders. Young consumers may not yet have conformed to cultural norms, indeed, they may be rebelling against them. This fact, combined with shared universal needs, desires and fantasies (for name brands, novelty, entertainment, and trendy and image-oriented products), make it possible to reach the global teen segment with a unified marketing programme. This segment is attractive both in terms of its size (about 1.3 billion) and its multi billion dollar purchasing power. Coca-Cola, Benetton, Swatch and Sony are some of the companies pursuing the global teenage segment. The global telecommunications revolution is a critical driving force behind the emergence of this segment. Global media such as MTV are perfect vehicles for reaching this segment. Satellites such as AsiaSatI are beaming Western programming and commercials to millions of viewers in China, India and other countries.

However, targeting young people as a global segment needs to be handled with care. Grey International's survey 'Teens 2000' on Austrian youngsters between 15 and 19 draws a picture of differing lifestyles within this age group. They represent 8.2 per cent of Austria's total population and have about €1 billion of free spending money at their disposal. With regard to lifestyle and brand preferences, significant differences occurred in this age group. The so-called *Fun-Freaks* regard their clique more highly than their family, as they live very much in the present. Their leisure time is filled with trendy sports, action movies, horror and comedies. They choose brands such as Burton, Cannondale, Vision or Stüssy. The *Nonchalants* live according to the principle 'Hopefully, there will never be a war again, and I am allowed to go to the next concert by the Backstreet Boys'. Nike, Swatch and Chiemsee are found in their shopping baskets. *Outlaws* show the most extreme patterns. Permanently in search of innovations, desperately avoiding to be perceived as mainstream seems to be their credo. Small, trendy labels which change rapidly are preferred. The – in the view of their parents – classic teenagers perceive their parents as role models and preferably read comics. These *Playkids* like brands such as Sony, Adidas and Oilily.[11]

Another global segment is the so-called elite. These are older, more affluent consumers who are well travelled and have the money to spend on prestigious products with an image of exclusivity. This segment's needs and wants are spread over various product categories: durable goods (luxury automobiles), non-durables (upscale beverages such as rare wines and champagne), and financial services (American Express gold and platinum cards). Technological change in telecommunications makes it easier to reach the global elite segment. Global telemarketing is a viable option today as AT&T International 800 services are available in more than 40 countries. Increased reliance on catalogue marketing by upscale retailers such as Harrods, Laura Ashley and Ferragamo has also yielded impressive results.

In business-to-business marketing, demographic variables such as industry or firm size may be used for creating different customer segments. Using the computer industry as an example, it makes sense to distinguish customer segments according to industry, as different industries have different requirements for their computer systems. Banks or insurance companies have to handle large databases safely and reliably. In educational institutions, user friendliness and use by customers of different computer literacy are key features. Industry classification systems may serve as helpful tools in this context.

Ownership may also serve as a feasible criterion for market segmentation. The requirements of government institutions (tendering, legal requirements, etc.) differ considerable from privately or publicly held institutions. A large multinational doing business in medical imaging (e.g. x-rays, computed axial tomography (CAT) scan, magnetic resonance imaging (MRI)) decided to segment the market by the health care delivery system: national research and teaching hospitals, government hospitals, and so on. It then rolled out a campaign that was regional, national and finally global, which was tailored for each different type of health care delivery. This horizontal segmentation approach worked as well in markets outside the home-country launch market as it did in the home country.[12]

Firm size also represents a suitable way to segment customers. As a rule, smaller firms have different needs than larger ones. They require smaller volumes, have budgetary restrictions and use external expertise more often than larger firms.[13]

Psychographic segmentation

Psychographic segmentation groups customers based on their attitudes, values and lifestyle. The latter may be defined as the consumer behaviour which the target group displays, and the values and attitudes, which lead to this particular behaviour. Thus, lifestyle is always related to specific product categories. The consumers' lifestyles are measured through extensive item batteries which cover *activities*, *interests* and *opinions* (AIO studies). The lifestyle surveys by the Research Institute of Social Change (RISC), the Centre de Communication Avancé (CCA) and the Values and Life Styles (VALS) by SRI International are among the most well known.[14]

Porsche AG, the German sports-car maker, turned to psychographics after watching world-wide sales decline from 50,000 units in 1986 to about 14,000 in 1993. Its US subsidiary, Porsche Cars North America, already had a clear demographic profile of its customers: 40+-year-old male college graduates whose annual income exceeded €170,000. A psychographic study showed that, demographics aside, Porsche buyers could be divided into five distinct categories (see Table 7.1). *Top Guns*, for example, buy Porsches and expect to be noticed; for *Proud Patrons* and *Fantasists*, on the other hand, such conspicuous consumption is irrelevant. Porsche will use the profiles to develop advertising tailored to each type. Notes Richard Ford, Porsche vice president of sales and marketing, 'We were selling to people whose profiles were diametrically opposed. You wouldn't want to tell an elitist how good he looks in the car or how fast he could go.' Results have been promising. Porsche's US sales improved nearly 50 per cent in 1994.[15]

One early application of psychographics outside the United States focused on value orientations of consumers in the United Kingdom, France and Germany. Although the study was limited in scope, the researcher concluded that 'the underlying values structures in each country appeared to bear sufficient similarity to warrant a common overall communications strategy'.[16] SRI International has recently conducted psychographic analyses of the Japanese market. Broader-scope studies have been undertaken by several global advertising agencies, including Backer, Spielvogel and Bates Worldwide (BSB), D'arcy Massius Benton and Bowles (DMBB), and Young and Rubicam (Y&R).[17] These analyses offer a detailed understanding of various segments, including the global teenager and global elite discussed above.

Backer Spielvogel and Bates's Global Scan

Global Scan is a study that encompasses 18 countries, mostly located in the Triad. To identify attitudes that could help explain and predict purchase behaviour for different

Table 7.1 Psychographic profiles of Porsche's American customers

Category	% of all owners	Description
Top Guns	27%	Driven and ambitious; care about power and control; expect to be noticed
Elitists	24%	Old money; a car – even an expensive one – is just a car, not an extension of one's personality
Proud patrons	23%	Ownership is what counts; a car is a trophy, a reward for working hard; being noticed doesn't matter
Bon vivants	17%	Cosmopolitan jet setters and thrill seekers; car heightens excitement
Fantasists	9%	Car represents a form of escape; don't care about impressing others; may even feel guilty about owning car

product categories, the researchers studied consumer attitudes and values, as well as media viewership/readership, buying patterns and product use. The survey attempts to identify both country-specific and global attitudinal attributes. Sample statements are 'The harder you push, the farther you get', and 'I never have enough time or money'. Combining all the country data yielded a segmentation study known as *Target Scan*, a description of five global psychographic segments that BSB claims represent 95 per cent of the adult populations in the 18 countries surveyed (see Figure 7.2). BSB has labelled the segments as Strivers, Achievers, Pressured, Traditionals and Adapters.

- *Strivers* (26 per cent). This segment consists of young people with a median age of 31 who live hectic, on-the-go lives. Driven to achieve success, they are materialistic pleasure seekers for whom time and money are in short supply.
- *Achievers* (22 per cent). Older than the Strivers, the affluent, assertive Achievers, are upwardly mobile and already have attained a good measure of success. Achievers are status-conscious consumers for whom quality is important.
- *Pressured* (13 per cent). The Pressured segment, largely comprising women, cuts across age groups and is characterised by constant financial and family pressures. Life's problems overwhelm the members of this segment.
- *Adapters* (18 per cent). This segment is composed of older people who are content with their lives and who manage to maintain their values while keeping open minds when faced with change.
- *Traditionals* (16 per cent). This segment is 'rooted to the past' and clings to the country's heritage and cultural values.

Global Scan is a helpful tool for identifying consumer similarities across national boundaries, as well as highlighting differences between segments in different countries. For example, in the United States, the 75 million baby boomers help swell the ranks of Strivers and Achievers to nearly half the population. In Germany, on the other hand, the Striver segment is older and comprises a smaller proportion of the population. *Global Scan* has also pinpointed important differences between Americans and Canadians, who are often considered to be part of the same geographic segment of North America.

Figure 7.2 The target groups of BSB's Global Scan

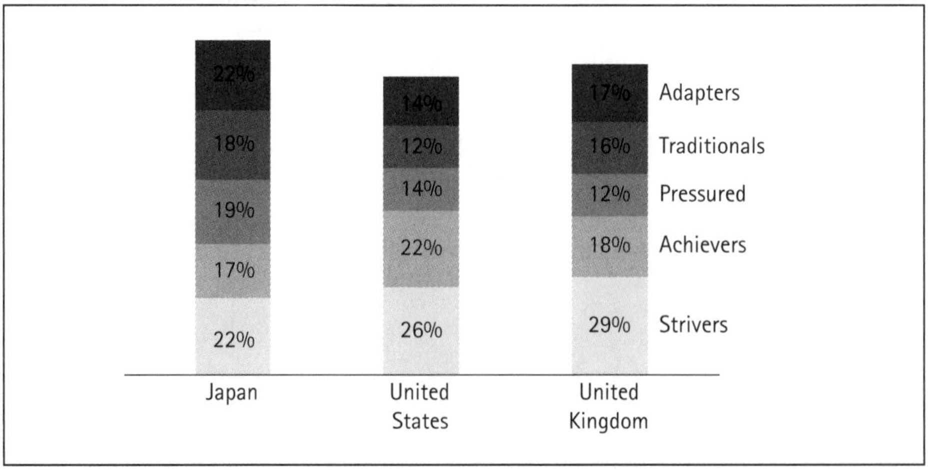

Similarly, *Global Scan* revealed marked differences between the circumstances in which Strivers find themselves in different countries. In the United States, Strivers are chronically short of both time and money, whereas Japanese Strivers have ample monetary resources. These differences translate directly into different preferences. US Strivers buy cars that are fun, stylish, and represent good value. Japanese Strivers view cars as an extension of their homes and will accessorise them with lavish features such as curtains and high-end stereo systems. This implies that different advertising appeals would be necessary when targeting Strivers in the two countries.

D'arcy Massius Benton & Bowles's Euroconsumer study

DMBB's research team focused on Europe and produced a 15-country study titled 'The Euroconsumer: Marketing myth or cultural certainty?' The researchers identified four lifestyle groups: Successful Idealists, Affluent Materialists, Comfortable Belongers and Disaffected Survivors. The first two groups represent the elite, the latter two, mainstream European consumers.

● *Successful idealists.* Comprising from 5 to 20 per cent of the population, this segment consists of persons who have achieved professional and material success while maintaining commitment to abstract or socially responsible ideals.
● *Affluent materialists.* These status-conscious 'up-and-comers', many of whom are business professionals, use conspicuous consumption to communicate their success to others.
● *Comfortable belongers.* Comprising one quarter to one half of a country's population, this group, like Global Scan's Adapters and Traditionals, is conservative and most comfortable with the familiar. Belongers are content with the comfort of home, family, friends and community.
● *Disaffected survivors.* Lacking power and affluence, this segment harbours little hope for upward mobility and tends to be either resentful or resigned. This segment is concentrated in high-crime urban inner city-type neighbourhoods. Despite Disaffected Survivors' lack of societal status, their attitudes nevertheless tend to affect the rest of society.

DMBB has also recently completed a psychographic profile of the Russian market. The study divides Russians into five categories, based on their outlook, behaviour and openness to Western products. The categories include Kuptsy, Cossacks, Students, Business Executives, and 'Russian Souls'. Members of the largest group, the Kuptsy (the label comes from the Russian word for 'merchant'), theoretically prefer Russian products but look down on mass-produced goods of inferior quality. Kuptsy are most likely to admire automobiles and stereo equipment from countries with good reputations for engineering, such as Germany and Scandinavia. Nigel Clarke, the author of the study, notes that segmentation and targeting are appropriate in Russia, despite the fact that its broad consumer market is still in its infancy. 'If you're dealing with a market as different as Russia is, even if you want to go "broad", it's best to think: "Which group would go most for my brand? Where is my natural centre of gravity?" '[18]

Young & Rubicam's Cross-Cultural Consumer Characterizations (4Cs)

Young & Rubicam's 4Cs is a 20-country psychographic segmentation study focusing on goals, motivations, and values that help to determine consumer choice. The research is based on the assumption that 'there are underlying psychological

217

processes involved in human behaviour that are culture-free and so basic that they can be found all over the globe.'[19]

Three overall groupings can be further subdivided into a total of seven segments: Constrained (Resigned Poor and Struggling Poor), Middle Majority (Mainstreamers, Aspirers and Succeeders), and Innovators (Transitionals and Reformers). The goals, motivations, and values of these segments range from 'survival', 'given up', and 'subsistence' (Resigned Poor) to 'social betterment', 'social conscience' and 'social altruism' (Reformers). Table 7.2 shows some of the attitudinal, work, lifestyle and purchase behaviour characteristics of the seven groups.

Combining the 4Cs data for a particular country with other data permits Y&R to predict product and category purchase behaviour for the various segments. Yet, as noted above in the discussion of *Global Scan*, marketers at global companies that are Y&R clients are cautioned not to assume that they can develop one strategy or one commercial to be used to reach a particular segment across cultures. As a Y&R staffer notes, 'As you get closer to the executional level, you need to be acutely sensitive to cultural differences. But at the origin, it's of enormous benefit to be able to think about people who share common values across cultures.'[20]

Eurostyles

The Eurostyles developed by the Centre de Comunication Avancé (CCA) represent a European, cross-national lifestyle typology. Since 1989, the Europanel Group carries out surveys in 15 European countries and gathers information on the following topics: demographic features of European consumers, current purchasing patterns, attitudes and motivations, moods and emotions. Based on this data pool, 16 types of consumers were identified, which are universal across borders. Figure 7.3 provides an

Table 7.2 Y&R'S 4CS

Attitudes	Work	Lifestyle	Purchase behaviour
Resigned Poor			
Unhappy	Labour	Shut-in	Staples
Distrustful	Unskilled	Television	Price
Struggling Poor			
Unhappy	Labour	Sports	Price
Dissatisfied	Craftsmen	Television	Discount stores
Mainstreamers			
Happy	Craftsmen	Family	Habit
Belong	Teaching	Gardening	Brand loyal
Aspirers			
Unhappy	Sales	Trendy sports	Conspicuous consumption
Ambitious	White collar	Fashion magazines	Credit
Succeeders			
Happy	Managerial	Travel	Luxury
Industrious	Professional	Dining out	Quality
Transitionals			
Rebellious	Student	Arts/crafts	Impulse
Liberal	Health field	Special interest magazines	Unique products
Reformers			
Inner growth	Professional	Reading	Ecology
Improve world	Entrepreneur	Cultural events	Home-made/grown

Figure 7.3 Europanel's Eurostyles

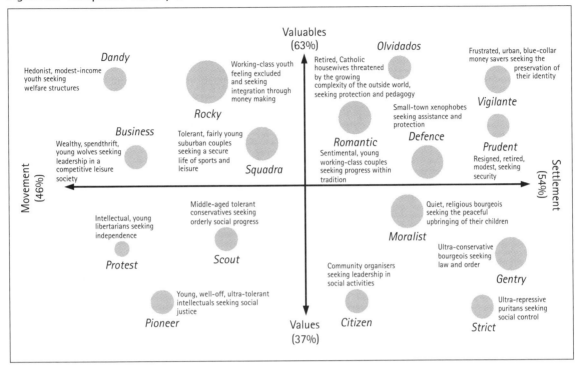

* The percentages in brackets indicate the share of this type compared to the European total population.
Source: Adapted from Josef Mazanec, 'Exporting Eurostyles to the USA', *International Journal of Contemporary Hospitality Management*, 5,4 (1993): p. 4.

overview of the 16 Eurostyle-types on the dimensions values and valuables, movement and settlement. The dimension 'settlement' encompasses values such as maintaining one's own position and social status, clinging to tradition and habits. In contrast, 'movement' covers values such as dynamism, criticism, scepticism towards authorities and law. The dimension 'valuables' is oriented towards material values on one end, and immaterial values on the other end.[21]

The size of the different segments varies across countries. The most widespread type are the Rocky (13.5 per cent), the Defence (8.5 per cent) and the Romantic (7.8 per cent). Rockies are found particularly in countries such as the Netherlands, Great Britain, France and Switzerland. In contrast, Moralists and Romantics dominate in Germany, Austria, Belgium and Switzerland.

In business-to-business marketing, psychographic variables are used for segmenting as well. They are particularly relevant, when it comes to personal features of employees involved in the decision-making process and the composition and co-ordination within the buying centre.[22]

Behaviour segmentation

Behaviour segmentation focuses on whether people buy and use a product, as well as how often and how much they use it. Consumers can be categorised in terms of usage rates for example, heavy, medium, light and nonuser. Consumers can also be segmented according to user status: potential users, nonusers, ex-users, regulars,

GLOBAL PERSPECTIVE

Going global – how market research firms follow their customers

Not only manufacturers of goods and services focus on the question how to address customers worldwide. Also, companies who supply the information necessary to take these decisions follow their example. As lifestyles and other buyer-related information turned out to be critical for targeted marketing activities, many manufacturers do not want to live without this information on their international markets.

For that reason, market research firms are identifying new markets for their services so that the battle over lucrative markets is meanwhile in full swing. Names such as Experian, Claritas or CACI which are familiar to American consumers, receive an indifferent shrug from their European counterparts. But these times will soon be over. The market research company Experian has selected the Australian market as a foreign market to target first. A database covering lifestyle and purchasing patterns of more than 3.5 million Australian consumers was already established. It is assumed that Australia will provide further insights into other markets in the Pacific Rim area.

The European market is another high potential for lifestyle data. Claritas, whose product Prizm is widely used in the US, has now established databases in countries such as France, the Netherlands, Switzerland and Sweden. Italy and Spain will be next. Experian offers consumer-related information in France, Germany, Greece and Denmark, to name a few. Equifax Europe has launched its product MicroVision in Spain, where 38 million consumers may be separated into 11 main and 32 sub-categories with respect to their lifestyle. These types reach from 'entrepreneurial elite' to 'small agrarians' (a type which does not exist in the UK, but which is very common in France and Southern Europe). The British subsidiary of US-based CACI (which has developed the most frequently cited lifestyle typology Acorn; for further detail see http://www.demographics.caci.com/Databases/ACORN.html) offers a similar service with its 'Lifestyles UK'. Forty-four million consumers can be grouped into segments using 300 lifestyle variables. Among these variables are features such as number of credit cards, travel and leisure patterns, use of computer games and calling habits.

However, entering European markets is not all that easy. One of the key obstacles are restrictive regulations concerning data protection. An issue of particular debate is the written consent of consumers that their personal data may be processed for commercial use. Additionally, the way the data are processed raised concern among Europe's legal experts. In order to handle the enormous data volumes efficiently, questionnaires are usually processed in low-wage countries such as the Philippines. For confidentiality reasons, European consumer protection agencies are anything but happy with this procedure. In case their opinion prevails, market research firms will have to deal with a considerable increase in their cost structure.

An approach which is becoming more and more popular is to combine lifestyle-related data with geographic information on the consumer. This combination offers a wide spectrum of direct marketing applications. In the Netherlands, Experian set up a data base of publicly available data such as car ownership and other consumption statistics and combined it with lifestyle data and purchasing patterns. Additionally, this information was linked to 280,000 postal codes. On average, 16 households are summed up under one postal code.

Yet things don't get easier! The postal code system is not differentiated in all European countries. While in the UK 1.6 million postal codes are available for categorising, France only has 3,000. In addition, the existence of publicly accessible data may raise problems. In Germany, consumption data is provided only every 10 years within the micro census. As the micro census relies on the competence of the *Länder*, this leads to a situation where data requested and collection methods are far from being uniform across the states. Market research companies see themselves confronted with the fact that they have to collect their own data, which can be quite costly.

GLOBAL PERSPECTIVE continued

However, government institutions also see their time coming. In order to participate in the lucrative market of providing consumer data, the Swedish Statistical Bureau decided to sell information directly to corporate customers. As a result, the CACI decided to withdraw from the Swedish market. The additional competition and the small market potential of Sweden's 9 million inhabitants would not justify investments.

Food for thought

- Is it more difficult for service companies than for manufacturing companies to internationalise their activities? Argue your point with reference to Experian.
- Why is lifestyle data, on its own or in combination with other information such as consumption or geographic patterns, so important to consumer goods companies?

Source: David Reed, 'LifestyleData: desperately seeking a lifestyle data currency', *Precision Marketing*, 20 October 1997. http://www.experian.com/, http://www.wigeogis.at/, http://www.caci.co.uk/

first-timers, and users of competitors' products. Campbell Soup Company has targeted China for the simple reason that the Chinese have the highest per capita consumption of soup in the world.[23] Similarly, the tobacco companies are targeting China because the Chinese are heavy smokers.

In 1993, Tambrands Inc., marketers of Tampax brand tampons, launched a €17 million global advertising effort in North America, Eastern and Western Europe, Latin America and the Pacific Rim. The campaign had two strategic purposes directly related to usage rates and user status. One ad was designed to show women new times and ways to use tampons. It included advice from gynaecologists that tampons can safely be worn overnight, a creative appeal reflecting research showing that two thirds of tampon users do not use them at night. Other creative executions featured stylish women who scoff at sanitary pads – which Tambrands does not make. This message may be particularly effective in reaching nonusers in overseas markets, where tampon use is not as high as in the United States.[24]

Telecommunication companies also use behaviour segmentation to group their customers. Routinely, they collect a huge amount of data such as number and length of telephone calls, amount of calls at different day times, payment patterns and lifestyle indicators. This potential remained unused for a long time, until the idea come up to filter out different needs of different customer groups. While up to then customers were usually divided into business and private customers, the information analysed now allows much more specific distinctions. This results in better service, new products, tailored tariff systems and, in the end, a closer customer relationship. Data mining experts such as Olivier Suard, consultant at Kenan Systems, try to calm down concerned consumer protection activists. In his statement he stresses the importance of aggregate data for marketing activities: 'it helps to know that, for example, owners of mobile phones under the age of 25 like to use their integrated voice-mail box a lot. But I am not sure that anyone is interested who Fred Smith called yesterday – particularly if you consider the cost necessary to retrieve this information.'[25]

Benefit segmentation

Global benefit segmentation focuses on the numerator of the value equation – the 'B' in $V = B/P$. As today their basic needs are satisfied, consumers want to achieve higher goals with their consumption and thus expect additional value from their decisions. The Swedish car manufacturer Volvo covers a car's basic benefit with its products – movement. Yet movement is not the only benefit which consumers can draw from their Volvo. Volvo addresses the target group of consumers who see a top priority in their family's and their personal safety. Customers who look for superior engine power and status may tend more towards a BMW, for example. The issue of benefit segmentation becomes difficult, when benefit attributes, which at an earlier stage lead to a unique product offer, turn into standard features. Volvo encountered this difficult situation in the US, where sales sagged. The same applies to Apple Computers, whose computers stood out for their user friendliness. They

 EUROPEAN FOCUS

Segmenting and targeting à la Viennoise!

Not only marketing departments think about how to define target groups and to position the company's product in the competitive environment. In Vienna's coffee shops, this has been a hot issue since the 17th century.

It all started on 12 August 1683, when Georg Franz Kolschitzky was honoured for his services as a messenger during the Turkish siege of Vienna. As a reward, he asked for two bags of coffee beans and the permission to roast them and serve them as hot coffee to Viennese customers. For generations, waiters and waitresses have been training the art of targeting and positioning their products and service. As a result, over the centuries extensive knowledge was developed and passed on: demographic variables, customer motives, benefits expected and usage patterns. The following gives a typology of Viennese coffee shop customers.

The *Hesitant*: his/her behaviour is characterised by extensive pondering and discussions with regard to their consumption. Usually, the hesitant comes alone or in twos. The order is hardly audible. For a waiter a true challenge! To satisfy the customer, a lot of information has to be implied. So mistakes are likely to occur. If the hesitant gets a mélange (coffee with milk and milk foam) instead of the – whispered – Einspänner (black coffee with a bonnet of whipped cream), the 'manufacturer' will not be confronted with rage, but with a more subtle sanction – a smaller tip.

The *Garrulous Gourmet*: at first sight he/she appears easygoing – happy with all and everything! However, this overall happiness wants to be shared. A clever waiter will approach such a customer with empathy. To safeguard the customer's happiness, the menu is discussed extensively. Orders placed are changed and adapted various times. In the end, this guest is enchanted with the perfect service and rewards it – with a considerable tip and continued visits.

The *Gentleman*: in this case, the waiter deals with a pro. Courtesy, prompt service and good product quality are an absolute must. The perfect waiter satisfies the guest's needs and wants speedily and quietly.

Marketing experts will identify many more target groups. A field trip to Vienna and its coffee shops would certainly pay off!

PS: The typology described is applicable to male as well as female coffee shop guests. Since Jovanni Milan opened his coffee shop to women at the end of the 18th century, equal rights are not an issue!

Food for thought

- Draw up a similar typology for customers of Irish pubs. What are the similarities and differences compared to the typology of Viennese coffee shop customers?
- Which steps are involved in developing buyer typologies based on empirical data? Compile a list of tasks required.

Source: Hildegard Heczko, 'Die Gunst des Kellners', *Der Standard*, 13/14 March 1999, p. A16. http://www.tourist-net.co.at/coffee/coffee3.htm.

saw themselves confronted with Microsoft's products promising exactly the same benefit.

Increasingly, consumers buy branded products to achieve a variety of objectives. The reason lies in the different, often conflicting roles and role expectations that consumers have to comply with today. Harley-Davidson decided to segment its market based on benefits expected. In order to achieve their job goals, managers have to comply with the expectation of being target-oriented conformists. So, during the working week they hide their quest for individuality and freedom. At weekends they can finally unleash their neglected individuality and rebellious spirit by taking a ride on their Harley. For this reason, this target group is sometimes also called 'Rolex Riders'. This key benefit is also reflected in communication activities. To complete the temporary change from a button-down shirt to a Hell's Angel, Harley-Davidson offers accessories such as temporary tattoos and riveted leather jackets. Similarly, manufacturers of SUVs (sports utility vehicles) such as Rover or Chrysler segment their markets.[26]

This approach can achieve excellent results by virtue of marketers' superior understanding of the problem a product solves or the benefit it offers, regardless of geography. For example, Nestlé discovered that cat owners' attitudes toward feeding their pets are the same everywhere. In response, a pan-European campaign was created for Friskies dry cat food. The appeal was that dry cat food better suits a cat's universally recognised independent nature.

Key points

- Market segmentation is the process of subdividing a market into distinct subsets of customers that behave in the same way or have similar needs.

- As in the national context, there are different approaches in international market segmentation.

- When using geographic segmentation, different countries are clustered into target groups according to their geographic closeness or distance.

- Demographic segmentation is based on the quantitative features of a population such as age, gender, income, education or profession. In business-to-business marketing, customers are segmented according to firm size, industry or ownership structure.

- Psychographic segmentation groups consumers based on their attitudes, values and lifestyles.

- When the behaviour segmentation approach is applied, consumers who use a product in the same way or intensity comprise one target group.

- Benefit segmentation is based on the fact that customers in a target group are most likely related in the expectations they have from the product.

GLOBAL TARGETING

As discussed earlier, segmenting is the process by which marketers identify groups of consumers with similar wants and needs. Targeting is the act of evaluating and comparing the identified groups and then selecting one or more of them as the prospect(s) with the highest potential. A marketing mix is then devised that will provide the organisation with the best return on sales while simultaneously creating the maximum amount of value to consumers.

Criteria for targeting

The three basic criteria for assessing opportunity in global target markets are the same as in single-country targeting: current size of the segment and anticipated growth potential; competition; and compatibility with the company's overall objectives and the feasibility of successfully reaching a designated target.

Current segment size and growth potential

The question arises, whether the market segment targeted currently will be large enough that it presents a company with the opportunity to make a profit. If it is not large enough or profitable enough today, it might have high growth potential in the future so that it is attractive in terms of a company's long-term strategy. Indeed, one of the advantages of targeting a market segment globally is that, whereas the segment in a single-country market might be too small, even a narrow segment can be served profitably with a standardised product if the segment exists in several countries.[27] The billion-plus members of the global 'MTV Generation' constitute a huge market that, by virtue of its size, is extremely attractive to many companies.

China represents an individual geographic market that offers attractive opportunities in many industries. Consider the growth opportunity in financial services, for example. There are currently only about three million credit cards in circulation, mostly used by businesses. Low product saturation levels are also found for personal computers; there is one computer for every 6,000 people. The ratio in the United States is one computer for every four people. The opportunity for automobile manufacturers is even greater. China has 1.2 million passenger cars, one car for every 20,000 Chinese. Only 60,000 of those cars are owned by private citizens.

The sports utility vehicle (SUV) segment of the US auto market is a textbook example of a growth segment. SUV sales grew by nearly 35 per cent between 1990 and 1994; by the end of 1997, American families bought more SUVs, minivans and pick-ups than cars. This was the first time that these vehicles have surpassed cars in sales since a brief period at the end of the Second World War when cars were not available. One industry expert predicted that light trucks would represent 55 per cent of family vehicle sales by 2002. In addition to the Big Three US car manufacturers, competitors from Japan, Europe, Korea and even China are entering the market. The SUV segment is growing outside the United States as well; Chrysler builds a right-hand drive Jeep Cherokee for the Japanese market. In 1994, Chrysler sold 10,000 Cherokees in Japan, more than double the number in 1993.[28]

Competitive intensity and potential competition

A market or market segment characterised by strong competition may be a segment to avoid. However, Kodak's position as the undisputed leader in the €2 billion colour film market did not deter Fuji from launching a competitive offensive. In addition to offering traditional types of 35mm film at prices below Kodak's, Fuji quickly made inroads by introducing a number of new film products targeted at the 'advanced amateur' segment that Kodak had neglected. Despite its early successes, after nearly two decades of effort, Fuji's US market share has been in the 10 to 16 per cent range. Part of the problem is Kodak's distribution clout: Kodak is well entrenched in supermarket and drugstore chains, where Fuji must also jostle with other newcomers such as Konica and Polaroid. In addition, Kodak has agreements with dozens of American amusement parks guaranteeing that only Kodak film will be sold on the premises. Fuji is also developing its market in Europe, where Kodak commands 'only' 40 per cent of the colour film market. Fuji currently enjoys 25 per cent of the European market, compared with 10 per cent a decade ago. Meanwhile, Kodak has spent half a billion dollars in Japan, the world's second-largest market for photographic supplies; its market share there currently stands at about 10 per cent.[29]

Compatibility and feasibility

If a global target market is judged to be large enough, and if strong competitors are either absent or not deemed to represent insurmountable obstacles, then the final consideration is whether a company can and should target that market. In many cases, reaching global market segments requires considerable resources such as expenditures for distribution and travel by company personnel. Another question is whether the pursuit of a particular segment is compatible with the company's overall goals and established sources of competitive advantage. Although Pepsi was firmly entrenched in the Russian market, having entered in 1972, Coke waited 15 years to make its first move in Russia and 20 years before it decided to make major investments. At the time of Coke's entry, Pepsi had 100 per cent of the Russian cola market. This would appear to be a difficult position to challenge, but because of the size of the Coke investment and the skilful execution of its investment moves in Russia, by 1996 Coke's market share had reached 50 per cent.[30]

Selecting a global target market strategy

If, after evaluating the identified segments in terms of the three criteria presented above, a decision is made to proceed, an appropriate targeting strategy must be developed. There are three basic categories of target marketing strategies: standardised marketing, concentrated marketing, and differentiated marketing.

Standardised global marketing

Standardised global marketing is analogous to mass marketing in a single country. It involves creating the same marketing mix for a broad market of potential buyers. This strategy calls for extensive distribution in the maximum number of retail outlets. The appeal of standardised global marketing is clear: greater sales volume, lower production costs, and greater profitability. The same is true of standardised global communications: lower production costs and, if done well, higher quality and greater effectiveness of marketing communications.

Executives at Revlon International recently adopted a standardised strategy when they announced their intention of making Revlon a global name. President Paul Block declared, 'All Revlon North American advertising for all products, whether they are cosmetics, skincare, hair care, or Almay, will now be used world-wide.'[31] The global theme is keyed to a 'Shake Your Body' campaign. Revlon's strategy calls for developing the huge consumer markets emerging in Central and Eastern Europe, including Hungary and the former Soviet republics.

Concentrated global marketing

The second global targeting strategy involves devising a marketing mix to reach a single segment of the global market. In cosmetics, this approach has been used successfully by House of Lauder, Chanel and other cosmetics houses that target the upscale, prestige segment of the market. This is the strategy employed by the hidden champions of global marketing: companies that most people have never heard of that have adopted strategies of concentrated marketing on a global scale. These companies define their markets narrowly. They go for global depth rather than national breadth.

GLOBAL PERSPECTIVE

Targeting adventure seekers with an American classic

Over the past decade, savvy export marketing has enabled Harley-Davidson to dramatically increase world-wide sales of its heavyweight motorcycles. Export sales increased from 3,000 motorcycles in 1983 to 15,000 units for the 1990 model year. By 1996, non-US sales exceeded €340 million, up from €100 million in 1989. From Australia to Germany to Mexico City, Harley enthusiasts are paying the equivalent of up to €22,000 to own an American-built classic. In many countries, dealers must put would-be buyers on a six-month waiting list because of high demand.

Harley's international success comes after years of neglecting overseas markets. Early on, the company was basically involved in export selling, symbolised by its underdeveloped dealer network. Moreover, print advertising simply used word-for-word translations of the US ads. By the late 1980s, after recruiting dealers in the important Japanese and European markets, company executives discovered a basic principle of global marketing. 'As the saying goes, we needed to think global but act local,' said Jerry G. Wilke, vice president for world-wide marketing. Harley began to adapt its international marketing, making it more responsive to local conditions.

In Japan, for example, Harley's rugged image and high quality helped make it the best-selling imported motorcycle. Still, Toshifumi Okui, president of Harley's Japanese division, was not satisfied. He worried that the tag line from the US ads, 'One steady constant in an increasingly screwed-up world', did not connect with Japanese riders. Okui finally convinced Milwaukee to allow him to launch a Japan-only advertising campaign, juxtaposing images from both Japan and America, such as American cyclists passing a rickshaw carrying a geisha. After learning that riders in Tokyo consider fashion and customised bikes to be essential, Harley opened two stores specialising in clothes and bike accessories.

Harley discovered that in Europe an 'evening out' means something different than it does in America. The company sponsored a rally in France, where beer and live rock music were available until midnight. Recalls Wilke, 'People asked us why we were ending the rally just as the evening was starting. So I had to go persuade the band to keep playing and reopen the bar until 3 or 4 a.m.' Still, rallies are less common in Europe than in the United States, so Harley encourages its dealers to hold open houses at their dealerships.

While biking through Europe, Wilke also learned that German bikers often travel at speeds exceeding 100 miles per hour. Now, the company is investigating design changes to create a smoother ride at autobahn speeds. Harley's German marketing effort may also begin focusing on accessories to increase rider protection. Despite high levels of demand, the company intentionally limits production increases in order to uphold Harley's recent improvements in quality and to keep the product supply limited in relation to demand. Harley is still careful to make home-country customers a higher priority than those living abroad; thus, only 30 per cent of its production goes outside the United States. The Harley shortage seems to suit company executives just fine. Notes Harley's James H. Patterson, 'Enough motorcycles is too many motorcycles.'

Food for thought

- How important is it for Harley-Davidson to manufacture the motorcycles in the US? How should HQ in Milwaukee respond to a Japanese suggestion to build the motorbikes in Asia?
- Which management challenges arise for Harley-Davidson from the need to offer clothes and bike accessories in Japan?

Source: Kevin Kelly and Karen Lowry Miller, 'The rumble heard round the world: Harleys', *Business Week*, 24 May 1993, pp. 58, 60. Robert L. Rose, 'Vrooming back: After nearly stalling, Harley-Davidson finds new crowd of riders', *Wall Street Journal*, 31 August 1991, pp. A1, A6. John Holusha, 'How Harley outfoxed Japan with exports', *New York Times*, 12 August 1990, p. F5. Robert C. Reid, 'How Harley beat back the Japanese', *Fortune*, 25 September 1989, p. 155 ff. Harley-Davidson 1996 Annual Report.

For example, Winterhalter (a German company) is a hidden champion in the dishwasher market, but the company has never sold a dishwasher to a consumer. It has also never sold a dishwasher to a hospital, school, company or any other organisation. It focuses exclusively on dishwashers for hotels and restaurants. It offers dishwashers, water conditioners, detergents and service. Jüergen Winterhalter commented in reference to the company's narrow market definition: 'This narrowing of our market definition was the most important strategic decision we ever made. It is the very foundation of our success in the past decade.'[32]

Differentiated global marketing

The third target marketing strategy is a variation of concentrated global marketing. It entails targeting two or more distinct market segments with different marketing mixes. This strategy allows a company to achieve wider market coverage. For example, in the SUV segment described earlier, Rover has a €42,500+ Range Rover at the high end of the market and a scaled-down version, the Land Rover Discoverer, is priced at under €30,000 which competes directly with the Jeep Grand Cherokee. These are two different segments, and Rover has a concentrated strategy for each.

One of the world masters of differentiated global marketing is SMH, the Swiss Watch Company. SMH offers watches ranging from the Swatch fashion accessory watch at €43 world-wide to the €85,000+ Blancpain. Although the research and development (R&D) and manufacturing at SMH are integrated and serve the entire product line, each SMH brand is managed by a completely separate organisation that targets a concentrated, narrow segment in the global market.

In the cosmetics industry, Unilever NV and Cosmair Inc. pursue differentiated global marketing strategies by targeting both ends of the perfume market. Unilever targets the luxury market with Calvin Klein and Elizabeth Taylor's Passion; Wind Song and Brut are its mass-market brands. Cosmair sells Trésor and Giorgio Armani Gió to the upper end of the market and Gloria Vanderbilt to the lower end. Mass marketer Procter & Gamble (P&G), known for its Old Spice and Incognito brands, also embarked on this strategy with its 1991 acquisition of Revlon's EuroCos, marketers of Hugo Boss for men and Laura Biagiotti's Roma perfume. Now, P&G is launching a new prestige fragrance, Venezia, in the United States and nine European countries.[33]

Key points

- After defining potential global target groups, a company needs to decide which target group(s) specifically shall be chosen for future marketing activities.

- As in the national context, the following selection criteria apply: actual size and potential growth of the market segment, competitive intensity and new potential competitors, compatibility and feasibility with respect to the corporate objectives and resources.

- When the most attractive segments are chosen, the question of the most suitable marketing strategy arises.

- In case a firm follows a standardised, global marketing strategy, this implies that a world-wide standardised marketing mix is applied to all target groups.

- Under a differentiated marketing strategy, a marketing mix specific to each of the global target groups is developed.

- A concentrated marketing strategy means focusing the marketing mix on a single global market segment.

GLOBAL PRODUCT POSITIONING

Positioning is the location of your product in the mind of your customer. Thus, one of the most powerful tools of marketing is not something that a marketer can do to the product or to any element of the marketing mix: Positioning is what happens in the mind of the customer. The position that a product occupies in the mind of a customer depends on a host of variables, many of which are controlled by the marketer.

To graphically reproduce the mental map of consumers, a two-dimensional diagram appears helpful. Customers place the main products on the market within this diagram to the extent of how these products fit their key demands. The following example (see Figure 7.4) shows the positioning map of US fast food restaurants. The dimensions which were considered relevant for a purchasing decision were the number of locations and cleanliness.[34]

After the global market has been segmented and one or more segments have been targeted, it is essential to plan a way to reach the target(s). To achieve this task, marketers use positioning. In today's global market environment, many companies find it increasingly important to have a unified global positioning strategy. For example, Chase Manhattan Bank launched a €64 million global advertising campaign geared to the theme 'profit from experience'. According to Aubrey Hawes, a vice president and corporate director of marketing for the bank, Chase's business and private banking clients 'span the globe and travel the globe. They can only know one Chase in their minds, so why should we try to confuse them?'

Figure 7.4 Positioning map of American fast-food restaurants in the mind of consumers

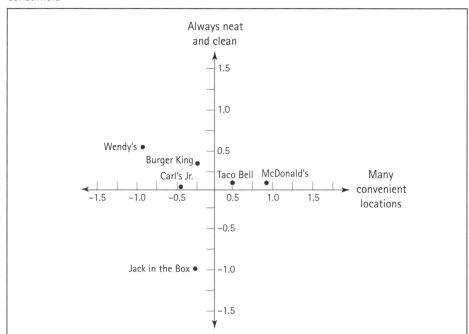

Source: adapted from James H. Myers, *Segmentation and Positioning for Strategic Marketing Decisions* (Chicago: American Marketing Association, 1996).

The question comes up whether global positioning works for all products. One study suggests that global positioning is most effective for product categories that approach either end of a 'high-touch/high-tech' continuum.[35] Both ends of the continuum are characterised by high levels of customer involvement and by a shared 'language' among consumers.

High-tech positioning

Personal computers, video and stereo equipment, and automobiles are examples of product categories in which high-tech positioning has proven effective. Such products are frequently purchased on the basis of concrete product features, although image may also be important. Buyers typically already possess or wish to acquire considerable technical information. High-tech products may be divided into three categories: technical products, special-interest products, and demonstrable products.

- *Technical products*: Computers, chemicals, tyres and financial services are just a sample of the product categories whose buyers have specialised needs, require a great deal of product information, and share a common 'language'. Computer buyers in Russia and the United States are equally knowledgeable about '486 microprocessors, 80-meg hard drives, and 8 meg of RAM (random access memory)'. Marketing communications for high-tech products should be informative and emphasise features.
- *Special-interest products*: Although less technical and more leisure or recreation oriented, special-interest products are also characterised by a shared experience and high involvement among users. Again, the common language and symbols associated with such products can transcend language and cultural barriers. Fuji bicycles, Adidas sports equipment, and Canon cameras are examples of successful global special-interest products.
- *Products that demonstrate well*: Products that 'speak for themselves' in advertising of features and benefits can also travel well. The Polaroid instant camera is an example of a highly demonstrable and very successful global product.

High-touch positioning

Marketing of high-touch products requires less emphasis on specialised information and more emphasis on image. Like high-tech products, however, high-touch categories are highly involving for consumers. Buyers of high-touch products also share a common language and set of symbols relating to themes of wealth, materialism and romance. The three categories of high-touch products are products that solve a common problem, global village products, and products with a universal theme.

- *Products that solve a common problem*: At the other end of the price spectrum from high-tech, products in this category provide benefits linked to 'life's little moments'. Ads that show friends talking over a cup of coffee in a café or quenching thirst with a soft drink during a day at the beach put the product at the centre of everyday life and communicate the benefit offered in a way that is understood world-wide.
- *Global village products*: Chanel fragrances, designer fashions, mineral water and pizza are all examples of products whose positioning is strongly cosmopolitan in nature. Fragrances and fashions have travelled as a result of growing world-wide

interest in high-quality, highly visible, high-priced products that often enhance social status. However, the lower-priced food products just mentioned show that the global village category encompasses a broad price spectrum.

In global markets, products may have a global appeal by virtue of their country of origin. The 'American-ness' of Levis, Marlboro and Harley-Davidson enhances their appeal to cosmopolitans around the world. In consumer electronics, Sony is a name synonymous with vaunted Japanese quality; in automobiles, Mercedes is the embodiment of legendary German engineering.

- *Products that use universal themes*: As noted earlier, some advertising themes and product appeals are thought to be basic enough that they are truly transnational. Additional themes are materialism (keyed to images of well-being or status), heroism (themes include rugged individuals or self-sacrifice), play (leisure/recreation), and procreation (images of courtship and romance).

It should be noted that some products can be positioned in more than one way, within either the high-tech or high-touch poles of the continuum. A sophisticated camera, for example, could simultaneously be classified as technical and special interest. Other products may be positioned in a bipolar fashion, that is, as both high-tech and high-touch. For example, Bang & Olufsen consumer electronics, by virtue of their design elegance, are perceived as both high-tech and high-touch.

Key points

- **Positioning describes the process of anchoring a product or product range in the customer's mental map. When companies are globally active, the question arises whether they can take advantage of a globally uniform product positioning strategy. This is the case for products which may be found at either end of the so-called high-tech/high-touch continuum.**

- **While the positioning of high-tech products requires an emphasis on technical features, high-touch products are primarily positioned based on their image.**

- **Both product categories are characterised by the high involvement of their consumers and a common 'shared' language.**

Summary

The global environment must be analysed before a company pursues expansion into new geographic markets. Through global market segmentation, the similarities and differences of potential buying customers can be identified and grouped. Demographics, psychographics, behavioural characteristics, and benefits sought are common attributes used to segment world markets. After marketers have identified segments, the next step is targeting. The identified groups are evaluated and compared; the prospect(s) with the greatest potential is selected from them. The groups are evaluated on the basis of several factors: segment size and growth potential, competition, and compatibility and feasibility. After evaluating the identified segments, marketers must decide on an appropriate targeting strategy. The three basic categories of global target marketing strategies are standardised marketing, concentrated marketing and differentiated marketing. Finally, companies must plan a way to reach their chosen target market(s) by determining the best positioning for their product offerings. Here, marketers devise an appropriate marketing mix to fix the product in the mind of the potential buyers in the target market. High-tech and high-touch positioning are two strategies that can work well for a global product.

Concepts and definitions

Global market segmentation	Describes the division of a global market into market segments, also called target markets or target segments. Each of these market segments may be attracted by a specifically designed marketing mix to optimally suit the needs and wants of this segment.
Segmentation approaches	There are different approaches to market segmentation: geographic segmentation describes an approach whereby markets in the same geographic region are pulled together to one market segment. Demographic segmentation uses demographic variables such as age or income to classify customers. Using a psychographic approach, customers are categorised based on their attitudes, values and lifestyle. Behaviour segmentation forms market segments based on the usage behaviour of the consumer. Benefit segmentation uses different customer expectations as to the benefit of a product to form different market segments.
Criteria for selecting global target groups	The selection of which market segments will be targeted may be based on the following criteria: actual and potential size of the segment, competitive intensity and potential competitors and compatibility and feasibility with the company's resources and objectives.
Global target market strategies	There are three basic categories of target marketing strategies: (i) standardised global marketing, which applies the same marketing mix to all target groups; (ii) differentiated global marketing in which marketing strategies are customised to the different target groups; and (iii) concentrated global marketing, which focuses on a single, global market segment.
Global product positioning	Positioning is the location of a product in the consumer's mind. Whether a global product positioning strategy is suitable depends on the product category the product belongs to. Global positioning is most effective for product categories that approach either end of a 'high tech/high touch' continuum. Both ends of the continuum are characterised by high levels of customer involvement and by a shared 'language' among consumers.
High-tech positioning	Technical products such as computers or chemicals, special-interest products such as sporting goods, and products that can be demonstrated easily (e.g. polaroid cameras) are particularly suited for global positioning. These products are often purchased on the basis of concrete product features. Buyers typically already possess or wish to acquire considerable technical information.
High-touch positioning	In the case of high-touch products, the emphasis lies more on the product's image, while specialised information appears of minor relevance. High-touch products comprise products that solve a common problem (e.g., soft drinks), global village products such as cosmetics or fashion and products that use universal themes.

Discussion questions

1 What is a global market segment? Pick a market that you know something about, and describe the global segments for this market.

2 Identify the major geographic and demographic segments in global markets.

3 Gillette has recently introduced its new Mach III shaving system. Describe the global strategy that Gillette has adopted for Mach III.

4 Nissan has launched a new model in Europe with the advertising message that the car has been designed and manufactured in Japan and road tested and refined to meet the demanding needs of American markets. How would you describe the positioning of this new model in Europe?

Webmistress's hotspots

Homepage of Volkswagen
Here you find an overview of VW's TV spots, which are currently broadcast on the New Beetle and other VW cars.
http://www3.vw.com/vwworld/museum.htm

Homepage of Georgia Tech
For 10 years, the Graphic, Visualization and Usability Center at Georgia Tech University has been carrying out Internet-based surveys on internet usage patterns. Here you find a profile of the typical Internet user.
http://www.cc.gatech.edu/gvu/user surveys/

Homepage of the market research company SRI International
Here you can find which different VALS types can be distinguished and how they can be profiled.
http://future.sri.com/vals/valsindex.html

Homepage of Claritas
At this site, you find company examples of how lifestyle databases from Claritas are used for marketing activities.
http://www.claritas.co.uk/v4/index.htm

Suggested reading

Alster, Judith and Holly Gallo, 'Corporate strategies for global competitive advantage', Reader's Digest Association Conference Board, Working Papers no. 996, 1992.

Cavusgil, S. Tamer, 'Knowledge development in international marketing', *Journal of International Marketing*, 6, 2 (1998): pp.103–112.

Garland, Barbara C. and Marti J. Rhea, 'American consumers: profile of an import preference segment', *Akron Business and Economic Review*, 19, 2 (1988): pp. 20–29.

Green, Paul E. and Abba M. Krieger, 'Segmenting markets with conjoint analysis', *Journal of Marketing*, 55, 4 (October 1991): pp. 20–31.

Hassan, Salah S. and Roger D. Blackwell, *Global Marketing*. Orlando, FL: The Dryden Press, 1994.

Hout, Thomas, Michael E. Porter and Eeleen Rudden, 'How global companies win out', *Harvard Business Review* (September/October 1982): pp. 98–108.

Miles, Gregory L., 'Think global, go intermodal', *International Business* (March 1993): pp. 61 ff.

Morwitz, Vicki G. and David Schmittlein, 'Using segmentation to improve sales forecasts based on purchase intent: Which 'intenders' actually buy?', *Journal of*

Marketing Research, 29, 4 (November 1992): pp. 391–405.

Piirto, Rebecca, *Beyond Mind Games: The Marketing Power of Psychographics*. Ithaca, NY: American Demographics Books, 1991.

Prokesch, S.E., 'Competing on customer service: An interview with British Airways' Sir Colin Marshall', *Harvard Business Review* (November/December 1995): pp. 100–116.

Raju, P.S., 'Consumer behavior in global markets: The A-B-C-D paradigm and its application to Eastern Europe and the Third World', *Journal of Consumer Marketing*, 12, 5 (1995): pp. 37–56.

Simon, Herman, *Hidden Champions: Lessons from 500 of the World's Best Unknown Companies*. Boston, MA: Harvard Business School Press, 1996.

Sonnenberg, Frank K., *Marketing to Win: Strategies for Building Competitive Advantage in Service Industries*. New York: HarperBusiness, 1990.

Taylor, William, 'Message and muscle: an interview with Swatch Titan Nicolas Hayek', *Harvard Business Review*, 71 (March–April 1993): pp. 99–110.

Trout, Jack and Steve Rivkin, *The New Positioning: The Latest on the World's #1 Business Strategy*. New York: McGraw-Hill, 1996.

Wolfe, Bonnie Heineman, 'Finding the international niche: A "How to" for American Small Business', *Business Horizons*, 34, 2 (1991): pp. 13–17.

Womack, James P., Daniel T. Jones and Daniel Roos, *The Machine That Changed the World*. New York: HarperCollins, 1990.

Notes

1. Greg Farrell, 'Getting the bugs out', *Brandweek*, 6 April 1998, p. 30. 'VW's US comeback rides on restyled Beetle', *Wall Street Journal*, 6 May 1997, p. B1. Dagmar Mussey and Laurel Wentz, 'The New Beetle storms Europe: will it succeed?', *Advertising Age*, 23 November 1998, p. 10. Edmund Chew, 'New Beetle enters into the unknown', *Automotive News Europe*, 9 November 1998, p. 12. Jean Halliday, 'Auburn, Michigan: Steve Wilhite, Volkswagen', *Advertising Age International Supplement*, 14 December 1998, p. 12. Andreas Stockinger, 'Und plötzlich ist die Welt wieder rund!', *Der Standard*, 15 February 1999, p. 32.

2. Peter Bennett, D., *Dictionary of Marketing Terms* (Chicago: American Marketing Association, 1995).

3. Salah S. Hassan and Lea Prevel Katsanis, 'Identification of global consumer segments: A behavioral framework', *Journal of International Consumer Marketing*, 3, 2 (1992): p. 17.

4. John K. Ryans Jr., 'Is it too soon to put a tiger in every tank?' *Columbia Journal of World Business*, March–April (1969): p. 73.

5. Arthur C. Fatt, 'The danger of "Local" international advertising', *Journal of Marketing*, January (1967).

6. Theodore Levitt, 'The globalization of markets', *Harvard Business Review*, May–June (1983): p. 92.

7. Teresa J. Domzal and Lynette Unger, 'Emerging positioning strategies in global marketing', *Journal of Consumer Marketing*, 4, 4 (1987): pp. 26–27.

8. Valerie Reitman, 'Enticed by visions of enormous numbers, more Western marketers move into China', *Wall Street Journal*, 12 July 1993, pp. B1, B6.

9. John Bussey, 'India's market reform requires perspective', *Wall Street Journal*, 8 May 1994, p. A1. Miriam Jordan, 'In India, luxury is within reach of many', *Wall Street Journal*, 17 October 1995, p. A1.

10. Marcus W. Brauchli, 'Star struck: a satellite TV system is quickly moving Asia into the global village', *Wall Street Journal*, 10 May 1993, pp. A1, A8.

11. Fritz Luger, 'Statt Rebellion zählt nur Lust am Konsum', *Der Standard*, 11/12 October 1997, p. 25.

12. Interview with Nicholas F. Rossiello, Vice President Marketing and Sales, AFP Imaging Corporation, Elmsford, NY, 30.10.1996.

13. James H. Myers, *Segmentation and Positioning for Strategic Marketing Decisions* (Chicago: American Marketing Association, 1996).

14. Karen Brunso and Klaus G. Grunert, 'Cross-cultural similarities and differences in shopping for food', *Journal of Business Research*, 42 (1998): pp. 145–150.

15. Alex Taylor III, 'Porsche slices up its buyers', *Fortune*, 16 January 1995, p. 24.

16. Alfred S. Boote, 'Psychographic segmentation in Europe', *Journal of Advertising Research*, 22, 6 (1982): p. 25.

17. The following discussion is adapted from Rebecca Piirto, *Beyond Mind Games: The Marketing Power of Psychographics* (Ithaca: American Demographics Books, 1991).

18. Stuart Elliot, 'Figuring out the Russian consumer', *New York Times*, 1 April 1992, pp. C1, C19.

19. Rebecca Piirto, *Beyond Mind Games: The Marketing Power of Psychographics* (Ithaca: American Demographics Books, 1991), p. 161.

20. Rebecca Piirto, *Beyond Mind Games: The Marketing Power of Psychographics*, (Ithaca: American Demographics Books, 1991), p. 165

21. Josef Mazanec, 'Exporting Eurostyles to the USA', *International Journal of Contemporary Management*, 5,

4 (1993): pp. 3–9. Ralph Kreutzer, 'Länder-übergreifende Segmentierungskonzepte – Antwort auf die Globalisierung der Märkte', *Jahrbuch der Absatz- und Verbrauchsforschung*, 37, (1991): pp. 4–27. S. Kramer, *Europäische Life-Style – Analysen zur Verhaltensprognose von Konsumenten*, (Hamburg: Kovacs, 1991). Europanel, 'Eurostyles – Eine europaweite Landkarte mit 16 sozio-kulturellen Typen', *Marketing Journal*, 22 (1989): pp. 106–111.

22. Peter J. LaPlaca, 'Contributions to marketing theory and practice from *Industrial Marketing Management*', *Industrial Marketing Management*, 38, (1997): pp. 179–198.

23. Adam Heller, 'A recipe for success?', *China Business Review*, July–August (1993): p. 30.

24. Laura Bird, 'Tambrands plans global ad campaign', *Wall Street Journal*, 22 June 1993, p. B8. Dyan Machan, 'Will the Chinese use tampons?,' *Forbes*, 16 January 1995, p. 86.

25. George Cole, 'Operators are getting to know all about you', *The Economist*, 18 November 1998.

26. Gregory Carpenter and Alice Tybout, 'Meeting the challenge of the postmodern consumer', *Financial Times*, 5 October 1998.

27. Michael E. Porter, 'The strategic role of international marketing', *Journal of Consumer Marketing*, 3, 2 (1986): p. 21.

28. Andrew Pollack, 'Jeep is giving Chrysler a success story in Japan', *New York Times*, 26 April 1994, p. C1.

29. Clare Ansberry, 'Uphill Battle: Eastman Kodak Co. has arduous struggle to regain lost edge', *Wall Street Journal*, 2 April 1987, pp. 1, 12.

30. Interview with Oleg Smirnoff, former Marketing Manager at PepsiCola Int'l, New York, 31.10.1996.

31. Pat Sloan, 'Revlon eyes global image', *Advertising Age*, 1 January 1993, p. 1.

32. Hermann Simon, *Die heimlichen Gewinner* (Frankfurt: Campus Verlag, 1996).

33. Gabriella Stern, 'Procter senses opportunity in posh perfume' ,*Wall Street Journal*, 9 July 1993, pp. B1, B5.

34. James H. Myers, *Segmentation and Positioning for Strategic Marketing Decisions* (Chicago: American Marketing Association, 1996), S. 187.

35. Teresa J. Domzal, and Lynette Unger, 'Emerging positioning strategies in global marketing', *Journal of Consumer Marketing*, 4, 4 (1987): pp. 26–27.

Integrating brand strategies after an acquisition: Schwarzkopf & Henkel cosmetics

In 1997, Henkel owned a total of 330 companies and had nearly 55,000 employees in over 60 countries. It generated sales of DM20.1 billion (about €10.28 billion) through its six product market sectors Adhesives, Detergents/Household Cleansers, Cosmetics/Toiletries, Surface Technologies, Chemical Products and Industrial and Institutional Hygiene.

The Cosmetics/Toiletries sector generated sales of DM2.97 billion in 1997. Here activities are dominated by the need to integrate a former competitor (Hans Schwarzkopf GmbH). The shares of Schwarzkopf (a descendant of the company founder) initially derived from Hoechst AG (1995) and Schwarzkopf was then bought out by Henkel in 1996. In its last year as a separate company, Hans Schwarzkopf GmbH achieved world sales of over DM 1 billion and had a workforce of more than 4,000 employees.

Following the acquistion of Schwarzkopf by Henkel the branded articles business in the Cosmetics/Toiletries sector, which includes the strategic business units Body Care, Oral Hygiene, Skin Care and Fragrances, has been regrouped as Schwarzkopf & Henkel Cosmetics (SHC). The hair salon business, however, is represented by Schwarzkopf Professional. SHC's international alignment is reflected in over 50 affiliated companies in 44 countries.

Following the acquisition, SHC faced problems in the hair-care sector. They needed to reorganise the marketing of three main brands, one, Poly Kur, which originated with Henkel and two, Gliss Kur and Schauma, which had been part of the Schwarzkopf portfolio. They needed to avoid mutual interference on the market and to achieve the best possible exploitation of market potential. The relevant decisions relating to mid-1997 (i.e. the period roughly six months after finalisation of the acquisition) focus on designing their future brand strategy, including implementation in terms of marketing policy and international marketing considerations. Brand policy considerations centre around the necessity to analyse respective brand positioning of the three products and to draft design recommendations on the basis of these analyses.

The positioning of a brand is the position it occupies in the eyes of consumers in comparison with ideal and competing brands.

- Analysing the actual position involves identifying the position of real and ideal brands in terms of criteria governing the decision to buy, as subjectively perceived by consumers in a multi-dimensional awareness and evaluation context.
- This is followed by the specification of the target positioning, the most essential aspect of which is the position assessed by the consumers as ideal (ideal brand).
- Depending on the position of a company's brand in relation to the ideal brand, efforts can then be focused on reinforcing or shifting the actual brand position nearer to the ideal brand.
- In principle, it would also be conceivable to influence the ideal requirements to bring them into line with the company's brand.

So far as competitors are concerned, this decision-making problem can be expressed as the choice between a profiling strategy (to distinguish oneself from the competition by a unique selling proposition and to occupy a positioning niche) and an imitative or 'me too' strategy.

- The first is the brand price positioning (pricing).
- The second is the performance basis. This can stress the 'natural quality' i.e. when hair problems are solved by products which provide more gentle, mild care through vegetable ingredients. Another option would be to offer 'high tech' products which provide a pronounced 'technical' repair performance on the basis of scientific know-how.
- The third evaluation dimension is the perceived degree of specialisation of the brand, as reflected in the differentiation of the products offered. This is determined on the one hand by the breadth of the product range, i.e. the number and types of product variants for different hair types and problems (e.g. fine, dry/stressed, permed/dyed hair), and on the other hand by the depth of the range represented by the care performance intensity of the

number and types of application varieties for hair problems (instant repair treatment, pack, thermal pack, revitalising care, etc.). Brands occupying a specialist position are those which not only provide products for a great many hair types and problems, but also offer a large number of differentiated application varieties for problem hair (with graduated action intensity). The general brands focus on normal hair-care (e.g. family products), with a small number of product variants and application varieties.

Figure 1 illustrates the positioning of Gliss Kur, Poly Kur and Schauma in 1997 in comparison with competing and ideal brands in terms of the feature dimensions explained above. The positions assessed as ideal are based on SHC Management estimates. Note that their market research shows that performance basis is less significant in terms of decision to buy than the other two dimensions. This is shown by the different degrees of shading in the figure.

The figure shows a clear relationship between source and perceived quality. Consumers are basically prepared to pay high prices for what they perceive as special care performance. The various positions of the three ideal brands relate to different market segments as possible target groups.

● In the zone around ideal brand I, the predominant group comprises hair-care consumers looking for a reasonably priced general brand for themselves or their families.

● The ideal brand II segment relates to persons (especially women) aged between 20 and 40 in the middle income bracket who prefer uncomplicated but effective hair-care.

● Ideal brand III mainly relates to women in the higher income bracket who expect more in terms of hair-care performance. The age of these women also ranges widely (between 20 and 55).

Ideal brand II is of particular interest because demographic studies in most European countries show that the proportion of the population over 40 years of age will increase sharply in the future. SHC market research studies also indicate that this age group has high purchasing power and that it will probably develop increased awareness of appearance and health in the coming years. Promising products in this segment will have to cater to the special problems of older people, e.g. less resilient or thinning hair, and hair loss. It is apparent that increasing numbers of people are now ready to use a more technological type of product in the hair-segment.

So far as SHC brands are concerned, Figure 1 also shows that, following the acquisition, Henkel now has two brands with similar positioning: Gliss Kur and Poly Kur. Schauma is quite differently positioned.

Figure 1 Actual brand positions, Henkel and other cosmetic/toiletries, mid-1997

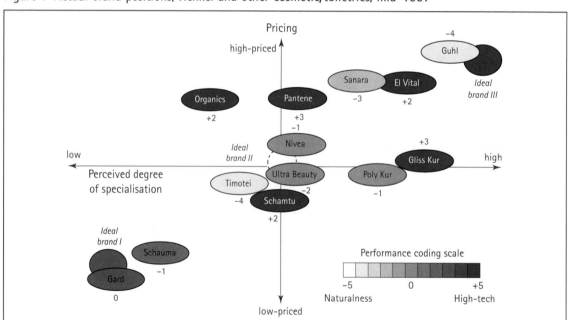

As a result, this case will concentrage mainly on problems relating to the Gliss Kur and Poly Kur brands.

As far as the performance basis is concerned, Gliss Kur (the original Schwarzkopf brand) and Poly Kur (the original Henkel brand) occupy different positions, since Gliss Kur focuses more on the high-tech aspects of the product, whereas Poly Kur is characterized by its natural quality. However, it should be remembered that due to several relaunches and repositioning campaigns in the years prior to Henkel's acquisition of Schwarzkopf – some of which tended towards increased high-tech competence – Poly Kur lines are not clearly perceived as being natural care products. Poly Kur still conjures up technical associations. Gliss Kur, on the other hand, is a highly specialized brand which has consistently been engineered as a high-tech product promising consumers high competence based on outstanding, scientifically substantiated hair repair performance.

In terms of pricing, both brands are situated in the medium price range, though consumers do not rate Poly Kur's price/performance ratio as excellent as that of Gliss Kur. SHC experts estimate that consumers associate Gliss Kur with a high level of treatment competence and will therefore be more willing to accept higher prices without switching to other brands. This willingness is not as pronounced in the case of Poly Kur.

The very similar degree of specialisation is due to the similarity of the assortment structure of Gliss Kur and Poly Kur in the segments of shampoos, care products (conditioners), conventional hair treatments (e.g. packs), and special treatments (e.g. hair-end fluids). The vast breadth and above all the depth of the assortment confers on both brands the position of a hair-care specialist in the treatment segment. Poly Kur has a slightly wider range for many of the relatively normal hair types but a slightly narrower range of special treatments. Gliss Kur's assortment includes highly differentiated products for hair types and focuses on special applications for different, but mostly problem hair. The unique selling proposition of the Gliss Kur brand stems from this differentiation. Poly Kur, on the other hand, is mainly oriented toward uncomplicated care for a wide variety of hair types.

In summary, as a result of consistent brand management, Gliss Kur is reckoned to have significantly higher competence in the repair and special treatments segment for different types of problem hair. For some time now, SHC has been considering introduc-

ing special products to meet the specific care needs of older people. Figure 2 illustrates the Gliss Kur and Poly Kur assortment structures graphically after the Schwarzkopf acquisition. As the figure shows, they overlap to a considerable extent.

Figure 2 Assortment structure of Gliss Kur and Poly Kur after the Henkel/Schwarzkopf acquisition (1997)

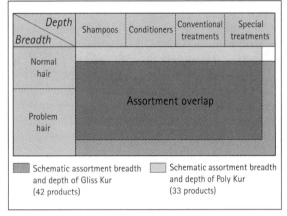

Source: Schwarzkopf & Henkel, in-house.

If one looks at the marketing mix design, it can be seen that product policy specifications for Poly Kur include the use of formulations incorporating vegetable ingredients, but without any consistent reflection of this in the packaging design.

Over a long period, the bottles used for conditioners and shampoos, for example, tended to have a rectangular outline. Only relatively recently has an attempt been made to give the bottles a more 'natural' character by adding the picture of a leaf. In contrast, Gliss Kur products include substances claimed to provide chemical repair performance, which has been stressed since 1996 by the keywords 'Hair Repair Complex'. Packaging for Gliss Kur products consistently features a pictorial motif of stylised hair repair.

The idea of introducing products catering to the hair problems of the 40-plus age group is currently being deliberated. Within the scope of a new concept called the 'Age Repair 40+' line, formulations are being developed which will include vita proteins (vitamin-protein complexes) as ingredients. Initial market research results indicate a high level of acceptance for this care line.

When communicating for Poly Kur products, the focus since the last repositioning has concentrated on natural care properties. The Gliss Kur brand is now increasingly targeting demanding consumers with a high interest in cosmetics (this being partly due to the great similarity with the Poly Kur target group). The intention is to draw these consumers' attention to the fact that, with problem hair, the 'Hair Repair Complex' is the only alternative to cutting the hair. This is underlined in communication by a visual message, with scissors symbolising the drastic last resort.

As already described, product pricing is basically similar for both brands, with Gliss Kur commanding slightly higher prices. The explanation given by SHC experts for the particularly pronounced price acceptance for a special care line for older people is the higher purchasing power of this target group and their tendency to pay more for special performance. The distribution policy for Gliss Kur and Poly Kur focuses on wide distribution of the products in both cases, with special emphasis on chemists and specialised retailers.

At the international level, Gliss Kur and Poly Kur products are mainly sold in Western Europe with inroads now also being made in Eastern Europe countries. The findings presented here come from in-house work by SHC on its products (1998). Apart from a few countries such as Russia and Poland, where special circumstances prevail due to the economic development in these countries, the target countries are generally similar in terms of economic factors (e.g. gross domestic product, purchasing power, competition and media situation), legal and political considerations (e.g. laws, regulations), geographical conditions (e.g. climate, topography), technological fundaments of production, as well as socio-cultural factors (e.g. consumer habits and attitudes to cosmetic articles). For example, the attitude to using hair-care products is usually rather uncomplicated as regards the potential benefits obtained through using these products (healthy hair, personal attractiveness, etc.). In this context, however, SHC market research results indicate that the picture of a sophisticated, experienced

consumer of hair-care products is more typical of German-speaking than French-speaking countries.

In the period after the acquisition, SHC noted that Gliss Kur and Poly Kur were not developing as desired on the market and that there was interdependence in both entrepreneurial planning and market-oriented implementation. Product management is therefore faced with the problem of designing virtually the same concepts for two similarly positioned, but practically competing brands. The sales department cannot find sufficient arguments to push distribution of both brands in the trade. This is particularly the case in the special treatments segment where the products are essentially similar.

Gliss Kur and Poly Kur also compete in terms of consumer preference, since the specialist positioning plays a greater role in the decision to buy than questions of natural quality or scientific care performance. Considerable substitution to the debit of Poly Kur is therefore probable, and this is worsened by the similarity of the Gliss Kur and Poly Kur target groups. SHC has decided, however, to maintain both brands. Its problem is therefore how to develop a new brand policy for them.

Discussion questions

1 Devise a suitable new (target) positioning for the two brands, referring to the three positioning dimensions mentioned above.

2 Explain the consequences of the new positioning for the assortment structures of Gliss Kur and Poly Kur, making suggestions for an appropriate breadth and depth of the brands' assortment (with regard to their intended degree of specialisation).

3 What conclusions can be drawn from the proposed positioning for the implementation in terms of marketing measures?

Source: C. Phillips, A. Pruyn and M.P. Kestemenont *Understanding Marketing, A European Casebook* (Wiley, 2000).

Oriflame

INTRODUCTION
This case will give you a general overview of the Swedish cosmetic company, Oriflame International SA, with concentration on the impressive development of Oriflame's entry into Eastern and Central Europe. A special focus will be directed toward Oriflame's operations in Poland.

COMPANY PROFILE
Oriflame was founded in Sweden in 1967 by brothers Jonas and Robert af Jochnick and Bengt Hellsten. In 1972, the parent company, Oriflame International SA (OISA), Luxembourg, was established. In 1982, OISA became listed on the London Stock Exchange.

Oriflame's specific market concept, which involves direct sales, also allowed for rapid market development outside the Nordic area. The company is currently represented in 42 countries in Europe, the Far East, Australia and the Americas.

In 1987, the mail order operation was expanded following the introduction of the Vevay brand name. In 1992, the natural cosmetics company Fleur de Santé became affiliated with the group. ACO Hud was acquired in 1992 and is Sweden's best-known brand name in skin care products. The products are retailed through Swedish, Norwegian and Icelandic pharmacies.

Oriflame develops and produces its own naturally based products in its manufacturing plant in Ireland where the Group's research laboratories are also located.

Oriflame Eastern Europe SA (ORESA), which is managed from Brussels, was established in 1990 with the objective of penetrating Eastern European markets.

In 1994, direct sales accounted for 83 per cent of the Group's sales (ORESA and OISA). Oriflame is represented by sales companies in 42 countries, of which 29 are wholly owned and mainly located in Europe. Oriflame has licensees operating in a further 13 countries. The organisational structure of a country sales company is shown in Figure 1.

THE MARKET
The market for cosmetic products is developing positively with recent growth averaging around 4 per cent per year by volume, although, as with other consumer industries, growth in 1992–1993 decreased as a consequence of the general economic recession.

The company has experienced steady growth in sales since the start in 1967 with, in June 1994, sales totalling $230 million for the group. The increase has been particularly significant in Europe with the establishment of new operations in Central and Eastern Europe. This growth is also explained by the fact that people are becoming more discerning about how they buy things. Many people find visiting a department store tiresome and impersonal. The current trend is a return to personal service, care and attention. Combine that with Oriflame's commitment to offering value for money with a full 100 per cent money back guarantee and the current sales growth is explained.

In addition to Europe, major growth has come from South and Central America. Oriflame's operations on the South American continent are directed from Chile, where the success of the local operation continues.

The global market for cosmetics and toiletries (C&T) is mature, and growth through the year 2000 is projected to reach the modest rate of 3 per cent annually. Europe accounts for 37 per cent of overall sales and is the major single market for C&T products. The growth rate in the region is among the strongest of any in the world when the results from Eastern Europe are considered. By contrast, the US market is saturated and growth is slow.

In the global market for C&T, skin care is a large sector in most countries, except in the United States where skin care is less developed than in Europe in terms of user penetration. One key trend is the launch of products that are marketed as having benefits to the skin which are not just cosmetic. This trend can be seen across the cosmetic markets and indicates that demand is becoming more sophisticated. It usually involves a close association with health benefits. These therapeutic cosmetics, 'cosmeceuticals', are expected to become a major growth area in the skin care market. The cosmetics industry has been very active in the development of such products in recent years, spending heavily on research and development (R&D) and often transferring medical research to cosmetic products.

Although there is a continuous search for innovation in the C&T sector, the lack of legal protection in such forms as patents adds a factor of increased risk and hinders the potential for return on capital.

Figure 1 Organisational structure of sales company

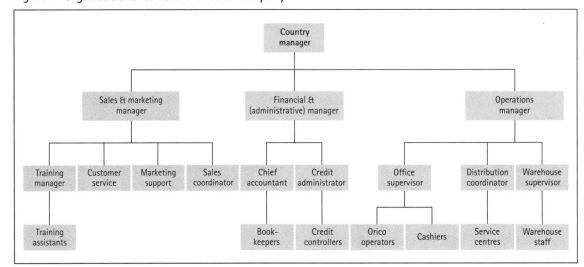

Pan-European sales of skin care lines increased by 8 to 10 per cent during 1992. The growth trend continues in the area of anti-aging products, with the quality demands on effective long-lasting moisturisers rising. The public's increasing concern about environmental pollution and the link to the harmful effects of the sun's ultraviolet rays is also of great interest to the industry.

Body care products continue to perform well in Europe, but market penetration levels are relatively low compared to the sun care market.

Cosmetics sold through direct selling methods make up the following percentages of the following markets: Sweden (20), United Kingdom (15), Finland (13), France (7), Denmark (11), Eastern Europe (11), Spain (7), Holland (6), Norway (4), other (13).

Overall, direct sales of cosmetics account for 10 to 15 per cent of the entire cosmetics market.

THE DIRECT-SELLING INDUSTRY

Direct selling, which was already a substantial industry in the United States by 1920, is defined by the Direct Selling Association as follows:

The selling of consumer goods direct to private individuals, in their homes and places of work, through transactions initiated and concluded by a salesperson. Direct selling has several advantages over shop retailing, not only for the customer, but also for the manufacturer. The customer can pick up the products at a service centre or have them delivered at home. The manufacturer does not have to

support advertising costs to attract its customers. The distributors play a double role, being both customers and sales people in the recruitment of new customers.

In July 1994, the World Federation of Direct Selling Association indicated that direct selling was a $60 billion industry in the world, with 30 million people involved in this activity each year. As an example, the United States counted 5 million to 7 million people in direct selling and Japan more than 2 million. Most people who sell direct do it not only because they like the products and want to increase their income, but also because it is a good opportunity for them to develop an independent activity. Direct sales is now a global activity, with many new players competing with traditional companies.

Most of today's successful direct selling companies use a sales system called network marketing or multi-level marketing. An article in *The Wall Street Journal* described Network Marketing in the following way:

Network marketing is a sales system which totally omits the stores. Networks sell all kinds of products: from pens or toothpaste to computers, cars, and even houses. These products are usually 15–50 per cent cheaper than those purchased in the stores. By the end of this century, we will be buying 50–60 per cent of all the products and services in this way.

The rules are about the same everywhere. An authorised distributor delivers the company's products directly to the customer's house. His first clients are his family and friends. A distributor buys the products at a price which is 20–30 per cent cheaper than the price the customer will later pay for them. The difference is where his profit is. If he wants to make more, he recruits new sales agents. Depending on the number of people he recruits and on the volume of goods he and the recruits buy, he receives a commission and a bonus. Sometimes it can be a prize, a nice trip abroad, sometimes even a retirement pension. Those who recruit the biggest number of new agents make the most. The company also makes money because it has no such costs as rent or a lease. It would have to pay for all of this if it sold its goods in the stores.

Oriflame is one of the main direct sales companies in many of its markets and the largest direct sales company in Scandinavia and in Central and Eastern Europe.

ORIFLAME

Direct selling

Conventional selling involves moving a product through a hierarchy of middlemen from the manufacturer to the end customer. All these middlemen – wholesalers, retailers and jobbers – earn a profit from handling the product. In a direct-selling environment, these positions are not necessary and profits are instead shared among the distributors. These cost cuttings also give Oriflame the possibility to sell a higher-quality product at lower, more competitive prices.

Oriflame's responsibility in the markets in which it operates is to package the products and handle the financing and data processing, warehousing, shipping and marketing, as well as creating training programmes and materials to support the independent distributors.

The Oriflame distributors offer unique, value-added services such as cosmetics consultancy in their customers' homes or offices. It is company policy that prospective customers (1) are not subject to 'pressure selling' nor are they obliged to purchase; (2) receive free skin analysis and personalised advice on proper skin care; and (3) are offered free ongoing after-sales service.

Oriflame has 300,000 distributors world-wide. Distributors usually have other jobs; thus, their involvement with Oriflame is sometimes only a hobby. Historically, distributors have been paid strictly on commission, and their primary sales tool has been sales catalogues provided by Oriflame. (More

than 12 million catalogues in 17 languages are distributed every year.)

Oriflame's selling method consists of selling a wide range of the highest-quality cosmetics to consumers on a person-to-person basis, backed by a unique, multilevel marketing plan.

Distributors get their catalogues every two to four weeks and use them to sell to friends, relatives and colleagues – normally, their primary customer base. Distributors order products they sell from the catalogues, receive bundled shipments from Oriflame, and then pass products on to individual customers.

Oriflame is now implementing and expanding a new (for them) marketing method. This involves the distributor's building up a sales network and receiving a bonus or commission on the sales made by each individual recruited to be a distributor, as well as on the sales made by the recruits. This system, often called multilevel marketing, can offer career opportunities for current 'hobbyists' because the system permits 'main source' levels of income. The method has worked most successfully for Oriflame in Latin American and several Eastern European countries. Distributors in these countries often enjoy incomes well above national averages. Catalogues are an integral part of this system, but are issued less frequently. Over time, Oriflame will adapt this method for use in its traditional Western European markets.

Oriflame has never been successful in the German and US markets despite several start-up attempts. Direct sales accounted for 83 per cent of Oriflame's sales in 1994 compared with 70 per cent in 1994. It has been decided by the Board of Directors that Oriflame's future direction will be in the field of direct selling. This is where the company has its highest potential. (See appendix at the end of this case for further explanations of the marketing plan.)

Other activities

Mail order at Oriflame can be divided into two types. The first is by direct customer purchase of specially selected products appearing in sales catalogues that are distributed 10 to 12 times a year. This method is referred to as the positive option.

The second category of mail-order sales is based on the book club type of system. Subscribers/members/customers are offered specially composed packages through a brochure. The parcel is sent to the customers unless they actively inform the company that they do not wish to receive it (negative option).

The mail-order market accounts for around 5 per cent of the total cosmetics market. The market is expanding, especially in the Nordic area. The activities in Eastern Europe have a major potential as the time is right for this concept and strong development is anticipated generally. The market as a whole is subject to tough competition from companies such as Yves Rocher.

The mail-order market within the Oriflame Group is composed of Oriflame's operation in Denmark – Vevay's cosmetic club and Fleur de Santé's natural cosmetics. In 1992, the mail-order operations were combined to form a division within the Oriflame group.

The mail-order operations started in Denmark in 1978 with Oriflame's cosmetics club. Today, Oriflame in Denmark has around 100,000 members and sales of around $8 million.

Vevay was founded in Sweden in 1987. Since then, operations have expanded to Norway, Finland and Denmark and during 1993 ORESA started up its own operations in Poland, Hungary and the Czech Republic. Vevay has around 120,000 members and sales of around $4 million.

Fleur de Santé has been an associate company of Oriflame since May 1992 (36 per cent ownership). The company, located in Malmo, has a turnover of around $15 million in Sweden, Norway, and Finland. In August 1992, Oriflame acquired the distribution rights for Fleur de Santé in Eastern Europe. A company was started in the Czech Republic in February 1993.

Mail order in 1994 accounted for 7 per cent of total Oriflame sales.

ACO

The ACO company evolved from the Swedish pharmacy operations, and the name ACO dates back to 1939. In connection with the nationalisation of Swedish pharmacies in 1972, ACO was transferred to the government-owned pharmaceuticals company, Kabi Vitrum. Oriflame acquired ACO on 1 January 1992.

ACO's main market is Sweden, where the products are sold through pharmacies. ACO is the best-known brand name for skin care products in Sweden. Its main products are creams, lotions, sun care products and hand care products.

The ACO products exist within the low and average price ranges, whereas the Nordic Light products compete with exclusive prestige brands.

The growth in sales during the year has mainly been through new products or recently introduced products as well as sun care products. Sales increased

to $24 million. ACO accounted for 10 per cent of total Oriflame sales.

Manufacturing

At the end of 1977, Oriflame's Board of Directors decided to build a production plant on the outskirts of Dublin, Ireland. The plant was completed two years later, in July 1979, following extensive project work, including transfers of technology from former subcontractors. The building covered 2,800 square metres for production, research laboratories and quality control. Extensions were made in 1980, 1989, 1991–1992, and 1992–1993. The current extensions now have been completed and have increased the capacity for filling from 22 million to approximately 40 million units. This, of course, includes the ACO equipment transferred from Stockholm. In 1993, the factory covered 11,000 square metres for production, research laboratories, and quality control. The plant is one of Europe's most modern cosmetic manufacturing units and is well equipped with high-technology production equipment.

All Oriflame products undergo strict physical, chemical and microbiological control before reaching the customer. The objective is that the customer should be able to rely on the product to provide long-term quality, regardless of how it was purchased.

In order to attain this objective, all deliveries of raw materials and packaging are tested according to a strict specification before they enter the production process. An overriding priority is to offer consumer products that meet the highest safety and quality standards. The water used is tested daily to guarantee a high degree of microbiological purity.

Research and product development in the Dublin plant is actively concentrated on developing new cosmetic formulations in line with the market demands and expectations. In production and development, products and packaging are tested continuously for microbiological stability and quality of packaging. The production philosophy, including packaging, is to concentrate on new consumer demands such as biodegradability, recycling, and the absence of animal raw materials.

The Research and Development Department has generated over 100 new products for Oriflame, Vevay, Fleur de Santé, and ACO in 1994.

Oriflame results

In 1993 and 1994, the Oriflame Group results were as follows:

	1994 ($ 000)	1993 ($ 000)
Sales	232,137	192,406
Operating profit	36,192	31,431
Profit before tax	37,206	31,556
Profit after tax	28,676	23,522
Capital expenditure	20,349	13,822
Profit margin %	16	16.4
Equity/assets ratio (%)	57	55
Return on net capital employed (%)	32	36
Gearing (%)	14	31
Employees	1,328	1,148

Exchange rate $ = 1.56

ORIFLAME EASTERN EUROPE

Decision to start

When Oriflame decided, in 1990, to create Oriflame Eastern Europe, Jonas af Jochnick called back to Europe a young Swedish manager, Sven Mattsson, who at the time was managing director for the operations in the Philippines. The year before, af Jochnick had resigned from his position as Oriflame chairman in order to devote more time to look at new marketing opportunities, particularly in Eastern Europe. Af Jochnick, together with Mattsson and a secretary, opened an office in Brussels for the new company, ORESA. The objective was to exploit business opportunities for the direct selling of cosmetic products in Eastern Europe, with initial emphasis on Czechoslovakia, Hungary and Poland. In Eastern Europe, Oriflame targets for the later stage of its development were Bulgaria, Romania, the Soviet Union and Yugoslavia.

On 10 July 1990, af Jochnick was appointed Chairman of ORESA. In a letter to Oriflame shareholders, he wrote:

The opening up of the Eastern European markets offers new and exciting opportunities to establish business activities in these countries. There is a strong ambition and commitment by the new democratically elected governments in some of these countries to develop their markets along the lines of Western-style market economies, and legislation is being proposed or passed in a number of Eastern European countries to encourage foreign investment.

In particular the Directors of ORESA believe that opportunities exist for companies:

1 which are active in the consumer goods areas;
2 which are prepared to re-invest cash and profits in the local markets and which are in a position to wait a considerable period before remitting profits;
3 with the resources to establish or invest in local manufacture;
4 which are willing to invest in the development and professional training of local nationals as future management.

Currently there is a high degree of uncertainty as to where and how quickly these opportunities will develop since definite legal frameworks have not yet been established in all the countries in Eastern Europe. It is therefore impossible to predict with any degree of certainty what financial returns can be expected or the timing of such returns.

Investment in these countries must instead be based on the belief that the recent political changes are irreversible and that there will remain a strong commitment to develop these economies with policies based on Western economic principles. I believe that for the companies which take the initiative early and take a long-term view, future reward and returns should far exceed what can be expected from mature markets in the West.

The initial objective of ORESA was to establish sales organizations in Czechoslovakia, Hungary and Poland, using the well-proven direct-selling techniques already used by the company in its existing markets. The techniques seemed particularly well suited to these countries due to the highly undeveloped retail distribution networks found there at that time.

ORESA was also examining the possibility of entering into joint-venture arrangements with existing cosmetic manufacturers in each of these countries to enable products to be sourced locally. In the longer term, manufacturing for export of cosmetic products in Eastern Europe was envisaged.

Development 1990–1994 (Table 1)

The first country that Oriflame entered was Czechoslovakia. Eliska Wescia, a woman of Czech origin living in Malmö, was made an offer to return to Prague. She accepted and first sales were made in December 1990. A 100-square-metre office was opened and after three months, $300,000 worth of sales had been made. Sales were growing so fast that the company had to stop recruiting for a while to establish a warehouse and find new office facilities. In

Table 1 Sales statistics

Country: Czech Republic*	1991	Start: December 1990 1992	1993	1994
Total sales (US$ thousands)	4,526	12,684	12,758	13,700
Active file count	2,320	7,629	12,494	18,804
Activity %/month (average)	74%	81%	68%	61%
Sales/active/month (US$ average)	490	138	125	112
No. of employees	9	33	51	61
Office space (square metres)	300	300	450	600
Warehouse space (square metres)	600	660	700	1,000
No. of service centres		16	17	21
Advertising spending (US$ thousands)		15	378	400

Country: Slovakia	Start: January 1993 1993	1994
Total sales (US$ thousands)	3,197	6,400
Active file count	3,795	9,090
Activity %/month (average)	66%	59%
Sales/active/month (US$ average)	180	90
No. of employees	10	30
Office space (square metres)	280	550
Warehouse space (square metres)	0	600
No. of service centres	0	6
Advertising spending (US$ thousands)	23.5	89

Country: Hungary	1991	Start: May 1991 1992	1993	1994
Total sales (US$ thousands)	1,400	6,500	9,500	13,500
Active file count	3,602	13,442	18,933	23,285
Activity %/month (average)	65%	62%	53%	50%
Sales/active/month (US$ average)	133	100	81	93
No. of employees	14	35	60	75
Office space (square metres)	60	180	280	400
Warehouse space (square metres)	50	700	1,200	1,200
No. of service centres	0	1	4	9
Advertising spending (US$ thousands)	0	20	275	250

Country: Turkey	1991	Start: April 1992 1992	1993	1994
Total sales (US$ thousands)		1,278	9,933	12,900
Active file count		2,523	16,224	28,550
Activity %/month (average)		83.7%	61.7%	47.4%
Sales/active/month (US$ average)		289	167	98
No. of employees		11	37	74
Office space (square metres)		350	450	750
Warehouse space (square metres)		100	800	1,500
No. of service centres		1	4	9
Advertising spending (US$ thousands)		8.7	44.4	70.3

Country: Greece	1991	Start: May 1993		1994
		1992	1993	
Total sales (US$ thousands)			554	1,845
Active file count			819	3,048
Activity %/month (average)			89%	66%
Sales/active/month (US$ average)			218	196
No. of employees			11	26
Office space (square metres)			280	480
Warehouse space (square metres)			200	300
No. of service centres			1	3
Advertising spending (US$ thousands)			22	50

Country: Bulgaria	1991	Start: August 1994		1994
		1992	1993	
Total sales (US$ thousands)				810
Active file count				2,450
Activity %/month (average)				93%
Sales/active/month (US$ average)				200
No. of employees				15
Office space (square metres)				400
Warehouse space (square metres)				600
No. of service centres				0
Advertising spending (US$ thousands)				2

* Czechoslovakia split into two nations – the Czech Republic and Slovakia – 1 January 1993. During 1993 and most of 1994, warehousing was handled by Czech sales company fulfilment.

1994, Oriflame had a 600-square-metre office in Prague with a 1,000-square-metre warehouse, and 15 service centres spread over the country.

In Poland, the company recruited the first 12 distributors in March 1991. They ordered, among themselves, $20,000 in the first two weeks and are still today among the leaders in the Polish network. A Polish citizen who had spent two years in Iran and who was fluent in English was recruited as country manager.

In Hungary, where competitors like Avon and Amway were already established, Sven Mattsson was general manager of Oriflame until the company found a Swede with a Hungarian background, Thomas Grünwald, to assume responsibility for Hungary in May 1991, which was when the first Oriflame products were sold. At the beginning, sales did not develop as fast as in Poland and Czechoslovakia. However, three years later, sales were developing faster in Hungary (plus 38 per cent) than in the Czech Republic (plus 15 per cent) or in Poland, which had only a small increase. Mattsson says, 'This can partly be explained by the fact that Oriflame naturally offers the best service level within the capi-

tal region. Approximately 25 per cent of the Hungarian population lives in the Budapest area, a figure which is much higher then the other bordering countries. Local management has also been very successful in working with leaders of the network.' In 1994, Oriflame had 75 employees in Hungary.

In April 1992, Oriflame started operations in Turkey. The company had great hopes for this more Western market where well-trained managers were available and where everything seemed to be a lot smoother and easier, in spite of a lot of red tape and bureaucracy. This was nothing compared with what the company had experienced in Eastern Europe up to now. The initial investment was paid back after three months of operations. In December 1992, Oriflame sales were $450,000. Turkish distributors appeared to be entrepreneurial and cooperative.

The operations have been greatly helped by the country's well-developed infrastructure (banking, telecommunications, etc.). Oriflame's high expectations were not met in 1994 because of the economic crisis Turkey faced during the year. In March, the dollar value moved from 14,000 to 40,000 Turkish liras over a few days. Sales dropped 40 per cent below forecast, but Sven Mattsson remained optimistic about the medium and long-term future. In January 1995, Oriflame Turkey opened a new 1,200-square-metre office and a 2,000-square-metre warehouse near the Istanbul airport.

In May 1993, Oriflame started its sales in Greece, a member country of the European Union with no import duties. Oriflame had to pay 12 per cent duties for the Czech Republic and from 10 to 50 per cent for Hungary and 20 per cent for Turkey. In 1994, Oriflame Greece showed profit.

In Bulgaria, Oriflame opened a 400-square-metre office and a 600-square-metre warehouse in August 1994. Success was immediate, and the company experienced its biggest initial growth, with distributors placing an average monthly order of $250 in this country where the average income is only about $80 per month.

In Russia, Ukraine and Latvia, ORESA has, since 1991, sold its products wholesale to retail outlets as high inflation, inadequate banking systems, and a relatively undeveloped infrastructure have made it difficult to use the traditional Oriflame concept of selling through distributors. However, the company is now ready to adopt direct sales there, implementing the same Marketing Plan as in other Eastern European countries. A Swedish manager, Fredrik Ekman, moved to Moscow in October 1993.

From 1991 to 1995, ORESA increased its staff and office facilities in Brussels. In 1995, the head office was staffed by 30 people, ensuring centralised functions such as Operations and Marketing, Finance, Supply, Business Development, and Legal Affairs (see Figure 2).

In 1995, ORESA planned to open sales companies in Romania and Lithuania. A relaunch of Oriflame's activities in Germany took place during the course of 1995. Oriflame Germany is being managed from Brussels.

A 10,000-square-metre ultramodern manufacturing plant, located in Warsaw, was due to start operating in mid-1995. This involved a total investment of approximately US$ 20 million.

As Sven Mattsson likes to say, 'Our initial aim was to start with Czechoslovakia and then to follow with Poland and Hungary and other markets according to our success in established markets, but also according to available management resources. Our ambition is to become market leaders, both in the direct selling industry as well as the cosmetic industry and to capitalize on all the advantages which result from being the first on a market.'

ORIFLAME IN POLAND

Decision to start

In December 1990, Edward Zieba, who had worked for a state chemical company in Poland and who had spent three years in Iran with a construction company, was recruited by Oriflame with the objective of starting operations in Warsaw. During that month, he had long discussions at the Brussels headquarters of ORESA and visited the Oriflame produc-

Figure 2 **Oriflame Eastern Europe organisation**

tion plant in Ireland and the emerging sales company in Czechoslovakia. During the first months of 1991, Zieba became very sceptical about the development of Oriflame in Poland with direct-selling techniques and a multilevel approach, which had never been used in his country.

'I really thought at that time that it could not possibly work in Poland. Our mentality is too different and what we have lived through over past decades left little hope of implementing such methods with success. I had accepted the job because I treated it as something new and exciting, but I was very doubtful,' commented Zieba to the case writer during his visit to Oriflame Warsaw in May 1994.

Oriflame started its operation in Poland in March 1991. At that time, Zieba gathered some 20 of his friends with their spouses for a cosy party during which he did not speak about Oriflame but only displayed some products on a table in the kitchen. After a while, all of those gathered there started asking questions. At the end of the evening, he gave a few samples to those interested (all of them) while briefly explaining the opportunity of the Oriflame marketing plan. Although the quality of the products was fully recognised, each of the guests appeared concerned about the selling method. Three years later, in 1994, eight of them were selling Oriflame products as their only professional activity and were at the epicentre of several different networks of thousands of distributors.

Products and pricing

Initially, a selection of 100 items was offered. One year later, the number increased to 150. Oriflame cosmetics are gentle but effective. They are produced from nonirritant, natural plant extracts and protect the skin against the harmful effects of pollution and stress. Oriflame products link the best of nature with the best of science to achieve the highest quality.

A first product selection was made by the Marketing Department in Brussels and one of Zieba's first assignments was to propose local pricing. Oriflame generally sells in local currency. At a later stage, free choice was given with regard to new introductions and discontinuations. Our intention was and still is to offer the most comprehensive range of skin care, colour and fragrance products in the Polish market. The first months clearly showed that consumer habits differ in many areas from what we are used to in western countries.

Since conception, product price positioning has been one of the most important issues and intensive market studies are continuously carried out in this area. 'It is necessary to keep on top of a rapidly changing economic environment. At an early stage it was decided to offer very competitive prices in order to attract millions of new customers rather than selling a limited number of items with traditionally high margins.'

Merchandise support

Twice a year, Oriflame issues 380,000 copies of its catalogue, showing 250 products classified in the following categories: skin care, body care, family favourites, colour, cosmetics, women's fragrance and men's fragrance. Prices are not printed in the catalogue but on a separate loose sheet. Oriflame prints all its catalogues in Sweden, using the same catalogue in nine different countries. Translation and typesetting of the texts is made in each country before the printing. One of the difficulties the company has to face is product sales forecasts, which have to be made 15 months in advance.

Three catalogues, a product guide, information on the Marketing Plan, samples and some real products are all in the starter kit that any new distributor has to buy at the cost of $28 in order to start their business. Additional catalogues can be acquired at cost by the distributors. The company decided that the catalogues should always pass through the distributors and would never be sent directly by the company to a prospective consumer.

We see a catalogue as a major marketing tool and there is a lot of effort going into the preparation of every issue. I do not think that one cannot overestimate its impact on the company image, product awareness, and finally on sales. We are still investing considerable amounts of money into it and experimenting with its look and content. It is one of the best investments.

Operations

When Oriflame started operating in Warsaw from a rented villa, people were lining up for hours in the street to buy some of the first product range. Rapidly, 70 per cent of the products were out of stock, and the company decided to stop recruiting new distributors for three months. That time was used to reorganise all distribution procedures and open some service centres.

In March 1992, Oriflame Poland purchased Kamelia, a cooperative that produced cosmetic products in Ursus, a suburb of Warsaw, later followed by the installation of packaging facilities in the old factory. By April 1992, Bozona Karpinska had joined the company as operations manager in charge of distributors, warehouses and customer service.

In 1993, 12 service centres were opened, most of them in rented villas throughout the country, to allow distributors to come and pick up the merchandise. In 1994, Oriflame had created a total of 18 centres, 10 of which were company owned; the others were on an agreement basis with different entrepreneurs. A new warehouse has been completed along with new pick and pack facilities for a few thousand orders per day.

In 1994, Oriflame Poland employed 150 people, all of them of Polish origin. The distribution network counted over 50,000 registered members.

By 1995, Oriflame was selling a range of 200 products, 60 per cent of which were filled and packed in Ursus, with the remaining 40 per cent coming from the factory in Ireland.

On 31 January 1995, a daily newspaper published in Warsaw printed an article that said: 'Swedish company Oriflame was the first direct selling company in our market (1991). According to Oriflame management, the speed of turnover growth and network development in Poland is the most remarkable in the 27 years' history of the company.'

Advertising and public relations

In 1993, it became evident that Oriflame was aiming toward a mass market with its sales volume and, therefore, the company decided to invest into both advertising and public relations (PR) activities to strengthen its brand awareness. The first successful advertising campaign was run in the autumn of 1993, followed by spring and autumn of 1994. The media used were mainly public TV and all segments of women's magazines. The advertising budget for 1994 was almost $700,000, of which 70 per cent was spent on TV.

Below-the-line activities included not only traditional PR but also exhibitions and company promotional days in all major cities in the country, with an estimated audience of 300,000. Frequent contacts with the press resulted in broad media coverage, with little negative comment.

The Oriflame distributors

When a new distributor registers with Oriflame, he or she can generally place orders on credit up to US$500, the average order being $100. Given the state of the bank system, which was still very poor in 1994, distributors' cash payment facilities are organised in all service centres across the country.

In December 1994, Oriflame Poland had built a network of 50,000 active distributors (placing orders at least once during the preceding three months) plus 30,000 nonactive distributors (no orders in the last three months). One distributor, Jerzy Ruggier, a student at Warsaw University, explains: 'I know that I have to create a place for my job. I learned responsibility. It is important for me to sell high-quality products, to be honest, and not to break the rules. It is a way to start a small business and to help people to understand the new laws and taxes.' Another distributor, Joanna Szablinska, had set an objective for herself: 'I wanted to become a Sapphire Director and buy a new car, an Alpha Romeo. Oriflame is a way of socialising, something which gives you the opportunity to learn how to make safe contacts with other people and buy some luxury in different forms.'

Of the 573 distributors who have reached the director level and beyond, 90 per cent of them devoted all their working time to Oriflame. Another several hundred are making a living that is far beyond average standards in Poland. The Oriflame network consists of some 75 per cent of women and 25 per cent of men, the majority being 25 to 35 years old. Bert Wozciech, after three years as area manager for Benetton in Poland, joined Oriflame as training manager for the whole network. Since 1993, he has organised training sessions for the directors. Every Monday at 4:30 p.m. in Warsaw, he conducted, in a lawyers' club, a seminar on motivation, which was free of charge and open to any active or prospective distributor who wished to attend.

In May 1994, Edward Zieba commented on the Oriflame situation in Poland:

We want to intensify our support because we do not only want to do business but also develop social life and the individual distributor. We do not want to give only more money to the distributors, we want to develop a club, to make the distributors more able to meet other people and belong to something special. . . .

The years of rapid growth are over but I am convinced that in 3 years from now we will have at least 100,000 active distributors.

Table 2 Sales statistics

Country: Poland	1991	1992	1993	1994
Total sales (US$ thousands)	2,250	21,566	35,390	37,180
Active file count	1,782	24,101	38,925	45,020
Activity %/month (average)	84	65	58	53
Sales/active/month (US$ average)	355	288	161	118
No. of employees	14	81	130	154
Office space (square metres)	130	600	800	1,000
Warehouse space (square metres)	100	900	1,100	2,400
No. of service centres	0	2	14	18
Advertising spending (US$ thousands)	0	20	320	700

Competition

In 1994, it was estimated that over a million Poles were working for different networks in direct-selling, multinational companies such as Avon, Amway, Zepter, Oriflame, Herbalife, and so on. Two of them, Amway and Zepter, were described as follows.

Amway, one of the world's largest and most dynamic direct-sales companies, has been active in Poland since 1992. Although Amway came to the Polish market relatively late, it now boasts the largest network of sales agents. In the opinion of the Amway bosses, Poland is their best market, both in terms of the number of distributors and in terms of sales. In the world, Amway has more than two million distributors, who sell about 400 of the company's own products and a few thousand products manufactured by other firms from which Amway has acquired selling rights. Its total annual sales amount in 1994 was $4 billion. In Poland, the monthly turnover is about $30 million zloty. In 1992–1993, Amway managed to build a network of 100,000 distributors. An Amway executive stated: 'Poland is our best market in both sales and number of distributors in relation to its population.' Amway distributors are not employees of the company but are independent entrepreneurs who have their own businesses. So far, Amway in Poland sells about 20 products: laundry detergents, dishwashing liquids, care cosmetics and personal hygiene products. The big advantage of the Amway products is that they can be returned even after they are taken out of the packaging.

Amway is not just cosmetics. It is also the author of a television serial, Bliznes Start. This programme talks not only about the basics of entrepreneurship and a free market economy, it also presents people – Polish businessmen.

In Sweden, Amway differs from its Swedish competitor in that, at the moment, it has no plans to start production. The only products Amway buys from Polish companies are advertising gadgets: bags, balloons, and so forth. Total sales for 1994 were estimated to be $28 million.

Zepter is a Swiss–Austrian firm, which for the past year has been selling kitchen utensils. The demonstrations of its products take place in private homes. Using the products purchased by the owner of the house, the person making the presentation demonstrates the advantages of using the Zepter pots and pans, which are expensive by Polish standards. Zepter products can also be purchased by instalments. One becomes the owner of the chrome–nickel pots, pans, and silverware or 24-carat gold-plated coffee set only after the last instalment is paid. In 1993, Zepter had 25,000 distributors in Poland but, as the company's representative assures us, sales grow monthly.

Oriflame manufacturing in Poland

The high demand for natural skin care and make-up products in Poland inclined the Oriflame corporate management to make the investment at Ursus. 'We see Poland as a very big and important market for our products, a market which is still growing. We believe it is a prudent decision to broaden our activities here by building an ultramodern factory,' said Jonas af Jochnick, the company's founder and president, during a press conference at Oriflame headquarters.

The $20 million manufacturing plant was due to start operating during 1995. It is a state-of-the-art production equipment and complete research and laboratory facility, which will make it the most modern cosmetics factory in Poland. Products will be made from the same ingredients and under the same strict quality control as in all other Oriflame plants. All production processes will be environmentally safe.

Poland is the second country where Oriflame cosmetics will be manufactured. Part of the production will be exported to neighbouring countries. More than 300 people will be employed full-time once the new plant is operational.

KEY FACTORS IN ORIFLAME'S SUCCESS

Looking back over the years from 1990 onward and the development of Oriflame in Eastern European markets, Sven Mattsson identified these key factors to the company's success.

- *Local management*. Since the beginning, in 1990, Oriflame developed a local management policy. Sending expatriates to do the job, even if they had a solid knowledge and experience of both the company's products and the local culture, was never considered as an appropriate solution. In each country, the company recruits a local manager and staff, spending a lot of time during interviews explaining the nature and spirit of the free market economy, the direct-selling method and the Oriflame Marketing Plan.
- *Marketing plan*. The marketing plan itself is considered one of the main assets of the company. Support, guidance and training were supplied from Brussels, with staff spending a great amount of effort and time helping local markets. The marketing plan, called 'The Success Plan' was the same for each country, with minor adaptations where required.

  Mattsson summarises the Oriflame concept, 'Oriflame considers itself as a company offering two kinds of products. First, a concrete one, originating from the product range of 200 products displayed in a catalogue with a pricing policy that favoured volume rather than margins. Second, a more intangible product, which originated from the business opportunity offered to each distributor to develop their own business.'
- *PR and advertising*. Investing in PR has always been considered important. This is especially true of former communist countries who have long forgotten the knowledge and practice of a free market economy. Oriflame was spending approximately $45,000 per year in each country for PR and is planning to increase it in the coming years. A considerable amount was invested in 'above the line' advertising to capitalise on the relative inexperience of media purchasing during 1991 to 1993. 'Oriflame has reached 80 per cent awareness in Poland, the Czech Republic and Hungary, which is definitely partly due to successful advertising cam-

paigns during the past years,' says Mattsson. Oriflame used a mix of TV commercials, printed advertisements and billboards.
- *Product and price*. Out of the range of approximately 200 products, the company manufactures about 65 per cent; the remaining 35 per cent come from subcontractors. Oriflame cosmetics are made from pure, natural ingredients. As Jonas af Jochnick explained, 'The company is dedicated to ensuring that our customers receive the highest-quality products at reasonable prices each time they purchase Oriflame cosmetics.' 'Our aim is to have our products priced below our international competitors and at the same time be considered as an alternative to cheap local products,' says Mattsson.
- *Distribution*. In order to facilitate the distributor's activity, the company has created in each country several service centres. This further improves the lead time between order and delivery. In 1994, Poland had 18 service centres; the Czech Republic and Slovakia, 20; Hungary, 9; Turkey, 9; and Greece, 3. The aim has been to give a 48-hour service turnaround throughout the country, with a 24-hour service in the capitals. 'Our distribution strategy has proven to be very successful. As in all areas of life today, speed and accuracy are very important and this is especially true for direct selling.'

STRATEGIC ISSUES

After four years of activity in Eastern Europe, results have been well beyond early expectations. Sven Mattsson is now facing various issues that will influence the recommendations he will make to Jonas af Jochnick and the ORESA board for the future.

- How far should the company go to increase its service to the distributors who, of course, appreciate very much having products available as fast as possible? Moving the products faster always means higher costs. How much value should be attributed to distributor convenience? Should an inventory of the whole Oriflame product range be kept at each service centre?
- Should the company invest in advertising campaigns? How important is the advertising for a direct-selling company to keep the awareness high? Is it worthwhile continuing when the increased media prices are taken into consideration?
- Should the company enlarge its product range with noncosmetic products to increase sales and possibly to attract new distributors?
- A few countries into which Oriflame is considering

expanding and where it is conducting marketing research still have high inflation rates. What kind of specific pricing and product policy would the company need to implement in order to ensure a minimum risk for its investment?

- Should the company go for local management or expatriates? What kind of management is needed for starting up a new, more distant sales company? What kind of management is required when the company enters into a more mature stage?

APPENDIX

The marketing plan: an overview

To become an Oriflame distributor, a candidate should be sponsored by an existing registered Oriflame distributor. Products are sold directly to the consumer by independent distributors who are not employed by Oriflame.

There are no exclusive territories or franchises available under the Oriflame policy. Any distributor is free to conduct his or her business in any area of the country. No distributor shall sell, demonstrate, or display Oriflame products in any retail outlet.

Oriflame recommends a markup of 30 per cent on all products purchased at distributor price. The distributor's income is based on a monthly accumulation of points. All products are assigned two sets of numbers: bonus points (BP), which normally remains a constant number, and business volume (BV), which is a monetary value that changes if prices change. In general, the value of the BV equals the distributor price (DP), excluding value-added tax (VAT).

The total BP of all the products a distributor buys and sells during the course of a month will determine

Monthly BP	Monthly performance discount – percentage of BV
10,000 +	21%
6,600–9,999	18%
4,000–6,599	15%
2,400–3,999	12%
1,200–2,399	9%
600–1,199	6%
200–599	3%

the distributor's performance discount percentage. The monthly performance discount is based not only on his or her own business volume, but also on the business volume generated by any distributors who have been sponsored by him or her.

The monthly performance discount is added to the 30 per cent markup, the maximum being 21 per cent, equivalent to 10,000 BP per month. Distributors can also earn a further 1 per cent or 4 per cent bonus if they meet certain criteria. Cash awards from $3,000 to $20,000 can be earned when reaching the higher titles in the marketing plan.

If a customer is not satisfied, the products are replaced or refunded through the '100% customer satisfaction guarantee'.

The available credit per order is $500. All outstanding payments must be made before a next order is placed, or within 30 days from the date of invoice. Payments can be made at the Oriflame head office, at some Oriflame service centres, at the post office, or by bank transfer. Orders can be made at service centres or by mail or fax by using a distributor order form.

Source: The case was written by Nathalie Rouvier and Vahid Bafandi under the supervision of Professor Dominique Xardel, ESSEC, Cergy Pontoise, France. It is intended as a basis for class discussion rather than to illustrate either effective or ineffective handling of management situations. © D. Xardel 1998. Used by permission.

Rocking the boat at MTV: dealing with market fragmentation

There are two things you need to know about MTV. The first, and this is the good news, is that MTV just might be the best idea for a TV network ever invented. That's because in its original and pure form, MTV filled hour after hour of airtime with music videos supplied by record companies to promote their artists. What a concept! A network of commercials, interrupted only by more commercials and an occasional promotion. But the bad news is this: the channel must be constantly

refreshed to stay current because pop music devours its young at a fearful pace.

To stay fresh, MTV is currently undergoing its most sweeping overhaul of the decade. The CEO intends to drive earnings by stretching and spinning the MTV and Nickelodeon brands into as many as a dozen new cable networks, feature films, online content, records, toys, clothes, books, and especially global markets. The results so far look promising, but there's always the danger that corporate pressures to exploit the brands could strain management, alienate consumers, or worst of all, leave those inside MTV Networks feeling as if they're no longer working in a hip, happening place but merely toiling for another money-hungry media giant like Fox, say, or Disney. Says Jeff Dunn, the chief operating officer of Nickelodeon: 'How to maintain our guerrilla flavor when we've become the great corporate moneymaker is a real challenge.' Even Dunn, a preppy, Harvard-trained MBA, says that if the 'suits' take over, MTV Networks is in trouble. (Marc Gunther, *Fortune,* 27 October 1997).

Back in the 1980s, Mark Knopfler of Dire Straits sang 'I want my MTV', and since then millions of people around the world have been granted this request. Launched in the USA in 1981, MTV was the first 24-hour music television network in the world, and has been the international leader ever since. It was the first network to have a presence on all five continents and currently reaches half of the television-owning households in the world. MTV is available to 298 million households in 82 countries around the globe, either via cable or by satellite.

MTV's first international move was the launch of MTV Networks Europe in 1987. During the first ten years, its philosophy was decidedly 'global'. Bill Roedy, head of MTV's international activities, strongly believed in an internationally standardised product and sought to create one network that would serve the entire continent from its base in London. In his view, the 18- to 24-year-olds that form the core of MTV's audience did not differ significantly from country to country, and would be attracted to the global youth culture projected by MTV. However, it did not take long for local competitors to emerge, such as VIVA in Germany and Video Music in Italy, and these channels cut deeply into MTV's market share. Advertisers also complained that they did not need to reach a pan-European audience, but were more interested in national ones. Both pressures prompted Roedy to abandon his pan-European network in 1996 and to move towards more localisation. His response has been to split the network into five services: MTV in the UK and Ireland, MTV Central (Austria, Germany and Switzerland), MTV Southern (Italy), MTV Nordic (Sweden, Finland, Norway and Denmark), and MTV Europe (35 countries including Spain, France, Belgium, the Netherlands, Greece, Israel and Eastern Europe). Within each of the five broadcasting areas MTV's 'feed' can be split yet further, to allow for adver-

tising focused on even smaller geographic territories. As of January 1999, MTV reaches approximately 62 million households across Europe, roughly the same number of households as it reaches in the USA.

After gaining experience in Europe, MTV started a Portuguese-language MTV Brasil in 1990. The next step was to expand to the rest of the continent by launching MTV Networks Latin America in 1993. This Spanish-language network offers two separate services. The northern feed, coming from Mexico City, is directed towards Bolivia, Colombia, Ecuador, Venezuela, Central America, the Caribbean, Mexico and parts of the USA. The southern feed, originating from Buenos Aires, is distributed to Argentina, Chile, Paraguay, Peru and Uruguay. In all, 25 million households across Latin America have access to MTV.

The next step was to launch MTV Networks Asia with its headquarters in Singapore in 1995. Its first service was the Chinese-language MTV Mandarin, which is transmitted via satellite to China, Taiwan, Brunei, Singapore and South Korea. The English-language MTV Southeast Asia was started almost simultaneously to serve the Philippines, Malaysia, Brunei, Hong Kong, Indonesia, Papua New Guinea, Singapore, South Korea, Thailand and Vietnam. In 1996 the English-language MTV India was added, reaching India, Bangladesh, Nepal, Sri Lanka, Pakistan and the Middle East. Together, over 100 million households across Asia can tune in to MTV.

Most recent moves have been the launch of MTV Australia in 1997 and MTV Russia in 1998. The latter is particularly remarkable, as MTV is the first Western television network to create a customised service for the Russian market. The Russian-language programming is made in Moscow and is broadcast 'free-as-air' in most of the country's large cities.

A large part of MTV's success is attributable to the network's ability to understand, follow and even shape the volatile audience of teens and twenty-somethings in a way that suit-and-tie-wearing executives at stuffier networks have found difficult to imitate. MTV has consistently been able to strike a chord with the fickle group of young adults, who appreciate its unpredictable and irreverent approach. By being at the forefront of new trends, MTV has become essential for those who want to know what is fashionable. This has made MTV more than a TV channel – it is a part of the youth culture. While focused on the group of 18- to 24-year-olds, MTV picks up many viewers in the 12- to 17-year-old segment, who can't wait to be 18, and among the 25- to 34-year-old group, who want to stay young as long as possible. In most countries, few other networks have catered to these specific segments, and this has opened the door for MTV's entrance into the market.

However, in broadcasting, good channel format and a receptive target audience are not enough to guarantee success. It also depends on a network's ability to manage relationships with a number of key external stakeholders:

- *First, a channel needs suppliers – someone must provide MTV with videos.* At this moment, the record companies produce these highly expensive videos as promotional devices to sell their CDs and supply them free of cost to music channels. But while both sides benefit from this relationship, it places the record companies in a relatively dependent position. If MTV decides not to broadcast a new video, record companies have few alternatives. Unsurprisingly, the record companies would be happy if MTV had more competitors. It is not a good omen for MTV that its leading challenger in Germany, VIVA, was initiated by the record companies PolyGram, EMI Music, Sony and Time Warner.
- *Secondly, advertisers are essential to the survival of a TV channel.* Most commercial broadcasters do not rely an viewers to pay for the programmes watched (either by subscription or pay as you view), but largely finance operations out of advertising revenues. This is also true for MTV, which is heavily dependent on attracting enough advertisers interested in its youth segment. Some advertisers have become whole-hearted partners of MTV. For instance, PepsiCo has a long-term relationship with MTV, with the intention of co-promoting both brands and reinforcing each other's positions world-wide. However, there are not very many companies that want the international advertising that MTV is so good at offering outside of the USA. Furthermore, many advertisers in the USA would not mind some competition for MTV, to keep advertising prices down.
- *A third success factor for TV channels is distribution.* Programmes need to reach viewers' TV sets, either by satellite, cable or through the airwaves. Transmitting via satellite is relatively simple. Satellite 'slots' can be rented from third parties and viewers can receive transmissions with a dish. However, in most countries the number of households with a dish is quite low, given the high initial cost, ranging from €1,000 to €3,000. Because of this most commercial channels prefer distribution via cable systems, which have a high level of pen-

etration in most developed economies. Yet getting cable operators to carry a channel often proves to be an arduous task. Most cable operators have small regional monopolies and need to be convinced of the need to make extra costs to carry an additional channel. Many cable systems are technically limited to a fixed number of channels and therefore they need to drop an existing broadcaster before a new channel can be accommodated. This gives cable companies quite a bit of power, leading operators in some countries to demand that commercial channels pay for a slot on the cable.

Although MTV has been at the top of the charts for more than 15 years, other channels have been steadily rising in the ratings and challenge MTV's virtual ownership of the youth market. In the USA, real competition has only recently emerged. The Canadian network MuchMusic launched a channel in the USA in 1994 and by 1997 was also present in Mexico, Argentina and Finland. The Box, a channel that allows viewers to call in and select the videos to be played, has been doing moderately well, expanding from the USA to the UK, the Netherlands, Argentina, Peru and Chile. MOR Music Television is a music-shopping network that combines videos with merchandising breaks. Besides these general music channels, MTV is facing a number of competitors focusing on only one type of music. BET on Jazz, Black Entertainment Television, The Nashville Network, Country Music Television, The Gospel Network and Z Music (Christian) may all draw viewers away from MTV.

Outside its home base, competition varies by country, but is becoming fierce in a number of mature markets. For instance, in Germany MTV has lost its top spot to VIVA, which employs German-speaking DJs and mixes international and local music. The same is true in the Netherlands, where a local player, The Music Factory, is knocking MTV off front stage. In the UK, The Box pulled ahead of MTV in 1997 and a new entrant, UK Play, has launched an assault. In all these cases the competitive advantage of MTV's new rivals is their ability to tailor programming to the demands of the local market.

Taken together, these developments form a rather tricky strategic problem for MTV. As the market for music television is maturing, it seems to be fragmenting. The market seems to be disintegrating into niches along musical and geographic lines. Competitors are focusing on one type of music or one country, out-specialising the generalist MTV.

So far, MTV's response has been to follow the trend towards narrower target audiences and more specific programming content. Internationally, MTV seems to be moving further and further away from its strategy of international standardisation, towards localised programming with an international flavour. As for segmentation along musical lines, MTV is endeavouring to offer a broad range of different formats to cover different musical tastes. MTV's oldest spinoff is VH-1, which is also a 24 hours a day music channel, directed towards an audience of 25- to 40-year-olds, who want a mix of 'classics' and easily digestible contemporary music. VH-1 is doing well in the USA and has been moving abroad in the last few years. It is now more popular than MTV in the UK. Another move has been the launch of M2 in the US market in August 1996. M2 is an all-video channel that closely resembles the early free-form MTV, before it began running more long-form non-music programmes. Industry analysts remark that even if M2 does not break even, it might block the way for new competitors and should satisfy record companies' complaints that MTV does not offer enough airtime to new acts.

MTV's latest move has been to spawn a new range of MTV brand extensions. MTV Extra has been created with the intention of focusing on playing independent rock. MTV Base is a channel playing soul and rap, and VH-1 Classics plays pop and rock from the late 1970s and early 1980s. One of the critical factors that will determine these channels' success is whether advertisers are willing to buy airtime. Nielsen ratings are usually important for determining advertising spending, but these ratings are notoriously unable to track the viewing and channel surfing behaviour of the young music audience, rendering them quite unreliable. Advertisers must therefore be willing to place 'trust' in MTV's ability to reach, and connect with, the intended target audience.

In the medium to long term, the most important factor in determining whether MTV remains successful might be its ability to constantly renew itself and remain youthful. It is hard work staying at the cutting edge of pop culture. It requires constant undermining of everything that has become established. MTV has now become part of the music establishment – but it cannot permit itself to act as such. It must ride the next wave of youth culture. The struggle continues. At the moment the average age of MTV employees is 28 years and there are more people with nose rings than neckties. The only corporate dress code, jokes CEO Tom Freston, is 'no full-frontal nudity'. Nevertheless, as the company grows and new channels are added, the threat of becoming a regular corporation increases. Add to this the pressure from MTV's owner, the media giant Viacom, to exploit the MTV brand through films, records, toys, clothes, books and other merchandising, and the threat of becoming an ordinary company becomes apparent. Or as the employee quoted at the beginning of this case put it: 'How to maintain our guerrilla flavor when we've become the great corporate moneymaker is a real challenge.'

Whether MTV's moves towards localisation and brand extensions will prove to be the best possible response to the fragmentation of the music television market remains to be seen. And whether MTV's company culture can retain its youthful rebelliousness and creativity as the company grows is also an issue on the minds of the company's top management. In short, MTV has some difficult nuts to crack which is not exactly what Mark Knopfler meant when he sang about getting 'your money for nothing and your chicks for free'.

Discussion questions

1 What are the advantages gained by MTV by being a global player? How strong are the pressures for further localisation of MTV's services?

2 How can MTV balance the demands of global operations and local responsiveness?

3 Which 'musical segments' do you recognise in your national market?

4 In which segments is MTV vulnerable to new specialist music channels?

5 How can MTV convince advertisers of their reach, given the unreliability of the Nielsen ratings?

6 How should MTV respond to possible fragmentation and specialist competition?

7 How should MTV respond to new media, in particular to broadcasting via the Internet?

8 How should MTV be organised to operate in all of these countries, segments and media, while remaining young, rebellious and innovative?

Source: C. Phillips, A. Pruyn and M.P. Kestemenont, *Understanding Marketing, A European Casebook* (Wiley, 2000).

PART IV

Global marketing strategy

CHAPTER 8

Market selection and market entry alternatives – exporting

No nation is ever ruined by trade.
BENJAMIN FRANKLIN

The World can be Changed. The Future is not Destiny.
ROBERT JUNGK

Chapter objectives

After reading this chapter, you will know:

- Which criteria are suitable for the selection of foreign target markets.
- How these criteria are analysed and applied in a systematic manner.
- Which market entry alternatives are available to companies and how they decide the most appropriate one.
- The different forms of exporting.
- When to go for direct rather than indirect exporting.
- How governments influence export activities of firms.
- How to recognise export activities as a process developing over time.
- Different ways of export financing and methods of payment.

Why is this important? Here are three situations in which you would need an understanding of the above issues:

- You are looking for an approach to systematically analyse the pros and cons of different markets in order to arrive at a market selection decision.
- You have decided on exporting as the most suitable market entry alternative for your foreign activities. Now you want more detail on government assistance and export finance.
- You have decided to export your products but are uncertain about the most suitable form of exporting.

Practice link

In Germany, foreign activities are a way of life for the *Mittelstand*, 2.5 million small and mid-sized companies that generate two thirds of Germany's gross national product (GNP) and account for 30 per cent of exports. For companies such as J.N. Eberle, steel-maker, Trumpf, a machine tool manufacturer, and J. Eberspächer, which makes auto exhaust systems, international sales account for as much as 40 per cent of total sales. *Mittelstand* owner-managers target global niche markets and prosper by focusing on quality, innovation, and investing heavily in research and development. For example, the chief executive of G.W. Barth, a company that manufactures cocoa-bean roasting machines, invested nearly €1.7 million in infrared technology that reduced temperature variances. The company's global market share stands at 70 per cent, a threefold increase in a 10-year period, as Ghirardelli Chocolate, Hershey Foods, and other companies have snapped up Barth's roasters. At ABM Baumüller, a manufacturer of motors and other components for cranes, a major investment in technology allows the company to tailor products to customer needs by means of flexible manufacturing. New automated production equipment was installed that allows changeover to different products in a matter of seconds. Two-thirds of all envelopes produced worldwide are estimated to be made on machines made by Winkler & Dünnebier. The German company manufactures some of the most complex machines for producing envelopes, turning out 25 envelopes per second in up to 22,000 variants. Winkler & Dünnebier's business is not only envelopes; the company is also world-leader in equipment to produce paper-based hygiene products.[1] The story is repeated throughout Germany; as a result, in industry after industry, the *Mittelstand* is world-class in foreign activities.[2]

The success of the *Mittelstand* serves as a reminder of the impact international activities can have on a country's economy. It also demonstrates the difference between international selling and international marketing. International selling does not involve tailoring the product, the price, or the promotional material to suit the requirements of global markets. The only marketing mix element that differs is the place – that is, the country where the product is sold. This selling approach may work for some products or services; for unique products with little or no international competition, such an approach is possible. Similarly, companies new to international markets may initially experience success with selling. Even today, the managerial mindset in many companies still favours international selling. However, as companies mature in the global marketplace or as new competitors enter the picture, it becomes necessary to engage in international marketing.

International marketing targets the customer in the context of the total market environment. The international marketer does not take the domestic product 'as is' and simply sells it to international customers. To the international marketer, the product offered in the home market is a starting point. It is modified as needed to meet the preferences of international target markets. Similarly, the international marketer sets prices to fit the marketing strategy and does not merely extend home-country pricing to the target market. Despite the cost incurred in international preparation, transportation and financing, successful companies strive for an internationally competitive price. Finally, the export marketer also adjusts strategies and plans for communications and distribution to fit the market. In other words, effective communication about product features or uses to buyers in export markets may require creating brochures with different copy, photographs or artwork. As an internationally successful manager noted, 'We have to approach the international market with marketing literature as opposed to sales literature.'

Export marketing is the integrated marketing of goods and services that are destined for customers in international markets. Export marketing requires

1 An understanding of the target market environment.
2 The use of marketing research and the identification of market potential.
3 Decisions concerning product design, pricing, distribution and channels, advertising and communications – the marketing mix.

Topics 1 and 2 listed above were covered in preceding chapters. The following chapters are devoted to the marketing mix. The purpose of this chapter is to provide a guideline to how companies can select high-potential target markets. First, it outlines which criteria and tools can be used to identify promising markets. After relevant target markets are selected, a company needs to decide on how to enter these markets. In general, there are two options: operate from the home market or establish a business overseas. Depending on the strategic intention a company holds with respect to its international operations, it will decide on one or the other. Finally, exporting in its various forms is presented as a way to enter and serve foreign markets.

SELECTING FOREIGN MARKETS

The decision as to which foreign markets to address should be based on a number of criteria: the potential market size, the product fit, additional costs, to name but a few. Each criterion has to be evaluated carefully, as it may constitute either an incentive or a barrier to successfully entering a foreign market. While the importance of selection criteria may vary across companies and foreign markets, they can in principle be grouped into five broad categories: (1) market-related characteristics, such as product fit, market size and potential, (2) cost-related aspects, such as transportation costs, (3) the regulatory framework, such as political environment, and (4) tariffs, duties and non-tariff trade barriers.

When it comes to the question which criteria to use for market selection, empirical analyses have provided some answers. The question regarding which specific variables are applied in country selection depends very much on a firm's specific portfolio of resources and capabilities as well as on its international objectives. Generally, however, companies set similar priorities as to the importance of selection criteria. Market-related characteristics are judged to be the most important followed by cost-related and regulatory influences. Finally, it has to be noted that the importance of certain characteristics varies across industries. A generalised recommendation on which criteria to select has therefore to be treated with caution.[3] Notwithstanding these limitations, the selection process should begin with a product-market profile, i.e. the establishment of key factors influencing sales and profitability of the product in question.

MARKET SELECTION CRITERIA

If a company is getting started for the first time in international activities, its product-market profile will have to be based on its experience in the home market. The basic questions to be answered can be summarised as the nine Ws:

1 Who buys our product?
2 Who does not buy our product?
3 What need or function does our product serve?
4 What problem does our product solve?
5 What are customers currently buying to satisfy the need and/or solve the problem for which our product is targeted?
6 What price are they paying for the products they are currently buying?
7 When is our product purchased?
8 Where is our product purchased?
9 Why is our product purchased?

Any company must answer these critical questions if it is going to be successful in export markets. Each answer provides an input into decisions concerning the four Ps. Remember, the general rule in marketing is that, if a company wants to penetrate an existing market, it must offer more value than its competitors, such as better benefits, lower prices, or both. Once a company has created a product-market profile, the next step in choosing a foreign target market is to appraise possible markets. The following criteria should be assessed: market potential, market access as expressed through regulations such as tariffs and duties as well as non-tariff trade barriers, shipping costs, or product fit.

Market potential

What is the basic market potential for the product? To answer this question, searching a library or the Internet are good places to start. Numerous international and national organisations such as the United Nations (UN), the OECD or the European Union publish helpful information. Other valuable sources of information are the national and international statistical bureaus, such as the US Census Bureau, the German Statistisches Bundesamt or the European EUROSTAT. Also the national Ministries of Foreign Affairs and related organisations provide information on business and industries abroad.

Whatever source of information is used, the ultimate goal is to determine the major factors affecting demand for a product. Then, using the tools and techniques described in the previous chapter and available data, it is possible to arrive at a rough estimate of total potential demand for the product in one or more particular international markets. National income is often a good starting indicator on which to base demand estimates. Additional statistical measures will considerably sharpen the estimate of total demand. For example, when estimating the demand for automobile tyres, data on the total number of cars registered in any country in the world should be easy to obtain. This data, combined with data on petrol consumption, should permit estimation of the total mileage driven in the target market. When this figure is combined with tyre life predictions, it is a straightforward matter to calculate demand estimates.

Tariffs and duties

Even though the market potential of a foreign target market may appear promising, a second criterion, market access considerations, needs to be taken into account. Whether a market is freely accessible depends on a set of national controls that apply to merchandise sold into the foreign target market. These controls include items such as import tariffs and duties, non-tariff trade barriers such as import restrictions or quotas, foreign exchange regulations, or preference arrangements. These topics are discussed in more detail in the following sections.

Tariffs and duties as an important aspect of a foreign country's regulatory environment may influence market selection either positively or negatively. Before the Second World War specific duties were widely used, and the tariffs of many countries, particularly those in Europe and Latin America, were extremely complex. Between 1959 and 1988, tariff administration was simplified by the use of the Brussels nomenclature (BTN). This nomenclature was worked out by an international committee of experts under the sponsorship of the Customs Cooperation Council, now World Customs Organization (WCO), which in 1955 produced a convention that took effect in 1959.

The rules of this convention were used by most General Agreement of Tariffs and Trade (GATT) member countries until the Harmonized Tariff System (HTS) went into effect in January 1989. The Harmonized Tariff System was adopted by more than 65 countries and provides a standardised classification system for all products.[4] This makes it easier for buyers and sellers to determine export classifications.

In spite of the progress made in simplifying tariff procedures, the task of administrating a tariff presents an enormous problem. People working with imports and exports must familiarise themselves with the different classifications and use them accurately. Even a tariff schedule of several thousand items cannot clearly describe every product traded globally. The introduction of new products and new materials used in manufacturing processes creates new problems. Often, determining the rate on a particular article requires assessing how the item is used or determining its main component material. Two or more alternative classifications may have to be considered.

The classification of a product can make a substantial difference in the duty applied. Under the BTN, it was sometimes possible to seek a more favourable classification to minimise the duty levied in the importing country. For example, an importer of semi-finished products was able to secure a lower tariff rate by calling its product a pump housing, a casing with some internal components, instead of a pump. Under the HTS, however, 'a pump is a pump'; the manufacturer is forced to import the casings with fewer working parts and do more finishing in the target market to maintain the lower import rates.

Tariff systems and customs valuation

Tariff systems provide either a single rate of duty for each item applicable to all countries, or two or more rates, applicable to different countries or groups of countries. Tariffs are usually grouped into three classifications: single-column tariffs, two-column tariffs, and preferential tariffs. The *single-column tariff* is the simplest type of tariff and consists of a schedule of duties in which the rate applies to imports from all countries on the same basis.

Under the *two-column tariff*, the initial single column of duties is supplemented by a second column showing reduced rates as determined through tariff negotiations with other countries. Rates agreed upon by convention are supplied to all countries enjoying most favoured nation (MFN) status within the framework of the WTO. Under the WTO, nations agree to apply their most favourable tariff or lowest tariff rate to all nations, subject to some exceptions, that are signatories to the WTO. The status of most favoured nation is thus more a political than an economic tool. For example, the United States threatened China with the loss of MFN status because of alleged human rights violations. The loss of MFN could have a significant impact on its trade with the United States. The landed prices of Chinese products would rise by 60 to 100 per cent or more, which would price them out of the market. Table 8.1 illustrates what a change in tariffs could mean to China.

A *preferential tariff* is a reduced tariff rate applied to imports from certain countries. The WTO prohibits the use of preferential tariffs with three major exceptions. First, historical preference arrangements such as the British Commonwealth preferences, and similar arrangements that existed before the WTO are exempt. Second, preference schemes that are part of a formal economic integration treaty, such as free trade areas or common markets, are excluded. Third, industrial countries are permitted to grant preferential market access to companies based in less developed countries.

Under WTO regulations, the primary basis of customs valuation is known as *transaction value*. As the name implies, transaction value is defined as the actual individual transaction price paid by the buyer to the seller of the goods being valued. In

Table 8.1 Tariff rates, MFN vs. non–MFN

	MFN	*Non-MFN*
Gold jewellery such as plated neckchains	6.5%	80%
Screws, lock washers, miscellaneous iron/steel parts	5.8%	35%

Source: US Customs Service.

instances in which the buyer and seller are related parties (for example, when a company purchases parts from its manufacturing subsidiaries abroad), customs authorities have the right to scrutinise the transfer price to make sure it is a fair reflection of market value. If there is no established transaction value for the goods, alternative methods are used to compute the customs value, which sometimes result in increased values and, consequently, increased duties.

Types of duties

Customs duties are divided into two categories. They may be calculated either as a percentage of the value of the goods (ad valorem duty), as a specific amount per unit (specific duty), or as a combination of both of these methods.

Ad valorem duties are expressed as a percentage of the value of goods. The definition of customs value varies from country to country. Therefore, firms are well advised to secure information about the valuation practices applied to products in the country of destination. A uniform basis for the valuation of goods for customs purposes was elaborated by the Customs Cooperation Council in Brussels and was adopted in 1953. In countries adhering to HTS conventions on customs valuation, the customs value is landed CIF[5] cost at the port of entry. *Specific duties* are expressed as a specific amount of currency per unit of weight, volume, length, or number of other units of measurement. Specific duties are usually expressed in the currency of the importing country, but there are exceptions, particularly in countries that have experienced sustained inflation.

In the case of *alternative duties*, both ad valorem and specific duties are set out in the custom tariff for a given product. Normally, the applicable rate is the one that yields the higher amount of duty, although there are cases in which the lower is specified. *Compound or mixed duties* provide for specific plus ad valorem rates to be levied on the same articles.

To offset the impact of dumping, which is the sale of merchandise in export markets at unfair prices to the harm of the local economy, most countries have introduced *antidumping duties*. Such duties take the form of special additional import charges equal to the dumping margin. *Countervailing duties* (CVDs) are additional duties levied to offset subsidies granted in the exporting country. Subsidies and countervailing measures received a great deal of attention during the Uruguay GATT negotiations.

Several countries, including Sweden and some other members of the EU, apply a system of *variable import levies* to certain categories of imported agricultural products. In instances in which the prices of imported products would undercut those of domestic products, the effect of these levies would be to raise the price of imported products to the domestic price level. Temporary import surcharges follow a similar objective: to provide additional protection for local industry and, in particular, in response to balance-of-payments deficits.

Theoretically, these duties equal various national taxes such as value-added or sales tax. Under WTO regulations, these tariffs may not lead to additional protection for local manufacturers or subsidise firms' international activities. A major objective of the GATT's Uruguay Round was to improve market access for foreign companies. One of the key obstacles in this endeavour were tariffs, which rendered foreign products considerably more expensive and thus drove them out of the market. As negotiations were successful, tariffs for many product categories were reduced or entirely eliminated. Exports of electronics products to the EU, which have been subject to tariff barriers, 14 per cent for semiconductors and 4 per cent for computer components, are now exempt from tariffs. However, a lot of work still has to be done. Even in industrialised countries such as the European Union or the US, heavy duties are still imposed on various product categories. In the European Union, trucks are subject to a tariff of 22 per cent, in the US 25 per cent. Particularly high tariffs are imposed on agricultural products, which are especially protected in many countries. In the EU, duties on fruit juice vary from 46 per cent to 215 per cent. The US impose a tariff of 132 per cent on peanut butter.[6]

While tariffs came under extensive scrutiny during GATT negotiations, antidumping regulations still enjoy great popularity when it comes to protecting home markets. This is even more the case now, as the WTO allows antidumping duties under certain circumstances: when foreign products (a) are sold at more favourable prices than in the home market, (b) are sold below production costs, or (c) local manufacturers provide evidence of damage to themselves, such as a decrease in sales. This renders antidumping measures not only a legal but also a very flexible instrument. Antidumping duties have turned out to be very persistent. Despite rapidly changing market situations, they are routinely revised only every five years. At the same time, they increase prices on imported products significantly. In the European Union, antidumping duties accounted for a 29 per cent mark-up on average. US customers have to take a mark-up of 57 per cent. In the case of supercomputers produced by the Japanese NEC, US authorities added antidumping duties of 454 per cent (!). When it comes to introducing new antidumping duties, the US leads the ranking. In 1998 alone, 25 new cases were registered, compared to 16 in 1997. The EU, however, does not lag behind in this respect. At present, the EU is investigating 13 petitions against steel manufacturers from Slovenia to South Korea. Companies from industries such as consumer electronics, textiles and forestry have announced that they are going to file complaints against their foreign competitors.[7]

Non-tariff barriers

A non-tariff trade barrier (NTB) is any measure, other than a tariff, that is a deterrent or obstacle to the sale of products in a foreign market. The five major types of NTBs, or hidden trade barrier, as they are sometimes called, are discussed next.

Quotas and trade control

Quotas are government-imposed limits or restrictions on the number of units or the total value of a particular product or product category that can be imported. The trade distortion caused by a quota is even more severe than a tariff because once the quota has been reached, market price mechanisms are not allowed to operate. The phrase 'state trade controls' refers to the practice of monopolising trade in certain commodities. In the former Soviet Union, all commodities were monopolised. However, there are also many examples of non-Communist government monopolies. The Swedish government, for example, controls the import of all alcoholic beverages and tobacco products and the French government controls all imports of coal. After the European Union limited the import of Ukrainian steel to 233,000 tonnes, the US followed in 1997 with a reduction to 500,000 tonnes. These amounts equalled one third of Ukraine's steel export volume. The US justified its move as a protection of the domestic steel industry. The market share of Ukrainian steel in the US was said to amount to more than 10 per cent.[8]

In addition to governmental import regulations, so-called *voluntary restraints* were established in international trade. Under such an arrangement, importers voluntarily agree to restrict imports to a certain amount. Some Southeast Asian and Third World countries have accepted such restrictions for their exports of textile products to the US; Japan 'voluntarily' restrained its exports of cars and TVs to the US. In the light of these agreements, some critics have raised concerns against this managed trade rather than free trade.

Discriminatory procurement policies

These can take the form of government rules and administrative regulations, as well as formal or informal company policies, that discriminate against foreign suppliers. For example, the Buy American Act of 1933 stipulates that US federal agencies must buy articles produced in the United States unless domestically produced goods are not available, the cost is unreasonable, or if purchasing US materials would be inconsistent with the public interest.

Restrictive customs procedures

The rules and regulations for classifying and valuing commodities as a basis for levying import duties can be administered in a way that makes compliance difficult and expensive. For example, a product might be classified by the British Customs Authorities under a certain harmonised number; Canadian customs may disagree. The British exporter may have to attend a hearing with Canadian customs officials to reach an agreement. Such delays cost time and money for both the importer and exporter.

Selective monetary controls and discriminatory exchange rate policies

Discriminatory exchange rate policies distort trade in much the same way as selective import duties and export subsidies. For example, many countries from time to time require importers to place on deposit, at no interest, an amount equal to the value of imported goods. In effect, these regulations raise the price of foreign goods by the cost of money for the term of the required deposit.

Restrictive administrative and technical regulations

These include antidumping regulations, size regulations, and safety and health regulations. Some of these regulations are intended to keep out foreign goods, while others are directed toward legitimate domestic objectives. For example, despite a GATT agreement concerning technical barriers to trade, Japan used technical standards unrelated to performance to bar US forest products from its market. Safety and pollution regulations for automobiles, on the other hand, are motivated almost entirely by legitimate concerns about highway safety and pollution. However, an effect of these regulations has been to make it so expensive to comply with safety requirements that some automakers have withdrawn from certain markets. Volkswagen, for example, no longer sells diesel automobiles in the United States for this reason.

Another example of a restrictive technical regulation is found in Germany, which requires that imports of feed meal contain only 5 per cent fat. Wellens & Company, a US-based firm, produces a feed meal that contains about 10 per cent fat, and, according to the company president, 'We simply don't sell any to the Germans. To change the meal's fat content would involve special machinery which would greatly increase production costs; it simply wouldn't be worth it.' Wellens expects several other

Western European countries to adopt the 5 per cent regulation, which the company claims does nothing for the animal's health.

As discussed previously, there is a growing trend to remove all such restrictive trade barriers on a regional basis. The creation of the European Union represents a major milestone in this respect. A key goal of the EU is to have one standard for all of Europe for such things as automobile safety, drug testing and certification, food and product quality controls, and professional licensing to facilitate trade and commerce. The creation of a single North American market consisting of the United States, Canada and Mexico is also aimed at the removal of barriers to trade.

Shipping cost

Costs incurred during preparation for foreign markets and shipping costs can affect the market potential for a product. If a similar product is already being manufactured in the target market, shipping costs may render the imported product non-competitive. It is important to investigate alternative modes of shipping as well as ways to differentiate a product to offset the price disadvantage.

Product fit

With information on market potential, cost of access to the market, and local competition, the next step is to decide how well a company's product fits the market in question. In general, a product fits a market if it satisfies the following criteria: (1) the product is likely to appeal to customers in the potential market; (2) the product will not require more adaptation than is economically justifiable by the expected sales volume; (3) import restrictions and/or high tariffs do not exclude or make the product so expensive in the target market as to effectively eliminate demand; (4) shipping costs to the target market are in line with the requirements for competitive price; and (5) the cost of assembling sales literature, catalogues, and technical bulletins is feasible in view of the market potential. The last factor is particularly important in selling highly technical products.

A MARKET SELECTION MODEL

Following the identification of the relevant market selection criteria and the collection of the respective information on different target markets, the task is to systematically track down the most promising foreign markets.

In this respect, a very common approach is a multi-stage selection process. At each stage in the filtering process, the number of potential target countries is narrowed down. During this process, selection criteria become increasingly stringent. Thus, at the end, only countries which comply with all requirements remain as target markets. Figure 8.1 illustrates this stepwise procedure graphically.

Scoring models provide a means to systematise the country selection process. Based on their international experience and the information gathered on different target markets, managers may develop a decision matrix. Figure 8.2 provides an example of such a selection model. On one side, it lists the selection criteria and weighs these criteria according to their importance for their specific business. On the other side, it gives the prospective target markets. Estimates are given on each country's perform-

Figure 8.1 **A multi-stage selection process**

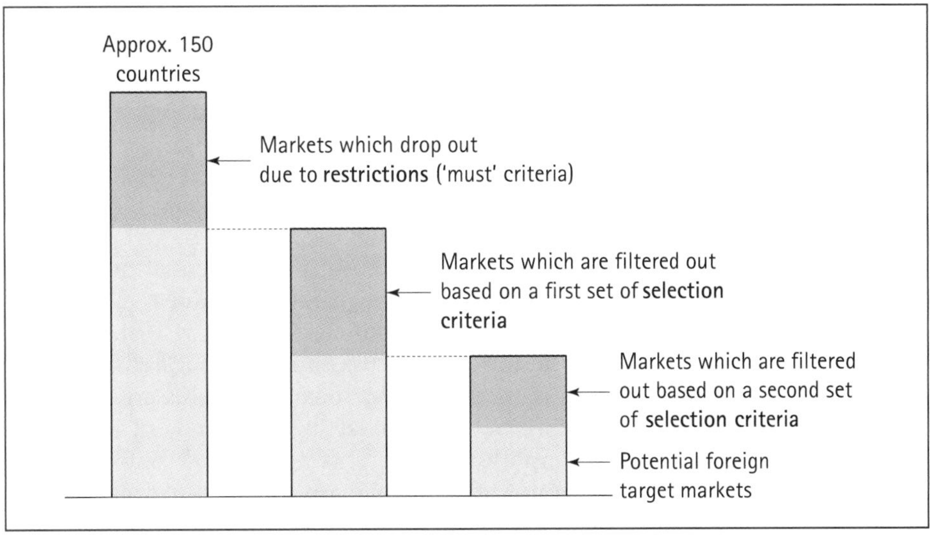

Source: adapted from D.J.G. Schneider and R.U. Müller, *Datenbankgestützte Marktselektion: Eine methodische Basis für Internationalisierungs-strategien* (Stuttgart, 1989).

ance on the different selection criteria. By multiplying estimates and weights and adding them up, a final summated score for each country is obtained. The country with the highest score is identified as the most promising foreign target market.[9]

Figure 8.2 **A scoring model for international market selection**

Selection criteria	1 Market potential		2 Tariffs		3 Non-tariff barriers		4 Product fit		5 Competitive intensity		6 Shipping costs		Summated score	
Weights	W = 15		W = 5		W = 17		W = 25		W = 22		W = 16		Max 400 P.	Rank
Countries	E	W×E	E	W×E	E	W×E	E	W×E	E	W×E	E	W×E		
Denmark	2	30	2	10	1.5	25	3.5	87	0.5	11	3.5	56	219	4
Sweden	3.5	52	4	20	3.5	59	25	62	2	44	3	48	285	2
Norway	2	30	3	15	2	34	3.5	87	1	22	2.5	40	228	3
Finland	4	60	4	20	3.5	59	3	75	4	88	1.5	29	326	1
Portugal	0	0	3	15	1	17	0.5	12	2	44	2	32	120	5
Germany														
Austria														
Spain ⋮														

W = Weights of selection criteria
E = Estimates (0 = very bad conditions; 1 = bad conditions; 2 = acceptable conditions; 3 = favourable conditions; 4 = very favourable conditions)
W×E = weighted estimate

267

However, this 'objective' procedure shall not obscure the fact that it was derived through subjective estimates. In order to reduce personal biases, it may be useful to use as much secondary information as possible and to engage different raters.

According to the model outlined in Figure 8.2, Finland appears as the most suitable country for the fictitious company's market selection.

VISITING THE POTENTIAL MARKET

After the research effort has zeroed in on potential markets, there is no substitute for a personal visit to size up the market firsthand and begin the development of an actual export marketing programme. A market visit should do several things. First, it should confirm (or contradict) assumptions regarding market potential. A second major purpose is to gather additional data necessary to reach the final go/no go decision regarding an export marketing programme. There are certain kinds of information that simply cannot be obtained from secondary sources. For example, an export manager or international marketing manager may have a list of potential distributors. He or she may have corresponded with distributors on the list and formed some tentative idea of whether they meet the company's international criteria. It is difficult, however, to negotiate a suitable arrangement with international distributors without actually meeting face to face to allow each side of the contract to appraise the capabilities and character of the other party. A third reason for a visit to the export market is to develop a marketing plan in co-operation with the local agent or distributor. Agreement should be reached on necessary product modifications, pricing, advertising and promotion expenditures, and a distribution plan. If the plan calls for investment, agreement on the allocation of costs must also be reached.

One way to visit a potential market is through a trade show or a government sponsored trade mission. Hundreds of trade fairs, usually organised around a product, a group of products, or activity, are held in major markets.

Key points

- Selecting appropriate foreign markets is a key task in a firm's international process.

- The decision which foreign market(s) to address is based on a number of criteria such as potential market size, the product fit, competitive activities and additional costs.

- The number and weight attached to specific selection criteria depends very much on the industry in which a firm is active.

- To systematise the decision process, scoring models may be used. They allow a stepwise decision-making and thus reduce the complexity of country selection.

- After promising foreign target markets have been tracked down, international marketers are well advised to visit these new markets. Visits during trade shows or trade missions allow a double-check of secondary information gathered and enable personal contacts with potential partners abroad.

By attending trade shows and missions, company representatives can conduct market assessment, develop or expand markets, find distributors or agents, or locate potential end users (i.e. engage in direct selling). Perhaps most important, by attending a trade show, it is possible to learn a great deal about competitors' technology, pricing, and the depth of their market penetration. For example, while walking around the exhibit hall, one can gather literature about products that often contains strategically useful technological information. Overall, company managers or sales personnel should be able to get a good general impression of competitors in the marketplace while at the same time trying to sell their own company's product.

DIFFERENT MODES OF MARKET ENTRY

After a company has decided which foreign target markets are promising, it needs to think about how to enter these markets. The decision on entry into a specific market entry is influenced by three key factors: (1) how many resources and what investment are necessary to enter the market, (2) to what extent can the manufacturer control corporate activities in the foreign market, and (3) how much knowledge can the manufacturer gain about the foreign market by this market entry alternative.[10]

If a company does not want to engage or does not have extensive resources for its international activities, it may choose a market entry alternative based on exporting goods produced in the home country through, for example, an independent distributor abroad. The advantage of the agent/distributor option is that it requires little investment. It is a pay-as-you-go option. The disadvantage of this option is that it does not create a company presence in the market and it does not give a company control over its marketing effort. In addition, agents and distributors are not necessarily a no-investment option. If the manufacturer has deep pockets, any termination of an agency or distributorship agreement may lead to a claim by the agent or distributor for lost profits and damages. A written contract with a no-cause termination clause is no guarantee of protection from an agent/distributor lawsuit because agents and distributors may press claims on the grounds of a breach of good faith.

In case a company wants to monitor marketing activities in the foreign market more closely or wants to obtain market presence, it is well advised to choose a suitable market entry alternative such as subsidiaries, joint ventures or strategic partnerships. However, a better presence in the foreign market and closer control go in line with higher investments into labour, materials, capital, land and transportation.

If a company decides to produce outside the home market, it has a choice of buying, building or renting its own manufacturing plant or signing a local licensing partner. A licensing partner may be in a position to add production to an existing plant with less investment than the manufacturer would require to achieve the same volume of production.

In some economically less developed markets, the choice of producing abroad may be involuntary, as government regulations require a certain degree of local content. In most industrialised countries, this choice is entirely up to a firm's economic considerations. In many countries, companies combine the company-owned marketing subsidiary with agents and distributors. This option gives the company local presence and control of the marketing effort and, where cost effective, takes advantage of distributor and agent capabilities. The local presence of the company can provide a much better communications link with the regional and world headquarters and, if

EUROPEAN FOCUS

The world of Wolford

It all started in Bregenz on the Austrian side of Lake Constance. From here Wolford, manufacturer of luxury products for leg and body wear, set out to conquer the world. Meanwhile, more than 1,000 employees and over 200 boutiques across the globe achieve sales of about €150 million. A key success factor: the company's foreign market operations.

Early on, the management came to the conclusion that the Austrian market was too small for Wolford's exclusive products, so the company sought out market opportunities abroad. Now the company achieves more than 90 per cent of its sales outside of Austria. When entering new markets, Wolford applies different strategies. In markets which are of limited strategic importance or where the market potential remains unclear, Wolford relies on the expertise and the know-how of foreign partners in an export contract. Brazil may serve as an example for this approach. In 1998, a local partner was trusted with the exclusive distribution of Wolford products. Markets which appear of strategic importance to the firm, such as Germany or the UK, are usually entered through a foreign subsidiary wholly-owned by Wolford. Today, there are wholly-owned subsidiaries in Switzerland, Germany, France, the UK, Spain, Italy, Japan and Scandinavia. New subsidiaries are also planned in China and the Netherlands.

Wolford's foreign operations may serve as a suitable example of how a firm's strategy to approach foreign markets may change over time. Looking at the US operation, Wolford's stepwise market entry approach can be outlined very well. When Wolford started to market its products in the US, the firm found itself confronted with a difficult situation: US female consumers did not give a lot of attention to the product area Wolford was doing business in.

Even more important for a producer of luxury goods, they were not willing to spend a lot of money on exquisite hosiery. Consequently, Wolford had to invest intensively in 'customer education' to increase the consumers' awareness. Similarly to Brazil, Wolford started out with choosing a local distribution partner in the US – Easton International. The reasons for this approach were lower up-front investments and the ability to take advantage of Easton's market know-how. When the US market developed increasingly well, Wolford decided to terminate the agreement with Easton International. In order to obtain better control and more market presence, Wolford opted for a company-owned subsidiary and franchisees. This switch ensured that Wolford's aim of building up a strong luxury brand with a premium-pricing strategy would not be thwarted by conflicting interests of independent distributors. And the overwhelming success proves Wolford's approach is right! In 1997, US sales of €10 million already accounted for 6 per cent of total sales, and significant increases are forecast. However, Wolford's success has now also induced its US competitors, such as fashion designers Donna Karan or Calvin Klein, to address the luxury leg and body wear.

Food for thought

- Contrast the advantages and disadvantages of using local distributors, franchisees and company owned subsidiaries for Wolford's international market expansion.
- What are the potential dangers for Wolford when using a stepwise market entry approach, such as the one described for the US?

Source: 'Wolford', *Advertising Age, International Supplement*, December 1996, p. i4; 'Wolford', *Euromarketing*, 23 April 1996, p. 5; 'Wolford to start US unit', *Women's Wear Daily*, 29 April 1996, p. 18; 'Wolford plans giant strides in the US', *Women's Wear Daily*, 6 January 1997, p. 11; 'Wolford keeps opening new doors', *Women's Wear Daily*, 10 February 1998, p. 4; 'Europe's second act in hosiery', *Women's Wear Daily*, 28 December 1998, p. 10; 'Wolford to step downtown this fall', *Women's Wear Daily*, 24 August 1998, p. 6ff.

Figure 8.3 Market entry alternatives

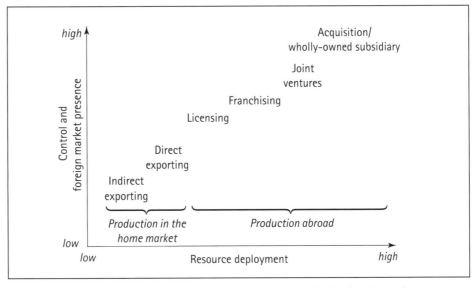

Source: Adapted from Günther Müller-Stewens and Christoph Lechner, 'Unternehmensindividuelle und gastlandbezogene Einflußfaktoren der Markteintrittsformen'. In Klaus Macharzina and Michael-Jörg Oesterle (eds), *Handbuch Internationales Management* (Wiesbaden: Gabler, 1997), p. 237; Gunter Stahr, *Auslandsmarketing*, Vol. 1 (Stuttgart: Kohlhammer, 1979), p. 162.

it is well executed, ensure that the company's effort reflects the fullest potential of the company's ability to execute a global strategy with local responsiveness.

Figure 8.3 provides an overview of different market entry alternatives.

EXPORTING

If a company decides to manufacture at home and serve foreign markets with these products, it has two alternatives to address these markets: indirect and direct exporting. As outlined above, the decision is influenced by the three key factors: necessary investment, market presence and control.

Indirect exporting

Many companies, particularly at the beginning of their international activities, decide to take the easier route of handling their foreign business: indirect exporting. Under indirect exporting, a partner in the manufacturer's home country takes over all activities related to the foreign markets. There are numerous export services providers to choose from. These include export trading companies (ETCs), export management companies (EMCs), export merchants, export brokers, combination export managers, manufacturer's export representatives or commission agents, and export distributors. However, because these terms and labels may be used inconsistently, a manufacturer is urged to check and confirm the services performed by a particular independent export organisation.

A typical export service provider acts as the export department for several unrelated companies that lack export experience. Export service providers perform a variety of services, including marketing research, channel selection, arranging financing and shipping, and documentation. According to a survey of US-based EMCs, the most important activities for export success are marketing information gathering, communication with markets, setting prices, and ensuring parts availability. The same survey ranked export activities in terms of degree of difficulty; analysing political risk, sales force management, setting pricing, and obtaining financial information were deemed most difficult to accomplish.[11]

Direct exporting

Another option to organise distribution into foreign markets is direct exporting. Contrary to indirect exporting, this approach requires a more extensive commitment of funds, but in turn provides the manufacturer with better control and market presence. The key question in this respect is to what extent the manufacturer wants to participate in the distribution activities. Basically, there are two options: direct market representation and independent representation.

Direct market representation

There are two major advantages to direct representation in a market: control and communications. Direct representation allows decisions concerning programme development, resource allocation, or price changes to be implemented unilaterally. Moreover, when a product is not yet established in a market, special efforts are necessary to achieve sales. The advantage of direct representation is that these special efforts are ensured by the marketer's investment. With indirect or independent representation, such efforts and investment are often not forthcoming; in many cases, there is simply not enough incentive for independents to invest significant time and money in representing a product. The other great advantage to direct representation is that the possibilities for feedback and information from the market are much greater. This information can vastly improve export marketing decisions concerning product, price, communications and distribution.

Direct representation does not mean that the exporter is selling directly to the consumer or customer. In most cases, direct representation involves selling to wholesalers or retailers. For example, the major automobile exporters in Germany and Japan rely on direct representation in the US market in the form of their distributing agencies, which are owned and controlled by the manufacturing organisation. The distributing agencies then sell products to franchised dealers.

Independent representation

In smaller markets, it is usually not feasible to establish direct representation because the low sales volume does not justify the cost. Even in larger markets, a small manufacturer usually lacks adequate sales volume to justify the cost of direct representation. Whenever sales volume is small, use of an independent distributor is an effective method of sales distribution. Finding good distributors can be the key to export success.

Piggyback marketing

Piggyback marketing, or the use of a mother hen salesforce, is an innovation in international distribution that has received much attention in recent years. This is an arrangement whereby one manufacturer obtains distribution of products through another's distribution channels. Both parties can benefit. The active distribution partner makes fuller use of its distribution system capacity and thereby increases the revenues generated by the system. The manufacturer using the piggyback arrangement does so at a cost that is much lower than that required for any direct arrangement. Successful piggyback marketing requires that the combined product lines be complementary. They must appeal to the same customer, and they must not be competitive with each other. If these requirements are met, the piggyback arrangement can be a very effective way of fully utilising an international channel system to the advantage of both parties. A case in point is the Kauai Kookie Kompany, whose owners observed Japanese tourists stocking up on cookies before returning home from Hawaii. Now the cookies are sold in a piggyback arrangement with travel agencies in Japan. The cookies can be purchased from a catalogue after travellers have returned home, thus reducing the amount of baggage.[12]

Exporting – a developmental process

Research has shown that exporting is essentially a developmental process that can be divided into the following distinct stages.[13]

1 The firm is unwilling to export; it will not even fill an unsolicited export order. This may be due to perceived lack of time ('too busy to fill the order'), or to apathy or ignorance.
2 The firm fills unsolicited export orders but does not pursue orders. Such a firm would be an export seller.
3 The firm explores the feasibility of exporting (this stage may bypass stage 2).
4 The firm exports to one or more markets on a trial basis.
5 The firm is an experienced exporter to one or more markets.
6 After this success, the firm pursues country or region focused marketing based on certain criteria (e.g. all countries where English is spoken, all countries where it is not necessary to transport by water).
7 The firm evaluates the global market potential before screening for the best target markets to include in its marketing strategy and plan. All markets, domestic and international, are regarded as equally worthy of consideration.

The probability that a firm will advance from one stage to the next depends on different factors. Moving from stage 2 to stage 3 depends on management's attitude toward the attractiveness of exporting and its confidence in the firm's ability to compete internationally. However, commitment is the most important aspect of a company's international orientation. Before a firm can reach stage 4, it must receive and respond to unsolicited export orders. The quality and dynamism of management are important factors that can lead to such orders. Success in stage 4 can lead a firm to stages 5 and 6. A company that reaches stage 7 is a mature, geocentric enterprise that is relating global resources to global opportunity. To reach this stage requires management with vision and commitment.

One study noted that export procedural expertise and sufficient corporate resources are required for successful exporting. An interesting finding was that even the most experienced exporters express a lack of confidence in their knowledge about shipping arrangements, payment procedures, and regulations. The study also showed that, although profitability is an important expected benefit of exporting, other advantages include increased flexibility and resiliency and improved ability to deal with sales

GLOBAL PERSPECTIVE

Born global?

So-called 'born globals' do not follow the traditional developmental process outlined above. Many different terms have been coined for this type of enterprise such as global start-ups or international new ventures. They all have one thing in common: they are small firms which at a very early stage of their business already target international markets. Born globals are innovative and take advantage of revolutionary, new technologies to excel in service to their customers. Typically, born globals understand the world as one big market. So in most cases, after two years in business they achieve more than a quarter of their sales in foreign markets.

When considering the prevalent theory that views globalisation as a question of firm size and, related to that, economies of scale, then born globals are a phenomenon which should not exist. In fact, small companies are often said to be losing in global competition due to their limited resources.

The British company ComponentSource is a typical born global. The firm specialises in selling software components. Even before starting the business it was evident that globalising the firm's activity was an absolute necessity. The company's customers, software developers across the globe, simply expected these tools to be sold world-wide in the same way their products are. And the success is remarkable! Today, CD-ROMs with software tools

developed by ComponentSource's customers are part of Microsoft's Visual Basic Development Tool Box.

Wave System is a pioneering company in this sense as well. For its business, metering systems for databases, globalisation is not an option but a necessity. As a manager put it: 'For us, globalisation is our reality. It would be much weirder, if you asked me how we were going to stay local. Our customers as well as communication and information technologies force us to be global.'

Irrespective of the industry, born globals stand out for one key characteristic: from the very beginning, they have a global vision guiding their activities.

Food for thought

- Are all companies selling their goods or services on the Web automatically global companies? Why? Why not?
- It is questionable whether one should call an Austrian software company founded two years ago and achieving 25 per cent of its sales in Germany a 'born global'. How then would you define 'born global' companies? Draw up a list of criteria such companies should fulfil.

Source: Katherine Campbell, 'The global company', *Financial Times*, 24 October 1997; Tage Koed Madsen and Per Servais, 'The internationalization of born globals – an evolutionary process?', *International Business Review*, 6 (1997), pp. 561–583; Gary A. Knight and S. Tamer Cavusgil, 'The born global firm: a challenge to traditional internationalization theory', *Advances in International Marketing*, Jai Press, 1996; Benjamin M. Oviatt and Patricia McDougall, 'Global start-ups: entrepreneurs on a global stage', *Academy of Management Executive*, 9, 2 (1995): pp. 30–44.

fluctuations in the home market. Whereas research generally supports the proposition that the probability of being an exporter increases with firm size, it is less clear that export intensity, the ratio of export sales to total sales, is positively correlated with firm size. Table 8.2 summarises some of the export-related problems that a company typically faces.[14]

National policies governing exports and imports

Exports are of major importance to the global as well as national economies. Since the 1950s, the global exchange of goods has increased sixteenfold. World-wide exports have risen from 7 per cent to 15 per cent of global GNP.[15] In 1997, the WTO recorded

Table 8.2 Export-related problems

Logistics	Servicing Exports
1 Arranging transportation	12 Providing parts availability
2 Transport rate determination	13 Providing repair service
3 Handling documentation	14 Providing technical advice
4 Obtaining financial information	15 Providing warehousing
5 Distribution co-ordination	**Sales Promotion**
6 Packaging	16 Advertising
7 Obtaining insurance	17 Sales effort
Legal Procedure	18 Marketing information
8 Government red tape	**Foreign Market Intelligence**
9 Product liability	19 Locating markets
10 Licensing	20 Trade restrictions
11 Customs/Duty	21 Competition overseas

an increase of world-wide exports of goods by 9.5 per cent. This represents the second highest growth rate over the last 20 years. Overall, global exports of goods and services amount to €5.5 trillion. Table 8.3 provides an overview of the leading exporting and importing nations.[16]

The US ranks first in exports as well as imports, followed by Germany and Japan.[17] Despite, or perhaps because of this importance, national policies toward exports and imports can be summarised in one word: schizophrenic. For centuries, the nation-states of the world have combined two opposing policy attitudes toward the movement of goods across national boundaries. Nations take steps to encourage exports by outright subsidy and by indirect measures. The latter include tax rebates and extensive government support programmes in the area of promotion and producer education. The flow of goods in the other direction, imports, is generally restricted by national policy. Measures such as tariffs, import control, and a host of non-tariff barriers are designed to limit the inward flow of goods. Thus, the international situation is a combination of measures designed to simultaneously encourage exports and restrict imports.

The import of foreign cheese to the US illustrates this perfectly. On the one hand, the US dairy industry is greatly shielded from imports. Cheese is a protected product through access controls that have the flavour of Catch-22. A company cannot import

Table 8.3 The world's leading exporting and importing nations

Exporters	Value (in € billion)	Share of total world-wide exports (%)	Importers	Value (in € billion)	Share of total world-wide exports (%)
1 US	584.4	12.6	US	762.8	16.1
2 Germany	434.1	9.4	Germany	374.5	7.9
3 Japan	357.2	7.7	Japan	287.1	6.0
4 France	244.2	5.3	UK	307.2	5.5
5 UK	237.6	5.1	France	260.6	4.8
6 Italy	202.7	4.4	Hong Kong, China	177.1	3.7
7 Canada	181.9	3.9	Italy	177.1	3.7
8 The Netherlands	164.1	3.5	Canada	170.5	3.6

cheese into the United States unless it has done so in the past, and quantities are determined by lottery. On the other hand, the US government actively pursued Japan to open its rice markets to US producers. This effort finally met with success in 1993.

To see the tremendous results that can come from a government-encouraged export strategy, consider Japan, Singapore, Korea, and the so-called greater China or China Triangle market, which includes Taiwan, Hong Kong and the People's Republic of China. In a mere three decades, Japan totally recovered from the destruction of the Second World War and became an economic superpower as a direct result of export-led growth strategies pursued by Japanese companies and encouraged by the Ministry for International Trade and Industry (MITI). The 'four tigers', Singapore, Korea, Taiwan and Hong Kong, have been inspired by the Japanese experience and all have export-based economies. China is a 'fifth tiger', booming along with 10 per cent growth and low inflation. China has attracted enormous sums of foreign investment from companies in the Triad and from overseas Chinese in the region who set up production facilities to support local sales as well as exports to world markets.

Government programmes supporting exports

Any government concerned with trade deficits or economic development should focus attention on educating uninvolved firms about the potential gains from exporting. This is true at the national, regional and local government levels. There are three commonly used governmental activities designed to support export activities of national firms. Tax incentives treat earnings from export activities preferentially either by applying a lower rate to earnings from these activities, or by providing a refund of taxes already paid on income associated with exporting. The tax benefits offered by export-conscious governments include varying degrees of tax exemption or tax deferral on export income, accelerated depreciation of export-related assets, and generous tax treatment of overseas market development activities. Naturally, in many cases, the actual treatment of export-related income is even more favourable than tax statutes would imply.

Governments also support export performance by providing outright subsidies, which are direct or indirect financial contributions that benefit producers. Export subsidies can severely distort trade patterns when less competitive but subsidised producers displace competitive producers in world markets. Export subsidies to support agricultural trade will be reduced under the World Trade Organization (WTO). The third support area is governmental assistance to exporters. Assistance may also be oriented toward export promotion. Government agencies at various levels often take the lead in setting up trade fairs and trade missions designed to promote sales to foreign customers.

Key points

- After a company has selected potential foreign markets, it has to decide how to enter these markets.

- A market entry decision is influenced by three key factors: (1) how many resources and what investment are necessary to enter the market, (2) how much control of activities in the foreign market is desired, and (3) how much market knowledge can the manufacturer gain by a specific market entry alternative.

Key points	• If a company does not want to engage extensive resources abroad, it may choose a market entry alternative based on exporting goods produced in the home market. In case a company wants to monitor marketing activities in the foreign market more closely or wants to obtain market presence, market entry alternatives such as wholly-owned subsidiaries, joint ventures or strategic partnerships are advisable.
	• Due to its limited resources deployment, exporting is the choice of market entry for companies which are in the early stage of their foreign activities. The more experienced firms become, the more they will switch to resource-intensive forms of market entry.
	• Under indirect exporting, a partner in the manufacturer's home country, such as an export trading company or an export management company, takes over all activities related to the foreign market. This partner basically serves as an 'external export department'.
	• With direct exporting, a company installs either a direct representation or an indirect one, such as a distributor. Direct exporting provides a company with better control and market presence in the foreign market, however, at the expense of higher cost.
	• So-called 'born globals' do not follow the traditional development process of internationalisation. Typically, born globals are small and they target foreign markets at a very early stage of their business. For them, operating internationally is not an option but a necessity.

EXPORT FINANCING/METHODS OF PAYMENT

The decision as to the appropriate method of payment for a given international sale is a basic credit decision. A number of factors must be considered, including currency availability in the buyer's country, creditworthiness of the buyer, and the seller's relationship to the buyer. Finance managers at companies that have never exported often express concern regarding payment. Many chief financial officers (CFOs) with international experience know that a comparison of international receivables with domestic receivables often demonstrates that there is less problem collecting on international sales than on domestic sales, provided the proper financial instruments are used. The reason is simple: as explained below, a letter of credit can be used to guarantee payment for a product. Domestic sales, on the other hand, are usually conducted on an open account basis. Collecting thus hinges on the creditworthiness of the buyer. After an exporter and importer have established a good working relationship, and the finance manager's level of confidence increases, it may be possible to move to a documentary collection or open account method of payment. Different methods for arranging payment for export sales to buyers abroad are outlined in Figure 8.4 and are explained in the following.

Non-documentary payments

There are a number of conditions that may prompt the exporter to request cash payment, in whole or in part, in advance of shipment. Examples include times when

Figure 8.4 Different methods of export financing

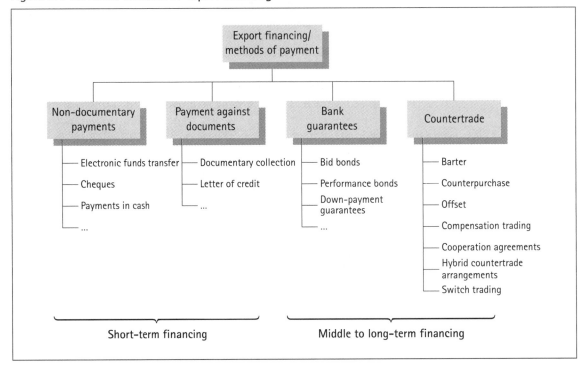

credit risks abroad are high, when exchange restrictions within the country of destination may delay return of funds for an unreasonable period, or when, for any other reason, the exporter may be unwilling to sell on credit terms. Because of competition and restrictions against cash payment in many countries, the volume of business handled on a cash-in-advance basis is small.

Sales on open account

Open account terms generally prevail in areas where exchange controls are minimal and exporters have had long-standing relations with good buyers. Open account terms also prevail when sales are made to branches or subsidiaries of the exporter. The main objection to open account sales is the absence of a tangible obligation. Normally, if a time draft is drawn and is dishonoured after acceptance, it can be used as a basis of legal action, whereas in the case of a dishonoured open account transaction, the legal procedure may be more complicated.

Sales on a consignment basis

As in the case of sales on open account, no tangible obligation is created by consignment sales. In countries with free ports or free trade zones, it can be arranged to have consigned merchandise placed under bonded warehouse control in the name of a foreign bank. Sales can then be arranged by the selling agent and arrangements made to release partial lots out of the consigned stock against regular payment terms. The merchandise is not cleared through customs until after the sale has been completed.

Payments against documents

In case the relationship between international buyer and seller is not yet longstanding, a more secure form of payment than cash in advance may seem appropriate.

Documentary collection (drafts)

A documentary collection is a method of payment using a bill of exchange, also known as a draft. A bill of exchange is a negotiable instrument which is easily transferable from one party to another.

A documentary draft is an important instrument in an export transaction. With a documentary draft, the documents that are required to clear the goods through customs and convey title, plus other important shipping documents, are sent to a bank in the importer's country. The draft is presented to the importer along with these documents, which are delivered against the importer's honouring of the draft.

Letter of credit

Letters of credit are widely used as a payment method in international export trade. Excluding advance payment terms, a letter of credit offers the exporter the best assurance of being paid for products sold internationally. That assurance arises from the fact that the payment obligation under a letter of credit lies with the buyer's bank and not the buyer.

There are various types of letters of credit. However, a letter of credit is essentially a letter by which a bank substitutes its creditworthiness for that of the buyer. A letter of credit can be considered a conditional guarantee issued by the bank on behalf of the buyer to a seller, assuring payment if the seller complies with the terms set forth in the letter of credit. For importers, however, the letter is more expensive because funds might have to be deposited in their bank to secure the credit line. If a letter of credit is selected as payment method, the exporter ordinarily receives payment at the time shipping documents are presented to the bank negotiating the letter of credit in the seller's country. Figure 8.5 provides a schematic overview of the main steps involved in an export transaction supported by a letter of credit: (1) exporter and importer agree on the sales of goods, (2) the importer asks his bank to open a letter

Figure 8.5 Main steps in a letter of credit

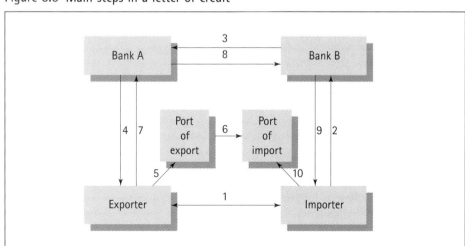

of credit, (3) the importer's bank advises the exporter's bank that a letter of credit has been opened, (4) the exporter's bank lets the exporter know that a letter of credit has been opened, (5) the exporter passes the goods to the shipper and obtains the necessary documentation (e.g. bill of lading), (6) the goods are shipped to the port of import, (7) the exporter hands the ownership documents to his bank, (8) the document are passed to the importer's bank, (9) the importer receives the ownership documents, providing he already deposited the value of the letter of credit at his bank or the bank has granted him a credit line, (10) with the ownership documents in hand, the importer is now able to collect the goods from the port.

Bank guarantees

Bank guarantees are a suitable export financing tool when it comes to long-term contracts. A long-term financial time frame is particularly common in investment goods industries. In practice, there are different types of bank guarantees. Bank guarantees generally serve the purpose of damage protection, which arises for example by a partner not living up to certain agreements. There are various forms of bank guarantees, two of them are described below. A bid bond is a guarantee, where the bank guarantees a foreign manufacturer that the bank's client will carry out the purchase on the condition that the manufacturer won the tender. Under a performance bond, a bank guarantees that its client will perform the contract. The amount guaranteed lies between 10 and 20 per cent of the total amount contracted.

In most countries that support foreign trade relations, the government institutions are installed to provide exporters with similar types of guarantees. These governmental guarantees are particularly helpful to small and medium-sized businesses which would otherwise have difficulties in handling their export financing.[18]

Countertrade[19]

Some exporters finance international transactions by taking full or partial payment in some form other than money. A number of alternative finance methods, known as countertrade, are widely used. In a countertrade transaction, a sale results in products flowing in one direction to a buyer; a separate stream of products and services, often flowing in the opposite direction, is also created. Countertrade generally involves a seller from the West and a buyer in a developing country. For example, the countries in the former Soviet bloc have historically relied heavily on countertrade. This approach reached a peak in popularity in the mid-1980s. Countertrade expands when hard currency is scarce. Exchange controls may prevent a company from expatriating earnings; the company may be forced to spend money in-country for products that are then exported and sold in third-country markets.

Two categories of countertrade are discussed next. Barter falls into one category. The mixed forms of countertrade, including counterpurchase, offset, compensation trading and co-operation agreements, belong in a separate category. They incorporate a real distinction from barter, because money or credit is involved in the transaction.

Simple barter

Simple barter is a direct exchange of goods or services between two parties. Although no money is involved, both partners construct an approximate shadow price for products flowing in each direction. For example, General Electric (GE) sold a turbine generator to Romania in the late 1970s. For payment, GE Trading Company accepted €130 million in chemicals, metals, nails, and other products, which it then sold on the world market. The most high-profile company that has been involved in barter deals is PepsiCo, Inc., which has done business in the Soviet market for over 20 years. Russia and other Commonwealth of Independent States (CIS) countries paid Pepsi for soft-drink syrup concentrate with Stolichnaya vodka that was in turn exported to the United States by Pepsi's PepsiCo Wines & Spirits subsidiary and marketed by M. Henri Wines.

Counterpurchase

This form of countertrade, also termed parallel trading or parallel barter, is distinguished from other forms in that each delivery in an exchange is paid for in cash. For example, Rockwell International sold a printing press to Zimbabwe for €7 million. The deal went through, however, only after Rockwell agreed to purchase €7 million in ferrochrome and nickel from Zimbabwe, which it subsequently sold on the world market.

The Rockwell–Zimbabwe deal illustrates several aspects of counterpurchase. Generally, products offered by the foreign principal are not related to the Western firm's exports and thus cannot be used directly by the firm. In most counterpurchase transactions, two separate contracts are signed. In one, the supplier agrees to sell products for a cash settlement (the original sales contract); in the other, the supplier agrees to purchase and market unrelated products from the buyer (a separate, parallel contract). The value of the counterpurchase generally represents a set percentage, and sometimes the full value, of the products sold to the foreign principal. When the Western supplier sells these goods, the trading cycle is complete.

Offset

Offset is a technique whereby the government in the country of import seeks to recover large sums of hard currency spent on expensive purchases such as military aircraft or telecommunications systems. In effect, the government is saying, 'If you want us to spend government money on your products, you must export products from our country.'[20] On occasion, offset may also involve co-operation in manufacturing or some form of technology transfer. For example, a foreign principal may include requirements to place subcontracts locally and/or to arrange local assembly or manufacturing equal to a certain percentage of the contract value. The commitment to local assembly or manufacturing under the supplier's specifications is commonly termed a co-production agreement, which is tied to the offset but does not, in itself, represent a type of countertrade.

Offset may be distinguished from counterpurchase because the latter is characterised by smaller deals over shorter periods of time.[21] Another major distinction between offset and other forms of countertrade is that the agreement is not contractual but reflects a memorandum of understanding that sets out the value of products to be offset and the time period for completing the transaction. In addition, there is no penalty on the supplier for nonperformance. Some highly competitive sales have required offsets exceeding 100 per cent of the valuation of the original sale.

Compensation trading

This form of countertrade is also called buyback and involves two separate and parallel contracts. In one contract, the supplier agrees to build a plant or provide plant equipment, patents or licences, or technical, managerial or distribution expertise for a hard currency down-payment at the time of delivery. In the other contract, the supplier company agrees to take payment in the form of the plant's output equal to its investment (minus interest) for a period of as many as 20 years.

Essentially, the success of compensation trading rests on the willingness of each firm to be both a buyer and a seller. The People's Republic of China has used compensation trading extensively. Egypt also used this approach to develop an aluminium plant. A Swiss company, Aluswiss, built the plant and also exports alumina (an oxide of aluminium found in bauxite and clay) to Egypt. Aluswiss takes back a percentage of the finished aluminium produced at the plant as partial payment for building the plant. As this example shows, compensation differs from counterpurchase in that the technology or capital supplied is related to the output produced.[22] In counterpurchase, the goods taken by the supplier typically cannot be used directly in its business activities.

Co-operation agreements

Co-operation agreements meet the needs of Western firms doing business with non-market economies, which are reluctant to link selling and buying. What distinguishes these arrangements from other types of countertrade is the specialisation of each Western firm for either buying or selling, not both. Each of the three forms of co-operation agreements represents an increasingly complex accommodation to the needs of trading partners. They include co-operation and simple barter (triangular deals); co-operation and counterpurchase; and co-operation, counterpurchase, and credit by a bank.

Hybrid countertrade arrangements

Hybrid forms of countertrade are becoming more prevalent in trading arrangements. For example, the investment performance contract in Third World markets is an additional condition of offset arrangements. Countries such as Brazil, Mexico and even Canada now make official approval of investment proposals contingent on commitments by the investors to export. As a second example, 'project accompaniment' typifies an arrangement in which a Western supplier is encouraged to buy a greater volume and/or wider range of products, compared with the countertrade commitment. Project accompaniment has surfaced as a condition to the exchange of industrial goods by the West for oil from Middle Eastern producers.

Key points

- The decision as to the appropriate method of payment of a given international sale is a basic credit decision.

- While domestic sales are usually conducted on an open account basis, foreign sales often require more caution and attention.

- Internationally active firms may choose from a variety of methods of payment, such as non-documentary payments, where the exporter requests cash payment, payment against documents, such as by letter of credit or documentary collection, bank guarantees and countertrade.

- A widely used tool of payment is a letter of credit, which essentially substitutes a bank's creditworthiness for that of the buyer. It can be considered a conditional guarantee issued by the bank on behalf of the buyer to a seller, assuring payment if the seller complies with the terms set forth in the letter of credit.

Key points	• Countertrade is an alternative finance method, where full or partial payment is taken in some form other than money. Countertrade can take on various forms, such simple barter, counterpurchase, offset, compensation trading, co-operation agreements or hybrid countertrade arrangements. It flourishes when hard currency is scarce.

Summary

This chapter provides an overview of how a company may select potential foreign markets. The export market choice should be based on a thorough evaluation of criteria which influence the potential success abroad. Among these criteria are the market potential, market access, shipping costs or product fit, to name but a few. To systematise the decision making, a scoring model may be applied. Ultimately, a visit to the potential foreign market is highly advisable before developing an export programme.

Once the potential foreign target market is selected, a company has to decide on how to enter this market. There are different options at hand. The choice of which one is the most suitable depends on three key factors: (1) how many resources and what investment are necessary to enter the market, (2) to what extent can the manufacturer control corporate activities in the foreign market, and (3) how much market knowledge can the manufacturer gain by a specific market entry alternative.

In case a company does not want to engage extensive resources abroad, it may choose a market entry alternative based on exporting goods produced in the home market. If it wants to monitor marketing activities in the foreign market more closely or wants to obtain market presence, a market entry alternative such as wholly-owned subsidiary, a joint venture or a strategic partnership is advisable.

Due to its limited resources deployment, exporting is the choice of market entry for companies which are in the early stage of their foreign activities. They may either choose indirect exporting, where an external partner takes over all activities related to the foreign market, or direct exporting, where the company installs a direct representation in the foreign market or employs a foreign distributor.

Exporters must also have a thorough understanding of international financial instruments, non-documentary and documentary payments such as the frequently used letter of credit, bank guarantees and countertrade. Barter and countertrade are methods of making sales to customers who do not have access to hard currency but are prepared to make payment in some form other than money.

Concepts and definitions

Market selection   Deals with the issue of which foreign market(s) to target. A systematic decision should be based on a number of market selection criteria which influence the firm's sales and profitability. Among these criteria are market potential, tariffs and duties, non-tariff barriers and shipping costs, to name but a few. The nature, number and significance of these criteria to foreign market selection may vary from industry to industry.

Tracking down the most promising foreign market(s), is usually achieved through a filtering process using selection criteria such as those mentioned above. To systematise the decision further, scoring models weighing criteria and ranking countries may be used.

Tariffs and duties Are part of a set of national controls that apply to merchandise sold into the foreign target market. Duties are divided into three categories. They may be calculated either as a percentage of the value of the goods (ad valorem duty), as a specific amount per unit (specific duty) or as a combination of both.

Harmonised tariff system (HTS) A convention signed by most WTO members. It aims to harmonise product classification systems and facilitate tariff procedures.

Most favoured nation (MFN) This clause implies that a country imposes the most favourable tariff rate on imports from countries it has agreed to consider 'most-favoured nations'.

Non–tariff barriers (NTB) Any measure other than a tariff that is a deterrent or obstacle to the sale of products in a foreign market is defined as non-tariff barrier. Among the major NTBs are

- *Quotas*: governmental limits or restrictions on the number of units or the total value of a particular product or product category that can be imported.
- *Discriminatory procurement procedures*: administrative regulations to buy domestic goods rather than imported products, unless the domestic goods are not available or unreasonably expensive.
- *Restrictive customs procedures*: purposefully complicate customs rules and regulations on foreign supplies to render compliance extremely difficult and complex to exporters.
- *Selective monetary controls*: to prevent imports from coming into the country, some countries require importers to place on deposit an amount equal to the value of imported goods.
- *Restrictive administrative and technical regulations:* regulations on safety and health issues or technical specifications may be designed in a way that they intentionally keep out foreign products.

Different modes of market entry After selecting a foreign target market, a decision has to be reached on how to enter the market. In principle, a firm has various entry modes to choose from, such as export, licensing, franchising, joint ventures or wholly-owned subsidiaries. Three key factors influence the choice of a specific market entry alternative: (1) resources and investment necessary, (2) degree of control of foreign market activities and (3) the desired market presence.

Indirect exporting Under indirect exporting, a manufacturer engages an external partner, such as an export management company, to handle his export activities. The export management company serves as an 'export department' for several independent companies. Particularly for internationally less experienced firms, indirect exporting provides a suitable way to engage in international marketing. The resources and investment necessary and the risk incurred are limited. However, indirect exporting does not provide the manufacturer with control of foreign market activities or with an immediate market presence in the foreign market.

Direct exporting In contrast to indirect exporting, the manufacturer achieves more control and market presence at the expense of higher investment. Direct exporting may take three forms: (1) direct market representation: a manufacturer engages a company representative to establish/support contacts in the foreign market, or (2) independent representation: a manufacturer installs an independent agent or distributor in the foreign target market, and (3) piggyback marketing, where one manufacturer obtains distribution of products through another's distribution channels.

Born globals
Born globals or global start-ups or international new ventures as they are often called do not follow the traditional development process of stepwise increasing their international activities. Even at a very early stage of being in business, they consider the world as their market and obtain a quarter or even more of their total sales internationally.

Discussion questions

1 What criteria should be assessed when evaluating potential export markets?

2 How do governments attempt to influence exports? Discuss typical support measures.

3 What are the various types of duties of which export marketers should be aware?

4 How would you describe a born global? What does it take for a company to be a born global?

5 What is the difference between barter and countertrade? Why do companies barter?

Webmistress's hotspots

Homepage of the Bundesstelle für Außenhandelsinformationen (BFAI)
Many governments try to assist their internationally active firms with valuable information. Under http://www.bfai.com/, you can see what kind of information is typically provided (e.g. an industry report on Hungary's cooling system business).

Homepage of the Delegation of the European Commission in Japan
There is a widespread opinion in the business community that Japan is a difficult market to export to. Therefore, the EU has opened a bureau in Japan offering services such as training programmes and information to manufacturers interested in exporting to Japan. On this homepage, you find some information on the Delegation's activities.
http://www.jpn.cec.eu.int/english/eu-relations/

Homepage of the UK Institute of Export
The British Institute of Export provides a wide variety of support to its individual members and corporate partners. Beside educational activities, it offers a fee-based Export Market Information Research Service (EMIRS) as well as many useful web links for exporters.
http://www.export.org.uk/institute/

Homepage of the Michigan State University's International Business Resources
This award-winning website is a very comprehensive compilation of information related to international business topics. You may find links to leading international journals and magazines from all over the world, international trade information, statistical data, regional and country information, international trade information and so on.
http://ciber.bus.msu.edu/busres.html

Homepage of DEG – Deutsche Investitions- und EntwicklungsGmbH
The DEG, government-related consulting institution, supports companies in their foreign activities, particularly in economically less developed countries. They offer project management as well as financial engineering support. If you want to learn more about their service, please check out their website!
http://www.deginvest.de/german/flash/1/

Suggested readings

Aulakh, P., and M. Kotabe, 'Antecedents and performance implications of channel integration in foreign markets', *Journal of International Business Studies*, 28 (first quarter 1997): pp. 145–175.

Bello, D.C. and R. Lohtia, 'Export channel design: the use of foreign distributors and agents', *Journal of the Academy of Marketing Science*, 23, 2 (1995): pp. 83–93.

Bilkey, Warren J., 'Attempted integration of the literature on the export behaviour of firms', *Journal of International Business Studies*, 8, 1 (1978): pp. 33–46.

Bonaccorsi, Andrea, 'What do we know about exporting by small italian exporting firms?', *Journal of International Marketing*, 1, 3 (1993): pp. 49–76.

Bonaccorsi, Andrea, 'On the relationship between firm size and export intensity', *Journal of International Business Studies*, 23, 4 (fourth quarter 1992): pp. 605–636.

Branch, Alan E., *Elements of Export Marketing Management*. London: Chapman and Hall, 1990.

Cavusgil, S. Tamer and V.H. Kirpalani, 'Introducing products into export markets: success factors', *Journal of Business Research*, 27, 1 (May 1993): pp. 1–15.

Cavusgil, S. Tamer, Shaoming Zou and G.M. Naidu, 'Product and promotion adaptation in export ventures: an empirical investigation', *Journal of International Business Studies*, 24, 3 (third quarter 1993): pp. 449–464.

Chae, M.S. and J.S. Hill, 'The hazards of strategic planning for global markets', *Long Range Planning*, 29, 6 (1996): pp. 880–891.

Chan, T.S. 'Emerging trends in export channel strategy: an investigation of Hong Kong and Singaporean firms', *European Journal of Marketing*, 26, 3 (1992): pp. 18–26.

Craig, C.S. and S.P. Douglas, 'Developing strategies for global markets: an evolutionary perspective', *Columbia Journal of World Business*, 1 (Spring 1996): pp. 70–81.

Das, M., 'Successful and unsuccessful exporters from developing countries', *European Journal of Marketing*, 28, 12 (1994): pp. 19–33.

Davis, Edward W., 'Global outsourcing: have US managers thrown the baby out with the bath water?', *Business Horizons*, 35, 4 (July–August 1992): pp. 58–65.

Dominguez, Luis V. and Carlos G. Gequeira, 'Strategic options for LDC exports to developed countries', *International Marketing Review*, 8, 5 (1991): pp. 27–43.

Gilmore, W.S. and J.C. Camillus, 'Do your planning processes meet the reality test?', *Long Range Planning*, 29, 6 (1996): pp. 869–879.

Gordon, John S., *Profitable Exporting: A Complete Guide to Marketing Your Products Abroad*. New York: Wiley, 1993.

Holden, A.C., 'The Repositioning of Ex-Im Bank', *Columbia Journal of World Business* (Spring 1996): pp. 82–93.

Holden, A.C. and J. DiLorenzo-Aiss, 'State agencies link with Eximbank to overcome the difficulty of obtaining adequate export finance', *Multinational Business Review*, 4, 2 (1996): pp. 13–20.

Howard, Donald G., 'The role of export management companies in global marketing', *Journal of Global Marketing*, 8, 1 (1994): pp. 95–110.

Iansiti, M. and A. MacCormack, 'Developing products on Internet time', *Harvard Business Review* (September–October 1997): pp. 108–117.

Johnson, Thomas E., *Export/Import Procedure and Documentation*. New York: AMACOM, 1991.

Katsikeas, Constantine S., 'Perceived export problems and export involvement: the case of Greek exporting manufacturers', *Journal of Global Marketing*, 7, 4 (1994): pp. 95–110.

Katsikeas, Constantine S. and Nigel F. Piercy, 'Long-term export stimuli and firm characteristics in a European LDC', *Journal of International Marketing*, 1, 3 (1993): pp. 23–48.

Kim, C.K. and J.Y. Chung, 'Brand popularity, country image and market share: an empirical study', *Journal of International Business Studies*, 28, 2 (1997): pp. 361–386.

Koh, Anthony C., James Chow and Sasithorn Smittivate, 'The practice of international marketing research by Thai exporters', *Journal of Global Marketing*, 7, 2 (1993): pp. 7–26.

Korth, Christopher M., 'Managerial barriers to US exports', *Business Horizons*, 34, 2 (March/April 1991): pp. 18–26.

Kostecki, Michel M., 'Marketing strategies between dumping and anti-dumping action', *European Journal of Marketing*, 25, 12 (1992): pp. 7–19.

Kotabe, Masaaki and Michael R. Czinkota, 'State government promotion of manufacturing exports: a gap analysis', *Journal of International Business Studies*, 23, 4 (fourth quarter 1992): pp. 637–658.

Leonidou, Leonidas C., 'Empirical research on export barriers: review, assessment and synthesis', *Journal of International Marketing*, 3, 1 (1995): pp. 29–44.

Leonidou, L.C. and C.S. Katsikeas, 'The export development process: an integrative review of empirical models', *Journal of International Business Studies*, 27 (September 1996): p. 517.

Liang, N. and A. Parkhe, 'Importer behavior: the neglected counterpart of international exchange', *Journal of International Business Studies*, 28 (third quarter 1997): pp. 495–530.

Louter, Pieter J., Cok Ouwerkerk and Ben A. Bakker, 'An inquiry into successful exporting', *European Journal of Marketing*, 25, 6 (1991): pp. 7–23.

Maggiori, Herman J., *How to Make the World Your Market: The International Sales and Marketing Handbook*. Los Angeles: Burning Gate Press, 1992.

Mahone, Charlie E., Jr, 'Penetrating export markets: the role of firm size', *Journal of Global Marketing*, 7, 3 (1994): pp. 133–148.

Murray, Janet Y., Masaaki Kotabe and Albert Wildt, 'Strategic and financial performance implications of global sourcing strategy: a contingency analysis', *Journal of International Business Studies*, 26, 1 (1995): pp. 181–202.

Namiki, Nobuaki, 'A taxonomic analysis of export marketing strategy: an exploratory study of US exporters of electronics products', *Journal of Global Marketing*, 8, 1 (1994): pp. 27–50.

Parke, David, 'US national security export controls: implications for global competitiveness of US high-tech firms', *Strategic Management Journal*, 13, 1 (January 1992): pp. 47–66.

Pattison, Joseph E., *Acquiring the Future: America's Survival and Success in the Global Economy*. Homewood, IL: Dow Jones–Irwin, 1990.

Rao, C.P., M. Krishna Erramilli and Gopala K. Ganesh, 'Impact of domestic recession on export marketing behavior', *International Marketing Review*, 7, 2 (1990): pp. 54–65.

Raven, Peter V., Jim M. McCullough and Patriya S. Tansuhaj, 'Environmental influences and decision-making uncertainty in export channels: effects on satisfaction and performance', *Journal of International Marketing*, 2, 3 (1994): pp. 37–60.

Raynauld, Andre, *Financing Exports to Developing Countries*. Paris: Development Centre of the Organization for Economic Cooperation and Development, 1992.

Reich, Michael R., 'Why the Japanese don't export more pharmaceuticals: health policy as industrial policy', *California Management Review*, 32, 2 (Winter 1990): pp. 124–150.

Robock, Stefan H., 'The export myopia of US multinationals: an overlooked opportunity for creating US manufacturing jobs', *Columbia Journal of World Business*, 28, 2 (Summer 1993): pp. 24–32.

Rossen, Philip J. and Stan D. Reid (eds), *Managing Export Entry and Expansion*. New York: Praeger, 1987.

Rynning, Marjo-Riitta and Otto Andersen, 'Structural and behavioral predictors of export adoption: a Norwegian study', *Journal of International Marketing*, 2, 1 (1994): pp. 73–90.

Samiee, Saeed, 'Strategic considerations of the EC 1992 plan for small exporters', *Business Horizons*, 22, 2 (March–April 1990): pp. 48–52.

Schaffer, Matt, *Winning the Countertrade War: New Export Strategies for America*. New York: Wiley, 1989.

Seringhaus, F.H. Rolf, 'A comparison of export marketing behavior of Canadian and Austrian high-tech firms', *Journal of International Marketing*, 1, 4 (1993): pp. 49–70.

Seringhaus, F.H. Rolf, 'Export promotion in developing countries: status and prospects', *Journal of Global Marketing*, 6, 4 (1993): pp. 7–32.

Singer, Thoman Owen and Michael R. Czinkota, 'Factors associated with effective use of export assistance', *Journal of International Marketing*, 2, 1 (1994): pp. 53–72.

Swamidass, Paul M., 'Import sourcing dynamics: an integrative perspective', *Journal of International Business Studies*, 24, 4 (fourth quarter 1993): pp. 671–692.

Terpstra, Vern and Chow-Ming Joseph Yu, 'Export trading companies: an American trade failure?' *Journal of Global Marketing*, 6, 3 (1992): pp. 29–54.

US Department of Commerce, *A Basic Guide to Exporting*. Washington, DC: US Department of Commerce, 1992.

US Department of Commerce, *Toward a National Export Strategy: US Exports = US Jobs: Reports to the United States Congress*. Washington, DC: Trade Promotion Co-ordinating Committee, 1993.

Venedikian, Harry M., *Export–Import Financing*. New York: Wiley, 1992.

Verzariu, Pompiliu, *Countertrade, Barter and Offsets: New Strategies for Profit in International Trade*. New York: McGraw-Hill, 1985.

Wichmann, H.J., 'Private and public trading companies within the Pacific Rim nations', *Journal of Small Business* (January 1997): pp. 62–65.

Yip, George S., 'Global strategy as a factor in Japanese success', *The International Executive*, 38, 1 (January/February 1996): pp. 145–167.

Notes

1. Peter Marsh, 'The rocket science of innovation', *Financial Times*, 23 September 1999.

2. Gail E. Schares and John Templeman, 'Think small: the export lessons to be learned from Germany's midsize companies', *Business Week*, 4 November 1994, pp. 58–60ff.

3. Karl Heinrich Oppenländer. 'Einflußfaktoren der internationalen Standortwahl.' In *Handbuch Internationales Management*, ed. Klaus Macharzina and Michael-Jörg Oesterle (Wiesbaden: Gabler, 1997), pp. 210–230.

4. Thomas E. Johnson, *Export/Import Procedure and Documentation* (New York: AMACOM, 1991).

5. C(ost).I(nsurance).F(reight). Landed: implies that the seller has to cover the costs and freight necessary to bring the goods to the named port of destination. This also includes insurance against the risk of loss and damage to the goods during transport. The term 'landed' indicates that unloading costs, including lighterage and wharfage, are borne by the seller.

6. 'Border battles: conventional trade barriers are coming down, but not quickly enough', *The Economist*, 3 October 1998, pp. 6–10.

7. 'Unfair protectionism: Protectionism is on the rise in a new guise: anti-dumping cases are multiplying in America, Europe and around the world', *The Economist*, 7 November 1998, pp. 75–76.

8. 'Ukraine steel producers out in the cold', *Financial Times*, 15 January 1998.

9. Hans Günther Meissner, *Strategisches Internationales Marketing* (München: Oldenbourg, 1995).

10. Günter Müller-Stewens and Christoph Lechner. 'Unternehmensindividuelle und gastlandbezogene Einflußfaktoren der Markteintrittsform'. In *Handbuch Internationales Management*, ed. Klaus Macharzina and Michael-Jörg Oesterle (Wiesbaden: Gabler, 1997), pp. 231–252.

11. Donald G. Howard, 'The role of export management companies in global marketing', *Journal of Global Marketing*, 8, 1 (1994): pp. 95–110.

12. Jack G. Kaikati, 'Don't crack the Japanese distribution system – just circumvent it', *Columbia Journal of World Business*, 28, 2 (1993): p. 41.

13. This section relies heavily on Warren J. Bilkey, 'Attempted integration of the literature of the export behavior of firms', *Journal of International Business Studies*, 9, Spring–Summer (1978): pp. 33–46. The stages are based on Rogers' adoption process (Everett M. Rodgers, *Diffusion of Innovations* (New York: Free Press, 1962)).

14. Masaaki Kotabe and Michael R. Czinkota, 'State government promotion of manufacturing exports: a gap analysis', *Journal of International Business Studies*, 23, 4 (1992): pp. 637–658.

15. 'Schools brief: trade winds', *The Economist*, 8 November 1997.

16. 'World trade growth accelerated in 1997, despite turmoil in some Asian financial markets' (World Trade Organization, 1998).

17. 'For richer, for poorer', *The Economist*, 18 March 1995, p. 9.

18. Hans Dietmar Sauer, 'Formen der Finanzierung von Exportgeschäften.' In *Handbuch Internationales Management*, ed. Klaus Macharzina and Michael-Jörg Oesterle (Wiesbaden: Gabler, 1997), pp. 421–437.

19. Many of the examples in the following section are adapted from Matt Schaffer, *Winning the Countertrade War: New Export Strategies for America* (New York: Wiley, 1989).

20. Matt Schaffer, 'Countertrade as an export strategy', *Journal of Business Strategy*, 11, 3 (1990).

21. Patricia Daily and S.M. Ghazanfar, 'Countertrade: help or hindrance to less-developed countries?', *The Journal of Social, Political, and Economic Studies*, 18, 1 (1993): p. 65.

22. Patricia Daily and S.M. Ghazanfar, 'Countertrade: help or hindrance to less-developed countries?' , *The Journal of Social, Political, and Economic Studies*, 18, 1 (1993): p. 66.

CHAPTER 9

Production abroad and strategic alliances

The world is changing and we can't do business the way we used to. We used to be very much a company that didn't look much beyond Germany. But the globalisation of the industry has meant that we had to expand into the United States and other parts of the world. There is no choice.
HORST URBAN, CONTINENTAL AG

In a complex, uncertain world filled with dangerous opponents, it is best not to go it alone.
KENICHI OHMAE

Alliances as a broad-based strategy will only ensure a company's mediocrity, not its international leadership.
MICHAEL PORTER

After reading this chapter, you will know:

- Different market entry and expansion alternatives involving production abroad.
- How and when to engage in licensing, franchising, joint ventures or establishing subsidiaries.
- Success factors and problems of strategic alliances.
- Key characteristics of Japanese *keiretsu* and their effects on competition.
- New forms of strategic alliances such as virtual enterprises.

Why is this important? Here are three situations in which you would need an understanding of the above issues:

- You have decided to intensify your commitment to foreign markets. In order to obtain a solid market presence and good control over foreign operations, you want to know which market expansion alternatives would suit your intentions.
- In the international arena, you are facing Japanese competitors. A profound understanding of *keiretsu* will help you to anticipate actions and reactions of your Japanese competitors.
- You are looking for international co-operations that allow you to produce in markets formerly addressed through exporting.

Practice link

It is little wonder that most of the world's leading automakers have set their sights on Brazil. An enormous population and a rapidly growing economy represent an attractive market potential compared to saturated markets like Europe or the US. Nearly 2 million vehicles were sold in Brazil in 1996, and analysts predict that sales could reach 3 million units by 2000. To serve this market, car manufacturers are busy establishing and extending their local production capacities. Brazil represents Volkswagen AG's largest market outside of Germany. VW Brasil operates seven plants, including a lean-production truck plant in Resende that produces nearly half a million vehicles annually. VW's sister company Audi just recently opened its €600 million state-of-the-art production facility in Curitiba. The Curitiba plant is among the 10 most productive plants in the company. In Anchieta, where more than 3,000 VW Golf and Audi A3 cars leave the belts monthly, the management is thinking intensively about modernising the facilities. More than 40 years ago, the Brazilian government invested heavily in the industrialisation and subsidised this location with its money. However, the competitive pressure is high. Fiat, Brazil's number two producer, has spent €850 million to increase production. Its rugged new Palio 'world car' has been a hot seller since its introduction in 1996. American producers are also in the market. General Motors (GM) produces Blazers in São José dos Campos. GM has earmarked €1.1 billion for three new plants, including a €510 million state-of-the-art small car works in the Southern Brazil city of Rio Grande do Sul. Ford has invested more than €850 million in a plant in São Bernardo do Campo that produces Fiesta subcompacts and the new Ka minicar. Chrysler has a production facility in Campo Largo and also participates in a small-displacement engine manufacturing joint venture with BMW.

Surprisingly, Japan's automakers have been relatively slow to develop the market. Toyota is a minor player, and Honda's €85 million plant produces only 15,000 Civics each year. New investments are in the pipeline. Mercedes-Benz opened its first production plant in April 1999, Ford and GM are planning new facilities.[1]

While the traditional way of running production facilities was to form a subsidiary, lately new forms of organising and managing foreign activities have been developed. For its new €1 billion production plant, Ford ties in its suppliers more intensively. Ford plans to share production activities with its suppliers. Jobs such as the production of body parts and paintwork are provided by suppliers in the same location as Ford carries out the remaining activities. Based on this principle, Volkswagen has already successfully outsourced the final car mounting. Other manufacturers are thinking about similar systems.[2]

In this chapter, alternative ways to organise and manage overseas production are discussed and the various demands placed on strategic alliances are considered. The chapter closes with a look at Japanese *keiretsu*, relationship enterprises and virtual organisations.

PRODUCTION ABROAD

Besides conventional exporting, foreign activities can be organised in different ways. The advantage of the agent/distributor option is the fact that it requires little investment. It is a pay-as-you-go option. The disadvantage of this option is that it does not create a company presence in the market and does not give a company control over marketing effort. Also, controlling operations is rather difficult. In many countries, companies combine the company-owned marketing subsidiary with agents and distributors. This option gives the company local presence and control of its marketing. The local presence of the company can provide a much better communications link with regional and world headquarters and, if well executed, ensures that the company implements a global strategy with local responsiveness. The available alternatives for serving overseas markets trade off ownership and investment with control, as shown in Figure 9.1.

Figure 9.1 Ownership and control

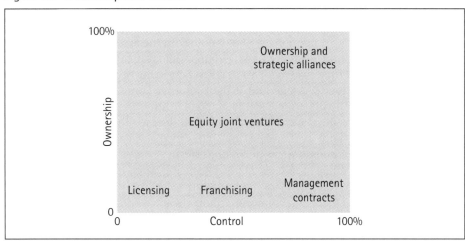

There are different varieties of ownership and control, which range from management contracts to subsidiaries with 100 per cent ownership to global strategic partnerships. In China, Procter & Gamble (P&G) operates with a combination of joint ventures and its own company presence, with P&G marketing executives directing the company's China strategy. This approach has enabled P&G to increase its share of the urban shampoo market to 60 per cent as compared to 9 per cent for Unilever. P&G has invested heavily in market research, advertising, and distribution, and in creating its own command presence in the market. As a result of these initiatives, Head & Shoulders, P&G's brand, is China's fastest growing hair care brand.[3]

Although in theory, it is possible to obtain ownership without control and control without ownership, a higher share of ownership tends to go along with increased control (see Figure 9.1). Companies which have founded subsidiaries have control over every business aspect in this firm, such as personnel management, financial and marketing activities. Within a joint venture, this is not always the case, as the control is divided among the owners. Licensing and franchising allow reasonable control with comparably little investment.

Licensing

Licensing can be defined as a contractual arrangement whereby one company (the licensor) makes an asset available to another company (the licensee) in exchange for royalties, licence fees, or some other form of compensation.[4] The licensed asset may be a patent, trade secret, or company name. Licensing is a form of global market entry and expansion strategy with considerable appeal. A company with advanced technology, know-how, or a strong brand image can use licensing agreements to supplement its bottom-line profitability with little initial investment. Licensing can offer an attractive return on investment for the life of the agreement, providing the necessary performance clauses are in the contract. The only cost is the cost of signing the agreement and of policing its implementation. Contrary to pure contract manufacturing, the licensor does, as a rule, not guarantee to take a certain amount of products produced, and the licensee is in charge of marketing the products at his own risk.

Of course, anything so easily attained has its disadvantages and risks. The principal disadvantage of licensing is that it can be a very limited form of participation. When licensing technology or know-how, the licensor has to live with the threat of limited control. Potential returns from marketing and manufacturing may be lost, and the agreement may have a short life if the licensee develops its own know-how and capability to stay abreast of technology in the area of the licensed product. Even more distressing, licensees have a troublesome way of turning themselves into competitors or industry leaders. This is especially true because licensing enables a company to borrow, leverage and exploit another company's resources. In Japan, for example, Meiji Milk produced and marketed Lady Borden premium ice cream under a licensing agreement with Borden, Inc. Meiji learned important skills in dairy product processing and, as the expiration dates of the licensing contracts drew near, rolled out its own premium ice cream brands.[5]

Perhaps the most famous licensing fiasco dates back to the mid-1950s, when Sony cofounder Masaru Ibuka obtained a licensing agreement for the transistor from AT&T's Bell Laboratories. Ibuka dreamed of using transistors to make small, battery-powered radios. Bell engineers informed Ibuka that it was impossible to manufacture transistors that could handle the high frequencies required for a radio; they advised him to try making hearing aids. Undeterred, Ibuka presented the challenge to his Japanese engineers, who spent many months improving high-frequency output. Sony was not the first company to unveil a transistor radio; an American-built product, the Regency, featured transistors from Texas Instruments and a colourful plastic case. However, it was Sony's high quality, distinctive approach to styling and its marketing savvy that ultimately translated into world-wide success.

Conversely, the failure to seize an opportunity to license can also lead to dire consequences. In the mid-1980s, Apple Computer chairman John Sculley decided against licensing Apple's famed operating system. Such a move would have allowed other computer manufacturers to produce Macintosh-compatible units. Meanwhile, Microsoft's growing world dominance in computer operating systems and applications got a boost from Windows, which featured a Mac-like graphical interface. Apple belatedly reversed direction and licensed its operating system, first to Power Computing Corporation in December 1994, then to IBM and Motorola. The Mac clones have been very popular; Power Computing shipped 170,000 Macintosh clones in 1996, and in 1997 the Mac clones had captured over 25 per cent of the Mac market. Despite these actions, the global market share for Macintosh and Mac clones has slipped below 5 per cent. Apple's failure to license its technology in the pre-Windows era ultimately cost the company over €106 billion (the market capitalisation of Microsoft, the company that won the operating system war).

As the Borden and transistor stories make clear, companies may find that the up-front, easy money obtained from licensing turns out to be a very expensive source of revenue. To prevent a licensor/competitor from gaining unilateral benefit, licensing agreements should provide for a cross-technology exchange between all parties. At the absolute minimum, any company that plans to remain in business must ensure that its license agreements provide for full cross-licensing – that is, the licensee shares its developments with the licensor. In this manner, licensing agreements may create an access to new markets and open the door to low-risk manufacturing relationships. They can also speed diffusion of new products or technologies.

When companies do decide to license, they should sign agreements that anticipate more extensive market participation in the future. Insofar as is possible, a company should keep options and paths open for other forms of market participation. One path is joint venture with the licensee.

Trademarks can be an important part of the creation and protection of opportunities for lucrative licences.[6] Image-oriented companies such as Coca-Cola and Disney, as well as designers like Pierre Cardin, license their trademarked names and logos to overseas producers of clothing, toys and watches. Business is booming. The top tier names are expanding their fee income by 15 per cent a year and more. When licensing a trademark, the challenge is to maintain and enhance the brand equity of the marque. This means that licensees must be carefully selected and supervised. A bad licensee can seriously depreciate the value of a marque by turning out merchandise or services that do not meet up to the standard of the marque.

Franchising

Franchising is a special form of licensing. The difference is that franchising is a more extensive transfer of know-how. The franchisor provides the franchise with an entire business concept, which comprises a successful product and marketing package as well as managerial fundamentals. Franchising represents a relatively quick way of entering and expanding into foreign markets, as the franchisor incurs only little expenses. At the same time, contractual agreements provide the franchisor with an extensive influence on the franchisee's operations. These measures safeguard the development of an internationally uniform brand image. In general, franchising entails little financial resources from the franchisor, but offers him a high degree of control and market know-how.

In particular, US restaurant and hotel chains have discovered the opportunities of franchising as a tool for internationalisation. Inspired by success stories such as McDonald's or Pizza Hut, other restaurant chains such as T.G.I. Friday's or the Hard Rock Café are tackling the European market. Together with its British master franchisee Whitbread PLC, Hard Rock Café opened more than 50 restaurants in 26 European countries. After its debut in London, Hard Rock Cafés can be found in Belgium, Denmark, France, Germany, Scotland, Spain and Sweden.[7] When asked about their experiences in Europe, most US franchisors name high wages and real estate prices as major problems. One finding, however, is shared by all of them: each country and every master franchisee are different. This cultural diversity is often underestimated and not always easy to handle. Flexibility is therefore a key success factor. Despite the luring opportunities of franchising, experts advise caution. Companies internationalising need to be quite clear of how much involvement international activities require. A second aspect is the selection of potential franchisees. Often, the search for and the selection of franchisees is undertaken too carelessly. Finally, all partners should be aware of the fact that an international relationship between franchisor and franchisee requires time to develop. Experts estimate that it takes at least a time span of one year to identify a suitable franchisee. For professional support, they advise to consult banks and foreign chambers of commerce.[8]

European companies too use franchising as a tool to internationalise, and quite successfully, as evidenced by Benetton or Body Shop. The Italian firm Figurella runs more than 120 locations in Italy and is expanding greatly throughout Europe. Equally successful, the French coiffeurs Jacques Dessange and Jean-Louis David pursue their internationalisation through franchising. The traditional German toy manufacturer Margarete Steiff GmbH also uses franchising for its internationalisation. Starting in Austria in 2000, soft toys with the famous button in their ears will be offered by franchisees in so-called 'Steiff-Galeries'. Plans to expand into the US and the UK are already evolving.[9]

European companies are currently conquering the US market in their key franchising domain: fast food. Two German franchisors, Prostmahlzeit with its potato dishes, and Schweinske, which specialises in pork dishes, have set foot in the US markets with their first franchisees. The Spanish company Telepizza, which co-operates more than 200 franchisees in Spain, has teamed up with more than 50 franchisees abroad, some of them in the US.[10]

Joint ventures

A joint venture with a local partner represents a more extensive form of participation in foreign markets than either exporting or licensing. The advantages of this strategy include the sharing of risk and the ability to combine different value chain strengths, for example international marketing capability and manufacturing. One company might have in-depth knowledge of a local market, an extensive distribution system, or access to low-cost labour or raw materials. Such a company might link up with a foreign partner possessing considerable know-how in the area of technology, manufacturing and process applications. Companies that lack sufficient capital resources might seek partners to jointly finance a project. Finally, a joint venture may be the only way to enter a country or region if government bid award practices routinely favour local companies or if laws prohibit foreign control but permit joint ventures.

Joint ventures offer particularly attractive opportunities for market entry and expansion, when the economic and political environment in the target country is rather volatile. In Russia, firms actively participating in joint ventures target small to midsize companies, which can adapt rapidly in a still unstable environment. One study noted that of the 6,000 joint ventures registered in Russia since 1987, 20 per cent are up and running. Most of the joint ventures studied were initiated by the Western partner. The major business activities were evenly divided between services and manufacturing. Some were targeted at Westerners in Russia, for example, hotel, exhibition and legal services. Others targeted the domestic market in computer software and systems, telecommunications, music recording, architecture and medicine. Others focused on both markets: engineering, retail distribution, dentistry, security services, business consulting, banking, construction, and the leasing of construction equipment. Most of the manufacturing ventures were initially limited to assembly work but have moved on to producing components in Russia. The activities range from computer manufacturing to fish processing. Some of the joint ventures combined manufacturing and services; for example, there is a camera company that both sells and services the equipment it makes.

A case study set in Hungary demonstrates how joint ventures may be used to the advantage of both partners. Digital's joint venture agreement with the Hungarian Research Institute for Physics and the state-supervised computer systems design firm Szamalk is a case in point. Though the venture was formed so Digital would be able to sell and service its equipment in Hungary, the underlying importance of the venture was to stop cloning of Digital's computers by Central European firms.

Because of these clear advantages, especially in emerging markets, the conventional wisdom is that a joint venture is the only way to go. Not all agree with this 'wisdom'. In China, the situation is changing rapidly, and today companies should think beyond joint ventures with a well-connected local partner and consider the alternative of a wholly-owned foreign enterprise. In China, both alternatives are substantially the same in terms of taxation and corporate liability. They operate under similar rules and regulations. There are some technical differences, but the bottom line is that the wholly-owned subsidiary takes less time to establish than a joint venture and does not require a board of directors.

Today, there is a shift on the part of foreign investors in China from the joint venture to the wholly-owned subsidiary. The reasons are fundamental: investors achieve greater flexibility and control with a wholly-owned subsidiary, and the government is becoming more concerned about what a company brings to the country in terms of jobs, technology, and know-how than it is about how its deals are structured.

In China, as everywhere, each case must be decided on its merits. Two questions must be answered in every case: What does each partner bring to the deal, and what are the interests and capabilities of the partners going forward. The fact is that joint ventures are hard to sustain even in stable environments because the partners in a joint venture have different capabilities, resources, visions and interests. In fast-growing and fast-changing environments, it is much more difficult to sustain joint ventures. In China, for example, access to markets has been hindered by what foreign investors thought was the essential success factor in China: guanxi (relationships). In fact, what many investors have discovered is that China is a big country and the scope of their partner's guanxi is limited. Many investors have discovered to their disappointment that their partner lacked the guanxi needed to move forward. A wholly-owned subsidiary can retain agents and advisors to assist it in acquiring the land, materials, approvals and services that it needs to do business in China.[11]

Some major joint venture alliances are outlined in Table 9.1.

It is possible to use a joint venture as a source of supply for third-country markets. This must be carefully thought out in advance. One of the main reasons for joint venture 'divorce' is disagreement about third-country markets in which partners face each other as actual or potential competitors. To avoid this, it is essential to work out a plan for approaching third-country markets as part of the venture agreement.

The disadvantages of joint venturing can be significant. Joint venture partners must share rewards as well as risks. The main disadvantage of this global expansion strategy is that a company incurs very significant costs associated with control and co-ordination issues that arise when working with a partner. Also, as noted above with licensing, a dynamic joint venture partner can evolve into a stronger competitor. In some instances, country-specific restrictions limit the share of capital help by foreign companies. Cross-cultural differences in managerial attitudes and behaviour can present formidable challenges as well.

James River's European joint venture, for example, brought together 13 companies from 10 countries. Major problems included computer systems and measures of production efficiency; Jamont uses committees to solve these and other problems as they arise. For example, agreement had to be reached on a standardised table napkin size; for some country markets, 30 by 30 centimetres was the norm; for others, 35 by 35 centimetres was preferred.[12]

Difficulties such as those outlined above are so serious that, according to one study of 170 multinational firms, more than one third of 1,100 joint ventures were unstable, ending in 'divorce' or a significant increase in the US firm's power over its partner.[13] Another researcher found that numerous joint ventures with Japanese

Table 9.1 Market entry and expansion by joint venture

Companies involved	Purpose of joint venture
GM, Toyota	New United Motors Manufacturing, Inc. (NUMMI), a jointly operated plant in Freemont, California
Ford, Mazda	Joint Venture (Production) in Flat Rock, Michigan
AT&T, NEC	AT&T provides CAD technology in exchange for NEC's advanced logic chips
AT&T, Mitsubishi Electric	AT&T manufactures and markets Mitsubishi's memory chips in exchange for the technology used to design them
Texas Instruments, Kobe Steel	Joint effort making logic semiconductors in Japan
IBM, Siemens AG	Joint effort making logic semiconductors in Japan
Bosch, Kia	Production Joint Venture MOST (Motor Systems & Technology), manufacturing sensory and test equipment
Goodyear, Sumitomo	Joint Venture (one company in the US, one in Europe, two in Japan) co-ordinating global sourcing and technology transfer in tyre manufacturing

Source: Adapted from Bernard Wysocki, 'Global reach: Cross-border alliances become favorite way to crack new markets', *The Wall Street Journal*, 26 March 1990, pp. A1, A12; John Griffiths, 'Goodyear and Sumitomo', *Financial Times*, 4 February 1999: Haig Simonian, 'Bosch to control Kia Venture', *Financial Times*, 17 December 1997.

High potentials in China and India – opportunities or risks?

For car manufacturers, China as well as India represent markets with considerable potential. For that reason, the 'Who is Who' of car manufacturing is active in these markets. Large amounts of money are invested in joint ventures and subsidiaries to conquer the market. In India, foreign company activities were facilitated, after legal restrictions were removed in 1991. Manufacturers such as GM, Ford, Daimler Chrysler, Peugeot, Fiat or Daewoo are present in India with considerable financial investments. The majority of cars sold in the Indian market are not imported, but produced locally. In many cases, a manufacturer decides in favour of joint ventures with local partners. Mercedes Benz produces its model E-220 in a joint venture with India's Tata Group, Suzuki its compact car with Marutl Udyog. A market of 950 million consumers offers a rewarding target for corporate activities.

Beside India, China is another large market of the future for car manufacturers. Growth rates are enormous. Compared to 1985, production increased 78 times from 5,000 to 389,000 cars. At present, about 3 million cars have private owners. Industry experts

estimate that the market volume will increase to 5–6 million cars in 2010. If these forecasts manifest themselves, China would be the fourth largest car market after the US, Europe and Japan. Volkswagen (VW) runs the largest and most successful venture in China. In a joint venture with Shanghai Automotive Industry Corporation (SAIC), 200,000 cars of the type Santana are produced per year. Also, VW co-operates in the production of the model Jetta with First Auto Works (FAW) in Changchun. Chrylser's joint venture with Beijing Auto Works was founded at the beginning of the 1980s and produces Jeep Cherokees. New investments are in the pipeline. GM entered a joint venture with SAIC in 1997 with a value of more than €1.3 billion. Under this co-operation, Buick Sedans for government use are produced.

Despite the general enthusiasm about China's opportunities, this market holds a number of obstacles and difficulties for those who want to enter the Chinese market. The Chinese government does not allow foreign investors to hold the majority in a joint venture. Also, it reserves itself the right to set

Foreign car manufacturers in China	Investments (€ millions)	Ownership (%)	Production capacity (in 1,000 pcs.)	Actual production output in 1997 (in 1,000 pcs.)
Volkswagen Shangai	288	50	250	230
Volkswagen Changchun	437	40	150	45
VW total	725			
Peugeot-Citroen Wuhan	263	25	150	28
Peugeot-Citroen Guangzhou*	85	30	50	1.6
Peugeot-Citroen total	348			
General Motors Shanghai	700	50	100	**
General Motors Shenyang *	25	30	30	0
General Motors total	725			
Chrysler Beijing (approx.)	132 ***	42	100	52
Chrysler total	132			
Plans cancelled				
Daimler-Benz Guangdong-Hainan	416	na	100	0
Daimler-Benz Family Car China	680	na	250	0
Daimler-Benz total	1,096			

*Production put on hold   ** Estimate based on registered capital of €53 million   *** Start in 1999
Source: 'Stalling in China', The Economist, 347, 8067, 10 April 1998.

GLOBAL PERSPECTIVE continued

production output and product prices. Official statements by top politicians may make one wonder. Only recently, a FAW representative told a Chinese magazine: 'We no longer want to be the extended arm of foreign car manufacturers. If we look at South Korea or Japan, we are totally convinced that we will achieve the same goals.' The reaction of government officials did not take long. In order to achieve more favourable import tariffs of 37.5 per cent on parts, manufacturers must reach a local content of at least 40 per cent. As a consequence, most of the big manufacturers increased their local content to more than 80 per cent.

However, the economic landscape also provides many examples of stalled projects. In 1997, Peugeot dissolved a joint venture in Guangzhou. Mercedes-Benz too looks back on a turbulent history in China. With great enthusiasm, the company provided 1994 investments amounting to €680 million. These funds were designated to a production facility for a Chinese family car based on Mercedes'

A-Klasse. In 1995, the Chinese Prime Minister Jian Zemin signed a contract on a planned joint venture. Within this project, €850 million would be invested into the manufacturing of Minivans and engines together with Nanfang South China Motor Corporation. The contract was celebrated as a victory for Mercedes, particularly as the company was preferred against GM. Two years later however, the implementation was still far from being satisfying. Jürgen Hubbert, Member of the Board at Mercedes Benz, has some advice for firms which want to become actively involved in China: 'Whenever you finalise a project, you are only at the beginning.'

Food for thought

- In your view, what are the major country specific risks for a car company investing in markets like India or China?
- Draw up a list of factors that could be used when assessing the market potential of cars in India and China?

Source: Vasuki Rao, 'India ignites the interest of global auto industry', *Journal of Commerce*, 411 (1997): pp. 3A; James Harding, 'Long march to mass market', *Financial Times* (25 June 1997), p. 13; James Cox, 'Chinese auto industry stumbles', *USA Today*, 16 December 1996, p. 9B; John Templeman, 'How Mercedes trumped Chrysler in China', *Business Week* (31 July 1995), pp. 50–51; 'Shifting gears – Part 2 of 2', *China Business Review*, 24 (6): p. 15ff; 'Stalling in China: Daimler-Benz', *The Economist*, 347, 8064 , 18 April 1998.

companies were either liquidated or transferred to the Japanese interest. The most fundamental problem was the different benefits that each side expected to receive.[14]

In a joint venture, the real payoff is from learning skills from the partner, rather than just getting product to sell while avoiding investment. Yet, compared to American and European firms, Japanese and Korean firms seem to excel in their ability to leverage new knowledge that comes out of a joint venture. For example, Toyota learned many new things from its partnership with GM about US supply and transportation and managing American workers that have been subsequently applied at its Camry plant in Kentucky. However, some American managers involved in the venture complained that the manufacturing expertise they gained was not applied broadly throughout GM. This complaint has validity to the extent that GM has missed opportunities to leverage new learning. Still, many companies have achieved great successes pursuing joint ventures. Gillette, for example, has used this strategy to introduce its shaving products in the Middle East and Africa.

Wholly-owned subsidiaries/acquisition

After companies gain experience outside the home country via exporting or licensing and joint ventures, the time comes for many companies when a more extensive form of participation in global markets is wanted. The desire for control and ownership of operations outside the home country drives the decision to invest. Foreign direct investment (FDI) figures record investment flows as companies invest in or acquire plant, equipment or other assets outside the home country. By definition, direct investment presumes that the investor has control or significant influence over the investment, as opposed to portfolio investment in which it is assumed that the investor does not have significant influence or control. The operational definition of direct investment is ownership of 20 per cent or more of the equity of a company. According to UNCTAD estimates, world-wide direct investment totalled €360 billion in 1997, a 19 per cent increase to the year before.

Table 9.2 comprises a list of companies which are ranked based on their foreign direct investments.

United Parcel Service (UPS) recently announced plans to invest more than €850 million in Europe over five years; Ford Motor Company is building a €425 million factory in Thailand; South Korea's LG Electronics purchased a 58 per cent stake in Zenith Electronics. Each of these represents foreign direct investment.

The most extensive form of participation in global markets is 100 per cent ownership, which may be achieved by start-up or acquisition. Ownership requires the greatest commitment of capital and managerial effort and offers the fullest means of participating in a market. Companies may move from licensing or joint venture strategies to ownership in order to achieve faster expansion in a market, greater control, or higher profits. In 1991, for example, Ralston Purina ended a 20-year joint venture with a Japanese company to start its own pet-food subsidiary. Monsanto Company and Bayer AG, the German pharmaceutical company, are two other companies that have also recently disbanded partnerships in favour of wholly owned subsidiaries in Japan.[15] In many countries, government restrictions may prevent majority or 100 per cent ownership by foreign companies.

Table 9.2 Ranking of international companies based on their FDI

Rank	Company	Country
1	General Electric	US
2	Shell, Royal Dutch	UK/The Netherlands
3	Ford Motor Company	US
4	EXXON Corporation	US
5	General Motors	US
6	IBM	US
7	Toyota	Japan
8	Volkswagen Gruppe	Germany
9	Mitsubishi	Japan
10	Mobil Corporation	US
11	Nestlé SA	Switzerland
12	Asea Brown Boveri (ABB)	Switzerland/Sweden
13	Elf Aquitaine SA	France
14	Bayer AG	Germany
15	Hoechst AG	Germany
16	Nissan Motor Co. Ltd.	Japan
17	FIAT Spa	Italy
18	Unilever	The Netherlands/UK
19	Daimler-Benz AG	Germany
20	Philips Electronics NV	The Netherlands

Source: UNCTAD, World Investment Report 1998 (New York, 1999).

Courage pays: Ford bets on Jaguar

In 1989, the Ford Motor Company acquired Jaguar PLC of Coventry, England, for €2.2 billion. L. Lindsay Halstead, chairman of Ford of Europe, called the Jaguar acquisition the fulfilment of 'a long-time strategic objective of entering the luxury car market in a significant way'. Ford lacked a high-end luxury model for both the US and European markets, and the company was betting it could take a nameplate highly valued for exclusivity and sell it to more people by launching a new, less expensive line of Jaguars. The management was quite aware of the fact that this could be quite risky. While the Ford name is synonymous with bread and butter, Jaguar has a truly exclusive position in customers' minds.

In 1988, its best sales year, Jaguar sold just under 50,000 cars world-wide. Ford set an objective of producing 150,000 cars by the end of the decade, two thirds of which would be the lower-priced sporty sedan. Ford also targeted 1992 as the year Jaguar would show a positive cash flow. Unfortunately, the Jaguar acquisition coincided with the global recession that hurt sales in Japan, Germany and the United States. To make matters worse, a 10 per cent luxury tax imposed in the United States scared off potential buyers. By 1991, Jaguar sales slipped to 25,676 cars.

Ford must also deal with other challenges. Although Jaguar's classy image and racing heritage are prized attributes, the cars were also legendary for their unreliability. Gears sometimes did not shift, headlights did not light, and the brakes had been known to catch fire. Part of the problem could be traced to manufacturing, where there were 2,500 defects per 100 cars produced in 1990. By 1992, that number had been reduced to 500 defects per 100 cars.

Ford has been forced to invest heavily to update and upgrade Jaguar's plant facilities and improve productivity. As a benchmark, Ford's manufacturing experts know that German luxury car makers can build a car in 80 hours; the Japanese need only 20 hours. If Jaguar is ever to achieve world-class status, the assembly time of 110 hours per car must be drastically reduced.

Ironically, die-hard Jaguar loyalists, customers whose continued support Jaguar desperately needs, are giving the new, improved Jaguars mixed reviews. It seems that many Jaguar owners enjoy the misery brought on by an unreliable car. In fact, Jaguar clubs in the United States bestow 'Cat Bite' awards on members with the best tales of woe. According to these owners, the new Ford-era cars 'lack mystique'.

Some observers question the wisdom of Ford's purchase, expressing doubts that Ford will ever break even on its investment. Ford's Japanese competitors including Honda, Nissan and Toyota have allocated their financial resources differently. They have made major investments to launch new nameplates and upgrade their dealer organisations. Infiniti, Lexus, and other new luxury sedans are winning new buyers with high quality, high performance and outstanding dealer service. Publicly, Ford is confident its multibillion-dollar bet will pay off. As chairman Halstead said in 1990, 'We're happy we made the purchase. It was a long-term vision. We don't expect results overnight.'

1998 brought the first good news. Although Jaguar did not entirely reach its highflying objectives of 50,000 cars sold, the trends were definitely very positive.

Food for thought

- Do you think Ford would have been served better by investing into 'new nameplates' (as for example Toyota did) instead of purchasing Jaguar? Why? Why not?
- Why was Ford so keen to enter the high-end luxury car market?

Source: Joann S. Lublin and Craig Forman, 'Going upscale: Ford snares Jaguar, but $2.5 billion is high price for prestige', *The Wall Street Journal*, 3 November 1989, pp. A1, A4; Steven Prokesch, 'Jaguar battle at a turning point', *The New York Times*, 29 October 1990, p. C1; Steven Prokesch, 'Ford's Jaguar bet: payoff isn't close', *The New York Times*, 21 April 1992, p. C1; Robert Johnson, 'Jaguar owners love company and sharing their horror stories', *The Wall Street Journal*, 28 September 1993, p. A1; 'Rough ride: luxury cars were once a cosy money spinner for a few car companies', *The Economist*, 14 November 1998.

Large-scale direct expansion by means of establishing new facilities can be expensive and require a major commitment of managerial time and energy. Alternatively, acquisition is an instantaneous and sometimes less expensive approach to market entry. Although full ownership can yield the additional advantage of avoiding communication and conflict-of-interest problems that may arise with a joint venture or production partner, acquisitions still present the demanding and challenging task of integrating the acquired company into the world-wide organisation and co-ordinating activities. The decision to invest abroad, whether by expansion or acquisition, sometimes clashes with short-term profitability goals. This is an especially important issue for publicly held companies. Despite these challenges, there is an increasing trend toward foreign investment by companies.

Table 9.3 lists some examples, grouped by industry, of companies that have pursued global expansion via acquisition. Table 9.4 shows incoming and outgoing European FDI by source and target country.

Several of the advantages of joint venture alliances also apply to ownership, including access to markets and avoidance of tariff or quota barriers. Like joint ventures, ownership also permits important technology experience transfers and provides a company with access to new manufacturing techniques. For example, the Stanley Works, a toolmaker with headquarters in New Britain, Connecticut, has bought more than a dozen companies since 1986, among them Taiwan's National Hand Tool/Chiro company, a socket wrench manufacturer and developer of a cold forming process that speeds up production and reduces waste. Stanley is now using the technology in the manufacture of other tools. This example clearly shows the value of global cross-fertilisation and blended technology as a key benefit of globalisation.[16]

The alternatives discussed earlier – licensing, joint ventures and ownership – are in fact points along a continuum of alternative strategies or tools for global market entry and expansion. The overall design of a company's global strategy may call for combinations of exporting/importing, licensing, joint ventures and ownership among different operating units. Such is the case in Japan for Borden, Inc.; it is ending licensing and joint venture arrangements for branded food products and setting up its own

Table 9.3 Market entry and expansion by acquisition

Product category/industry	Acquiring company	Target
Apparel, personal care and food products	Sara Lee Corp. (US) Sandoz AG (Switzerland)	Douwe Egberts (coffee and tea), Dim (hosiery), and other companies with total sales in excess of €850 million in seven different countries; Gerber (1994)
Automotive tyres	Bridgestone Corporation (Japan)	Firestone Tire and Rubber Company (1988; €2.5 billion)
	Continental AG (Germany)	General Tire (1987)
	Pirelli SpA (Italy)	Armstrong Tire (1988)
	Michelin (France)	Uniroyal/Goodrich (1990; €1.3 billion)
Media and entertainment	Sony (Japan)	CBS Records (€1.7 billion, 1987); Columbia Pictures (€2.9 billion, 1989)
	Matsushita (Japan)	MCA/Universal (€5.6 billion, 1990)
Consumer electronics	Thomson SA (France)	GE's consumer electronics business, GE's RCA subsidiary; Telefunken (Germany)

Table 9.4 European FDI – incoming and outgoing funds by source and target country (1998; in € million)

	Funds invested in						Funds coming from					
1998	World	EU	Extra EU	US	Japan	Canada	1998	World	EU	Extra EU	US	Japan	Canada
EU	–	–	191,640	112,470	1,010	2,740	EU	–	–	94,300	59,400	2,420	710
B/L	20,652	16,712	3,940	475	4	1,290	B/L	18,667	12,331	6,336	3,733	–111	136
DK	3,454	3,294	160	–667	40	13	DK	5,761	1,147	4,614	3,640	0	0
D	74,349	22,635	51,713	39,603	131	216	D	17,766	15,130	2,636	2,749	48	–95
E	16,430	4,849	11,612	115	–1	625	E	10,104	9,006	1,098	626	–46	2
F	34,334	15,753	18,581	6,417	60	212	F	24,577	19,684	4,894	3,882	103	290
IRL	1,917	941	976	981	–	–	IRL	6,247	3,190	3,058	3,251	–	–
I	10,787	5,667	5,120	1,777	70	118	I	2,332	2,125	200	–258	69	7
NL	34,243	16,598	17,645	6,821	–64	608	NL	28,477	11,454	17,022	13,339	186	66
A	2,181	1,062	1,119	–6	2	19	A	4,207	3,720	486	55	0	146
P	2,394	948	1,446	58	0	0	P	1,029	485	543	201	4	2
FIN	19,707	18,479	1,228	810	17	0	FIN	8,692	8,607	85	26	48	0
SE	18,887	9,540	9,347	2,163	20	136	SE	16,812	12,864	3,948	683	–91	199
UK	78,849	10,100	68,749	53,922	736	–498	UK	48,930	–306	49,238	27,469	2,195	–69

Source: Eurostat News Release, Nr. 60/99, 1 July 1999.

production, distribution, and marketing capabilities for dairy products. Meanwhile, in non-food products, Borden has maintained joint venture relationships with Japanese partners in flexible packaging and foundry materials.[17]

Key points

- Companies which strive for profound market knowledge and better control of their foreign activities can choose from different market entry and expansion alternatives.

- The main alternatives involving overseas production are licensing, franchising, joint ventures, wholly-owned subsidiaries or acquisitions as well as new forms of strategic alliances.

- Improved control and more intensive market contact tend to demand a higher equity investment.

DEMANDS ON STRATEGIC ALLIANCES

The recent changes in the political, economic, socio-cultural and technological environments of the global firm have combined to change the relative importance of strategic alliances. Trade barriers have fallen, markets have globalised, consumer needs and wants have converged, product life cycles have shortened, and new communications technologies and trends have emerged. These developments provide unprecedented market opportunities, but also present strong strategic implications for the global organisation and new challenges for the global marketer. Once thought of only as joint ventures with the more dominant party reaping most of the benefits (or losses) of the partnership, cross-border alliances are taking on surprising new configurations and even more surprising players. For its global communication services project 'Iridium' (see Global Perspective), Motorola, a leading manufacturer of cellular phones and pagers, decided to pursue competitive collaboration with other firms, some of which are rivals.

Every company faces a business environment characterised by unprecedented degrees of dynamism, turbulence and unpredictability. Today's firm must be equipped to respond to mounting economic and political pressures. Reaction time has been sharply cut by advances in technology. The firm of tomorrow must be ready to do whatever it takes to ensure that it is creating unique value for customers and that it has a competitive advantage.

Strategic alliances and, as the example of 'Iridium' demonstrates, sometimes even competitive collaborations offer significant advantages. However, this need not necessarily be the case for every business situation. The following section will address the fundamental issues: whether to co-operate and when to co-operate.

The terminology used to describe the new forms of co-operation strategies varies widely. The phrases collaborative agreements, strategic alliances, strategic international alliances, and global strategic partnerships (GSPs) are frequently used to refer to linkages between companies that jointly pursue a common goal. A broad spectrum of interfirm agreements, including joint ventures, can be covered by this terminology. However, the strategic alliances discussed in this chapter exhibit three characteristics:[18]

1 The participants remain independent subsequent to the formation of the alliance.
2 The participants share the benefits of the alliance as well as control over the performance of assigned tasks.
3 The participants make ongoing contributions in technology, products and other key strategic areas.

According to estimates, the number of strategic alliances has been growing at a rate of 20 to 30 per cent since the mid-1980s. The upward trend for GSPs comes in part at the expense of traditional cross-border mergers and acquisitions.[19]

Roland Smith, chairman of British Aerospace, offers a straightforward reason why a firm would enter into a GSP: 'A partnership is one of the quickest and cheapest ways to develop a global strategy.'[20] Like traditional joint ventures, GSPs have some disadvantages. Each partner must be willing to sacrifice some control, and there are potential risks associated with strengthening a competitor from another country. Despite these drawbacks, GSPs are attractive for several reasons. First, high product development costs may force a company to seek partners; this was part of the rationale for Boeing's partnership with a Japanese consortium to develop a new jet aircraft, the 777. Second, the technology requirements of many contemporary products mean that an individual company may lack the skills, capital, or know-how to go it alone.[21] Eli Lilly, for example, entered a strategic alliance with an American and a British partner to develop a new drug against thrombosis. Independently, Bristol-Myers Squibb and Rhone-Poulenc teamed up with the same US company to develop a new combination drug.[22] Also, partnerships may be the best means of securing access to national and regional markets. They provide important learning opportunities. Gary Hamel, Professor at the London Business School, has observed that the partner that proves to be the fastest learner can ultimately dominate the relationship.[23]

GSPs and joint ventures differ in significant ways. Traditional joint ventures are basically alliances focusing on a single national market or a specific problem. A true global strategic partnership is different.[24] It is distinguished by the following six attributes:

GLOBAL PERSPECTIVE

Iridium

Motorola thinks the future of telephone communications is up in the air – literally. The company has embarked on an ambitious programme called Iridium, at the heart of which is a network of 66 powerful, low-orbit satellites. Iridium will allow Motorola to offer global personal communication services that will supplement, and perhaps render obsolete, ground-based wire and cellular telephone services. Iridium's first customers will probably be globetrotting business executives who need to send and receive voice messages and data. The needs of business travellers may be just the beginning: 90 per cent of the world's population lacks access to telephones. Iridium could bring telephone service to rural areas in South America, Africa and Asia without wires. Given the high cost, this picture still belongs to the future. Iridium's first customers have to pay the considerable amount of €2,500 for the cellular phone and €2.5 and more per minute in talk fees.

With an investment of €2.9 billion, Iridium was too costly to be tackled by Motorola alone. Therefore, Motorola partnered with more than a dozen companies from various parts of the world, each with a specific strength. Taytheon, Martin Marietta and Siemens AG stepped in as strategic partners. Lockheed, for example, will build the satellites. Some partners will be responsible for connecting calls in specific geographic regions. The Vebacom GmbH, a subsidiary of Germany's Veba AG, will provide service in Northern and Western Europe. Other participants include Krunichev Enterprise, a Russian rocket manufacturer, and Great Wall Industry Corporation, which is affiliated with the Chinese army.

Industry observers note that Iridium must overcome some major hurdles if it is to succeed. For one thing, Iridium is just one of several competing telephone and data systems being developed.

Competitors such as Globalstar or ICO Communications did not want to lag behind in this lucrative market. However, they too had to face major setbacks. Globalstar had to watch some of its satellites going down in the Kasachian desert after a failing mission into orbit. And ICO Communications was still looking for potential partners. The second problem consisted of finding investors who would be willing to share the high risk. In 1995, Iridium had to withdraw an offer of €255 million *junk bonds*, after investors wanted to see a return rate of more than 25 per cent.

Iridium has been operating since 1 November 1998, and its first moves were anything but successful. At 12,000 the number of customers lagged far behind targets. Investors expected to see 27,000 Iridium customers. The blame was said to be technical problems. Kyocera, supplier of the cellular phones, encountered production problems, software bugs resulted in transmission problems. The transmission of communications was of low quality and frequently interrupted. Also, marketing flaws and deficient sales activities were held responsible for the low customer acquisition rate. The more than 200 partners did not display the commitment they were expected to. The difficult financial situation led to the fact that in 1999 new talks with supporting banks had to be conducted.

At Iridium, the management is still confident: the question is not whether Iridium will be a success, but when.

Food for thought

- What are the main reasons behind Iridium's lack of success to date?
- How do you judge the future potential of Iridium? Would you invest your personal money into the venture?

Source: Jeff Cole, 'Star wars: in new space race, companies are seeking dollars from heaven', *The Wall Street Journal*, 10 October 1995, pp. A1, A12; Harlan S. Byrne, 'Far out', *Barron's* (19 June 1995), pp. 31–35; Joe Flowers, 'Iridium, Parts I and II', *Wired* (Fall 1993); Quentin Hardy, 'Iridium pulls $300 million bond offer; analysts cite concerns about projects', *The Wall Street Journal*, 22 September 1995, p. B5; Nancy Hass, 'Preemptive strike', *Financial World* (14 September 1993), pp. 36–39; Rob Frieden, 'Satellite-based personal communications services', *Telecommunications* (December 1993), pp. 25–28; Christopher Price, 'New industry gets a fillip after price after setbacks: global mobile', *Financial Times*, 18 November 1998; 'Mobile phone campaign fails to conquer world', *The Times*, 21 January 1999; Christopher Price, 'Iridium wins time on debt', *Financial Times*, 30 March 1999; Christopher Price, 'Motorola pledges support for Iridium', *Financial Times*, 20 March 1999.

1 Two or more companies develop a joint long-term strategy aimed at achieving world leadership by pursuing cost leadership, differentiation or a combination of the two and by creating a variety, needs or access-based position or a combination of the three.

2 The relationship is reciprocal. Each partner possesses specific strengths that it shares with the other; learning must take place on both sides.

3 The partners' vision and efforts are truly global, extending beyond home countries and the home regions to the rest of the world.

4 If the relationship is organised along horizontal lines, continual transfer of resources laterally between partners is required, with technology sharing and resource pooling representing norms.

5 If the relationship is along vertical lines, both parties to the relationship must understand their core strengths and be able to defend their competitive position against the possibility of either a forward or backward integration move by their vertical partner, and they must work together to create a unique value for the customers of the downstream partner in the value chain.

6 When competing in markets excluded from the partnership, the participants retain their national and ideological identities.

The Iridium programme embodies several prerequisites that experts believe are the hallmarks of good alliances. Motorola is forming an alliance to exploit a unique strength, namely, its leadership in wireless communications. The Iridium alliance partners all possess unique strengths of their own. It is unlikely that any of the partners has the ability or the desire to acquire Motorola's unique strength. Finally, rather than focusing on a particular market or product, Iridium is an alliance based on skills, know-how and technology.[25]

Companies like Nike and Gallo have perfected the way to employ strategic partnerships. Nike, the world's largest sports equipment seller, does not manufacture a single shoe. It rather concentrates on its key strengths: marketing and sales. Gallo, the largest wine company on earth, does not grow a single grape, and Boeing, the pre-eminent aircraft manufacturer, makes little more than cockpits and wings.[26] While outsourcing manufacturing for many companies might be a tactical response dedicated to some immediate cost savings, it is clear that Nike, Gallo and Boeing put significant thought into establishing their supply chains, and that they could view their supplier arrangements as strategic. In fact, Nike's ability to outsource its manufacturing to multiple low-cost producers in the Far East has been a critical component of its success. Although these vertical arrangements may be critically important to the success of the firm, they are not alliances unless the partners are linked in a long-term relationship. If they are not, then they are simply supply agreements.

The strategic alliances between McDonald's, Disney and Coca-Cola are based on the idea to merge the firms' different key competencies in order to join forces in times of globalisation. In 1997, McDonald's and Disney entered a formal strategic alliance for 10 years. Their first joint project was the launch of Disney's film production *Flubber*, which was accompanied by special products and sales promotion at McDonald's. *Armaggedon* was supported through special 'Astromenus'. In contrast to the partnership with Disney, the co-operation with Coca-Cola is grounded on a 'shared vision and a good deal for trust'. Coke not only exclusively supplies McDonald's, but also offers sales promotion in the form of self-service stations shaped as a large Coke bottle. In addition, Coke, which is present in twice as many countries as McDonald's, offers support in the internationalisation process of the hamburger company. What makes the three so successful in their co-operation: all three of them are market leaders in their industry.[27]

An example of a strategic relationship of partners along vertical lines is in *lean manufacturing*. For instance, an assembler of an automobile relies on suppliers not only to build but also to design key components of the automobile. This kind of co-operation can lead to shorter design cycles, superior quality and lower costs but it will not occur unless there is a mutual commitment to work together and a confidence on both sides that the two parties will not invade each other's domain. This kind of co-operation can strengthen the competitive advantage of each of the partners by enabling them to identify and concentrate on their core strengths.

Success factors

Assuming that a proposed alliance meets the six prerequisites just outlined, it is necessary to consider the following six basic factors that are deemed to have significant impact on the success of GSPs.[28]

1 *Mission.* Successful GSPs create win–win situations, in which participants pursue objectives on the basis of mutual need or advantage.
2 *Strategy.* A company may establish separate GSPs with different partners; strategy must be thought out up-front to avoid conflicts.
3 *Governance.* Discussion and consensus must be the norms. Partners must be viewed as equals.
4 *Culture.* Personal chemistry is important, as is the successful development of a shared set of values. The failure of a partnership between Britain's General Electric Company and Siemens AG was blamed in part on the fact that the former was run by finance-oriented executives and the latter by engineers.
5 *Organisation.* Innovative structures and designs may be needed to offset the complexity of multicountry management.
6 *Management.* GSPs invariably involve a different type of decision making. Potentially divisive issues must be identified in advance and clear, unitary lines of authority established that will result in commitment by all partners.[29]

The issue of learning deserves special attention. One team of researchers notes the following:

> The challenge is to share enough skills to create advantage vis-à-vis companies outside the alliance while preventing a wholesale transfer of core skills to the partner. This is a very thin line to walk. Companies must carefully select what skills and technologies they pass to their partners. They must develop safeguards against unintended, informal transfers of information. To restrict transparency, some companies have established what they call a 'zone of co-operation'. Similar to a communications department, this team is designed to work as gatekeeper. It is in charge of requests to enter into contact with certain employees or to receive information. Under this system, the unintentional transfer of know-how is reduced significantly.[30]

A report by McKinsey and company shed additional light on the specific problems of alliances using partnerships between Western and Japanese firms.[31] Often, problems between partners had less to do with objective levels of performance than with a feeling of mutual disillusionment and missed opportunity. The study identified four common problem areas in alliances gone wrong. The first problem was that each partner had a different dream; the Japanese partner saw itself emerging from the alliance as a leader in its business or entering new sectors and building a new basis for the future, while the Western partner sought relatively quick and risk-free financial returns. Said one Japanese manager, 'Our partner came in looking for a return. They got it. Now they complain that they didn't build a business. But that isn't what they set out to create.'

A second area of concern is the balance between partners. Each must contribute to the alliance, and each must depend on the other to a degree that justifies partici-pation in the alliance. The most attractive partner in the short run is likely to be a company that is already established and competent in the business with the need to master, say, some new technological skills. The best long-term partner, however, is likely to be a less competent player or even one from outside the industry.

Another common cause of problems is frictional loss, caused by differences in man-agement philosophy, expectations and approaches. All functions within the alliance may be affected, and performance is likely to suffer as a consequence. Speaking of his Japanese counterpart, a Western businessperson said, 'Our partner just wanted to go ahead and invest without considering whether there would be a return or not.' The Japanese partner stated that 'The foreign partner took so long to decide on obvious points that we were always too slow.' Such differences often cause much frustration and time-consuming debates, which stifle decision making.

Last, the study found that short-term goals can result in the foreign partner's limit-ing the number of people allocated to the joint venture. Those involved in the ven-ture may perform only two- or three-year assignments. The result is corporate amnesia, that is, little or no corporate memory is built up on how to compete in Japan. The original goals of the venture will be lost as each new group of managers take their turn. When taken collectively, these four problems will almost ensure that the Japanese partner will be the only one in it for the long haul.

Case examples of partnerships

CFM International/GE/Snecma – a success story

Commercial Fan Moteur (CFM) International, a partnership between General Electric's (GE's) jet engine division and Snecma, a government-owned French aero-space company, is a frequently cited example of a successful GSP. GE was motivated in part by the desire to gain access to the European market so it could sell engines to Airbus Industrie; also, the €680 million in development costs was more than GE could risk on its own. While GE focused on system design and high-tech work, the French side handled fans, boosters and other components. The partnership resulted in the development of a highly successful new engine that, to date, has generated tens of billions of € in sales to 125 different customers.

The alliance got off to a strong start because of the personal chemistry between two top executives, GE's Gerhard Neumann and the late General René Ravaud of Snecma. The partnership thrives despite each side's differing views regarding gov-ernance, management and organisation. Brian Rowe, senior vice president of GE's engine group, has noted that the French like to bring in senior executives from outside the industry, whereas GE prefers to bring in experienced people from within the organisation. Also, the French prefer to approach problem solving with copious amounts of data, whereas Americans may take a more intuitive approach.[32]

AT&T/Olivetti – a failure

In theory, the partnership in the mid-1980s between AT&T and Italy's Olivetti appeared to be a winner. The collective mission was to capture a major share of the global market for information processing and communications.[33] Olivetti had what appeared to be a strong presence in the European office equipment market. AT&T executives, having just presided over the divestiture of their company's regional telephone units, had set their sights on overseas growth, with Europe as the starting point. AT&T promised its partner €220 million and access to microprocessor and telecommunications technology. The partnership called for AT&T to sell Olivetti's personal computers in the US; Olivetti, in turn, would sell AT&T computers and switching equipment in Europe. Underpinning the alliance was the expectation that synergies would result from the pairing of companies from different industries – communications and computers.

Unfortunately, that vision was nothing more than a hope. There was no real strength in Olivetti in the computer market, and Olivetti had no experience or capability in communications equipment. Tensions ran high when sales did not reach expected levels. AT&T group executive Robert Kavner cited communication and cultural differences as being important factors leading to the breakdown of the alliance. 'I don't think we or Olivetti spent enough time understanding behaviour patterns,' Kavner said. 'We knew the culture was different but we never really penetrated. We would get angry, and they would get upset.'[34] In 1989, AT&T cashed in its Olivetti stake for a share in the parent company Compagnie Industriali Riunite SpA (CIR). In 1993, citing a decline in CIR's value, AT&T sold its remaining stake.

Boeing/Japan – a controversy

GSPs have been the target of criticism in some circles. Critics warn that employees of a company that becomes reliant on outside suppliers for critical components will lose expertise and experience erosion of their engineering skills. Such criticism is often directed at GSPs involving US and Japanese firms. For example, a proposed alliance between Boeing and a Japanese consortium to build a new fuel-efficient airliner, the 7J7, generated a great deal of controversy. The project's €3.4 billion price tag was too high for Boeing to shoulder alone. The Japanese were to contribute between €850 million and €1.7 billion; in return, they would get a chance to learn manufacturing and marketing techniques from Boeing. Although the 7J7 project was shelved in 1988, a new wide-body aircraft, the 777, was developed with about 20 per cent of the work subcontracted out to Mitsubishi, Fuji, and Kawasaki.[35]

Critics envision a scenario in which the Japanese use what they learn to build their own aircraft and compete directly with Boeing in the future. One team of researchers has developed a framework outlining the stages that a company can go through as it becomes increasingly dependent on partnerships.[36]

- *Stage One:* Outsourcing of assembly for inexpensive labour.
- *Stage Two:* Outsourcing of low-value components to reduce product price.
- *Stage Three:* Growing levels of value-added components move abroad.
- *Stage Four:* Manufacturing skills, designs and functionally related technologies move abroad.
- *Stage Five:* Disciplines related to quality, precision manufacturing, testing and future avenues of product derivatives leave.

- *Stage Six:* Core skills surrounding components, miniaturisation and complex systems integration move abroad.
- *Stage Seven:* Competitor learns the entire spectrum of skills related to the underlying core competence.

The next stage is obvious. The partner now has the complete manufacturing skill set and capability and may decide to push for forward integration, that is, to move closer to the customer by introducing its own brand into the marketplace.

Key points

- A strategic alliance can be defined as a form of co-operation, where (i) the partners remain independent even after entering the alliance, (ii) the partners share the benefits, risks as well as the control in the alliance and (iii) they provide technologies, products and other strategic resources for the partnership.
- The success factors of strategic alliances are a shared vision and shared goals, a clear separation between co-operation and competition, discussion and consensus as key characteristics in co-operation, a shared value system and the will to work together.

Co-operative strategies in Japan: *keiretsu*

Japan's *keiretsu* represent a special category of co-operative strategy. A *keiretsu* is an interbusiness alliance or enterprise group that, in the words of one observer, 'resembles a fighting clan in which business families join together to vie for market share'.[37] *Keiretsu* exist in a broad spectrum of markets, including the capital market, primary goods markets and component parts markets.[38] *Keiretsu* relationships are often cemented by bank ownership of large blocks of stock as well as cross-ownership of stock between a company and its buyers and non-financial suppliers. Further, *keiretsu* executives can legally sit on each other's boards, as well as share information and co-ordinate prices in closed-door meetings of 'presidents' councils'. Thus, some people interpret *keiretsu* essentially as cartels that have the government's blessing.

Some observers have disputed charges that *keiretsu* have an impact on market relationships in Japan, claiming instead that the groups primarily serve a social function. Others acknowledge the past significance of preferential trading patterns associated with *keiretsu* but assert that the latter's influence is now weakening. It is beyond the scope of this chapter to address these issues in detail, but there can be no doubt that, for companies competing with the Japanese or wishing to enter the Japanese market, a general understanding of *keiretsu* is crucial. Imagine, for example, what it would mean in Germany if an automaker (e.g. Daimler-Chrysler or BMW), an electrical products company (Siemens), a steel maker (Thyssen), and a software company (SAP or Debis) were interconnected, rather than separate, firms. Global competition in the era of *keiretsu* means competition exists not only among products, but between different systems of corporate governance and industrial organisation.[39]

Some of Japan's largest and most well-known companies are in the centre of a *keiretsu*. For example, the Mitsui Group and Mitsubishi Group are organised around big trading companies. These two, together with the Sumitomo, Fuyo, Sanwa and DKB groups make up the 'big six' *keiretsu*. Each group strives for a strong position in each major sector of the Japanese economy. Annual revenues in each group are in the € hundreds of billions.[40] In absolute terms, *keiretsu* constitute less than 0.01 per cent of all Japanese companies. However, they account for an astonishing 78 per cent of

Figure 9.2 Mitsubishi Group's *keiretsu* structure

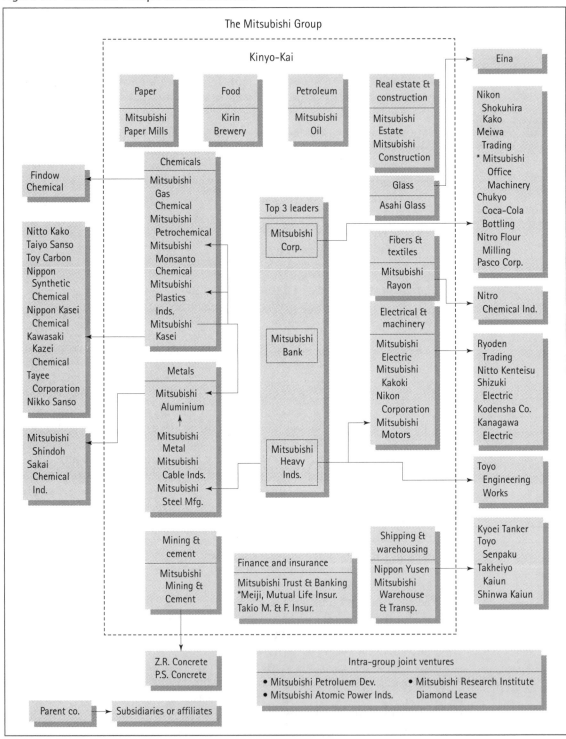

Source: Courtesy of the Mitsubishi Group, from T.M. Collins and T.L. Doorley, *Teaming Up for the 90s: A Guide to International Joint Ventures and Strategic Alliances* (New York: Deloitte & Touche, 1991).

the market valuation of shares on the Tokyo Stock Exchange, a third of Japan's business capital and approximately one quarter of its sales.[41] These alliances can effectively block foreign suppliers from entering the market and result in higher prices to Japanese consumers, while at the same time resulting in corporate stability, risk sharing and long-term employment. The Mitsubishi Group's *keiretsu* structure is shown in detail in Figure 9.2.

In addition to the big six, several other *keiretsu* have formed, bringing new configurations to the basic forms described above. Vertical supply and distribution *keiretsu* are alliances between manufacturers and retailers. For example, Matsushita controls a chain of 25,000 National stores in Japan through which it sells its Panasonic, Technics and Quasar brands. About half of Matsushita's domestic sales are generated through the National chain, 50 to 80 per cent of whose inventory consists of Matsushita's brands. Japan's other major consumer electronics manufacturers, including Toshiba and Hitachi, have similar alliances (Sony's chain of stores is much smaller and weaker by comparison). All are fierce competitors in the Japanese market.[42]

Another type of manufacturing *keiretsu* outside the big six consists of vertical hierarchical alliances between assembly companies and suppliers and component manufacturers. Intergroup operations and systems are closely integrated, with suppliers receiving long-term contracts. Toyota, for example, has a network of about 175 primary and 4,000 secondary suppliers. One supplier is Koito. Toyota owns about one fifth of Koito's shares and buys about half of its production. The net result of this arrangement is that Toyota produces about 25 per cent of the sales value of its cars, compared with 50 per cent for GM. Manufacturing *keiretsu* show the gains that can result from an optimal balance of supplier and buyer power. Because Toyota buys a given component from several suppliers (some are in the *keiretsu*, some are independent), discipline is imposed down the network. Also, since Toyota's suppliers do not work exclusively for Toyota, they have an incentive to be flexible and adaptable.[43]

The practices described above lead to the question of whether or not *keiretsu* violate antitrust laws. As many observers have noted, the Japanese government frequently puts the interests of producers ahead of the interests of consumers. In fact, the *keiretsu* were formed in the early 1950s as regroupings of four large conglomerates – *zaibatsu* – that dominated the Japanese economy until 1945. They were dissolved after the occupational forces introduced antitrust as part of the reconstruction. Today, Japan's Fair Trade Commission appears to favour harmony rather than pursuing anticompetitive behaviour.[44]

Prestowitz provides the following example to show how *keiretsu* relationships have the potential to impact US businesses. In the early 1980s, Nissan was in the market for a supercomputer to use in car design. Two vendors under consideration were Cray, the world-wide leader in supercomputers at the time and Hitachi, which had no functional product to offer. When it appeared that the purchase of a Cray computer was pending, Hitachi executives called for solidarity – both Nissan and Hitachi were members of the same big six *keiretsu*, the Fuyo Group. Hitachi essentially mandated that Nissan show preference to Hitachi, a situation that rankled US trade officials. Meanwhile, a coalition within Nissan was pushing for a Cray computer. Ultimately, thanks to US pressure on both Nissan and the Japanese government, the business went to Cray. Prestowitz describes the Japanese attitude towards this type of business practice:

It respects mutual obligation by providing a cushion against shocks. Today Nissan may buy a Hitachi computer. Tomorrow it may ask Hitachi to take some of its redundant workers. The slightly lesser performance it may get from the Hitachi computer is balanced against the broader considerations. Moreover, because the decision to buy Hitachi would be a favour, it would bind Hitachi closer and guarantee slavish service and future Hitachi loyalty to Nissan products. This attitude of sticking together is what the Japanese mean by the long-term view; it is what enables them to withstand shocks and to survive over the long term.[45]

Foreign companies have reason to be concerned with *keiretsu* outside the Japanese market as well. *Keiretsu* relationships are crossing the Pacific and directly affecting overseas markets. According to data compiled by Dodwell Marketing Consultants, in California alone *keiretsu* own more than half of the Japanese-affiliated manufacturing facilities. Illinois-based Tenneco Automotive, a maker of shock absorbers and exhaust systems, does a great deal of world-wide business with the Mazda *keiretsu*. In 1990, however, Mazda dropped Tenneco as a supplier to its US plant in Kentucky. Part of the business was shifted to Tokico Manufacturing, a Japanese transplant and a member of the Mazda *keiretsu*. A non-*keiretsu* Japanese company, KYB Industries, was also made a vendor. A Japanese auto executive explained the rationale behind the change: 'First choice is a *keiretsu* company, second choice is a Japanese supplier, third is a local company.'[46]

However, the power of *keiretsu* does not seem invincible. The continuing recession and financial crisis in Japan led to the fact that many of the large *keiretsus* entered into severe troubles. The Mitsubishi Group, one of Japan's largest and most powerful *keiretsus*, suffered heavy financial losses. The Fuyo Group is, as the Japanese press puts it nobly, 'in difficulties'. A company of the group, the car manufacturer Nissan, closed the financial year 1998 with a profit 80 per cent below target. The damages that *keiretsu* encountered are basically routed in their own strengths. The close relationship between companies has delayed significant restructuring processes, as managers are guided to follow the Group's strategies.[47]

Beyond strategic alliances

The *relationship enterprise* is said to be the next stage of evolution of the strategic alliance. Groupings of firms in different industries and countries will be held together by common goals that encourage them to act almost as a single firm. Cyrus Freidheim, vice chairman of the Booz, Allen & Hamilton consulting firm, recently outlined an alliance that, in his opinion, might be representative of an early reliance enterprise. He suggests that, within the next few decades, Boeing, British Airways, Siemens, TNT and Snecma might jointly build several new airports in China. As part of the package, British Airways and TNT would be granted preferential routes and landing slots, the Chinese government would contract to buy all its aircraft from Boeing/Snecma, and Siemens would provide air traffic control systems for all ten airports.[48]

More than the simple strategic alliances we know today, relationship enterprises will be super alliances among global giants, with revenues approaching €1 trillion. They would be able to draw on extensive cash resources, circumvent antitrust barriers and, with home bases in all major markets, enjoy the political advantage of being a 'local' firm almost anywhere. This type of alliance is not driven simply by technological change but by the political necessity of having multiple home bases.

Another perspective on the future of co-operative strategies envisions the emergence of the *virtual corporation*. (The term virtual is borrowed from computer science;

some computers feature virtual memory that allows them to function as though they have more storage capacity than is actually built into their memory chips.) As described in a *Business Week* cover story, the virtual corporation 'will seem to be a single entity with vast capabilities but will really be the result of numerous collaborations assembled only when they're needed.'[49]

On a global level, the virtual corporation could combine the twin competencies of cost effectiveness and responsiveness; thus, it could pursue the 'think global, act local' philosophy with ease. This reflects the trend toward mass customisation. The same forces that are driving the formation of the digital *keiretsu* described earlier, high-speed communication networks, for example, are embodied in the virtual corporation. As noted by Davidow and Malone, 'The success of a virtual corporation will depend on its ability to gather and integrate a massive flow of information throughout its organisational components and intelligently act upon that information.'[50]

Why has the virtual corporation suddenly burst onto the scene? Previously, firms lacked the technology to facilitate this type of data management. Today, distributed databases, networks, and open systems make possible the kinds of data flows required for the virtual corporation. In particular, these data flows permit supply-chain management. Ford provides an interesting example of how technology is improving information flows among the far-flung operations of a single company. Ford's €5 billion world car, known as the Mercury Mystique and Ford Contour in the United States and the Mondeo in Europe, was developed, using an international communications network linking computer workstations of designers and engineers on three continents.[51]

Key points

- A Japanese *keiretsu* is a special form of co-operation and strategic alliance where different companies or company groups are intensively intertwined.

- Very often, foreign competitors interpret *keiretsu* relations essentially as cartels which dominate the market and restrict competition.

- Information and communication technologies as well as globalisation have fostered new forms of strategic alliances.

- Virtual enterprises may be characterised as multiple co-operations which are employed only when needed.

Summary

Companies can choose among a wide range of alternatives when deciding how to participate in markets around the world. Exporting, licensing, joint ventures and ownership each represent distinct advantages and disadvantages. The choice depends in part on how a firm configures its value chain. Licensing is a good strategy for increasing the bottom line with little investment. It can be a suitable choice for a company with advanced technology or a strong brand image. Joint ventures offer companies the opportunity to share risk and combine value chain strengths. Companies considering joint ventures must plan carefully and communicate with partners to avoid 'divorce'. Ownership, through start-up or acquisition, can require a major commitment of resources, but can offer the benefits of full control.

Changes in the political, economic, sociocultural and technological environments are leading to new strategies in global competition. Co-operative strategies include global strategic partnerships, the Japanese *keiretsu*, or virtual enterprises. These alliances have become more important as companies need to share the high cost of product development, pool skills and know-how, gain access to markets, and find new opportunities for organisational learning.

Concepts and definitions

Production abroad
: When a company wants to extend its engagements abroad beyond mere exporting, it can choose from different market expansion alternatives. They encompass licensing, franchising, joint ventures, subsidiaries/acquisitions and various forms of strategic alliances. These alternatives tend to provide a firm with better control and a more intensive access to foreign markets than exporting, but usually also require higher investments.

Licensing
: Licensing can be defined as a contractual arrangement whereby one company (the licensor) makes an asset available to another company (the licensee) in exchange for royalties, licence fees, or some other form of compensation. The licensed asset may be a patent, trade secret or company name.

Franchising
: Franchising is a form of licensing, which goes far beyond conventional licensing. The franchisor provides the franchisee with an extensive company concept, which comprises a successful product and marketing concept as well as the fundamentals of managing such a business.

Joint venture
: A joint venture is a company run by two partner firms, for example a foreign and a local partner. Their influence on decision making depends primarily on the degree of ownership in the joint company. A joint venture offers a good opportunity to build on local know-how. In addition, joint ventures find greater acceptance from local authorities.

Subsidiary/ acquisition
: The most extensive engagement abroad is a subsidiary, which may either be established through the formation of a new facility (green field investment) or through the acquisition of an existing firm. Under this arrangement, a company has complete decision power and control over its foreign activities.

keiretsu
: Japan's *keiretsu* represent a special category of co-operative strategy. A *keiretsu* is an interbusiness alliance or enterprise group. Foreign competitors frequently assert that these close relations essentially represent cartels which dominate the market and restrict competition.

Virtual enterprise
: A virtual enterprise may be described as an alliance (often cross-border) based on several co-operations which are activated only on demand. Over the last years, the communication and information technologies have accelerated the foundation of such co-operations.

Discussion questions

1 A company wants to expand its foreign activities. The management strives for more control. Which alternatives for the market entry or expansion can they choose from?

2 The Managing Director (MD) of XYZ Manufacturing Company of Manchester, England, comes to you with a licence offer from a company in Osaka. In return for sharing the company's patents and know-how, the Japanese company will pay a licence fee of 5 per cent of the ex-factory price of all products sold based on the English company's licence. The MD wants your advice. What would you tell him?

3 What are five attributes that distinguish GSPs from traditional joint ventures?

4 What are *keiretsu*? How do these forms of industrial structures affect companies that compete with Japan or that are trying to enter the Japanese market?

5 The opening chapter quotations present opposing views about the value and wisdom of strategic alliances. Which do you agree with?

Webmistress's hotspots

Homepage of the International Franchise Association
If you want to become a franchisee, you find more than 1,000 interesting offers from all over the world in the virtual 'Franchise Mall'.
http://www.franchise.org/

Website about joint ventures in China
This site provides information about the legal framework in China, useful for example, if you want to engage in a local joint venture.
http://www.chinatoday.com/law/a01.htm

Homepage of Iridium
Here you find more information how Iridium works. Also, you will get some more facts on the development of this unique alliance under Motorola's leadership.
http://www.iridium.com/

Homepage of Jaguar
On the official Jaguar site, you will not only find interesting information on Jaguar's history and product portfolio, but also about the company's future in Formula One racing.
http://www.jaguar.com/

Homepage of LIMA
The International Licensing Industry Merchandisers' Association (LIMA) is a non-profit organisation of licensors. It aims to enforce the legal rights of its members world-wide. Beside legal support, this organisation provides information on relevant aspects of international licensing.
http://www.licensing.org/

Suggested readings

Adler, Paul S., 'Time-and-motion regained', *Harvard Business Review*, 71, 1 (January/February 1993): pp. 97–108.

Adler, Paul S. and Robert E. Cole, 'Designed for learning: a tale of two auto plants', *Sloan Management Review*, 34, 3 (Spring 1993): pp. 85–94.

Agarwal, Sanjeev, 'Socio-cultural distance and the choice of joint venture: a contingency perspective', *Journal of International Marketing*, 2, 2 (1994): pp. 63–80.

Agarwal, Sanjeev and Sridhar N. Ramaswami, 'Choice of foreign market entry mode: impact of ownership, location and internalization factors', *Journal of*

International Business Studies, 23, 1 (First Quarter 1992): pp. 1–27.

Ali, Abbas J. and Robert C. Camp, 'The relevance of firm size and international business experience to market entry strategies', *Journal of Global Marketing*, 6, 4 (1993): pp. 91–112.

Atuahene-Gime, Kwaku, 'International licensing of technology: an empirical study of the differences between licensee and non-licensee firms', *Journal of International Marketing*, 1, 2 (1993): pp. 71–88.

Beamish, Paul W., 'The characteristics of joint ventures in the People's Republic of China', *Journal of International Marketing*, 1, 2 (1993): pp. 29–48

Badaracco, Joseph L. Jr, 'Alliances speed knowledge transfer', *Planning Review*, 19, 2 (March/April 1991): pp. 10–16.

Bell, Brian, 'Two separate teams should be set up to facilitate strategic alliances', *Journal of Business Strategy*, 11, 6 (November/December 1990): pp. 63–64.

Berlew, F. Kingston, 'The joint venture – a way into foreign markets', *Harvard Business Review* (July/August 1984): pp. 48–54.

Bleeke, Joel and David Ernst, 'Is your strategic alliance really a sale?' *Harvard Business Review*, 73, 1 (January/February 1995): pp. 97–105.

Bleeke, Joel and David Ernst, 'The way to win in cross-border alliances', *Harvard Business Review*, 69, 6 (November/December 1991): pp. 127–135.

Bleeke, Joel and David Ernst, *Collaborating to Compete*. Somerset, NJ: John Wiley, 1991.

Blodgett, Linda Longfellow, 'Research notes and communications factors in the instability of international joint ventures: an event historical analysis', *Strategic Management Journal*, 13, 6 (September 1992): pp. 475–481.

Campbell, Dennis, Louis Lafili and McGeorge School of Law, *Distributorship, Agency and Franchising in an International Arena: Europe, the United States, Japan and Latin America*. Boston: Kluwer Law and Taxation Publishers, 1990.

Carter, John D., Robert Frank Cushman and C. Scott Hartz. *The Handbook of Joint Venturing*. Homewood, IL: Dow Jones–Irwin, 1988.

Chan, Peng S. and Robert T. Justis, 'Developing a global business strategy vision for the next decade and beyond', *Journal of Management Development*, 10, 2 (1991): pp. 38–45.

Contractor, Farok and Peter Lorange, *Cooperative Strategies in International Business*. Cambridge, MA: Ballinger, 1987.

Darnall, Robert J., 'Inland Steel's joint venture from competitive gap to competitive advantage', *Planning Review*, 18, 5 (September/October 1990): pp. 10–14.

Davidow, William H. and Michael S. Malone, *The Virtual Corporation*. New York: HarperBusiness, 1993.

Dyer, Jeffrey H. and William G. Ouchi, 'Japanese-style

partnerships: giving companies a competitive edge', *Sloan Management Review* (Fall 1993): pp. 51–63.

Egelhoff, William G., 'Great strategy or great strategy implementation – two ways of competing in global markets', *Sloan Management Review*, 34, 2 (Winter 1993): pp. 37–50.

Enen, Jack, *Venturing Abroad: International Business Expansion Via Joint Ventures*. Blue Ridge Summit, PA: Liberty Hall Press, 1991.

Erdmann, Peter B., 'When businesses cross international borders: strategic alliances and their alternatives', *Columbia Journal of World Business*, 28, 2 (Summer 1993): pp. 107–108.

Fedor, Kenneth J. and William B. Werther, Jr, 'Making sense of cultural factors in international alliances', *Organizational Dynamics*, 24, 4 (Spring 1995): pp. 33–48.

Ferguson, Charles H., 'Computers and the coming of the US keiretsu', *Harvard Business Review*, 68, 4 (July/August 1990): pp. 55–70.

Flanagan, Patrick, 'Strategic alliances keep customers plugged in', *Management Review*, 82, 3 (March 1993): pp. 24–26.

Frey, S.C.J. and M.M. Schlosser, 'ABB and Ford: creating value through cooperation', *Sloan Management Review* (Fall 1993): pp. 65–72.

Fruin, Mark, *The Japanese Enterprise System*. Oxford: Oxford University Press, 1992.

Gates, Stephen, *Strategic Alliances: Guidelines for Successful Management*. New York: Conference Board, 1993.

Gerlach, Michael L., *Alliance Capitalism: The Social Organization of Japanese Business*. Berkeley: University of California Press, 1992.

Gillespie, Ian, *Joint Ventures*. London: Eurostudy, 1990.

Gomes-Casseres, Benjamin, 'Joint ventures in the face of global competition', *Sloan Management Review*, 30, 3 (Spring 1989): pp. 17–26.

Grant, Robert M., R. Krishnan, Abraham B. Shani and Ron Baer, 'Appropriate manufacturing technology: a strategic approach', *Sloan Management Review*, 33, 1 (Fall 1991): pp. 43–54.

Haigh, Robert W., 'Building a strategic alliance – The Hermosillo experience as a Ford–Mazda proving ground', *Columbia Journal of World Business*, 27, 1 (Spring 1992): pp. 60–74.

Hamel, Gary and C. K. Prahalad, 'Do you really have a global strategy?', *Harvard Business Review* (July–August 1985): pp. 139–148.

Hamel, Gary, Yves L. Doz and C. K. Prahalad, 'Collaborate with your competitors – and win', *Harvard Business Review*, 67, 1 (January/February 1989): pp. 133–139.

Harrigan, Kathryn Rudie, 'Joint ventures and global strategies', *Columbia Journal of World Business* (Summer 1984): pp. 7–16.

Hill, Charles W. L., Peter Hwang and W. Chan Kim, 'An eclectic theory of the choice of international entry mode', *Strategic Management Journal*, 11, 2 (1990): pp. 117–128.

Hwang, Peter, Williams P. Burgers and W. Chan Kim, 'Global diversification strategy and corporate profit performance', *Strategic Management Journal*, 10, 1 (January/February 1989): pp. 45–57.

James, Harvey S. and Murray L. Weidenbaum. *When Businesses Cross International Borders: Strategic Alliances and Their Alternatives*. Westport, CT: Praeger, 1993.

Jarillo, J. Carlos and Howard H. Stevenson, 'Co-operative strategies – the payoffs and the pitfalls', *Long Range Planning*, 24, 1 (February 1991): pp. 64–70.

Johnston, Gerald A., 'The yin and the yang: Cooperation and competition in international business', *Executive Speeches*, 7, 6 (June/July 1993): pp. 15–17.

Jones, Kevin K. and Walter E. Schill, 'Allying for advantage', *The McKinsey Quarterly*, 3 (1991): pp. 73–101.

Jorde, Thomas M. and David J. Teece, 'Competition and cooperation: striking the right balance', *California Management Review*, 31, 3 (Spring 1989): pp. 25–37.

Ketelhohn, Werner, 'What do we mean by cooperative advantage?' *European Management Journal*, 11, 1 (March 1993): pp. 30–37.

Kim, W. Chan and Peter Hwang, 'Global strategy and multinationals' entry mode choice', *Journal of International Business Studies*, 23, 1 (first quarter 1992): pp. 29–54.

Klein, Saul and Jehiel Zif, 'Global versus local strategic alliances', *Journal of Global Marketing*, 8, 1 (1994): pp. 51–72.

Kodama, Fumio, 'Technology fusion and the new R&D', *Harvard Business Review*, 70, 4 (July/August 1992): pp. 70–78.

Kogut, Bruce, 'Designing global strategies: comparative and competitive value-added chains', *Sloan Management Review* (Summer 1985): pp. 17–27.

Kogut, Bruce, 'Designing global strategies: profiting from operational flexibility', *Sloan Management Review* (Fall 1985): pp. 27–38.

Kruytbosch, Carla, 'Let's make a deal', *International Business*, 6, 3 (March 1993): pp. 92–96.

Lawrence, Paul and Charalambos Vlachoutsicos, 'Joint ventures in Russia: put the locals in charge', *Harvard Business Review*, 71, 1 (January/February 1993): pp. 44–51.

Lei, David, 'Offensive and defensive uses of alliances', *Long Range Planning*, 25, 6 (December 1992): pp. 10–17.

Lei, David and John W. Slocum Jr, 'Global strategy, competence-building and strategic alliances', *California Management Review*, 35, 1 (Fall 1992): pp. 81–97.

Lewis, Jordan D., 'Competitive alliances redefine companies', *Management Review*, 80, 4 (April 1991): pp. 14–18.

Lewis, Jordan D., 'The new power of strategic alliances',

Planning Review, 20, 5 (September/October 1992): pp. 45–46.

Lewis, Jordan D., *Partnerships for Profit: Structuring and Managing Strategic Alliances*. New York: Free Press (1990).

Lindsey, Jennifer, *Joint Ventures and Corporate Partnerships: A Step-by-Step Guide to Forming Strategic Business Alliances*. Chicago: Probus, 1989.

Lodge, George and Richard Walton, 'The American corporation and its new relationships', *California Management Review*, 31, 3 (Spring 1989): pp. 9–24.

Lorange, Peter, 'Interactive strategic alliances and partnerships', *Long Range Planning*, 29, 4 (1996): pp. 581–584.

Lorange, Peter and Johan Roos, 'Why some strategic alliances succeed and others fail', *Journal of Business Strategy*, 12, 1 (January/February 1991): pp. 25–30.

Lorange, Peter and Johan Roos, *Strategic Alliances: Formation, Implementation and Evolution*. Cambridge, MA: Blackwell, 1992.

Luo, Yadong, 'Evaluating the performance of strategic alliances in China', *Long Range Planning*, 29, 4 (1996): pp. 534–542.

Lynch, Robert, *The Practical Guide to Joint Ventures and Corporate Alliances: How to Form, How to Organize, How to Operate*. New York: Wiley, 1989.

Madhok, Anoop, 'Revisiting multinational firms' tolerance for joint ventures: a trust-based approach', *Journal of International Business Studies*, 26, 1 (first quarter 1995): pp. 117–138.

McCaffrey, Roger A. and Thomas A. Meyer, *An Executive's Guide to Licensing*. Homewood, IL: Dow Jones–Irwin, 1989.

McDougall, Patricia, 'New venture strategies: an empirical identification of eight "archetypes" of competitive strategies for entry', *Strategic Management Journal*, 11, 6 (October 1990): pp. 447–467.

McMillan, John, 'Managing suppliers: incentive systems in Japanese and US industry', *California Management Review*, 32, 4 (Summer 1990): pp. 38–55.

Michelet, Robert and Rosemary Remacle, 'Forming successful strategic marketing alliances in Europe', *Journal of European Business*, 4, 1 (September/October 1992): pp. 11–15.

Miller, Danny, 'The generic strategy trap', *Journal of Business Strategy*, 13, 1 (January/February 1992): pp. 37–41.

Morrison, Allen J. and Kendall Roth, 'A taxonomy of business-level strategies in global industries', *Strategic Management Journal*, 13, 6 (September 1992): pp. 399–417.

Mowery, David C. and David J. Teece, 'Japan's growing capabilities in industrial technology: implications for US managers and policymakers', *California Management Review*, 35, 2 (1993): pp. 9–34.

Murray, Edwin A. Jr and John F. Mahon, 'Strategic

alliances: gateway to the new Europe?' *Long Range Planning*, 26, 4 (August 1993): pp. 102–111.

Nadel, Jack, *Cracking the Global Market: How to Do Business around the Corner and around the World*. New York: American Management Association, 1987.

Negandi, Anant R. and Peter A. Donhowe, 'It's time to explore new global trade options', *Journal of Business Strategy*, 10, 1 (January/February 1991): pp. 27–31.

Newman, Victor and Kazem Chaharbaghi, 'Strategic alliances in fast-moving markets', *Long Range Planning*, 29, 6 (1996): pp. 850–856.

Niland, Powell, 'Case study – US–Japanese joint venture: New United Motor Manufacturing, Inc. (NUMMI)', *Planning Review*, 17, 1 (January/February 1989): pp. 40–45.

Ohmae, Kenichi, 'The global logic of strategic alliances', *Harvard Business Review*, 67 (March/April 1989): pp. 143–154.

Olson, Philip D., 'Choices for innovation-minded corporations', *Journal of Business Strategy*, 11, 1 (January/February 1990): pp. 42–46.

O'Reilly, Anthony J.F., 'Leading a global strategic charge', *Journal of Business Strategy*, 12, 4 (1991): pp. 10–13.

Osland, Gregory E., 'Successful operating strategies in the performance of US–China joint ventures', *Journal of International Marketing*, 32, 4 (1994): pp. 53–78.

Oster, Sharon, *Modern Competitive Analysis*. New York: Oxford University Press, 1990.

Pant, P. Narayan and Vasant G. Rajadhyaksha, 'Partnership with an Asian family business – what every multinational corporation should know', *Long Range Planning*, 29, 6 (1996): pp. 812–820.

Parkhe, Arvind, 'Interfirm diversity, organizational learning and longevity in global strategic alliances', *Journal of International Business Studies*, 22, 4 (Fourth Quarter 1991): pp. 579–601.

Perlmutter, H.V. and D.A. Heenan, 'Cooperate to compete globally', *Harvard Business Review* (March/April 1986): pp. 136–152.

Perlmutter, Howard V. and David A. Heenan, 'How multinational should your top managers be?' *Harvard Business Review* (November/December, 1974): pp. 121–132.

Quelch, John A. and James E. Austin, 'Should multinationals invest in Africa?' *Sloan Management Review*, 4, 3 (Spring 1993): pp. 107–119.

Rabstejnek, George, 'Let's go back to the basics of global strategy', *Journal of Business Strategy*, 10, 5 (September/October 1989): pp. 32–35.

Robert, Michel, 'The do's and don'ts of strategic alliances', *Journal of Business Strategy*, 13, 2 (March/April 1992): pp. 50–53.

Robert, Michel. *Strategy Pure and Simple: How Winning CEOs Outthink Their Competition*. New York: McGraw-Hill, 1993.

Robertson, Thomas S., 'How to reduce market pen-etration cycle times', *Sloan Management Review* (Fall 1993): pp. 87–96.

Root, Franklin R., *Entry Strategies for International Markets*. New York: Lexington Books, 1994.

Rosow, Jerome M., *The Global Marketplace*. New York: Facts on File, 1988.

Schill, Ronald L. and David N. McArthur, 'Redefining the strategic competitive unit: towards a new global marketing paradigm?' *International Marketing Review*, 9, 3 (1992): pp. 5–24.

Schoemaker, Paul J. H., 'How to link strategic vision to core capabilities', *Sloan Management Review*, 34, 1 (Fall 1992): pp. 67–81.

Sherman, Andrew, *Franchising and Licensing: Two Ways to Build Your Business*. New York: American Management Association, 1991.

Spencer, William J. and Peter Grindley, 'SEMATECH after five years', *California Management Review* (Summer 1993): pp. 9–35.

Spinks, Stephen O. and Robert C. Stanley, 'Joint ventures under EC antitrust and merger control rules: concentrative or cooperative?' *Journal of European Business*, 2, 4 (March/April 1991): pp. 29–34.

Starr, Martin Kenneth, *Global Corporate Alliances and the Competitive Edge: Strategies and Tactics for Management*. New York: Quorum Books, 1991.

Thakar, Manab and Luis Ma. R. Calingo, 'Strategic thinking is hip, but does it make a difference?' *Business Horizons*, 35, 5 (September/October 1992): pp. 47–54.

Treece, David J. (ed), *The Competitive Challenge: Strategies for Industrial Innovation and Renewal*. Cambridge, MA: Ballinger Publishing, 1987.

Vanhonacker, Wilfried, 'Entering China: an unconventional approach', *Harvard Business Review*, 75 (March/April 1997): pp. 130–140.

Van Fleet, Mark, 'Two sources of overseas investment and export expertise', *Journal of Business Strategy*, 2, 6 (November/December 1991): pp. 62–63.

Van Wolferen, Karel G., 'The Japan problem', *Foreign Affairs* (Winter 1986): pp. 288–303.

Voss, Bristol, 'Strategic federations frequently falter in Far East', *Journal of Business Strategy*, 14, 4 (July/August 1993): p. 6.

Wever, Kirsten S. and Christopher S. Allen, 'Is Germany a model for managers?' *Harvard Business Review*, 70, 5 (September/October 1992): pp. 36–43.

Yablonsky, Dennis, 'The US West/Carnegie Group strategic alliance', *Planning Review*, 18, 5 (September/October 1990): pp. 18–19.

Yavas, Ugur, Dogan Eroglu and Sevgin Eroglu, 'Sources and management of conflict: the case of Saudi–US joint ventures', *Journal of International Marketing*, 2, 3 (1994): pp. 61–82.

Yip, George S., *Total Global Strategy: Managing for Worldwide Competitive Advantage*. Upper Saddle River, NJ: Prentice Hall, 1992.

Yoshida, Kosaku, 'New economic principles in America – competition and cooperation: a comparative study of the US and Japan', *Columbia Journal of World Business*, 26, 4 (Winter 1992): pp. 30–44.

Yoshino, Michael Y. and U. Srinivasa Rangan, *Strategic Alliances: An Entrepreneurial Approach to Globalization*. Boston: Harvard Business School Press, 1995.

Notes

1. John Barham, 'A leaner, simpler production: Management Volkswagen', *Financial Times*, 11 June 1999.
2. Tim Burt, John Griffiths, and Nikki Tait, 'Ford's full service', *Financial Times*, 9 August 1999.
3. 'Annual Report', 10: Procter & Gamble Company, 1995.
4. F.R. Root, *Entry Strategies for International Markets* (New York: Lexington Books, 1994).
5. Yumiko Ono, 'Borden's breakup with Meiji Milk shows how a Japanese partnership can curdle', *Wall Street Journal*, 21 February 1991, p. B1.
6. Conversation between Prof. Warren J. Keegan and E.M. Lang, CEO at REFAC Technology Development Corporation, 122 East 42nd Street, New York, NY.
7. Jack Hayes, 'Love American style: European market embraces US restaurant chains', *Nation's Restaurant News*, 17 August 1998, pp. 47ff.
8. 'Going global: Trend of the '90s', *Franchise Times*, September 1997, p. 3ff. Ian Jones, 'What to do (or not to do) about going international', *World Trade*, 10, 2 (1997): pp. 76–78.
9. Ingrid Puschautz, 'Bären-Offensive mit neuen Steiff-Galerien', *Wirtschaftsblatt*, 22 September 1999, p. D5.
10. Julie Bennett, 'What's hot worldwide', *Franchise Times*, September 1997, p. 13.
11. For an excellent brief supporting wholly-owned subsidiaries see Wilfried Vanhonacker, 'Entering China: an unconventional approach', *Harvard Business Review*, March–April (1997): pp. 130–140.
12. James Guyon, 'A joint-venture papermaker casts net across Europe', *Wall Street Journal*, 7 December 1992, p. B6.
13. Lawrence G. Franko, 'Joint venture divorce in the multinational company', *Columbia Journal of World Business*, May–June (1971): pp. 13–22.
14. W. Wright, 'Joint venture problems in Japan', *Columbia Journal of World Business*, Summer (1979): pp. 74–80; W. Wright and C.S. Russell, 'Joint venture in developing countries: reality and responses', *Columbia Journal of World Business*, Summer (1975): pp. 74–80.
15. Yumiko Ono, 'Borden's breakup with Meiji Milk shows how a Japanese partnership can curdle', *Wall Street Journal*, 21 February 1991, p. B1.
16. Louis Uchitelle, 'The Stanley Works goes global', *New York Times*, 23 July 1989, pp. 1, 10.
17. 'Annual Report', 13: Borden Inc., 1990.
18. Michael A. Yoshino, and U. Srinivasa Rangan, *Strategic Alliances: An Entrepreneurial Approach to Globalization* (Boston: Harvard Business School Press, 1995). Riad Ajami and Dara Khambata, 'Global strategic alliances: the new transnationals', *Journal of Global Marketing*, 5, 1/2 (1991): pp. 55–59 address this aspect from a different perspective.
19. Carla Kruytbosch, 'Let's make a deal', *International Business*, March (1993): p. 92.
20. Jeremy Main, 'Making global alliances work', *Fortune*, 17 December 1990, p. 121.
21. Kenichi Ohmae, 'The global logic of strategic alliances', *Harvard Business Review*, March–April (1989): p. 145.
22. 'Annual report: Top 50 pharmaceutical companies', *Med Ad News*, September 1998, pp. 150ff. 'Bristol-Myers Squibb Co', *PharmaBusiness*, November 1998, pp. 65ff.
23. Jeremy Main, 'Making global alliances work', *Fortune*, 17 December 1990, p. 121.
24. Howard Perlmutter and David Heenan, 'Cooperate to compete globally', *Harvard Business Review*, March–April (1986): p. 137.
25. Adapted from Michel Robert, *Strategy Pure & Simple: How Winning CEOs Outthink Their Competition* (New York: McGraw-Hill, 1993).
26. James Brian Quinn, 'Strategic outsourcing', *Sloan Management Review*, Summer (1994).
27. 'The science of alliance', *The Economist*, 4 April 1998.
28. Howard Perlmutter and David Heenan, 'Cooperate to compete globally', *Harvard Business Review*, March–April (1986): p. 137.
29. Howard Perlmutter and David Heenan, 'Cooperate to compete globally', *Harvard Business Review*, March–April (1986): p. 138.
30. Gary Hamel, Yves L. Doz and C.K. Prahalad, 'Collaborate with your competitors – and win', *Harvard Business Review*, January–February (1989): p. 136.
31. Kevin K. Jones and Walter E. Schill, 'Allying for advantage', *The McKinsey Quarterly*, 3 (1991): pp. 73–101.
32. Bernard Wysocki, 'Global reach: cross border alliances become favorite way to crack new markets', *Wall Street Journal*, 26 March 1990, p. A 12.
33. Howard Perlmutter and David Heenan, 'Cooperate to compete globally', *Harvard Business Review*, March–April (1986): p. 145.

34. Bernard Wysocki, 'Global reach: cross border alliances become favorite way to crack new markets', *Wall Street Journal*, 26 March 1990, p. A 12.

35. John Holusha, 'Pushing the envelope at Boeing', *New York Times*, 10 November 1991, pp. 1, 6.

36. David Lei and John W. Jr. Slocum, 'Global strategy, competence-building and strategic alliances', *California Management Review*, Fall (1992): pp. 81–97.

37. Robert L. Cutts, 'Capitalism in Japan: cartels and keiretsu', *Harvard Business Review*, July–August (1992): p. 49.

38. Michael L. Gerlach, 'Twilight of the Keiretsu? A critical assessment', *Journal of Japanese Studies*, 18, 1 (1992): p. 79.

39. Ronald J. Gilson and Mark J. Roe, 'Understanding the Japanese Keiretsu: Overlaps between corporate governance and industrial organization', *Yale Law Journal*, 102, 4 (1993): p. 883.

40. Clyde V. Prestowitz, *Trading Places: How We Are Giving Our Future to Japan and How to Reclaim It* (New York: Basic Books, 1989), p. 296.

41. Carla Rappoport, 'Why Japan keeps on winning', *Fortune*, 15 July 1991, p. 76.

42. The importance of the chain stores is eroding due to increasing sales at mass merchandisers not under the manufacturer's control.

43. 'Japanology Inc. – Surfy', *The Economist*, 6 March 1993, p. 15.

44. Carla Rappoport, 'Why Japan keeps on winning', *Fortune*, 15 July 1991, p. 84

45. Clyde V. Prestowitz, *Trading Places: How We Are Giving Our Future to Japan and How to Reclaim It* (New York: Basic Books, 1989), pp. 299–300. For years, Prestowitz has argued that Japan's industry structure – keiretsu included – gives its companies unfair advantages. A more moderate view might be that any business decision must have an economic justification. Thus, a moderate would caution against overstating the effect of keiretsu.

46. Carla Rappoport, 'Why Japan keeps on winning', *Fortune*, 15 July 1991, pp. 76, p. 80

47. 'The diamonds lose their sparkle: Mitsubishi misery', *The Economist*, 9 May 1998; Alexandra Harney, 'Close links – a barrier for predators: Japan', *The Financial Times*, 1 March 1999; Clyde Prestowitz, 'The Japan that can say yes', *The Financial Times*, 4 March 1999.

48. 'The global firm: R.I.P', *The Economist*, 6 February 1993, p. 69.

49. John Byrne, 'The virtual corporation', *Business Week*, 8 February 1993, p. 103.

50. William H. Davidow and Michael S. Malone, *The Virtual Corporation: Structuring and Revitalising the Corporation for the 21st Century* (New York: Harper Business, 1993) p. 59.

51. Julie Edelson Halpert, 'One car, worldwide, with strings pulled from Michigan', *New York Times*, 29 August 1993, p. 7.

CHAPTER 10

Global competition and strategy

Competition is embedded in the instinct of entrepreneurs.
JOHN KENNETH GALBRAITH[1]

After reading this chapter, you will know:

- The importance of corporate strategies for the overall performance of a company.
- The determinants for selecting, creating and pursuing a particular strategy.
- The different levels of examining corporate strategy and the competitive position of a firm.
- Why different companies pursue different strategies.

Why is this important? Here are three situations in which you would need an understanding of the above issues:

- You might be asked to provide an analysis of the strategic positioning of your company referring to the particular national context or the particular industry your firm belongs to.
- You might start your own business and have to decide which strategy to pursue, taking into consideration your firm's external and internal environment.
- Your company might be threatened by fierce competition. It is your task to decide which steps to undertake to ensure your company's competitiveness.

Practice link

From its home base in Sweden, IKEA has become a €3.4 billion global home-furnishing powerhouse. With 140 stores in 28 countries,[2] the company's success reflects founder Ingvar Kamprad's vision of selling a wide range of stylish, functional home furnishings at prices so low that the majority of people can afford to buy them. The store exteriors are painted bright blue and yellow – Sweden's national colours. Shoppers view furniture on the main floor in scores of realistic settings arranged throughout cavernous showrooms. In a departure from standard industry practice, IKEA's furniture bears names such as 'Ivar' and 'Sten' instead of model numbers. At IKEA, shopping is very much a self-service activity; after browsing and writing down the names of desired items, shoppers pick up their furniture on the lower level. There they find boxes containing the furniture in kit form; one of the cornerstones of IKEA's strategy is having customers take their purchases home in their own vehicles and assemble the furniture themselves. The lower level of a typical IKEA store also contains a restaurant, a grocery store called the Swede Shop, a supervised play area for children, and a baby care room.

The bottom line for IKEA is that the company creates a unique value for customers. Instead of salespersons, a limited number of display items, and a catalogue to order from, IKEA offers informative displays and product information for everything it sells. In a traditional furniture store, you place an order and wait weeks or months for delivery. At IKEA, you make a purchase and take it with you. Traditional furniture is assembled and ready to use. IKEA furniture is sold in kit form ready to assemble. The traditional store offers salespersons or consultants, assembled and ready to use product, delivery and higher prices. IKEA offers rock bottom prices.

IKEA is focused on the young customer or the young at heart. The core market is the customer with a limited budget who appreciates IKEA's product line, displays and prices. Because IKEA knows the needs and wants of this market segment, it has been successful in serving customers not only in Sweden where the company was founded, but also globally. IKEA's success in crossing borders has been instrumental in changing furniture retailing from a multidomestic industry to a global one.

The essence of global marketing strategy is in successfully relating the strengths of an organisation to its environment. As the horizons of marketers have expanded from domestic to global markets, so too have the horizons of competitors. The reality in almost every industry today, including home furnishings, is global competition. This fact of life puts an organisation under increasing pressure to master techniques for conducting industry analysis, competitor analysis, understanding competitive advantage at both the industry and national levels, and developing and maintaining competitive advantage. These topics are covered in detail in this chapter.

DIMENSIONS OF GLOBAL COMPETITION

A company's success in global markets is determined by its ability to establish sustainable competitive advantages. However, competitiveness, especially of a sustainable nature, can only be reached by following a consistent, well-defined strategy.

To understand the key drivers behind global competition, different levels of strategic analyses and aggregation have to be undertaken. First of all, competitive analyses need to focus on a national level. These analyses not only support the identification of characteristics shaping the competitiveness of a nation, but also help in understanding the environment in which firms compete in their global industries.

Secondly, the forces influencing competition in an industry should be examined. In this context, industries are defined as those firms that produce products or services that are close substitutes for each other.

Thirdly, analyses of a firm's competitive position *within* a particular industry are of importance. Strategic groups may be identified and group maps might support companies in positioning themselves within an industry and may facilitate the development and choice of a particular strategy.

Finally, the competitive advantages of individual companies have to be taken into consideration. In this context, our discussion will focus on generic strategies, strategic intent and hypercompetition.

NATIONAL COMPETITIVE ADVANTAGES

The national environment appears to play an important role in shaping a company's success in global markets. Why else, for example, is the United States the home base for the leading competitors in PCs, software, credit cards and films? Why is Germany the home of so many world leaders in printing presses, chemicals and luxury cars? Why are so many leading pharmaceutical, chocolate/confectionery and trading companies located in Switzerland? Why are the world leaders in consumer electronics home-based in Japan?

According to Michael E. Porter, the presence or absence of particular attributes in individual countries influences industry development. Porter describes these attributes – i.e. factor conditions, demand conditions, related and supporting industry, and firm structure and rivalry – in terms of a national diamond (see Figure 10.1). The diamond shapes the environment in which firms compete in their global industries.

Figure 10.1 Determinants of national advantage[3]

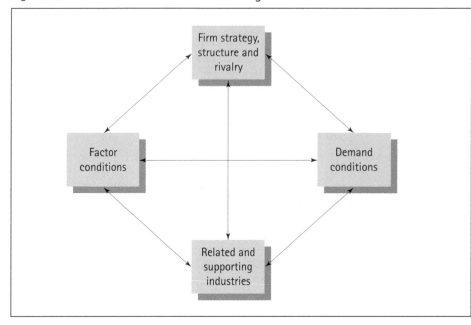

Source: Michael E. Porter, *The Competitive Advantage of Nations* (New York: Free Press, 1990), p. 72.

Factor conditions

The phrase factor conditions refers to a country's endowment with resources. Factor resources may have been created or inherited, and are divided into five categories: human, physical, knowledge, capital and infrastructure.

Human resources

The quantity of workers available, the skills possessed by these workers, wage levels, and the overall work ethic of the workforce together constitute a nation's human resource factors. Countries with a plentiful supply of low-wage labour have an obvious advantage in the current production of labour-intensive products. This advantage may disappear if wages increase and production moves to another country. However, low-wage countries may be at a disadvantage when it comes to the production of sophisticated products requiring highly skilled workers capable of working without extensive supervision.

Physical resources

The availability, quantity, quality, and cost of land, water, minerals and other natural endowments determine a country's physical resources. A country's size and location are also included in this category, because proximity to markets and sources of supply, as well as transportation costs, are strategic considerations. These factors are obviously important advantages or disadvantages to industries dependent on natural resources.

Knowledge resources

The availability, within a nation, of a significant population with scientific, technical and market-related knowledge means a nation is endowed with knowledge resources.

The presence of these factors is usually a function of the educational orientation of the society as well as the number of research facilities and universities, both government and private, operating in the country. These factors are important to success in sophisticated products and services, and to doing business in sophisticated markets. This factor relates directly to Germany's leadership in chemicals; for some 150 years, Germany has been home to top university chemistry programmes, advanced scientific journals, and apprenticeship programmes.

Capital resources

Countries vary in the availability, amount, cost and types of capital available to the country's industries. The nation's savings rate, interest rates, tax laws and government deficits all affect the availability of this factor. The advantage to industries with low capital costs versus those located in nations with relatively high costs is sometimes decisive. Firms paying high capital costs are frequently unable to stay in a market in which the competition comes from a nation with low capital costs. The firms with the low cost of capital can keep their prices low and force the firms paying high costs to either accept low returns on investment or leave the industry. The globalisation of world capital markets is changing the manner in which capital is deployed. Investors can now send their capital to nations or markets with the best risk/return profile. Global firms will increasingly be following capital to the best places, rather than operating in nations where capital is scarce or expensive.

Infrastructure resources

Infrastructure includes a nation's banking system, health care system, transportation system and communications system, as well as the availability and cost of using these systems. More sophisticated industries are more dependent on advanced infrastructures for success.

Alternative categorisation of factors

Factors can be further classified as either *basic factors*, such as natural resources and labour, or *advanced factors*, such as highly educated personnel and modern data communications infrastructure. Basic factors do not lead to sustainable international competitive advantage. For example, cheap labour is a transient national advantage that erodes as a nation's economy improves and average national income increases relative to other countries. Advanced factors, which lead to sustainable competitive advantage, are scarcer and require sustained investment. For example, the existence of a labour force of trained artisans offers Italy a basis of sustained competitive advantage in the Italian tile industry.

Another categorisation of factors differentiates between *generalised factors*, such a suitable highway system, and *specialised factors*, such as focused educational systems. Generalised factors are precedents required for competitive advantage; however, sustainable advantage requires the development of specialised factors. For example, the competitive advantage of the Japanese robotics industry is fueled by extensive university robotics courses and programmes that graduate robotics skilled trainees of the highest calibre.

Competitive advantage may also be created indirectly by nations that have selective factor *disadvantages*. For example, the absence of suitable labour may force firms to develop forms of mechanisation that give the nation's firms an advantage. Scarcity of raw materials may motivate firms to develop new materials. For example, Japan, faced with scarce raw materials, developed an industrial ceramics industry that leads the world in innovation.

Demand conditions

The nature of home-market demand conditions for the firm's or industry's products and services are important because they determine the rate and nature of improvement and innovation by the firms in the nation. These are the factors that either train firms for world-class competition or fail to adequately prepare them to compete in the global marketplace. Three characteristics of home demand are particularly important to creation of competitive advantage: (1) the composition of home demand, (2) the size and pattern of growth of home demand, and (3) the means by which a nation's home demand pulls the nation's products and services into foreign markets.

The composition of home demand determines how firms perceive, interpret and respond to buyer needs. Competitive advantage can be achieved when the home demand sets the quality standard and gives local firms a better picture of buyer needs, at an earlier time, than is available to foreign rivals. This advantage is enhanced when home buyers pressure the nation's firms to innovate quickly and frequently. The basis for advantage is the fact that the nation's firms can stay ahead of the market when firms are more sensitive to and more responsive to home demand and when that demand, in turn, reflects or anticipates world demand.

The size and pattern of growth of home demand are important only if the composition of the home demand is sophisticated and anticipates foreign demand. Large home markets offer opportunities to achieve economies of scale and learning while dealing with familiar, comfortable markets. There is less apprehension about investing in large-scale production facilities and expensive R&D programmes when the home market is sufficient to absorb the increased capacity. If the home demand accurately reflects or anticipates foreign demand, and if the firms do not become content with serving the home market, the existence of large-scale facilities and programmes will be an advantage in global competition.

Rapid home-market growth is another incentive to invest in and adopt new technologies faster, and to build large, efficient facilities. The best example of this is Japan, where rapid home-market growth provided the incentive for Japanese firms to invest heavily in modern, automated facilities. Early home demand, especially if it anticipates international demand, gives local firms the advantage of getting established in an industry sooner than foreign rivals. Equally important is early market saturation, which puts pressure on a company to expand into international markets and innovate. Market saturation is especially important if it coincides with rapid growth in foreign markets.

The means by which a nation's products and services are pushed or pulled into foreign countries is the third aspect of demand conditions. The issue here is whether a nation's people and businesses go abroad and then demand the nation's products and services in those second countries. The automobile industry discovered a promising market in East Europe. Amongst others, companies such as Scania, Volvo, Navistar, Renault, Volkswagen and Ford have entered Poland. This also led to investments by many car component manufacturers which followed into Poland and will also have a remarkable and prosperous effect on the development of the spare parts industry in this country.[4]

A related issue is whether foreigners come to a nation for training, pleasure, business or research. After returning home, they are likely to demand the products and services with which they became familiar while abroad. Similar effects can result from professional, scientific and political relationships between nations. Those involved in the relationships begin to demand the products and services of the recognised leaders.

It is the interplay of demand conditions that contributes to competitive advantage. Of special importance are those conditions that lead to initial and continuing incentives to invest and innovate, and to continuing competition in increasingly sophisticated markets.

Related and supporting industries

A nation has an advantage when it is home to internationally competitive industries in fields that are related to, or in direct support of, other industries. Internationally competitive supplier industries provide inputs to downstream industries that are likely to be internationally competitive in terms of technological innovation, price and quality. Access is a function of proximity both in terms of physical distance and cultural similarity. It is not the inputs themselves that give advantage. It is the contact and co-ordination with the suppliers that allows the firm the opportunity to structure the value chain so that linkages with suppliers are optimised. These opportunities may not be available to foreign firms.

Similar advantages accrue when there are internationally competitive and related industries in a nation that co-ordinate and share value chain activities. A clear example of this is opportunities for sharing between computer hardware manufacturers and software developers. Related industries also create pull-through opportunities as described earlier. Porter notes that the development of the Swiss pharmaceuticals industry can be attributed in part to Switzerland's large synthetic dye industry; the discovery of the therapeutic effects of dyes in turn led to the development of pharmaceutical companies.[5]

Firm strategy, structure and rivalry

Differences in management styles, organisational skills and strategic perspectives create advantages and disadvantages for firms competing in different types of industries, as do differences in the intensity of domestic rivalry. In Germany, for example, company structure and management style tends to be hierarchical. Managers tend to come from technical backgrounds, and to be most successful when dealing with industries that demand highly disciplined structures, such as chemicals and precision machinery. Italian firms, however, tend to look like, and be run like, small family businesses that stress customised rather than standardised products, niche markets and substantial flexibility in meeting market demands.

Capital markets and attitudes toward investments are important components of national environments. For example, the majority of shares of US publicly held companies are owned by institutional investors such as mutual funds and pension plans. These investors will buy and sell shares to reduce risk and increase return, rather than get involved in an individual company's operations. These very mobile investors drive managers to operate with a short-term focus on quarterly and annual results. This fluid capital market structure will provide funds for new growth industries and rapidly expanding markets in which there are expectations of early returns. On the other hand, US capital markets do not encourage more mature industries in which return on investment is lower and patient searching for innovations is required. Many other countries have an opposite orientation. For example, in Japan, banks are allowed to take equity stakes in the companies to which they loan money and provide other profitable banking services. These banks take a longer-term view than stock markets and are less concerned about short-term results.

Perhaps the most powerful influence on competitive advantage comes from domestic rivalry. Domestic rivalry keeps an industry dynamic and creates continual pressure to improve and innovate. Local rivalry forces firms to develop new products, improve existing ones, lower costs and prices, develop new technologies, and improve quality and service. Rivalry with foreign firms lacks this intensity. Domestic rivals have to fight each other not just for market share, but also for employee talent, R&D breakthroughs, and prestige in the home market. Eventually, strong domestic rivalry will push firms to seek international markets to support expansions in scale and R&D investments, as Japan amply demonstrates. The absence of significant domestic rivalry will create complacency in the home firms and eventually cause them to become non-competitive in the world markets.

It is not the number of domestic rivals that is important; rather, it is the intensity of the competition and the quality of the competitors that make the difference. It is also important that there be a fairly high rate of new business formations to create new competitors and safeguard against the older companies' becoming comfortable with their market positions and products and services. New entrants bring new per-

EUROPEAN FOCUS

Romania – an attractive location

With the 1997 relaxation of rules on foreign investment, Romania appears to be a promising business environment for the future.

According to a study by the consulting firm Roland Berger & Partner, there are several factors which make Romania an attractive location compared with most other regional markets.

First of all, labour costs are low with an average monthly wage of around €128 and social security levies at 32 per cent. There is also lack of saturation from foreign investors, and the imbalance of supply and demand is largely in favour of the supply side. Another helpful feature can be seen in the readiness of the Romanian development agency and privatisation bodies to assist would-be investors. The size of the market, the relative ease with which foreigners can learn Romanian and the flexibility and pragmatism of the labour force complete the positive picture.

However, there is also a negative side to the story.

Risk factors such as high and unpredictable inflation, bureaucratic officialdom and the hostility of employees of recently privatised establishments have to be taken into account!

Romania is expected to attract significant inflows of investment. Currently, the largest investor is Daewoo, the Korean conglomerate, with an investment value of €212 million. This is followed by Coca-Cola, Shell, New Holland, Molino Holding, Amoco and Credit Lyonnaise.

Food for thought

● How could you apply Porter's diamond model to evaluate Romania's national competitive advantage?

● How important are labour costs as a determinant of foreign direct investment for car manufacturers? Compare labour costs with other factors driving foreign investment decisions.

Source: 'Romanian FDI boom?', *Newsletter*, 17, 13 (20 June 1997): p. 9.

spectives and new methods. They frequently define and serve new market segments that established companies have failed to recognise.

Other forces acting on the diamond

Two additional elements of Porter's model to consider in the evaluation of national competitive advantage are *chance* and *government*. In addition, there are *non-market forces* that are part of the environment and that should be considered as an expansion of or supplement to government and chance.

Chance

Chance events play a role in shaping the competitive environment. Chance events are occurrences that are beyond the control of firms, industries, and usually governments. Included in this category are such things as wars and their aftermath, major technological breakthroughs, sudden dramatic shifts in factor or input cost (e.g. the oil crises), dramatic swings in exchange rates, and so on.

Chance events are important because they create major discontinuities in technologies that allow nations and firms that were not competitive to leapfrog over old competitors and become competitive, even leaders, in the changed industry. For example, the development of microelectronics allowed many Japanese firms to overtake American and German firms in industries that had been based on electromechanical technologies: areas traditionally dominated by the Americans and Germans.

From a systemic perspective, the role of chance events lies in the fact that they alter conditions in the diamond shown in Figure 10.1. The nation with the most favourable diamond, however, will be the one most likely to take advantage of these events and convert them into competitive advantages. The Japanese pharma market currently faces major changes. Not only is the population declining, but also disease patterns are changing. National health expenditure per capita increases and product range broadens. These changes constitute a remarkable chance for national and especially international competition. However, the major challenge, which foreign companies are faced with in the first place, is to get access to the Japanese market.[6] It remains to be seen whether these opportunities will be exploited by foreign competition or whether the particular national diamond is favourable enough. The German life insurance industry, too, forces major changes on national and international competition. This particular market is experiencing pressure from increasing competition, deregulations as well as changing consumer preferences, products and distribution. So far company agents represented the main channels to end-consumer markets. However, changes provide an opportunity for national and foreign brokers, banks and direct investment companies.[7] Which nation will be successful will be determined by the respective national diamond.

Government

Although it is often argued that government is a major determinant of national competitive advantage, the fact is that government is not a determinant, but rather an influence on determinants. Government influences determinants by virtue of its role as a buyer of products and services and by its role as a maker of policies on labour, education, capital formation, natural resources and product standards. It also influences determinants by its role as a regulator of commerce, for example, by telling banks and telephone companies what they can and cannot do.

By reinforcing positive determinants of competitive advantage in an industry, government can improve the competitive position of the nation's firms. Governments devise legal systems that influence competitive advantages by means of tariff and non-tariff barriers and laws requiring local content and labour. In other words, government can improve or lessen competitive advantage but cannot create it.

Other non-market factors

In addition to government and chance, there are other non-market forces that affect the strategy system. The non-market forces include interest groups, activists, and the public, in addition to government. These non-market forces are part of a non-economic strategy system that operates on the basis of social, political and legal forces that interact in the non-market environment of the firm.[8] An understanding of these forces is especially complicated and critical to the success of global strategies that are implemented in many different countries and cultures. The non-market environment differs from the market environment in many ways. For example, the market environment is principally one involving economic exchange, whereas the non-market environment includes regulatory bodies, interest groups, and others whose interest may not be driven by economic motives and often involve political motives. For example, in some countries, environmental groups have promoted regulations that dramatically increase capital and operating costs for businesses that operate manufacturing plants. In the pharmaceutical industry, religious groups have impeded progress in genetic research. Competing companies operating in different national or geographic markets that do not have these limitations or costs have a competitive advantage.

Interplay between the system determinants

It is important to view the determinants of national competitive advantage as an interactive system in which activity in any one of the four points of the diamond impacts on all the others and vice versa. The influences on the development of related and supporting industries is depicted in Figure 10.2, while the influence on domestic rivalry is shown in Figure 10.3.

Other researchers have challenged Porter's thesis that a firm's home-base country is the main source of core competencies and innovation. For example, Professor Alan Rugman of the Templeton College, University of Oxford, argues that the success of companies based in small economies such as Canada and New Zealand stems from the diamonds found in a particular host country or countries. For example, a company based in a European Union (EU) nation may rely on the national diamond of one of the 14 other EU members. Similarly, one impact of the North American Free Trade Agreement (NAFTA) on Canadian firms is to make the US diamond relevant to competency creation. Rugman argues that, in such cases, the distinction between the home nation and host nation becomes blurred. He proposes that Canadian managers must look to a double diamond depicted in Figure 10.4 and assess the attributes of both Canada and the US when formulating corporate strategy.[9]

Figure 10.2 Influences on the development of related and supporting industries

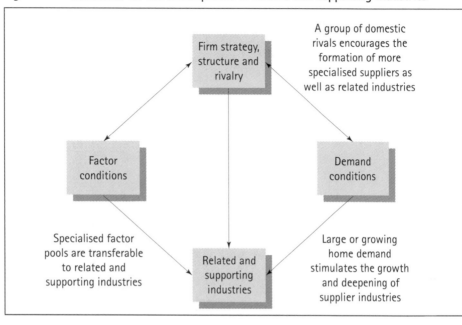

Source: Michael E. Porter, *The Competitive Advantage of Nations* (New York: Free Press, 1990), p. 139.

Figure 10.3 Influences on domestic rivalry

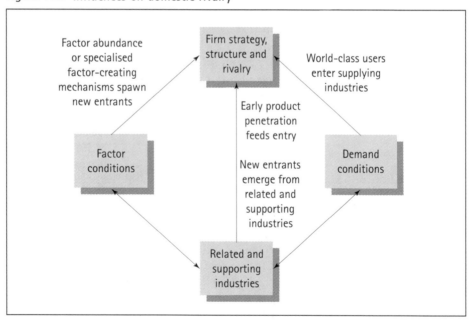

Source: Michael E. Porter, *The Competitive Advantage of Nations* (New York: Free Press, 1990), p. 141.

Figure 10.4 The complete system

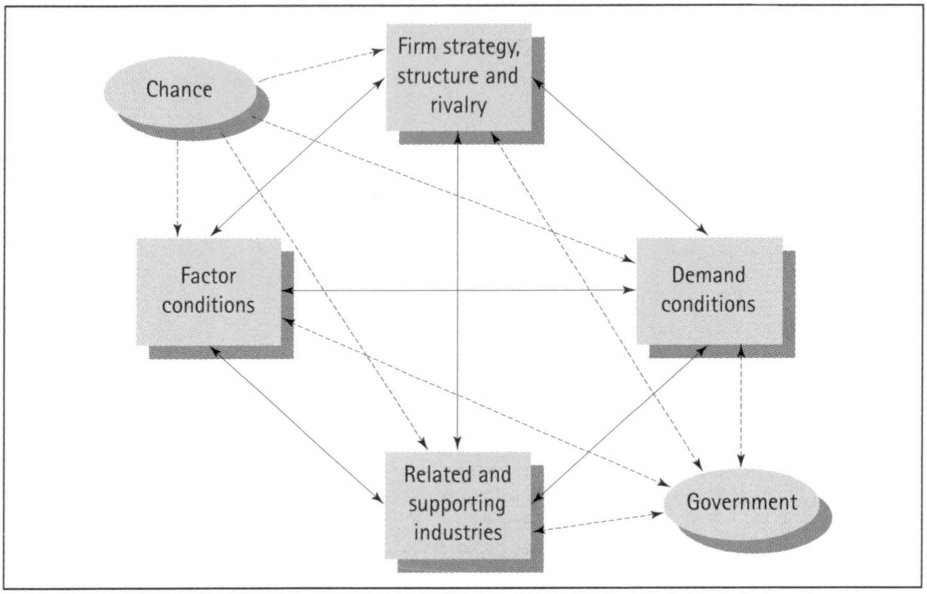

Source: Michael E. Porter, *The Competitive Advantage of Nations* (New York: Free Press, 1990), p. 127.

Key points	
	• A company's success in global markets is heavily influenced by its national environment.
	• According to Porter, the national industrial environment is shaped by four factors representing the so-called national diamond: factor conditions, demand conditions, related and supporting industries as well as firm structure and rivalry.
	• Besides these four factors, chance events, government and non-market factors such as interest groups, activists and the public are major determinants of national competitive advantage.
	• It is important to recognise that the national diamond constitutes an interactive system with each attribute impacting on all the others and vice versa.

INDUSTRY ANALYSIS

Five forces model

A useful way of gaining insight into the nature of competition is through industry analysis. As a working definition, an industry can be defined as a 'group of firms that produce products that are close substitutes for each other'. In any industry, competition works to drive down the rate of return on invested capital toward the rate that would be earned in the economist's perfectly competitive industry. Rates of return that are greater than this so-called competitive rate will stimulate an inflow of capital either from new entrants or from existing competitors making additional investment. Rates of return below this competitive rate will result in withdrawal from the industry and a decline in the levels of activity and competition.

According to Michael E. Porter of Harvard University, a leading theorist of com-

Figure 10.5 Forces influencing competition in an industry

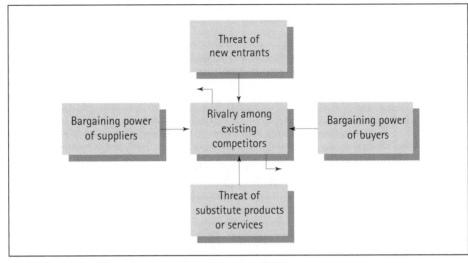

Source: Michael E. Porter, *Competitive Strategy* (New York: Free Press, 1980), p. 4.

petitive strategy, there are five forces influencing competition in an industry (see Figure 10.5): the threat of new entrants; the threat of substitute products or services; the bargaining power of suppliers; the bargaining power of buyers; and the competitive rivalry between current members of the industry. In industries such as soft drinks, pharmaceuticals and cosmetics, a favourable combination of the five forces has resulted in attractive returns for competitors. However, pressure from any of the forces can reduce or limit profitability, as evidenced by the recent fortunes of some competitors in the personal computer (PC) and semiconductor industries. A discussion of each of the five forces follows.

Threat of new entrants

New entrants to an industry bring new capacity, a desire to gain market share and position, and, very often, new approaches to serving customer needs. The decision to become a new entrant in an industry is often accompanied by a major commitment of resources. New players push prices downward and squeeze margins, resulting in reduced industry profitability. Porter describes eight major sources of barriers to entry, the presence or absence of which determine the extent of the threat of new industry entrants.[10]

The first barrier, *economies of scale*, refers to the decline in per unit product costs as the absolute volume of production per period increases. Although the concept of scale economies is frequently associated with manufacturing, it is also applicable to research and development (R&D), general administration, marketing, and other business functions. France Telecom and Deutsche Telekom have entered a joint venture operation called ThinkOne. This co-operation enables efficient use of synergies and economies of scale resulting in innovative services for their customers and greater survivability in an increasingly competitive market.[11] The Chinese and the Indian markets for light commercial vehicles, on the other hand, are swamped by a large number of small producers, who will have to close down their production or enter alliances with large partners, as they are not able to create sufficient economies of scale.[12] When existing firms in an industry achieve significant economies of scale, it becomes difficult for potential new entrants to be competitive.

Product differentiation, the second major entry barrier, is the extent of a product's perceived uniqueness – in other words, whether or not it is a commodity. High levels of product differentiation and brand loyalty, whether the result of physical product attributes or effective marketing communication, 'raise the bar' for would-be industry entrants. Absence of these barriers, on the other hand, constitutes a great opportunity for foreign competition. Currently, companies like Estee Lauder, L'Oreal, Beiersdorfer, Unilever and Procter & Gamble take their chance on the markets of Eastern Europe. Especially in the skin care sector, industry turns out to be very competitive. This is reflected in high advertising budgets, various product launches and brand extensions. The current situation enables these companies to build market share and brand loyalty in immature markets.[13]

A third entry barrier relates to *capital requirements*. Capital is required not only for manufacturing facilities (fixed capital) but also for financing R&D, advertising, field sales and service, customer credit, and inventories (working capital). The enormous capital requirements in such industries as pharmaceuticals, mainframe computers, chemicals and mineral extraction present formidable entry barriers.

A fourth barrier to entry are one-time *switching costs* caused by the need to change suppliers and products. These might include retraining, ancillary equipment costs, the cost of evaluating a new source, and so on. The perceived cost to customers, of switching to a new competitor's product, may present an insurmountable obstacle preventing industry newcomers from achieving success. For example, Microsoft's huge installed base of PC operating systems and applications presents a formidable entry barrier.

A fifth barrier to entry is access to *distribution channels*. To the extent that channels are full, expensive to enter, or unavailable, the cost of entry is substantially increased because a new entrant must create and establish new channels. Some Western companies have encountered this barrier in Japan.

Government policy is frequently a major entry barrier. In some cases, the government will restrict competitive entry. This is true in a number of industries, especially those in the low, lower-middle and upper-middle income categories, that have been designated as national industries by their respective governments. Japan's postwar industrialisation strategy was based on a policy of preserving and protecting national industries in their development and growth phases. China is following a policy today of requiring foreign investors in many industries to join with local partners in their Chinese investments. In telecommunications, for example, it is not possible to invest in China without a partner.

Established firms may also enjoy *cost advantages independent of the scale economies* that present barriers to entry. Access to raw materials, favourable locations and government subsidies are several examples.

Finally, expected *competitor response* can be a major entry barrier. If new entrants expect existing competitors to respond strongly to entry, their expectations about the rewards of entry will certainly be affected. A potential competitor's belief that entry into an industry or market will be an unpleasant experience may serve as a strong deterrent. Bruce Henderson, former president of the Boston Consulting Group, used the term *brinkmanship* to describe a recommended approach for deterring competitive entry. Brinkmanship occurs when industry leaders convince potential competitors that any market entry effort will be countered with vigorous and unpleasant responses.

Threat of substitute products

A second force influencing competition in an industry is the threat of substitute products. The availability of substitute products places limits on the prices market leaders can charge in an industry; high prices may induce buyers to switch to the substitute.

For example, G.D. Searle enjoyed near-monopoly profits on sales of its Nutrasweet brand aspartame sweetener, thanks to patent protection and a track record for quality and safety. As patents expired around the world (the US patent expired in December 1992), Nutrasweet was forced to cut prices to preserve market share. Besides facing a threat from makers of generic aspartame, a new generation of artificial sweeteners is waiting in the wings. One product, Johnson & Johnson's sucralose, offers the benefit of longer shelf life compared to aspartame.[14] For the first time, the availability of substitute products represented a significant negative competitive force for Nutrasweet.

Bargaining power of suppliers

If suppliers have enough leverage over industry firms, they can raise prices high enough to significantly influence the profitability of the industry. Several factors influence supplier bargaining power:

1 Suppliers will have the advantage if they are large and relatively few in number.
2 When the suppliers' products or services are important inputs to user firms, are highly differentiated, or carry switching costs, the suppliers will have considerable leverage over buyers.
3 Suppliers will also enjoy bargaining power if their business is not threatened by alternative products.
4 The willingness and ability of suppliers to develop their own products and brand names if they are unable to get satisfactory terms from industry buyers will influence their power.

Bargaining power of buyers

The ultimate aim of industrial customers is to pay the lowest possible price to obtain the products or services that they use as inputs. Usually, therefore, the buyers' best interests are served if they can drive down profitability in the supplier industry. The following are conditions under which buyers can exert power over suppliers:

1 When they purchase in such large quantities that supplier firms depend on the buyers' business for survival.
2 When the supplier's products are viewed as commodities – that is, as standard or undifferentiated – buyers are likely to bargain hard for low prices, because many supplier firms can meet their needs.
3 When the supplier's industry's products or services represent a significant portion of the buying firms' costs.
4 When the buyer is willing to achieve backward vertical integration.

The example of Nutrasweet illustrates the positive and negative influences of the dynamic between buyer and seller. Soft drink bottlers such as PepsiCo and Coca-Cola are major buyers of Nutrasweet, which historically was the most expensive ingredient in diet soft drinks. As Nutrasweet's patents expired, the soft drink giants' bargaining power increased as they sought sharply lower prices for this key ingredient. While the soft drink makers buy in large quantities, Nutrasweet is used in more than 5,000 products – a fact that diminishes buyer power by reducing the leverage of one or a few buyers. Conversely, Coca-Cola's buyer power was also enhanced when it developed and patented its own low-calorie sweetener.

Rivalry among competitors

Rivalry among firms refers to all the actions taken by firms in the industry to improve their positions and gain advantage over each other. Rivalry manifests itself in price competition, advertising battles, product positioning, and attempts at differentiation. To the extent that rivalry among firms forces companies to innovate and/or rationalise costs, it can be a positive force. To the extent that it drives down prices, and therefore profitability, it creates instability and negatively influences the attractiveness of the industry. Several factors can create intense rivalry:

1 Once an industry becomes mature, firms focus on market share and how it can be gained at the expense of others.
2 Industries characterised by high fixed costs are always under pressure to keep production at full capacity to cover the fixed costs. Once the industry accumulates excess capacity, the drive to fill capacity will push prices and profitability down.
3 A lack of differentiation or an absence of switching costs, encourages buyers to treat the products or services as commodities and shop for the best prices. Again, there is downward pressure on prices and profitability.
4 Firms with high strategic stakes in achieving success in an industry generally are destabilising because they may be willing to accept unreasonably low profit margins to establish themselves, hold position, or expand.

ANALYSIS OF INDUSTRY GROUPS[15]

So far, the discussion on competitive advantage has focused on the national context and on an industry as a whole. However, as the airline business illustrates, different groups of firms pursue different competitive strategies within an industry. British Airways, for example, is changing its sales focus to target first- and business-class travellers instead of economy.[16] Lufthansa is cutting commissions in the UK. This procedure is part of a European wide strategy which focuses on reducing distribution costs and expanding its direct sales.[17] Alitalia hopes to expand its 33 per cent market share by increasing its network and improving its service.[18] All these examples clearly show that, although belonging to the same industry, companies pursue individual strategies.

Individual strategies evolve by adopting competitive strategies along differing dimensions. The following dimensions usually capture the possible differences among a firm's strategic options in a given industry:

● Specialisation constitutes an important dimension referring to the width of a company's product line, the target customer segments, and the geographic markets severed. Brand identification, channel selection, product quality and cost position represent further dimensions that enable companies to build their competitive strategy. Some companies seek to develop brand identification directly with the ultimate customer instead of supporting distribution channels.

- Technological leadership, vertical integration, leverage, as well as the relationship with the parent company, home and host government constitute critical elements in developing a firm's strategy.
- A company's strategic position can involve a number of these dimensions which are related to each other.

Although strategic positions are developed individually for each company, one is likely to find groups of companies following the same strategic dimensions within an industry: so-called strategic groups.

Strategic groups

A strategic group is the group of firms in an industry which follows the same or a similar strategy along important strategic dimensions.[19] Take for example, Ricardo.de, an internet auction house. Since it was launched on 25 August 1998 it has attracted more than 220,000 registered users. In its financial year ending 30 June 2000, the company expects a turnover of €1.2 million.[20] This very successful business model has its forerunner in the USA: eBay. Launched in 1995, eBay provides an on-line forum for Web users to trade personal items in an auction format. The service enables users to browse through listed items in a user-friendly, fully-automated environment available 24 hours a day, seven days a week. After only two months of operation the company had more than one million registered users and more than 600,000 auctions in 1,085 categories.[21] Clearly, Ricardo.de is trying to emulate eBay's strategy in Germany. Strategic groups evolve for several reasons; be it initial strengths or weaknesses, choice of entry time or a firm's historical background. Members of a strategic group often obtain similar market share and react to environmental events in a similar way. Strategic groups are not equivalent to segmentation strategies or market segments. Rather, they are defined on the basis of a broader conception of strategic posture.

Taking into account the underlying strategic dimensions and the fact, that these groups are likely to react similarly to environmental events, strategic groups can be analysed and monitored. Figure 10.6 illustrates this point and shows a strategic group map for a hypothetical industry along the dimensions 'vertical integration' and 'specialisation'. Group A represents a strategic group offering a full line of products with moderate quality. This group is further characterised by a high level of vertical integration, low manufacturing costs as well as low service. Group B, on the other hand, only offers a narrow line of high price, high technology, high quality products. The level of vertical integration is very low. Group C is positioned somewhere in-between those two extremes. It provides the consumer with a moderate line of low quality, low price products, however, it offers a very high level of customer service. Group D is similar to Group A in terms of 'vertical integration' but offers only a narrow product line.

Characteristics of strategic groups

When defining strategic groups, it is also important to take into account a company's relationship to its parent (where applicable), as each of the different types of firms are managed with somewhat different objectives. The same applies for a firm's relationship to its home and host government.

Figure 10.6 A map of strategic groups in a hypothetical industry

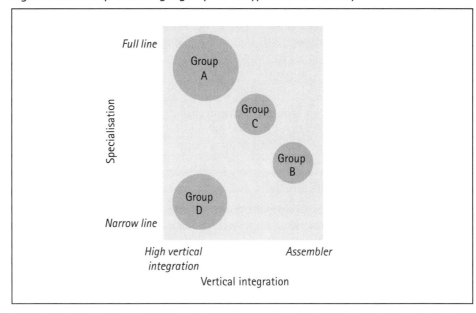

Source: Adapted from Michael E. Porter, *Competitive Strategy – Techniques for Analysing Industries and Competitors* (New York: Free Press, 1980), p. 131.

Mobility barriers[22]

Although certain entry barriers such as access to distribution channels or capital requirements apply to an industry as a whole, each strategic group is also characterised by a special set of entry barriers. As these barriers not only limit access to a specific industry but also switching between strategic groups, they are referred to as mobility barriers. Again, Lufthansa functions as an example. In order to be competitive on short-haul German and European routes, Lufthansa is poised to plan a separate airline which offers low costs without any frills. This specific strategic model is adopted from British Airways which owns a separate carrier termed 'Go' and KLM, which operates a budget carrier called 'Buzzaway'. However, it's not only BA who is pursuing this particular strategy. Budget airline Eurowings can be found in the same strategic group. However, the following statements clearly illustrate the mobility barriers Lufthansa will face when trying to enter this particular strategic group. Eurowings spokesman: 'If the airline operated at a low cost, then it would be a serious threat. But we cannot imagine it would be so flexible.' Deutsche BA spokesman: 'We see ourselves as the main competitor to Lufthansa with our frequencies and services, and the new low-cost carrier would not affect our routes much.'[23]

The above quotes also imply that overcoming mobility barriers is not only risky, but also costly. The cost of overcoming mobility barriers might exceed the additional profits gained by joining a particular strategic group.

Overall, mobility barriers constitute the major reason, why some firms in an industry are persistently more profitable than others and why successful models are not simply imitated by competition.

Bargaining power[24]

Another important characteristic of strategic groups is their varying level of bargaining power with consumers and suppliers. Two reasons are responsible for this: The strategies pursued may yield differing degrees of vulnerability to common suppliers or buyers; or they might involve contact with different suppliers and buyers with varying levels of bargaining power. Swiss Air, for example, has been known to show an aloof attitude with travel agencies and tour operators. Now, with the company seeing through its new strategy of cutting costs and strengthening ties with other carriers as well as with travel agents, this attitude has changed dramatically. Travel agents and tour operators now find more willingness for negotiation and dialogue from the airline. Moreover, the alliance with Delta has facilitated and eased communication between Swiss Air and the agency community.[25]

Threat of substitutes[26]

Strategic groups face different levels of exposure to substitute products depending on their strategic focus. Companies focusing on serving special customer needs will be less vulnerable to substitutes than companies which solely build their competitive advantage on low prices. Swiss Air has cultivated an image of being independent, devoted to high quality and good food, expensive fares and a cachet that comes with being Swiss. This makes it a favourable carrier for international travellers; however, in terms of impact on the bottom line, this particular strategy has not worked out in favour of Swiss Air.[27] It can be assumed that airlines offering less expensive fares attract customers for short-distance flights.

Rivalry among firms[28]

As mentioned above (see Firm strategy, structure and rivalry) domestic rivalry keeps an industry dynamic and creates continual pressure to improve and innovate. The same can be applied to industries. The presence of several strategic groups will often affect the level of rivalry in an industry. However, not all strategic groups within an industry will face the same degree of competitive rivalry. Swiss Air, for example has been operating in a marketplace less competitive than the rest of Europe or the United States. Now, with the industry becoming global, they can no longer put up with high costs and inflexible work rules.[29]

The degree of competition between strategic groups in an industry is determined by four factors: the extent to which target groups overlap, the degree of product differentiation, the number of strategic groups and their relative sizes and the extent to which strategies differ. These four determinants cannot be seen independently. Rather, they interrelate to determine the pattern of rivalry for customers among strategic groups in an industry.[30]

The strategic group map

Strategic groups can be displayed graphically in a two-dimensional map (illustrated in Figure 10.6). The dimensions used as axes have to be selected with respect to the particular firm and industry. Although the map is limited to two dimensions, it provides a company with a useful analytical tool. Having developed a strategic group map enables a company to identify mobility barriers and marginal groups, to analyse trends, to predict reactions and, last but not least, to chart the directions of strategic groups. Moreover, these maps can also support the company's choice of which strategic group to compete in; in short, which competitive strategy to pursue.

Key points	• Individual strategies evolve by adopting competitive strategies along differing dimensions.
	• A group of firms within an industry following the same or a similar strategy along these dimensions is called a strategic group.
	• Strategic groups are characterised by four distinct factors: the extent of mobility barriers protecting the company's strategic group, the bargaining power of the firms in the strategic group, its vulnerability to substitute products and the degree of exposure to rivalry from other groups.
	• A strategic group map provides a useful analytical tool for companies.

COMPETITIVE ADVANTAGE OF INDIVIDUAL COMPANIES

Having discussed the key national characteristics which determine the global success of companies located in the respective markets (the national diamond), analysed the forces which influence competition within an industry (five forces model) as well as the importance and implications of strategic groups, we now focus on individual companies.

Strategy is integrated action in pursuit of competitive advantage.[31] Successful strategy requires an understanding of the unique value that will be the source of the firm's competitive advantage. Firms ultimately succeed because of their ability to carry out specific activities or groups of activities better than their competitors. These activities enable the firm to create unique value for their customers. It is this value that is central to achieving and sustaining competitive advantage. This unique value must be something that competitors will not be able to match easily. The uniqueness and magnitude of the customer value created by a firm's strategy is ultimately determined by customer perception. Operating results such as sales and profits are measures that depend on the level of psychological value created for customers. The greater the perceived consumer value, the stronger the competitive advantage, and the better the strategy. A firm may market a better mousetrap, but the ultimate success of the product depends on customers deciding for themselves whether to buy it. Value is like beauty, it is in the eye of the beholder. In sum, competitive advantage is achieved by creating more value than the competition, and value is defined by customer perception.

Three different models of competitive advantage have received considerable attention. The first offers generic strategies, which are four alternative positions that organisations can seek in order to offer superior value and achieve competitive advantage. According to the second model, the generic strategies alone do not explain the astonishing success of many Japanese companies in recent years. A more recent model, based on the concept of strategic intent, proposes four different sources of competitive advantage. Finally, building on the second model, a more dynamic perspective referred to as hypercompetition has been developed. All three models are discussed below.

Generic strategies for creating competitive advantage

In addition to the five forces model of industry competition, Porter developed a framework of so-called generic business strategies based on two sources of competitive advantage: low cost and differentiation. Figure 10.7 shows that the combination

Figure 10.7 Generic competitive strategies

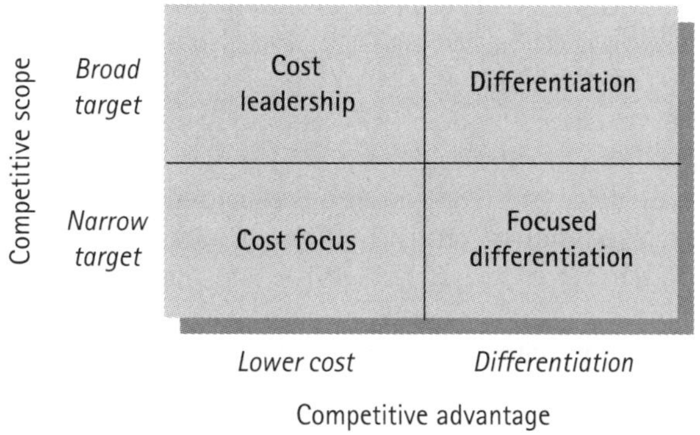

Source: Michael E. Porter, *The Competitive Advantage of Nations* (New York: Free Press, 1990), p. 39.

of these two sources with the scope of the target market served (narrow or broad) or product mix width (narrow or wide) yields four generic strategies: cost leadership, product differentiation, focused differentiation, and cost focus.

Generic strategies aiming at the achievement of competitive advantage demand that the firm make choices. The choices concern the position it seeks to attain from which to offer unique value (based on cost or differentiation) and the market scope or product mix width within which competitive advantage will be attained.[32] The nature of the choice between positions and market scope is a gamble and involves risk. By choosing a given generic strategy, a firm always risks making the wrong choice. The broad market strategies are as follows.

Cost–leadership advantage

When the unique value delivered by a firm is based on its position as the industry's low-cost producer, in broadly defined markets or across a wide mix of products, a cost-leadership advantage occurs. This strategy has become increasingly popular in recent years as a result of the popularisation of the experience curve concept. A firm that bases its competitive strategy on overall cost leadership must construct the most efficient facilities (in terms of scale or technology) and obtain the largest share of market so that its cost per unit is the lowest in the industry. These advantages, in turn, give the producer a substantial lead in terms of experience with building the product. Experience then leads to more refinements of the entire process of production, delivery and service, which leads to further cost reductions.

Whatever its source, cost-leadership advantage can be the basis for offering lower prices (and more value) to customers in the late, more competitive stages of the product life cycle.

A lot of companies pursue active strategies to attain cost leadership in their markets. For example, the UK-based group Unichem has merged with France's Alliance Sante to form Alliance Unichem. The merger makes the new company the largest drug wholesaler in the UK, Italy and Portugal, and the second largest in France. Europe-wide, Gehe still holds the number one position not only in terms of market share, but also in terms of cost leadership. However, should Alliance Unichem be able to overcome the difficulties involved in the merger and realise all cost reductions, Gehe's dominant position in Europe will be under pressure.[33] Another example is Shell Chemicals, which implemented a strategic cost leadership programme. This particular programme represents the result of a study reviewing Shell Chemicals' business on a global basis, which found Shell's costs to be higher than those of other major top firms.[34]

Differentiation

When a firm's product delivers unique value because of an actual or perceived uniqueness in a broad market, it is said to have a differentiation advantage. This can be an extremely effective strategy for defending market position and obtaining above-average financial returns; unique products often command premium price.

Take, for example, Jet Service, the leading French courier company for overnight handling of documents and packages up to 30 kg. With its outstanding delivery system, it holds one quarter of the market. In the European market, the company has more than 130 collection and delivery centres, known as Jet Points. The system uses hand-held computers with integrated barcode scanners to track packages and improve vehicle utilisation. As Jet Services has a strong position in the pharmaceutical and medical sector, it uses refrigerator barcodes to track temperature sensitive packages in order to provide customers with unique and critical value added.[35]

Narrow target strategies

The preceding discussion of cost leadership and differentiation considered only the impact on broad markets. By contrast, strategies to achieve a narrow focus advantage target a narrowly defined market/customer. This advantage is based on an ability to create more customer value for a narrowly targeted segment and results from a better understanding of customer needs and wants. A narrow-focus strategy can be combined with either cost- or differentiation-advantage strategies. In other words, whereas cost focus means offering a narrow target market low prices, a firm pursuing focused differentiation will offer a narrow target market the perception of product uniqueness at a premium price.

Focused differentiation

The German Mittelstand companies have been extremely successful pursuing focused differentiation strategies backed by a strong export effort. The world of high-end audio equipment offers another example of focused differentiation. A few hundred companies, in the United States and elsewhere, make speakers and amplifiers and related hi-fi gear that cost thousands of dollars per component. Although audio components as a whole represent a €17.8 billion market worldwide, annual sales in the high-end segment are only €848 million. In Japan alone, discriminating audiophiles purchase €170 million in high-end audio equipment each year. Increases in disposable income in Japan and other Pacific Rim countries have provided opportunities for overseas consumer electronics companies.[36]

Cost focus

The final strategy is cost focus, when a firm's lower cost position enables it to offer a narrow target market lower prices than the competition. In the shipbuilding industry, for example, Polish and Chinese shipyards offer simple, standard vessel types at low prices that reflect low production costs.[37]

Playing the spread[38]

Porter's framework has been further refined by Day, who argues that the choice

Figure 10.8 Generic competitive strategies – additional dimensions

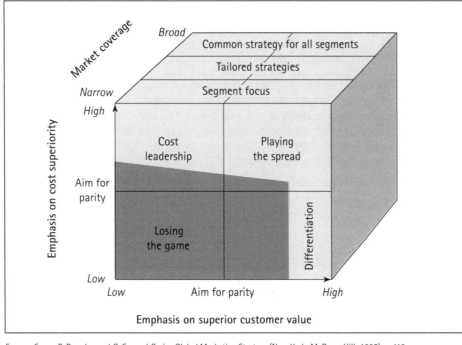

Source: Susan P. Douglas and C. Samuel Craig, *Global Marketing Strategy* (New York: McGraw-Hill, 1995), p. 112.

between differentiation and lowest delivered cost is not necessarily mutually exclusive. The strategy where improved product quality and customer value may lead to lower costs is termed *playing the spread*. Lower unit costs due to scale economies result from a higher market share, which again is an outcome of improved product quality.

Figure 10.8 shows the three underlying dimensions of the refined model: emphasis on customer value, emphasis on costs and emphasis on scope of market coverage. Day initially developed his framework in relation to domestic markets. However, it can also be applied to international markets.

The three dimensions enable a broad array of possible strategies based on core competence and selected market. However, some combinations are more favourable than others. A company offering moderate prices, but no clear differentiation of its products bears the risk to be outperformed by competition superior in costs or differentiation.

Key points

- Competitive advantage stems from a unique value that companies provide for their customers.

- According to Porter, there are two sources of competitive advantage: low cost and differentiation.

- By combining these two sources with the scope of markets served or the product mix width deployed, four generic strategies evolve: cost leadership, product differentiation, focused differentiation and cost focus.

- Day argues that no choice has to be made between the two sources of competitive advantage. The strategy where improved product quality and customer value may lead to lower costs is termed *playing the spread*.

Strategic intent

An alternative framework for understanding competitive advantage focuses on competitiveness as a function of the pace at which a company implants new advantages deep within its organisation. This framework identifies strategic intent, growing out of ambition and obsession with winning, as the means for achieving competitive advantage. Writing in the *Harvard Business Review*, Hamel and Prahalad note:

> Few competitive advantages are long lasting. Keeping score of existing advantages is not the same as building new advantages. The essence of strategy lies in creating tomorrow's competitive advantages faster than competitors mimic the ones you possess today. An organisation's capacity to improve existing skills and learn new ones is the most defensible competitive advantage of all.[39]

This approach is founded on the principles of W.E. Deming, who stressed that a company must commit itself to continuing improvement in order to be a winner in a competitive struggle.

Layers of advantage

A company faces less risk in competitive encounters if it has a wide portfolio of advantages. Successful companies steadily build such portfolios by establishing layers of advantage on top of one another. Komatsu is an excellent example of this approach. Another is the TV industry in Japan. By 1970, Japan was not only the world's largest producer of black-and-white TV sets but was also well on its way to becoming the leader in producing colour sets. The main competitive advantage for such companies as Matsushita at that time was low labour costs.

Because they realised that their cost advantage could be temporary, the Japanese also added additional layers of quality and reliability advantages by building plants large enough to serve world markets. Much of this output did not carry the manufacturer's brand name. For example, Matsushita Electric sold products to other companies such as RCA that marketed them under their own brand names. Matsushita was pursuing a simple idea: a product sold was a product sold, no matter whose label it carried.[40]

In order to build the next layer of advantage, the Japanese spent the 1970s investing heavily in marketing channels and Japanese brand names to gain recognition. This strategy added yet another layer of competitive advantage: the global brand franchise – that is, a global customer base. By the late 1970s, channels and brand awareness were established well enough to support the introduction of new products that could benefit from global marketing – video cassette recorders (VCRs) and photocopy machines, for example. Finally, many companies have invested in regional manufacturing so their products can be differentiated and better adapted to customer needs in individual markets.

The process of building layers illustrates how a company can move along the value chain to strengthen competitive advantage. The Japanese began with manufacturing (an upstream value activity) and moved on to marketing (a downstream value activity) and then back upstream to basic R&D. All of these sources of competitive advantage represent mutually desirable layers that are accumulated over time.

Loose bricks

A second approach takes advantage of the loose bricks left in the defensive walls of competitors whose attention is narrowly focused on a market segment or a geo-

Formule 1

In the mid-80s, the French budget hotel industry was suffering from stagnation and overcapacity. In order to overcome this situation, top management at Accor challenged its managers to forget everything they knew about the existing rules, practices and traditions of the industry.

In 1985 Accor launched a line of budget hotels called Formule 1. At that time, there were only two distinct market segments in the budget hotel industry. One segment represented no-star and one-star hotels, whose average price per room was between €9.15 and €13.7. Customers were attracted to these hotels only because of the low price. The other segment consisted of two-star hotels with an average price per room of €30.5. Customers who expected a better sleeping environment would have to pay for it.

In a first step, Accor's managers began by identifying what customers of all budget hotels – no-star, one-star and two-star hotels wanted: a good night's sleep for a low price. By emphasising those widely shared needs, Accor's managers saw the opportunity to overcome the compromise that the customers were forced to make. Four questions helped them to create a new business model:

- Which of the factors the industry took for granted should be eliminated?
- Which of the factors should be reduced well below the industry standard?
- Which factors should be raised well above the industry standard?
- Which factors had to be created that were never offered before by the industry?

The first question helps management to decide whether the factors that companies compete on actually deliver value to customers. Firms focusing on benchmarking often take factors for granted, even though they have no value or even detract from value; change management is widely neglected. The second question helps managers to determine whether products and services have been over-designed in the race to match and beat competitors. In a third step, compromises imposed on the customer from industry are discovered and eliminated. The last question helps managers to discover totally new sources of value for the customer.

Proceeding through the different stages enabled Accor's management to come up with a totally new concept for a hotel, which led to the launch of Formule 1. Accor started by eliminating such standard hotel features as costly restaurants and appealing lounges. Although this might lead to the loss of some customers, Accor was convinced that most people could do without those features. Other dimensions overserving customers were reduced, too: receptionists are on hand only during peak check-in and check-out hours. Automated teller machines serve customers at other times. Rooms are small and equipped only with a bed, no stationery, no desks or decorations. There are only a few shelves and a pole for clothing. The rooms themselves constitute modular blocks manufactured in a factory, resulting in economies of scale in production, high quality control and good installation.

Pursuing this totally new strategy has enabled Accor to cut costs dramatically, and even more importantly expand its market share. With Formule 1 competition has become irrelevant. At last count, market share in France was greater than the sum of the five next-largest players.

Food for thought

- What is the role of benchmarking in strategy development? Discuss the key advantages and limitations.
- Should Formule 1 attempt to gain fresh competitive insights by looking at other industries than the hotel industry? What type of comparisons would you envisage?

Source: W. Chan Kim and Renée Mauborgne, 'Value innovation: the strategic logic of high growth', *Harvard Business Review* (January–February 1997): pp. 103–112.

GLOBAL PERSPECTIVE

Swatch – changing the rules for the second time?

By 1967, Switzerland's share of the world market, which in 1952 stood at 56 per cent, had fallen to a mere 20 per cent of the finished watch segment, while world production had grown from 61 million to 320 million pieces and movements annually. The Swiss, once the industry's leaders in innovation, had fallen behind, although they were the first to introduce the model of an electronic wristwatch. However, they dismissed the new technology as a fad and continued to rely on their mechanical time-pieces where most of their research efforts were concentrated.

One company, however, managed to break out of this vicious circle by employing a totally new concept unheard of so far within the watch industry: ETA with its concept for Swatch watches.

In contrast to common practices, it was not the product, its styling and technical value that were focused on, but its brand name. Unlike ordinary watches, Swatch was positioned as a high-fashion accessory for fashion conscious people between 18 and 30. However, it turned out that a wide range of people outside this target group also bought Swatch. A Zurich-based designer, Jean Robert, was responsible for the innovative style of the product.

As a high-fashion item, Swatch watches were not sold through drugstores and mass retailers. Department stores, chic boutiques and jewellery shops served as distribution channels. Extensive training of retailers' sales personnel and attractive distributors' margins combined with innovative advertising ensured the unique positioning of the product. The unisex models differed in the colour of the cases and straps, and the dial design was based on a constant technical concept.

Swatch has earned a reputation as being innovative over the last twenty years. However, the successful business model no longer holds and the Swatch brand no longer represents a phenomenon. Although financial figures are still revealing a healthy turnover – a rise of 7.5 per cent to €210 million in 1998 – Swatch is struggling to reposition itself by branching out into new technologies and into retail stores of its own.

There is a widespread belief within the industry that the Swatch Group is reaching saturation point with its brands. As with many innovators, Swatch has lost much of its reputation for breaking new ground. Although there is little doubt that watches will stay the company's core business, the Swatch Group is looking elsewhere to build commercial growth. The company has expanded into the Internet, car and telecom industries.

In Finland, Swatch has joined an initiative with Schlumberger, a smart card firm. The common project deals with integration of Schlumberger's contactless smart card technology into a next-generation watch produced by Swatch. Bus users are able to wave their watches as they board the bus rather than deal with money to pay for their ticket. Similar projects have been undertaken in Australia. The so-called 'Swatch Access', already used for ski lift access, not only keeps time, but eventually will be used to withdraw cash and pay bills, as a public transport ticket, as a gateway to loyalty and incentive programmes, as a substitute for membership cards and as a key to electronic security doors.

In the telecommunications field, Swatch has launched the new Cordless II Answer DECT phone. The telephone includes a digital answering machine that can store up to 22 minutes of messages and is available in three different colours. A luxury mobile set is also offered. These devices follow the Beep Box, a numeric pager shaped as a circle.

Some of the newest markets targeted evolve from the e-commerce business. Swatch has developed the 'Swatch Internet Time', which is intended to take the difficulty out of dealing with multiple time zones on the Internet. The new system divides a day into beats and features instead of time zones. One of the latest products is a watch enabling the wearer to check his/her e-mail messages.

In addition, the company is opening new stores or buying back franchises. Swatch plans to own 500 outlets around the world by the year 2000.

Whether the new strategy pays off and provides Swatch with a revival of its success story remains to be seen.

GLOBAL PERSPECTIVE continued

Food for thought

- What are the key marketing implications of the decision to position Swatch watches as a high-fashion accessory?

- Which potential problems should be considered when extending the Swatch brand to other product categories, such as telephones, pagers, fragrances or cars?

Source: Arieh A. Ullmann 'The Swatch in 1993', *Casestudy* (1993), State University of New York at Binghamton; Sylvia Dennis, 'Finland bus travelers use watch-based e-ticketing' *Newsbytes News Network*, 18 December 1998; Martyn Williams, 'Swatch redefines time for Internet world', *Newsbytes News Network*, 22 November 1998; Anonymous, 'Swatch creates round flex-based pager', *Radio Communications Report*, 9 November 1998, p. 34; Kristi Ellis and Wendy Hessen, 'Swatch at 15: a new identity', *Women's Wear Daily*, 176 (3), 1959, p. 16; Anonymous, 'Every second counts as Swatch gets smart', *Electronic Payments International*, September 1997, p. 9; Hank Kim, 'Mercury rising at watch shoot', *AdWeek East*, 25 August 1997, p. 3; Anonymous, 'The Future is DECT', *Mobile & Cellular Magazine*, August 1997, p. 26; Paul Edwards, 'Can Swatch keep up with changing times?', *Marketing Week*, 15 July 1999, p. 21; Laura Randall, 'Swatch unveils plans for e-mail watch', *Newsbytes News Network*, 12 July 1999; Anonymous, 'Swatch ticks toward Web, telecoms, cars', *Wall Street Journal Europe*, 5 June 1999, p. 4; Anonymous, 'Swatch grows in US', *Women's Wear Daily*, 1 March 1999, p. 12; Keith Flamer, 'Can Swatch bring back the good times?', *Jewelers' Circular-Keystone*, December 1998, pp. 66ff.

graphic area. Global distribution has been identified to be a major loose brick with many companies.[41] This is especially true for an Internet-driven market place. E-commerce represents a threat to store-based retailers as it allows aggressive competition on price and convenience. Waterstone's, for example, plans to launch its own online bookshop to compete with already established Internet bookshops such as Amazon.com. Another example would be Marks & Spencer, which has set up a considerable mail-order system in an attempt to stay competitive.[42]

Changing the rules

A third approach involves changing the so-called rules of engagement and refusing to play by the rules set by industry leaders. Swatch is one example which gained widespread success and recognition by changing the rules set by the Swiss watch industry (see the Global Perspective).

Collaborating

A final source of competitive advantage is using know-how developed by other companies. Such collaboration may take the form of licensing agreements, joint ventures and partnerships.

The German electricity market will undergo major restructuring due to its new energy law which will introduce competition to all levels. Four success factors have been identified which will enable companies offering electricity to compete and survive in this rapidly changing and evolving market. Knowledge about the market and its participants, efficiency at all tiers of the value chain, a marketing mix tailored to the market as well as speed and flexibility in serving the market are said to be essential. According to forecasts, only 100 or fewer of the currently existing 1,000 German utilities will survive the initial phase of competition. Other parts of the energy industry now also seek to improve their prospects by various types of co-operative ventures. One example are project-related co-operative ventures such as a crude oil refinery of Neustadt GmbH & Co. OHG, a joint venture of Agip, BP, Mobil and Ruhr Oil. Another example is provided by the Europe-wide ROUTEX, which combines the petroleum companies Aral, BP, Mobil, Statoil and IP.[43]

Hypercompetition

In a recent book, Dartmouth College professor Richard D'Aveni suggests that the Porter strategy frameworks fail to adequately address the dynamics of competition in the 21st century.[44] D'Aveni notes that, in today's business environment, market stability is undermined by short product life cycles, short product design cycles, new technologies and globalisation. The result is an escalation and acceleration of competitive forces. In light of these changes, D'Aveni believes the goal of strategy has shifted from sustaining to disrupting advantages. The limitation of the Porter models, D'Aveni argues, is that they provide a snapshot of competition at a given point in time. In other words, they are static models.

Acknowledging that Hamel and Prahalad broke new ground in recognising that few advantages are sustainable, D'Aveni aims to build on their work to shape 'a truly dynamic approach to the creation and destruction of traditional advantages'. D'Aveni uses the term hypercompetition to describe a dynamic, competitive world in which no action or advantage can be sustained for long. In such a world, D'Aveni argues, 'everything changes' because of the dynamic manoeuvring and strategic interactions by hypercompetitive firms such as Microsoft and Gillette. According to D'Aveni's model, competition unfolds in a series of dynamic strategic interactions in four arenas: cost–quality, timing and know-how, entry barriers, and deep pockets. Each of these arenas is 'continuously destroyed and recreated by the dynamic manoeuvring of hypercompetitive firms'. According to D'Aveni, the only source of a truly sustainable competitive advantage is a company's ability to manage its dynamic strategic interactions with competitors' frequent movements that maintain a relative position of strength in each of the four arenas. The irony and paradox of this model is that, in order to achieve a sustainable advantage, companies must seek a series of unsustainable advantages! D'Aveni is in agreement with Peter Drucker, who has long counselled that the role of marketing is innovation and the creation of new markets. Innovation begins with abandonment of the old and obsolete. In Drucker's words, 'Innovative organisations spend neither time nor resources on defending yesterday. Systematic abandonment of yesterday alone can transfer the resources ... for work on the new.'[45]

D'Aveni urges managers to reconsider and reevaluate the use of what he believes are old strategic tools and maxims. He warns of the dangers of commitment to a given strategy or course of action. The flexible, unpredictable player may have an advantage over the inflexible, committed opponent. D'Aveni notes that, in hypercompetition, pursuit of generic strategies results in short-term advantage at best. The winning companies are the ones that successfully move up the ladder of escalating competition, not the ones that lock into a fixed position. D'Aveni also is critical of the five forces model. The best entry barrier, he argues, is maintaining the initiative, not mounting a defensive attempt to exclude new entrants.

Key points

- Hamel and Prahalad's framework for understanding competitive advantage emphasises competitiveness as a function of the pace at which a company implants new advantages deep within the organisation.

- Four approaches to gaining sustainable competitive advantages are introduced: build several layers of advantage, find loose bricks left in the defensive wall of competitiors, change the rules set by industry leaders and collaborate.

- D'Aveni argues that the only true competitive advantage is a firm's ability to manage its dynamic strategic interactions with competitors' frequent moves. This is especially true for four different areas: cost-quality, timing and know-how, entry barriers and deep pockets.

Summary

In this chapter, we focus on factors helping industries and countries achieve competitive advantage.

Porter has described four determinants of national advantage. Factor conditions include human, physical, knowledge, capital, and infrastructure resources. Demand conditions include the composition, size and growth pattern of home demand. The rate of home-market growth and the means by which a nation's products are pulled into foreign markets also affect demand conditions. The final two determinants are the presence of related and supporting industries and the nature of firm strategy, structure, and rivalry. Porter notes that chance and government also influence a nation's competitive advantage.

Looking at the competitiveness of an industry Porter's five forces model views industry competition as a function of the threat of new entrants, the threat of substitutes, the bargaining power of suppliers and buyers, and rivalry among existing competitors. Porter's positions can be used by managers to understand how to combine activities to create unique value, the source of competitive advantage.

Within an industry, groups of companies may follow the same or similar strategies along important strategic dimensions. These groups are referred to as strategic groups. Strategic groups within an industry can be illustrated in a map functioning as a useful strategic tool.

Finally, focusing on the individual strategy of a company, an understanding of the unique source of a firm's competitive advantage proves to be of great importance. Porter's model of competitive advantage of individual firms identifies four alternative generic strategies, that organisations can pursue in order to provide their customers with superior value.

Hamel and Prahalad have proposed an alternative framework for pursuing competitive advantage, growing out of a firm's strategic intent and use of competitive innovation. A firm can build layers of advantage, search for loose bricks in a competitor's defensive walls, change the rules of engagement, or collaborate with competitors and utilise their technology and know-how. This framework is not necessarily inconsistent with the positions proposed by Porter. The concepts proposed by Hamel and Prahalad, as well as D'Aveni, stress the dynamic environment. Strategic positions have shorter lives than in the past and may have to be supplemented or abandoned faster than ever before.

Concepts and definitions

The national diamond	The national diamond consists of four attributes interacting with each other: Factor conditions, demand conditions, related and supporting industries, firm strategy, structure and rivalry. According to Porter, these attributes determine a company's success in global markets.[46]
Five forces model	According to Porter, there are five forces influencing competition in an industry: (1) the threat of new entrants, (2) the bargaining power of suppliers, (3) the bargaining power of buyers, (4) the threat of substitute products or services, and (5) the rivalry among existing competitors.[47]
Generic strategies	Porter identified so-called generic business strategies based on two sources of competitive advantage: low cost and differentiation. Combined with the scope of the target market served (narrow or broad) or the width of the product mix (narrow or wide) four generic strategies have been identified: cost leadership, product differentiation, focused differentiation and cost focus.[48]
Playing the spread	Day argues that the basic sources of competitive advantage, low cost and differentiation, are not necessarily mutually exclusive. The author termed a strategy where improved product quality and customer value may lead to lower costs, 'playing the spread'.[49]
Strategic groups	A strategic group constitutes a group of companies in an industry following the same or a similar strategy.[50]
Hypercompetition	The term hypercompetition describes a dynamic, competitive world, in which no action or advantage can be sustained for long. According to D'Aveni, a company must seek a series of unsustainable advantages in order to be competitive in the areas cost-quality, timing and know-how, entry barriers and deep pockets. D'Aveni argues that the flexible, unpredictable player will have an advantage over the inflexible, committed opponent.[51]

Discussion questions

1 How can a company measure its competitive advantage? How does a firm know if it is gaining or losing competitive advantage?

2 Outline Porter's 'five forces' model of industry competition. How are the various barriers of entry relevant to global marketing?

3 Give an example of a company that illustrates each of the four generic strategies that can lead to competitive advantage: overall cost leadership, cost focus, differentiation, and focused differentiation.

4 What are the three strategic positions identified by Michael Porter? Identify a company example for each position.

5 What is the relationship, if any, between Porter's four generic strategies and his three strategic positions?

6 Briefly describe Hamel and Prahalad's framework for competitive advantage.

7 How can a nation achieve competitive advantage?

8 Do you agree with D'Aveni that no action or strategic advantage can be sustained for long? Why? Why not?

IKEA homepage

The IKEA homepage gives you the opportunity to 'surf' the company from different perspectives. You are able to choose between a global site and specific country sites. The latter enables you to find the IKEA store next to you and to get familiar with products, special offers and news referring to this particular location.
http://www.ikea.com/

VW homepage

When entering the VW homepage you will find funny gags like the TURBONIUM as well as useful information about the company, its products, its services and its stores.
http://www.volkswagen.com/

Lufthansa

Visit the Lufthansa homepage, select a language and your country site. By doing so, you will be able to find out more (among other things) about the Star Alliance or let the Travel Assistant help you to choose, book and pay for your flight ... maybe to your favourite holiday location?
http://www.lufthansa.com/

SWATCH homepage

The SWATCH homepage will not only provide you with the up-to-date catalogue of products, but will also enable you to find the nearest shop with help of the store locator. Furthermore the Euro converter and Internet time will facilitate doing shopping and business in the global world of the WWW.
http://www.swatch.com/

Ricardo.de

On the Ricardo.de homepage you will have access to three different categories: ricardo live, ricardo nonstop and ricardo private. Via ricardo live you can take part in an online auction with live moderation. Ricardo nonstop enables you to purchase 24 hours, seven days a week and, finally, ricardo private gives you the opportunity to open your own auction.
http://www.ricardo.de/

eBay

Again, an online auction! 3,456,220 items are displayed in over 2,500 categories ... you can bid, you can sell and you can win. Try it and see for yourself.
http://www.ebay.com/

Suggested readings

Aharoni, Yair, 'The state-owned enterprise as a competitor in international markets', *Columbia Journal of World Business*, Spring (1980): pp. 14–22.

Baron, David P., 'The nonmarket strategy system', *Sloan Management Review*, 37, 1 (1995): pp. 73–85.

Bartmess, Andrew, and Keith Cerny, 'Building competitive advantage through a global network of capabilities', *California Management Review*, 35, 2 (1993): pp. 78–103.

Brouthers, Lancer Eliot and Steve Werner, 'Are the Japanese good global competitors?', *Columbia Journal of World Business*, Fall (1990): pp. 5–11.

Calantone, Roger J. and C. Anthony DiBenedetto, 'Defensive marketing in globally competitive industrial markets', *Columbia Journal of World Business*, 23, 3 (1988): pp. 3–14.

D'Aveni, Richard, *Hypercompetition: Managing the Dynamics of Strategic Maneuvering*. New York: Free Press, 1994.

Day, George, *Market Driven Strategy: Processes for Creating Value*. New York: Free Press, 1990.

Dertouzos, Michael L., Richard K. Lester and Robert M. Solow, *Made in America: Regaining the Competitive Edge*. New York: HarperCollins, 1989.

Douglas, Susan P. and C. Samuel Craig, *Global Marketing Strategy*. New York: McGraw-Hill, 1995.

Egelhoff, William G., 'Great strategy of great strategy implementation – two ways of competing in global markets', *Sloan Management Review*, 34, 2 (1993): pp. 37–50.

Garsombke, Diane J., 'International competitor analysis', *Planning Review*, 17, 3 (1989): pp. 42–47.

Ghoshal, Sumantra and D. Eleanor Westney, 'Global competition: confront your rivals on their home turf', *Harvard Business Review*, 71, 3 (1993): p. 10.

Ghoshal, Sumantra and D. Eleanor Westney, 'Organizing competitor analysis systems', *Strategic Management Journal*, 12, 1 (1991): pp. 17–31.

Hamel, Gary and C.K. Prahalad, 'The core competence of the corporation', *Harvard Business Review*, May–June (1990): pp. 79–91.

Hamel, G. and C.K. Prahalad, 'Do you really have a global strategy?' *Harvard Business Review*, March–April (1985): pp. 73–93.

Hamel, Gary and C.K. Prahalad, 'Strategic intent', *Harvard Business Review*, May–June (1989): p. 69.

Henzler, Herbert A., 'The new era of Eurocapitalism', *Harvard Business Review*, 70, 4 (1992): pp. 57–68.

Jacquemin, Alexis, 'The international dimension of European competition policy', *Journal of Common Market Studies*, 31, 1 (1993): pp. 91–101.

Koch, A., 'International competitiveness and the competence-based competition', *Conference Proceeding: Third International Workshop on Competence-Based Competition*, Ghent 1995.

Lorange, Peter and Johan Roos, 'Why some strategic alliances succeed and others fail', *Journal of Business Strategy*, 12, 1 (1991): pp. 25–30.

Moore, Geoffrey A., *The Death of Competition: Leadership & Strategy in The Age of Business Ecosystems*. New York: HarperBusiness, 1996.

Porter, Michael E., *The Competitive Advantage of Nations*. New York: Free Press, 1990.

Porter, Michael E., *Competitive Advantage: Creating and Sustaining Superior Performance*. New York: Free Press, 1985.

Porter, Michael E., *Competitive Strategy – Techniques for Analysing Industries and Competitors*. New York: The Free Press, 1980.

Porter, Michael E., 'What is strategy?' *Harvard Business Review*, November/December (1996): pp. 60–78.

Robert, Michel M., 'Attack competitors by changing the game rules', *Journal of Business Strategy*, 12, 5 (1991): pp. 53–56.

Rugman, Alan M. and Alain Verbeke, 'Foreign subsidiaries and multinational strategic management: an extension and correction of Porter's single diamond framework', *Management International Review*, 33, 2 (1993): pp. 71–84.

Schill, Roland L. and David N. McArthur, 'Redefining the strategic competitive unit: towards a new global marketing paradigm?' *International Marketing Review*, 34, 1 (1992): pp. 5–24.

Notes

1. Bodo Harenberg, *Harenberg Lexikon der Sprichwörter & Zitate* (Dortmund: Harenberg Kommunikation, 1997).
2. http://www.ikea.com/content/main.asp?tab=5.
3. Michael E. Porter, *The Competitive Advantage of Nations* (New York: Free Press, 1990).
4. Information Online Ltd, 'East European component developments: findings at idea forum in Budapest', *Automotive Components Analysis*, 21, 9 (1995).
5. Michael E. Porter, *The Competitive Advantage of Nations* (New York: Free Press, 1990).
6. Reed Maurer, 'How to crack the Japanese pharma market', *Marketletter*, 19 October (1998).
7. Sorcha Corcoran, 'Backs to the wall', *Life Insurance International*, August (1998): p. 12.
8. David P. Baron, 'The nonmarket strategy system', *Sloan Management Review*, 37, 1 (1995): pp. 73–85.
9. Alan M. Rugman and Alain Verbeke, 'Foreign subsidiaries and multinational strategic management: an extension and correction of Porter's single diamond framework', *Management International Review*, 33, 2 (1993): pp. 71–84.
10. Michael E. Porter, *Competitive Strategy – Techniques for Analysing Industries and Competitors* (New York: The Free Press, 1980).
11. Sylvia Dennis, 'France Telecom, Deutsche Telecom create ThinkOne joint venture', *Newsbytes News Network*, 2 December 1998.
12. Knight-Ridder, 'Global demand for light commercial vehicles tails off', *The European*, 16 November 1998.
13. Anonymous, 'State of the skin care industry in

Eastern Europe', *Drug & Cosmetic Industry*, 163, 3 (1998): pp. 20ff.

14. Shapiro Eben, 'Nutrasweet's race with the calendar', *The New York Times*, 8 April (1992): p. C1.

15. Michael E. Porter, *Competitive Strategy – Techniques for Analysing Industries and Competitors* (New York: The Free Press, 1980).

16. Anonymous, 'BA targets premium business', *Travel Trade Gazette UK & Ireland*, 9 December 1998, p. 3.

17. Anonymous, 'Lufthansa to swing UK axe', *Travel Trade Gazette UK & Ireland*, 9 December 1998, p. 1.

18. James Ruggia, 'A new face', *Travel Agent*, 292, 11 (1998): pp. 56ff.

19. Michael E. Porter, *Competitive Strategy – Techniques for Analysing Industries and Competitors* (New York: The Free Press, 1980).

20. Anonymous, 'Kunden billig abzuholen', *Presse*, 5 October 1999, p. 21.

21. Michael Gannon, 'eBay Inc.', *Venture Capital Journal*, 1 November 1998.

22. Michael E. Porter, *Competitive Strategy – Techniques for Analysing Industries and Competitors* (New York: The Free Press, 1980).

23. Paul Needham, 'Lufthansa low-cost line will threaten Eurowings', *Travel Trade Gazette Europe*, 26 February 1998, p. 16.

24. Michael E. Porter, *Competitive Strategy – Techniques for Analysing Industries and Competitors* (New York: The Free Press, 1980).

25. Elaine X. Grant, 'Swiss skies brighten', *Travel Agent*, 291, 5 (1998): pp. 30–31.

26. Michael E. Porter, *Competitive Strategy – Techniques for Analysing Industries and Competitors* (New York: The Free Press, 1980).

27. Elaine X. Grant, 'Swiss skies brighten', *Travel Agent*, 291, 5 (1998): pp. 30–31.

28. Michael E. Porter, *Competitive Strategy – Techniques for Analysing Industries and Competitors* (New York: The Free Press, 1980).

29. Elaine X. Grant, 'Swiss skies brighten', *Travel Agent*, 291, 5 (1998): pp. 30–31.

30. Michael E. Porter, *Competitive Strategy – Techniques for Analysing Industries and Competitors* (New York: The Free Press, 1980).

31. George Day, *Market Driven Strategy: Processes for Creating Value* (New York: Free Press, 1990).

32. Michael E. Porter, *The Competitive Advantage of Nations* (New York: Free Press, 1990).

33. Anonymous, 'Alliance Unichem poses threat to Gehe's position', *Newsletter*, 1 December 1997.

34. Anonymous, 'New Asian Century (2)', *Japan Chemical Week*, 8 July 1999, p. 7.

35. Graham Look, 'Portable computers enhance logistics for French courier', *Automatic ID News Europe*, 7, 8 (1998): p. 16.

36. Jared Sandberg, 'High-end audio entices music lovers', *The Wall Street Journal*, 12 February (1993): p. B1.

37. Michael E. Porter, *The Competitive Advantage of Nations* (New York: Free Press, 1990).

38. George Day, *Market Driven Strategy: Processes for Creating Value* (New York: Free Press, 1990).

39. Gary Hamel and C.K. Prahalad, 'Strategic intent', *Harvard Business Review*, May–June (1989): p. 69; Gary Hamel and C.K. Prahalad, 'The core competence of the corporation', *Harvard Business Review*, May–June (1990): pp. 79–91.

40. James Lardner, *Fast Forward. Hollywood, The Japanese and the VCR Wars* (New York: New American Library, 1987).

41. G. Hamel and C.K. Prahalad, 'Do you really have a global strategy?', *Harvard Business Review*, March–April (1985): pp. 73–93.

42. Stephen Burden, 'Current trends and issues in the retail sector', *European Venture Capital Journal*, October (1998): pp. 31ff.

43. Peter Preusser, 'Competition and the structure of the German electricity market', *Power Economics*, 2, 7 (1998): pp. 23ff.

44. Richard D'Aveni, *Hypercompetition: Managing the Dynamics of Strategic Maneuvering* (New York: Free Press, 1994).

45. Peter Drucker, *On the Profession of Management* (Boston, MA: Harvard Business School Publishing, 1988).

46. Michael E. Porter, *The Competitive Advantage of Nations* (New York: Free Press, 1990).

47. Michael E. Porter, *Competitive Strategy – Techniques for Analysing Industries and Competitors* (New York: The Free Press, 1980).

48. Michael E. Porter, *The Competitive Advantage of Nations* (New York: Free Press, 1990).

49. George Day, *Market Driven Strategy: Processes for Creating Value* (New York: Free Press, 1990).

50. Michael E. Porter, *Competitive Strategy – Techniques for Analysing Industries and Competitiors* (New York: The Free Press, 1980).

51. Richard D'Aveni, *Hypercompetition: Managing the Dynamics of Strategic Maneuvering* (New York: Free Press, 1994).

Czech beer goes world-wide

Let us take the example of the most successful brand of Czech beer (from the daily *Hospodarske Noviny,* 24 September 1997): Budvar has nearly doubled its production in the last few years. The Budejovice brewery received the Giovanni Marcora international prize from the European Union.

Ceske Budejovice (Budweiser) – in four years Budweiser Budvar nearly doubled its production from 590,000 hectolitres (hl) in 1992 to 1.026 million hl in 1996. Exports of beer in this period grew from 362,000 to 495,000 hl. In the first half of 1997, the brewery produced 531,710 hl of beer, which is 6.2 per cent more than the same period in 1996. Its export represented a growth of 12.9 per cent. In total, in 1997 Budvar sold about 600,000 hl of beer abroad from an anticipated production of 1.150 million hl. In six months of 1997 sales rose by CZK936 million (about €17 million), which is 17.8 per cent more than in the same period in 1996. The profit increased by about CZK240 million.

Economic manager of the Ceske Budejovice brewery Petr Jansky considers the growth of exports a permanent feature, in spite of the fact that the European beer market is oversaturated. At the beginning of the 1990s, the company exported to 18 countries, but by 1997 the figure was 48 countries. Jansky predicted that by the end of that year (1997), the number of countries would reach 50. For example, the company exported 220,000 hl of beer to Germany in 1996. Among foreign brands, Budvar came in at third place directly behind the Danish brands Tuborg and Fax. Tuborg (460,000 hl), however, has most of its so-called exports executed by its own brewery in Monchengladbach. According to Jansky, it is necessary to exercise patience, because results will not be apparent immediately. 'In Britain, we are selling 100,000 hectalitres (hl) this year, whereas years ago we began with only a few thousand hl. A similar situation is taking place now in Russia. Last year we sold less than 4000 hl. This year we are selling more than 25,000 hl, and we predict that in following period it will be 100,000 hl of beer,' he said.

Jansky added that Budvar received the Giovanni Marcora prize for the year 1996, awarded by the agricultural commission of the European Union, for being the most progressive company in foodstuffs, agriculture and ecology. 'In the context of prizes which we have received in the past few years, this affair departs from the norm. The company did not get the prize – as it received prizes in previous years – for the quality of its product, but rather for the overall level of operations and dynamic progress,' said Jansky. He also called attention to the fact that only current member states of the European Union had received such an award up until then.

The production of beer has a long and illustrious history in the Czech Republic. The first brew of the 'Pilsner type', the beer which later became popular with beer drinkers world-wide as the PILS beer and which owes its name to the town of Pilsner (Plzen), was produced in that town in 1842. Since then, Czech beer of the Pilsner variety has developed a world-class reputation for superior quality. Another well-known brand was born in the country. In 1895 a joint-stock brewery – today's Budweiser Budvar – was founded in the town of Budweis (Ceske Budejovice). That company nowadays uses the internationally protected trademarks Budweiser beer and Budweiser Budvar.

Although all the ingredients for Czech world-class beer production remain (intense competition, world-class products and suppliers, and discriminating home demand), the lustre of the beer industry was tarnished by the legacy of communist rule and central planning. Central planning meant that the beer sector, in common with others, was plagued by under-investment and the uneconomic allocation of resources. Pilsner Urquell and Budvar were in fact the only products for which the central planners provided export support. Further, at the end of the 1980s, the market for Czech beer in Central and Eastern Europe (CEE) collapsed under the strain of tariffs and other protective trade barriers.

However, the Czech beer sector is in the middle of a dramatic transition and renaissance. Beer producers have made significant investments in new production equipment and technology. Marketing and distribution investments are on the rise and are increasingly important as customer needs and distribution channels change. Beer producers compete with each other for domestic market share. Competitive pressure will intensify. During this industry turmoil, some beer producers have been attaining positions of export leadership while others are forced to leave the market.

Profitability throughout the sector has been negatively affected by a shift away from premium beer, stagnation in domestic sales, artificially low prices and low levels of exports. Fierce competition, low operating margins, and trade barriers have compelled breweries to reduce costs and build a low-cost production base. Ironically, the difficult competitive environment has made Czech beer producers internationally price-competitive. In addition, low industry profitability since privatisation has forced breweries to restructure. Continued industry restructuring and consolidation are anticipated. It will become increasingly harder for small and medium-sized breweries to remain in business and it is anticipated that consolidation will accelerate to finish around the millennium.

In 1996, production of beer in the Czech Republic was 18.24 million hl. Total domestic consumption was more than 16.5 million hl and exports stood at 1.8 million hl. The six largest companies produced more than 12.7 million of beer, accounting for 69.8 per cent of total domestic capacity. Products from the largest breweries took 67.4 per cent of domestic consumption. Their share of Czech exports was 92 per cent.

The Czech Republic still has the world's highest per capita consumption of beer (160 litres per year). Table 1 compares consumption in several countries. The data show that, although countries such as Denmark and Germany also have high per capita beer consumption, they cannot rival the Czech Republic! Some countries such as China and Italy have extremely low consumption by any standards.

It is predicted that overall domestic consumption will stagnate and/or gradually decline following changes in lifestyle in the coming years. In addition, potential consumers with improving purchasing power may shift from standard to premium beers and the shift to this heavier and more expensive version will not necessarily lead to higher consumption levels. Lower class, low-income consumers will most likely continue to prefer cheap beers, as they will remain highly price-sensitive. Czechs drink most beer at weekends, but overall beer consumption is still relatively high on workdays. Approximately 50 per cent of adults (over 18 years) drink more than one beer (0.5 litres) a day.

Three big breweries have export potential: Budweiser Budvar, Pilsner Urquell and Prague Breweries, the last of which has a strong foreign investor (it has had a joint venture with UK Bass since 1994). The export figures for Czech beers grow every year. Budweiser Budvar is the largest exporter. It increased its exports for the first six months of 1997 by 13 per cent over the same period in 1996. Pilsner Urquell also registered an increase in exports, and its goal is to regularly increase its yearly exports by roughly a fifth. Finally, Prague Breweries are the fastest growing exporter in the Czech Republic, with growth of 23 per cent per annum, owing in particular to its support from Bass (Table 2).

Looking at Czech beers in foreign markets, we can also see expansion. In the German market, for example, according to data compiled by the Union of German Breweries, the most successful foreign brand was Tuborg (Denmark) with 460,000 hl, followed by Fax (Denmark) and Budvar, both with 220,000 hl. Pilsner Urquell and Staropramen (a brand from Prague Breweries) both had 60,000 hl and tied in eighth place. Total imports of beer into Germany increased in 1996 against the previous year by 7 per cent, and according to exporters it could attain up to 10 per cent of total consumption. Nevertheless there is a common problem for all exporters: the strong brand loyalty of local consumers in beer segments, which is demonstrated in Table 3.

Table 1 Average annual per capita beer consumption in selected countries, 1998

	(Litres)
Czech Republic	160
Germany	137
Denmark	125
UK	101
Italy	25
China	12

Source: Bass 1998.

Table 2 Export volumes by groups in 1997

	(Hectolitres)
Budweiser Budvar	540,262
Pilsner Urquell	457,871
Prague Breweries	419,239

Source: Prague Breweries 1998.

Table 3 Imported beers as a percentage of total local consumption in selected countries

	1996	*1998**	*2000**
Belgium	5.6	5.9	6.0
Czech Republic	0.4	0.4	0.4
Hungary	1.9	1.8	2.4
Germany	2.8	3.5	4.2
Poland	0.5	0.4	0.9
Austria	4.8	5.2	5.6
Slovakia	13.2	9.6	9.3

* Estimate
Source: Canodead Ltd in *Hospodarske Noviny*, 17 February 1998.

Table 3 shows the small proportion of beer imported in the large traditional markets. One way of dealing with this is to enter new markets and Czech breweries consider Russia a (good) prospective market. It is one of the biggest consumers of hard alcohol in the world – but perhaps they can be persuaded to drink beer. Consumers still prefer vodka but it is predicted that little by little new consumption habits will assert themselves, and there is evidence of a slight switch to light alcohol drinks. This could mean a great opportunity for Czech beers.

Czech beer prices when compared internationally are extremely low. Those low prices are artificial – another legacy of the planned system. Up to now price increases implemented by brewers have been below inflation (currently around 10 per cent per year). This is changing, however: in 1998, an annual price hike of up to 3 per cent or more over inflation was expected.

Since the Velvet Revolution, the Czech brewing sector has generally underperformed with respect to exports. However, we have seen a strong recovery in sales to the traditional CEE markets. Experts give a conservative forecast of an average annual export growth rate of at least 10 per cent through the year 2000, when exports should reach 3–6 million hectolitres. Figure 1 shows export destinations for Czech beer in 1996.

The use of exporting as an entry strategy for beer can be complicated by trade barriers (tariffs, taxes on consumption, quotas, etc.). The Slovak government has, for example, introduced quotas for imports of Czech beers in order to protect their local producers. This means Czech breweries will need to use techniques other than traditional sales methods in order to emerge in foreign markets. An article from the daily *MF Dues* (12 September 1997) shows they intend to do this.

Figure 1 Where did Czech breweries export to in 1996?

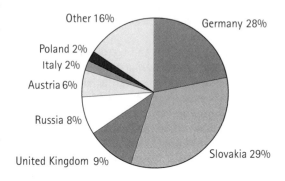

Source: *Vyzkumy ustav pivovarsky a sladarsky,* 1997.

BREWERIES WANT TO EXPAND PRODUCTION ABROAD

Thanks to their extraordinary success in the past few years, the strongest domestic breweries will begin to produce their own brands directly in foreign countries. This route is led by Pilsner Urquell, though even Budweiser Budvar is thinking about moving its breweries abroad. (Budvar was the largest exporter in 1997.) Breweries at least partly want to move away from the trade barriers that restrict imports of beer to, for example, Slovakia or Russia.

'Originally, we were proud that Budvar would produce only in (the city of) Ceske Budejovice (Budweiser). Now, however, we are thinking about selling the brewing licence abroad,' said Robert Chart, sales director of the Budweiser Company.

Pilsner Urquell already has experience with producing beer abroad. In July 1997 it began licensing the production of its Gambrinus brand in the Lithuanaian brewery Ragutis. The company is preparing a similar project in Saransko (Russia) and in Zlaty Bazant (Slovakia). Pilsner Urquell even looks to the South American markets.

The Pilsner brewery, which exports approximately one-tenth of production, believes in a further reinforcement of its positions abroad through a connection with the second domestic brewery Radegast. Nomura, which is trying to enter these two companies, intends export expansion for both into the eastern market.

Prague Breweries will also make use of a connection with a foreign partner. The British brewery concern Bass, which is its majority shareholder, is establishing the beers Staropramen and Vratislavice in the British Isles. For example, Vratislavice 12º, under the name

Czech Lager, is currently available in all Tesco super-markets. Staropramen entered the British market in 1993 thanks to Bass, and since that time sales have grown continuously. Last year, for example, roughly 40,000 hl of Smichov beer was sold in the UK.

'In the first six months of this year, the sales of Staropramen in Great Britain grew 23 per cent against the same period last year,' said Prague Breweries spokeswoman Diana Dobálová (*MF Dues*, September 1997).

Discussion questions

1 What are the main arguments of Czech brewers for foreign market entry?

2 Analyse the market environment for breweries in your country; describe existing competitor positions. Draw a perceptual map.

3 Find an ideal position for a Czech brand, define the proper marketing strategy, and outline the marketing plan to reach that position.

4 Define the key success factors for the new entrant, and recommend the mode of entry for Czech breweries.

Source: Phillips, C., Pruyn, A. and Kestemenot, M.P., *Understanding Marketing, A European Casebook* (Wiley, 2000).

Norsk Hydro fertilisers in the US: entering a highly competitive market

Case A: 1970–1975

At the beginning of 1970, the sales manager of Norsk Hydro felt an urgent need for more efficient marketing of calcium nitrate in the United States. A preliminary market appraisal indicated a considerable potential for growth, while sales had been stagnating for several years. Contacts with farmers and marketing channels had revealed unsatisfactory knowledge of the Hydro company, its agents and the 'Viking Ship' brand. The problem required high priority, as stocks of calcium nitrate were piling up and the US was the main market for it.

In case A, a study of the market potential, the US marketing practices and the agent's mode of operation is presented as the background for discussing choice of market representation and distribution network, and choice of promotional programme.

COMPANY BACKGROUND

Norsk Hydro was founded in 1905 for the purpose of producing and selling fertilisers. The basic idea was to use inexpensive hydro-electric power from Norwegian waterfalls to bind nitrogen from the air. A leading businessman in Oslo, Sam Eyde, had established contacts with scientists in several countries, especially with Professor Kristian Birkeland in Trondheim. Working on an idea from a British scientist, they developed a process which seemed promising for large-scale industrial production. Capital was provided from Sweden, Germany and France and technological support was found, mainly in Germany.

Through times of severe competition, international over-capacity, conflicts with capital owners, two world wars etc., Hydro matured into the leading industrial enterprise in Norway. Particularly since 1950, Hydro had tried to diversify into new fields. One line of thought was to look for products where the cheap electric power could continue to form a competitive edge, for instance in the production of aluminium and magnesium. Another line pointed towards employment of the general chemical know-how which had been accumulated, for instance in the production of plastics.

In the 1960s, Hydro joined the search for oil in the North Sea with remarkable success, which in turn led the company into the petrochemical industry.

By this stage Hydro had acquired a strategic importance for Norway, and the state bought up a majority shareholding, a significant portion of which was owned in France at the time.

DIVISIONAL BACKGROUND

Throughout the years when fertilisers were its main field of activity, Hydro had a function-oriented organisation. The new ventures were handled by project

357

groups directly responsible to the top management. As the new activities grew in size and complexity, drastic organisational changes were needed. In 1965 it was decided to develop a divisionalised structure in which each product group should be run as a business on its own within general frameworks established by a central management committee assisted by a limited staff of specialists.

The fertilisers were combined with feedstuff and other agricultural products into a 'Nitrogen Division'. Around 1970, the N-division was still the company's main breadwinner. The production of fertilisers took place in several locations along the Norwegian coast and in Telemark. Hydro had also ventured into production investments in other countries, notably in Qatar, and this was looked upon as a promising line of expansion.

The sales of the N-division were organised on a regional basis with five sales areas. The three most important were Norway, Denmark and Sweden. They were all looked upon as parts of the home market and absorbed around 80 per cent of the sales. The remaining two sales areas were markets beyond Suez and Rest-Europe/USA.

EXPORT BACKGROUND

From the start, Hydro had been oriented towards international markets. The scale of investment and production exceeded by far the market potential in Norway alone. However, fertilisers turned out to be problematic to sell internationally. Most countries wanted their own production facilities and there had been periods of severe overcapacity. In times of war fertilisers were considered strategic goods, and political interests had to be taken into account. Fertilisers also proved to be very sensitive to fluctuating business cycles.

For these and other reasons, the main producers in Western Europe established vehicles for 'sales collaboration'. Vis-à-vis countries with centralised buying they tried to bargain as a group; in other cases they tried to reduce costs by coordinating stocks, transport, etc. Such collaboration was regulated by long-term agreements which secured participants a market share, but prevented expansion of the more dynamic firms.

The US market was somewhat different, giving more scope for active business. American farmers had increased their use of fertilisers year by year and in several periods the local production capacity had been insufficient. Some kinds of fertilisers were not produced locally at all, for instance calcium nitrate. In general, agricultural equipment was marketed in a 'modern' way with emphasis on product innovation and active promotion through a variety of channels and media.

PRODUCT BACKGROUND

The Nordic markets mainly demanded a so-called 'complex fertiliser' which combined nutritional chemicals, for instance nitrogen, phosphorus and potassium. Such a product was expensive to buy, but gave good results and saved labour costs. Production followed the so-called 'Odda Process', an important characteristic of which was that it yielded considerable quantities of calcium nitrate as a by-product. In fact, the profitability of fertiliser production was to some extent dependent on good prices for this by-product.

For many years, calcium nitrate had found a good market in the Nordic countries. However, demand had declined and stocks had been piling up. There was a possibility of converting calcium nitrate into other types of fertilisers, but this would require considerable investments, increase production costs and take at least one or two years.

Calcium nitrate was a relatively simple type of fertiliser with limestone as its main ingredient. Research in many countries had proved it to have several valuable effects. The quality of the soil could be improved by modifying its chemical characteristics, making it more porous and helping the diffusion of humidity. As to effects on the crop, calcium nitrate could, under favourable conditions, increase the volume almost as much as the 'complex fertiliser'. It could also prevent plant diseases that resulted in brown leaves, spotted fruits, harsh taste etc.

A rather similar type of fertiliser was the so-called Chile saltpetre, taken from natural deposits in South America. However, there was a crucial difference: instead of calcium, it had sodium as its main base and research reports had indicated that this gave less beneficial effects, especially on the quality of the soil.

MARKETING IN THE US

Exports of fertilisers to the US started in 1947 through an agent called Wilson & Geo. Meyer & Co (WGM) in San Francisco. WGM had been selling chemicals on the West Coast since 1850. They had concentrated on what they called chemical specialties, mainly to farmers. WGM pointed out to the Hydro management that fertilisers could be transported by ship from

Norway cheaply enough to be competitive, at least in central coastal areas. Hydro decided to test the idea and a rather loose agreement was set up, covering calcium nitrate for the western regions.

WGM impressed Hydro with their active marketing. WGM represented eight to ten manufacturing firms (no direct competitors to Hydro) and seemed to have well-planned sales cycles for each of them. They developed their sales force to ten well-trained salesmen who visited wholesalers and retailers regularly and also, when time permitted, farmers and their organisations. The internal administration and the physical distribution of goods seemed to function well (50 people). Since 1964 the turnover had been relatively stable, around 30,000 tons of calcium nitrate per year. Hydro represented around 40 per cent of the total WGM turnover.

On the East Coast, selling had started in 1968 through Hydro's own New York office. Because of limited staff, most of the selling was done by local agents in the major agricultural regions. However, modest results had been achieved (around 6,000 tons per year) and several agents had been replaced. WGM had aired an interest in taking charge of the East Coast as well, and to try this idea they might take over Florida.

A preliminary market study, carried out by the New York office, indicated a potential of 150,000 tons of calcium nitrate in the WGM areas. There was no US production as the manufacturers had chosen other types of fertilisers and other processes than Hydro. The main competitor was undoubtedly the Chile saltpetre which for 30 years had been established under the 'Bulldog' brand. The annual imports of Chile saltpetre to the US were around 300,000 tons per year.

WGM'S PROMOTIONAL EFFORTS

For the first 20 years, WGM had operated very independently. After all, the exports of calcium nitrate to the US were not a major issue for Hydro, and its limited marketing staff had other things to look after. WGM had developed a philosophy whereby they selected specialised market segments with limited competition and tried to build up strong positions there. For calcium nitrate, they had concentrated on farmers who had vegetables, fruit or tobacco as their main fields of activity.

WGM asserted that selling a fertiliser was in many ways 'a brand operation', where preferences had to be built up amongst the final consumers. The strong position of the Bulldog brand seemed to support this

view. WGM had chosen the name 'Viking Ship', which corresponded to the visual symbol of the Hydro company. The full product name was 'Viking Ship Calcium Nitrate'. In all printed material, Hydro was referred to as manufacturer and WGM as distributor.

In order to build up brand awareness and preference, several media were used. The main medium was professional magazines for farmers, especially those who claimed readership amongst growers of vegetables, fruit and tobacco. During the seasons, whole-page advertisements were inserted in almost every issue of the three major magazines. Local radio was also an important medium, and short messages were broadcast in evening hours when farmers were known to be listening.

WGM had also prepared colourful pamphlets and display material which were mainly distributed through the salesmen and their contacts. The salesmen were instructed to be active personal advocates for the WGM products vis-à-vis trade channels, and at regular sales conferences they were briefed by their sales manager on the latest product news.

As to the content of the advertising, WGM had tried to develop a short and clear message about the Hydro fertiliser. Farmers were known to spend limited time reading their magazines. They had modest educational backgrounds and were reported to shun complicated technical information.

The cost of promotion had to be covered by WGM's agent commission. WGM had complained that this gave little scope for active marketing. They had indicated that either the commission would have to be raised or Hydro would have to pay an advertising allowance. However, according to the contract, Hydro found that WGM were responsible for all sales activities. Within the Hydro management there had also been aired doubts 'whether fertilisers should really be sold as soap'.

A major problem for WGM representatives had been to secure a free flow of goods through the distribution channels. American manufacturers of fertilisers etc. had gained a considerable influence over wholesalers and retailers through long-term loans. For this reason, and because the Viking Ship fertiliser was a small product, the dealers were reluctant to stock it regularly in sufficient quantities. WGM representatives had to work hard to keep up a kind of 'transit sales', helping the dealers to deliver goods which had already been ordered by the farmers. The salesmen had reported less problems with this in areas where advertising had been concentrated.

MARKETING INFORMATION

Throughout his 15 years with Hydro, Sales Manager Hans Hansen had been in sporadic contact with the US market. Only since the divisionalisation in 1965, however, had he been able to concentrate a major part of his attention on this market. He had visited WGM several times for shorter periods. In tune with the company's greater interest for mercantile functions, Hansen wanted to develop a deeper understanding of the US operation. Hansen was himself trained as a sales analyst and administrator and felt the need for more agricultural competence in his staff. A young agriculturist, Jens Jensen, was appointed in 1969 and after a briefing period he was sent to the US for three months. His task was to make a study of the fertiliser market in general and Hydro's position in particular. Jensen travelled with WGM's representatives, but also made extensive contacts on his own, especially with those engaged in agriculture.

As to the farmers, Jensen found that the knowledge of Hydro and its calcium nitrate was very low. The Viking Ship brand was considered a rather one-sided source of nitrogen, and nitrogen could be acquired more cheaply through urea. Farmers who were better informed preferred Chile saltpetre because they knew it so well and felt they could trust it. Jensen had also received several complaints against Hydro's fertiliser because of hygroscopicity/clotting under open air stocking. There were also complaints about blocking of tubes and nozzles, probably because of insufficient cleaning.

The trade channels were better informed through personal contacts with WGM representatives. However, they showed little motivation for passing their information on to the farmers. It seemed fairly obvious that the dealers gave preferential treatment to American products. And after all, who were WGM and Hydro? What did Vikings from the cold north know about farming in the US? Besides, was there any incentive in promoting the Viking Ship brand? If you succeeded in building sales for such an unknown brand, somebody else would immediately cut prices and reap the benefits. Moreover, WGM quoted the same prices to everybody. Shouldn't there be some extras for dealers who really intended to promote the brand and bought large quantities?

As to professional groups (researchers, teachers, consultants, advisors etc.), Jensen was welcomed both in universities and farmers' organisations. He felt that they spoke the same language and that he could bring news from European agriculture. In fact, he got the impression that there was little contact amongst the US groups and that he could – in a small way – help to bridge information gaps. Jensen found several reports on calcium nitrate, partly unpublished, which coincided with Hydro's own findings. However, this type of fertiliser was considered fairly unimportant and it seemed low in priority for research funding. Publishing alternatives seemed limited, and the researchers were not interested in writing popular stuff for the farmers' magazines.

Jensen confirmed the preliminary estimate of the sales potential, but asserted strongly that a major sales increase would need a drastic change in people's knowledge of and attitudes towards the product.

Discussion questions

1 Should Hydro's fertiliser business on the US West Coast be continued?

2 Supposing that exports of calcium nitrate to small and specialised farmers were to be continued, what market representation and distribution network should be developed?

3 What should a promotional programme targeting the West Coast farmers look like?

Source: Larsen, H.H., *Cases in Marketing*, Sage Publishers, 1997.

Case B: 1980–1995

From Case A we know the start-up problems facing the firm on the US West Coast during the 1970s. We shall now re-enter the US fertiliser scene and discuss Hydro's strategic challenges from 1980 onwards. For each major challenge, the market background and Hydro's choices will be briefly described. We deliber-ately avoid details, as the teaching objective is to focus on the strategic essence of a firm's long-term internationalisation.

At the Hydro headquarters, people were generally pleased in 1993. During the past 20 years, Hydro had grown from a marginal exporter to become one of the larger suppliers of fertilisers to the North American market. At this point, Gerd Petersen, who had been with the company for ten years, was asked to review and analyse the development of Hydro's activities in this market so far. What was done well? What could have been done differently? The company was also interested in an assessment of Hydro's current position in this market. Were there other ways to organise the company's activities in the United States? Should one make changes in the current position and what, if anything, should be done for the future? The management wanted a thorough analysis of the wisdom of past decisions, and how to proceed for further growth for the future.

Gerd tried to envisage what alternative options Hydro had at each stage. She needed to discuss the pros and cons and try to see the rationale behind Hydro's decisions. To support her evaluation, Gerd consulted what her textbooks had to say about the firm's process of internationalisation. She also sought examples from local firms which might confirm or challenge Hydro's pattern of decisions. Gerd knew that the management were considering her for a top management position and the outcome of this decision was partly riding on her analysis and recommendations.

She realised that she did not have all the information she needed in order to make her analysis complete, but for now she would do her best with what she had and make a list of the items about which she would have to seek out additional information, at some point in the future.

EXPANSION OF THE WEST COAST OPERATION

During the 1970s, the West Coast operation was turned into a success. The market potential of 150,000 tons of calcium nitrate was efficiently tapped, and both sales income and profits grew. Distribution channels were developed and motivated through better information, training, delivery services etc. A new pricing and rebate system made it more worthwhile to distribute the Viking Ship products.

As to marketing communication with end users – the small and specialised farmers – a protracted disagreement between Hydro and the San Francisco agent (WGM) caused advertising to fluctuate between scientific documentation and emotional messages. The Viking Ship name and symbol were heavily criticised but had to be kept because of Hydro's global investments in this 'branding' policy. In spite of the marketing success, Hydro felt that one major issue

remained unsolved – their rather weak control of long-term strategy, marketing planning/implementation and client feedback. WGM was certainly cooperative, but had other product markets to look after. Around 1970, Hydro had approached the agent about the possibility of their buying a share of WGM, say around 50 per cent. The proposition was turned down flatly by Mr G. Meyer: 'I opened the profitable US market for you over 20 years ago, and now you try to outmanoeuvre me. Instead, you should show some appreciation by letting my firm cover our target groups all over the US!'

In fact, Hydro had contemplated doing just that. Apart from the control aspect, they felt that the West Coast operation had developed into a highly professional marketing set-up with a deep understanding of US farming, distribution channels, competition and marketing practices.

Gradually, WGM's attitude towards joint ownership turned more positive. People on both sides got to know each other better. Mr G. Meyers was growing older, his sons had been trained by Hydro in Norway and could more easily see that a partial Hydro takeover could have positive effects both professionally and for the WGM owners.

Finally, in 1985 an agreement was reached whereby Hydro took over 50 per cent of the shares in WGM. A new, professional board was elected, comprising both WGM and Hydro representatives together with local business people with relevant experience from US marketing.

The new company retained the WGM name, to capitalise on its goodwill in the agribusiness world. (Internally, the term 'Hydro/WGM' was used to remind everybody of the change.) Now the road was open for WGM to expand to other regions of the US. Some changes had to be made in WGM's portfolio of non-Hydro products. This was by far outweighed by the expansion of Hydro sales.

In all new regions, WGM's 'classical' marketing procedure was followed. The target groups – small and specialised farmers – were carefully studied, so were the distribution channels, and a painstaking, personal networking took place. When distribution was secured, promotion started in highly select media with proven coverage and impact on both end users and middlemen. Opinion leaders were mobilised in farmers' unions/clubs, among agricultural researchers and writers, public farming advisors etc.

Today, WGM is Hydro's undisputed, nationwide marketing organisation for small and specialised farmers. Young Hydro trainees are being 'brought up' there, to take the valuable US experience to other marketplaces. The WGM experience also plays a central part in Hydro's international 'Fertiliser Academy' discussed below.

ENTERING THE BULK FERTILISER MARKET

During the 1970s, repeated discussions had taken place at the Hydro headquarters in Oslo on the pros and cons of entering the big, 'industrial' market for fertilisers in the US. The size of this market was tempting, in fact the biggest and most professional fertiliser marketplace in the world. However, the competition was very tough indeed, both from locally produced and imported products, and margins were cut to the bone. A number of product types – other than calcium nitrate – would be requested by producers of corn, soybeans, wheat, potatoes etc. The marketing infrastructure for big, bulk deliveries would have to comprise large landing, unloading and stocking facilities in central harbours, regional distribution centres, a fleet of tank lorries etc.

It seemed fairly obvious that this type of business was outside WGM's range of resources and competence. A better option might be another type of organisation, specialised for this type of 'giant' marketing. For Hydro to start this from scratch looked rather slow and cumbersome. Quicker and more efficient might be to acquire – or cooperate with – an existing US company. But the entry ticket would in that case carry a high price and considerable risks.

The solution came in 1988 as a side effect of Hydro's European strategy. Hydro had, for a number of years, aimed at becoming a market leader in all major fertiliser arenas, first of all in Western Europe. To achieve this, Hydro had started an acquisition campaign, taking over majority positions in leading local manufacturing firms.

One of Hydro's acquisitions was Nederlandse Stikstof Maatschappij (NSM) in Terneuzen, near the Dutch/Belgian border. This company had an asset which looked particularly tempting to Hydro: a well-established marketing set-up in the US called Transnitro – specially aimed at big, industrial farming. Transnitro had an efficient head office in New York and a nationwide network for stocking/distributing large quantities of bulk fertilisers.

Of course, this asset brought the price of NSM up considerably, but Hydro found that Transnitro could give them the desired quick and efficient inroad in the US bulk market. And from day one they would be

in the driver's seat, controlling strategy, marketing planning/implementation and client contact and feedback. This might also enhance Hydro's global competitiveness, for instance by sharpening its ability to operate in markets with really tough rivalry and small profit margins.

The takeover was implemented rather quickly, building on the existing management cadres and their relationship with NSM. Some Hydro officials were gradually introduced in the set-up to promote a stepwise merging of Transnitro into the Hydro world.

Today, therefore, Hydro covers the important US fertiliser market with two wholly owned marketing organisations: WGM for specialised farming, where fertilisers are bought in smaller quantities; and Transnitro for large, industrial farming, where fertilisers are bought in bulk.

Thus, marketing was well taken care of, based on products imported from Europe. But other strategic issues were waiting around the corner . . .

DIRECT INVESTMENT IN LOCAL PRODUCTION?

When Hydro started their internationalisation, the production of fertilisers was localised in Norway and based on the use of hydroelectric power. During the post-war years, however, a number of competitive forces had changed.

- New technology had made the use of hydroelectricity less decisive.
- Production costs had been lowered and transportation costs had become relatively more important.
- Market integration, like the EU, had made foreign ownership of industrial plants more acceptable.
- Political attitudes in many countries favoured local production of 'strategic' goods like fertilisers.

Hydro's first move towards international relocation took place around 1970. The Arab countries had gained power and wealth via OPEC and were seeking investments which could increase their inhabitants' welfare in the long term. The sheikdom of Qatar wanted to develop fertiliser production in a joint venture with a Western firm, and Hydro was chosen as partner.

Despite political risk, strain on management capacity etc., Hydro took the challenge. They found the Qatar operation interesting *per se,* and saw it also as a future supplier of markets east of Suez. It could also offer good training for personnel, useful for further international moves.

The pioneering Qatar establishment gave good results and sharpened Hydro's appetite for foreign direct investments. Gradually, a strategy emerged where Hydro was seen as the world's largest producer and exporter of fertilisers. They decided to invest heavily in a global network of production and marketing units, and saw acquisition of foreign companies and plants as the main mode of operation.

The strategy was first implemented in Western Europe. Companies and factories were bought in major markets like the UK, France, Germany and the Netherlands (NSM). As mentioned above, the latter was of particular importance for the US, because of its bulk marketing set-up there for 'industrial farming' (Transnitro).

Around 1990, the question of having production facilities in the US became rather pressing. The two marketing organisations there functioned well and sold record volumes every year. Efficient deliveries were difficult to achieve based only on large transatlantic shipments. With increasing tonnage coming in, the landing/unloading and stocking capacity might have to be expanded. Last, but not least, clients still showed some preference for US-made products.

Hydro considered several alternatives for the start-up of fertiliser production in the US. A green-field establishment might mobilise the latest achievements in Hydro's production technology. A quicker solution might be to acquire one of the existing operators an the US market. Systematic searching for candidates was carried through according to requirements such as size, location, technology, environmental issues, profitability, market reputation, management resources etc.

Gradually, the search zoomed in on one of the US's largest regional, cooperative groups – Farmland Industries – with headquarters in Kansas City. Farmland had an annual turnover of US$3.5–4 billions in terms of fertilisers, oil products, feedstuff and food articles in 19 states. Farmland's production facilities were located in Green Bay, Florida. They had been built around 1970 and had later undergone considerable modernisation. Thereby, some environmental problems had been reduced or eliminated.

Negotiations led to a joint venture agreement whereby Hydro bought a 50 per cent share in Farmland's fertiliser plant. Farmland would run the production, while Hydro would do the marketing. Of special importance for Hydro was the fact that Farmland's products were phosphate-based, supplementing Hydro's nitrogen-based products, thereby covering a wider range of client needs. Hydro also gained access to natural deposits of phosphate close to Green Bay.

COORDINATION OF US FERTILISER BUSINESS

We have now seen how Hydro's US fertiliser business developed over 45 years to the point where it covered both large and small farming operations

- in most US states
- with a wide range of products
- distributed through many channels
- by many organisational units
- located in diverse areas
- with varying degrees of overlapping
- and interdependent activities.

This complex situation, rather typical for firms diversifying and going international, called for measures that could foster better coordination and efficiency.

Top management of Hydro's world-wide businesses (fertilisers, light metals, oil and gas etc.) were located in Oslo. The basic idea was to have a lean, tightly knit management team to draw up global policies and structures, and leave as much as possible of the operative business to the substructures of the company. The main substructures were product group divisions with global responsibility. The divisional top management was also located in Oslo, to secure close contact between all sectors on the general management level.

The product group divisions were subdivided in various ways. For instance, the Aluminium Division was subdivided according to the further refinement of the metal: one subdivision looked after the rolling into plates for packaging etc., another was responsible for extrusion into building products etc., while a third worked with machining into car equipment etc. The aluminium extrusion business had developed a new organisational structure to promote better international market orientation: its headquarters had been moved out of Norway to Lausanne in Switzerland. From there, the top management could stay in close, personal touch with the operating units all over Europe. It was also easier to recruit top international businessmen to Lausanne than to Oslo, thus developing a highly competent milieu which might also be used for training young, aspiring internationalists.

Against this background, Hydro discussed the build-up of the agribusiness. The Nordic and West

European markets were still dominant, and represented a 'home' market; other markets were grouped under the term 'Hydro Agri International'. The top management should remain in Oslo, and delegation should be achieved through a geographic/regional subdivision.

One of these was to be 'Hydro Agri North America', HANA for short. HANA should report to Hydro Agri International in Oslo on major, strategic issues, but be responsible for all aspects/functions of the operational business (sourcing/production, logistics, marketing, administration etc.). HANA's headquarters was located to Tampa, Florida. Its first general manager was a Norwegian with wide experience from agribusiness in many parts of the world. Most of the staff, however, were recruited in the US, mainly from Hydro's units there, to secure two-way cultural understanding and market orientation.

From the start, HANA had more than enough to look after: the two marketing organisations, WGM and Transnitro, had to be streamlined and trained to cover new products from Farmland and others. Hydro's entry into production and other types of sourcing required better logistics. Operating within a joint venture also called for top management attention.

Thus, a new structure for better US agribusiness coordination gradually emerged. It was supplemented with management development efforts, both centrally and locally. The central Oslo management started the 'Hydro Fertiliser Academy' with the aim of offering teaching programmes for the commercial side of the business. People from all parts of the world could be selected for training, as well as agents and their representatives.

FUTURE HQ–SUBSIDIARY RELATIONSHIPS

Textbooks tend to give limited attention to the development of the HQ–subsidiary relationship. However, this is an extremely important aspect of the process of internationalisation. Lack of fit between 'foreign' activities and 'home' strategy and structure often creates problems, conflicts and retarded international expansion.

Without pretending a generally valid description of an 'unhealthy' development, we shall point at some risks. First, let us look at the HQ.

- The home top management tend to keep the reins too tight. They are sceptical towards the local (provincial?) managers 'out there'. Do they really have a holistic view of the company or division?

Can they be trusted not to indulge in some crazy local activity, contradicting central policy?

- As a compromise between centralisation and delegation to operating units, a regional 'sub-headquarters' may be established for groups of markets which are geographically/culturally/commercially related. But still, the 'home' HQ feels that it must be in control and asks for all kinds of reporting and even inspection. An unofficial, dual management network may develop, creating confusion, obstruction and loss of efficiency.

- Another compromise is for the home HQ to delegate in the line relationships, and develop central service and advisory staffs to be drawn upon by the subsidiaries. If these staffs are clever enough always to be in front with respect to, for instance, marketing issues, they may be respected and listened to. If not, they may represent a source of irritation, bureaucracy and unnecessary costs.

Turning now to the subsidiaries, many dangers are lurking under the surface even there:

- When the subsidiaries are newly established, they tend to be very obedient. They owe everything to the home HQ – resources, competence, technology, management systems etc. Often, the first subsidiary managers are recruited from the home base, and bring with them the rules of good behaviour from there – even if they need not be locally palatable.

- As subsidiaries mature, they tend to develop 'teenager' opposition: 'Back home, they don't really trust us. They doubt whether we really understand the world (our market) and can do sensible planning on our own. They question our economic responsibility, and show irritation every time we need fresh capital.'

- At a later stage, 'home' managers may be replaced by locally recruited people. The teenager opposition may now be strengthened by cultural misconceptions. In the local business milieu, it may be degrading to receive too much instruction from the HQ, especially if that instruction comes from someone lower in the hierarchy like a sales manager, not to mention a subordinate staff person. This may be a threat to a desired macho image, and contacts homewards may therefore be minimised.

Gerd Petersen thought these descriptions were somewhat caricatured. But, she did see how perceived power bases change along with the process of internationalisation. She realised that she needed to take another look at the HQ–subsidiary relationship, among other things. It was not an easy task that Gerd had been given. Many things had happened over the past several years, and the information available to her was not complete. But, eager to meet the challenge and hoping for a promotion, she set out to do her analysis of the past, the present and the future for Hydro in the United States. With hard work and some luck, she also hoped for a future as head of Hydro's US operations . . .

Discussion questions

1 Should Hydro aim also at the big 'industrial' farmers, buying fertilisers in bulk, and should they build market position from scratch or buy themselves into an existing sales and distribution set-up?

2 At what stage should Hydro go into production of fertilisers in the US?

3 Should Hydro choose a green-field approach or try acquisition of a US manufacturer, perhaps as a joint venture?

4 Supposing that Hydro's US fertiliser business has become big and profitable, but also highly diversified, how could better coordination be achieved?

Source: Larsen, H.H., *Cases in Marketing*, Sage Publishers, 1997.

PART V

Creating global marketing programmes

CHAPTER 11

Product and service decisions

The prospects for American car manufacturers in Europe would appear to be good if they will meet the conditions and requirements of these various countries but to attempt to do so on the lines on which business is done in America would make it a fruitless task.

JAMES COUZENS, OFFICER OF THE FORD MOTOR COMPANY, 1907

The market for IBM computers or Toshiba laptops is not defined by geographic borders but by the inherent appeal of the product to users, regardless of where they live.

KENICHI OHMAE, EX-MCKINSEY CONSULTANT, MANAGEMENT GURU & JAPANESE POLITICIAN, 1989

After reading this chapter, you will know:

- The differences between services and products as well as the strategic implications of these differences in the global marketplace.
- How global products and services differ from global brands.
- Several alternatives for positioning products and services on a global scale.
- The importance of saturation levels in global markets.
- Factors in product and service design that determine success in global marketing.
- Strategic alternatives for geographic expansion.
- Why the continuous development and introduction of new products in a global market are keys to survival and growth.

Why is this important? Here are three situations in which you would need an understanding of the above issues:

- You are entering the Asian market and need to strike a balance between the payoff from adopting products and services to local market preferences and the cost advantages that come from concentrating resources on a limited number of standardised products or services.
- Your company offers successful global products and services. These products and services, however, do not carry the same name and are positioned differently from country to country. You have to decide whether the global products and services should be turned into a global brand or not.
- You are the product manager responsible for the global launch of a new portable CD player and have to decide whether you should position the product on 'high-touch' or 'high-tech'.

Practice link

Founded by Anita Roddick, who in 1976 identified a niche in the cosmetics market for naturally-based products with minimal packaging, The Body Shop has evolved into a world-wide network of more than 1,500 retail stores in 47 countries.[1]

In 1988, the company decided to enter the $12 billion US cosmetics market. Under the direction of a British expatriate, who was previously the president of Unilever's fragrance subsidiary, 12 company-owned shops were opened on the East Coast. In mid-1990, the company began franchising, and by year's end, 37 shops had been opened.[2]

The US market, however, has never been very inviting for the company and its products. From the beginning The Body Shop had to deal with a different set of challenges. First, environmental concern, a key factor in the company's product and service offering, had been less of a public issue in the United States, and it was not certain that the company's strong brand image and unfamiliar practices would appeal to Americans. Anita Roddick was also amazed by how constrained business was in the US. The Food and Drug registrations, the various state and city regulations, and the lawyers horror stories all made Roddick nervous about her decision. Under warnings about product liability and the likelihood of litigation, she was advised not to offer a refill service in the United States. Lawyers also convinced her to drop her 'Against

Animal Testing' logo on products for fear of retribution by the cosmetics industry. Finally, The Body Shop's global success had not gone unnoticed in the cosmetics industry. Betting on the growth of the 'green consumer' population, many leading firms, such as Revlon or Esteé Lauder, were introducing 'natural' lines, and revamping the look and marketing pitch of their products.[3, 4, 5]

Selling its cosmetic products in the US market has remained a challenge for The Body Shop. In 1999 the company had to close three warehouses and 11 stores. It bought back 28 stores from franchisees, reorganised its central office and created a product and marketing team especially for the US market. As CEO, Patrick Gournay, remarked: 'Although the 1999 trading result in the USA did not meet our expectations, we have set ourselves some aggressive targets ... we are working hard to tailor our product and marketing offer to the US market.'[6]

In the following, the complexity of global product and service decisions will be discussed in detail. The chapter opens with a description of the basic concepts of products and services. Subsequently, different strategies to position products and services in the global market are outlined. In addition, important product and service design considerations are presented and strategic alternatives for geographic expansion developed. The chapter ends with a discussion of the new product and service development process in global marketing.

BASIC CONCEPT OF PRODUCTS AND SERVICES

The introduction to global product and service decisions opens with a brief review of product and service concepts. All basic concepts are fully applicable to global marketing. Additional concepts that apply specifically to global marketing are then discussed in more detail.

Products: definition and classification

What is a product? On the surface, this seems like a simple question with an obvious answer. A product can be defined in terms of its tangible, physical attributes – such things as weight, dimensions, and materials. Thus, a Volkswagen Golf could be defined as 1,169 kg of metal or plastic, measuring 4.15 m long, 1.73 m wide, and 1.43 m high. However, any description limited to physical attributes gives an incomplete account of the benefits a product provides. At a minimum, car buyers expect an automobile to provide safe, comfortable transportation, derived from physical features such as air bags and adjustable seats. However, marketers cannot ignore status, mystique and other intangible product attributes that a particular model of automobile may provide. Indeed, major segments of the auto market are developed around these intangible attributes.

Similarly, Porsche drivers get much more than basic transportation from their beloved cars. A Porsche is a lifestyle product. Even people who drive their Porsche to work are driving because it is a form of lifestyle. Clearly, there is literally a world of difference between the need served by a car to the lifestyle driver and the driver who is using the car as a form of transportation. Some companies like Porsche are focused on the lifestyle driver whereas others, like DaimlerChrysler, sell to lifestyle drivers and to the basic transportation market. Porsche is selling a social and personal experience. When one buys a Porsche, one is eligible to become a member of one of approximately 360 regionally organised Porsche Clubs world-wide. New Porsche Clubs are being founded in greater numbers which further spread a positive Porsche Club spirit through their many driving and social events.[7]

Honda is an example of an activity-based strategy company. If you can power it with a motor, Honda will make it, from 50 to 5,000cc, from a few thousand Euro to 75,000 Euro, from the transportation market in the developing world to the recreation market in any country.

A product, then, can be defined as a collection of physical, psychological and symbolic attributes that collectively yield satisfaction, or benefits, to a buyer or user.

A number of frameworks for classifying products have been developed. A frequently used classification is based on users and distinguishes between consumer and industrial goods. Both types of goods, in turn, can be further classified on the basis of other criteria, such as how they are purchased (convenience, preference, shopping and speciality goods) and their life span (durable, nondurable and disposable).[8] These and other classification frameworks developed for domestic marketing are fully applicable to global marketing.

Services: characteristics and categories

Services can be defined as intangible benefits purchased by customers that do not involve ownership. Besides being intangible, three other characteristics distinguish services from products: variability, perishability and simultaneous production and consumption.

Whereas products can be examined before purchase and be compared to competitive offerings, customers cannot feel, see, or smell services before they are purchased. For example, one will only figure out how enjoyable flying with Virgin Airlines is when actually sitting in the plane. Since services rely primarily on people to provide them, services are usually much more variable than products. One might have a flawless flight with Virgin Airlines on one occasion, but have the baggage lost the next time. Another distinction between services and products is perishability. If services are

Figure 11.1 Product–service continuum

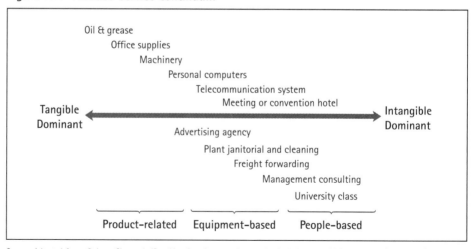

Source: Adapted from: G. Lynn Shostack, 'Breaking free from product marketing', *Journal of Marketing*, 41 (April 1997): p. 77.

not consumed when offered, they immediately go to waste. The empty seat in the airline jet cannot be stored in inventory. If it is not filled, its value is lost. Unlike products, which are produced, sold and consumed, services are often sold first, then produced and consumed simultaneously. A consumer buying an airline ticket or a movie ticket, will consume these services at the same time as they are produced.

The risks and opportunities in the global marketplace vary according to the type of service offered. Therefore, it is important to categorise services by considering a product-service continuum where the basic underlying variable is tangibility. As Donald Cowell suggests, 'What is significant about services, where they are objects being marketed, is the relative dominance of intangible attributes in the make-up of the "service product". Services are a special kind of product. They may require special understanding and special marketing efforts.'[9] Figure 11.1 illustrates the product–service continuum and further classifies services into product related, equipment-based and people-based services.

The more tangible, product-related services play a supporting role to products. Every new Volkswagen in the UK, for example, is not only covered by a three-year unlimited mileage warranty, but also by a one-year roadside assistance programme. Dell's general three-year warranty, as another example, provides free post-sale service support to purchasers of computers. In a competitive environment, service support can be the determining factor in a product's success. One talks about equipment-based services, when service is the primary offering and products play a supportive role because they are needed to deliver the service. An example is T-Online, Deutsche Telekom's Internet unit and Germany's largest Internet provider that went public in April 2000. People-based services are primary service offerings that rely on people rather than equipment for delivery. Doctors, lawyers, management consultants and university professors are typical examples. The concept of tangibility is useful for global marketers because many international offerings are composed of product and service combinations. The key task for managers is to evaluate carefully which elements of the offering dominate from the customer's point of view. The more the market offering is characterised by intangible elements, the more difficult it is to apply the standard marketing processes that were developed for products.[10]

Products and services: national, international and global

Many companies find that, as a result of expanding existing businesses or acquiring a new business, they have products or services for sale in a single national market. For example, Kraft Foods at one time found itself in the chewing-gum business in France, the ice-cream business in Brazil, and the pasta business in Italy. Although each of these unrelated businesses was, in isolation, quite profitable, the scale of each was too small to justify heavy expenditures on R&D, let alone marketing, production and financial management from international headquarters. An important question regarding any product or service is whether it has the potential for expansion into other markets. The answer will depend on the company's goals and objectives and on the assessment of the opportunities to hand.

Managers run the risk of committing two types of errors regarding product decisions in global marketing. One error is to fall victim to the 'not invented here' (NIH) syndrome, ignoring product or service decisions made by subsidiary or affiliate managers. Managers who behave in this way are essentially abandoning any effort to leverage product and service policy outside the home-country market. The other error has been to impose product or service decision policy on all affiliated companies on the assumption that what is right for customers in the home market must also be right for customers everywhere. Volkswagen has learned the consequences of this latter error. VW saw its position in the US import market erode from leader to also-ran in the 1980s. Although the company once sold more cars in the United States than all other foreign automakers combined, VW had less than a 2 per cent market share in the United States in 1990. One industry observer summed up the company's main mistake this way: 'Volkswagen has thought that what works in Germany should work in the United States.' Volkswagen opened a design studio in Los Angeles, hoping to become better attuned to the tastes of American car buyers. The New Beetle was designed in this studio and Volkswagen's imports into the US market increased by 43 per cent in 1999 and VW came back to a 4.4 per cent market share.[11, 12]

The three product and service categories in the local-to-global continuum – national, international and global – are described in the following section.

National or local products and services

A national product or service is one that, in the context of a particular company, is offered in a single national market. Sometimes national products or services appear when a global company caters to the needs and preferences of particular country markets. For example, McDonald's developed McAroni, a salad with pasta, for sale only in Sweden.

Such an example notwithstanding, there are several reasons why national products or services – even those that are quite profitable – may represent a substantial opportunity cost to a company. First, the existence of a single national business does not provide an opportunity to develop and utilise global leverage from headquarters in marketing, R&D and production. Second, the local product or service does not allow for the transfer and application of experience gained in one market to other markets. One of the major tools available to the multicountry marketer is comparative analysis. By definition, single-country marketers cannot avail themselves of this tool. A third shortcoming of single-country product or service is the lack of transferability of managerial expertise acquired in the single-product/service area. Managers who gain experience with local products or services can utilise their product experience only in the one market in which the product or service is sold. Similarly, any manager coming from outside the market in which the single product or service is sold will lack experience in the single-product/service business. For these reasons, purely local products and services should generally be viewed as less attractive than products or services with international or global potential.

International products and services

International or regional products and services are offered in multinational, regional markets. A classic international product would be the Asian product, offered throughout Asia but not in the rest of the world. An example for an Asian product is McDonald's 'Noodle Soup'. Offered in most Asian markets, it is clearly an international product. However, unlike the 'Big Mac', for example, it is not a global product.

MCC's Smart is another example of an international product. The small city-coupé is only offered in Germany, Switzerland, Austria, Italy, France, Spain, Belgium, Luxembourg and the Netherlands.

GLOBAL PERSPECTIVE

Developing a 'world car' ...

In 1993, Ford Motor launched its mid-size 'world car' Mondeo in Europe, and in the summer of 1994 the car succeeded the Ford Tempo and Mercury Topaz in the US. Mondeo was said to represent a truly international effort, a first in the history of Ford. Three different engineering centres took part: Detroit designed the V-6 engine and the automatic transmission, as well as the heating and air-conditioning units; Dunton (UK) developed the interior, the steering, the suspension, the electronics and the four-cylinder engine; and, finally, Cologne (Germany) performed the structural engineering. The project was managed by an Englishman, located in Cologne, but final responsibility rested at Ford headquarters in Dearborn, Michigan.

In all, the company spent some €3 billion on developing the new car, i.e. twice as much as was spent on the previous successes, Taurus and Sable. Also, it took some eight years, twice as long as usual, to move from initial idea to first sale. Ford had to harmonise divergent American and European engineering standards and fly hundreds of people back and forth across the Atlantic. In addition to the extreme costs of coordination, the company mentioned a number of other reasons for the high expenditures and long development time: expensive retooling and renovations at nine large factories, late changes in design and component upgrading, and expensive defects in pilot production.

Nevertheless, the development of the world car – one of the most complex global car projects ever attempted – has been a success. The Mondeo has been praised by industry experts, was awarded the 'European Car of the Year' award in 1993, and had strong sales. Ford is convinced that it is possible to create a 'universal design' for cars. According to Fritz Mayhew of Ford Motor, the differences in automobile design now are driven more by driving conditions and the way people use vehicles than by aesthetic design judgements. Designers must be aware of different uses of products, cultural conditions and product regulations, such as electrical standards and ergonomic standards, around the world.

Source: 'Will the third time be the charm?', *Forbes*, 15 July 1993, p. 54; 'Ford's $6 billion baby', *Fortune*, 28 June 1993, pp. 76–81; 'Ford's new Model T', *Financial World*, 9 November 1993, pp. 38–41; 'Enter the McFord', *The Economist*, 23 July 1994 (322); 'Ford launches its global cars', *Production*, September 1994, pp. 62–64; 'Machine dreams', *Brandweek*, 26 April 1993, pp. 16–24.

Global products and services and global brands

Global products and services are offered in global markets. They are international and multiregional. A true global product or service is offered in the Triad, in every world region, and in countries at every stage of development. Some global products or services were designed to meet the needs of a global market; others were designed to meet the needs of a national market but also, happily, meet the needs of a global market.

Note that a product or service is not a brand. For example, change management and process reengineering are a category of global service; Arthur Andersen and McKinsey are global brands. Or take portable personal sound or personal stereos: they are a category of global products; Sony is a global brand. A global brand, like a national or international brand, is a symbol about which customers have beliefs or perceptions. Many companies, including Sony, make personal stereos. Sony created the category more than 10 years ago, when it introduced the Walkman. It is important to

Table 11.1 Nissan marques in various markets

Model/ Type	Europe	North America	Japan	Latin America
A 32	Maxima QX	Infiniti I30	Cefiro	Maxima
D 21	Pickup	Nissan Truck	Datsun	Nissan Pickup
H 41	Cabstar	–	Atlas	Cabstar Atlas
S 14	200 SX	240 SX	Silvia	200SX
B 14	Sunny	Sentra Sedan	Sunny	Sentra

understand that global brands must be created by marketers; a global brand name can be used as an umbrella for introducing new products or services. Although Sony, as noted above, markets a number of local products, the company also has a stellar track record both as a global brand and a manufacturer of global products.

A global brand has a similar image, similar positioning, and is guided by the same strategic principles. However, the marketing mix for a global brand may vary from country to country. That means that the product or service, price, promotion and place (channels of distribution) may vary from country to country. Indeed, if one tracks the examples Marlboro, Coke, Sony, Mercedes and Avon one will indeed find that the marketing mix for these products varies from country to country. The Mercedes, which is exclusively a luxury car in the United States, is also a strong competitor in the taxi market in Europe. Avon, which is a premium-priced and packaged cosmetic line in Japan, is popularly priced in the rest of the world. In spite of these variations in marketing mix, each of these products is a world or global brand.

A global product or service differs from a global brand in one important respect: it does not carry the same name and image from country to country. Like the global brand, however, it is guided by the same strategic principles, is similarly positioned,

Table 11.2 Top 60 rankings of global brands

The world's top 60 brands		
1. Coca-Cola	21. Heinz	41. Colgate
2. Microsoft	22. BMW	42. Hertz
3. IBM	23. Xerox	43. IKEA
4. General Electric	24. Honda	44. Chanel
5. Ford	25. Citibank	45. BP
6. Disney	26. Dell	46. Bacardi
7. Intel	27. Budweiser	47. Burger King
8. McDonald's	28. Nike	48. Moet & Chandon
9. AT&T	29. Gap	49. Shell
10. Marlboro	30. Kelloggs	50. Rolex
11. Nokia	31. Volkswagen	51. Smirnoff
12. Mercedes	32. Pepsi-Cola	52. Heineken
13. Nescafé	33. Kleenex	53. Yahoo!
14. Hewlett-Packard	34. Wrigley's	54. Ralph Lauren
15. Gillette	35. AOL	55. Johnnie Walker
16. Kodak	36. Apple	56. Pampers
17. Ericsson	37. Louis Vuitton	57. Amazon.com
18. Sony	38. Barbie	58. Hilton
19. Amex	39. Motorola	59. Guinness
20. Toyota	40. Adidas	60. Marriott

and may have a marketing mix that varies from country to country. Whenever a company finds itself with global products or services, it faces an issue: should the global product or service be turned into a global brand? This requires that the name and image of the product or service be standardised. One of the biggest examples of this move was Nissan's decision to drop the Datsun marque in Europe and the United States and to adopt various model names for Nissan's world-wide product line. Table 11.1 shows some examples of the numerous marques that Nissan utilised prior to this decision.

Table 11.2 shows a ranking of the top 60 global brands. It was compiled by Interbrand, a leading brand consultancy, in association with Citibank to enable companies and investors to assess the contribution that brands make to the business and, ultimately, their role in delivering long-term shareholder value. A significant feature of the table is the inclusion of corporate brands – Microsoft, Disney, AT&T (second, sixth and ninth, respectively) – in the top ten, compared with product brands such as Coke or Marlboro (tenth). This reflects an increasing number of companies that view themselves more as relationship businesses than as product businesses.[13]

When an industry globalises, companies are under pressure to develop global products or services. A major driver for the globalisation of products is the cost of product R&D. As competition intensifies, companies discover that they can reduce the cost of R&D for a product by developing a global product design. Even products such as automobiles, which must meet national safety and pollution standards, are under pressure to become global: With a global product or service, companies can offer an adaptation of a global design instead of a unique national design in each country.

Mars, Inc. confronted the global brand issue with its chocolate-covered caramel bar that sold under a variety of national brand names such as Snickers in Germany or the United States and Marathon in the United Kingdom. Mars decided to transform the candy bar – a global product – into a global brand. This decision entailed some risk, such as the possibility that consumers in the United Kingdom would associate the name Snickers with knickers, the British slang for a woman's undergarment. Mars also changed the name of its successful European chocolate biscuit from Raider to Twix, the same name used in the United States. In both instances, a single brand name gives Mars the opportunity to leverage all of its product communications across national boundaries. In doing this, managers must now think globally about the positioning of Snickers and Twix, something that they were not obliged to do when the candy products were marketed under different national brand names.

Coke is arguably the quintessential global product and global brand. Coke's positioning and strategy are the same in all countries; it projects a global image of fun, good times and enjoyment. Coke is 'the real thing'. There is only one Coke. It is unique. It is a brilliant example of marketing differentiation. The essence of discrimination is to show the difference between your products and other competing products and services.

This positioning is a considerable accomplishment when considering the fact that Coke is a low/no-tech product. It is flavoured, carbonated, sweetened water in a plastic, glass or metal container. The company's strategy is to make sure that the product is within arm's reach of desire. However, the marketing mix for Coke varies. The product itself is adapted to suit local tastes; for example, Coke increases the sweetness of its beverages in the Middle East, where customers prefer a sweeter drink. Also, prices may vary to suit local competitive conditions, and the channels of distribution may differ. However, the basic, underlying, strategic principles that guide the management of the brand are the same world-wide. Only an ideologue would insist that a global product cannot be adapted to meet local preferences; certainly, no company building a global brand needs to limit itself to absolute marketing mix uniformity. The issue is not exact uniformity, but rather offering essentially the same value. As discussed in the next few chapters, other elements of the marketing mix for example, price, communications appeal and media strategy, and distribution channels may also vary.

Global marketers should systematically identify and assess opportunities for developing global brands. Creating a global brand requires a different type of marketing effort including a higher degree of up-front creative vision than that required to create one or more national brands. On the other hand, the ongoing effort to maintain brand awareness is less for a leading global brand than it is for a collection of local brands. What criteria do marketers use to decide whether to establish global brands? One expert has argued that the decision must be 'determined by bottom-up consumer-driven considerations, not by top-down manufacturer-driven business convenience'.[14] A major determinant of success will be whether the marketing effort is starting from scratch with a 'blank slate', or whether the task is to reposition or rename an existing local brand in an attempt to create a global brand. Starting with a blank slate is vastly easier than repositioning existing brands. Still, Mars and many companies have succeeded in transforming local brands into international or global brands. Today, there are thousands of global brands, and every day the list grows longer.

Key points

- Services differ from products most strongly in their intangibility, their perishability, their variability, and the fact that production and consumption are usually simultaneous.

- Products and services can be offered in a single national market, in multinational or regional markets, or in global markets.

- With a global product or service, companies can offer an adaptation of a global design instead of a unique national design in each country.

- Global brands are guided by the same strategic principles, have the same name and similar images, and generally follow a similar positioning (examples: BMW, Volvo, Coke).

POSITIONING OF PRODUCTS AND SERVICES

The positioning of products and services is a communications strategy based on the notion of mental 'space'. Positioning refers to the act of locating a brand in customers' minds over and against other products in terms of product or service attributes and benefits that the brand does and does not offer. The word, first formally used in 1969 by Ries and Trout in an article that appeared in *Industrial Marketing*, describes a strategy for 'staking out turf' or 'filling a slot' in the mind of target customers.[15]

Several general strategies have been suggested for positioning products or services: positioning by attribute or benefit, quality/price, use or application, and use/user.[16] Two additional strategies, high-tech and high-touch, have been suggested for global products.

Attribute or benefit

A frequently used positioning strategy exploits a particular product attribute, benefit, or feature. In global marketing, the fact that a product is imported can itself represent a benefit positioning. Economy, reliability and durability are other frequently used attribute/benefit positions. Volvo automobiles are known for solid construction that offer safety in the event of a crash. In the ongoing credit card wars, VISA's advertising focuses on the benefit of world-wide merchant acceptance.

Quality/price

This strategy can be thought of in terms of a continuum from high fashion/quality and high price to good value (rather than low quality) at a low price.[17] The American Express Card, for example, has traditionally been positioned as an upscale card whose prestige justifies higher annual fees than VISA or EUROCARD/MasterCard.

Use/user

Positioning can also be achieved by describing how a product or service is used or associating a product or service with a user or class of users the same way in every market. For example, Benetton uses the same positioning for its clothing when it targets the global youth market. Marlboro's extraordinary success as a global brand is due in part to the product's association with cowboys – the archetypal symbol of rugged independence, freedom, space, and Americana – and transformation advertising that targets urban smokers. As Clive Chajet, a corporate and brand identity expert, explains, 'The cowboy is as enduring an icon as you can have. And the stronger your brand image, regardless of the environment in which you compete, the better off you are.'[18] Why choose Marlboro instead of another brand? Smoking Marlboro is a way of getting in touch with a powerful urge to be free and independent. Lack of physical space may be a reflection of the Marlboro user's own sense of 'macho-ness' or a symbol of freedom and independence. The message is reinforced in advertising with an image carefully calculated to appeal to the universal human desire for those things and urges smokers to 'join that rugged, independent cowboy in the Old West!' The advertising succeeds because it is very well done and, evidently, addresses a deep, powerful, need that is found around the globe.[19] Not surprisingly, Marlboro is the most popular cigarette brand in the former Soviet Union.

MCC Smart used the slogan 'Reduced to the MAX' to attract a new segment of young and dynamic automobile buyers. Harley-Davidson has successfully broadened its image to reach a new class of motorcycle enthusiast: aging baby boomer professionals who wanted to adopt an outlaw persona on weekends. An ad for the upscale Range Rover showing the sports utility vehicle on a mountaintop has the headline, 'The real reason many CEOs are unavailable for comment.'

Can global positioning work for all products and services? One study suggests that global positioning is most effective for product and service categories that approach either end of a 'high-touch/high-tech' continuum.[20] Both ends of the continuum are characterised by high levels of customer involvement and by a shared language among consumers.

High-tech positioning

Personal computers, video and stereo equipment, and automobiles are product categories for which high-tech positioning has proven effective. Such products are frequently purchased on the basis of physical product features, although image may also be important. Buyers typically already possess – or wish to acquire – considerable technical information. High-tech products may be divided into three categories: technical products, special interest products and demonstrable products.

Computers, chemicals, tyres and financial services are technical products in the sense that buyers have specialised needs, require a great deal of product information, and share a common language. Computer buyers in Russia and Spain are equally knowledgeable about Pentium microprocessors, hard drives and random access memory (RAM) requirements. Marketing communications for high-tech products should be informative and emphasise features.

Special-interest products also are characterised by a shared experience and high involvement among users, although they are less technical and more leisure or recreation oriented. Again, the common language and symbols associated with such products can transcend language and cultural barriers. Adidas and Nike sports equipment, Canon cameras, and TVs from Philips are examples of successful global special-interest products.

High-touch positioning

Marketing of high-touch products requires less emphasis on specialised information and more emphasis on image. Like high-tech products, however, high-touch categories are highly involving for consumers. Buyers of high-touch products also share a common language and set of symbols relating to themes of wealth, materialism and romance. There are three categories of high-touch products: products that solve a common problem, global village products, and products with a universal theme. At the other end of the price spectrum from high-tech, high-touch products that can solve a problem often provide benefits linked to 'life's little moments'. Ads that show friends talking over a cup of coffee in a cafe or quenching thirst with a soft drink during a day at the beach put the product at the centre of everyday life and communicate the benefit offered in a way that is understood world-wide. Upscale fragrances and designer fashions are examples of products whose positioning is strongly cosmopolitan in nature. Fragrances and fashions have travelled as a result of growing world-wide interest in high-quality, highly visible, high-priced products that often enhance social status.

Products may have a global appeal by virtue of their country of origin. The Americanness of Levis, Marlboro and Harley-Davidson enhances their appeal to cosmopolitans around the world and offers opportunities for benefit positioning. In consumer electronics, Sony is a name synonymous with vaunted Japanese quality; in automobiles, Mercedes is the embodiment of legendary German engineering.

Some products can be positioned in more than one way, within either the high-tech or high-touch poles of the continuum. A sophisticated camera, for example, could simultaneously be classified as technical and special interest. Other products may be positioned in a bipolar fashion, that is, as both high-tech and high-touch. For example, Bang & Olufsen consumer electronics products, by virtue of their design elegance, are perceived as both high-tech and high-touch.

Key points	• Products or services positioned by attribute or benefit exploit a particular product attribute, benefit or feature (Volvo = safety).
	• Products or services positioned by quality/price exploit the common perception that a high price is analogue to high quality (American Express Card = expensive, but high quality, high prestige).
	• Products or services positioned by use/user associate the product or service with a user or class of users (Marlboro = be free and independent as the cowboys are).
	• Products or services positioned 'high-tech', are purchased on the basis of physical product features and image (WAP cellular phones).
	• Products or services positioned 'high-touch' share a common language and set of symbols relating to the themes of wealth, materialism and romance (Volkswagen's New Beetle).

PRODUCT SATURATION LEVELS IN GLOBAL MARKETS

Many factors determine a product's market potential. In general, product saturation levels, or the percentage of potential buyers or households who own a particular product, increase as national income per capita increases. However, for markets in which income is sufficient to enable consumers to buy a particular product, other factors must be considered. For example, the sale of air conditioners is explained by income and climate. In a low-income country, many people cannot afford an air conditioner no matter how hot it is. Affluent people in a northern climate can easily afford an air conditioner but have no need for one.

During the 1960s, the ownership of electric vacuum cleaners in the European market ranged from a high of 95 per cent of households in the Netherlands to a low of 7 per cent of households in Italy. The differences in ownership of this appliance are explained only partially by income. A much more important factor in explaining ownership levels is the type of floor covering used in the homes of the country. Almost every home in the Netherlands contains rugs, whereas in Italy the use of rugs is uncommon. This illustrates the importance of need in determining the sales potential for a product. Thus, in addition to attitudes toward cleanliness, the presence or absence of a particular companion product is very significant for electric vacuum cleaners. If Italians had more carpets covering their floors, the saturation level for vacuum cleaners would be higher.

The existence of wide disparities in the demand for a product from one market to the next is an indication of the possible potential for that product in the low-saturation-level market. For example, a major new product category in the United States in the early 1980s was mousse, a hair grooming product for women that is more flexible than stiff, dry hair spray. This product had been available in Europe for 25 years prior to its introduction in the United States. The success of the product in Europe was a clear signal of market potential. Indeed, it is more than likely that this opportunity could have been tapped earlier. Every company should have an active global scanning system to identify potential market opportunities based on demand disparities.

PRODUCT AND SERVICE DESIGN CONSIDERATIONS

Product and service design is a key factor in determining success in global marketing. Should a company adapt a design for various national markets or offer a single design to the global market? In some instances, making a design change may increase sales. However, the benefits of such potential sales increases must be weighed against the cost of changing a product's or service's design and testing it in the market. Global marketers need to consider four factors when making product or service design decisions: preferences, costs, laws and regulations, and compatibility.

Preferences

There are marked and important differences in preferences around the world for factors such as design or taste. Marketers who ignore preferences do so at their own peril. The Chrysler Neon for example, launched in January 1994, has been an incredible success in the US. Car magazines hailed the Neon as America's best subcompact and dealers had three times as many orders for the Neon as Chrysler had been able to build. The same car, however, failed to repeat its American success when exported to Europe, where it seemed expensive, noisy and under-powered compared with the local competition, such as Volkswagen's Golf.

Sometimes, a design that is successful in one world region does meet with success in the rest of the world. BMW and Mercedes dominate the luxury car market in Europe and are strong competitors in the rest of the world, with exactly the same design. In effect, these companies have a world design. The other global luxury car manufacturers are Japanese, and they have expressed their flattery and appreciation for the appeal of the BMW and Mercedes look by styling cars that are influenced by the BMW and Mercedes line and design philosophy. If imitation is the most sincere form of flattery, BMW and Mercedes have been honoured by their competition.

Costs

In approaching the issue of product or service design, company managers must consider cost factors. Of course, the actual cost of producing the product or creating a service will create a cost floor. Other design-related costs – whether incurred by the manufacturer or the end user – must also be considered. Earlier in this chapter, we noted that the cost of repair services varies around the world and has an impact on product design. A classic example of how labour cost affects product decisions were the contrasting approaches to aircraft design adopted by the British and the Americans. The British approach, which resulted in the Comet, was to place the engine inside the wing. This design meant lower wind resistance and therefore greater fuel economy. A disadvantage of the design was less accessible engines than externally mounted ones, meaning they were more time consuming to maintain and repair. The American approach to the question of engine location was to hang the engines from the wings at the expense of efficiency and fuel economy to gain a more accessible engine and, therefore, to reduce the amount of time required for engine maintenance and repair. Both approaches to engine location were rational. The British approach took into account the relatively lower cost of the labour required for engine repair, and the American approach took into account the relatively high cost of labour for engine repair in the United States.

Laws and regulations

Compliance with laws and regulations in different countries has a direct impact on product and service design decisions, frequently leading to design adaptations that increase costs. This may be seen especially clearly in Europe, where one impetus for the creation of the single market was to dismantle regulatory and legal barriers particularly in the areas of technical standards and health and safety standards that prevented pan-European sales of standardised products. In the food industry, for example, there were 200 legal and regulatory barriers to cross-border trade within the European Union (EU) in 10 food categories. Among these were prohibitions or taxes on products with certain ingredients, and different packaging and labelling laws. The removal of these barriers has largely reduced the need to adapt product and service designs and has resulted in the creation of standardised Euro-products.

Compatibility

The last product design issue that must be addressed by company managers is product or service compatibility with the environment in which it is used. A simple thing like failing to translate the user's manual into various languages can hurt sales. Also, electrical systems range from 50 to 230 volts and from 50 to 60 cycles. This means that the design of any product powered by electricity must be compatible with the power system in the country of use.

Manufacturers of televisions and video equipment find that the world is a very incompatible place for reasons besides those related to electricity. Three different TV broadcast and video systems are found in the world today: the French SECAM system, the German PAL system, and the US NTSC system. Companies that are targeting global markets design multisystem TVs and VCRs that allow users to simply flip a switch for proper operation with any system. Companies that are not aiming for the global market design products that comply with a single set of technical requirements.

Measuring systems do not demand compatibility, but the absence of compatibility in measuring systems can create product resistance. The lack of compatibility is a particular danger for the United States, which is the only nonmetric country in the world. Products calibrated in inches and pounds are at a competitive disadvantage in metric markets. When companies integrate their worldwide manufacturing and design activity, the metric-English measuring system conflict requires expensive conversion and harmonisation efforts.

Key points

- Product or service design is a critical success factor in global marketing. The key question is whether to adapt a design for various national markets, or to offer a single design to the global market.
- The following factors have to be considered when making product or service design decisions:
  - Preferences: there might be significant differences in preferences around the world for factors such as design or taste.
  - Cost: different categories of cost might be perceived differently in various national markets.
  - Laws and regulations: compliance with laws and regulations might directly impact design decisions.
  - Compatibility: products and services must be in compliance with the environment in which they are used.

ATTITUDES TOWARD COUNTRY OF ORIGIN

One of the facts of life in global marketing is the existence of stereotyped attitudes toward foreign products or services. Stereotyped attitudes may either favour or hinder the marketer's efforts. On the positive side, as one marketing expert pointed out, 'German is synonymous with quality engineering, Italian is synonymous with style, and French is synonymous with chic.'[21] However, no country has a monopoly on a favourable foreign reputation for its products and services or a universally inferior reputation. Similarly, individual citizens in a given country are likely to differ in terms of both the importance they ascribe to a product's or service's country of origin and their perceptions of different countries.

If a country's manufacturers produce quality products that are nonetheless perceived as being of low quality, there are two alternatives. One is to attempt to hide or disguise the foreign origin of the product. Package, label and product design can minimise evidence of foreign sourcing. A brand policy of using local names will contribute to a domestic identity. The other alternative is to continue the foreign identification of the product and attempt to change consumer or customer attitudes toward the product. Over time, as consumers experience higher quality, the perception will change and adjust. Unfortunately, this might be a long process as perceptions of quality often lag behind reality.

In some market segments, foreign products have a substantial advantage over their domestic counterparts simply because they are foreign. This appears to be the case with beer in the United States. In one study, subjects who were asked to indicate taste preference for beer in a blind test indicated a preference for domestic beers over imports. The same subjects were then asked to indicate preference ratings for beers in an open test with labels attached. In this test, the subjects preferred imported beer.

It is a happy situation for the global marketer when foreign origin has a positive influence on perceptions of quality. One way to reinforce foreign preference is by charging a premium price for the foreign product to take advantage of consumer tendencies to associate price and quality. The relative position of imported beer in the US premium-priced beer market is an excellent example of this positioning strategy. Similarly, Anheuser-Busch is enjoying great success with its Budweiser brand in Europe. In Britain, where it is positioned as a super-premium beer, a six-pack of Bud sells for about twice the US price.

GEOGRAPHIC EXPANSION – STRATEGIC ALTERNATIVES

Companies can grow in three different ways. The traditional methods of market expansion – further penetration of existing markets to increase market share and extension of the product or service line into new market areas in a single national market – are both available in domestic operations. In addition, a company can expand by extending its existing operations into new countries and areas of the world. The latter method, geographic expansion, is one of the major opportunities of global marketing. To pursue geographic expansion effectively, a framework for considering alternatives is required. When a company has a product/market base, it can select from four strategic options to extend this base into other geographic markets (Figure 11.2). Alternatively, it can design an entirely new product or service designed for global markets.

Figure 11.2 Global product planning: strategic alternatives for expanding into global markets

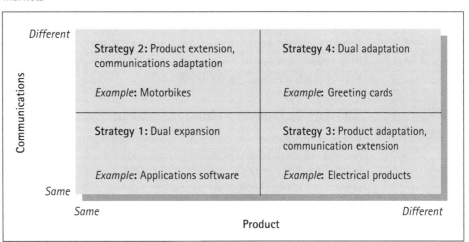

Strategy 1: Product/communication extension (dual extension)

Many companies employ product/communication extension as a strategy for pursuing opportunities outside the home market. Under the right conditions, this is the easiest product marketing strategy and, in many instances, the most profitable one as well. Companies pursuing this strategy sell exactly the same product or service, with the same advertising and promotional appeals as used in the home country, in some or all world-market countries or segments. Note that this strategy is utilised by companies at different stages of the globalisation process. The critical difference is one of execution and mindset. For some companies, the dual extension strategy grows out of an ethnocentric orientation; these companies are making the assumption that all markets are alike. More experienced companies do not make such assumptions; the company's geocentric orientation allows it to thoroughly understand its markets and consciously take advantage of similarities in world markets.

Some marketers have learned the hard way that the dual extension approach does not work in every market. When Campbell Soup tried to sell its tomato soup in the United Kingdom, it discovered, after substantial losses, that the English prefer a more bitter taste than Americans. Happily, Campbell learned its lesson and subsequently succeeded in Japan by offering seven soup varieties for example, corn potage, designed specifically for the Japanese markets. Another US company spent several million Euros in an unsuccessful effort to capture the British cake mix market. It offered fancy US-style cake mixes with frosting. After the product was launched, the company discovered that the British consume their cake at tea time. The cake they prefer is dry, spongy and suitable for being picked up with the left hand while the right manages a cup of tea. A second US company hoping to sell cake mixes in the United Kingdom assembled a panel of housewives and asked them to bake their favourite cake. Having learned about British cake preferences, this company created a dry, spongy cake mix product and acquired a major share of the British market.

The product/communication extension strategy has an enormous appeal to global companies because of the cost savings associated with this approach. The two most obvious sources of savings are manufacturing economies of scale and elimination of

385

duplicate product R&D costs. Also important are the substantial economies associated with standardisation of marketing communications. For a company with world-wide operations, the cost of preparing separate print and TV ads for each market can be enormous. Although these cost savings are important, they should not distract executives from the more important objective of maximum profit performance, which may require the use of an adaptation or invention strategy. As we have seen, product extension, in spite of its immediate cost savings, may in fact result in market failure.

Strategy 2: Product extension/communication adaptation

When a product or service fills a different need, appeals to a different segment, or serves a different function under conditions of use that are the same or similar to those in the domestic market, the only adjustment that may be required is in marketing communications. Motor bikes are examples of products that have been marketed with this approach. They satisfy recreation needs in Europe but serve as basic or urban transportation in many other countries. Similarly, outboard marine motors are usually sold to a recreation market in the high-income countries, whereas the same motors in most lower-income countries are mainly sold to fishing and transportation fleets. Other examples are companies that decided to market their line of home lawn and garden power equipment in less developed countries (LDCs) as agricultural implements.

As these examples show, the product extension/communication adaptation strategy – either by design or by accident – results in product transformation. The same physical product ends up serving a different function or use than that for which it was originally designed or created.

The appeal of the product extension/communications adaptation strategy is its relatively low cost of implementation. Because the product in this strategy is unchanged, R&D, tooling, manufacturing set-up, and inventory costs associated with additions to the product line are avoided. The only costs of this approach are in identifying different product functions and revising marketing communications (including advertising, sales promotion, and point-of-sale material) around the newly identified function.

Strategy 3: Product adaptation/communication extension

A third approach to global product and service planning is to extend, without change, the basic home-market communications strategy while adapting the product or service to local use or preference conditions. Exxon/ Esso adheres to this strategy. It adapts its gasoline formulations to meet the weather conditions prevailing in different markets while extending the basic communications appeal without change.

There are many other examples of products that have been adjusted to perform the same function around the globe under different environmental conditions. Soap and detergent manufacturers have adjusted their product formulations to meet local water and washing equipment conditions with no change in their basic communications approach. Household appliances have been scaled to sizes appropriate to different use environments, and food products, by virtue of their potentially high degree of environmental sensitivity, are often adapted. Mueslix, for example, is a European cereal that was pioneered by Kellogg's Swiss division. Kellogg's brought the Mueslix name and product concept to the United States but completely changed the formulation and nature of the product.

Strategy 4: Dual adaptation

Sometimes, when comparing a new geographic market to the home market, marketers discover that environmental conditions or consumer preferences differ. The same may be true of the function a product serves or consumer receptivity to advertising appeals. In essence, this is a combination of the market conditions of strategies 2 and 3.

Unilever's experience with fabric softener in Europe exemplifies the classic multinational road to adaptation. For years, the product was sold in 10 countries under seven different brand names, with different bottles and marketing strategies. Unilever's decentralised structure meant that product and marketing decisions were left to country managers. They chose names that had local-language appeal and selected package designs to fit local tastes. Today, rival Procter & Gamble is introducing competitive products with a pan-European strategy of standardised products with single names, suggesting that the European market is more similar than Unilever assumed. In response, Unilever's European brand managers are attempting to move gradually toward standardisation.[22]

Hallmark, American Greetings, and other US-based greeting card manufacturers have faced genuine market condition and preference differences in Europe, where the function of a greeting card is to provide a space for the sender to write an individual message. In contrast, US cards contain a prepared message, known in the greeting card industry as sentiment. In European stores, cards are handled frequently by customers, a practice that makes it necessary to wrap greeting cards in cellophane. Thus, American manufacturers pursuing an adjustment strategy have changed both their product and their marketing communications in response to this set of environmental differences.

Sometimes, a company will draw on all four of these strategies simultaneously when marketing a given product in different parts of the world. For example, H. J. Heinz utilises a mix of strategies in its ketchup marketing. Whereas a dual extension strategy works in England, spicier, hotter formulations are also popular in Central Europe and Sweden. Ads in France featured a cowboy lassoing a bottle of ketchup and thus reminded consumers of the product's American heritage. Swedish ads conveyed a more cosmopolitan message; by promoting Heinz as 'the taste of the big world' and featuring well-known landmarks such as the Eiffel Tower, the ads disguised the product's origins.[23]

Strategy 5: Product invention

Adaptation strategies are effective approaches to international (stage two) and multinational (stage three) marketing, but they may not respond to global market opportunities. They do not respond to the situation in markets where customers do not have the purchasing power to buy either the existing or adapted product. This latter situation applies to the LDCs of the world, which are home to roughly three-quarters of the world's population. When potential customers have limited purchasing power, a company may need to develop an entirely new service or product, designed to satisfy the need or want at a price that is within the reach of the potential customer. Invention is a demanding but potentially rewarding product and service strategy for reaching mass markets in LDCs.

The winners in global competition are the companies that can develop products or services offering the most benefits, which in turn create the greatest value for buyers.

In some instances, value is not defined in terms of performance, but rather in terms of customer perception. The latter is as important for an expensive perfume or champagne as it is for an inexpensive soft drink. Product and service quality is essential, indeed, it is frequently a given, but it is also necessary to support the product or service quality with imaginative, value-creating advertising and marketing communications. Most industry experts believe that a global appeal and a global advertising campaign are more effective in creating the perception of value than a series of separate national campaigns.

Colgate pursued this strategy in developing Total, a new toothpaste brand whose formulation, imagery, and ultimate consumer appeal were designed from the ground up to translate across national boundaries. The product was tested in six countries, each of which had a different cultural profile: the Philippines, Australia, Colombia, Greece, Portugal and the United Kingdom. Total is now sold in 75 countries and generates €80 million in revenues. According to John Steel, senior vice president for global business development at Colgate, Total's success resulted from the application of a fundamental marketing principle: Consumers are the ones who make or break brands. 'There ain't no consumers at 300 Park Avenue,' he says, referring to company headquarters. Steel explains, 'You get a lot more benefit and you can do a lot more with a global brand than you can a local brand. You can bring the best advertising talent from the world to a problem. You can bring the best research brains, the best leverage of your organisation onto something that is truly global. Then all your R&D pays off, the huge packaging costs pay off, the advertising pays off, and you can leverage the organisation all at once.'[24]

How to choose a strategy

Most companies seek a product or service strategy that optimises company profits over the long term. Which strategy for global markets best achieves this goal? There is, unfortunately, no general answer to this question. Rather, the answer depends on the specific product–market–company mix.

In terms of cultural sensitivity, consumer products and services are generally more sensitive than industrial products or services. Another rule of thumb is that food products frequently exhibit the highest degree of cultural sensitivity. What this means to managers is that some products or services, by their nature, are likely to demand significant adaptation. Others require only partial adaptation, and still others are best left unchanged.

To sum up, the choice of product and communications strategy in international marketing is a function of three key factors: (1) the product or service itself, defined in terms of the function or need it serves; (2) the market, defined in terms of the conditions under which the product or service is used, the preferences of potential customers, and the ability to buy the products or services in question; and (3) the costs of adaptation and manufacture to the company considering these product/communications approaches. Only after analysis of the product/market fit and of company capabilities and costs can executives choose the most profitable international strategy.

Key points	
	• Growing through **market expansion** means to further penetrate existing markets to increase market share or to extend the product or service lines into new market segments in a single national market.
	• Growing through **geographic expansion** means to extend a firm's existing operations into new countries and areas of the world.
	• The easiest and often most profitable strategy of geographic expansion is the 'Dual Extension': companies sell exactly the same product or service abroad, with the same advertising and promotional appeals as used in the home country.
	• Opposite to the 'Dual Extension' strategy is the 'Dual Adaptation' strategy. It is used when environmental conditions, consumer preferences and consumer receptivity to advertising and promotional appeals in new geographic markets differ significantly from these factors in the home market. Here, companies must adapt the product or service as well as the marketing communication.

NEW PRODUCTS AND SERVICES IN GLOBAL MARKETING

It is widely acknowledged that a constant supply of new products and services and their successful introduction into the market are keys to a firm's survival and growth. Studies, however, have shown that more than 50 per cent of all new products and services fail in the commercialisation process. Why do so many new products fail? In some cases, the product development process is flawed. In others, the product concept is very poorly backed by market research. In some others, it is the launch process and its execution that is at fault. In any case, the failure statistic highlights the need for close management attention to the new product or service development and commercialisation process.

What is a new product or service? Newness can be assessed in the context of the product itself, the organisation, and the market. The product or service may be an entirely new invention or innovation, for example, the video cassette recorder (VCR) or the compact disc. It may be a line extension (a modification of an existing product) such as Diet Coke. Newness may also be organisational, as when a company acquires an already existing product or service with which it has no previous experience. Finally, an existing product or service that is not new to a company may be new to a particular market.

Identifying new-product ideas

The starting point for an effective world-wide new-product or service programme is an information system that seeks new-product or new-service ideas from all potentially useful sources and channels. Those ideas relevant to the company undergo screening at decision centres within the organisation. There are many sources of new-product or new-service ideas, including customers, suppliers, competitors, company salespeople, distributors and agents, subsidiary executives, headquarters executives, documentary sources (for example, information service reports and publications), and, finally, actual first-hand observation of the market environment.

EUROPEAN FOCUS

Building the world's largest aircraft ...

When it comes to new products, few businesses are more perilous than making civil aircraft. Aeroplanes cost billions to develop and are designed to last a generation. Boeing bet the company when it launched the 747, spending €1 billion on the project, 2.5 times the value of the firm. Boeing's rivals, Lockheed and McDonnell Douglas, bet heavily too and lost. Their widebody jets, the Tristar and the DC 10, never earned a penny. Lockheed quit the civil-jet business and McDonnell Douglas was taken over by Boeing.

In 1970, a consortium of European companies founded Airbus Industrie and marked a turning point in the international aviation industry. Over the past 20 years the European consortium has encroached on Boeing's dominant market share. Boeing used to account for well over two-thirds of orders, but in 1999 Airbus gained 55 per cent of all orders announced in that year. Boeing reigns supreme only with the largest 747s.

Until recently, Airbus had been content to attack the 747 from below, with bigger versions of its long-range A340. The latest, soon to go into production, can carry 385 passengers. Virgin Atlantic will have an A340 with bedrooms below the main deck, where passengers can sleep on the night flight that it is starting between London and Buenos Aires.

But Airbus is determined also to launch an attack from above. Noel Forgeard, CEO of Airbus, estimates that over the next 20 years there is a market for 1,400 'super-jumbos' that are equipped to carry 550–660 passengers. Hence Airbus, which is owned by France's Aerospatiale, Germany's DaimlerChrysler Aerospace, British Aerospace and Spain's CASA, is stepping up work on its super-jumbo, the A3XX. In all, the partners and the consortium headquarters in Toulouse have 1,000 staff working on the design of this huge double-decker. And Airbus lobbyists are starting to ask their governments for loans to help launch the aircraft. Of the €5 billion that it will cost to get the A3XX off the ground, a third is supposed to come from Airbus; a third from associates, including Italy's Alenia, Sweden's Saab Aircraft and a Japanese company; and the remaining third from European governments. Under an agreement signed with the United States in 1992, governments can finance up to that portion of the launch cost of a new aircraft.

The production of the A3XX could start by the end of 2000 and the earliest an A3XX could take wing would be in 2005. The launch timetable, however, has slipped, as nervousness about the slump in Asian travel has given airlines cold feet. Boeing appreciates those delays: after all, any delay in the A3XX provides Boeing with more years of near-monopoly profits.

Source: 'For their next trick: Airbus may be about to challenge the Jumbo Jet's 30-year-old monopoly', *The Economist*, 27 March 1999; Airbus Industrie, 'Another record year for Airbus Industrie', *Internet Document*, http://www.airbus.com/about.html; 'How Airbus could rule the skies', *Business Week*, 2 August 1999; 'Up, up, and away at least for Airbus?', *Business Week*, 9 February 1998.

The international new–product department

As previously noted, a high volume of information flow is required to scan adequately for new-product opportunities, and considerable effort is subsequently required to screen these opportunities to identify candidates for product development. An organisational design for addressing these requirements is a new-product department. The function of such a department is fourfold: (1) to ensure that all relevant information sources are continuously tapped for new-product ideas; (2) to screen these ideas to identify candidates for investigation; (3) to investigate and analyse selected new-product ideas; and (4) to ensure that the organisation commits resources to the most likely new-product candidates and is continuously involved in an orderly programme of new-product introduction and development on a world-wide basis.

With the enormous number of possible new products, most companies establish screening grids to focus on those ideas that are most appropriate for investigation. The following questions are relevant to this task:

1 How big is the market for this product at various prices?
2 What are the likely competitive moves in response to our activity with this product?
3 Can we market the product through our existing structure? If not, what changes and what costs will be required to make the changes?
4 Given estimates of potential demand for this product at specified prices with estimated levels of competition, can we source the product at a cost that will yield an adequate profit?
5 Does this product fit our strategic development plan?
   (a) Is the product consistent with our overall goals and objectives?
   (b) Is the product consistent with our available resources?
   (c) Is the product consistent with our management structure?
   (d) Does the product have adequate global potential?

Testing new products and services in national markets

The major lesson of new-product or service introduction outside the home market has been that whenever a product or service interacts with human, mechanical, or chemical elements, there is the potential for a surprising and unexpected incompatibility. Since virtually every product or service matches this description, it is important to test a product or service under actual market conditions before proceeding with full-scale introduction. A test does not necessarily involve a full-scale test-marketing effort. It may simply involve observing the actual use of the product or application of a service in the target market.

Key points

- New products and services can be classified as:
  - New to the consumer and new to the company (product or service innovation)
  - New to the consumer but not new to the company (product/service or line extension)
  - Not new to the consumer but new to the company (new product or service duplication)

- The new-product development process consists of four critical steps: first, the permanent identification of new-product ideas. Second, the screening of these ideas and the identification of promising candidates for further investigation. Third, the stringent investigation and analysis of the selected new-product ideas. Fourth, the organisation of sufficient resources.

- To test a product or service under actual market conditions before proceeding with a full-scale introduction is, in global markets, even more important than in local or national markets.

Summary

Products and services are the most important elements of a marketing programme. Global marketers face the challenge of formulating a coherent global product or service strategy for their companies. Product or service strategy requires an evaluation of the basic needs and conditions of use in the company's existing and proposed markets. Whenever possible, opportunities to market global products or services should be given precedence over opportunities to market local or international products.

Marketers must consider four factors when designing products or services for global markets: preferences, costs, regulations, and compatibility. Attitudes toward the country of origin must also be taken into account. Five strategic alternatives are open to companies pursuing geographic expansion: product/communications extension; product extension/communications adaptation; product adaptation/communications extension; dual adaptation; and product invention. Global competition has created pressure on companies to excel at product and service development. There are different definitions of what constitutes a new product or service; the most difficult type of new-product or service launch is clearly one involving an entirely new product or service in a market in which a company has little or no experience. Successful global product or service launches require leverage. An organisation must accumulate and disseminate knowledge concerning past practices, both successful and unsuccessful. Opportunities for comparative analysis further enhance the effectiveness of marketing planning activities within the global system.

Concepts and definitions

Product	Products can be defined as a collection of physical, psychological and symbolic attributes that collectively yield satisfaction, or benefits, to a buyer or user.
Service	Services can be defined as intangible benefits purchased by customers that do not involve ownership.
Characteristics of services	*Intangibility:* Services are frequently consumed rather than possessed.
	Perishability: Services cannot be stored.
	Variability: Services are often custom-made and the quality depends primarily on the people who provide them.
	Simultaneous production and consumption: For many service offerings, the time of production is very close or simultaneous to the time of consumption.
National, international, global products or services	*National products or services*: Products or services that, in the context of a particular company, are offered in a single national market.
	International products or services: Products or services that are offered in multinational, regional markets.
	Global products or services: Products or services that are offered in the global market. They are international and multiregional.

Global brands	Both global products or services as well as global brands are offered in global markets. However, only global brands carry the same name and image from country to country. A global brand is therefore always a global product or service. A global product or service, in contrast, is not always a global brand.
Positioning	The act of locating a brand in customers' minds over and against other products in terms of attributes and benefits that the brand does and does not offer.
Country of origin effects	Describe the influence that a product's country of origin ('Made in *country*') has on the quality perceptions of the product.

Discussion questions

1 What are the differences between services and products? What are the strategic implications of these differences?

2 What is the difference between a product or service and a brand?

3 What are the differences among a local, an international, and a global product or brand? Cite examples.

4 What criteria should global marketers consider when making product or service design decisions?

5 How can buyer attitudes about a product's country of origin affect marketing strategy?

6 Identify several global brands. What are some of the reasons for the global success of the brands you chose?

7 Briefly describe various combinations of product/communication strategies available to global marketers. When is it appropriate to use each?

Webmistress's hotspots

Netscape Yellow Pages
Here you can find businesses in 144 countries around the world as well as links to most country's yellow pages.
http://www.netscape.com/netcenter/yellowpages.html

Europages: the European Business Directory
This page provides information on 500,000 companies in 30 European countries. You can search by product/service or by company name. You can also browse though company catalogues sorted by industry.
http://www.europages.com/

Homepage of Trade Show Central
TSCentral's homepage provides a comprehensive resource to locate trade shows and exhibitions all over the world.
http://www.tscentral.com/

Webpage of USITC – industry information (United States International Trade Commission)
Sorted by industry/product you will find here a variety of links, for example, to

government sources, industry databases, patent information, industry/product-related publications and associations.
http://www.usitc.gov/tr/INDUSTR2.HTM

Homepage of KOMPASS
This business-to-business search engine offers information on 1.5 million companies, 23 million key product and service references, 2.9 million executive names, as well as 600,000 trade and brand names in close to 70 countries.
http://www.kompass.com/

Suggested readings

Carpano, Claudio and J. James Chrisman, 'Performance implications of international product strategies and the integration of marketing activities', *Journal of International Marketing*, 3, 1 (1995): pp. 9–28.

Chao, Paul, 'Partitioning country of origin effects: consumer evaluations of a hybrid product', *Journal of International Business Studies*, 24, 2 (Second Quarter 1993): pp. 291–306.

Cordell, Victor V., 'Effects of consumer preferences for foreign sourced products', *Journal of International Business Studies*, 23, 2 (Second Quarter 1992): pp. 251–270.

Drucker, Peter, 'The discipline of innovation', *Harvard Business Review*, 76, 6 (1998): pp. 149–157.

Du Preez, Johann P., Adamantios Diamantopoulos and Bodo B. Schlegelmilch, 'Product standardization and attribute saliency: a three-product empirical comparison', *Journal of International Marketing*, 2, 1 (1994): pp. 7–28.

Elliott, Gregory R. and Ross C. Cameron, 'Consumer perception of product quality and the country-of-origin effect', *Journal of International Marketing*, 2, 2 (1994): pp. 49–62.

Faulds, David J., Orlen Grunewald and Denise Johnson, 'A cross national investigation of the relationship between the price and quality of consumer products: 1970–1990', *Journal of Global Marketing*, 8, 1 (1994): pp. 7–26.

Freker, Jack, 'High-tech, high-touch builds customer loyalty', *Telemarketing & Call Center Solutions*, 16, 8 (1998): pp. 50–52.

Handfield, Robert B., Gary L. Ragatz, Kenneth J. Petersen and Robert M. Monczka, 'Involving suppliers in new product development', *California Management Review*, 42, 1 (Fall 1999): pp. 59–82.

Hill, John S. and William L. James, 'Product and promotion transfers in consumer goods multinationals', *International Marketing Review*, 8, 2 (1991): pp. 6–17.

Hill, John S. and Up Kwon, 'Product mixes in US Multinationals: an empirical study', *Journal of Global Marketing*, 6, 3 (1992): pp. 55–73.

Hulland, John S., 'The effects of country-of-brand and brand name on product evaluation and consideration: a cross-country comparison', *Journal of International Consumer Marketing*, 11, 1 (1999): pp. 23–40.

Johansson, Johny K., Ilkka A. Ronkainen and Michael R. Czinkota, 'Negative country-of-origin effects: the case of the new Russia', *Journal of International Business Studies*, 25, 1 (First Quarter 1994): pp. 157–176.

Keegan, Warren J., Sandra Moriarty and Tom Duncan, *Marketing*. Vol. 2. Upper Saddle River, NJ: Prentice Hall, 1995.

Keltner, Brent, David Finegold, Geoff Mason and Karin Wagner, 'Market segmentation strategies and service sector productivity', *California Management Review*, 41, 4 (Summer 1999): pp. 81–102.

Kim, W. Chan and Renee Mauborgne, 'Creating new market space', *Harvard Business Review*, 77, 1 (January/February 1999): pp. 83–93.

Kotabe, Masaaki, 'Corporate product policy and innovative behavior of European and Japanese multinational: an empirical investigation', *Journal of Marketing*, 54, 2 (April 1990): pp. 19–23.

Kuczmarski, Thomas D., *Managing new products: the power of innovation*. Upper Saddle River, NJ: Prentice Hall, 1992, p. 254.

Maas, Judith, 'Customer service: extraordinary results at Southwest Airlines, Charles Schwaab, Land's End, American Express, Staples and USAA', *Sloan Management Review*, 40, 1 (Fall 1998): p. 105.

Maas, Judith, 'Discovering the soul of service: the nine drivers of sustainable business success', *Sloan Management Review*, 40, 3 (Spring 1999): pp. 151–152.

Macrae, Chris, *World Class Brands*. Reading, MA: Addison-Wesley, 1991.

Mathe, Herve and Teo Forcht Dagi, 'Harnessing technology in global service businesses', *Long Range Planning*, 29, 4 (1996): pp. 449–461.

Meyer, Marc and Arthur DeTore, 'Product development for services', *Academy of Management Executive*, 13, 3 (1999): pp. 64–76.

Moskowitz, Howard R. and Samuel Rabino, 'Sensory segmentation: an organizing principle for international product concept generation', *Journal of Global Marketing*, 8, 1 (1994): pp. 73–94.

Ogbuehi, Alphonso O. and Ralph A. Bellas Jr, 'Decentralized R&D for global product development: strategic implications for the multinational corporation', *International Marketing Review*, 9, 5 (1992): pp. 60–70.

Papadopoulos, Nicolas and Louise A. Heslop, *Product-Country Images: Impact and Role in International Marketing*. New York: International Business Press, 1993.

Prasad, V. Kanti and G. M. Naidu, 'Perspectives and preparedness regarding ISO-9000 international quality standards', *Journal of International Marketing*, 2, 2 (1994): pp. 81–98.

Quelch, John, Robert Buzzell and Eric Salama, *The marketing challenge of Europe 1992*. Reading, MA: Addison-Wesley, 1992, p. 71.

Roche, Eileen, 'Product development', *Harvard Business Review*, 77, 1 (1999): pp. 21–24.

Rosenthal, Stephen R., *Effective Product Design and Development: How to Cut Lead Time and Increase Customer Satisfaction*. Homewood, IL: Business One Irwin, 1992.

Roth, Martin S., 'Effects of global market conditions on brand image customization and brand performance', *Journal of Advertising*, 24 (Winter 1995): pp. 55–77.

Roth, Martin S. and Jean B. Romeo, 'Matching product category and country image perceptions: a framework for managing country-of-origin effects', *Journal of International Business Studies*, 23, 3 (Third Quarter 1992): pp. 477–498.

Samiee, Saeed, 'Customer evaluation of products in a global market', *Journal of International Business Studies*, 25, 3 (Third Quarter 1994): pp. 579–604.

Schilling, Melissa A. and Charles W. L. Hill, 'Managing the new product development process: strategic imperatives', *Academy of Management Executive*, 12, 3 (1998): pp. 67–81.

Schneider, Benjamin and David E. Bowen, 'Understanding customer delight and outrage', *Sloan Management Review*, 41, 1 (1999): pp. 35–45.

Tax, Stephen S. and Stephen W. Brown, 'Recovering and learning from service failure', *Sloan Management Review*, 40, 1 (Fall 1998): pp. 75–88.

Tersine, Richard and Michael Harvey, 'Global customization of markets has arrived', *European Management Journal*, 16, 1 (1998): pp. 79–90.

Tse, David K. and Gerald Gorn, 'An experiment on the salience of country-of-origin in the era of global brands', *Journal of International Marketing*, 1, 1 (1993): pp. 57–76.

Tse, David K. and Wei-na Lee, 'Removing negative country images: effects of decomposition, branding and product experience', *Journal of International Marketing*, 1, 4 (1993): pp. 25–48.

Ulgado, Francis M. and Moonku Lee, 'Consumer evaluations of bi-national products in the global market', *Journal of International Marketing*, 1, 3 (1993): pp. 5–22.

Verona, Gianmario, 'A resource-based view of product development', *Academy of Management Review*, 24, 1 (1999): pp. 132–142.

Voss, Kevin E. and Patriya Tansuhaj, 'A consumer perspective on foreign market entry: building brands through brand alliances', *Journal of International Consumer Marketing*, 11, 2 (1999): pp. 39–58.

Witt, Jerome and C. P. Rao, 'The impact of global sourcing on consumers: country-of-origin effects on perceived risk', *Journal of Global Marketing*, 6, 3 (1992): pp. 105–128.

Notes

1. http://www.int.the-body-shop.com/aboutus/ra99.pdf (cited May 2000).
2. Christopher A. Barlett, Kenton Elderkin and Krista McQuade, 'The Body Shop International', *Harvard Business School Case Study* (1991): pp. 2–4.
3. Christopher A. Barlett, Kenton Elderkin and Krista McQuade, 'The Body Shop International', *Harvard Business School Case Study* (1991): pp. 2–4.
4. Tara Rummell, 'What's new at The Body Shop?', *Global Cosmetic Industry*, 165, 5 (November 1999): pp. 16–18.
5. Christina Robb, 'Whole-earth beauty', *The Boston Globe* 15 September 1990, p. 15.
6. http://www.int.the-body-shop.com/aboutus/ra99.pdf (cited May 2000).
7. http://www.porsche.com/german/veranstaltungen/clubs/default.htm (cited April 2000).
8. Warren J. Keegan, Sandra Moriarty and Tom Duncan, *Marketing* (Upper Saddle River, NJ: Prentice Hall, 1995).
9. Donald Cowell, *The Marketing of Services*, (London: Heinemann, 1984), p. 35.
10. Henry Assael, *Marketing: Principles & Strategies* (Fort Worth: Dryden Press, 1993).
11. Steven Greenhouse, 'Carl Hahn's East German homecoming', *The New York Times*, 23 September 1990, p. 6.
12. http://www.volkswagen-ir.de/deutsch/01/index.html (cited May 2000).
13. http://www.interbrand.com/valuebrands.html (cited May 2000).

14. A.E. Pitcher, 'The role of branding in international advertising', *International Journal of Advertising*, 4, (1985): p. 244.

15. Al Ries and Jack Trout, *Positioning: The Battle for Your Mind*, 44 (New York: Warner Books), 1982.

16. David A. Aaker and Gary Shansby, 'Positioning your product', *Business Horizons* (May–June 1982): pp. 18–23.

17. David A. Aaker and Gary Shansby, 'Positioning your product', *Business Horizons* (May–June 1982): pp. 18–23.

18. Stuart Elliot, 'Uncle Sam is no match for the Marlboro man', *The New York Times*, 27 August 1995, p. 11.

19. Jagdish N. Shet, *Winning Back Your Market*, 158 (New York: Wiley, 1985).

20. Teresa J. Domzal and Lynette Unger, 'Emerging positioning strategies in global marketing', *Journal of Consumer Marketing* (Fall 1987): pp. 27–37.

21. Dana Milbank, 'Made in America becomes a boast in Europe', *The Wall Street Journal*, 19 January 1994, p. B1.

22. E.S. Browning, 'In pursuit of the elusive Euroconsumer', *The Wall Street Journal* (23 April 1992): p. B2.

23. Gabriele Stern, 'Heinz aims to export taste for ketchup', *The Wall Street Journal* (23 April 1992): pp. B1, B9.

24. P. Weisz, 'Border crossings: Brands unify image to counter cult of culture', *Brandweek*, 31 October 1994, p. 24.

CHAPTER 12

Global pricing

The real price of everything is the toil and trouble of acquiring it.
ADAM SMITH, WEALTH OF NATIONS, 1776

CHAPTER OBJECTIVES

After reading this chapter, you will know:

- The complexity of international price setting.
- Which external and internal factors influence international pricing.
- The different approaches to setting prices in an international context.
- Factors promoting or inhibiting international price standardisation.
- How to react to dumping prices by one of your competitors.
- The key issues involved in transfer pricing and the role tax authorities play in different countries.

Why is this important? Here are three situations in which you would need an understanding of the above issues:

- You are operating in a highly inflationary business environment and you have to set your prices so that they meet both customer demand and your corporate goals.
- You are entering the international arena or a specific foreign market. Thus, you want to know what different approaches there are to calculate your sales price.
- You are co-ordinating the flow of revenues between different operating units within an MNC. You will have to determine a 'fair' transfer price and need to co-operate with tax authorities on these issues.

Practice link

Many clothing retailers such as Hennes & Mauritz and The Gap have discovered the Web as a sales outlet. Hardly any of them, however, are selling internationally. The reason: pricing! Prices across countries still differ as a result of different market conditions such as different tax rates or transportation costs. The Internet will erode these differences and lead to a more standardised approach. Looking at book and music sales for example, most European Internet buyers are attracted by high price differentials between Europe and the US. Similarly, with clothing prices in the US being substantially lower than in Europe, Internet shopping would undercut The Gap retail outlets' prices in the UK for example by 30 to 50 per cent. [1]

Brioni, the famous Italian manufacturer of high-class men's wear, did not worry about these issues. When the Italian lira was devalued, considerable price differences across markets were the result. Instead of standardising prices to the same level, Brioni decided to do nothing. As Brioni's customers either did not perceive the enormous price differences across markets or simply did not want to invest into sourcing from a different country, Brioni's move harmed neither its reputation nor its sales volume.[2]

One of the most challenging tasks in global business is establishing and setting prices for international markets. A closer look unveils the complexity of global price setting. Pricing systems and policies have to deal with uniquely global constraints. External factors such as fluctuating exchange rates, international transportation costs, middlemen in elongated international channels of distribution and the demands of global accounts for equal price treatment regardless of location have to be taken into account. In addition to the diversity of national markets in the three basic dimensions – cost, competition and demand – the international executive is also confronted by conflicting governmental tax policies and claims as well as various types of price controls. These include dumping legislation, resale price maintenance legislation, price ceilings and general reviews of price levels.

Also, there are important internal organisational considerations besides cost. Within a typical corporation, there are many interest groups and, frequently, conflicting price objectives. Divisional vice presidents, regional executives and country managers are each concerned about profitability at their respective organisational levels. Similarly, the director of international marketing seeks competitive prices in world markets. The controller and financial vice president are also concerned about profits. The manufacturing vice president seeks long runs for maximum manufacturing efficiency. The tax manager is concerned about compliance with government transfer pricing legislation and company counsel is concerned about the antitrust implications of international pricing practices. Compounding the problem is the rapidly changing global marketplace and the inaccurate and distorted nature of much of the available information regarding demand. In many parts of the world, external market information is distorted and inaccurate. It is often not possible to obtain the definitive and precise information that would be the basis of an optimal price.

At the same time, sub-optimal pricing decisions may have a devastating effect on other marketing aspects. The customers' perception of value might become distorted due to different price levels in different countries, sales forces may lose motivation, promotional spending may need to be restricted, etc. and above all, a company's profitability may be affected.[3] So not only are there numerous variables to be taken into account, the variables are also constantly changing. Simple decision rules no longer work under these constraints.

Numerous empirical studies show that managers are quite aware of the prominent position of pricing in the international marketing mix. When it came to rank the most difficult issues in global marketing, 81 per cent of the US and 78 per cent of the European managers questioned ranked international price setting as the by far the most intricate problem, followed by establishing adequate product quality.[4] In some studies, only achieving suitable product quality was ranked more important than price setting.[5]

In the following, the multi-faceted international pricing decisions will be outlined in more detail. The chapter opens with an overview of environmental factors influencing price decisions. It is outlined in what way currency fluctuations, inflation, government controls and subsidies, as well as competitive behaviour and market demand impact a firm's price setting. Subsequently, different pricing approaches for international markets are presented. Basically, a company may choose between a rigid or flexible cost-plus strategy as well as a dynamic incremental pricing approach, depending on its international experience and objectives. Another important issue in international price setting is whether to standardise or differentiate prices across international markets. Pro and cons will be outlined. The chapter ends with the discussion of special problems/issues in international pricing such as dumping, grey markets and transfer pricing.

ENVIRONMENTAL INFLUENCES ON PRICING DECISIONS

Global marketers must deal with a number of environmental considerations when making pricing decisions. Among these are currency fluctuations, inflation, government controls and subsidies, competitive behaviour and market demand. Some of these factors work in conjunction with others; for example, inflation may be accompanied by government controls. Each consideration is discussed in detail below.

Currency fluctuations

Fluctuating currency values are a fact of life in international business. The marketer must decide what to do about this fact. Are price adjustments appropriate when currencies strengthen or weaken? There are two extreme positions; one is to fix the price of products in country target markets. If this is done, any appreciation or depreciation of the value of the currency in the country of production will lead to gains or losses for the seller. The other extreme position is to fix the price of products in home-country currency. If this is done, any appreciation or depreciation of the home country currency will result in price increases or decreases for customers, with no immediate consequences for the seller.

In practice, companies rarely assume either of these extreme positions. Pricing decisions should be consistent with the company's overall business and marketing strategy: if the strategy is long term, then it makes no sense to give up market share in order to maintain export margins. When currency fluctuations result in appreciation in the value of the currency of a country that is an exporter, wise companies do two things: they accept that currency fluctuations may unfavourably impact operating margins and they double their efforts to reduce costs. In the short run, lower margins enable them to hold prices in target markets and in the longer run, driving down costs enables them to improve operating margins.

Table 12.1 International pricing strategies under varying currency conditions

When the domestic currency is weak	*When the domestic currency is strong*
● Stress price benefits	● Engage in non-price competition by improving quality, delivery and after-sale service
● Expand product line and add more costly features	● Improve productivity and engage in vigorous cost reduction
● Shift sourcing/manufacturing to domestic market	● Shift sourcing and manufacturing overseas
● Exploit export opportunities in all markets	● Give priority to exports to countries with relatively strong currencies
● Use a full-costing approach, but employ marginal-cost pricing to penetrate new or competitive markets	● Trim profit margins and use marginal-cost pricing
● Speed repatriation of foreign-earned income and collections	● Keep the foreign-earned income in host country; slow down collections
● Minimise expenditures in local or host-country currency	● Maximise expenditures in local or host-country currency
● Buy needed services (advertising, insurance, transportation, etc.) in the domestic market	● Buy needed services abroad and pay for the in local currencies
● Bill foreign customers in their own currency	● Bill foreign customers in the domestic currency

Source: S. Tamer Cavusgil, 'Pricing for global markets', *Columbia Journal of World Business*, Winter 1996: p. 69.

For companies that are in a strong, competitive market position, price increases can be passed on to customers without significant decreases in sales volume. In more competitive market situations, companies in a strong-currency country will often absorb any price increase by maintaining international market prices at pre-revaluation levels. In actual practice, a manufacturer and its distributor may work together to maintain market share in international markets. Either party, or both, may choose to take a lower profit percentage. The distributor may also choose to purchase more product to achieve volume discounts; another alternative is to maintain leaner inventories if the manufacturer can provide just-in-time delivery. By using these approaches, it is possible to remain price competitive in markets in which currency devaluation in the importing country is a price consideration.

Table 12.1 provides a more detailed overview of how a company can react, if its international business activities suffer from volatile currency conditions.

If a country's currency weakens relative to a trading partner's currency, a producer in a weak-currency country can cut export prices to hold market share or leave prices alone for healthier profit margins. BMW experienced these problems in the 1980s, when exchange rates of DM to $ changed considerably. Table 12.2 visualises this classical dilemma.

Many sales are contracts to supply goods or services over time. When these contracts are between parties in two countries, the problem of exchange rate fluctuations and exchange risk must be addressed. In this case, an exchange rate clause may solve some problems.

An exchange rate clause allows the buyer and seller to agree to supply and purchase at fixed prices in each company's national currency. If the exchange rate fluctuates within a specified range, say plus or minus 5 per cent, the fluctuations do not affect the pricing agreement that is spelled out in the exchange rate clause. Small fluctuations in exchange rates are not a problem for most buyers and sellers. Exchange rate clauses are designed to protect both the buyer and the seller from unforeseen large swings in currencies.

The basic design of an exchange rate clause is straightforward: review exchange rates periodically (this is determined by the parties; any interval is possible, but most clauses specify a monthly or quarterly review) and compare the daily average during the review period and the initial base average. If the comparison produces exchange rate fluctuations that are outside the agreed range of fluctuation, an adjustment is made to align prices with the new exchange rate if the fluctuation is within some range. If the fluctuation is greater than some limit, the parties agree to discuss and negotiate new prices.

In other words, the clause accepts the foreign exchange market's effect on currency value, but only if it is within a certain range of 5 to 10 per cent. Any fluctuation within the range does not affect pricing and any fluctuation outside the range specified opens up a re-negotiation of prices.

Table 12.2 **Exchange rates and pricing: BMW in the US**

	1986 BMW 528i	*1992 BMW 528i*	*Change in %*
Exchange rate	3.59 DM	1.59DM	(56%)
Price	$ 30,000	$ 42,500	+42%
DM sales	107,700 DM	67,575 DM	(37%)

To achieve 1986 profit levels, the car would have to cost $67,800 (i.e. a 226 per cent price increase)!

Inflation

Inflation, or a persistent upward change in price levels, is a world-wide phenomenon. Inflation requires periodic price adjustments. These adjustments are necessitated by rising costs that must be covered by increased selling prices. An essential requirement when pricing in an inflationary environment is the maintenance of operating profit margins. Regardless of cost accounting practices, if a company maintains its margins, it has effectively protected itself from the effects of inflation. To keep up with inflation in Peru, for example, Procter & Gamble at one time resorted to biweekly increases in detergent prices of 20 per cent to 30 per cent.[6]

Within the scope of this chapter, it is possible only to touch on the many accounting issues and conventions relating to price adjustments in international markets. In particular, it is worth noting that the traditional FIFO (first-in, first-out) costing method is hardly appropriate for an inflationary situation. A more appropriate accounting practice under conditions of rising prices is the LIFO (last-in, first-out) method, which takes the most recent raw material acquisition price and uses it as the basis for costing the product sold. In highly inflationary environments, historical approaches are less appropriate costing methods than replacement cost. The latter amounts to a next-in, first-out approach. Although this method does not conform to generally accepted accounting principles (GAAP), it is used to estimate future prices that will be paid for raw and component materials. These replacement costs can then be used to set prices. This approach is useful in managerial decision making, but it cannot be used in financial statements. Regardless of the accounting methods used, an essential requirement under inflationary conditions of any costing system is that it maintains gross and operating profit margins. Managerial actions can maintain these margins subject to the following constraints.

Government controls and subsidies

If government action limits the freedom of management to adjust prices, the maintenance of margins is definitely compromised. Under certain conditions, government action is a real threat to the profitability of a subsidiary operation. In a country that is undergoing severe financial difficulties and is in the midst of a financial crisis (e.g. a foreign exchange shortage caused in part by runaway inflation), government officials are under pressure to take some type of action.

For example, Procter & Gamble (P&G) encountered strict price controls in Venezuela in the late 1980s. Despite increases in the cost of raw materials, P&G was granted only about 50 per cent of the price increases it requested; even then, months passed before permission to raise prices was forthcoming. As a result, by 1988 detergent prices in Venezuela were less than what they were in other countries.[7]

In some cases, governments will take expedient steps rather than getting at the underlying causes of inflation and foreign exchange shortages. Such steps might include the use of broad or selective price controls. When selective controls are imposed, foreign companies are more vulnerable to control than local businesses, particularly if the outsiders lack the political influence over government decision making possessed by local managers.

Government control can also take the form of prior cash deposit requirements imposed on importers. This is a requirement that a company has to tie up funds in the form of a non-interest-bearing deposit for a specified period of time if it wishes to import products. Such requirements clearly create an incentive for a company to minimise the price of the imported product; lower prices mean smaller deposits. Other government requirements that affect the pricing decision are profit transfer rules that restrict the conditions under which profits can be transferred out of a country. Under such rules, a high transfer price paid for imported goods by an affiliated company can be interpreted as a device for transferring profits out of a country.

Government subsidies can also force a company to make strategic use of sourcing to be price competitive. In many countries, government subsidies to the agricultural sector make it difficult for foreign marketers of processed food to compete on price when exporting there. In case a foreign manufacturer from a country, where the product group in question is not subsidised, exports to a market, for example the European Union, where domestic producers receive subsidies, his prices will not be competitive. One way out of this dilemma is sourcing within the market or region in question. In the EU for example, by sourcing a product in France for resale in the Netherlands, a company can take advantage of lower costs derived from subsidies and eliminated price escalation due to tariffs and duties.

Competitive behaviour and market demand

Pricing decisions are bounded not only by cost, but also by the nature of demand and competitive action. A company producing a specialised product, or a product with a clear technological advantage over competitive products, has more flexibility in price setting than in a more competitive environment. Pricing then is often reduced to a static role in the marketing mix. The contrary is true, when a company encounters fierce competition in a market. Particularly aggressive competitors may use predatory pricing to drive other manufacturers out of the market.[8] Genuine predatory pricing is extremely rare, because it assumes the unlikely capability of a single producer to dominate a world market. However, the reproach of predatory pricing has been used as a suitable excuse for anti-dumping sanctions. Under the title of predatory pricing, national governments can impose duties on cheap imports that they judge as being dumped into their markets. In the 1990s, the Canadian subsidiary of the US baby food manufacturer Gerber Inc. suffered from government measures against its purported predatory pricing practices. Canada's International Trade Tribunal forced Gerber to raise its prices sharply, after it sold baby food at about 33 cents a jar, about 10 cents less than its major competitor HJ Heinz Canada Ltd. This price level was considered predatory and entailed the Court's demand for a 60 per cent price increase. As a result, Gerber lost its customer base almost entirely to its main competitor. The victims of this retaliatory measure were Canadian customers who were deprived of lower priced access to quality food.[9]

If competitors do not adjust their prices in response to rising costs, management – even if acutely aware of the effect of rising costs on operating margins – will be severely constrained in its ability to adjust prices accordingly. Conversely, if competitors are manufacturing or sourcing in a lower-cost country, it may be necessary to cut prices to stay competitive.

The interplay of these factors is reflected in the pricing policies adopted by companies. With increasing globalisation, there is greater competitive pressure on companies to restrain price increases. In a globalised industry, companies must compete with companies from all over the world. The car industry is a good example: the fierce struggle for market share by American, European, Japanese and Korean companies makes it difficult for any company to raise prices. If a manufacturer does raise prices, it is important to make sure that the increase does not put the company's product out of line with competitive alternatives.[10]

Key points	
	• International price setting is a process influenced by a large number of external and internal variables.
	• Among the most important external variables are currency fluctuations, inflation, government controls and subsidies, competitive behaviour and market demand.
	• Currency fluctuations may lead either to additional profit or loss for a firm. If a country's currency weakens relative to a trading partner's currency, a producer in a weak-currency country can cut export prices to hold market share or leave prices unchanged for healthier profit margins. In case the currency gets stronger, the reverse applies.
	• Inflation – the persistent upward change in price levels – may require periodic price adjustments for a company. The attention lies on maintaining operating profit margins.
	• Under certain circumstances, price control is taken out of the hands of a company. In countries, which are undergoing severe financial difficulties, governments may restrict price increases or prescribe fixed prices.

DIFFERENT APPROACHES TO INTERNATIONAL PRICE SETTING

Basically, companies active in international markets have three different options in how to set prices for foreign markets: (i) the approach of rigid cost-plus pricing, (ii) flexible cost-plus pricing and (iii) dynamic incremental pricing.

The selection which pricing option is used depends very much on the management's attitude towards international activities as well as its experience on international markets. So the inexperienced or part-time exporter does not usually go to all the effort to determine the best price for a product in international markets, but tries to recover the maximum revenue from each export venture. Such a company will frequently use the much simpler approach of rigid cost-plus pricing. As managers gain experience and become more sophisticated in their approach, however, they realize that the factors identified above should be considered when making pricing decisions. Eventually, they usually apply flexible cost-plus pricing and later on dynamic incremental pricing.

Rigid cost-plus pricing

Companies new to exporting frequently use a strategy known as cost-plus pricing to gain a toehold in the global marketplace. Cost-plus pricing requires adding up all the costs involved in getting the product to where it must go, plus shipping and ancillary charges and a profit percentage. The obvious advantage of using this method is its low threshold: it is relatively easy to arrive at a quote, assuming that accounting costs are readily available. The disadvantage of using historical accounting costs to arrive at a price is that this approach completely ignores demand and competitive conditions in target markets. However, novice exporters often do not care. They are reactively responding to global market opportunities, not proactively seeking them.

Often rigid cost-plus pricing results in either too low or too high prices in the light of market and competitive conditions. The latter phenomenon is also often called price escalation. Price escalation is the increase in a product's price as transportation, duty and distributor margins are added to the factory price. Figure 12.1 illustrates the mechanism of price escalation in international markets.

A European manufacturer of household cleaning products intended to export products to South America. The escalation of the C.I.F. price to the retail shelf in South America, with transportation, import duties and taxes, wholesaler and distributor margins, retail margins and VAT turned out to be in excess of 300 per cent! In many cases, this will price the exporter's products out of the market and render an export venture a failure.

The global marketer has several options when addressing the problem of price escalation. The choices are dictated in part by product and market competition. Marketers of domestically manufactured finished products may be forced to switch to lower-income, lower-wage countries for the sourcing of certain components or even of finished goods to keep costs and prices competitive. The athletic footwear industry is an example of an industry in which the leading companies have opted for low-income, low-wage country sourcing of their production. The low-wage strategy option should never become a formula, however. The problem with moving production to a low-wage country is that it provides a one-time advantage. This is no substitute for ongoing creativity in creating value. High-income countries are the home of thriving manufacturing operations run by companies that have been creative in figuring out ways to drive down the cost of labour as a percentage of total costs and in how to create a unique value. The Swiss watch industry, which owns the world's luxury watch

Figure 12.1 An example of international price escalation

	Street price for foreign markets	Street price for domestic market
Price ex works	100	100
+ Transportation, duties, taxes (10% for international sales, +5% for domestic sales)	+10	+5
Sub-total	110	105
+ International distributor's margin (30%)	35	
Sub-total	145	
+ National distributor margin (30%)	45	30
Sub-total	190	135
National retail margin (30%)	60	40
Sub-total	250	175
+ VAT (20%)	50	35
Total	300	210

business, did not achieve and maintain its pre-eminence by chasing cheap labour: it continues to succeed because it has focused on creating a unique value for its customers.

Another option is to source 100 per cent of a finished product offshore near or in local markets. The manufacturer could enter into a licensing arrangement, a joint venture, or a technology transfer agreement. With this option, the manufacturer has a presence in the market it is trying to penetrate; price escalation due to high manufacturing costs and transportation charges in the home market are no longer an issue. In 1992, IKEA, the Swedish home furnishing company, sourced 50 per cent of its products abroad, compared with only 10 per cent in 1989.[11] Daimler-Chrysler built a manufacturing plant in Tuscaloosa, US, to build its new sport utility vehicle. BMW has a plant in Spartanburg, where it manufactures two-seater sport car vehicles for the world markets.[12]

The third option is a thorough audit of the distribution structure in the target markets. A rationalisation of the distribution structure can substantially reduce the total mark-ups required to achieve distribution in international markets. Rationalisation may include selecting new intermediaries, assigning new responsibilities to old intermediaries, or establishing direct marketing operations such as selling on the web. For example, Toys 'R' Us has invaded the Japanese toy market because it bypassed layers of distribution and adopted a warehouse style of selling similar to its approach in other markets. Toys 'R' Us has been viewed as a test case of the ability of Western retailers, discounters, in particular – to change the rules of Japanese distribution.

Flexible cost-plus pricing

Under the approach of flexible cost-plus pricing, prices are derived the same way as rigid cost-plus pricing. In this case however, price variations are allowed under special circumstances. If, for example, the nature of the customer, the size of the order or the intensity of local competition require more flexibility, prices are adjusted accordingly.

Although this price-setting approach allows a higher degree of freedom to adjust for local idiosyncrasies, the primary goal is still to maintain profit margins.[13]

This pricing approach may be used, if a company aims at holding its market share in foreign markets. In single-country marketing, this strategy often involves reacting to price adjustments by competitors. For example, when one airline announces special bargain fares, most competing carriers must match the offer or risk losing passengers. In global marketing, currency fluctuations often trigger price adjustments. In the mid to late 1980s, most world currencies were rather strong compared to the US$. Companies based in Japan, Germany, France and elsewhere had to attempt to hold the line on US prices. Needless to say, adjusting prices to fit the competitive situation may mean lower profit margins. When Max Imgruth, head of Charles Jourdan USA, vetoed double-digit price increases for the company's shoes in 1992, he noted, 'The American consumer is not going to swallow those price increases.' Speaking of his company, he lamented, 'We're taking a tremendous hit. We're living on air and inspiration.' Now that the US$ appreciated against most other currencies, US firms reversely have these problems. If US-based companies marketing internationally maintain their price levels, currency translations tied to the strong dollar would have automatically increased the price of many products. As a result, companies would price themselves out of many international markets. To avoid this, companies may set prices based not their home currency price translated at the current exchange rate but, rather, on the competitive situation in each market and the ability and willingness of customers to pay.

Dynamic incremental pricing

This pricing option is based on the idea that fixed costs emerge regardless of whether the company is internationally successful or not. Its primary goal is thus to regain at least variable and international marketing and promotion costs in export ventures. As to the overhead, they are only partly added. This practice allows a company to sell at very competitive prices.

Therefore, this strategy is also known as penetration pricing. Penetration pricing uses price as a competitive weapon to gain market position. Over the past few decades, Asian MNCs have successfully used this pricing option to penetrate European and US markets. It should be noted that a first-time exporter is unlikely to use penetration pricing. The reason is simple: penetration pricing often means that the product may be sold at a loss for a certain length of time. Sometimes, this puts incremental pricing close to the air of dumping, which will be reverberated through legal sanctions in most countries. ·

Companies that are new to exporting cannot absorb such losses. They are not likely to have the marketing system in place (including transportation, distribution and sales organisations) that allows global companies like Sony to make effective use of a penetration strategy. However, a company whose product is not patentable may wish to use penetration pricing to achieve market saturation before the product is copied by competitors.

When Sony developed the portable compact disc player in the mid-1980s, the cost per unit at initial sales volumes was estimated to exceed €500. Since this was a 'no-go' price in Sony's international target markets, Akio Morita instructed management to price the unit in the €250 range to achieve penetration. Sony anticipated the sales volume to be expected in these markets would lead to scale economies and lower costs sufficient to achieve a profit at this lower price range.

Dynamic incremental pricing, however, also works in a different direction. While under penetration pricing, prices start low and are increased incrementally, market skimming introduces the product into a market at a relatively high price, which is then lowered over a period of time. The market skimming pricing strategy is a deliberate attempt to reach a market segment that is willing to pay a premium price for a product. In such instances, the product must create high value for buyers. This pricing strategy is often used in the introductory phase of the product life cycle, when both production capacity and competition are limited. By setting a deliberately high price, demand is limited to early adopters who are willing and able to pay the price. One goal of this pricing strategy is to maximise revenue on limited volume and to match demand to available supply. Another goal of market skimming pricing is to reinforce customers' perceptions of high product value. When this is done, the price is part of the total product positioning strategy.

When Sony first began selling Betamax video cassette recorders (VCRs) in the 1970s, it used a skimming strategy. Under the impression of the €1,099 price tag, a top manager recalls:

> It was fantastic, really. When you have a new product that is as jazzy as a videotape recorder, you really skim off the cream of the consuming public. The Betamax was selling for over a thousand €. But there were so many wealthy people who wanted to be the first in the neighbourhood that it just went whoof – like a vacuum. It flew off the shelf.[14]

STANDARDISATION VERSUS DIFFERENTIATION IN INTERNATIONAL PRICING

Beside the discussed approaches to international price setting, an important question is whether prices should be standardised across markets or differentiated between international markets. A price differentiation may occur due to different levels of production or distribution costs. Also, strategic considerations may lead a company to set different prices in international markets. For example, in order to compensate for the effect of different levels of competitive intensity or tax differences, it may make sense to charge different prices across borders.[15]

In practice, companies act far from consistent. Samli and Jacobs studied the pricing practices of US multinational firms.[16] Based on a mail survey, they concluded that 70 per cent of the firms in their sample of the top 350 of the Fortune 500 largest industrial companies and the 100 largest US multinational companies standardised their prices, whereas 30 per cent used variable pricing in world markets. Another study, however, provides an entirely different picture. A survey among German companies indicated that about 70 per cent of all companies in the sample use a differentiated strategy.[17]

Under certain circumstances, a firm uses pricing to aid its cross-subsidisation strategies. Cross-subsidisation means that a company uses financial resources accumulated in one part of the world to fight a competitive battle in another. A classic example is the price battle between Michelin and Goodyear in the 1970s. The French tyre company Michelin used its strong profit base in Europe to attack its major competitor Goodyear in its home market, the US. Compared to Goodyear and its leading

Figure 12.2 **Influences on price standardisation vs. differentiation**

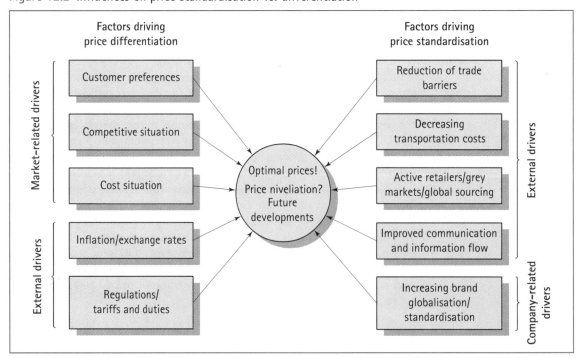

Source: Hermann Simon and Robert J. Dolan, *Profit durch Power Pricing* (Campus, Frankfurt, 1997), p. 168.

market position, Michelin had little to lose when it reduced prices in the US. It used its strong profit background to 'cross-subsidise' its activities in the US market. Eventually, Goodyear retaliated in the same way in the European market and the price war came to an end.[18]

Figure 12.2 provides a list of factors impinging on whether to charge different or standardised prices. According to Simon and Dolan, the decision to differentiate or standardise prices across borders is influenced by four drivers. A careful consideration of each factor and its applicability for the current pricing decision may finally lead to the most suitable alternative.[19] Generally speaking, the forces supporting price harmonisation appear to be stronger at present and their importance is likely to increase further in the future. Particularly, within economic regions, such as the European Union, price differentials between markets will be hard to maintain. While today, price differentials across the EU are still considerable, experts are convinced that they will shortly belong to the past. A recent survey showed that the price of a basket of 53 goods varied across the EU on average by 24 per cent from the mean – almost twice as much as within the US. Experts emphasise that price harmonisation within the EU will be the logical development in the next years.[20]

Companies may find themselves in an awkward situation: while actual price differences – due to differences in production or distribution costs – may appear justified, price standardisation will very likely increase as outlined before. How will companies now be able to prevent prices standardising at the lowest level possible? One answer may be found in so-called international price corridors. These price corridors will work particularly well in regions with intensive economic interaction, where market transparency is high and goods may flow freely across borders, as in the European Union for example.

Figure 12.3 delineates how a price corridor may work.

An international price corridor may serve as a compromise between unprofitably low uniform prices and country-specific differentiated prices. The price corridor aims to render arbitrage unattractive. Arbitrage is defined as the difference between prices for the same product in different markets. As will be described later, arbitrage will lead to grey markets or parallel imports, where traders take advantage of low prices for a given product in one market and then sell the goods in markets with a high price level.[21]

Figure 12.3 **An international price corridor**

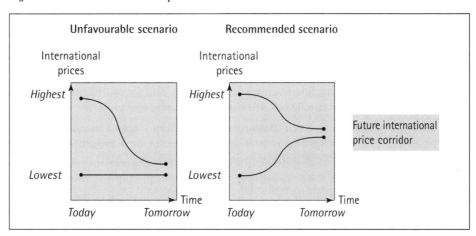

Source: Hermann Simon and Robert J. Dolan, *Profit durch Power Pricing* (Campus, Frankfurt, 1997), p. 176.

409

Figure 12.4 **A decision-making framework for international pricing**

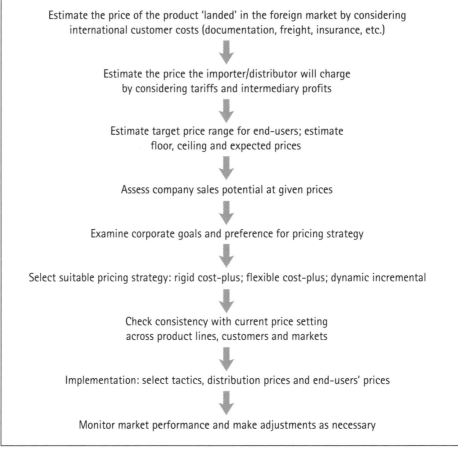

Source: S. Tamer Cavusgil, 'Pricing for global markets', *Columbia Journal of World Business* (Winter 1996), p. 73.

To assist companies faced with the task of international price setting, Figure 12.4 may serve as a guideline for the international price setting process. In a step-wise hands-on approach, this framework will allow firms to derive at suitable international prices.

Key points

- When determining an international price, a company has three different options: (i) rigid-cost plus pricing, (ii) flexible cost-plus pricing and (iii) dynamic incremental pricing. The three alternatives may be distinguished by the flexibility they permit and the costs they include.

- In times of increasing transparency across markets – due to communication technologies such as the Internet or a common currency, e.g. the Euro – price differentiation across markets is hard to maintain.

- To avoid levelling out prices on a uniform low base, companies have the possibility to use a price corridor. A price corridor defines the range within which prices across borders may vary. The price corridor needs to be set in a way that it prevents arbitrage, i.e. taking advantage of price differences.

DUMPING

Dumping is an important global pricing issue. If a company exports a product at a price lower than the price it normally charges in its own home market, it is said to be dumping the product. The question arises whether this practice is unfair competition. According to the WTO, opinions differ, but many governments take action against dumping in order to defend their domestic industries. The WTO agreement does not pass judgement. Its focus is on how governments can or cannot react to dumping – it disciplines anti-dumping actions in a document often called the 'Anti-Dumping Agreement'. Under this agreement, a government may impose sanctions, if it is able to show that dumping is taking place. The extent of dumping (how much lower the export price is compared to the exporter's home market price – the product's 'normal value') has to be calculated and must show that the dumping is causing injury. If the investigation shows dumping is taking place and domestic industry is being hurt, the exporting company can undertake to raise its price to an agreed level in order to avoid anti-dumping import duty.[22]

As the nature of these issues and regulations suggest, some countries use dumping legislation as a legitimate device to protect local enterprise from predatory pricing practices by foreign companies. In other nations, the regulations are used as protectionist measures to limit foreign competition in a market. The rationale for dumping legislation is that dumping is harmful to the orderly development of enterprise within an economy. Few economists would object to long-run or continuous dumping. If this were done, it would be an opportunity for a country to take advantage of a low-cost source of a particular good and to specialise in other areas. However, continuous dumping rarely occurs. The type of dumping practised by most companies is sporadic and unpredictable and does not provide a reliable basis for national economic planning. Instead, it may hurt domestic enterprise.

The last few years have seen a great incidence of antidumping investigation and penalties, imposed primarily in the EU, the US, Canada and Australia. These investigations often take a very long time, to an extent that the delay may even be lethal to the accusing company. An excellent example in this respect is the US-based company Smith Corona. It filed an antidumping complaint against Brother Industries of Japan in 1974 and was involved in dumping-related litigation until the day it declared bankruptcy. One of the lessons from this saga is that it can take years to get relief from the International Trade Commission. Smith Corona had to re-file its original complaint; the ITC finally found in its favour in 1980, ordering a 48.7 per cent duty on imports of portable typewriters. However, the duties only applied to typewriters; Brother responded by designing new products with chip-based memory functions. Because this new product was no longer classified as a typewriter – rather, it was a word processor – Brother effectively side-stepped the duties. Brother also began assembling typewriters and word processors from imported parts in a plant in Tennessee. This example shows to what lengths a company will go to get around dumping regulations; Brother used both product innovation and a new sourcing strategy. Finally, in an ironic twist, Brother turned the tables on Smith Corona by accusing the latter of dumping. The rationale: many of Smith Corona's typewriters are imported from a plant in Singapore; Brother pointed to its own US plant as evidence that it was the true US producer![23]

Companies concerned with running foul of antidumping legislation have developed a number of approaches for avoiding the dumping laws. One approach is to differentiate the product sold from that in the home market. An example of this is an auto accessory that one company packaged with a wrench and an instruction book, thereby changing the accessory to a tool. The tariff rate in the export market happened to be lower on tools and the company also acquired immunity from antidumping laws because the package was not comparable to competing goods in the target market. Another approach is to make non-price-competitive adjustments in arrangements with affiliates and distributors. For example, credit can be extended and essentially have the same effect as a price reduction.

GREY MARKETS AND PARALLEL IMPORTS

For many people, the phrase black market conjures up images of a shadowy, underground economy in which goods are bought and sold in back alleys without the knowledge of government authorities. For better or for worse, global marketing has a distinctive colour on its palette: grey. Grey marketing is the distribution of trademarked products in a country through channels unauthorised by the trademark owner. Or to put it differently: grey marketers sell unauthorised imports of goods into a market with a sales price less than the one offered by authorised distributors. Basically, they take advantage of price differences between markets, by re-importing branded merchandise from low-price into high-price markets.[24] This practice is also known as parallel importing. While there are different ways of parallel importing, their impact remains the same: reduced or cannibalised sales for the producer in high-price countries and troubles with authorised sales channels.[25]

The UK car market, for example, has seen an increasing number of cars coming in through parallel imports over the last decade. Particularly, Japan is a source for parallel car imports, as it is the largest market driving on the left. The cars sold may be either new ones from Japanese dealers who are pushed hard to reach their sales targets, or used cars, which did not undergo or pass the expensive third-year inspection in Japan. In 1998, it was estimated that some 80,000 UK registrations stem from grey market channels.[26]

Parallel imports also occurred with French champagne sold in the United States and in the European market for pharmaceuticals, in which prices vary widely from country to country.[27] In the United Kingdom and the Netherlands, for example, parallel imports account for as much as 10 per cent of the sales of some pharmaceutical brands. In the UK, the market for parallel imports of drugs grew from about €280 million in 1996 to €350 million in 1997, representing 5 per cent of the total drug market. Other estimates are even higher: according to these sources, 10–15 per cent of pharmaceuticals sold in the UK in 1999 stem from parallel importing, amounting to €825 million.[28] The large pharmaceutical company Glaxo Wellcome found its own way to curb parallel imports. In Spain, which is known as a market with rather low prices for pharmaceutical products, two different price lists were introduced: one with the – low – domestic price and one with higher prices relevant to export markets and 'priced to real economic criteria'. To ensure what Glaxo calls 'correct distribution practices', the company forced its distributors to comply with these price regulations. Disregarding the rules would result in detrimental consequences such as supply blockages. The Spanish government warned Glaxo not to let this step lead to shortages in the supply of pharmaceuticals, otherwise the company would have to suffer dire consequences.[29] Later that year, the European Commission became formally involved in the case by

EUROPEAN FOCUS

In the name of the people ...

... of the European Union, the European Court of Justice reached a memorable verdict on parallel imports. The case has been going on for quite some time, creating a lot of controversy and debate. The background: in 1995, an Austrian retailer, Hartlauer, selling consumer electronics and glasses at bargain prices, bought 21,000 spectacle frames in Bulgaria. The problem: these frames stemmed from an outdated collection by *Silhouette* and were sold to a trading company in Bulgaria under the constraint that the frames could be sold only there or in the states of the former Soviet Union. A classic case of parallel importing! *Silhouette* found itself in a position to defend its upmarket brand and sued *Hartlauer* to stop advertising the sale of the designer spectacle frames at extraordinary low prices. The European Court of Justice decided in favour of Silhouette and prohibited Hartlauer from selling the re-imported frames.

The ruling had far reaching implications, as other manufacturers exert pressure on parallel importers. Honda UK threatened dealers with legal actions, in case they would not cease trading Honda motorcycles sourced from outside the EU. Honda argues that grey market imports may harm customer safety. Usually, Honda's motorcycles arrive in the UK partially knocked-down and putting them together needed particular care and know-how. Among the dealers threatened with legal action is Granby Motors, which was a franchised Honda dealer until one year ago. Granby and his colleagues all belong to the Association of Parallel Importers

which aims at guaranteeing high standards. While its legal arguments might have been in line with court rulings, Honda found it very hard to proceed with its claims in public without being seen as anything else than anti-competitive.

The EU ruling also fuelled several actions pending again Britain's biggest supermarket chain Tesco. The company came under fire for selling designer products such as Levi's Jeans famous model 501 for €45, almost half the price charged in authorised outlets. Another US manufacturer, Guess?, is seeking legal action against Tesco for selling its T-shirts imported from sources other than the original manufacturer. A large company such as Tesco appears not to be worried by legal threats. Such uproar offers excellent value-for-money publicity and a quiet retreat is always possible when turbulence dies down.

As to the market impact, opinions are divided: while critics fear the damages in brand image and the loss of profits to importers, others assume that discrimination is a way to raise profits at the expense of consumers.

Food for thought

- Does the decision of the European Court of Justice harm the consumer? What are the key arguments for and against permitting parallel imports?
- Arguing from the perspective of an internationally renowned brand, which problems might be caused by parallel imports?

Source: 'Die weltweite Erschöpfung des Rechts aus einer Marke ist mit dem Gemeinschaftsrecht unvereinbar', *Pressemitteilung Nr, 49/98 des Europäischen Gerichtshofes,* 16 July 1998, http://curia.eu.int/de/cp/cp98/cp9849de.html; 'Hartlauer verliert Streit um Silhouette-Fassungen', *Die Presse,* 17.7.1998; 'A grey area: parellel imports in the EU', *The Economist,* 13 June 1998; Kevin Ash, 'Honda's legal case for higher profits', *The Daily Telegraph,* 19 December 1998; 'When grey is good: the European Union should be encouraging "grey" imports, not banning them', *The Economist,* 22 August 1998; 'A grey market: shopping – parallel imports under attack', *The Economist,* 5 December 1998.

sending a 'statement of objections' to Glaxo. It stated that Glaxo's practice would thwart the free flow of goods within the EU.[30]

As the Silhouette ruling shows, the EU takes a differentiated approach to grey markets, following manufacturers' considerations. Manufacturers put forward numerous arguments to fight parallel imports. They point out that parallel imports may result in a loss of consumer confidence and trust in branded goods. Not only will this discourage them from investment in their brand, but parallel imports may also expose consumers to piracy and fraud. A deeper look, however, provides a more differentiated picture. There are marketplaces where parallel importing is allowed: in the US and within EU borders and obviously this does not appear to harm consumers. On the contrary, increased competition leads to lower prices. Above all, advocates of legalising grey markets put forward that the parallel imports of genuine Nike sportswear, for example, does not mean allowing in counterfeits as well.[31]

TRANSFER PRICING

Transfer pricing refers the pricing of goods and services bought and sold by operating units or divisions of a single company. In other words, transfer pricing concerns intra-corporate exchanges – transactions between buyers and sellers that have the same corporate parent. For example, Toyota subsidiaries sell to and buy from, each other. The same is true of other companies operating globally. As companies expand and create decentralised operations, profit centres become an increasingly important component in the overall corporate financial picture. Appropriate intra-corporate transfer pricing systems and policies are required to ensure profitability at each level. When a company extends its operations across national boundaries, transfer pricing takes on new dimensions and complications. In determining transfer prices to subsidiaries, global companies must address a number of issues, including taxes, duties and tariffs, country profit transfer rules, conflicting objectives of joint venture partners and government regulations. Figure 12.5 illustrates the principles of transfer pricing and demonstrates the scope for profit increases through transfer price manipulation.

There are three major alternative approaches to transfer pricing. The approach used

Figure 12.5 Basic principles of transfer pricing

Country X (high tax)		Transfer price manipulation	
'Ex factory' costs	100		100
Tranfer price ('arm's length') to subsidiary in market Z	120	Artificially low transfer price	105
Profit	20		5
Local tax (50%)	10		2.5
Net profit	10		2.5
Country Z (low tax)			
Buys from X	120		105
Duty (20%)	24		21
Cost warehouse	144		126
Sells at (marketable price)	160		160
Profit	16		34
Tax (5%)	0.8		1.7
Net profit	15.2		32.3
Corporate net profit (2 markets)	25.2		34.8
Government tax/duty	34.8		25.2

will vary with the nature of the firm, products, markets and the historical circumstances of each case. The alternatives are: (1) cost-based transfer pricing, (2) market-based transfer pricing and (3) negotiated prices.

Cost-based transfer pricing

Because companies define costs differently, some companies using the cost-based approach may arrive at transfer prices that reflect variable and fixed manufacturing costs only. Alternatively, transfer prices may be based on full costs, including overhead costs from marketing, research and development (R&D) and other functional areas. The way costs are defined may have an impact on tariffs and duties of sales to affiliates and subsidiaries by global companies.

Cost-plus pricing is a variation of the cost-based approach. Companies that follow the cost-plus pricing method are taking the position that profit must be shown for any product or service at every stage of movement through the corporate system. In such an instance, transfer prices may be set at a certain percentage of fixed costs, such as '110 per cent of cost'. While cost-plus pricing may result in a price that is completely unrelated to competitive or demand conditions in international markets, many exporters use this approach successfully.

Market–based transfer price

A market-based transfer price is derived from the price required to be competitive in the international market. The constraint on this price is cost. However, as noted above, there is a considerable degree of variation in how costs are defined. Because costs generally decline with volume, a decision must be made regarding whether to price on the basis of current or planned volume levels. To use market-based transfer prices to enter a new market that is too small to support local manufacturing, third-country sourcing may be required. This enables a company to establish its name or franchise in the market without committing to a major capital investment.

Negotiated transfer prices

A third alternative is to allow the organisation's affiliates to negotiate transfer prices among themselves. In some instances, the final transfer price may reflect costs and market prices, but this is not a requirement.[32] The gold standard of negotiated transfer prices is known as an arm's-length price: the price that two independent, unrelated entities would negotiate. Table 12.3 summarises the results of various studies comparing transfer pricing methods by country.

Table 12.3 Transfer pricing methods for selected countries

Methods	United States	Canada	Japan	United Kingdom
1. Cost-based	46%	33%	41%	38%
2. Market-price-based	35%	37%	37%	31%
3. Negotiated	14%	26%	22%	20%
4. Other	5%	4%	0%	11%
	100%	100%	100%	100%

Source: Adapted from Charles T. Horngren and George Foster, *Cost Accounting: A Managerial Approach* (Upper Saddle River, NJ: Prentice Hall, 1991), p. 866.

GLOBAL PERSPECTIVE

When the taxman rings twice ...

Transfer pricing issues increasingly keep CFOs awake at night, as national revenue services compete to secure what they belief as their 'fair share' of a multinational company's profit. As surveys show, transfer pricing is the single tax issue with top priority on the corporate financial agenda. A look back in history unveils the troubles: tax systems were developed after the Second World War, when cross-border movements in goods, capital and labour were relatively small. Now, firms and people are more mobile – and can exploit tax differences between countries.

Internationally active firms may design their products in one country, manufacture them in another and sell them in a third. This opens up the wonderful world of transfer pricing: in the intra-corporate component exchange, inflated prices are charged to a subsidiary in a high-tax country to move taxable profits to a subsidiary in a low-tax country.

As a result, governments are eager to tighten their laws against incorrect transfer pricing. The UK, for example, introduced the so-called Corporate Tax Self Assessment (CTSA). This means more sophisticated planning tools and increased planning efforts, as companies will have to predict profits, taxable profits, capital allowances, double tax relief and group tax issues. Clearly, the burden is on the taxpayer to get complex calculations correct. In order to alleviate companies somewhat, Germany and several other countries have begun to enter APAs (Advanced Pricing Agreements). Under such an agreement, companies are allowed to adjust their transfer pricing submission with fiscal authorities before filing the final documentation.

The consequences of failure can be dire: in Japan, a number of high-profile MNCs such as Monsanto, Baxter or Ciba lost their battle against local tax authorities. Consequently, heavy fines and additional back taxes have been levied.

The OECD too has agreed on transfer pricing guidelines based on the 'arm's length' principle. However, companies fear the devil in the detail and arbitrary rulings from local authorities. They

view with particular horror moves towards penalties up to 10 per cent based on the tax bill, which might even put some of them out of business.

Yet, discussions are far from over. Two recent developments will even spur tax authorities' attention: selling on the Internet and the Euro.

As the Internet increases mobility of capital and financial activity exponentially, tax authorities are struggling to see how they can protect tax bases against massive leakage. The traditional tax principles with respect to source, residence and permanent establishment appear more than inadequate to prevent virtual tax havens. The supply of products by the Internet raises fundamental questions for tax. Currently there is no real global consensus how and where e-commerce should be taxed. Often, this forces companies to pay multiple taxes on the same income, so as not to come into conflict with different local authorities.

The second significant impact on transfer pricing will be the Euro. Not only will the Euro change pricing practices in general – intra-corporate as well as market pricing. It will also bring about much more clarity as to the prevailing structures of corporate transfer pricing. Fiscal authorities throughout Europe – and in non-participating states – will find it much easier to challenge assumptions and attempt to secure for themselves a 'fairer share' of the tax paid.

However, one aspect remains undisputed: 'tax competition' between states and transfer pricing will be a constant subject of debate at international level.

Food for thought

- Describe three principal options a company has when setting transfer prices. Which factors constrain the choice of a transfer pricing option in practice?
- From the perspective of a domestic profit centre transferring semi-finished products to an overseas subsidiary in a low tax country, would you prefer high or low transfer prices? How does the

GLOBAL PERSPECTIVE continued

'ideal' transfer price (high or low) change when the transaction is viewed from the perspective of (1) the purchasing subsidiary, (2) corporate head- quarters, (3) the domestic tax authority and (4) the overseas tax authority?

Source: 'The tap runs dry: disappearing taxes', *The Economist*, 31 July 1997 (343/8019); 'Time to tackle the most taxing issue: transfer pricing', *Financial Times*, 24 September 1998; Jim Kelly, 'Company tax shake-up finds multinationals ill-prepared', *Financial Times*, 2 July 1998; Jim Kelly, 'Cyberspace threats to fiscal regimes', *Financial Times*, 24 September 1999; Paul Abrahams, 'Taxing in the extreme', *Financial Times*, 24 September 1999; Jim Kelly, 'New upheaval on the way: corporate self-assessment', *Financial Times*, 20 November 1998; Brad Rolph and Jay Niederhoffer, 'Transfer pricing and e-commerce', *International Tax Review*, September 1999, pp. 34–39; Conrad Young and Robert Tsang, 'E-commerce and EMU', *International Tax Review*, December 1998/January 1999, pp. 13–16.

Tax regulations and transfer prices

Because the global corporation conducts business in a world with different corporate tax rates, there is an incentive to maximise income in countries with the lowest tax rates and to minimise income in high-tax countries. Governments, naturally, are well aware of this situation. In recent years, many governments have tried to maximise national tax revenues by examining company returns and mandating reallocation of income and expenses.

Joint ventures present an incentive to set transfer prices at higher levels than would be used in sales to wholly owned affiliates, because a company's share of the joint venture earnings is less than 100 per cent. Any profits that occur in the joint venture must be shared. Tax audits are an important reason for working out an agreement that will also be acceptable to the tax authorities. The tax authorities' criterion of arm's-length prices is probably most appropriate for the majority of joint ventures.

To avoid potential conflict, companies with joint ventures should work out pricing agreements in advance that are acceptable to both sides. The following are several considerations for joint venture transfer pricing:[33]

1 The way in which transfer prices will be adjusted in response to exchange rate changes.
2 Expected reductions in manufacturing costs arising from learning-curve improvements and the way these will be reflected in transfer prices.
3 Shifts in the sourcing of products or components from parents to alternative sources.
4 The effects of competition on volume and overall margins.

However, transfer pricing to minimise tax liabilities can also lead to unexpected and undesired distortions. A classic example is a major US company with a decentralised, profit-centred organisation that promoted and gave frequent and substantial salary increases to its divisional manager in Switzerland. The reason for the manager's rapid rise was his outstanding profit record. His stellar numbers were picked up by the company's performance appraisal control system, which in turn triggered the salary and promotion actions. The problem in this company was that the financial control system had not been adjusted to recognise that a Swiss tax haven profit centre had been created. The manager's sky-high profits were simply the result of artificially low transfer pricing into the tax haven operations and artificially high transfer pricing out of the Swiss tax haven to operating subsidiaries. It took a team of outside consultants to discover the situation. In this case, the company's profit and loss records were a gross distortion of true operating results. The company had to adjust its control system and use different criteria to evaluate managerial performance in tax havens.

Corporate costs and profits are also affected by import duties. The higher the duty rate, the more desirable a low transfer price. The high duty creates an incentive to reduce transfer prices to minimise the customs duty. Duties in many industry sectors were substantially reduced or eliminated by the Uruguay round of WTO negotiations. Many companies tend to downplay the influence of taxes when developing pricing policies. There are a number of reasons for this. First, some companies consider tax savings to be trivial in comparison with the earnings that can be obtained by concentrating on effective systems of motivation and corporate resource allocation. Second, management may consider any effort at systematic tax minimisation to be unethical. Another argument is that a simple, consistent and straightforward pricing policy minimises the tax investigation problems that can develop if sharper pricing policies are pursued. According to this argument, the savings in executive time and the costs of outside counsel offset any additional taxes that might be paid using such an approach. Finally, after analysing the world-wide trend toward harmonisation of tax rates, many chief financial officers (CFOs) have concluded that any set of policies appropriate to a world characterised by wide differentials in tax rates will soon become obsolete. They have therefore concentrated on developing pricing policies that are appropriate for a world that is very rapidly evolving toward relatively similar tax rates.

Although a full treatment of tax issues is beyond the scope of this book, students should understand that a basic pricing question facing global marketers is, 'What can a company do in the international pricing area in the light of current tax law?'

Key points

- If a company exports a product at a price lower than the price it normally charges on its home market, it is said to be dumping the product into the foreign market. For the competitors in the market, this might lead to dire consequences, when consumers switch to cheaper products. As a result, the WTO has elaborate regulations on how to treat dumping. In same cases, however, dumping may also be used as a more 'elegant' way to ban competition from the home market.

- Grey markets are a consequence of parallel imports. Parallel imports occur when a person other than the trademark owner distributes trademarked products in a country through unauthorised channels. Grey marketers sell unauthorised imports of goods into a market with a sales price less than the one offered by authorised distributors, as they take advantage of price differences between markets.

- Transfer pricing refers to the pricing of goods and services bought and sold by operating units or divisions of a single company. It concerns intracorporate exchanges. Transfer prices have attracted growing interest from national tax services, as companies may sometimes use transfer prices to shift profits from high-tax to low-tax countries. Therefore, most local authorities require transfer prices to be at arm's length, meaning a price that two independent, unrelated entities would negotiate.

Summary

Pricing decisions are a critical element of the marketing mix that must reflect internal factors such as production or distribution costs and external factors like currency fluctuation, inflation, governmental influences as well as competitive pressure and customer demand in the markets under scrutiny. Each company must examine the market, the competition and its own costs and objectives and local and regional regulations and laws in setting prices that are consistent with the overall marketing strategy.

Basically, companies may use three different approaches to price setting. Under a rigid-cost plus pricing, which is used mostly by companies new to foreign business, all costs incurred in getting a product to an international market and its customers are taken into account. Flexible-cost plus pricing is based on the same principle. Prices may vary however, if the market situation in the country requires it. Dynamic incremental pricing – a strategy for internationally experienced companies – is based on the idea that a firm incurs fixed costs regardless of whether or not it is internationally active. Therefore, the bottom line in price setting are variable and international marketing and promotion costs. Overheads may be added, if the foreign market situation allows it.

Dumping – selling products in international markets at prices below those in the home country or below the cost of production – and parallel importing are two particularly contentious pricing issues. As a consequence, organisations like the WTO or the OECD have issued guidelines how to treat these problematic situations. Company managers who are transferring goods and services within a company across borders have to answer the question how to price such intra-corporate transactions. As companies sometimes use these transactions to transfer profits from a high-tax to a low-tax country, national tax services try to counteract. As a result, companies need to pay more and more attention to company profitability objectives that conform to tax regulations in individual country markets.

Concepts and definitions

Rigid cost–plus pricing

Rigid cost-plus pricing means adding up all the costs required to get the product to where it must go. This practice is frequently used by novices in the international arena who strive for full coverage of their export ventures.

Flexible cost–plus pricing

Prices are derived in the same way as in rigid cost-plus pricing. However, price variations are allowed under special circumstances, such as the nature of customers, national idiosyncrasies etc.

Dynamic incremental pricing

Describes a price-setting practice which is based on the idea that fixed costs emerge regardless of whether the company is successful or not. Therefore, international prices are based on variable and international marketing and promotion costs. Overheads are added if possible.

Price corridor

A price corridor is a way to differentiate prices between markets in a time of price harmonisation across borders. A price corridor has to be determined in a way that it renders arbitrage (taking advantage of price differences between markets) unattractive. Price corridors are likely to be important within the EU, when the Euro is in effect in everyday life.

Dumping	If a company exports a product at a price lower than the price it normally charges on its home market, it is said to be dumping the product.
Parallel imports	Parallel imports take advantage of price differences between markets, by re-importing branded merchandise from low-price into high-price markets.
Grey market	Is a market where trademarked products are distributed through channels unauthorised by the owner of the trademark.
Transfer pricing	Refers to the pricing of goods and services bought and sold by operating units or divisions of a single company.
Principle of arm's length	Is a way of establishing a transfer price between a company's operating units. The price shall amount to what two independent, unrelated entities would negotiate.

Discussion questions

1 What are the factors influencing international prices?

2 Define the various types of pricing strategies available to global marketers.

3 What is dumping? Is it an important trade issue or a red herring?

4 How would you describe a grey market? Which options do producers have to curb parallel imports?

5 What is a transfer price? What is the difference, if any, between a transfer price and a regular price? What are three methods for determining transfer prices?

6 What are the three alternative approaches to global pricing?

7 If you were responsible for marketing computed axial tomography (CAT) scanners world-wide and your sourcing country (location of manufacture) was experiencing a strong and appreciating currency against almost all other world currencies, what options are available for adjusting prices to take into account the strong currency situation?

Webmistress's hotspots

Homepage of the WTO document dissemination facility
If you want to find out how much import duty the European Community levied on polyester staple fibre from Belarus due to dumping accusation in 1997, you will find the answer here! (By the way, it was 43.5 per cent!) You may also find all sorts of useful information on dumping and how it is treated by the WTO!
http://www.wto.org/wto/ddf/ep/public.html under the document # G/ADP/N/22/EEC

Homepage of the OECD
Here you will find the OECD guidelines on transfer pricing.
http://www.oecd.org//daf/fa/tr–price/transfer.htm

Homepage of the EAIVT (European Association of Independent Vehicle Traders)
In case you intend to check out how to import your new car from another EU country, here you can find some basic information.
http://www.eaivt.com/public/pigb.htm

Homepage of Hartlauer

This page provides you with extensive information on the company whose practices lead to a ground-breaking judgement of the EU Court of Justice.

http://www.hartlauer.at

Homepage of the European Court of Justice

Here you can find the details on the Court's decision in the case Hartlauer vs. Silhouette.

http://curia.eu.int/de/cp/index98.htm

Suggested readings

Abdallah, Wagdy M., *International Transfer Pricing Policies: Decision Making Guidelines for Multinational Companies.* New York: Quorum Books, 1989.

Belz, Christian, 'Internationale Preisharmonisierung', *Thexis*, 2 (1997): pp. 26–30.

Cannon, Hugh M. and Fred W. Morgan, 'A strategic pricing framework', *Journal of Business and Industrial Marketing*, 6, 3, 4 (Summer/Fall 1991): pp. 59–70.

Cohen, Stephen S. and John Zysman, 'Countertrade, offsets, barter and buyouts', *California Management Review*, 28, 2 (1986): pp. 41–55.

Coopers & Lybrand, *International Transfer Pricing.* Oxfordshire: CCH Editions Limited, 1993.

Diller, Hermann, 'Die Preispolitik der internationalen Unternehmung', *WiST Wirtschaftswissenschaftliches Studium*, 16, 6 (1987): pp. 269–275.

Doorley, Thomas L., III and Timothy M. Collins, *Teaming up for the '90s: A Guide to International Joint Ventures and Strategic Alliances.* New York: Business One Irwin, 1991.

Eccles, Robert G., *The Transfer Pricing Problem: A Theory for Practice.* Lexington, MA: Lexington Books, 1985.

Faulds, David J., Orlen Grunewald and Denise Johnson, 'A cross-national investigation of the relationship between the price and quality of consumer products, 1970–1990', *Journal of Global Marketing*, 8, 1 (1994): pp. 7–25.

Gaul, Wolfgang and Ulrich Lutz, 'Pricing in international marketing and Western European economic integration', *Management International Review*, 34, 2 (1994): pp. 101–124.

Glicklich, Peter A. and Seth B. Goldstein, 'New transfer pricing regulations adhere more closely to an arm's-length standard', *Journal of Taxation*, 78, 5 (May 1993): pp. 306–314.

Lancioni, Richard and John Gattorna, 'Strategic value pricing: its role in international business', *International Journal of Physical Distribution and Logistics*, 22, 6 (1992): pp. 24–27.

Lutz, Ulrich, *Preispolitik im internationalen Marketing und westeuropäische Integration*, Frankfurt: Peter Lang Europäischer Verlag der Wissenschaften, 1994.

Marn, Michael V. and Robert L. Rosiello, 'Managing price, gaining profit', *Harvard Business Review*, 70, 5 (September/October 1992): pp. 84–94.

Nagle, Thomas T., *The Strategy and Tactics of Pricing: A Guide to Profitable Decision Making.* Upper Saddle River, NJ: Prentice Hall, 1987.

Organization for Economic Cooperation and Development, *Tax Aspects of Transfer Pricing Within Multinational Enterprises: The United States Proposed Regulations.* Paris: OECD, 1993.

Paun, Dorothy A., Larry D. Compeau and Shruv Grewal, 'A model of the influence of marketing objectives on pricing strategies in international countertrade', *Journal of Public Policy and Marketing*, 16 (Spring 1997): pp. 69–82.

Robert, Michel, *Strategy Pure and Simple: How Winning CEOs Outthink Their Competition.* New York: McGraw-Hill, 1993.

Samli, A. Coskun and Laurence Jacobs, 'Pricing practices of American multinational firms: standardization vs. localization dichotomy', *Journal of Global Marketing*, 8, 2 (1994): pp. 51–74.

Sander, M., *Internationales Preismanagement.* Heidelberg: Physica-Verlag, 1997.

Schuster, Falko, 'Barter arrangements with money: the modern form of compensation trading', *Columbia Journal of World Business* (Fall 1980): pp. 61–66.

Seymour, Daniel T., *The Pricing Decision.* Chicago: Probus Publishing, 1989.

Simon, Hermann, 'Pricing opportunities – and how to exploit them', *Sloan Management Review*, 33, 2 (Winter 1992): pp. 55–65.

Simon, Hermann and Carsten Wiese, 'Europäisches Preismanagement', *Marketing ZFP*, 4 (1992): pp. 246–256.

Simon, Hermann and Eckhard Kucher, 'The European pricing time bomb and how to cope with it', *European Management Journal*, 10, 2 (June 1992): pp. 136–145.

Simon, Hermann and Robert J. Dolan, *Profit durch Power Pricing – Strategien aktiver Preispolitik.* Frankfurt: Campus Verlag, 1997.

Sinclair, Stuart, 'A guide to global pricing', *Journal of Business Strategy*, 14, 3 (1993): pp. 16–19.

Williams, Jeffery R., 'How sustainable is your competitive advantage?' *California Management Review*, 34, 3 (Spring 1992): pp. 29–51.

Notes

1. 'The Gap sees the web as global retail channel', *Newsbytes News Network*, 25 May 1998. Vanessa Thorpe, 'Gap takes to the net in move to outsmart high-street rivalry', *The Independent*, 26 May 1998.

2. Hermann Simon and Robert J. Dolan, *Profit durch Power-Pricing* (Frankfurt: Campus, 1997): p. 171.

3. S.T. Cavusgil, 'Unraveling the mystique of export pricing', *Business Horizons* (1988): pp. 54–63.

4. H. Simon, *Preismanagement: Analyse, Strategie, Umsetzung* (Wiesbaden: Gabler Verlag, 1992). H. Simon, *Preismanagement kompakt – Probleme und Methoden des modernen Pricing* (Wiesbaden: Gabler Verlag, 1995).

5. N. Piercy, 'British export market selection and pricing', *Industrial Marketing Management*, 10 (1981): pp. 287–297. J.C. Baker and J.K. Ryans, Jr. 'Some aspects of international pricing: a neglected area of management policy.' In *European Marketing: a Guide to the New Opportunities*, ed. R. Lynch, pp. 264–270 (London: Kogan Page, 1973). M.B. Myers, 'The pricing of export products: why managers aren't satisfied with the results?', *Journal of World Business*, 32, 3 (1997): pp. 277–289.

6. Alecia Swasy, 'Foreign formula: Procter & Gamble fixes aim on tough market: the Latin Americans', *Wall Street Journal*, 15 June 1990, p. A7.

7. Alecia Swasy, 'Foreign formula: Procter & Gamble fixes aim on tough market: the Latin Americans', *Wall Street Journal*, 15 June 1990, p. A7.

8. S. Tamer Cavusgil, 'Pricing for global markets', *Columbia Journal of World Business*, Winter (1996): pp. 66–78.

9. Peter Morton, 'Ottawa battles over babies', *Financial Post*, 26 August 1998, p. 3.

10. Lucinda Harper and Fred R. Bleakley, 'Like old times: an era of low inflation changes the calculus for buyers and sellers', *The Wall Street Journal*, 14 January 1994, p. A1.

11. Joan E. Rigdon and Valerie Reitman, 'Pricing paradox: consumers still find imported bargains despite weak dollars', *Wall Street Journal*, 7 October 1992, pp. A1, A6.

12. Richard Wolffe, 'Vision remains more of a blueprint than a reality', *Financial Times*, 17 November 1998. Graham Bowley, 'Braced for tough times ahead', *Financial Times*, 17 December 1998.

13. S. Tamer Cavusgil, 'Pricing for global markets', *Columbia Journal of World Business*, Winter (1996): pp. 66–78.

14. James Lardner, *Fast Forward: Hollywood, The Japanese and the VCR Wars* (New York: New American Library, 1987).

15. Hermann Diller. 'Preisgestaltung bei internationaler Tätigkeit'. In *Handbuch der Internationalen Unternehmenstätigkeit*, ed. Brij Nino Kumar and Helmut Haussmann (München: C.H. Beck'sche Verlagsbuchhandlung, 1992), pp. 685–702.

16. A. Coskun Samli and Laurence Jacobs, 'Pricing practices of American multinational firms: standardization vs. localization dichotomy', *Journal of Global Marketing*, 8, 2 (1994): pp. 51–73.

17. Hermann Diller, 'Preisgestaltung bei internationaler Tätigkeit'. In *Handbuch der Internationalen Unternehmenstätigkeit*, ed. Brij Nino Kumar and Helmut Haussmann (München: C.H. Beck'sche Verlagsbuchhandlung, 1992), pp. 685–702.

18. Gary Hamel and C.K. Prahalad, 'Do you really have a global strategy', *Harvard Business Review*, July–August (1985): pp. 139–148.

19. Hermann Simon and Robert J. Dolan, *Profit durch Power-Pricing* (Frankfurt: Campus, 1997).

20. Wolfgang Gaul and Ulrich Lutz, 'Pricing in international marketing and Western European economic integration', *Management International Review*, 34, 2 (1994): pp. 101–124. Hermann Diller. 'Preisgestaltung bei internationaler Tätigkeit'. In *Handbuch der Internationalen Unternehmenstätigkeit*, ed. Brij Nino Kumar and Helmut Haussmann (München: C.H. Beck'sche Verlagsbuchhandlung, 1992), pp. 685–702. Brendan Menton, 'Gambling on Europe', *Business and Finance*, 3 December 1998.

21. Eckhard Kucher and Hermann Simon, 'Schwierige Balanceakte: Die Preispolitik in Europa', *Harvard Business Manager*, 4 (1993): pp. 46–57.

22. http://www.wto.org/wto/about/agmnts7.htm (cited 8 February 2000).

23. Eduardo Lachica, 'Legal swamp: anti-dumping pleas are almost useless, Smith Corona finds', *Wall Street Journal*, 18 June 1992, pp. A1, A8.

24. L.P. Bucklin, 'Modeling the international gray market for public policy decisions', *International Journal of Research in Marketing*, 10 (1990): pp. 387–405. S.Tamer Cavusgil and Ed Sikora, 'How multinationals can counter gray-market imports', *Columbia Journal of World Business*, November/December (1988): pp. 27–33. Matthew B. Myers, 'Incidents of gray market activity among US exporters', *Journal of International Business Studies*, 30, 1 (1999): pp. 105–126.

25. Gert Assmus and Carsten Wiese, 'How to address the gray market threat using price coordination', *Sloan Management Review*, Spring (1995): pp. 31–41.

26. John Griffiths, 'Auctioneer rejects plan to sell grey car imports', *Financial Times*, 16 November 1999. Bethan Hutton, 'Drivers chase the bargains', *Financial Times*, 16 September 1999.

27. Peggy E. Chaudry and Michael G. Walsh, 'Managing the gray market in the European Union: the case of the pharmaceutical industry', *Journal of International Marketing*, 3, 3 (1995): pp. 11–33.

28. 'Uniform EU drug pricing and parallel imports', *Marketletter*, 16 March 1998. 'Parallel trade in Europe: an acceptable aspect of the future market?', *Marketletter*, 12 April 1999.

29. David White, 'Spain warns Glaxo on pricing', *Financial Times*, 8 April 1998. 'Glaxo Wellcome Spain takes on wholesalers over pricing', *Marketletter*, 13 April 1998.

30. 'EC rejects Glaxo PI barrier', *Chemist & Druggist*, 24 July 1999; 'GW Spain takes on wholesalers over pricing', *Marketletter*, 13 April 1998

31. 'Hardly the full monty', *The Economist*, 27 February 1999, pp. 78ff.

32. Charles T. Horngren and George Foster, *Cost Accounting: A Managerial Approach* (Upper Saddle River: Prentice Hall, 1991), p. 856.

33. Timothy M. Collins and Thomas L. Doorley, *Teaming Up for the 90s: A Guide to International Joint Ventures and Strategic Alliances* (Homewood, IL: Business One Irwin, 1991), pp. 212–213.

CHAPTER 13

Global logistics and channel decisions

More flexibility is the command of the hour.
HELMUT KOHL, FORMER GERMAN CHANCELLOR

A long journey does not know any light weights.
CHINESE PROVERB

Overview

After reading this chapter, you will know:

● The complexity of global logistics.
● The key decisions within in-bound logistics and the factors impinging on these decisions, such as factor conditions, transport costs, country infrastructure, political risk, market access and currency issues.
● How out-bound logistics can be organised and which tasks need to be taken care of in this respect.
● Which characteristics influence the design of distribution channels for international markets.
● How new developments, such as globalisation in retailing or e-commerce, reshape international distribution.

Why is this important? Here are three situations in which you would need an understanding of the above issues:

● To supply your customers with the right product at the right time, you need to co-ordinate the material flow to your production facilities around the globe.
● You are setting up foreign operations and need to check how your products reach your customers and which distribution partners may help you in this process.
● You need to establish/change your international distribution channels and need guidance on which factors have an impact on these strategic decisions and how global trends will influence your distribution system.

Practice link

With 2,700 stores and more than 100,000 employees in 13 countries, Kingfisher is the UK's most international retail group. Under the brands of B&Q, Comet, Woolworths and Superdrug in the UK or Castorama and Darty in France, Kingfisher earns its money in DIY, electrical and general merchandise retailing. However, not only Kingfisher's sales are going international. Its sourcing is too!

In order to maintain a favourable market position in these countries, the product range and price points need to remain attractive to consumers. The latter is the business of Dido Harding, Director of Global Sourcing. She is expected to join buying efforts across Kingfisher's outlets and use the increased market power to negotiate globally with suppliers for more favourable conditions. The savings can then be reinvested in price cuts for consumers. Forecasts for this year predict cost savings of €42–58 million. By the end of 2004 the cost savings should have increased to €290 million.

For Harding, global sourcing means more than just getting better prices from suppliers. Kingfisher will also move toward more direct sourcing, meaning cutting out importers and wholesalers. Thus, a retractable knife, which used to cost €1.5, could now be sold at €0.66. In line with these developments, Kingfisher will increase staff in its Asian direct sourcing offices from 58 to 110. For the more remote future, Kingfisher is even thinking of moving more towards own-brand development.

Experts predict a bright future for retailers' global sourcing initiatives. While today only 10 per cent of a supermarket's product line is sourced globally, this ratio may easily be raised to one third five years from now. Yet, local manufacturers need not fear being overtaken: local tastes will still have to be catered for.

Additional support for global sourcing activities comes from information technologies. Increasingly, supplier–purchaser relationships are facilitated through the computer and the Internet, where specifications are posted electronically and pre-qualified vendors can bid for the job.[1]

This chapter opens with a general positioning of channel decisions and logistics within a company's value chain. In the following, the different distribution functions are outlined in detail, with special emphasis on how new trends will shape global logistics in future. The next section is devoted to global channel strategy. Key characteristics influencing the actual channel design will be discussed as well as global trends in channel design and strategy.

THE NATURE OF GLOBAL LOGISTICS AND CHANNEL DECISIONS

As in the national environment, international distribution encompasses two areas of responsibility: channel management and logistics. Channel management implies identifying, selecting and supporting distribution partners. Selecting the 'right' channel participants is crucial to international success. Distribution partners take over valuable support and information services towards customers. Thus, they bridge the gap between manufacturer and customer. Yet, manufacturers and channel members will only be successful in achieving their common goals, if the physical flow of goods

Figure 13.1 Distribution functions in the value chain

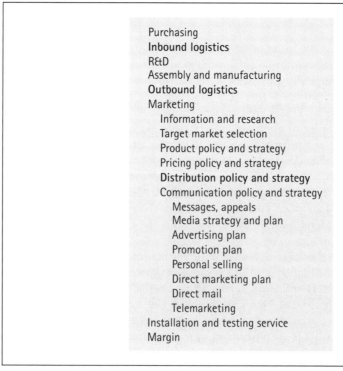

Purchasing
Inbound logistics
R&D
Assembly and manufacturing
Outbound logistics
Marketing
　Information and research
　Target market selection
　Product policy and strategy
　Pricing policy and strategy
　Distribution policy and strategy
　Communication policy and strategy
　　Messages, appeals
　　Media strategy and plan
　　Advertising plan
　　Promotion plan
　　Personal selling
　　Direct marketing plan
　　Direct mail
　　Telemarketing
Installation and testing service
Margin

corresponds to their activities. Global logistics is the means to ensure adequate supply, where the right products are made available to customers when and where they want them.

The value chain is a conceptual tool that provides a useful framework for integrating various organisational activities related to global distribution (see Figure 13.1).

Historically the responsibility for distribution activities was scattered throughout the value chain. The purchasing department would source materials and parts for production, the logistics department would take care of product shipment and the marketing department would select suitable distribution partners. Today, these functions are becoming increasingly intertwined.

For many companies, global sourcing is a first step towards producing abroad and establishing new distribution channels in foreign markets. For example, a company's global sourcing or in-bound logistics experts are not only searching for excellent materials and services at the best price. The supplier–purchaser relationships established within a sourcing context may be used for other purposes. Suppliers and manufacturers may reach a point where they decide to co-operate closer and target markets together. In this case, a joint venture or a strategic partnership between supplier and purchaser may also serve as a basis for foreign market access.[2]

Some companies even use logistic information for marketing purposes. Some car manufacturers, for example, keep customers informed about the current production status of their new car. This not only reduces the wait for customers psychologically, but also serves to intensify customer relationships.

In the following, we will take a closer look at the various functions of global distribution and the relevant marketing implications for a company.

IN-BOUND LOGISTICS: SOURCING DECISIONS

In-bound logistics describes the process of moving products and materials from suppliers to the factory. There are no simple rules to guide sourcing decisions. Indeed, the sourcing decision is one of the most complex and important decisions faced by a global company. Six factors must be taken into account in the sourcing decision:

1 Factor costs and conditions
2 Logistics (time required to fill orders, security and safety, and transportation costs)
3 Country infrastructure
4 Political risk
5 Market access (tariff and non-tariff barriers to trade)
6 Exchange rate, availability and convertibility of local money

Factor costs and conditions

Factor costs are land, labour and capital costs. Labour includes the cost of workers at every level: manufacturing and production, professional and technical, and management. Basic manufacturing direct labour costs today range from €0.40 per hour in economically less developed country to €5 to €20+ per hour in an industrialised country. In a longitudinal analysis, Table 13.1 shows indexes of hourly compensation costs for production workers in manufacturing for selected countries and regions. Note that manufacturing compensation costs in European countries, and in the Asian emerging countries in particular have increased relative to the US since 1980.

Table 13.1 Indexes of hourly compensation costs for production workers in manufacturing for selected countries: 1980 to 1994

Area or country	1980	1990	1991	1992	1993	1994	Area or country	1980	1990	1991	1992	1993	1994
United States	**100**	**100**	**100**	**100**	**100**	**100**	Austria[f]	90	119	116	126	122	127
Total[a]	67	83	86	88	86	88	Belgium	133	129	127	138	129	134
OECD[b]	77	94	97	99	96	99	Denmark	110	120	117	124	114	120
Europe	102	118	117	123	112	115	Finland	83	141	136	123	99	100
Asian newly industrialising economies[c]	12	25	28	30	31	34	Germany[gh]	125	147	146	157	154	160
Canada	88	106	110	105	98	92	Greece	38	45	44	46	41	(NA)
Mexico	22	11	12	14	15	15	Ireland	60	79	78	83	73	(NA)
Australia[d]	86	88	87	81	75	80	Italy	83	119	119	121	96	95
Hong Kong[e]	15	21	23	24	26	28	Luxembourg	121	110	108	117	111	(NA)
Israel	38	57	56	56	53	53	Netherlands	122	123	117	126	119	122
Japan	56	86	94	101	114	125	Norway	117	144	139	143	121	122
Korea, South	10	25	30	32	33	37	Portugal	21	25	27	32	27	27
New Zealand	54	56	54	49	48	52	Spain	60	76	78	83	69	67
Singapore	16	25	28	31	31	37	Sweden	127	140	142	152	106	110
Sri Lanka	2	2	3	2	3	(NA)	Switzerland	112	140	139	144	135	145
Taiwan	10	26	28	32	31	32	United Kingdom	77	85	88	89	75	80

NA = Not available.

Compensation costs include all pay made directly to the worker – pay for time worked and not worked (e.g. leave, except sick leave), other direct pay, employer expenditures for legally required insurance programmes and contractual and private benefit plans, and for some countries, other labour taxes. Data adjusted for exchange rates.

[a] the 24 foreign economies for which 1994 data were available
[b] Canada, Mexico, Australia, Japan, New Zealand and the European countries
[c] Hong Kong, South Korea, Singapore and Taiwan
[d] Includes non-production workers, except in managerial, executive, professional and higher supervisory positions
[e] Average of selected manufacturing industries
[f] Excludes workers in establishments considered handicraft manufacturers (including all printing and publishing and miscellaneous manufacturing in Austria)
[g] Includes workers in mining and electrical power plants
[h] Former West Germany

Notice in Table 13.1 that German hourly compensations costs for production workers in manufacturing were 160 per cent of those in the US, whereas those in Mexico were only 15 per cent of those in the US For Volkswagen (VW), the wage differential between Mexico and Germany, combined with the strength of the German Mark, dictated a Mexican manufacturing facility that builds Golf and Jetta models destined for the US market. Do lower wage rates demand that a company relocate its manufacturing to the low-wage country? Not necessarily! In Germany, VW Chairman Ferdinand Piech tried to improve his company's competitiveness by convincing unions to allow flexible work schedules. For example, during peak demand, employees would work six-day weeks; when demand slows, factories would produce cars only three days per week.

Moreover, wages are only one of the costs of production. Many other considerations enter into the sourcing decision, such as management's aspirations. For example, SMH assembles all of the watches it sells and it builds most of the components for the watches it assembles. It manufactures in Switzerland, the highest-income country in the world. SMH's Hayek decided that he wanted to manufacture in Switzerland in spite of the fact that a secretary in Switzerland makes more money than a chief engineer in Thailand. He did this by making a commitment to drive wage costs down to less than 10 per cent of total costs. At this level, wages rates are no longer a significant factor in competitiveness. As Hayek puts it, he does not care if his competitor's workers work for free! He will still win in a competitive marketplace because his value is so much greater.[3]

The other factors of production are land, materials and capital. The cost of these factors depends on their availability and relative abundance. Often, the differences in factor costs will offset each other so that, on balance, companies have a 'level field' in the competitive arena. For example, the United States has abundant land and Japan has abundant capital. These advantages partially offset each other. When this is the case, the critical factor is management, professional and worker team effectiveness.

World factor costs that affect manufacturing can be divided into three tiers. The first tier consists of the industrialised countries where factor costs are tending to equalise. The second tier consists of the industrialising countries – for example, Singapore and other Pacific Rim countries – that offer significant factor costs savings as well as an increasingly developed infrastructure and political stability, making them extremely attractive manufacturing locations. The third tier includes Russia and other countries that have not yet become significant locations for manufacturing activity. Third-tier countries present the combination of lower factor costs (especially wages) offset by limited infrastructure development and greater political uncertainty.

The application of advanced computer controls and other new manufacturing technologies has reduced the proportion of labour relative to capital for many businesses. In formulating a sourcing strategy, company managers and executives should also recognise the declining importance of direct manufacturing labour as a percentage of total product cost. The most advanced global companies are no longer blindly chasing cheap labour manufacturing locations because direct labour may be a very small percentage of the total.

When BMW took over Rover, UK managers and employees feared BMW might shift production to a lower-wage country than the UK. Looking into this decision in more detail, it quickly became clear that wage was not a suitable lever to reduce cost. The reason is that labour costs accounts only for a relatively small share of a car's total cost compared to other variables, namely 20 per cent.[4] Yet meanwhile, BMW decided to make a clear cut and is looking for potential buyers of the Rover operations, as restructuring efforts did not result in consolidation of Rover operations.[5]

As a result of the decreasing importance of labour costs in many industries, it may not be worthwhile to incur the costs and risks of establishing a manufacturing activity in a distant location. For example, the US based computer manufacturer Compaq had to decide whether to close plants in Houston and Scotland and contract out assembly work to the Far East. After determining that the human labour content in a personal computer (PC) is only about 15 minutes, the company opted to run Compaq's existing Houston factory 24 hours a day. Another decision was whether to source motherboards from a vendor in Asia. The firm calculated that Compaq could produce the boards, which account for 40 per cent of the cost of a PC, for €20 less than suppliers in the Far East. Manufacturing in Houston also saved two weeks in shipping time, which translated into inventory savings.[6]

Many companies have to their chagrin discovered that today's cheap factor costs can disappear as the law of supply and demand drives up wages and land prices. Many companies began sourcing in Japan in the 1950s. As wages and real estate costs increased, production was shifted to Hong Kong, then to Taiwan and Korea. During the 1970s and 1980s, production kept shifting to China, Indonesia, Thailand,

Malaysia, Bangladesh and Singapore. In recent years, the Far East, Costa Rica, the Dominican Republic, Guatemala, Honduras and Puerto Rico became more and more interesting for foreign production locations.[7]

Transport costs

In general, the greater the distance between the product source and the target market, the greater the time delay for delivery and the higher the transportation cost. However, innovation and new transportation technologies are cutting both time and dollar costs. To facilitate global delivery, transportation companies are forming alliances and becoming an important part of industry value systems. Manufacturers can take advantage of intermodal services that allow containers to be transferred between rail, boat, air and truck carriers. Today, transportation expenses for exports and imports represent approximately 5 per cent of total costs.

Fiat's international manufacturing network provides an excellent illustration of how companies can reconfigure inbound logistics in the value chain to support an overseas sourcing strategy. Fiat's plants are spanning Venezuela, Brazil, Argentina, Morocco, Poland, Turkey, South Africa and India as well as Italy. The objective is to deliver parts in synchronisation with production schedules across the different locations. To handle this demanding logistic job, a strategic alliance between several logistic service firms has been formed. The Italian logistics company Serra, familiar with Fiat's needs and philosophy, teamed up with the German Stute Verkehr, which brings in specific know-how in the implementation and control of terminal and sourcing operations. Their joint scope of service includes all aspects of vehicle component movement as well as inbound production flows and spare parts logistics. To support their operations, Serra Stute invited local logistics firms to co-operate in this venture.[8]

Country infrastructure

In order to present an attractive setting for a manufacturing operation, it is important that the country's infrastructure be sufficiently developed to support a manufacturing operation. The required infrastructure will vary from company to company, but minimally, it will include power, transportation and roads, communications, service and component suppliers, a labour pool, civil order and effective governance. In addition, a country must offer reliable access to foreign exchange for the purchase of necessary material and components from abroad as well as a physically secure setting where work can be done and product can be shipped to customers.

A country may have cheap labour, but does it have the necessary supporting services or infrastructure to support a manufacturing activity? Many countries offer these conditions, including Hong Kong, Taiwan and Singapore. There are also many other countries that do not, such as Lebanon, Uganda and El Salvador. One of the challenges of doing business in the new Russian market is an infrastructure that is woefully inadequate to handle the increased volume of shipments.

Political risk

Political risk, or the risk of a change in government policy that would adversely impact a company's ability to operate effectively and profitably, is a deterrent to

Internet – a gem in modern supply chain management?

The Internet has revolutionised the way we look at many things. This statement holds even more true for modern global logistics. When you think about how logistic procedures were handled in the past, phone, fax and paper dominated everyday work. Then computers entered offices and made things much easier. In supply chain management, EDI – electronic data interchange – is now an extensively used tool to send information such as orders, production schedules, forecasts and other similar input between organisations.

However, conventional EDI networks have some major drawbacks: they require sophisticated technological resources, which are quite easy to provide for large buyers but difficult to establish for small suppliers. The British retailer Sainsbury, for example, has 1,500 suppliers that do not use its EDI system, but instead rely on fax, phone or mail, when processing orders. The consequences are remarkable: 75,000 paper invoices have to be produced per month, requiring 70 personnel just to keep these orders running smoothly.

To reduce these costs, Sainsbury decided to implement a software package developed by the British e-commerce specialist Kewill. This software enables all aspects of buying to be conducted through a website on the Internet. Now all a Sainsbury supplier needs is a computer with Internet access at a monthly cost of about €50. Toys'R'Us has also announced the introduction of a similar system for its 500 suppliers in the UK, France and Germany. The French retailer Carrefour has also implemented its global supplier–buyer network based on the Internet.

What may seem fairly new to certain industries, has been everyday business for others for quite some time. The automobile manufacturers and their suppliers launched their own extranet – the Automotive Network Exchange. Sales over this Web-based network were reported to exceed €3.2 billion. Forecasts for the next 12 months project a volume of €8 billion in parts. Another example is the co-operation between the German-based international freight forwarder Schenker and Ford Motor Co. The 200,000 Ford vehicles per year built in 14 factories and shipped to 100 export markets around the world represent a logistical challenge. Ford now shares this challenge with its partner Schenker. Schenker not only co-ordinates the information and documentation flows for vehicle delivery, but offers Ford dealers the option of placing orders directly with Schenker via the Internet.

Food for thought

- How might web-based global logistics influence the competitiveness of retailers?
- Does global supply chain management weaken the role of intermediaries in a distribution channel? Why? Why not?

Source: Frook, John Evan and Richard Karpinski, 'Poised for critical mass', *Internetweek*, 11 January 1999 (747), pp. 14ff; Ginger Koloszyc, 'Supplier/buyer extranet simplifies global sourcing process', *Stores*, January 1999 (81/1), pp. 28–30; Rod Newing, 'Leaner, meaner – and more agile', *Financial Times*, 20 October 1999; Caroline Daniel, 'Keeping the wheels of e-commerce turning smoothly', *Financial Times*, 6 January 2000; John G. Parker, 'Schenker's baby', *Traffic World*, 31 January 2000 (261/5): pp. 15ff. André Versteeg, *Revolution im Einkauf*, Frankfurt: Campus Verlag, pp. 170ff.

investment in local sourcing. Conversely, the lower the level of political risk, the less likely it is that an investor will avoid a country or market. The difficulty of assessing political risk is inversely proportional to a country's stage of economic development: all other things being equal, the less developed a country, the more difficult it is to predict political risk. The political risk of the Triad countries, for example, is quite limited as compared to a less developed country in Africa, Latin America or Asia.

Market access

A key factor in locating production facilities is market access. If a country or a region limits market access because of local content laws, balance of payments problems, or any other reason, it may be necessary to establish a production facility within the country itself. China, for example, made it a policy to allow a foreign company's direct investment, only if investors would manufacture to a certain extent in China. Companies such as Ericsson, Motorola, Nokia, Siemens and others set up operations to comply with these rules. Meanwhile, these arrangements have got a new twist. As foreign companies are perceived too slow in transferring know-how and technology to their Chinese partners, China has tightened relevant regulations. The government is said to do everything to foster the development of a truly Chinese telecom business by, for example, imposing import quotas for mobile phones and raising the share of local equity in joint ventures. In the light of Chinese efforts to enter the WTO, however, these market access restrictions might soon be rendered obsolete.

Foreign exchange

In deciding where to locate a manufacturing activity, the cost of production supplied by a country source will be determined in part by the prevailing foreign exchange rate for the country's currency. Exchange rates are so volatile today that many companies pursue global sourcing strategies as a way of limiting exchange-related risk. At any point in time, what has been an attractive location for production may become much less attractive due to exchange rate fluctuation. For example, during the period from November 1996 to November 1997, the Turkish lira declined 89 per cent in value compared to the €. The prudent company will incorporate exchange volatility into its planning assumptions and be prepared to prosper under a variety of exchange rate relationships.

The dramatic shifts in price levels of commodities and currencies are a major characteristic of the world economy today. Such volatility argues for a sourcing strategy that provides alternative country options for supplying markets. Thus, if the €, the yen, or the dollar becomes seriously overvalued, a company with production capacity in other locations can achieve competitive advantage by shifting production among different sites.

The take-over of Rover's production plants in the UK raised serious concern for BMW's management, as losses were accumulating. One possible solution was to move sourcing overseas to benefit from favourable exchange rates. In the end, however, the BMW management turned this idea down as a short term measure, which would add complications by the demands of supply chain management and quality assurance.[9] As noted before, continuous losses forced BMW to look for potential buyers of Rover operations.

OUT-BOUND LOGISTICS

Outbound logistics is defined as moving products from the factory to customers. It involves aspects of transportation, inventory control, order processing and warehousing.

Transportation

Transportation decisions concern which of five methods a company should use to move its products: rail, truck, air, water or pipeline.

When contemplating market expansion outside the home country, management's inclination may be to configure these aspects of the value chain exactly as they are at home. However, this may not be the most effective solution because the organisation may lack the necessary skill and experience to conduct all value-chain activities in target markets. A company with home-market competitive advantages in both upstream activities and downstream activities – manufacturing and distribution, for example – may be forced to reconfigure distribution activities to successfully enter new global markets. For example, Wal-Mart's expansion into Mexico has been hampered by the fact that most Mexican suppliers ship directly to stores rather than to retailer warehouses and distribution centres. Thus, Wal-Mart lacks the control that is the key to its low prices in the United States. Notes Sam Dunn, director of administration for Wal-Mart de Mexico, 'The key to this market is distribution. The retailer who solves that will dominate.'[10]

3M does an excellent job of managing the physical distribution aspects of the value chain to support global export markets. In Europe, for example, 3M set up a distribution centre in Breda, the Netherlands, to receive containers from Norfolk, Virginia and other ports. Logistics managers convinced 3M to spend as much as €850 million per year for additional trucks to provide daily delivery service to each of 3M's 19 European subsidiaries. The outlay was approved after the managers demonstrated that savings could be achieved – due to lower inventories and faster deliveries – even if trucks were not filled to capacity.[11]

Laura Ashley, the global retailer of traditional English-style clothing for women, reconfigured its supply chain as well. The company has more than 500 company-owned retail stores around the world, supplying them with goods manufactured in 15 different countries. In the past, Laura Ashley's suppliers all sent goods to the company's distribution centre in Wales. This meant that blouses manufactured in Hong Kong were first sent to Wales; blouses bound for the company's Tokyo store then had to be sent back to the Far East. Not surprisingly, this was not an effective arrangement; Laura Ashley stores were typically sold out of 20 per cent of goods even though the company's warehouses were full. To cut costs and improve its inventory management, Laura Ashley has subcontracted physical distribution to FedEx's Business Logistics Service. FedEx's information system is tied in with the retail stores; when a Laura Ashley buyer orders blouses from Hong Kong, FedEx arranges shipment from the manufacturer directly to the stores.[12]

Inventory management

Proper inventory management ensures that a company neither runs out of manufacturing components or finished goods nor incurs the expense and risk of carrying excessive stocks of these items.

Order processing

Activities relating to order processing provide information inputs that are critical in fulfilling a customer's order. Order processing includes order entry, in which the order

A case of wine: adding utility through distribution channels

Each year, wine and spirits worth more than €1 billion are exported from France, Germany, Italy and other European countries to all parts of the world. Have you ever wondered how a case of wine finds its way from, say, France to your liquor store? In fact, after leaving the winery, the wine may pass through the hands of brokers, freight forwarders, shipping agents, export agents, shippers, importers, wholesalers and distributors before it finishes its journey at your local retailer.

In France, the structure of the wine industry is quite complex. An intermediary called a négociant plays an important role that varies according to region. Négociants sometimes act as brokers and have standing contracts to buy specified quantities of finished wine on behalf of importers in the various countries. The négociant also functions somewhat like a banker, paying the producer as much as 25 per cent in advance of delivery. Négociants may also buy grapes from growers to make their own wine, blending and bottling them under their own labels. Wine may be bottled and packed in cases by the producer or by the négociant.

Wine destined for France or other European markets travels by truck. If exported to more remote countries, a freight forwarder or shipping agent sends a truck to the winery to pick up the wine. There, the shipping agent consolidates various deliveries to fill a container for the shipping line of the importer's choosing. Shipping dates and rates will vary depending on the availability of containers. In general, a 20-foot container can hold 800 cases of wine; a single 40-foot container can take up to 1,300 cases. The weight of the wine is a consideration when determining how many cases to ship in a given container. Shipping wine is a challenging venture because of the volatile and perishable nature of the product. Proper storage and transportation are vital; light, heat and temperature fluctuations are wine's worst enemies. Ideally, wine should be kept at a constant temperature near 55 degrees. To prevent improper shipping from ruining a shipment, temperature-controlled containers (known as reefers) are often used, even though they add about €2 per case to the cost of the shipment. To further protect the wine, some importers avoid shipping during the hot summer months. Because ownership of the wine is transferred to the importer at the moment the wine leaves the French storage warehouse, it is important to insure the shipment. Wine shipments can even be insured against possible losses due to war and terrorism.

A trans-Atlantic trip to the US for example, takes a week or more. Once the wine enters the United States, it must clear US Customs. After it has cleared Customs, the wine is then shipped to the wholesaler's warehouse. After the wine has been unloaded at the warehouse, the distributor's sales staff arranges for the cases of wine to be delivered by truck or van to individual retailers.

There is as much variety among retail channels for wine as there is among wine producers. Outlets vary from 'mom and pop' grocery stores to wine sections in large supermarkets to huge wine and liquor discounters, with considerable variety in-between. In some stores, wine is stored and displayed haphazardly, often in sunny windows or near heating vents. Other stores go to great lengths to make sure that the wine is not ruined after its long journey in protective containers.

There are still other factors that have a major influence on sales. One is the marketing and merchandising skill of the retailer: point-of-sale recommendation from an informed retailer is important in selling fine wines. Also, the industry press can have a huge impact on sales. A good rating in special interest magazines can make the difference between obscurity and a sell-out in a particular wine.

Food for thought

- Which product specific factors determine the choice of physical distribution channels? Contrast wine with ice-cream.
- Which ideal characteristics would an Austrian wine exporter seek in a US importer?

is actually entered into a company's information system; order handling, which involves locating, assembling and moving products into distribution; and order delivery, the process by which products are made available to the customer.

Warehousing

Warehouses are used to store goods until they are sold; another type of facility, the distribution centre, is designed to efficiently receive goods from suppliers and then fill orders for individual stores. A company may have its own warehouses and distribution centre or pay a specialist to provide these facilities.

In terms of warehousing, the Internet will most likely change the way business is done. An example for these new developments is the UK's first e-commerce site in government. This site provides an excellent example of how the Internet revolutionises the logistics industry. To sell its multi-faceted information material in the UK, the Foreign Office engaged in a co-operation with a logistics company, MSAS Global Logistics. Instead of simply offering warehousing and delivery services, MSAS can look at the process from production to the customer, by using the Internet. In the case of the Foreign Office, MSAS not only runs the website for the government. Orders also go straight to MSAS and are then dispatched directly to customers. For the retail business, MSAS executives predict an increase in direct interactions between manufacturers, logistics operators and customers. In their view, the importance of warehouse management will grow, while at the same time the cost of property, staff and transport may be reduced.[13]

Key points

- To ensure a timely supply of customers with the right products, a company needs to make sure that the in-bound flow of materials into production and the out-bound flow of finished products is well co-ordinated.

- In-bound logistics or the management of product and material movement from the suppliers to the manufacturer is influenced by several factors: (i) factor costs and conditions, (ii) transport costs, (iii) country infrastructure, (iv) political risk, (v) market access and (vi) currency-related issues such as exchange rates, availability and convertibility of local money.

- Out-bound logistics means moving final products from the factory to customers. It involves aspects of transportation, inventory, control, order processing and warehousing.

INTERNATIONAL CHANNEL STRATEGIES

The purpose of marketing channels is to create utility for customers. The major categories of channel utility are place (the availability of a product or service in a location that is convenient to a potential customer); time (the availability of a product or service when desired by a customer); form (the product is processed, prepared and ready to use and in proper condition); and information (answers to questions and general communication about useful product features and benefits are available). Because these utilities can be a basic source of competitive advantage and product value, choosing a channel strategy is one of the key policy decisions marketing management must make.

Channel strategy in a global marketing programme must fit the company's competitive position and overall marketing objectives in each national market. If a company wants to enter a competitive market, it has two basic choices:

1 Direct involvement (its own sales force, retail stores, etc.)
2 Indirect involvement (independent agents, distributors, wholesalers).

The first choice requires the company to establish company-owned or franchised outlets. The second choice requires incentives to independent channel agents that will induce them to promote the company's product.

Decisions on product design, communication strategies and pricing require intensive thought and energy from a firm. However, these strategies will only become manifest, if the distribution system supports them. Selecting distribution channels not only implies selecting the 'right' channels, but also gaining channel access. Even though a suitable distribution channel/partner may have been identified, the potential partner may have established a relationship with a competitor already. If no contractual arrangement with your competitor exists, a company may convince the intermediary to switch. However, such a change is only likely if the distribution partner trades in a more attractive product and marketing package. Once-locked-up distribution channels may also open due to emerging distribution channels. Software developers, for example, once depended on restricted distribution channels to keep out potential competition. Now, in times of electronic commerce, new entrants may use the Internet's unlimited scope for their distribution activities.[14] The process of shaping international channels to fit overall company objectives is constrained by several factors: customers, products, middlemen and the environment. Important characteristics of each of these factors will be discussed in the following.

CHARACTERISTICS IMPACTING ON CHANNEL DESIGN AND STRATEGY

When it comes to designing an international distribution system, several factors have to be taken into account. Among these influences are customer, product, middleman and environmental characteristics. Each of these factors will be discussed in the following.

Customer characteristics

The characteristics of customers are an important influence on channel design. Their number, geographic distribution, income, shopping habits and reactions to different selling methods all vary from country to country and therefore require different channel approaches. Remember, channels create utility for customers.

In general, regardless of the stage of market development, the need for multiple channel intermediaries increases as the number of customers increases. The converse is also true: the need for channel intermediaries decreases as the number of customers decreases. For example, if there are only 10 customers for an industrial product in each national market, these 10 customers must be directly contacted by either the manufacturer or an agent. For mass-market products bought by millions of customers, retail distribution outlets or mail-order distribution is required. In a country with a large number of low-volume retailers, it is usually cheaper to reach them via wholesalers. Direct selling that bypasses wholesale intermediaries may be the most cost-effective means of serving large-volume retailers. These generalisations apply to all countries, regardless of stage of development; however, individual country customs will vary.

Customers' shopping habits, however, are also subject to changes. At present, Turkey is experiencing changes in food retailing which have already hit countries like Spain, Italy or France some time ago. Turkish consumers, who felt very comfortable with shopping in small 'mom and pop shops' at the corner of their street, now feel increasingly intrigued by shopping at supermarkets. For manufacturers, this represents a new trend, which is said to continue and will require adjustments. From 22 per cent in 1995, the market share of hyper- and supermarkets in Turkey climbed to 31 per cent in 1998 and is predicted to increase up to 43 per cent by 2003. And there is still room for expansion – supermarket penetration in Spain is at 76.4 per cent, in France and Germany at 93 per cent.[15]

Product characteristics

Certain product attributes such as degree of standardisation, perishability, bulk, service requirements and unit price have an important influence on channel design and strategy. Products with a high unit price, for example, are often sold through a company salesforce because the selling cost of this expensive distribution method is a small part of the total sale price. Moreover, the high cost of such products is usually associated with complexity or with product features that must be explained in some detail and this can be done most effectively by a controlled salesforce. For example, mainframe computers are expensive, complicated products that require both explanation and applications analysis focused on the customer's needs. A company-trained salesperson or sales engineer is well suited to the task of creating information utility for computer buyers.

Mainframe computers, photocopiers and other industrial products may require margins to cover the costs of expensive sales engineering. Other products require margins to provide a large monetary incentive to a direct salesforce. In many parts of the world, cosmetics are sold door to door; company representatives call on potential customers. The reps must create customer awareness of the value of cosmetics and evoke a feeling of need for this value that leads to a sale. The sales activity must be paid for. Companies using direct distribution for consumer products rely on wide gross selling margins to generate the revenue necessary to compensate salespeople. Amway and Avon are two companies that have succeeded in extending their direct sales systems globally.

Perishable products impose a special form of utility demands on channel members. Such products usually need relatively direct channels to ensure satisfactory condition at the time of customer purchase. In less developed countries, producers of vegetables, bread and other food products typically sell their goods in public marketplaces. In developed countries, perishable food products are distributed by controlled salesforces, and stock is checked by these sales distributor organisations to ensure that it is fresh and ready for purchase.

In 1991, Andersen Consulting assisted the Moscow Bread Company in improving its ability to distribute bread in the Russian capital. For Russians, bread is truly the staff of life, with consumers queuing up daily to buy fresh loaves at numerous shops and kiosks. Unfortunately, distribution was often hampered by excessive paperwork that resulted in the delivery of stale bread; Andersen found that as much as one third of the bread produced was wasted. The consulting team arrived at a simple solution: plastic bags to keep the bread fresh. The team found that, although 95 per cent of food is packaged in developed countries, the figure was only 2 per cent in the former Soviet Union, where open-air markets are the norm. Russian consumers responded favourably to the change; not only did the bags guarantee freshness and extend the shelf life of the bread by 600 per cent, the bags themselves created utility. In a country where such extras were virtually unknown, the bags constituted a reusable 'gift'.[16]

Bulky products usually require channel arrangements that minimise the shipping distances and the number of times products change hands between channel intermediaries before they reach the ultimate customer. Soft drinks and beer are examples of bulky products whose widespread availability is an important aspect of an effective marketing strategy.

Middleman characteristics

Channel strategy must recognise the characteristics of existing middlemen. Middlemen are in business to maximise their own profit and not that of the manufacturer. They are notorious for cherry picking, that is, the practice of taking orders from manufacturers whose products and brands are in demand to avoid any real selling effort for a manufacturer's products that may require push. This is a rational response by the middleman, but it can present a serious obstacle to the manufacturer attempting to break into a market with a new product. The cherry picker is not interested in building a market for a new product. This is a problem for the expanding international company. Frequently, a manufacturer with a new product or a product with a limited market share is forced to set up some arrangement for bypassing the cherry-picking segment of the channel. In some cases, manufacturers will set up an expensive direct distribution organisation to obtain a share of the market. When they finally obtain a share of the target market, they may abandon the direct distribution system for a more cost-effective intermediary system. The move does not mean that intermediaries are better than direct distribution. It is simply a response by a manufacturer to cost considerations and the newly acquired attractiveness of the company's product to independent distributors.

An alternative method of dealing with the cherry-picking problem does not require setting up an expensive direct salesforce. Rather, a company may decide to rely on a distributor's own sales force by subsidising the cost of the sales representatives the distributor has assigned to the company's products. This approach has the advantage of holding down costs by tying missionary and support selling in with the distributor's existing sales management team and physical distribution system. With this approach, it is possible to place managed direct-selling support and distribution support behind a product at the expense of only one salesperson per selling area. The distributor's incentive for co-operating in this kind of arrangement is that he or she obtains a free sales representative for a new product with the potential to be a profitable addition to his or her line. This co-operative arrangement is ideally suited to getting a new export-sourced product into distribution in a market.

Selection and care of distributors and agents

The selection of distributors and agents in a target market is a critically important task. A good commission agent or stocking distributor can make the difference between realising zero performance and performance that exceeds 200 per cent of

GLOBAL PERSPECTIVE

Distribution channels – A different perspective

In economically less developed countries, the conspicuous features of retail channels differ quite considerably from highly-developed ones. A remarkable number of people are engaged in selling very small quantities of merchandise. In Ethiopia and other East African countries, for example, an open window in the side of a building is likely to be a *souk*, a small walk-up store whose proprietor sells everything from toilet paper and playing cards to rice and eggs. To maximise sales, *souks* are strategically interspersed throughout neighbourhood areas. The proprietors know what customers want and need. For example, early in the day they may sell incense and a paper cone with enough coffee for the morning coffee ceremony. In the evening, cigarettes and gum may be in demand, especially if the *souk* is located near a neighbourhood nightclub. If a *souk* is closed, it is often possible to rouse the proprietor by knocking on the window, since the store also serves as the proprietor's domicile. Some *souk* owners will even provide 'kerb service' and bring items to a customer waiting in a car.

By comparison, government department stores in East Africa are less likely to display such a service orientation. Government stores may be stocked with mass quantities of items that are slow to sell. For example, the shelves may hold row after row of tinned tomatoes, even though fresh tomatoes are readily available year around in the market. Customers must go through several steps before actually taking possession of their purchases: determining what goods are available, making a purchase decision, moving to another area to pay, and finally, actually taking possession of the goods. This usually involves a substantial number of papers, seals and stamps, as well as interaction with two or three clerks. Clerk jobs are highly prized in countries where jobs are scarce; compared to the *souk* proprietor, who is willing to work from dawn to dusk, the government employee works from 9:00 a.m. to 5:00 p.m., with two hours off for lunch.

In Costa Rica, the privately owned *pulperia* is similar to the Western-style general store that was popular in the first part of the century. Customers enter the store, tell clerks what items are desired, and the clerks fetch the items – which may range from chicken feed to thumb tacks. A typical *pulperia* stocks staples such as sugar and flour in 50 kg bags, which the proprietor resells in smaller portions. Most *pulperias* have a refrigeration unit so they can sell ice-cream novelties; in areas where there is no electricity, the *pulperia* owner will use a generator to provide power for the refrigerator. *Pulperias* are serviced by a fleet of private wholesalers; on any given day, the soft drink truck, the candy truck, or the staples truck may make deliveries. The *pulperia* serves as a central gathering place for the neighbourhood and generally has a public telephone from which patrons can make calls for a fee. This attracts many people to the store in communities where there are few, if any, telephones.

Both the *souk* and the *pulperia* typically offer an informal system of credit. People who patronise these shops usually live in the neighbourhood and are known to the proprietor. Often, the proprietor will extend credit if he or she knows that a customer has suffered a setback such as loss of a job or a death in the family. Informally, the proprietors of private retail shops fulfil the role of a lender, especially for people who do not have access to credit through regular financial institutions.

Food for thought

- Do *souks* and *pulperias* have a future? Comment in the light of the small ethnic neighbourhood stores in the UK.
- What are the implications of a highly fragmented retail structure for the marketing of personal care products? Illustrate your answer with reference to soap.

Source: Private communication from Brian Larson of CARE Niger.

what is expected. At any point in time, some of any company's agents and distributors will be excellent, others will be satisfactory, and still others will be unsatisfactory and in need of replacement.

To find a good distributor, a firm can begin with a list provided by the home country's Ministry of Trade or Department of Commerce. The local chamber of commerce in a country can also provide lists, as can local trade associations. It is a waste of time to try to screen the list by mail. Go to the country and talk to end-users of the products you are selling and find out which distributors they prefer and why they prefer them or get this information from someone in the country who can do the research for you. If the product is a consumer product, go to the retail outlets and find out where consumers are buying products similar to your own and why. Two or three names will keep coming up. Go to these two or three and see which of them would be available to sign. Before signing, make sure there is someone in the organisation who will be the key person for your product. The key person is someone who will make it a personal objective to achieve success with your product.

This is the critical difference between the successful distributor and the worthless distributor. There must be a personal, individual commitment to the product. The second and related requirement for successful distributors or agents is that they must be successful with the product. Success means that they can sell the product and make money on it. In any case, the product must be designed and priced to be competitive in the target market. The distributor can assist in this process by providing information about customer wants and the competition and by promoting the product he or she represents.

Agent/distributor performance

The RF Division of Harris Corporation achieved great success in international markets with its short-wave radios. One of the reasons for its success was the quality of agents in key markets and their commitment to the Harris product. They were attracted to Harris because the company made a product that was as good as or better than any other product on the market. Also, Harris offered commissions of 33 per cent on all sales – at least 15 per cent higher than commissions offered by any other competitor. This was certainly one of the single most important factors in ensuring Harris's success. The generous commission motivated the agents to sell Harris products and provided the financial resources to support a strong marketing effort. There was of course a trade-off: Harris prices were higher, but in their target markets, this price effect was more than offset by the effectiveness of the higher margins.

Termination

The only way to keep a good distributor or agent is to work closely with him or her to ensure that he or she is making money on the product. Any distributor who does not make money on a line will drop it. It is really quite simple. In general, if a distributor is not working out, it is wise to terminate the agreement and find another one. Few companies are large enough to convert a mediocre distributor or agent into an effective business representative. Therefore, the two most important clauses in the distributor contract are the performance and cancellation clauses. Make sure they are written in a way that will make it possible to terminate the agreement. There is a myth that it is expensive or even impossible to terminate distributor and agent agreements. Some of the most successful global marketers have terminated hundreds of agreements and know success is based on their willingness to terminate if a distributor or agent does not perform. The key factor is performance: distributors who do not perform must either shape up or be replaced.

However, termination may result in legal adversity. In some countries, companies are exposed to courts that are blatantly corrupt. In Ecuador, for example, the courts have been handing down awards to terminated distributors of global companies that have been as high as 400 years of sales!

The Japanese importer and exclusive distributor of Porsche cars, Mizwa, announced legal action in Germany against Porsche, when the parent company tried to terminate the distribution contract after 45 years. Mizwa argued this termination would go against 'the basic principle of a sincere and loyal relationship'. The cancellation came after Porsche was dissatisfied with Mizwa's performance. Mizwa claimed that the economic downturn in Japan had caused slow sales and that current sales would exceed forecasts. A potential contract loss would have affected Mizwa pretty hard. The company had passed on distribution rights for Saab, which it usually marketed beside Porsche, to another firm and relied entirely on Porsche. Subsequently, Mizwa filed an injunction in a German court, which in the end was rejected. However, the two sides continued to negotiate and reached a new agreement. Porsche would take over imports to Japan through its new fully-owned subsidiary, as it has in other markets. Also, it would continue to sell to some Mizwa Motors dealerships, beside other independent operations.[17]

On the other hand, do not be deceived into thinking that termination is always going to be easy. Even if you have a termination clause, agents and distributors have rights in many jurisdictions that cannot be taken away by agreement. It is a rule of law that holds that if a distributor is acting in good faith on the assumption that his or her appointment as a distributor is going to continue, he or she has a right to sue a manufacturer for damages if the agreement is terminated.

Another rule for agreements is that you should be able to read and understand the agreement. If you cannot, insist that your attorney redraft the agreement in understandable language. If you cannot understand the agreement, you may find that it will come to haunt you. Whether you are an agent or a manufacturer, you should know what your rights and obligations are under your agreements.

Environmental characteristics

The general characteristics of the total environment are a major consideration in channel design. Because of the enormous variety of economic, social and political environments internationally, there is a need to delegate a large degree of independence to local operating management or agents. For example, the trend among consumers to shop in supermarkets rather than in small stores around the corner (as mentioned before) is not only a reflection of changing consumer tastes, but related to economic factors. As incomes are rising, large-capacity refrigerator/freezer units and automobiles become more easily available. So, many shoppers want to purchase a week's worth of groceries in one trip to the store. They have the money, ample storage space in the refrigerator, and the hauling capacity of the car to move this large quantity of food from the store to the home. The supermarket, because it is efficient, can fill the food shoppers' needs at lower prices than are found in butcher shops and other traditional full-service food stores. Additionally, supermarkets can offer more variety and a greater selection of merchandise than can smaller food stores, a fact that appeals to affluent consumers.

In some countries, political and legal requirements heavily influence the design of distribution channels. China, for example, does not allow foreign firms to own or manage distribution networks, wholesaling outlets or warehouses. So they have to employ local firms to handle importation and transportation logistics, and distributors or other intermediaries to deal with local customers. In the 1990s, the Chinese government loosened the regulations on manufacturing licences to foster local small business initiatives. As a result, a new quality of middlemen even in remote areas emerged. In the PC business, for example, these new entrepreneurs assemble PCs in the back room of their mom and pop shops and sell them to customers. To ascertain adequate quality standards, large foreign companies train their middlemen in product methods, technologies and systems to assist their grassroots efforts. This kind of co-operation may have its downsides in the future, as these new entrepreneurs use their product knowledge and technical skills for competing operations. However, legal restrictions for foreign companies in China may relax, as China is getting ready to enter the WTO. A bilateral agreement between China and the US grants foreign firms increasing participation in sales and distribution activities in China.[18]

Key points	
	• Channel strategy in a global marketing programme must fit the company's competitive position and overall marketing objectives in each national market in order to create utility for customers.
	• Several characteristics impact on channel design and strategy: (i) customer characteristics, such as their number, geographic distribution, income, shopping habits or their reactions to different selling methods, (ii) product characteristics such as perishability, service requirements or unit price, (iii) middleman characteristics, such as their attitude towards the manufacturer or (iv) environmental characteristics like economic, social and political macro-dimensions.
	• The art in designing an international distribution strategy is to combine local specificities with the need for standardisation to reap the benefits of being active globally.

GLOBAL TRENDS IN CHANNEL DESIGN AND STRATEGY

Over recent years, almost no other marketing instrument has seen more dramatic changes than distribution policy. Increasing globalisation as well as information and communication technologies have revolutionised the way products and services are sold. Some of the most important developments are outlined below.

Global retailing

Retailing has to some extent always been a global issue. For centuries, venturesome merchants have gone abroad both to obtain merchandise and ideas and to operate retail establishments. The development of trading company operations in Africa and Asia by British, French, Dutch, Belgian and German retailing organisations progressed extensively during the 19th and early 20th centuries. International trading and retail store operation were two of the economic pillars of the colonial system of that era. The big change taking place in international retailing today involves the gradual dis-

Carrefour SA – at the forefront of global retailing

It was in 1962, that Carrefour SA opened the first hypermarket in France. Part-supermarket, part department store, they offered their customers a wide array of product categories – groceries, toys, furniture, fast food and financial services – all under one roof. To protect this fragile blossom, the French government issued zoning laws that would keep competing stores from Carrefour's vicinity.

The rest is history. By the end of the 1990s, Carrefour was operating about 1,000 supermarkets in 20 countries and it is still continuing its global expansion. The new economic freedom in Central and Eastern Europe opened opportunities for expansion, as well as other regions on the globe. Carrefour started operations in Malaysia in 1994; Indonesia, Chile, Columbia and Chechnya are already serviced or will be in the near future. In China, where chain stores were unheard of, Carrefour was the first company to set up a hypermarket. An outlet in Beijing was opened in December 1995. Until then, food retailing was conducted largely either through small, collectively or individually owned 'mom and pop' stores or state-run open-air fresh food markets.

However, global distribution holds some challenges for Carrefour. For example, the local government in Buenos Aires has recently introduced new legislation limiting the expansion potential for large supermarkets. Instead, they favour discount stores which are already spreading throughout Buenos Aires. To stay competitive, Carrefour is planning to open Stoc and Comptoirs Modernes branches. In order to obtain all remaining shares in Comptoirs Modernes, Carrefour first had to award mandates for credit to Banque Nationale de Paris, Citibank and Paribas.

In Korea, Carrefour had to postpone its operation plans due to construction delays which were caused by complicated paperwork. And it is not only abroad that Carrefour faces difficulties. Concerns have been raised by the EU Competition Commission referring to antitrust issues prior to the acquisition of Promodes SA. Despite having to face major obstacles, world-wide effort seems worthwhile! Carrefour has gained reputation as a 'great credit story and one of the strongest corporate names in Europe – and the rest of the world'.

Food for thought

● Should the spread of hypermarkets be regulated more strongly to protect smaller local retailers? What are the pros and cons?
● Which factors should Carrefour SA take into account when selecting new country markets for their global expansion plans?

Source: 'Carrefour targets 25pc rise in sales for 1998', *Business Times*, 14 October 1998; 'Carrefour has entered the Czech market', *Hospordarske Noviny*, 16 November 1998, p. 11; 'Llegan lose hard discount', La Nacion, 22 September 1998, p. 3; 'Carrefour's jumbo to test appetite with lean pricing', *Euroweek*, 2 October 1998, pp. 34ff; 'Carrefour and Makro delay plans for opening new outlets', *Korea Economic Daily*, 17 June 1998; 'Carrefour acquisition hits snag', *MMM*, 17 3 (1999): p. 19; Richard Bowles, 'Food retailing takes off', *China Business Review*, 25 5 (1998): pp. 30ff.

solution of the colonial retailing structure and, in its place, the creation of international retailing organisations operating in the industrialised countries.

The status–quo of global retailing

Retail stores can be divided into categories according to the amount of square feet of floor space, the level of service offered, and width and depth of product offerings. In practice, stores have many different names in different countries, and definitions based on selling area also vary. A variety of terms is used to refer to large stores, including hypermarkets, mass merchandisers, discounters, supermarkets and superstores.

In general, countries in which the proportion of store numbers is low relative to their share of turnover are those that joined the supermarket revolution many years after it began. France, Belgium, Spain, Brazil and Colombia are some of the countries in which supermarket retailing sprang up as large, modern, highly efficient units were built. In Italy, where worker-protective legislation limiting the opening of large supermarkets is a factor, large surface stores grew in popularity more gradually. They have more than half of the grocery market share today, up from only 25 per cent several years ago. In other countries, supermarkets have existed for more than two decades. Some of the smaller units have been closed down, and new, very large stores have appeared in their place.

The large number of unsuccessful international retailing ventures suggests that anyone contemplating a move into international retailing should do so with a great deal of caution. The critical question for the would-be international retailer is, 'What advantages do we have relative to local competition?' The answer will often be 'Nothing', when local laws governing retailing practice are taken into account. In such cases, there is no reason to expect highly profitable operations to develop from a venture into international retailing.

On the other hand, the answer may indicate that potential advantages do exist. Basically, a retailer has two things to offer consumers. One is the selection of goods at a price, and the second is the overall manner in which the goods are offered in the store setting. This includes such things as the store site, parking facilities, in-store setting and customer service.

Global retailing not only offers new market potential, but also new revenue opportunities. Going global, retailers like Carrefour SA or Wal-Mart meet the same manufacturers in many countries. One global manufacturer of fast-moving consumer goods found that 10 per cent of its global business is done with Wal-Mart and 25 per cent with a handful of other global retailers. With a sophisticated global sourcing system in place, retailers can easily spot price differences across markets. Their global market power will serve them as a favourable position to start price negotiations.[19]

The future of global retailing

Finding familiar fast-food or hotel brands wherever we go internationally is no big surprise to many of us. Experts say that this feeling will be quite common in the near future, when it comes to global retailers. Estimates are that there will be a massive consolidation in retailing. The motto is 'it's either time to eat lunch or be lunch'. First moves in this directions may already be observed. The US retail giant Wal-Mart has bought the British Asda. The Dutch retailer Ahold is expanding globally and aims to team-up with Safeway and/or Sainsbury's. Carrefour and Promodes are joining forces and Tesco is still pondering. Compared to other industries, globalisation in retailing is lagging behind but speeding up considerably. While 10 years ago leading retailers achieved only 20 per cent of total sales from international operations, by now this ratio has increased to 50 per cent.

Experts believe that in the near future the 'superleague' in retailing will be dominated by four global retailers.[20] Table 13.2 provides an overview of this 'superleague' in global retailing.

Direct marketing

Direct marketing describes a distribution system, where sales to customers are carried

Table 13.2 The superleague in global retailing

Supermarket	Stores abroad
Ahold Including Spain, Poland, Czech Republic, US, Brazil and Argentina	1,720
Wal-Mart/ASDA Including Argentina, Brazil, Korea, Mexico, Germany, China and the UK	947
Carrefour Hypermarkets including Spain, Latin America, Asia and Central Europe*	234
Tesco Including Ireland, Hungary, Poland, Slovakia, Czech Republic, Thailand, Korea and Taiwan	109

* If deal with Promodes goes ahead, it will have over 9,000 stores in 26 countries.

Source: Alexandra Jardine, 'Retailers go on international shopping trip', *Marketing*, London, 20 January 2000, p. 15.

out via telephone, mail or door-to-door. The days of classical direct marketing are not over, even in times of the Internet. As a recent investigation shows, the good old door-to-door salesman – in most cases now a saleswoman – is alive and well. The one-on-one approach is still particularly effective for products which need demonstration or complex explanation, like cosmetics, household products or newer categories like nutritional supplements and lingerie.[21]

Direct marketing channels open also up opportunities for internationalisation even to smaller firms. An Bord Trachtala (ABT) – an Irish co-operative of more than 100 companies producing Irish crafts, giftware, fashions and other consumer goods – took such advantages. Due to their Irish ancestors, many US consumers are thrilled with Irish products, particularly around St Patrick's Day – celebrating Ireland's national saint. Until recently, ABT was selling through a number of ethnic stores across the US. Their market power and outreach, however, was quite limited. So some time ago, ABT joined forces with QVC, the US largest home-shopping TV channel. In an instance, ABT got access to an audience of 60 million households across the US, promoting 1,600 products a week, receiving 50,000 sales calls per hour and dispatching over 14,000 packages a day to customers. Sales figures for ABT are impressive. St Patrick's Day in 1997, which was devoted exclusively to Irish merchandise, generated revenues of €6 million – impossible with the previous sales network![22]

E-commerce and international distribution strategies

There is no advantage without disadvantage! This statement also holds true for manufacturers and retailers in electronic commerce. Shopping on the Internet is skyrocketing. Experts estimate that by 2003 sales of €1 trillion will be generated.[23]

The question arises how distribution systems can be designed under these new parameters. Figure 13.2 provides an overview of different distribution alternatives.

Basically, manufacturers have different choices on how to rearrange their distribution channels. They can decide to ignore online selling, which implies that everything stays the same. Given the enormous sales potential e-commerce offers, other alternatives may be more suitable. One reaction would be to shift a firm's sales entirely to the manufacturer. A successful example of this strategy is Dell Computer, for instance.

Figure 13.2 Alternative channel responses

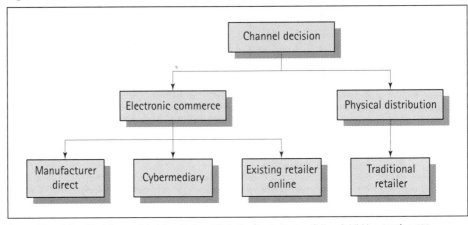

Source: Adapted from Ward Hanson, *Principles of Internet Marketing* (South-Western College Publishing, 2000): p. 376.

A different approach is to operate through existing retailers and their websites. If, for example, you have always dreamt of doing your grocery shopping in peace and quiet, without circling the parking lot for a suitable spot or waiting in line at the check-out seemingly for hours, then your time has come. A sales channel, which many thought might be irreplaceable – the grocery store – now gets competition from its virtual brother on the Internet. Online grocery shopping is not an easy task. While making the selection requires a mouseclick, the challenge lies in establishing a delivery network. So the volume generated through Internet sales was extremely critical to reach break-even. Some companies charge extra for perishable goods, tobacco or alcohol to cover their risk.[24]

One grocery retailer, however, merits the name 'e-tailer'. The British grocer Tesco is running its Internet home-shopping service extremely successfully. Around 300,000 registered customers generate sales of €3.5 million a week. In contrast to its competitors, which established highly automated new warehouses, Tesco takes advantage of its nearly 650 retail outlets across the country. For customers, this means a product range as wide as in-store and more convenient delivery times, as smaller vans are covering shorter distances. All in all, Tesco has performed extremely well in this area without heavy investments, what makes it one of the few profitable operators in grocery shopping over the Internet.[25]

Another approach to incorporate e-commerce into a firm's distribution channels is to choose a so-called cybermediary. A cybermediary is an online mediary which operates exclusively via the Internet.[26] Drugstore.com, a cybermediary for online drug sales, may serve as an example. Drugstore.com aims at customers who would be too embarrassed to ask their local pharmacist face-to-face for items such as birth control or incontinence products. Selling drugs over the Internet, however, is accompanied by several challenges: customers feeling ill might not want to wait until they receive the medication needed overnight. Drugstore.com therefore advises customers with acute pain to see their local doctor. Another issue is the sale of prescription drugs. Their offer at drugstore.com is restricted and will not save customers from seeing their local pharmacist. Yet, service opportunities for drugstore.com are wide open. Currently, drugstore.com offers advice on customer inquiries within one day, and more is still to come.[27]

Another example is Dressmart.com, an online men's clothing retailer for well-paid businessmen with little time to shop. Many companies already sell their own products to in-house staff. Dressmart.com takes advantage of such company intranets. It entered a deal with Ericsson, the Swedish Telecom company, to be featured on Ericsson's intranet. This deal gives Dressmart.com direct access to a workforce of 100,000 world-wide. Beside the effects of bargain-shopping online, Ericsson's management also sees an educational effect of the joint venture, as employees learn how to use the Internet for their purposes. The range of products offered in Dressmart's virtual fitting rooms consists of shirts, ties, shoes and accessories – all from well-known brands like Tiger, Jockey and Van Heusen. The reason behind: the clientele Dressmart's addresses does not try what they buy, as they know exactly what they want.[28]

It goes without saying that the new distribution channels within e-commerce are not applauded by everyone. Particularly traditional retail and distribution partners fear serious problems through channel conflicts. One question in this context is whether new sales are created or whether Internet sales simply cannibalise conventional distribution partners. Most likely the answer is the latter – at least in a national environment. Yet, it has to be noted that new opportunities arise from an on-line internationalisation of sales potential.[29]

However, as the following examples show, creative use of the Internet as sales tools may well support the manufacturer's and the traditional retailer's needs. Fashion manufacturers and retailers have discovered the Internet as a helpful sales tool for both parties. Karstadt, Esprit, Promodes and others use three-dimensional fashion sketches as a basis for a product catalogue. These sketches may be manipulated and rearranged to show how the garments will look like in the store. At store level, customers can use the system to search for special colours or styles to match with pieces bought last year and thus build a co-ordinated wardrobe.[30]

Despite the potential conflicts which may arise between traditional and electronic distribution channels, experts agree that there is no way back. Global e-commerce revenues are estimated to reach €350 billion by 2003 with a market share of 15–20 per cent in the world-wide retail sector.

On behalf of other industries, a global retailing expert provides a good summary: 'E-tailing will be a force, because, quite simply, the Net makes every retailer global. But retailers with physical stores have a unique advantage: they can establish an on-line strategy to complement their bricks-and-mortar presence in the market.'[31]

Key points

- **The design of distribution channels for international marketing has seen considerable changes over the last years. Several developments may be observed: a trend to globalisation of retailing operations, a rebirth of direct marketing activities even in times of the Internet and the effects of e-commerce on traditional distribution systems.**

- **While other industries have been going global for quite some time, retailing was still lagging somewhat behind. Yet times are changing. While 10 years ago, 20 per cent of total retail sales stemmed from international operations, this figure has risen to 50 per cent by now. Experts predict a continuation in this direction, which will bring along consolidation within the industry. In the near future, the global retailing business will be dominated by a superleague of transnational retail conglomerates.**

Key points

- Those who predicted decline in direct marketing, as e-commerce emerges, has been proven wrong. The one-on-one approach is still particularly effective for products which need demonstration or complex explanations. And there are still new product categories which rely increasingly on direct marketing, such as nutritional supplements or lingerie.

- E-commerce, the buzzword of the last decade, was predicted to revolutionise traditional sales channels. In most cases, this holds true. Yet, there are also success stories for traditional manufacturers and retailers, who have understood how to utilise the new tool for their and their customers' benefit.

Summary

Channel decisions are difficult to manage globally because of the variation in channel structures from country to country. Nevertheless, certain patterns of change associated with market development offer the astute global marketer the opportunity to create channel innovations and gain competitive advantage. The characteristics of customers, products, middlemen and environment all impact channel design and strategy. Consumer channels may be direct, via mail, door to door, the Internet, or direct factory/manufacturer outlets, or they may involve one or more levels of resellers. A combination of the manufacturer's salesforce, agents/brokers and wholesalers may also be used.

In economically developed countries, retail channels are characterised by the substitution of capital for labour. This is evident in self-service stores, which offers a wide range of items at relatively low gross margins. The opposite is true in economically less developed countries with abundant labour. Such countries disguise their unemployment in inefficient retail and wholesale channels suited to the needs of consumers; such channels may have gross margins that are 50 per cent lower than those in self-service stores in developed countries. A global marketer must either tailor the marketing programme to these different types of channels or introduce new retail concepts.

In the near future, retailing will see an increasing trend towards globalisation of operations. Experts say that only few transnational retail conglomerates will remain. The Internet is most likely fostering these developments, if retailers are able to offer added value to their customers. While the Internet may cannibalise to some extent traditional local distribution channels, it offers great opportunities for a firm's internationalisation at – in most cases – relatively low cost.

Transportation and physical distribution issues are critically important in global marketing because of the geographical distances involved in sourcing products and serving customers in different parts of the world. Today, many companies are reconfiguring their supply chains to cut costs and improve efficiency.

Concepts and definitions

In-bound logistics	Describes the process of moving products and materials from suppliers to the factory. Six factors must be taken into account in the sourcing decision: factor costs and con-

ditions, transport costs, country infrastructure, political risk, market access and currency issues.

Electronic data interchange (EDI)	EDI describes an IT network that co-ordinates information such as orders, production schedules, forecasts and other similar input between manufacturer and suppliers.
Out-bound logistics	Is defined as moving products from the factory to customers. It involves aspects of transportation, inventory control, order processing and warehousing.
Factors determining the design of international distribution channels	Several characteristics impact on channel design and strategy: (i) customer characteristics, such as their number, geographic distribution, income, shopping habits or their reactions to different selling methods, (ii) product characteristics such as perishability, service requirements or unit price, (iii) middleman characteristics, such as their attitude towards the manufacturer or (iv) environmental characteristics like economic, social and political dimensions.
E-tailing	Describes the increasing trend of retail operations globalising via the Internet. In this context, not only presenting a product range but selling it over the Internet gains increasing importance.
Cybermediary	A cybermediary is an online intermediary which operates exclusively via the Internet.

Discussion questions

1 In what ways can channel intermediaries create utility for buyers?

2 What factors influence the channel structures and strategies available to global marketers?

3 What is cherry picking? What approaches can be used to deal with this problem?

4. Briefly discuss the global issues associated with physical distribution and transportation logistics. Cite one example of a company that is making efficiency improvements in its physical distribution.

5 Design a distribution system for a new product (for example, a DIY kit to measure blood glucose level for people with diabetes) for different markets (in Asia, Europe etc.). How would you approach this challenge? What kind of decisions do you have to take? From whom would you get relevant information?

Webmistress's hotspots

Homepage of the UK's government first e-commerce site
Here you will find all sorts of publications of the Foreign Office, such as books, leaflets, videos, CD-Roms and much more.
http://www.informationfrombritain.com

Homepage of Dressmart.com
If you dread visits to the shopping mall for men's wear, here you find up-scale garments online.
http://www.dressmart.com

Homepage of Drugstore.com

Check out this website if you are looking for products to stock up your medical cabinet without leaving the house, or if you want to register for a trial of personal care products that you have always been interested in.
http://www.drugstore.com

Homepage of Tesco

You long for a bucket of ice cream with crunchy nuts and chunky caramel, but you are too lazy to drive over to your nearest supermarket, and you want it fast – delivered to your doorstep? You are in luck, if you are living in the UK – because then this website offers First Aid! If not, tough luck – but check out what you are missing!
http://www.tescodirect.com

Suggested readings

Alexander, Nicholas, *International Retailing*. Oxford, UK: Blackwell Business, 1997.

Allen, Randy L., 'The why and how of global retailing', *Business Quarterly*, 57, 4 (Summer 1993): pp. 117–122.

Bauer, P.T., *West African Trade*. Cambridge: Cambridge University Press, 1954.

Bello, Daniel C. and Ritu Lohtia, 'Export channel design: the use of foreign distributors and agents', *Journal of the Academy of Marketing Science*, 23, 2 (1995): pp. 83–93.

Bello, Daniel C., David J. Urban and Brohislaw J. Verhage, 'Evaluating export middlemen in alternative channel structures', *International Marketing Review*, 8, 5 (1991): pp. 49–64.

Carr, Mark, Arlene Hostrop and Daniel O'Connor, 'The new era of global retailing', *Journal of Business Strategy*, 19, 3 (1998): pp. 11–15.

Cavusgil, S. Tamer, 'The importance of distributor training at Caterpillar', *Industrial Marketing Management*, 19, 1 (February 1990): pp. 1–9.

Fernie, John, 'Distribution strategies for European retailers', *European Journal of Marketing*, 26, 8, 9 (1992): pp. 35–47.

Fields, George, *From Bonsai to Levi's: An Insider's Surprising Account of How the Japanese Live*. New York: Macmillan, 1983.

Frazier, Gary L., James D. Gill and Sudhir H. Kale, 'Dealer dependence levels and reciprocal actions in a channel of distribution in a developing country', *Journal of Marketing*, 53, 1 (January 1989): pp. 50–69.

Gentry, Julie R., Janjaap Semeijn and David B. Vellenga, 'The future of road haulage in the new European Union – 1995 and beyond', *The Logistics and Transportation Review*, 31, 2 (1995): pp. 145–160.

Hanson, Ward, *Principles of Internet Marketing*. Cincinnati: South Western College Publishing, 2000.

Harvey, Michael G. and Robert F. Lusch (eds), *Marketing Channels: Domestic and International Perspectives*. Norman, OK: Center for Economic & Management Research, 1982.

Helsell, Tina, 'China's middlemen – new paths to market', *China Business Review*, 27, 1 (2000): pp. 64–70.

Hill, John S., Richard R. Still and Unal O. Boya, 'Managing the multinational sales force', *International Marketing Review*, 8, 1 (1991): pp. 19–31.

Kaikati, Jack G, 'Don't crack the Japanese distribution system – just circumvent it', *Columbia Journal of World Business*, 28, 2 (Summer 1993): pp. 34–45.

Kale, Sudhir and Roger P. McIntyre, 'Distribution channel relationships in diverse cultures', *International Marketing Review*, 8, 3 (1991): pp. 311–345.

Klein, Saul, 'Selection of international marketing channels', *Journal of Global Marketing*, 4, 4 (1991): pp. 21–37.

Klein, Saul and Victor Roth, 'Satisfaction with international marketing channels', *Journal of the Academy of Marketing Science*, 21, 1 (Winter 1993): pp. 39–44.

Krokowski, Wilfried, *Globalisierung des Einkaufs*. Berlin: Springer, 1998.

Murphy, Paul R., James M. Daley and Douglas R. Dalenberg, 'Doing business in global markets: perspectives of international freight forwarders', *Journal of Global Marketing*, 6, 4 (1993): pp. 53–68.

Novich, Neil S., 'Leading-edge distribution strategies', *Journal of Business Strategy*, 11, 6 (November/December 1990): pp. 48–53.

Olsen, Janeen E. and Kent L. Granzin, 'Economic development and channel structure: a multinational study', *Journal of Macromarketing*, 10, 2 (Fall 1990): pp. 61–77.

Raguraman K. and Claire Chan, 'The development of sea-air intermodal transportation: an assessment of global trends', *The Logistics and Transportation Review*, 30, 4 (December 1994): pp. 379–396.

'Retail Marketing: International Perspectives', *The European Journal of Marketing*, 26, 8/9 (1992), special issue.

Rosenbloom, Bert, 'Motivating your international channel partners', *Business Horizons*, 33, 2 (March–April 1990): 53.

Sachdev, Harash J., Daniel C. Bello and Bruce K. Pilling, 'Control mechanisms within export channels of distribution', *Journal of Global Marketing*, 8, 2 (1994): pp. 31–50.

Samiee, Saeed, 'Retailing and channel considerations in developing countries: a review and research proposition', *Journal of Business Research*, 27, 2 (June 1993): pp. 103–129.

Sherwood, Charles and Robert Bruns, 'Solving international transportation problems', *Review of Business*, 14, 1 (Summer/Fall 1992): pp. 25–30.

Stern, Louis W. and Adel L. El-Ansary, *Marketing Channels*, 4th edn. Upper Saddle River, NJ: Prentice Hall, 1992.

Weigand, Robert E., 'Parallel import channels – options for preserving territorial integrity', *Columbia Journal of World Business*, 26, 1 (Spring 1991): pp. 53–60.

Notes

1. 'Shopping all over the world: retailers are trying to go global', *Business*, 19 June 1999; Susanna Voyle, 'Kingfisher's global sourcing aims', *Financial Times*, 21 January 2000; David Pyke, 'Strategies for global sourcing', *Financial Times*, 20 February 1998.

2. Wilfried Krokowski, *Globalisierung des Einkaufs*. Berlin: Springer, 1998; Ulli Arnold. 'Probleme der Beschaffung und Materialwirtschaft bei eigener Auslandsproduktion'. In *Handbuch der Internationalen Unternehmenstätigkeit*, ed. Brij Nino Kumar and Helmut Haussmann (München: Beck'sche Verlagsbuchhandlung, 1992), pp. 637–655; David Pyke, 'Strategies for global sourcing', *Financial Times*, 20 February 1998.

3. William Taylor, 'Message and muscle: an interview with Swatch Titan Nicolas Hayek', *Harvard Business Review*, 71, 2 (1993): pp. 99–110.

4. Juliette Jowit and Haig Simonian, 'BMW deal may not save car plant', *Financial Times*, 5 December 1998.

5. Uta Harnischfeger, 'BMW confirms sale of Rover', *Financial Times*, 16 March 2000.

6. Doron P. Levin, 'Compaq storms the PC heights from its factory floor', *New York Times*, 4 November 1994, p. 5.

7. Peter C.T. Elsworth, 'Can colors and stripes rescue Shrit makers from a slump?', *New York Times*, 17 March 1991, p. 5.

8. David Tinsley, 'Experts unite to target sector', *Lloyds List*, 25 October 1999.

9. Juliette Jowit and Haig Simonian, 'BMW deal may not save car plant', *Financial Times*, 5 December 1998.

10. Bob Ortega, 'Tough sale: Wal-Mart is slowed by problems of price and culture in Mexico', *The Wall Street Journal*, 28 July 1994, pp. A1, A5.

11. Robert L. Rose, 'Success abroad: 3M, by tiptoeing into foreign markets, became a big exporter', *Wall Street Journal*, 29 March 1991, p. A10.

12. Jack G. Kaikati, 'Don't crack the Japanese distribution system – just circumvent it', *Columbia Journal of World Business*, 28, 2 (1993): pp. 34–45.

13. Susanna Voyle, 'Distributors deliver government's first e-baby', *Financial Times*, 8 July 1999.

14. Allan Afuah, 'Technology approaches for the information age', *Financial Times*, 27 September 1999; Judith Chevalier, 'The pros and cons of entering a market', *Financial Times*, 1 November 1999.

15. Leyla Boulton, 'Big groups go shopping for revenue-rich retailers', *Financial Times*, 22 November 1999.

16. Andersen Consulting, *Case Study: Moscow Bread Company*, 1993.

17. 'Subaru dealers to handle Porsche sales', *Japan Industrial Journal*, 20 January 1998, p. 9; 'Porsche to control French distribution', *Automotive News Europe*, 22 June 1998, p. 30; Andrew Fisher, 'Dealership dispute settled', *Financial Times*, 21 January 1998; Michiyo Nakamoto, 'Challenge to Porsche from Japan importer', *Financial Times*, 16 October 1997.

18. Tina Helsell, 'China's middlemen – new paths to market', *China Business Review*, 27, 1 (2000): pp. 64–70.

19. Mark Carr, Arlene Hostrop and Daniel O'Connor, 'The new era of global retailing', *Journal of Business Strategy*, 19, 3 (1998): pp. 11–15.

20. Alexandra Jardine, 'Retailers go on international shopping trip', *Marketing*, 20 January 2000, pp. 15ff. 'Global retailing in the connected economy', *Chain Store Age Executive*, December 1999, pp. 69ff.

21. Richard Tomkins, 'The resurrection of a salesman', *Financial Times*, 16 October 1999, p. 9.

22. John Corrigan, 'Shopping on the box', *Business & Finance*, 24 April 1997.

23. Sean Dugan, 'The revenue factors: strategies for maximizing i-commerce success', *InfoWorld*, 4 October 1999, pp. 70ff.

24. Andrew Edgecliffe-Johnson, 'Groceries on the Net: virtually easy shopping', *Financial Times*, 23 Thursday 1999.

25. 'Tearaway Tesco', *The Economist*, 5 February 2000, p. 68.
26. Ward Hanson, *Principles of Internet Marketing* (Cincinnatti: South Western College Publishing, 2000).
27. Andrew Edgecliffe-Johnson, 'Online drugstore trades at 200% premium in latest Internet IPO', *Financial Times*, 29 July 1999.
28. Ashling O'Connor, 'Turn your office into an online workshop', *Financial Times*, 21 October 1999, p. 28.
29. Sean Dugan, 'The revenue factors: strategies for maximizing i-commerce success', *InfoWorld*, 4 October 1999, pp. 70ff.
30. Penelope Ody, 'Retailers keep an eye on business with new systems', *Financial Times*, 1 September 1999, p. v.
31. 'Global retailing in the connected economy', *Chain Store Age Executive*, December 1999, pp. 69ff.

CHAPTER 14

Global marketing communication

Eighteen-year-olds in Paris have more in common with 18-year-olds
in New York than with their own parents. They buy the same products,
go to the same movies, listen to the same music, sip the same colas.
Global advertising merely works on that premise.
WILLIAM ROEDY, DIRECTOR, MTV EUROPE

The advertising style of a country reflects the culture of that country.
MARIEKE DE MOOIJ

Advertising is the richest and most powerful form of communication in the world.
OLIVIERO TOSCANI, CREATIVE DIRECTOR, BENETTON

After reading this chapter, you will know:

- The elements and objectives of global marketing communication.
- Two contrasting positions regarding localisation or globalisation of advertising content.
- The characteristics of different advertising media and how information technology (IT) influences global advertising.
- Points to consider when selecting an advertising agency and creating a campaign for different cultural environments.

Why is this important? Here are three situations in which you would need an understanding of the above issues:

- You have to select suitable marketing communication instruments for a global company.
- You want to launch an advertising campaign in multiple-country markets, and have to select one or more advertising agencies.
- You are responsible for a global company's public relations.

Practice link

Benetton, well known for its controversial (often considered tasteless) advertisements which attract as much opprobrium as praise, spends only 4 per cent of sales revenue on marketing.[1] The headlines they produce are precisely the point. The company has turned the courting of controversy into a spectacularly successful marketing strategy. The campaigns in the 1980s, which played on themes of racial harmony, helped turn the firm into a powerful global brand. In the 1990s, when social issues became intentionally incendiary, sales grew by 25 per cent in 1990 (€1.44 billion in 1990) and another 15 per cent one year later.[2] Today, Benetton's annual turnover has reached about €2 billion.

The leading textile distribution company in Italy, Benetton was founded by Luciano Benetton and his brothers and sister in 1965. 'The campaign had to be different and it had to be international', he said, when he reviewed his advertising decision. Luciano Benetton also wanted to make people aware of the spirit of the company.[3] The communication philosophy of the Benetton group aims at developing a distinctive image targeted at a global consumer base and strives to make the most of its limited resources. Social issues, not clothes, play the leading part in the communication strategy. The aim is to promote discussion. This strategy almost always provokes reactions of outrage or praise. The picture of the dying AIDS victim was called 'obscene' by British magazine publishers such as IPC and EMAP and many publishers refused to run the photo. Others published it with stories describing the outrage of the advertising industry. On the other hand, some American gay activists say that the advert gave the issues involved a higher public profile.

Other communication activities of the Benetton group include sponsoring (Formula One racing), a large-format magazine sold in six bilingual editions in over 100 countries (dedicated to racial integration), and an international design school the company set up ('Fabrica'). To mark the 50th anniversary of the Declaration of the Human Rights, the United Nations Organisation invited Benetton to launch a world communications exercise. This is a striking endorsement of the value of Benetton's communication programmes.

Benetton group's 21 Investimenti, the industrial holding company controlled by Benetton, tripled its profits in 1998 (to a net profit of €19.83 billion). Benetton also invested in online shopping, namely in the Swedish company Boo.com, which claimed to be the 'first global sportswear shop'. Unfortunately, after just six months in operation, Boo.com went into liquidation in May 2000.[4,5]

Clearly, advertising, publicity and other forms of communication are critical tools in the global fashion war. Marketing communications – the promotion P of the marketing mix – refers to all forms of communication used by organisations to inform, remind, explain, persuade and influence the attitudes and buying behaviour of customers and other people. The primary purpose of marketing communications is to tell customers about the benefits and values that a product or service offers. The elements of the promotion mix are advertising, public relations, personal selling and sales promotion.

All of these elements can be utilised in global marketing, either alone or in varying combinations. The environment in which marketing communications programmes and strategies are implemented varies from country to country. The challenge of effectively communicating across borders is one reason Nike, Nestlé, Microsoft and other companies are embracing a concept known as integrated marketing communications (IMC). Adherence of an IMC approach explicitly recognises that the various elements of a company's communication strategy must be carefully coordinated.[6] In this chapter, advertising, public relations, sales promotion and personal selling will be examined from the perspective of the global marketer.

GLOBAL ADVERTISING AND BRANDING

Within different cultural environments, the global marketer has to pay attention to the interaction of the elements of the communication mix. He has to ascertain that all possible constraints (i.e. cultural diversity, media limitations, legal problems) are considered so that the right message is communicated and received by prospective consumers. Figure 14.1 shows how the elements of the communication process are influenced by different cultural environments (context A and context B). Each of them can affect the accuracy of the communication process. Furthermore, the model can be used to identify reasons for a failure. For example, media inadequacy (message may not get through, failure in step 3); different cultural interpretations (message not understood by audience, failure in step 4); or the needs and wants of the target market are not correctly assessed (message shows no effect on audience, failure in step 5).

Advertising may be defined as any sponsored, paid message placed in a mass medium. Global advertising refers to the use of the same advertising appeals, messages, art, copy, photographs, stories and video segments in multiple-country markets. A global company that has the ability to successfully transform a domestic campaign into a world-wide one, or to create a new global campaign from the ground up, has a critical advantage. There are powerful reasons for trying to create an effective global campaign. The creative process will force a company to determine whether there is a global market for its product. The first company to find a global market for any product is usually at an advantage over competitors making the same discovery later. The

Figure 14.1 The communication process

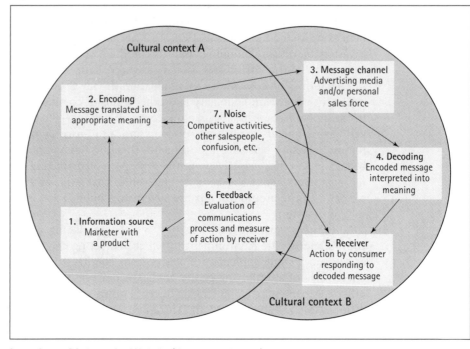

Source: Cateora, P.C., *International Marketing* (Homewood: Irwin, 1993), p. 522.

search for a global advertising campaign can be the cornerstone of the search for a coherent global strategy. Such a search should bring together everyone involved with the product to share information and leverage their experiences.

Since advertising is often designed to add psychological value to a product or brand, it plays a more important communication role in marketing consumer products than in marketing industrial products. Frequently purchased, low-cost products generally require heavy advertising support to remind consumers about the product. Not surprisingly, consumer products companies top the list of big global advertising spenders. Procter & Gamble, Unilever and Nestlé are just a few of the companies with significant global advertising expenditures. Advertising Age's ranking of global marketers in terms of advertising expenditures is shown in Table 14.1. The top 25 companies spent a total of €34.9 billion in 1997 world-wide.

There are several reasons for global advertising's growing popularity. Global campaigns attest to management's conviction that unified themes not only spur short-term sales but also help build long-term product identities and offer significant savings in production costs.[8] Europe is experiencing an internationalisation of brands as companies align themselves, buy up other companies, and get their pricing policies and production plans organised for a united region. From a marketing point of view, there is a great deal of activity going on that will make brands truly pan-European in a very short period of time.

The potential for effective global advertising also increases as companies recognise and embrace market segments crossing national boundaries; the youth culture, for example rather than ethnic or national culture. Athletic shoes and other clothing

Table 14.1 Top 25 global marketers, 1997 (€millions)[7]

Rank 1997	Rank 1996	Advertiser*	World-wide	Europe	US	Africa	Asia	Country count
1	1	Procter & Gamble Co.	4,881.63	1,624.66	2,327.06	9.25	477.76	63
2	2	Unilever	2,913.40	1,280.42	771.02	27.74	414.48	62
3	3	Nestlé	1,511.76	737.94	390.98	9.42	198.33	63
4	4	Toyota Motor Corp.	1,786.77	254.83	722.67	11.11	739.38	52
5	8	Coca-Cola Co.	1,473.67	371.22	602.97	4.24	209.28	61
6	10	General Motors Corp.	3,421.96	520.52	2,619.04	0.59	68.54	46
7	6	Volkswagen	935.76	628.00	173.82	5.77	35.12	44
8	5	PSA Peugeot Citroen	738.45	693.74	0.00	1.02	1.10	39
9	7	Nissan Motor Co.	1,198.65	220.39	463.26	5.17	476.41	50
10	12	Mars Inc.	1,255.31	615.27	521.70	0.00	81.95	38
11	11	Ford Motor Co.	1,786.52	491.08	1,087.35	4.07	87.21	47
12	17	Sony Corp.	1,312.40	322.10	659.55	0.51	258.65	53
13	20	L'Oreal	1,193.73	576.00	551.99	2.63	23.58	44
14	9	Philip Morris Cos.	2,450.74	440.18	1,813.50	0.51	86.10	52
15	13	Renault	593.73	550.55	0.00	0.00	0.00	36
16	19	Fiat	555.89	456.56	1.95	1.19	0.00	26
17	22	Honda Motor Co.	1,021.35	150.06	490.40	0.00	329.48	39
18	14	Henkel	525.18	524.25	0.00	0.00	0.93	25
19	18	McDonald's Corp.	1,396.05	243.89	883.67	0.42	189.09	49
20	15	Kao Corp.	525.10	0.00	29.61	0.00	495.49	9
21	16	Ferrero	481.16	448.84	16.46	0.00	6.96	31
22	23	BMW	599.15	373.93	136.49	2.80	76.60	39
23	21	Colgate-Palmolive	774.75	192.56	317.77	3.73	55.56	55
24	29	Danone Group	482.85	380.55	81.35	0.00	0.00	21
25	31	Johnson & Johnson	1,120.01	201.64	780.61	2.46	65.83	55

* Ranked by non-US ad spending

Source: *Advertising Age*, 'Ad Age Dataplace – top 100 global marketers 1997', (http://adage.com).

products, for instance, can be targeted to a world-wide segment of 18 to 25-year-old males. As noted in the quote at the beginning of this chapter, William Roedy, director of MTV Europe, sees clear implications of such product cultures for advertising. MTV is just one of the media vehicles that enable people virtually anywhere to see how the rest of the world lives and to learn about products that are popular in other cultures. Many human wants and desires are very similar if presented within recognisable experience situations. People everywhere want value, quality and the latest technology made available and affordable; everyone everywhere wants to be loved and respected, gets hungry, and so on.[9]

Global advertising also offers companies economies of scale in advertising as well as improved access to distribution channels. In cases in which shelf space is at a premium, as with food products, a company has to convince retailers to carry its products rather than those of competitors. A global brand supported by global advertising may be very attractive because, from the retailer's standpoint, a global brand is less likely to languish on the shelves. Landor Associates, a company specialising in brand identity and design, recently determined that Coke has the number one brand-awareness and esteem position in the United States, number two in Japan, and number six in Europe. However, standardisation is not always required or even advised. Nestlé's Nescafé is marketed as a global brand even though advertising messages and product formulation vary to suit cultural differences.

GLOBAL ADVERTISING CONTENT: THE EXTENSION VS ADAPTATION DEBATE

Communication experts generally agree that the overall requirements of effective communication and persuasion are fixed and do not vary from country to country. The same thing is true of the components of the communication process: The marketer's/sender's message must be encoded, conveyed via the appropriate channel(s), and decoded by the customer/receiver. Communication takes place only when meaning is transferred. Four major difficulties can compromise an organisation's attempt to communicate with customers in any location:

1 The message may not get through to the intended recipient. This problem may be the result of an advertiser's lack of knowledge about appropriate media for reaching certain types of audiences. For example, the effectiveness of television as a medium for reaching mass audiences will vary proportionately with the extent to which television viewing occurs within a country.
2 The message may reach the target audience but may not be understood or may even be misunderstood. This can be the result of an inadequate understanding of the target audience's level of sophistication or improper encoding.
3 The message may reach the target audience and may be understood but still may not induce the recipient to take the action desired by the sender. This could result from a lack of cultural knowledge about a target audience.
4 The effectiveness of the message can be impaired by noise. Noise in this case is an external influence such as competitive advertising, other sales personnel, and confusion at the receiving end, which can detract from the ultimate effectiveness of the communication.

The key question for global marketers is whether the specific advertising message and media strategy must be changed from region to region or country to country because of environmental requirements. Proponents of the 'one world, one voice' approach to global advertising believe that the era of the global village is fast approaching, and that tastes and preferences are converging world-wide. According to the standardisation argument, because people everywhere want the same products for the same reasons, companies can achieve great economies of scale by unifying advertising around the globe. Advertisers who follow the localised approach are sceptical of the global village argument. Rather, they assert that consumers still differ from country to country and must be reached by advertising tailored to their respective countries. Proponents of localisation point out that most blunders occur because advertisers have failed to understand and adapt to foreign cultures. Nick Brien, managing director of Leo Burnett, explains the situation this way:

> As the potency of traditional media declines on a daily basis, brand building locally becomes more costly and international brand building becomes more cost effective. The challenge for advertisers and agencies is finding ads which work in different countries and cultures. At the same time as this global tendency, there is a growing local tendency. It's becoming increasingly important to understand the requirements of both.[10]

During the 1950s, the widespread opinion of advertising professionals was that effective international advertising required assigning responsibility for campaign preparation to a local agency. In the early 1960s, this idea of local delegation was repeatedly challenged. For example, Eric Elinder, head of a Swedish advertising agency, wrote: 'Why should three artists in three different countries sit drawing the same electric iron and three copywriters write about what after all is largely the same copy for the same iron?'[11] Elinder argued that consumer differences between countries were diminishing and that he would more effectively serve a client's interest by putting top specialists to work who devise a strong international campaign. The campaign would then be presented with insignificant modifications that mainly entailed translating the copy into language well suited for a particular country.

At the beginning of the 1980s, Pierre Liotard-Vogt, former CEO of Nestlé, expressed similar views in an interview with *Advertising Age*:

> *Advertising Age*: Are food tastes and preferences different in each of the countries in which you do business?
>
> *Liotard-Vogt*: The two countries where we are selling perhaps the most instant coffee are England and Japan. Before the war they didn't drink coffee in those countries, and I heard people say that it wasn't any use to try to sell instant coffee to the English because they drink only tea and still less to the Japanese because they drink green tea and they're not interested in anything else. When I was very young, I lived in England and at that time, if you spoke to an Englishman about eating spaghetti or pizza or anything like that, he would just look at you and think that the stuff was perhaps food for Italians. Now on the corner of every road in London you find pizzerias and spaghetti houses. So I do not believe [preconceptions] about 'national tastes'. They are 'habits', and they're not the same. If you bring the public a different food, even if it is unknown initially, when they get used to it, they will enjoy it too.[12]

The standardisation-vs-localisation debate picked up tremendous momentum after the 1983 publication of Professor Ted Levitt's *Harvard Business Review* article entitled 'The Globalization of Markets'. However, in contrast to the view expounded by Levitt and Liotard-Vogt, some recent scholarly research suggests that the trend goes towards the increased use of localised international advertising. Kanso reached that conclusion in a study surveying two different groups of advertising managers, namely those taking localised approaches to overseas advertising and those taking standardised approaches.[13] Another finding was that managers attuned to cultural issues tended to prefer the localised approach, whereas managers less sensitive to cultural issues preferred a standardised approach. Bruce Steinberg, ad sales director for MTV Europe, has discovered that the people responsible for executing global campaigns locally can exhibit strong resistance to a global campaign. Steinberg sometimes has to visit as many as 20 marketing directors from the same company to get approval for a pan-European MTV ad.[14]

As Kanso correctly notes, the controversy over advertising approaches will probably continue for years to come. Localised and standardised advertising both have their place and both will continue to be used. Kanso's conclusion: what is needed for successful international advertising is a global commitment to local vision. In the final analysis, the decision whether to use a global or localised campaign depends on recognition by managers of the trade-offs involved. On the one hand, a global campaign will result in substantial benefits such as cost savings, increased control and the potential creative leverage of a global appeal. On the other hand, localised campaigns have the advantage of appeals that focus on the most important attributes of a product in each nation or culture. The question of when to use each approach depends on the product involved and a company's objectives in a particular market.

In Japan, for example, PepsiCo has achieved great success with a local campaign featuring 'Pepsiman', a superhero action figure. Prior to 1996, the ads shown in Japan were the same global spots used throughout the rest of the world. However, in Japan's €20.3 billion soft drink market, Pepsi trailed far behind Coca-Cola; Pepsi had a mere

GLOBAL PERSPECTIVE

Global campaigns for global products

Certain consumer products lend themselves to advertising extensions. If a product appeals to the same need around the world, there is a possibility of extending the appeal to that need. The list of products 'going global', once confined to a score of consumer and luxury goods, is growing. Global advertising is partly responsible for increased worldwide sales of disposable nappies, diamond watches, shampoos and athletic shoes. Some longtime global advertisers are benefiting from fresh campaigns. Jeans marketer Levi Strauss & Company racked up record sales in Europe in 1991 on the strength of a campaign extended unchanged to Europeans, Latin Americans and Australians. The basic issue is whether there is in fact a global market for the product. If the market is global, appeals can be standardised and extended. Soft drinks, Scotch whisky, Swiss watches and designer clothing are examples of product categories whose markets are truly global. For example, Seagram's recently ran a global campaign keyed to the theme line, 'There will always be a Chivas Regal'. The campaign ran in 34 countries and was translated into 15 languages. In 1991, Seagram's launched a global billboard campaign to enhance the universal appeal for Chivas. The theory: the rich all over will sip the brand, no matter where they made their fortune.

Gillette Company took a standardised 'one product/one brand name/one strategy' global approach when it introduced the Sensor razor in 1990. The campaign slogan was 'Gillette. The Best A Man Can Get', an appeal that was expected to cross boundaries with ease. Peter Hoffman, marketing vice president of the North Atlantic Shaving Group, noted in a press release: 'We are blessed with a product category where we're able to market shaving systems across multinational boundaries as if they were one country. Gillette Sensor is the trigger for a total Gillette megabrand strategy which will revolutionise the entire shaving market.' In the Japanese market, Gillette's standardised advertising campaign differs strikingly from that of arch-rival Schick. Prior to the Sensor launch, Gillette custommade advertising for the Japanese market; now, except that the phrase, 'The best a man can get', is translated into Japanese, the ads shown in Japan are the same as those shown in the United States and the rest of the world. Schick, meanwhile, uses Japanese actors in its ads.

Food for thought

- Which factors might lead a company to adapt the execution of adverts to local requirements, even if the product appeal is global?
- Draw up a list of cultural issues that might prevent the use of standardised advertising appeals.

3 per cent market share compared with Coke's 30 per cent share. The Pepsiman character was designed by local Japanese talent, but Industrial Light & Magic, the special-effects house owned by Star Wars creator George Lucas, was retained to give the TV spots a US-style high-tech edge. By breaking with its usual strategy of running global ads and increasing the ad budget by 50 per cent over 1995, Pepsi's 1996 sales in Japan rose by 14 per cent.[15]

McDonald's advertising has also enjoyed a surge of popularity in Japan, but for the opposite reason: McDonald's is including Japan in its global approach that invites consumers to associate the restaurant with family members interacting in various situations. Starting in 1996, McDonald's campaign in Japan depicted various aspects of fatherhood. One spot showed a father and son bicycling home with burgers and fries; another showed a father driving a vanful of boisterous kids to McDonald's for milkshakes. The ads come at a time when many Japanese 'salarymen' are reassessing the balance between work and family life. The campaign illustrates the use of localised global advertising; Japanese actors are used in the spots and local musicians composed music reminiscent of Japanese prime time TV shows.[16]

IMPACT OF INFORMATION TECHNOLOGY ON ADVERTISING

Today, the fragmentation of media is characteristic of advertising: Sergio Zyman, former marketing chief of Coca-Cola, stated that 'Technology has given people many more options than they had in the past' and 'Marketers increasingly need to find ways to speak to consumers individually, or in smaller and smaller groups.'[17] Talking to consumers one-to-one by telephone, mail or Internet opens ways of reaching audiences that can no longer be reached by mass media. The following section compares (Table 14.2) and discusses some advertising media and pays particular attention to the impact of information technology.

The use of direct marketing is growing rapidly in many parts of the world due to increased use of computer databases, credit cards and toll-free numbers, as well as changing lifestyles. Direct marketing is a system of marketing that integrates ordinarily separate marketing mix elements to sell directly to both consumers and other businesses, bypassing retail stores and personal sales calls. It uses a wide spectrum of media, including direct mail; telephone; broadcast, including television and radio; and print, including newspapers and magazines. Sales via the Internet are an expansion of direct marketing. Buitoni, an Italian pasta company owned by Nestlé, used direct marketing methods to build a base of loyal Buitoni customers: the Casa Buitoni Club. The strategy was to offer consumers a helpful authority on Italian food from which they could get advice on pasta. To obtain a database of consumers interested in getting involved in Italian cooking, Buitoni offered free recipe booklets in the press, through teletext or direct-response television to anyone interested. Altogether a database of more than 200,000 consumers was developed. Subsequently the households in the database were contacted and invited to join the Casa Buitoni Club. Membership benefits included toll-free lines, sweepstakes, gourmet-cooking weekends and so on. Through word-of-mouth and marketing efforts membership has grown constantly.[18]

The usage of direct mail, the most popular type of direct marketing, varies around the world based on literacy rates, level of acceptance, infrastructure and culture. In countries with low levels of literacy, a medium that requires reading is not effective. In other countries, the literacy rate may be high, but consumers are unfamiliar with direct mail and suspicious of products they cannot see.

The infrastructure of a country must be sufficiently developed to handle direct mail. The postal system must deliver mail on a timely basis and be free of corruption. In addition to the physical infrastructure, a system for developing databases, retrieving appropriate target names and tracking results is necessary. In one former Soviet republic, merchants were resistant to having their name and address publicly listed in a telephone directory. They feared that the local 'mafia' could readily use this information to extort protection money from these businesses.

Culture also plays a significant role in the decision to use direct mail. In Thailand, the local astrologer plays an important role in many business decisions. If the day that a direct mail campaign is scheduled to begin is not auspicious, the marketer may

Table 14.2 **Characteristics of different advertising media**

Medium	Types	Factors affecting rates	Advantages	Disadvantages
TV	Broadcast. Satellite. Cable.	Time of day. Audience size. Length of spot. Volume and frequency discounts.	Reaches large audience. Low cost per exposure. Highly visible. High prestige. Geographic selectivity. Socioeconomic selectivity.	High monetary costs. Highly perishable message. Size of audience not guaranteed. Amount of prime time limited.
Radio	AM. FM.	Time of day. Audience size. Length of spot. Volume and frequency discounts.	Low-cost broadcast medium. Messages can be quickly changed. Geographic selectivity. Socioeconomic selectivity.	Provides only audio messages. Short message life. Listeners' attention limited because of other activities while listening.
Internet	Web page. E-mail address.		Message can be changed quickly. Interactive. Visual presentation.	Difficult to get browsers to website.
Newspaper	National. Local. Morning. Evening. Sunday supplement. Weekly. Special.	Volume and frequency. Number of colours. Position in paper. Circulation level.	Almost everyone reads a newspaper. Selective for socio-economic groups. Geographic flexibility. Short lead time. Frequent publication. Merchandising service.	Short life. Limited reproduction capabilities. Large advertising volume limits exposure to any one advertisement.
Magazine	Consumer. Farm. Business. etc.	Circulation level. Cost of publishing. Type of audience. Volume and frequency. Size and position. Number of colours. Regional issues.	Socioeconomic selectivity. Good reproduction. Long life. Prestige. Read in leisurely manner.	High absolute monetary cost. Long lead time.
Direct mail	Letters. Catalogues. Price lists. Calendars. Brochures. Coupons. Circulars. Newsletters. Postcards. Booklets. Samples.	Cost of mailing lists. Postage. Production costs.	Highly selective. Little wasted circulation. Circulation controlled by advertiser. Personal. Stimulates action. Relatively easy to measure performance. Hidden from competitors.	Expensive. No editorial matter to attract readers. Considered junk mail by many. Criticised as invasion of privacy.
Outdoor	Posters. Painted displays. Spectaculars. Poster vans.	Location. Length of time. Land rental costs. Cost of production. Intensity of traffic.	Allows for repetition. Low cost. Message can be placed close to point of sale. Geographic selectivity. 24 hours a day.	Message must be short and simple. No socio-economic selectivity. Seldom attracts readers' full attention. Criticised for being traffic hazard and blight on countryside.

| Inside public transport | Buses. Underground. | Number of passengers. Size and position. | Low cost. Captive audience. Geographic selectivity. | Does not secure quick results. |
| Outside public transport | Buses. Taxi. | Number of advertisements. Size and position. | Low cost. Geographic selectivity. Reaches broad, diverse audience. | Lacks socioeconomic selectivity. Does not have high impact on readers. |

Source: J. O'Connor and E. Galvin, *Marketing and Information Technology* (London: Pitman Publishing, 1997), pp. 213–215.

delay the mailing until a more fortuitous day appears. Many developing countries and emerging markets are ignored for direct mail but have a lot of potential. Mexicans, for example, still receive very little direct mail and are not as jaded as consumers in the United States or Europe, who refer to direct mail as junk mail. Mexicans love bargains and are brand conscious and brand loyal. An added benefit to marketers is that postage and fulfilment costs are low. In a recent direct mail campaign, an automobile financing company, Gruppo Financiero Serfin, distributed 8,000 mail offers, had a 10 per cent response rate and converted 33 per cent of respondents.[19]

Direct-response advertising is more general than direct mail and involves media like television, radio, newspapers or magazines. The customer is usually asked to respond directly (via telephone). The increasing use of telephone for direct-response in TV commercials and print advertisements made it necessary to install call centres which handle the telephone calls. From an international marketer's point of view, it is interesting to note that such call centres can be placed outside a domestic market, as long as the operators can speak the language of the callers. In this way, it is possible to take advantage of lower labour costs.

Database marketing uses extensive lists of prospects and relevant demographic and psychographic information to narrow target markets to serious prospects and then to customise an offer to the prospect's interests. In the automobile market Porsche is known for its extensive database management initiatives among both prospective and current customers. The following two examples illustrate how databases with detailed information on customers can be developed. In Japan a bicycle manufacturer offered a fitting for a custom-made bicycle tailored to a customer's exact measurements. Having customers' measurements, as well as name and address provided by retailers, offered a major advantage for the company. A similar method has been used by Levi's. In addition to creating a positive perception among the jeans customers, Levi's obtained a number of personal data such as address, name and measurements.[20]

The application of IT is very visible within database marketing. Recently data warehousing has received a lot of attention. Data warehouses attempt to include all available information on customers from different sources. The data warehouse is the basis for e-business and customer relationship management.

Relationship marketing, often also viewed as ultimate database marketing, creates a series of one-to-one, long-term, profitable relationships with consumers. 'The longer a customer can be retained, the more profitable the customer becomes.'[21]

IT has also influenced television advertising. The main trends are more targeted messages, advertising-on-demand and pay-per-view. The more messages are targeted the more they reach specific audiences. Like special interest magazines which address a certain target group (e.g. golfers), developments in signal compression enable commercials in cable TV to reach specific consumer segments. Advertising-on-demand allows the audience to select advertisements individually (but also to suppress them automatically before they appear). For instance, before buying a car, one would like to watch all available commercials of cars. Finally, a trend is that TV viewers will be able to select any TV programme from a digital library. This includes also the selection of commercials and can be compared to reading a magazine.

Technology also makes it possible to target advertising messages in magazines and newspapers more selectively. Less cost-intensive and easier printing techniques, for example, enable the production of different editions, each addressing certain target audiences. One service offered by print media is to fax summaries or topics to consumers. The so-called 'electronic newspaper' allows consumers to create their own personal newspaper by selecting articles, information, etc. on a computer. Many articles from contemporary newspapers and magazines are already available on the Internet.

The Internet is a global vehicle, and predictions are that it will forever change marketing. The Internet offers new products and services simultaneously to consumers around the world, thus influencing the ways many goods are purchased, promoted and developed. Sequential new-product introduction by geographic area is not an option when marketing via the Internet. It has been argued that any company that establishes a site on the Internet automatically becomes a multinational company.[22] The Internet allows small companies to compete more easily and allows direct access to consumers in emerging markets. If you want to know where Ford automobiles may be purchased around the world, access their website (www.ford.com). If you want to learn more about the latest innovations from Nokia, the Finnish-based global manufacturer of cellular phones, access their website (www.nokia.com). If you find yourself in Japan and need some L.L. Bean shirts, order them through the L.L. Bean electronic catalogue rather than deal with the high-priced goods available in Japanese department stores. The product is shipped directly by the manufacturer through an international delivery service. This will greatly reduce the importance of intermediaries.

The Internet defies a narrow marketing classification. It is a product that provides varied electronic services such as home banking, but can also be used as a market research vehicle, an advertising vehicle, a public relations vehicle and a sales vehicle. Market researchers and students can search databases and find information about competition on their Web pages. Surveys, given the right target demographics, can be conducted via computer. Advertising and consumer promotions regularly appear on screen. Public relations, in the form of Web pages, can readily be presented. In some product categories, the computer can even replace retail outlets and sales personnel if so desired by a company.

With increasing use of the Internet, standardisation of prices around the world will become more of a reality for both consumer goods and particularly industrial goods that are available on the Internet. Pricing strategies for markets around the world vary according to the level of economic development within a country, the income distribution of the population, and a host of other factors. If the price of a Compaq laptop, a product that is standardised around the world, is less expensive if purchased in Indonesia, why should consumers purchase it in their home country? Pricing will become more transparent, because customers can easily shop the world for the best price for a specific product.

One of the key benefits of the Internet is the 'opportunity to access information and support faster, more cheaply, and more directly than existing communication systems like telephone, fax, mail and direct mail.'[23] The Internet has greatly reduced the cost of reaching consumers around the world. It provides two-way communication directly with consumers, no matter what country they reside in. This is especially helpful in international new-product development, in developing brand names and in launching products in new geographic markets.

There is also a variety of competitive information available on the Internet. Web pages may contain information on new products, pricing and sometimes even customer and client lists at no cost.

An accurate estimate of the number of people owning or having access to personal computers (PCs) and using the Internet is difficult to determine due to the explosive growth in the number of computers available at work and at home. By mid 1998, over 100 million people world-wide were using the Internet. The number of hosts is the highest in the United States, followed by the United Kingdom, Germany, Canada and Australia. In terms of hosts per 1,000 people, Finland ranks the highest, followed by the United States, Australia and New Zealand. In 1999, the Internet penetration in the United States was, for example, 33 per cent; in the United Kingdom the rate lay at about 20 per cent while in Germany and Italy, the Internet penetration was lower than 10 per cent (Germany 8.4 per cent; Italy 6.1 per cent).[24] Many companies are already into their second and third generation of websites, whereas other companies are just going online.

The increased use of the Internet has spawned new marketing terminology. For example, Evan I. Schwartz uses the term 'webonomics', which he defines as 'the study of production distribution and consumption of goods, services, and ideas over the World Wide Web.'[25]

Key points	• Marketing communications serve to tell consumers about the benefits and values a product or service offers.
	• Advertising is one element of marketing communications and refers to any sponsored or paid message. Global advertising uses the same advertising appeals, messages, art, copy, etc. in multiple-country markets.
	• The decision of whether to use a global or localised campaign depends on the recognition by managers of the trade-offs involved, the product involved and a company's objectives in a market.
	• Information technology (IT) enables global marketers to reach audiences that can no longer be reached by mass media.

SELECTING AN ADVERTISING AGENCY

Another global advertising issue companies face is whether to create ads in house, use an outside agency, or combine both strategies. For example, Chanel, Benetton and Diesel rely on in-house marketing and advertising staff. Coca-Cola has its own agency, Edge Creative, but also uses the services of outside agencies such as Leo Burnett. When one or more outside agencies is used, they can serve product accounts on a multicountry or even global basis. It is possible to select a local agency in each national market or an agency with both domestic and overseas offices. Today, however, there is a growing tendency for most companies to designate global agencies for product accounts in order to support the integration of the marketing and advertising functions. For example, in 1995, Colgate-Palmolive consolidated its €424.16 million in global billings with Young & Rubicam. Similarly, Bayer AG consolidated most of its €254.5 million consumer products advertising with BBDO Worldwide. Bayer had previously relied on 50 agencies around the globe. Agencies are aware of this trend and are themselves pursuing international acquisitions and joint ventures to extend their geographic reach and their ability to serve clients on a global account basis. The 25 largest global advertising organisations, ranked by 1998 gross income, are shown in Table 14.3.

The organisations identified in Table 14.3 may include one or more core advertising agencies as well as units specialising in direct marketing, public relations or research. The family tree of Adidas AG's advertising agency reflects the structure that is typical of agency ownership today. Leagas is owned by Abbott Mead Vickers/BBDO, which in turn is a unit of BBDO Worldwide, whose parent is the Omnicom Group.

In selecting an advertising agency, the following issues should be considered:

● *Company organisation.* Companies that are decentralised may want to leave the choice to the local subsidiary.
● *National responsiveness.* Is the global agency familiar with local culture and buying habits in a particular country, or should a local selection be made?

Table 14.3 World's top 25 advertising organisations 1998 (€millions)

Rank 1998	1997	Advertising organisation	Headquarters	World gross income
1	1	Omnicom Group	New York	4,082.02
2	2	Interpublic Group of Cos.	New York	3,651.51
3	3	WPP Group	London	3,526.21
4	4	Dentsu	Tokyo	1,515.06
5	5	Young & Rubicam	New York	1,408.09
6	7	Havas Advertising	Paris	1,101.01
7	6	True North Communications	Chicago	1,053.84
8	8	Grey Advertising	New York	1,052.23
9	9	Leo Burnett Co.	Chicago	805.72
10	12	Publicis	New York	788.92
11	13	Snyder Communications	Bethesda, Md.	767.03
12	11	MacManus Group	New York	728.86
13	10	Hakuhodo	Tokyo	623.33
14	14	Saatchi & Saatchi	New York	578.63
15	15	Cordiant Communications Group	London	511.69
16	17	TMP Worldwide	New York	294.70
17	16	Asatsu-DK	Tokyo	291.31
18	18	Carlson Marketing Group	Plymouth, Minn.	277.22
19	26	USWeb/CKS	Santa Clara	193.92
20	21	MA-LQ	Miles, Ill.	190.02
21	20	Daiko Advertising	Tokyo	143.11
22	19	Tokyo Agency	Tokyo	141.75
23	22	Dentsu, Young & Rubicam Partnerships	Singapore	123.43
24	28	Cyck-Simon	Gloucester, Mass.	116.98
25	27	Nelson Communications	New York	136.41

Source: 'World's top 50 advertising organizations', *Advertising Age*, 19 April 1999, p. s18.

Adidas

American athletic shoe companies are skilled global marketers. Reebok is the market leader in France, Spain and England and Nike is number one in many other European countries. Although advertising tag lines such as 'Just Do It' and 'Planet Reebok' are presented in English, other parts of the message are adapted to reflect cultural differences. In France, for example, violence in ads is unacceptable, so Reebok replaced boxing scenes with images of women running on a beach. Also, European participation in sports is lower than in America. Accordingly, Europeans are less likely to visit sporting goods stores. In France, Reebok shoes are now sold in nearly 1,000 traditional shoe stores.

Even in the face of such tough and growing competition, Adidas still enjoys high brand loyalty among older Europeans. The company recruits young people and pays them to wear Adidas shoes in public. They are also paid to work at sporting goods stores and promote Adidas products in other ways. Adidas also updated its image among younger European consumers by creating a new sport called Streetball. Ads airing on MTV Europe feature players outfitted in the company's new Streetball apparel line. Unlike its American rivals, Adidas does not utilise a global ad campaign.

The company does, however, maintain a single advertising agency, London-based Leagas Delany, for all its global markets. Bruce Haines, the agency's chief executive, notes, 'Adidas is structured by geographic territories and sports-based business units. We're anxious to make sure there's one hand writing one signature whatever the work, whatever the sport.' In a move that indicated optimism about Adidas's future, in 1995 Dreyfus's group raised its stake to full ownership. Meanwhile, Adidas was hard at work on a revolutionary new bare-footwear product. As Dreyfus said in an interview on CNN, 'The idea is there is nothing better than the foot as an instrument for running. The only problem is abrasion. So they are very revolutionary shoes and it will have a huge campaign behind it.'

The Adidas campaign in 1999, a global effort created by Amsterdam ad agency 180 Amsterdam, presented sport as something all people, from professional athletes to kids and everyone in between, can experience and enjoy. Adidas settled on the strategy reviving interest in the concepts of teamwork, fair play and excellence without attitude. The campaign subtly rebukes Nike's personal glory ethic while celebrating skilled, smart play.

In 1998 Adidas-Salomon achieved high growth rates despite a flat market. However, financial expenses relating to the acquisition of Salomon Worldwide in the same year (formerly the headquarters and holding organisation of the three brands Salomon, Taylor Made and Mavic) could not be offset by corresponding contributions to the result by the newly acquired brands. President Robert Louis-Dreyfus expected to be able to increase earnings in 1999.

Food for thought

- Why is it necessary to adapt advertising messages to different country markets for such universally used and accepted products as athletic shoes?
- Should Nike use its brand franchise for other products? Could you imagine Nike jeans, watches or soft drinks? What are the dangers and limitations of brand extensions?

Source: Dagmar Mussey, 'Adidas strides on its own path', *Advertising Age*, 13 February 1995, p. 6; Kevin Goldman, 'Adidas tries to fill its rivals' big shoes', *The Wall Street Journal*, 17 March 1994, p. B5; Joseph Pereira, 'Off and running: pushing US style, Nike and Reebok sell sneakers to Europe', *The Wall Street Journal*, 22 July 1993, pp. A1, A8; Stephen Barr, 'Adidas on the rebound', *CFO* (September 1991): pp. 48–56; Igor Reichlin, 'Where Nike and Reebok have plenty of running room', *Business Week*, 11 March 1991: pp. 56–60; Patrick Allossery, 'Adidas, the brand without attitude: A focus on sportsmanship takes on Nike's success-at-any-cost philosophy', *Financial Post*, 12 April 1999.

- *Area coverage*. Does the agency cover all relevant markets?
- *Buyer perception*. What kind of brand awareness does the company want to achieve? If the product needs a strong local identification, it would be best to select a national agency.

Despite an unmistakable trend toward using global agencies to support global marketing efforts, companies with geocentric orientations will adapt to the global market requirements and select the best agency or agencies accordingly. For example, Colgate acquired the Kolynos line of oral-care products in Latin America in the mid-1990s. McCann-Erickson Worldwide will be responsible for that account even though Young & Rubicam has the bulk of Colgate's business elsewhere.[26] Western agencies still find markets such as South Korea and Japan very complex. Similarly, Japanese and Korean agencies find it just as difficult to establish local agency presence in Western markets. Not surprisingly, as the Saturn unit of General Motors prepared for its 1997 entry into the Japanese market, it hired the Tokyo-based Dai-Ichi Kikaku as its agency.

ADVERTISING APPEALS AND PRODUCT CHARACTERISTICS

Advertising must communicate appeals that are relevant and effective in the target market environment. Because products are frequently at different stages in their life cycle in various national markets, and because of the basic cultural, social, and economic differences that exist in markets, the most effective appeal for a product may vary from market to market. Yet, global marketers should attempt to identify situations in which (1) potential cost reductions exist because of economies of scale; (2) barriers to standardisation such as cultural differences are not significant; and (3) products satisfy similar functional and emotional needs across different cultures.

Green, Cunningham and Cunningham conducted a cross-cultural study to determine the extent to which consumers of different nationalities use the same criteria to evaluate two common consumer products: soft drinks and toothpaste. Their subjects were college students from the United States, France, India and Brazil. Compared to France and India, the US sample placed more emphasis on the subjective and less on functional product attributes, and the Brazilian sample appeared even more concerned with the subjective attributes than did the US sample. The authors concluded that advertising messages should not use the same appeal for these countries if the advertiser is concerned with communicating the most important attributes of its product in each market.[27]

Effective advertising may also require developing different creative executions or presentations using a product's basic appeal or selling proposition as a point of departure. In other words, there can be differences between what one says and how one says it. If the creative execution in one key market is closely tied to a particular cultural attribute, the execution may have to be adapted to other markets. For example, the selling proposition for many products and services is fun or pleasure, and the creative presentation should show people having fun in a manner that is appropriate for a country or culture. Club Med attempted to use a unified global advertising campaign featuring beautiful photos of holidaymakers in revealing swimsuits. Many Americans, for whom modesty in public is important, saw the ads as risqué and titillating, with appeal only to 'swinging singles'. Europeans are accustomed to partial nudity on public beaches and did not consider the ads to be improper. Although Club

Med keyed its basic selling proposition to the theme 'The antidote to civilisation', the creative execution had to be brought in line with the tastes, perceptions and experiences of the American market.

According to one survey, experienced advertising executives indicated that strong selling propositions can be transferred more than 50 per cent of the time. An example of a selling proposal that transfers well is top quality. The promise of low price or of value for money regularly surmounts national barriers. In the same survey, most executives indicated that they did not believe that creative presentations travelled well. The obstacles are cultural barriers, communications barriers, legislative problems (for example, children cannot be used in France to merchandise products), competitive positions (the advertising strategy for a leading brand or product is normally quite different from that for a minor brand), and execution problems.

Food is the product category most likely to exhibit cultural sensitivity. Thus, marketers of food and food products must be alert to the need to localise their advertising. A good example of this is the recent effort by H.J. Heinz Company to develop the overseas market for ketchup. Heinz's strategy called for adapting both the product and advertising to target country tastes.[28] In Greece, for example, ads show ketchup being poured over pasta, eggs and cuts of meat. In Japan, they suggest using ketchup as an ingredient in Western-style food such as omelettes, sausages and pasta. Barry Tilley, London-based general manager of Heinz's Western Hemisphere trading division, says Heinz uses focus groups to determine what foreign consumers want in the way of taste and image. Americans like a relatively sweet ketchup, but Europeans prefer a spicier, more piquant variety. Significantly, Heinz's foreign marketing efforts are most successful when the company quickly adapts to local cultural preferences. In Sweden, the made-in-America theme is so muted in Heinz's ads that 'Swedes don't realise Heinz is American. They think it is German because of the name,' says Mr Tilley. In contrast to this, American themes still work well in Germany. Kraft and Heinz are trying to outdo each other with ads featuring strong American images. In one Heinz's TV ads, American football players in a restaurant become very angry when the 12 steaks they ordered arrive without ketchup. The ad ends happily, of course, with plenty of Heinz ketchup to go around.[29]

In general, the fewer the number of purchasers of a product, the less important advertising is as an element of the promotion mix. For example, successful marketing of expensive and technically complex industrial products generally requires a highly trained direct salesforce. The more sophisticated and technically complicated an industrial product is, the more necessary this becomes. For such products, there is no point in letting national agencies duplicate each other's efforts. Advertising of industrial products, computers and telecommunications equipment, for example, does play an important role in setting the stage for the work of the salesforce. A good advertising campaign can make it significantly easier for a salesperson to get in the door and, once inside, make the sale.

Key points	
	● **When selecting an advertising agency the company organisation, national responsiveness, area coverage and buyer perception should be considered.**
	● **The most effective appeal for a product may vary within different markets because of cultural, social and economic differences.**
	● **Global advertising may require developing different creative executions or they may be adapted to other markets.**

CREATING ADVERTISING

Art direction

Art direction is concerned with visual presentation, the body language of print and broadcast advertising. Some forms of visual presentation are universally understood. The US cosmetic company Revlon, for example, has used a French producer to develop television commercials in English and Spanish for use in international markets. These commercials, which are filmed in Parisian settings, communicate the universal appeals and specific advantages of Revlon products. By producing its ads in France, Revlon obtains effective television commercials at a much lower price than it would have to pay for similar-length commercials produced in the United States. PepsiCo has used four basic commercials to communicate its advertising themes. The basic setting of young people having fun at a party or on a beach has been adapted to reflect the general physical environment and racial characteristics of North America, South America, Europe, Africa and Asia. The music in these commercials has also been adapted to suit regional tastes, ranging from rock and roll in North America to bossa nova in Latin America to high life in Africa.

The international advertiser must make sure that visual executions are not inappropriately extended into markets. Benetton encountered a problem with its 'United Colors of Benetton' campaign (see Figure 14.2). The campaign appeared in 77 countries, primarily in print and on billboards. The art direction focused on striking, provocative interracial juxtapositions, a white hand and a black hand handcuffed together, for example. Another version of the campaign, depicting a black woman nursing a white baby, won advertising awards in France and Italy. However, because the image evoked the history of slavery in America, that particular creative execution was not used in the US market.

Copy

Translating copy, or the written text of an advertisement, has been the subject of great

Figure 14.2 Benetton's campaigns for racial equality

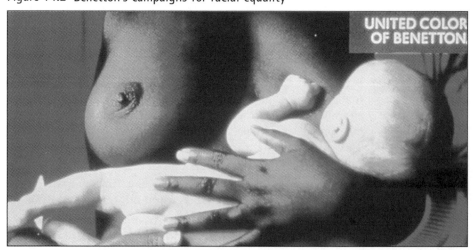

Oliviero Toscani took a photo of a black woman breast feeding a white child. Prizes and censorship arrived simultaneously. The photograph received the International Andy Award of Excellence in the United States.
Source: http://www.benetton.com/wws/aboutyou/ucdo/. Copyright: Benetton Group SpA.

debate in advertising circles. Copy should be relatively short and avoid slang or idioms. Because other languages frequently take more space to convey the same message, pictures and illustrations are used increasingly. More and more European and Japanese advertisements are purely visual, conveying a specific message and invoking the company name.[30] Low literacy rates in many countries seriously compromise the use of print as a communications device and require greater creativity in the use of audio-oriented media.

It is important to recognise overlap in the use of languages in many areas of the world (e.g. the EU, Latin America and North America). Capitalising on this, global advertisers can realise economies of scale in producing advertising copy with the same language and message for these markets. Of course, the success of this approach will depend in part on avoiding unintended ambiguity in the ad copy. On the other hand, in some situations ad copy must be translated into the local language. Advertising slogans often present the most difficult translation problems. The challenge of encoding and decoding slogans and tag lines in different national and cultural contexts can lead to hilarious errors. For example, Kentucky Fried Chicken's 'Finger-lickin' good' came out in Chinese as 'eat your fingers off'; the Asian version of Pepsi's 'Come Alive' copy line was rendered as a call to bring ancestors back from the grave.

Advertising executives may elect to prepare new copy for a foreign market in the language of the target country, or to translate the original copy into the target language. A third option is to leave some (or all) copy elements in the original (home-country) language. In choosing from among these alternatives, the advertiser must consider whether a translated message can be received and comprehended by the intended foreign audience. Anyone with a knowledge of foreign languages realises that the ability to think in that language facilitates accurate communication. One must understand the connotations of words, phrases and sentence structures, as well as their translated meaning, in order to be confident that a message will be understood correctly after it is received. The same principle applies to advertising, perhaps to an even greater degree. A copywriter who can think in the target language and understands the consumers in the target country will be able to create the most effective appeals, organise the ideas and craft the specific language, especially if colloquialisms, idioms or humour are involved. For example, in Southern China, McDonald's is careful not to advertise prices with multiple occurrences of the number four. The reason is simple: In Cantonese, the pronunciation of the word four is similar to that of the word 'death'.[31] In its efforts to develop a global brand image, Citicorp discovered that translations of its slogan 'Citi Never Sleeps' conveyed the meaning that Citibank had a sleeping disorder such as insomnia. Company executives decided to retain the slogan but use English throughout the world.[32]

When formulating television and print advertising for use in industrialised counties such as North America, Japan and the EU, the advertiser must recognise major style and content differences. Ads that strike viewers in some countries as irritating may not necessarily be perceived that way by viewers in other countries. American ads make frequent use of spokespersons and direct product comparisons, and use logical arguments to try to appeal to the reason of audiences. Japanese advertising is more image oriented and appeals to audience sentiment. In Japan, what is most important frequently is not what is stated explicitly but, rather, what is implied. Nike's US advertising is legendary for its irreverent, 'in your face' style and relies heavily on celebrity sports endorsers such as Michael Jordan. In other parts of the world, where soccer is the top sport, some Nike ads are considered to be in poor taste

Table 14.4 Advertising styles

Country	Style
America	Direct approach. Lecture or lesson format. Competitiveness. Data-based arguments. TV: verbal. Overstatement. Hard-selling. Use of power words (new, improved, the best, now, world-wide). Persuasive communication (facts, 'reason-why' arguments). Direct and indirect comparison (also competitive brands).
Great Britain	Shows individuals or couples. Young people teaching their parents. Class differences. Direct communication. Persuasiveness. Direct approach (comparison). Strong role differentiation (trend of reverse sexism). Humour and parody. Lesson format (presenter, testimonial).
Germany	Need for structure. Explicit language. Strong information orientation (direct, factual). Lesson format (presenter, testimonial). Important appeals are quality, technology and design, but also history and tradition. Attention to details. Winning is important. High regard for authority. High degree of freedom is not accepted.
Italy	Appeals are technology, design and quality. Conceptual thinking. Strong characteristic design, big ideas and affection for being theatrical. Respect for elders and educators. Sensuality is as much important as emotions. Strong role differentiation. Advertising execution is important (products as pieces of art).
Spain	Use of visual metaphors (concrete and abstract). Design- and art-orientated appeals. Innovation/stability paradox (desire for modernism but also sticking to tradition). Obedience to and respect for elders. Relations based on friendship and family. Tendency to decline authority. People appear in groups. Importance of dressing (to obtain a place in society). Feminine dimension (role of expert, provides unity in the family). Dignity and pride. Food and eating as expressions of 'good life'. Creativity (not hard work) as tool for success.
France	Need to be different. Theatrical and bizarre elements in advertising. Dramatic. Orientation toward image. Fantasy. Theatre and pleasure. Need to show emotions (drama-like). Addressing or lecturing in form of story. Song or word games. Entertainment through symbolism. Humour and drama. Appeals are beauty. Aesthetics. Image. Style. Extravagance. Elders teach the younger.
Belgium	See also France; direct address. Presenter and testimonial in combination with demonstration. Professional.
Holland	Obtrusive presenter perceived as authoritarian (uniforms, loud speech, experts). Direct presentation style. Presenters are typecast as a parody. Conformity/adventure paradox: leveling attitude but desire for adventure. Use of few power or magic words. Small role differentiation. Use of the word 'free'. Success can only be shown in understatements. Small children shown as independent. Sociability (feeling of care, warmth, being together with friends and loved ones). Entertainment form (use of humour).
Sweden	Feminine culture (men shown doing work in household). Entertainment form. Disrespect for authority. Tendency to get together for meetings (coffee is always served).
Poland	Respect for elders. Strong family values. Strong role differentiation. Demonstration and result orientation. Humour. Need for tradition (use of folklore, historical drama).
China	Indirect approach. Values are modernity, quality, technology, courtesy, respect for the elderly, etc. Use of special effects. Graphics and computer animation. Playing with words, characters and sounds.
Korea	Company more important than the brand. Confrontation is avoided. Strong need for harmony. Affiliation over competitiveness.

Source: Adapted from Marieke K. De Mooij, *Global Marketing and Advertising* (Thousand Oaks: Sage Publications, 1998).

and its pitchmen have less relevance. Nike has responded by adjusting its approach; notes Geoffrey Frost, director of global advertising, 'We have to root ourselves in the passions of other countries. It's part of our growing up.'[33]

Cultural considerations

Knowledge of cultural diversity, especially the symbolism associated with cultural traits, is essential when creating advertising. Local country managers will be able to share important information, such as when to use caution in advertising creativity. Use of colours and man–woman relationships can often be stumbling blocks. For example, white in Asia is associated with death. In Japan, intimate scenes between men and women are considered to be in bad taste; they are outlawed in Saudi Arabia. Veteran adman John O'Toole offers the following insights to global advertisers:

> Transplanted American creative people always want to photograph European men kissing women's hands. But they seldom know that the nose must never touch the hand or that this rite is reserved solely for married women. And how do you know that the woman in the photograph is married? By the ring on her left hand, of course. Well, in Spain, Denmark, Holland and Germany, Catholic women wear the wedding ring on the right hand.
>
> When photographing a couple entering a restaurant or theater, you show the woman preceding the man, correct? No. Not in Germany and France. And this would be laughable in Japan. Having someone in a commercial hold up his hand with the back of it to you, the viewer, and the fingers moving toward him should communicate 'come here'. In Italy it means 'good-bye'.[34]

The cultural environment influences advertising. The key concerns relate to values and motives, the advertising form and the execution of the advertising. Table 14.4 summarises some characteristics of advertising styles in different countries. The advertising styles reflect the cultural values.

Tamotsu Kishii identified seven characteristics that distinguish Japanese from American creative strategy.

1 Indirect rather than direct forms of expression are preferred in the messages. This avoidance of directness in expression is pervasive in all types of communication among the Japanese, including their advertising. Many television ads do not mention what is desirable about the brand in use and let the audience judge for themselves.
2 There is often little relationship between ad content and the advertised product.
3 Only brief dialogue or narration is used in television commercials, with minimal explanatory content. In the Japanese culture, the more one talks, the less others will perceive him or her trustworthy or self-confident. A 30-second advertisement for young menswear shows five models in varying and seasonal attire, ending with a brief statement from the narrator: 'Our life is a fashion show!'
4 Humour is used to create a bond of mutual feelings. Rather than slapstick, humorous dramatisations involve family members, neighbours and office colleagues.
5 Famous celebrities appear as close acquaintances or everyday people.
6 Priority is placed on company trust rather than product quality. Japanese tend to believe that if the firm is large and has a good image, the quality of its products should also be outstanding.
7 The product name is impressed on the viewer with short, 15-second commercials.[35]

Global media considerations

Media decisions

Although markets are becoming increasingly similar in industrial countries, the media environment still varies greatly (see also Table 14.5). This can have an impact on media decisions. For example, circulation figures of newspapers on a per capita basis cover a wide range. In Japan, where readership is high, one newspaper is in circulation for every two people. There are approximately 65 million newspapers in daily circulation in the United States, a per capita ratio of approximately one to four. In Latin America the ratio is one paper to 10 to 20 people and in Nigeria and Sweden one to 200 people.

Even when media availability is high, its use as an advertising vehicle may be limited. For example, in some European countries, television advertising either does not exist or is very limited, as in Denmark, Sweden and Norway. The time allowed for advertising each day on public networks varies from 12 minutes in Finland to 80 in Italy, with 12 minutes per hour per channel allowed in France and 20 in Switzerland, Germany and Austria. Regulations concerning content of commercials also vary, and there are long waiting periods in several countries before an advertiser can obtain broadcast time.

Table 14.5 Penetration of the information economy – selected countries

Countries	Daily newspapers[36]	Radios[37]	Television		Mobile phones[38]	Personal computers[39]	Internet hosts[40]
			Sets	Cable subscribers			
			per 1,000 people				per 10,000 people
	1996	1996	1997	1997	1997	1997	1998
Argentina	123	677	289	156.3	56	39.2	15.92
Australia	297	1,385	638	38.1	264	362.2	400.17
Austria	296	740	496	132	144	210.7	163.45
Belgium	160	792	510	361.8	95	235.3	150.65
Canada	157	1,078	708	261.4	139	270.6	335.96
China (Hong Kong)	739	695	412	61.5	343	230.8	108.02
Denmark	309	1,146	568	238.6	273	360.2	358.85
Finland	455	1,385	534	170	417	310.7	996.13
France	218	943	606	27.7	99	174.4	73.33
Germany	311	946	570	210.5	99	255.5	140.58
Greece	153	477	466	–	89	44.8	37.98
Ireland	150	703	455	147.4	146	241.3	121.85
Italy	104	874	483	0	204	113	55.69
Mexico	97	324	251	15.2	18	37.3	8.75
Netherlands	177	963	541	371.8	110	280.3	327.85
Norway	588	920	579	160.2	381	360.8	705.28
Portugal	75	306	523	38.5	152	74.4	45.34
Russian Federation	105	344	390	78.4	3	32	8.88
Saudi Arabia	57	319	260	–	17	43.6	0.02
Spain	99	328	506	10.8	110	122.1	61.9
Sweden	446	907	531	218.1	358	350.3	429.86
Switzerland	330	969	536	346	147	394.9	289.32
Turkey	109	178	286	8.1	26	20.7	4.30
United Kingdom	332	1,445	641	40.2	151	242.4	0.01
United States	215	2,115	847	245.9	206	406.7	975.94

Source: http://www.worldbank.org/data/wdi/pdfs/tab5–11.pdf.

In Saudi Arabia, where all advertising is subject to censorship, regulations prohibit a long list of subject matter, including the following:

- Advertisements of horoscope or fortune-telling books, publications, or magazines are prohibited.
- Advertisements that frighten or disturb children are to be avoided.
- Use of preludes to advertisements that appear to indicate a news item or official statement are to be avoided.
- Use of comparative advertising claims is prohibited.
- Noncensored films cannot be advertised.
- Women may appear only in those commercials that relate to family affairs, and their appearance must be in a decent manner that ensures their feminine dignity.
- Female children under six years of age may appear in commercials provided that their roles are limited to a childhood-like activity.
- Women should wear a long, suitable dress that fully covers their body except face and palms. Sweatsuits or similar garments are not allowed.[41]

Media vehicles and expenditures

As with all marketing decisions, advertisers must choose between global or local media vehicles. Global media consist primarily of cable television such as MTV, ITN and CNN, which are rapidly expanding, as well as regional editions of print publications. An exploding new global advertising medium is the World Wide Web. Any company, organisation, or individual can plant a flag on the Net, and establish a global presence!

Local media vehicles vary by country and consist of television, radio, newspapers, transit and outdoor. As might be expected, the largest per capita advertising expenditures occur mostly in the highly developed countries of the world. The lowest per capita expenditures are in the less developed countries. The high-income countries spend roughly 1.5 to 2.5 per cent of their gross national product (GNP) on advertising. In the low-income countries, expenditures range from less than 0.5 per cent to 1 per cent. The United States is by far the largest consumer of advertising in the world.

A key issue in advertising is media selection: print, broadcast, transit and so forth. Print advertising continues to be the number one advertising vehicle in most countries. However, spending on print media in the United States has been declining. The use of newspapers for print advertising is so varied around the world as to almost defy description. In Mexico, an advertiser that can pay for a full-page ad may get the front page, whereas in India, paper shortages may require booking an ad six months in advance.

In some countries, especially those where the electronic media are government owned, television and radio stations can broadcast only a restricted number of advertising messages. In Saudi Arabia, no commercial television advertising was allowed prior to May 1986; currently, ad content and visual presentation are restricted. In such countries, the proportion of advertising funds allocated to print is extremely high. In April 1995, Russia's national Channel 1 banned all commercial advertising; the ban was subsequently lifted.

As ownership of television sets increases in other areas of the world, such as Southeast Asia, television advertising will become more important as a communication vehicle.

Worldwide, radio continues to be a less important advertising medium than print and television. As a proportion of total measured media advertising expenditures, radio trails considerably behind both print, television and direct advertising. However, in countries where advertising budgets are limited, radio's enormous reach can provide a cost-effective means of communicating with a large consumer market. Also, radio can be effective in countries where literacy rates are low.

As countries add mass transportation systems and build and improve their road infrastructures, advertisers are utilising more indoor and outdoor posters and billboards to reach the buying public. Transit advertising was recently introduced in Russia, where drab streetcars and buses have been emblazoned with the bright colours of Western brands.

Key points	
	• The extension of visual executions should be appropriate in international markets.
	• The key concerns in advertising within different cultural environments relate to values and motives, the advertising form and the execution of the advertising.
	• The media penetration and regulation in different countries have an impact on media decisions.

PUBLIC RELATIONS

A company's public relations effort should foster goodwill and understanding among constituents both inside and outside the company. PR practitioners attempt to generate favourable publicity which, by definition, is a nonpaid form of communication. (In the PR world, publicity is sometimes referred to as earned media, whereas advertising and promotions are known as unearned media.) PR personnel also play a key role in responding to unflattering media reports or controversies that arise because of company activities in different parts of the globe. In such instances, PR's job is to make sure that the company responds promptly and gets its side of the story told. The basic tools of PR include news releases, newsletters, press conferences, tours of plants and other company facilities, articles in trade or professional journals, company publications and brochures, TV and radio talk show appearances by company personnel, special events and home pages on the Internet. As noted earlier, a company exerts complete control over the content of its advertising and pays for message placement in the media. However, the media typically receive far more press releases and other PR materials than they can use. Generally speaking, a company has little control over when, or if, a news story runs. The company cannot directly control the 'spin', slant or tone of the story. In addition to the examples discussed below, Table 14.6 summarises several instances of global publicity involving well-known firms.

Indeed, even in the field of PR itself, there are often great differences between theory and practice. One specific area of discourse is the notion of PR as a 'two-way symmetrical model' of communication that should occur between equal entities. This model holds that public relations efforts should be oriented toward social responsibility and problem solving, and be characterised by dialogue and harmonisation of interests. As such, the symmetrical model takes PR beyond an advocacy role that benefits the organisation. A similar model developed in Austria known as 'consensus-oriented public relations' supports the view that two-way symmetrical communication is more desirable and successful than asymmetrical PR. The two-way and

Table 14.6 Examples of global publicity

Company/brand (Home country)	Nature of publicity
Bruno Magli (Italy)	Markets shoes allegedly worn by O.J. Simpson on the night Nicole Simpson was murdered; widespread attention in newsreels and print media estimated to be worth €84.83 million. Shoe sales increased 50 per cent during the trial.
Nike (United States)	Victims of Heaven's Gate suicide cult wore Nikes when they died.
Mitsubishi (Japan)	Charges of sexual harassment at a plant in Illinois received widespread media coverage.
McDonald's (United States)	Plaintiff in the longest civil trial in British history. McDonald's charged two vegetarian activists with libel after the two distributed pamphlets calling McDonald's a 'multinational menace' that abused animals and workers. The defendants gained world-wide publicity for their cause.

consensus models are presumed to be especially effective in situations with a potential for conflict between differing parties. The issues pertaining to planning a hazardous waste landfill would be one example. However, as one expert has noted, implementation of these models remains problematic.[42]

PepsiCo made good use of integrated marketing communications when it undertook an ambitious global programme to revamp the packaging of its flagship cola. To raise awareness of its new blue can, Pepsi leased a Concorde jet and painted it in the new blue colour. Pepsi also garnered some 'free ink' by spending €4.24 million to film an ad with two Russian cosmonauts holding a giant replica of the new can while orbiting the earth in the Mir space station. As Massimo d'Amore, PepsiCo's head of international marketing, told reporters, 'Space is the ultimate frontier of global marketing. The cola wars have been fought all over the place, and it's time to take them to space.' It remains to be seen whether this effort will pay off in terms of increased brand loyalty.

IBM spent about €4.24 million to stage a rematch of a 1996 chess game between Gary Kasparov and a computer called Deep Blue. The match, which took place in New York City, was hailed as one of the best publicity stunts in recent years. To build visibility and interest, IBM purchased full-page newspaper ads, sent out numerous press releases, established an Internet site and purchased bus posters in Manhattan. The effort was a textbook study in integrated marketing communications; the match was widely covered by the world media. As Peter Harleman of Landor Associates, a corporate-identity firm, told *The Wall Street Journal*, 'Money almost can't buy the advertising [IBM] is getting out of this.' John Lister, of the Lister Butler brand identity consulting firm, agreed. 'They're doing a tremendous job of leveraging the brand in this. Not only do they have the IBM name attached to virtually every news report about, but they even branded their computer the corporate colour, blue.' Industry experts estimate that the match generated about €84.83 million in favourable earned media. IBM's Internet site provided live coverage and generated a million visits during a single match, a number which is believed to be a record for the World Wide Web.

EUROPEAN FOCUS

Elk-test (A-Class, Mercedes Benz)

'The elk (moose) suddenly stood in the middle of the street', reported a test driver of Mercedes-Benz just after an evasive manoeuvre in 1959. Thanks to the quick response of the driver and to the technique of the car nothing happened to the animal. But the incident gave the test its name: the elk-test (or moose test) was born. Many years later, in 1997, the existence of the moose was endangered, namely when Mercedes-Benz introduced the A-class. It was Robert Collin, writing for a Swedish automobile magazine, who discovered the weaknesses of the A-class. In an elk-test the Mercedes tipped over. From then onwards the A-class, a symbol for the strategic venture of Mercedes-Benz into a new product segment, was the focus of immense publicity. In the media, the event became the topic of the day. The first reaction of the company was rather weak. In a press conference, the responsible only promised to apply the Electronic Stability Program EPS as standard and to use new tyres. Experts predicted a loss of image for the brand and that it would be years until the brand recovered. In November 1997, Daimler-Benz announced that the delivery was halted for twelve weeks, because the undercarriage had to be redesigned completely. Daimler-Benz invested €1.27 billion in the A-class and the CEO,

Jürgen Schrempp, still expected to reach the sales goal of 200,000 vehicles per annum. After sales were suspended for three months, in February the retailers were supplied with the improved A-class. In a campaign the company advertised with mooses: for example soft toys were placed in Mercedes-Benz salesroom and advertisements showing elks and cars together were launched. To show the public the efforts that had been made to improve the security standard, the Daimler-Benz Group invited automobile magazine journalists for test drives. The Swedish journalist who caused the security concern and Niki Lauda, a famous Austrian Formula One driver, tested the car and confirmed the security system.

Food for thought

- Did Mercedes handle the 'elk-test' crises appropriately? Did the adverts including elks draw unnecessary attention to the initial technical problem?
- Select a recent corporate crisis and describe how the company responded to the crisis in its advertisements and/or PR.

Source: 'Mercedes: Rekord trotz Elchtest-Affäre', Der Standard, 14 January 1999, p. 26; 'Öffentlichkeitsarbeit: Nach dem 'Elch'-Test kommt der 'PR'-Test für Mercedes-Benz', http://www.Horizont.net, 5 November 1997; 'Mercedes kapituliert vor dem Elchtest', Der Standard, 12 November 1997, p. 19; http://www.mercedes-benz.com/d/cars/a-class/facts1.htm.

The publicity was especially gratifying to IBM officials because its problems with its much-ballyhooed information system at the 1996 Olympics resulted in a great deal of negative news coverage.[43]

Sometimes, publicity is generated when a company simply goes about the business of global marketing activities. Nike and other marketers have received a great deal of negative publicity regarding alleged sweatshop conditions in factories run by subcontractors. To date, Nike's public relations team has not done an effective job of counteracting the criticism by effectively communicating the positive economic impact Nike has had on the nations where its sneakers are manufactured. Volkswagen received a great deal of negative press coverage over a period of several months after its newly hired operations chief was accused of industrial espionage.

Once again McDonald's became a 'global target' of accusations by the People for the Ethical Treatment of Animals (Peta), a US organisation that wants the company to impose higher standards of animal welfare on its suppliers. For this purpose Peta advertises with the slogan 'Do you want your fries with *that*? McDonald's. Cruelty to go', by supporting it with terrible images like a flayed cow's head, dripping blood. Although most media owners rejected the advertisements, the protest group organised a world-wide action against McDonald's. As the official Internet site explains, McDonald's is only 'a symbol of all multinationals and big business relentlessly pursuing their profits at the expense of anything that stands in their way.' [44]

The ultimate test of an organisation's understanding of the power and importance of public relations occurs during a time of environmental turbulence, especially a potential or actual crisis. When disaster strikes, a company or industry often finds itself thrust into the spotlight. A company's swift and effective handling of communications during such times can have significant implications. The best response is to be forthright and direct, reassuring the public and providing the media with accurate information.

Any corporation that is conducting business outside its home country can utilise PR as boundary spanners between the company and employees, unions, shareholders, customers, the media, financial analysts, governments and suppliers. Although many companies have their own in-house PR staff, others may choose to engage the services of outside PR agencies. Some PR firms are associated with advertising organisations. Burston-Marsteller, for example, is a PR unit of Young & Rubicam, while Fleishman-Hillard is affiliated with D'Arcy Masius Benton & Bowles. Other PR firms, including the London-based Shandwick PLC and Edelman Public Relations Worldwide and Canada's Hill & Knowlton, are independent. Several independent PR firms in the United Kingdom, Germany, Italy, Spain, Austria and the Netherlands have joined together in a network known as Globalink. The purpose of the network is to provide members with various forms of assistance, such as press contacts, event planning, literature design and suggestions for tailoring global campaigns to local needs in a particular country or region. [45]

Sponsoring

Through sponsoring the target group is familiarised with a product, brand or company name. Sponsors aim to establish and consolidate the impression customers have of the enterprise and of brands. It is intended to transfer a distinct image and to build awareness. [46]

Typical events sponsored are sport events (75 per cent of sponsoring budget) and cultural events. Sport events like the Olympic Games become more and more attractive to marketers. In 1996, *The Times* magazine stated that 'The Olympic Games are universally acknowledged as the global media and marketing extravaganza. For top marketers, they offer brand values and unbeatable images'. [47] Rupert Murdoch's bid for the broadcast right of the Games Sydney 2000 (expected to be watched by 3.6 billion people) is about four times the sum paid by the European Broadcasting Union to screen the Olympic Games in 1996. Twenty years ago, the International Olympic Committee had great difficulties obtaining sponsor monies. Today, the Olympics stand for universally admired values such as excellence, success, international co-operation and peace.

A marketer aiming to transfer meanings from a sponsored event to its company or product must take care when selecting the most appropriate sponsoring events. It is particularly important to find similarities between the event and the company or product. The ice-cream brand Häagen-Dazs was launched by Grand Met in Europe at a price 30 per cent to 40 per cent higher than its closest competitors. Besides the unusual strategy (little advertising effort but opening of several posh ice-cream parlours in prominent locations) Häagen-Dazs was linked to arts sponsorship. At the Opera Factory's production of Don Giovanni in London, the high-priced ice-cream was even incorporated in the performance: 'When the Don called for sorbet, he received a container of Häagen-Dazs.' Within a few months, brand awareness reached more than 50 per cent in the United Kingdom.[48]

The growing role of public relations in global marketing communications

Public relations professionals with international responsibility must go beyond media relations and serve as more than a company mouthpiece; they are called on to simultaneously build consensus and understanding, create trust and harmony, articulate and influence public opinion, anticipate conflicts, and resolve disputes.[49] As companies become more involved in global marketing and the globalisation of industries continues, it is important that company managements recognise the value of international public relations. One recent study found that, internationally, PR expenditures are growing an average of 20 per cent annually. Fuelled by soaring foreign investment, industry privatisation and a boom in initial public offerings (IPOs), PR expenditures in India are reported to be growing by 200 per cent annually.

The number of international PR associations is growing as well. The new Austrian Public Relations Association is a case in point. Many European PR trade associations are part of the Confédération Européenne des Relations Publiques and the International Public Relations Association. Another factor fuelling the growth of international PR is increased governmental relations between countries. Governments, organisations and societies are dealing with broad-based issues of mutual concern such as the environment and world peace. Finally, the technology-driven communication revolution that has ushered in the information age makes public relations a profession with truly global reach. Faxes, satellites, high-speed modems and the Internet allow PR professionals to be in contact with media virtually anywhere in the world.

In spite of these technological advances, PR professionals must still build good personal working relationships with journalists and other media representatives as well as leaders of other primary constituencies. Therefore, strong interpersonal skills are needed. One of the most basic concepts of the practice of public relations is to know the audience. For the global PR practitioner, this means knowing the audiences in both the home country and the host country or countries. Specific skills needed include the ability to communicate in the language of the host country and familiarity with local customs. Obviously, a PR professional who is unable to speak the language of the host country will be unable to communicate directly with a large portion of an essential audience. Likewise, the PR professional working outside the home country must be sensitive to nonverbal communication issues in order to maintain good working relationships with host-country nationals. Commenting on the complexity of the international PR professional's job, one expert notes that, in general, audiences are 'increasingly more unfamiliar and more hostile, as well as more organised and powerful … more demanding, more sceptical and more diverse'. International PR practitioners can play an important role as 'bridges over the shrinking chasm of the global village'.[50]

How public relations practices differ around the world

Public relations practices in specific countries can be affected by cultural traditions, social and political contexts, and economic environments. As noted earlier, the mass media and the written word are important vehicles for information dissemination in many industrialised countries. In developing countries, however, the best way to communicate might be through the gongman, the town crier, the market square, or the chief's courts. In Ghana, dance, songs and storytelling are important communication channels. In India, where half of the population cannot read, writing press releases will not be the most effective way to communicate.[51]

Even in industrialised countries, there are some important differences between PR practices. In the United States, much of the news in a small, local newspaper is placed by means of the hometown news release. In Canada, on the other hand, large metropolitan population centers have combined with Canadian economic and climatic conditions to thwart the emergence of a local press. The dearth of small newspapers means that the practice of sending out hometown news releases is almost nonexistent.[52] In the United States, PR is increasingly viewed as a separate management function. In Europe, that perspective has not been widely accepted. PR professionals are viewed as part of the marketing function rather than distinct and separate specialists in a company. In Europe, fewer colleges and universities offer courses and degree programmes in public relations than in the United States. Also, European coursework in PR is more theoretical. In the United States, PR programmes are often part of mass communication or journalism schools and there is more emphasis on practical job skills.

A company that is ethnocentric in its approach to PR will extend home-country PR activities into host countries. The rationale behind this approach is that people everywhere are motivated and persuaded in much the same manner. Obviously, this approach does not take cultural considerations into account. A company adopting a polycentric approach to PR gives the host-country practitioner more leeway to incorporate local customs and practices into the PR effort. Although such an approach has the advantage of local responsiveness, the lack of global communication and coordination can lead to a PR disaster.[53]

In the autumn of 1994, computer chip maker Intel showed a poor understanding of public relations after a college professor discovered a technical defect in the company's flagship Pentium chip. The professor, Thomas Nicely, contacted Intel and asked for a replacement chip, but his request was refused. Intel acknowledged that Pentium had a flaw but insisted it would cause a computing error only once in 27,000 years. Having received no satisfaction from the semiconductor giant (Intel commands an 80 per cent share of the global semiconductor market), Nicely posted his complaint on the Internet. Word about the Pentium flaw and Intel's response spread quickly. Intel chief executive officer (CEO) Andrew Grove added fuel to the fire when he issued an apology via the Internet. Grove said, 'No chip is ever perfect,' and offered to replace defective chips if customers could prove they used computers to perform complicated mathematical calculations. Grove's lack of humility, coupled with revelations that the chipmaker itself had been aware of the Pentium flaw for months, only worsened the public's perception of the company. After weeks of negative publicity around the world, Intel finally announced that new Pentium chips would be available to anyone who requested them. The furore eventually died down without permanent damage to Intel's reputation.

Key points	
	• The main aim of PR is to generate favourable publicity which is a nonpaid form of communication.
	• In the field of PR itself there are two models of communication: a 'two-way symmetrical model' and a 'consensus-orientated model'.
	• Sponsoring leads to a distinct image and brand awareness.

SALES PROMOTION

Sales promotion refers to any consumer or trade programme of limited duration that adds tangible value to a product or brand. The tangible value created by the promotion may come in various forms, such as a price reduction or a 'buy one, get one free' offer. Mail-in refunds, samples and coupons are also commonly used. The purpose of a sales promotion may be to stimulate customers to sample a product or to increase consumer demand. Trade promotions are designed to increase product availability in distribution channels. Table 14.7 lists commonly used sales promotion tools and their objectives.

Many international managers have learned about promotion strategies and tactics by attending seminars such as those offered by the Promotional Marketing Association of America (PMAA). Sometimes, adaptation to country-specific conditions is required. According to Joseph Potacki, who teaches a Basics of Promotion seminar for the PMAA, the biggest difference between promotion in the United States and in other countries pertains to couponing. In the United States, couponing accounts for 70 per cent of consumer promotion spending. That percentage is much lower outside the United States. According to Potacki, 'It is far less – or nonexistent – in most other countries simply because the cultures don't accept couponing.'[54] Sales promotion in Europe is highly regulated, as shown in Table 14.8.

Table 14.7 **Sales promotion tools**

Tools	Objectives							
	Stimulate (trial) purchase	Encourage repeat purchase	Build distribution	Increase orders	Increase attractiveness/ perception of value packs	Attract attention	Provide information	Improve sales capabilities
Coupons	✓	✓						
Price-offs		✓						
Samples	✓		✓	✓				
In, on and near packs					✓			
Self-liquidating premiums	✓	✓						
Continuity premiums		✓						
Bonus packs		✓						
Contests and sweepstakes	✓			✓				
Displays						✓	✓	
Training							✓	✓
Events						✓	✓	
Trade show and exhibition	✓		✓			✓	✓	
Product demonstrations	✓		✓			✓	✓	

Source: Adapted from H. Muehlbacher, L. Dahringer and H. Leihs, *International Marketing. A Global Perspective* (London: Business Press, 1999), p. 769.

Table 14.8 Regulation of sales promotion in Europe

	UK	Ireland	Spain	Portugal	Greece	France	Italy	Netherlands	Denmark	Belgium	Germany	Luxembourg
In-pack premiums	P	P	P	P	P	M	P	M	M	M	M	N
Multiple-purchase offers	P	P	P	P	P	P	P	P	M	M	M	N
Extra product	P	P	P	P	P	P	P	M	P	M	M	P
Free product	P	P	P	P	P	P	P	P	P	M	P	P
Free mail-ins	P	P	P	P	P	P	P	P	M	M	N	M
With-purchase premiums	P	P	P	P	P	P	P	M	M	M	M	N
Cross-product offers	P	P	P	P	P	P	P	M	M	N	N	N
Collector devices	P	P	P	P	P	M	P	M	M	M	N	N
Competitions	P	P	P	P	P	M	P	M	M	P	M	M
Free drawings	P	P	P	P	P	P	P	N	N	N	N	N
Share-outs	P	P	P	P	P	M	M	N	N	N	N	N
Sweepstakes/lottery	M	M	M	M	M	M	M	M	N	M	M	N
Money-off vouchers	P	P	P	P	P	P	M	P	M	P	N	M
Money-off next purchases	P	P	P	P	P	P	M	P	N	P	N	N
Cash backs	P	P	P	P	P	P	N	P	P	P	M	N

P = Permitted, M = May be permitted, N = Not permitted.
Source: 'Europe's promotion maze', *Advertising Age*, 30 April 1990, p. 11.

Sales promotions are popular in Scandinavia because broadcast advertising is highly regulated. On the other hand, promotions in the Nordic countries are themselves subject to regulations. If such regulations are relaxed as the single market develops in Europe and regulations are harmonised, companies may be able to roll out pan-European promotions.

Companies must take extreme care when designing a sales promotion. A 1992 promotion sponsored by Maytag Corporation's Hoover European Appliance Group was a smashing success that turned into a financial and public relations fiasco. Over a period of several months, Hoover offered free round-trip airline tickets to the United States and Europe to purchasers of vacuum cleaners or other Hoover appliances. The promotion was designed to take advantage of low-cost, 'space available' tickets. Executives hoped that the cost of the tickets would be offset by commissions paid to Hoover when customers rented cars or booked hotel rooms. Finally, it was expected that a percentage of customers who bought appliances would fail to meet certain eligibility requirements and thus be denied free tickets.

In the United Kingdom, the word Hoover is both a brand name and a verb (as in, 'hoover the carpet'). The number of people who actually qualified for the free tickets, more than 200,000 in all, far exceeded company forecasts, while the number of car rentals and hotel bookings was lower than expected. Hoover was swamped by the volume of inquiries. Many customers were angered by long delays in responses to their requests for the tickets. The bottom line was that Hoover had failed to budget enough for the promotion, forcing Maytag CEO Leonard Hadley to take pretax charges of €64.98 million. In an effort to honour its commitment to Hoover customers, Maytag bought several thousand seats on various airlines. 'The Hoover name in the United Kingdom is valuable, and this investment in our customer base there is essential to our future,' Hadley said.

Hadley fired the president and director of marketing services at Hoover Europe and the vice president of marketing at Hoover UK. Fallout from the promotion became an ongoing PR nightmare, as headlines in the *London Daily Mail* trumpeted 'Hoover fiasco: Bosses sacked' and 'How Dumb Can You Get?' Meanwhile, complaints from angry Europeans poured into Maytag's Newton, Iowa, headquarters. A Hoover Holiday Pressure Group was rumoured to have thousands of members. Three people even travelled to Newton in an unsuccessful attempt to meet with CEO Hadley. By May 1995, Hadley was ready to throw in the towel. He decided to sell Hoover Europe to Italy's Candy SpA for €144.21 million. Hadley intends to refocus Maytag on the North American market.[55]

Although not all promotions have been successful, as the case of Hoover illustrates, sales promotions are an important element in the marketing mix. Promotions served in the past to boost sales. Since the customer (i.e. his activity) was unknown, the campaigns aimed at a wide audience with little differentiation. With available information about the customer (database), using information technology, marketers are now able to generate more accurate offers. The modern promotions are more effective because they relate directly to the customer's likes and lifestyle. One aspect of sales promotion is the launch of loyalty programmes to build strong relationships with existing customers. Distributing Tiger Tokens every time filling up a car with Esso was years ago a way to build up customer relationships. Nowadays many gas stations, supermarket chains or drugstores offer Clubcards which can be regarded as a means of winning customer loyalty. A further technical development of Clubcards, which basically include magnet stripes or bar codes, are Smart Cards. Smart Cards are equipped with a chip to store information about customers. The fact that many customers are concerned about giving often very personal information raises the need for data protection.[56]

Amazon.com, Inc., the largest virtual book and music store in the world, entered the European market in October 1998 with the launch of new websites for Germany (www.amazon.de) and the United Kingdom (www.amazon.co.uk). Amazon.com has not only been a forerunner in selling books, CDs or in offering free electronic greeting cards, it also invented a new marketing concept which can be called affiliate marketing or, as Amazon.com, Inc. calls it: *Associates Programme*. The Associates Programme is a scheme whereby owners of websites are able to earn extra money by offering books for sale by establishing links to the Amazon websites. In July 1999, the enrolment in the UK Associates Programme surpassed 10,000 member websites, including a number of charitable sites like the Royal National Institute for the Blind or the Children's Society.

PERSONAL SELLING

Personal selling is the fourth marketing communication tool discussed in this chapter. Selling is two-way, personal communication between a company representative and a potential customer as well as back to the company. The salesperson's job is to correctly understand the buyer's needs, match those needs to the company's product(s), and then persuade the customer to buy. Effective personal selling in a salesperson's home country requires building a relationship with the customer. Global marketing presents additional challenges because the buyer and seller may come from different national or cultural backgrounds. It is difficult to overstate the importance of a face-to-face, personal selling effort for industrial products in global markets. In 1993, a Malaysian developer, YTL Corp, sought bids on a €593.82 million contract for power-generation turbines. Siemens AG of Germany and General Electric (GE) were among the bidders. Datuk Francis Yeoh, managing director of YTL, requested meetings with top executives from both companies. 'I wanted to look them in the eye to see if we can do business,' Yeoh said. Siemens complied with the request; GE did not send an executive. Siemens was awarded the contract.[57]

The selling process is typically divided into several stages; prospecting, preapproach, approaching, presenting, problem solving, handling objections, closing the sale and following up. The relative importance of each stage can vary by country or region. Experienced sales reps know that persistence is one tactic often required to win an order. Persistence often means tenacity, as in 'don't take "no" for an answer'. However, in some countries, persistence means endurance, a willingness to patiently invest months or years before the effort results in an actual sale. For example, a company wishing to enter the Japanese market must be prepared for negotiations that could take from 3 to 10 years.

Prospecting is the process of identifying potential purchasers and assessing their probability of purchase. If VW wanted to sell vans in another country where they would be used as delivery vehicles, which businesses would need delivery vehicles? Which businesses have the financial resources to purchase such a van? Those businesses that match these two needs are better prospects than those that do not. Successful prospecting requires problem-solving techniques which involve understanding and matching the customer's needs and the company's products in developing a sales presentation.

The next two steps, the approach and the presentation, involve one or more meetings between seller and buyer. In global selling, it is absolutely essential for the salesperson to understand cultural norms and proper protocol. In some countries, the approach is drawn out as the buyer gets to know the salesperson on a personal level with no mention of the pending deal. In such instances, the presentation comes only after rapport has been firmly established.

During the presentation, the salesperson must deal with objections. Objections may be of a business or personal nature. A common theme in sales training is the notion of active listening. Naturally, in global sales, verbal and nonverbal communication barriers present special challenges for the salesperson. When objections are successfully overcome, the salesperson moves on to the close and asks for the order. A successful sale does not end there, however. The final step of the selling process involves following up with the customer to ensure his or her ongoing satisfaction with the purchase.

Technological changes influence the process of national and global personal selling. Some of the techniques described above (database marketing, Internet) enhance the success of the sale process. Many representatives use software programs that handle on-site analysis (i.e. financial), statistical process control, fax and/or electronic communication.[58] At Bell South (a telecommunications company) representatives meeting a prospect for the first time receive a customised set of selling suggestions via their personal computer.[59]

Salespersons in a global setting also need special knowledge about characteristics of the foreign country (language, culture). Training is often provided by the headquarters to improve the effectiveness of the salesforce. Training materials need to be translated into the languages of the individual countries to overcome language barriers.

Integrating all of the activities in marketing communications (direct marketing, personal selling, public relations, media advertising and promotions) provides synergies in persuasive impact and cost efficiencies, namely: 'Delivering the right message to the right customer decision maker at the right time'. For example, in the US Johnson & Johnson introduced Acuvue disposable contact lenses initially by an advertisement including a direct response inquiry. Simultaneously, eyecare professionals were contacted because they are essential mediators in the sale. On receipt of the customer inquiry, Johnson & Johnson passed the interest to the eyecare professionals (accompanied by a direct mail kit), who made an appointment with the customer. Then the professional informed Johnson & Johnson about the appointment who in turn sent the consumer a discount coupon good for an initial order. At the end of the sale, the company has a complete record including the customer's information and the identity of the eyecare professional.[60]

Key points

- Sales promotion adds tangible value to a product or brand.
- In some countries, sales promotion tools are strongly regulated.
- The personal selling process is divided into several stages and their importance can vary by country.
- Integrated marketing communications contain all elements of the marketing communication mix and provide synergies in persuasive impact and cost efficiency when all of the elements are carefully coordinated.

Summary

Marketing communications – the promotion P of the marketing mix – includes advertising, public relations, sales promotion and personal selling. Although marketers may identify opportunities for global advertising campaigns, local adaptation or distinct local campaigns may also be required. A powerful reason to try to create a global campaign is that the process forces a company to attempt to identify a global market for its product. In addition, the identification of global appeals and benefits forces a company to probe deeply to identify basic needs and buying motives. When creating advertising, care must be taken to ensure that the art direction and copy are appropriate for the intended audiences in target countries. Advertisers may place a single global agency in charge of world-wide advertising; it is also possible to use one or more agencies on a regional or local basis. Advertising intensity varies from country to country. The United States, for example, accounts for less than 25 per cent of gross world product but almost 50 per cent of world advertising expenditures. Media availability varies considerably from country to country. Television is the leading medium in many markets, but its availability for advertising is severely restricted or nonexistent in others. Public relations is another important tool in global marketing. Corporate communications must be designed to foster goodwill and provide accurate, timely information, especially in the event of a crisis.

Sales promotions must conform with regulations in each country market. An ill-designed promotion can result in unwanted publicity and lost customers. Finally, personal selling, or one-on-one communication, requires company representatives to be well versed in the culture of countries in which they do business. Behaviour in each stage of the selling process may have to be appropriately tailored to individual country requirements.

More recent additions to the international communication mix are direct marketing, database marketing and the Internet. Each technique is rapidly gaining acceptance around the world and can alter a company's marketing strategies for directly reaching the consumer.

Concepts and definitions

Advertising	Any sponsored, paid message that can be placed in a mass medium.
Database marketing	An interactive approach to marketing, which uses individually addressable marketing media and channels (such as mail, telephone and the salesforce). The media and channels extend help to a company's target audience, stimulate their demand, stay close to them by recording and keeping an electronic database memory of customer, prospect and all communication and commercial contacts. Database marketing helps to improve future contacts and ensures more realistic planning of marketing activities.
Direct marketing	A marketing system that integrates separate marketing mix elements to sell directly to both consumers and other businesses, bypassing retail stores and personal sales calls. Direct marketing uses a wide spectrum of media, including direct mail; telephone; broadcast, including television and radio; and print, including newspapers and magazines.
Global advertising	The use of the same advertising appeals, messages, art, copy, photographs, stories and video segments in multiple-country markets.
Marketing communications	Refers to all forms of communication used by organizations to inform, remind, explain, persuade and influence the attitudes and buying behaviour of customers and other people.
Personal selling	The selling process is typically divided into several stages: prospecting, preapproach, approaching, presenting, problem solving, handling objections, closing the sale, and following up.
Public relations	A nonpaid form of communication. PR's job is to make sure that the company responds promptly and gets its side of the story told. The basic tools of PR include news releases, newsletters, press conferences, tours of plants and other company facilities, articles in trade or professional journals, company publications and brochures, TV and radio talk show appearances by company personnel, special events, and home pages on the Internet.
Sales promotion	Refers to any consumer or trade programme of limited duration that adds tangible value to a product or brand.

Discussion questions

1 In what ways can global brands and global advertising campaigns benefit a company?

2 How does the standardised-versus-localised debate apply to advertising?

3 When creating advertising for world markets, what issues must art directors and copywriters take into account?

4 How do the media options available to advertisers vary in different parts of the world? What can advertisers do to cope with media limitations in certain countries?

5 What is the role of public relations in global marketing?

6 What is the role of sales promotion in the global marketing mix? How does it vary from one country to the next for the same product?

7 How does personal selling differ in international markets?

8 What are four considerations in selecting a direct mail strategy in a particular country?

9 What effect will the Internet have on international marketing communications?

Webmistress's hotspots

Homepage of the Omnicom Group
The corporate mission of the world's leading advertising organisation is 'to provide the strategic and financial support to help our companies achieve market leadership in their competitive arenas'. Find more information about Omnigroup at:
http://www.omnicomgroup.com/

Homepage of Ogilvy Public Relations Worldwide
Ogilvy Public Relations Worldwide is a global network of resources, talent and vision focused on achieving a client's goals: 'We believe in an informed, integrated and effective approach to communications strategy. One that produces success that endures. It's a high performance philosophy that generates consistent results.' More at:
http://www.ogilvypr.com/

Directory of public relations agencies and resources
Impulse Research is a full-service public opinion and marketing research firm, which provides a listing of important PR agencies all over the world:
http://www.impulse-research.com/prlist.html

Netdictionary
Netdictionary is an alphabetical reference guide to technical, cultural and humorous terms related to the Internet. Confused by the meaning of a cryptic networking term? Can't seem to make sense of a particular acronym? You've come to the right site:
http://www.netdictionary.com

Homepage of the International Olympic Committee
Welcome to the official sites of the International Olympic Committee (IOC)!
http://www.olympic.org/

Olympics and marketing
'Marketing has become an increasingly important issue for all of us within the Olympic Movement' – Juan Antonio Samaranch (President, International Olympic Committee). Find facts and figures on:
http://www.olympic.org/ioc/e/facts/marketing/mark–index–e.html

Suggested readings

Alden, Dana L., Wayne D. Hoyer and Chol Lee, 'Identifying global and culture-specific dimensions of humor in advertising: a multinational analysis', *Journal of Marketing*, 57, 2 (April 1993): pp. 64–75.

Andrews, J. Craig, Srinivas Durvasula and Richard G. Netemeyer, 'Testing the cross-national applicability of US and Russian advertising', *Journal of Advertising*, 23 (March 1994): pp. 71–82.

Banerjee, Anish, 'Transnational advertising development and management: an account planning approach and process framework', *International Journal of Advertising*, 13 (1994): pp. 95–124.

Botan, Carl, 'International public relations: critique and reformulation', *Public Relations Review*, 18, 2 (Summer 1992): pp. 149–159.

Bovet, Susan Fry, 'Building an international team', *Public Relations Journal* (August/September 1994): pp. 26–28ff.

Duncan, Thomas R. and Stephen E. Everett, 'Client perception of integrated marketing communications', *Journal of Advertising Research* (May/June 1993): pp. 119–122.

Epley, Joe S., 'Public relations in the global village: an American perspective', *Public Relations Review*, 18, 2 (Summer 1992): pp. 109–116.

Grunig, Larissa A., 'Strategic public relations constituencies on a global scale', *Public Relations Review* 18, 2 (Summer 1992): pp. 127–136.

Hanni, David A., John K. Rynas Jr and Ivan R. Vernon, 'Coordinating international advertising – The Goodyear case revisited for Latin America,' *Journal of International Marketing*, 3, 2 (1995): pp. 83–98.

Harris, Greg, 'International advertising standardization: what do the multinationals actually standardise?' *Journal of International Marketing*, 2, 4 (1994): pp. 13–30.

Haskett, James L., W. Earl Sasser Jr and Leonard A. Schlesinger, *The Service Profit Chain*. New York: Free Press, 1997.

Hiebert, Ray E., 'Advertising and public relations in transition from communism: the case of Hungary, 1989–1994', *Public Relations Review*, 20, 4 (Winter 1994): pp. 357–372.

Hill, John S. and Alan T. Shao, 'Agency participants in multi-country advertising: a preliminary examination of affiliate characteristics and environments', *Journal of International Marketing*, 2, 2 (1994): pp. 29–48.

Johansson, Johny K., 'The sense of "nonsense": Japanese TV advertising', *Journal of Advertising*, 23, 1 (March 1994): pp. 17–26.

Josephs, Ray and Juanita W. Josephs, 'Public relations, the UK way', *Public Relations Journal* (April 1994): pp. 14–18.

Kruckeberg, Dean, 'A global perspective on public relations ethics: the Middle East', *Public Relations Review*, 22, 2 (Summer 1996): pp. 181–189.

Leong, Siew Meng, Sween Hoon Ang and Leng Lai Tham, 'Increasing brand name recall in print advertising among Asians', *Journal of Advertising*, 25, 2 (1996): pp. 65–81.

Leslie, D.A., 'Global Scan: The globalisation of advertising agencies, concepts and campaigns', *Economic Geography*, 71, 4 (October 1995): pp. 402–426.

Lohtia, Ritu, Wesley J. Johnston and Linda Aab, 'Creating an effective print advertisement for the China market: analysis and advice', *Journal of Global Marketing*, 8, 2 (1994): pp. 7–30.

Luqmani, Mushtag, Ugur Yavas and Zahir Quraeshi, 'Advertising in Saudi Arabia: content and regulation', *International Marketing Review*, 6, 1 (1989): pp. 59–72.

Martin, Chuck, *The Digital Estate*. New York: McGraw-Hill, 1997.

Mathiesen, Michael, *Marketing on the Internet*, 2nd edn. Gulf Breeze, FL: Maximum Press, 1997.

McCullough, W.R., 'Global advertising which acts local: the IBM subtitles campaign', *Journal of Advertising Research*, 36, 3 (1996): pp. 11–15.

Mooij, Marieke K. De, *Advertising Worldwide: Concepts, Theories and Practice of International, Multinational and Global Advertising*, 2nd edn. Upper Saddle River, NJ: Prentice Hall, 1994.

Mueller, Barbara, *International Advertising: Communicating Across Cultures*. Belmont, CA: Wadsworth Publishing Company, 1995.

Mueller, Barbara, 'Standardisation vs. specialisation: an examination of westernisation in Japanese advertising', *Journal of Advertising Research* (1991): pp. 7–18.

Nessmann, Karl, 'Public relations in Europe: a comparison with the United States', *Public Relations Journal*, 21, 2 (Summer 1995): pp. 151–160.

Newsom, Doug and Bob Carrell, 'Professional public relations in India: need outstrips supply', *Public Relations Journal*, 20, 2 (Summer 1994): pp. 183–188.

Parameswaran, Ravi and R. Mohan Pisharodi, 'Facets of country of origin image: an empirical assessment', *Journal of Advertising*, 23, 1 (March 1994): pp. 43–56.

Pattinson, Hugh and Linden Brown, 'Chameleons in marketspace: industry transformation in the new electronic marketing environment', *Journal of Marketing Practice*, 2, 1 (1996): pp. 7–29.

Quelch, John A. and Lisa R. Klein, 'The Internet and international marketing', *Sloan Management Review*, 37, 3 (1996): p. 60.

Roth, Martin S., 'Depth versus breadth strategies for global brand image management', *Journal of Advertising*, 21, 2 (June 1992): pp. 25–36.

Schwartz, Evan I. *Webonomics*. New York: Broadway Books, 1997.

Sharpe, Melvin L., 'The impact of social and cultural conditioning on global public relations', *Public Relations Review*, 18, 2 (Summer 1992): pp. 103–107.

Shaver, Dick, *The Next Step in Database Marketing: Consumer Guided Marketing*. New York: Wiley, 1996.

Tansey, Richard and Michael R. Hyman, 'Dependency theory and the effects of advertising by foreign-based multinational corporations in Latin America', *Journal of Advertising*, 23, 1 (March 1994): pp. 27–42.

Taylor, Charles R., R. Dale Wilson and Gordon E. Miracle, 'The effect of brand differentiating messages on the effectiveness of Korean advertising', *Journal of International Marketing*, 2, 4 (1994): pp. 31–52.

Wells, Ludmilla Gricenko, 'Western concepts, Russian perspectives: meanings of advertising in the former Soviet Union', *Journal of Advertising*, 23, 1 (March 1994): pp. 83–95.

Zandpour, Fred, 'Global reach and local touch: achieving cultural fitness in TV advertising', *Journal of Advertising Research*, 34, 5 (September/October 1994): pp. 35–63.

Zavrl, Frani and Dejan Vercic, 'Performing public relations in central and eastern Europe', *International Public Relations Journal*, 18, 2 (1995): pp. 21–23.

Zhou, Nan and Russell W. Belk, 'China's advertising and the export marketing curve: the first decade', *Journal of Advertising Research*, 33, 6 (November–December 1993): pp. 50–66.

Notes

1. 'The next era: Benetton', *The Economist*, 23 April 1994.
2. 'More controversy, please, we're Italian – Benetton's latest outrage', *The Economist*, 1 February 1992.
3. F. Kennedy, 'How we met; Luciano Benetton and Oliviero Toscani', *Independent on Sunday*, 22 August 1999.
4. 'Bernard Arnault and Benetton invest in online shopping', *Les Echos*, 16 July 1999.
5. '21 Investimenti: Benetton triples profit', *La Stampa*, 29 May 1999.
6. Thomas R. Duncan and Stephen E. Everett, 'Client perception of integrated marketing communications', *Journal of Advertising Research*, May–June (1993): pp. 119–122.
7. 1996 rankings reflect data collected in 1998. Country count is the number of countries where spending was reported in 1997. Asia includes Australia and New Zealand. Primary data from AC Nielsen and its affiliates.
8. Ken Wells, 'Selling to the world: global ad campaigns after many missteps finally pay dividends', *The Wall Street Journal*, 27 August 1992, p. A8.
9. Dean M. Peebles, 'Executive insights: don't write off global advertising', *International Marketing Review*, 6, 1 (1989): pp. 73–78.
10. Meg Carter, 'Think globally, act locally', *Financial Times*, 30 June 1997, p. 12.
11. Elinder, Eric, 'International advertisers must devise universal ads, dump separate national ones, Swedish ad man avers', *Advertising Age*, 27 November 1961, p. 91.
12. 'A conversation with Nestlé's Pierre Liotard-Vogt', *Advertising Age*, 30 June 1980, p. 31.
13. Ali Kanso, 'International advertising strategies: global commitment to local vision', *Journal of Advertising Research*, January–February (1992): pp. 10–14.
14. Ken Wells, 'Selling to the world: global ad campaigns after many missteps finally pay dividends', *The Wall Street Journal*, 27 August 1992, p. A8.
15. Ono Yumiko, 'PepsiCo's pitch in Japan has new twist', *The Wall Street Journal*, 23 May 1997, p. B10.
16. Ono Yumiko, 'Japan warms to McDonald's doting dad ads', *The Wall Street Journal*, 8 May 1997, pp. B1, B12.
17. R. Tomkins, 'Commercial breakdown', *Financial Times*, 5 August 1999, p. 11.
18. E. Joachimsthaler and D.A. Aaker, 'Building brands without mass media', *Harvard Business Review*, January–February (1997): pp. 39–50.
19. Steven Soricillo, 'Mexico: Direct mail marketing across our border,' *Direct Marketing* (August 1996): p. 39.
20. D. Schmittlein, 'Mastering management – part 8 (5) – customers as strategic assets', *Financial Times*, 15 December 1995.
21. J. O'Connor and E. Galvin, *Marketing and Information Technology* (London: Pitman Publishing, 1997).
22. John A. Quelch and Lisa R. Klein, 'The Internet and international marketing', *Sloan Management Review*, 37, 3 (1996): p. 60.
23. Ibid.
24. *Advertising Age*, Ad age dataplace (http://adage.com/dataplace/).
25. Evan I. Schwartz, *Webonomics* (New York: Broadway Books, 1997).
26. Sally Goll Beatty, 'Young & Rubicam is only one for Colgate', *The Wall Street Journal*, 1 December 1995, p. B6.
27. Robert T. Green, William H. Cunningham and

Isabella C.M. Cunningham, 'The effectiveness of standardized global advertising', *Journal of Advertising*, (1975): pp. 25–30.

28. Gary Levin, 'Ads going global', *Advertising Age*, 22 July 1991, pp. 4, 42.

29. Gabriella Stern, 'Heinz aims to export taste for ketchup', *The Wall Street Journal*, 20 November 1992, p. B1.

30. Vern Terpstra and Ravi Sarathy, *International Marketing* (Orlando, FL: The Dryden Press, 1991).

31. Jeanne Whalen, 'McDonald's cooks worldwide growth', *Advertising Age International*, July–August (1995): p. I4.

32. Stephen E. Frank, 'Citicorp's big account is at stake as it seeks a global brand name', *The Wall Street Journal*, 9 January 1997, p. B6.

33. Roger Thurow, 'Shtick ball: in global drive, Nike finds its brash ways don't always pay off', *The Wall Street Journal*, 5 May 1997, p. A10.

34. John O'Toole, *The Trouble with Advertising* (New York: Chelsea House, 1980), pp. 209–210.

35. Anthony C. di Benedetto, Mariko Tamate and Rajan Chandran, 'Developing creative advertising strategy for the Japanese marketplace', *Journal of Advertising Research*, January–February (1992): pp. 39–48; Mary C. Gilly, 'Sex roles in advertising: a comparison of television advertisements in Australia, Mexico and the United States', *Journal of Marketing*, April (1988): pp. 75–85; Marc G. Weinberger and Harlan E. Spotts, 'A situation view of information content in TV advertising in the US and UK', *Journal of Advertising*, 53, January (1989): pp. 89–94.

36. Numbers of newspapers published at least four times a week.

37. Estimated number of radio receivers in use for broadcasts to the general public.

38. Refers to users of portable telephones subscribing to an automatic public mobile telephone service using cellular technology that provides access to the public switched telephone network.

39. Estimated number of self-contained computers designed to be used by a single individual.

40. Number of computers with active Internet Protocol (IP) addresses connected to the Internet. All hosts without a country code identification are assumed to be located in the United States.

41. 'National Trade Data Bank: The Export Connection, USDOC, International Trade Administration', *Market Research Reports*, 2 October 1992.

42. K. Nessmann, 'Public Relations in Europe: a comparison with the United States', *Public Relations Journal*, 21, 2 (1995): pp. 155–158.

43. Bart Ziegler, 'Checkmate! Deep Blue is IBM publicity coup', *The Wall Street Journal*, 9 May 1997, p. B1.

44. Richard Tomkins, 'When global leaders become global targets', *Financial Times*, 15 October 1999, pp. 24–25.

45. Joe Mullich, 'European firms seek alliances for global PR', *Business Marketing*, 79, August (1994): pp. 4, 31.

46. J. Kolarz-Lakenbacher and G. Reichlin-Meldegg, *Sponsoring* (Wien: Orac, 1995).

47. A. Mitchell, 'How the Olympics won the big prize. An amazing sponsorship rebirth', *The Times*, 24 January 1996.

48. E. Joachimsthaler and D.A. Aaker, 'Building brands without mass media', *Harvard Business Review*, January–February (1997): pp. 39–50.

49. K. Nessmann, 'Public relations in Europe: a comparison with the United States', *Public Relations Journal*, 21, 2 (1995): pp. 151–160.

50. Larissa A. Grunig, 'Strategic public relations constituencies on a global scale', *Public Relations Review*, 18, 2 (1992): p. 130.

51. Carl Botan, 'International public relations: Critique and reformulation', *Public Relations Review*, 18, 2 (1992): pp. 150–151.

52. Malvin L. Sharpe, 'The impact of social and cultural conditioning on global public relations', *Public Relations Review*, 18, 2 (1992): pp. 104–105.

53. Carl Botan, 'International public relations: critique and reformulation', *Public Relations Review*, 18, 2 (1992): p. 155.

54. Leslie Ryan, 'Sales promotion: made in America', *Brandweek*, 31 July 1995, p. 28.

55. Rick Jost, 'Maytag wrings out after flopped Hoover promotion', *The Des Moines Register*, 5 April 1993, p. 3B; Rick Jost, 'Mail flying in from Britons upset by Maytag promotion', *The Des Moines Register*, 11 July 1994, p. B3.

56. J. O'Connor and E. Galvin, *Marketing and Information Technology* (London: Pitman Publishing, 1997), p. 222.

57. Marcus W. Brauchli, 'Looking East: Asia, on the ascent, is learning to say no to "arrogant" West', *The Wall Street Journal*, 13 April 1994, pp. A1, A8.

58. M. Czinkota and I.A. Ronkainen, *Global Marketing* (Orlando, FL: Dryden Press, 1996).

59. D. Schmittlein, 'Mastering management – Part 8 (5) – Customers as strategic assets', *Financial Times*, 15 December 1995.

60. D. Schmittlein, 'Mastering management – Part 8 (5) – Customers as strategic assets', *Financial Times*, 15 December 1995.

The launch of GSM cellular telephones in South Africa

Driving to Jan Smuts Airport for yet another flight to Cape Town, Vodacom's Managing Director, Alan Knott-Craig contemplated the year ahead in anticipation of tomorrow's management strategy meeting. South Africa's cellular industry had not only recorded the world's fastest launch of a GSM cellular subscriber base, but had also become the world's fastest growing cellular market and the second largest GSM cellular subscriber base in the world in just one year. Such an achievement, during the transition to Mandela and De Klerk's new South Africa, surprised industry experts around the world. Solid market leaders with a 65 per cent estimated share, Knott-Craig's team would be contemplating the next phase of market growth and competitive strategy.

THE CELLULAR COMMUNICATIONS INDUSTRY

South Africa's cellular communications industry consisted of four main players: network operators, service providers, dealers, and equipment manufacturers.

Network operators

Vodacom and Mobile Telephone Networks (MTN) were awarded the first two network operator licences by the government regulator. The licences empowered each operator to set up and operate the network infrastructure necessary to provide national GSM digital cellular coverage. Although Europe's GSM digital cellular standard was more expensive than the analogue cellular standard most common to the United States, Britain, and other countries, GSM's many advanced capabilities such as fax and data transmission were leading to growing acceptance as a global standard. After many debates, the South African government specified the GSM standard. Vodacom and MTN were assigned separate frequencies for transmission and reception from the available radio frequency band. Some frequencies were reserved for a potential third network in the future.

The ownership of both network operators included international firms, government or quasi-governmental bodies and local black business consortia. Vodacom's relationship to Telkom, the state-owned, fixed-wire telephone monopoly, almost assured it of appointment as the first network operator.

Licences were awarded to both Vodacom and MTN on 30 September 1993 and they began building network infrastructure. However, due to the certainty that Vodacom or Telkom would be awarded at least one of the licences, MTN began building network infrastructure later and was well behind on 1 April 1994 when the test period began for a limited number of subscribers. Although MTN had made gains by the official launch date of 1 June 1994, it was clear that Vodacom remained ahead in many important geographic coverage areas.

The regulator levelled the playing field by requiring both network operators to allow 'roaming' during the test period and the first three months of normal operations. Roaming allowed an MTN subscriber to place calls in an area where only Vodacom base stations existed or where MTN base stations were operating at capacity when a subscriber call was placed. Similarly, Vodacom callers could place calls using the MTN infrastructure if Vodacom coverage was not available. The two networks agreed to cease roaming ahead of schedule in August 1994, except for emergency calls. Subscribers from either network could make a '112' emergency call on any network – even from phones without the Subscriber Identity Module (SIM) card inserted in the cellular phone. The SIM card was a smart card containing an integrated circuit chip to identify the caller at network-level for billing and administrative purposes.

The regulator allowed the network operators to set up and manage their own distribution channel. Following the international trend, both network operators appointed service providers.

Service providers

Service providers marketed network services and provided the bulk of customer care. Exclusive service providers acted on behalf of one network – dual service providers represented both – but in all cases a client wishing to subscribe to a cellular network was required to sign a contract with one of the network operators' appointed service providers. The South African Cellular Service Providers Association (SACSPA) was established to promote the interests of service providers and provided a forum for cooperating on matters of common concern such as fraud and bad debt. Both network operators encouraged service providers to become SACSPA members.

Service providers were responsible for the sale of handsets, car kits and other cellular equipment, airtime subscriptions, account billing and collection, and ongoing client service. Customers did not have any direct relationship with the network operators. The network operators billed service providers for total calls made by each subscriber (airtime) less a discount of approximately 25 per cent to 30 per cent (depending on the number of subscribers enrolled by the service provider and a loyalty bonus) plus a monthly subscription fee, which varied according to the tariff the customer chose. Certain incentive payments were also paid. Connection bonuses were paid for net new subscriptions signed by a service provider. Although these subsidies were confidential, the media regularly speculated that subsidies ranged from R500 to R2,000. Most media sources indicated that service providers used the subsidies to lower the price of cellular handsets. The loyalty bonuses were designed to entice dual service providers to concentrate business with one network and varied according to the proportion of a service provider's total subscribers using a particular network.

Network operators received and transmitted customer calls. Every time a cell phone was turned on, the Vodacom system would record the nearest base station(s). This allowed the placement of a call from any telephone or cellphone to interconnect into the appropriate switches for ultimate transmission to the cell user. Thus, a particular call might utilise not only Vodacom's equipment, but also equipment of Telkom. Vodacom's network equipment recorded the SIM card number, the number called, the cellular handset IMEI identification number, the starting and ending time of the call and the type of call for every call as part of a call data record (CDR). The network operators downloaded the resulting CDRs, and reports concerning calls, to service providers on multiple occasions during the day via node-to-node links. Data were formatted to be readable by the service providers' billing systems.

Service providers received the CDR transmissions and other reports for use with internal accounting and management software – the most important component being the billing system. Billing systems performed the mission-critical function of allocating CDRs to subscribers so subscribers were billed for calls placed. In addition, some billing systems offered integrated application processing capabilities that included issuance, activation and deactivation of handsets and SIM cards on the network as well as performance of certain record-keeping in customer care centres. The software used was complicated and most service providers procured the EPPIX billing system marketed by a UK firm that specialised in cellular billing systems. Other service providers formed strategic alliances with overseas service providers and adapted the partner's administrative systems and business strategies to the local market. A few service providers developed local administrative and billing systems. There was little standardisation of billing systems and even EPPIX installations could be configured quite differently. Vodacom's own information technology division was headquartered in Cape Town.

There was little doubt that all service providers had experienced administrative and financial difficulties that were exacerbated by the short notice many had received concerning their appointments. As a result, some service providers did not have billing systems up and running when the test period began.

Service providers were hard hit by the faster than expected growth, especially the financial management and management information departments. It was obvious that many were having difficulties getting costs under control. The first-year results announced by the two publicly traded service providers showed signs of the severe trading conditions. Knott-Craig had heard rumours that the published results were typical, perhaps better, than many privately held service providers, and he had heard the reverse. In any case, the persistent rumours that smaller service providers would not last six months had not been fulfilled, and the industry ended the first year with 17 service providers – the same number that had begun the year.

Vodacom owned a service provider – VODAC. MTN's major shareholders controlled another service provider, M-TEL. Suspicions of favouritism to these service providers tainted relationships with some service providers. The network operators' licences did not require them to use service providers, but Vodacom believed that service providers had been proven to speed market penetration around the world and the firm had committed to contracts with 11 service providers.

Dealers

Service providers often appointed dealers to sell airtime subscriptions on their behalf. Vodacom had gained an early competitive advantage when Teljoy and Vodac signed dealer agreements with certain major retail outlets and dealers. This had resulted in fast growth. Teljoy, the leading national TV rental chain with shops located in top retail sites, had become the world's second largest GSM cellular service provider and captured over one third of the South African market, largely as a result of its retail presence and extensive advertising prior to and during the launch of cellular. Teljoy had been advertising heavily in advance of the launch of national satellite TV in recent months.

Many dealers had come and gone during the first year. For some, this was an intentional strategy to take advantage of short-term opportunities created by the explosive launch. Others were undercapitalised, and service provider billing system problems allegedly held up incentive payments for too long to allow dealer survival in many cases.

International and local fraud syndicates had penetrated the dealer network, and the police had made many arrests. Service providers often used the full connection bonus payment and other promotional funds to subsidise the price of equipment sold on longer-term airtime subscriber contracts – often comparing the sale of R2,500 phones for little or nothing to the sale of razors below cost to promote usage of blades.

Posing as legitimate clients, fraud teams either bought cellular phones at the low, subsidised prices or stole them and exported them to other GSM countries. Theft of airtime represented a far greater hazard. Many 'phone shops' had been discovered in urban areas where local and international phone calls were sold at reduced rates. Call charges exceeding many thousands of Rands were sometimes completed before service providers became aware of the problem. Customers were reporting their cell phones stolen from restaurants, cafés and even from their bedside tables while they slept.

Fraud team links to African and Asian drug syndicates had been reported in the press. A 'phone shop' could quickly run up a R10,000 bill on a stolen SIM card in a weekend, offsetting the total monthly airtime (calls) revenue of more than 65 average subscribers. SACSPA had shared police evidence concerning the infiltration of the country by international fraud syndicates in anticipation of the 1995 Rugby World Cup (which South Africa later won). A classic tournament watched by billions around the world, this was the first time the World Cup had been held in one country and experts wondered if the police force was up to the challenge of international fraud teams.

Regulation

The Postmaster General was the official regulator of the telecommunications industry. Pallo Jordan, Minister of Posts, Telecommunications and Broadcasting, was responsible for the government's overall communications strategy. The Minister was rethinking telecommunications policy, and an extensive Green Paper had been circulated for discussion to the South African public and all interested parties. The continuation of Telkom's fixed wire telephone monopoly was debated in the Green Paper but seemed unlikely to change. The regulator had approved a number of Vodacom tariff plans. Service providers could not charge more than the regulated call tariffs, although they were free to discount any tariff.

Knott-Craig was conscious that the Vodacom and Telkom cultures were different due to the nature of the businesses but felt that certain aspects of culture were shared. He was particularly pleased that he could draw on Telkom and Vodafone technical expertise and business experience when required. However, the impression that Vodacom received special favours, either from Telkom or the Regulator, were a constant source of irritation that Knott-Craig was tired of denying. He also tired of rejecting allegations that Vodacom favoured Vodac or Teljoy over other service providers.

EQUIPMENT MANUFACTURERS

Equipment manufacturers participated in the industry in two ways: by supplying cellular base stations and infrastructure to network operators and by supplying cellular handsets and accessories to service providers and dealers. Nokia, Ericsson, Alcatel, Siemens, Panasonic, and Motorola were among the leading brands participating in the latter. Vodacom sourced base stations from Siemens and Alcatel while MTN's network standardised on Ericsson equipment.

Service providers felt that the equipment manufacturers were becoming problematic. Consumer dissatisfaction with manufacturers was a serious problem, according to the SACSPA. Some manufacturers were taking up to six months to repair handsets under warranty, and this necessitated significant investments in loan phones. No doubt, Motorola's decision to appoint major retailers as distributors would affect service providers, even though retailers would require a service provider to connect their subscribers to a network operator.

There was also a constant threat of stock shortages as new countries adopted the GSM standard. Many manufacturers shipped stock only after receiving a letter of credit and then shipped amounts less than those ordered by the major service providers. News of a Chinese consortium beginning the manufacture of GSM handsets had appeared in the South African business press. Manufacturers also were organised in a trade association, the CTMIA.

THE BUSINESS ENVIRONMENT

South Africa's cellular industry received a baptism of fire in its first year. Violence racked the country in the run-up to President Nelson Mandela's election on 29 April 1994. When the government announced that two network operators would be appointed, the appointment of a second network operator became highly politicised, delaying the appointment of a second network operator.

The first half of 1994 had been politically turbulent. There were constant rumours that right-wing or left-wing forces would attempt to sabotage the elections or overthrow the government if Nelson Mandela's African National Congress (ANC) won. Many skilled people were leaving the country and, paradoxically, many were returning. Some political parties spoke of privatising state-run monopolies, such as Telkom, and the parastatals controlling the transportation, iron and steel, and electrical distribution industries. Although these bodies represented a comparatively high percentage of GNP compared to other countries, ANC supporters such as the labour unions and the Communist Party of South Africa voiced disapproval of privatisation schemes. Some political parties were advocating that reconstruction and development required nothing less than a centrally planned Marxist/Leninist economy.

Cellular telephony was viewed with suspicion by many parties who viewed the proposed launch as a thinly disguised attempt to keep the control of telecommunications in the hands of the white minority. Thus, even though both licences were awarded on 30 September 1993, an agreement was reached with the African National Congress only on 22 October 1993. Equipment purchases and service provider appointments could only begin thereafter. South Africa traditionally comes to a standstill during the mid-December to mid-January Christmas break, and this created additional problems. Some service providers had been appointed as late as a few weeks prior to the April 1994 rollout to a limited subscriber base for testing.

Both licences required the network operators to subsidise cellular telephony in the historically disadvantaged communities. Both networks had initiated projects in this regard and appointed black-owned service providers. In addition, Vodacom and MTN were to engage in economic activities outside their mainstream business to the value of R1 billion to the government at the end of five years. Attempts to increase the historically disadvantaged population's access to telecommunications resulted in Vodacom's telephone shop, which was designed to house up to 10 cellular pay telephones. The shops also created much needed jobs. MTN could take credit for the invention of the world's first working GSM cellular pay phone in a similar project.

The market

South Africa blends First and Third World characteristics. First World shopping malls and business areas and Third World squatter shacks often coexist within kilometres. Urbanised areas generally have high economic activity and income, but rural areas are much poorer. Table 1 highlights some indicators of human and economic development.

Knott-Craig was concerned about the escalating violence in the country during early 1995. Violent crime had reached the levels experienced prior to the election in some areas, and the police were clearly experiencing difficulty in combating crime. Security had positive and negative impacts on cellular telephone usage. Security was a popular reason for buying a cellular phone and promotions featuring on-call security services by Autopage Cellular and Teljoy both seemed to have done well. However, it was far too early for reliable usage statistics to be available for subscribers interested in security.

The Government of National Unity was exceeding the expectations many held prior to the election. President Mandela was especially popular. However, ANC's Reconstruction and Development Programme was moving more slowly than expected, and President Mandela had recently ordered his cabinet to pursue economic growth with increased vigour. The school system was a particular worry for many people with school-aged children, and there was a perception that managerial and professional people with

Table 1 Selected development statistics for selected countries

	Population in 1992 (millions)	Gross Domestic Product in 1992 ($US millions)	Energy use per capita in 1992 (per capita kilowatts)	Telephone main lines in 1990 (in thousands)	Access to safe drinking water (%)	Crude birth rate in 1992 (per 1,000 population)	Human Development Index
United States	255.4	5,920,199	7,662	136,337		16	0.925
New Zealand	3.4	41,304	4,284	1,469	97	17	0.907
Korea	43.7	296,136	2,569	13,276	93	16	0.859
Chile	13.6	41,203	837	861	87	23	0.848
Mexico	85.0	329,011	1,525	5,355	89	28	0.804
South Africa	39.8	103,651	2,487	3,315		31	0.650
Indonesia	184.3	126,364	303	1,069	34	25	0.586
Kenya	25.7	6,884	223	183	49	37	0.434
Pakistan	119.3	41,904	92	843	72	40	0.393

Source: The World Bank, *World Development Report 1994: Infrastructure for Development* (New York: Oxford, 1994); except for Human Development Index, excerpted from United Nations Development Program, *Human Development Report 1994* (New York: Oxford).

children were leaving the country in record numbers, although official emigration statistics did not confirm this perception. There was a possibility that the stringent exchange controls placed on emigrating people may have had some impact on how many people actually reported immigration.

MARKETING

Achieving competitive advantage required careful analysis on the network operator and service provider tier. The nature of government regulation often made it difficult to differentiate a business in meaningful ways from one's competitor.

Product

Network coverage, that is, the area in which calls could be placed and received by cellular users, was a common way to differentiate cellular networks. With the exception of a difficult period of oversubscription during August and September 1994, Vodacom felt that its network covered a far larger area and boasted superior quality. Network quality was measured by counting calls dropped (disconnected due to some network problem) and consumer complaints about the quality of the audio transmission. Although MTN's network started building months after Vodacom, it was clear that MTN would catch up to Vodacom within the short term.

Promotion

The coverage advantage had been the focus of Vodacom's major selling effort masterminded by GM

Joan Joffe and was a major reason that two out of three subscribers had chosen Vodacom. The award-winning launch of GSM's cellular telephone in a South African TV advertisement focused on this coverage advantage. The R21 million measured ad spending placed the combined TV, press and radio spending in the top 20 South African companies' ad spending for 1994 – just behind MTN's R23 million. Service providers also promoted network brands in their own advertising and both networks enjoyed widespread brand awareness. Exact figures were unavailable but the combined advertising spending of the service providers probably exceeded R20 million.

Joffe was particularly proud of the recent promotions connected to Vodacom's sponsorship of the Rugby World Cup. Adverts had high recognition and had received high liking and noting scores. Market research indicated that the TV advertisements were particularly well-liked and Vodacom's share of purchase intent had increased significantly. Joffe could not say whether this was due to MTN's ongoing coverage problems or the promotional campaigns but believed it might be due to both.

MTN's advertising also had been very effective. Featuring a unique and humorous monotonic delivery by a male gravelly-voiced announcer, the TV and radio ad shared the advantages of having the magic of MTN's mobile communications at one's disposal. MTN positioned its brand as 'the better connection' and achieved high recognition and branding. The innovative use of an MTN airship also aided brand recognition.

Pricing

Government regulation affected pricing strategies most. Consumers generally judged two costs when considering adopting cellular telephony. Initial one-time costs included the cost of the cellular handset and any accessories (such as a hands-free car kit), the cost of the SIM card (R65.00), and the cost of activating the SIM card on the network (the connection fee R125.00). Ongoing costs included the monthly subscription (R125.00) and call charges (R1.10 per minute during peak hours and R.65 during off-peak hours). The average user received a monthly bill of R250 to R300.

Call charge tariffs, monthly subscription fees, SIM card charges and connection fees were regulated, and both network operators charged the same amounts. Network operators could ask for new tariffs to be approved but the other network was also free to apply to use the same new tariff immediately. Service providers were allowed to discount call tariffs in order to gain business. However, a discount of even 10 per cent of the call tariff would be reduced directly from the service provider's 25 per cent to 30 per cent of the total call charge – thus, a 10 per cent discount could result in almost a 40 per cent reduction in sales revenue at the service provider tier. SACSPA felt that such discounting would seriously jeopardise the long-term survival of the service provider tier, and there was some question as to how discounts could be applied without infringing on the network requirements for approval of new tariffs by the regulator. Indeed, one firm that was alleged to discount tariffs ran into financial trouble almost immediately. Some service providers were cleverly bundling packages with added-value emergency services and other augmented product offers that were clearly legal.

Both networks subsidised the cost of handsets. Initial subsidies did not affect the price of handsets significantly but, as competition heated up at the end of the first year, subsidies had increased to a very significant level. The large subsidies allowed service providers to sell low-end R1,500 handsets for almost nothing and to sell top-range handsets for as little as R2,000.00. Indeed, Autopage had bought up the total available stock of a new Alcatel handset that was offered with an added-value emergency services package free of charge to qualifying applicants. Free phones fuelled rapid growth but also created the problems noted earlier.

Distribution

The service provider distribution model was a cause of some concern. Vodafone was experimenting with a direct-to-market approach in the United Kingdom. The US model featured network operators and dealers. In the US model, dealers were marketing agents and the networks took total responsibility for the billing and customer service functions. Both approaches had been successful.

Most industry experts would attribute Vodacom's commanding market share to its superior network coverage and quality and its exclusive presence in leading retail outlets. Teljoy sold cellular subscriptions through its retail outlets located in most shopping mall locations across the country. In addition, exclusive service providers – primarily Teljoy and Vodac – had tied up exclusive dealerships with major retailers, office supply outlets, and dealers. MTN had also tied up exclusive agreements, but Knott-Craig, the Managing Director, was confident he had won the early rounds of this fight.

THE CURRENT SITUATION

As he thought about tomorrow's strategy meeting, Knott-Craig became frustrated at the traffic jam ahead on the way to the airport. It was not normally so crowded at this time of day on the R24 and, as he changed from the CD to hear the traffic report on Radio 702, the strategy meeting continued to dominate his thinking. The industry had exceeded forecasts of 100,000 subscribers and achieved 350,000 in its first year.

He sensed that new problems would require very different solutions to the past. It seemed certain that explosive growth would not be repeated but that the industry could achieve 1,000,000 subscribers by the end of the first three years. It seemed certain that the quality of new subscribers (as measured by average airtime and bad debt) would deteriorate as cellular usage expanded. New subscriptions had declined dramatically since both networks had reduced connection bonuses on 1 April 1995. Balancing the desirability for growth against the profitability required to satisfy shareholders and to make the RDP payment was not going to be easy.

Technologically, Knott-Craig planned for Vodacom to stay ahead. MTN had recently announced a host of value-added network services that allowed users to use a cellular phone as a pager or to call for a host of services, such as legal advice. Both networks had launched fax and data services and paging services at about the same time. Caller identification would also be available soon on both networks.

Teljoy had already taken the initiative to launch a 112 emergency service enhancement using the 911 number popularised by an American TV series shown on South African TV. Fax services were to be enhanced shortly. A fax would then be held similarly to voice mail to be retrieved later when desirable.

The traffic jam cleared as he passed a minor motor car accident on the freeway, and Knott-Craig could see the airport in the distance. He would arrive on time.

This case was prepared by Professor Steve Burgess of The School of Economic and Business Studies at the University of Witwatersrand as the basis for class discussion rather than to illustrate either effective or ineffective handling of an administrative situation.

Nokia and the cellular phone industry

In the early spring of 1994, Jorma Ollila, CEO of the Nokia group, looked back on a successful year where his company's cellular phone sales had increased by more than 70 per cent and his profits had more than doubled. In a growing market, the Finnish company had managed to increase its market share, moving up from a global market share of 13 per cent in early 1992 to 20 per cent at the end of 1993. Rapidly increasing development costs had forced many of Nokia's competitors to shut down or sell out to larger rivals. How could Nokia sustain its growth in such a turbulent industry? How could the management make decisions in light of such uncertainty?

EVOLUTION OF THE INDUSTRY

The mobile phone industry was born as a result of the need for professionals to contact others on the move. With only a restricted amount of the radio spectrum, it meant that an open broadcast system needed to squeeze every conversation out on the same limited bandwidth. The cellular breakthrough was achieved at AT&T's Bell laboratories in 1979, making it possible for the same tiny bandwidth to be used by thousands of individual, switched messages (see appendix). By the beginning of 1993, cellular service was in place in more than 90 countries.

There were several categories of products on the market for wireless communication. Mobile communication was, beside cellular telephones, largely represented by pagers, with an estimated 50 million subscribers[1] world-wide in 1993. The pagers can, like the cellular phones, also receive short messages in both data and voice. Computer companies like Apple, AT&T, IBM and AST Research introduced personal digital assistants (PDAs). These handheld, pen-based computers could send wireless facsimile and electronic mail and were expected to include voice communication eventually. The mode of communication used depended mainly on the complexity and urgency of the message. E-mail, pagers, computers, or facsimile did not provide instant confirmation that the message was received. This was possible only with the telephone.

The cellular telephone industry consisted, like the telecommunication industry, of production of phones, infrastructure, and operators of the infrastructure. Infrastructure refers to the transmitting towers, and the many categories of switching technology used to establish the connections. Motorola, Ericsson and Nokia were manufacturers of both infrastructure and cellular phones. The interdependency between these two sectors is very tight, as a feature developed for handsets only is functional if the infrastructure can accommodate it (see appendix). Operators of the cellular networks were often also those providing fixed wire telecommunication in a given area, although competitors were starting to make aggressive moves on that market. Well-known companies such as Sprint, AT&T, McCaw cellular, and most of the national operators in Europe were players in this arena.

The Nordic governments had chosen the NMT

(Nordic Mobile Telephone) 450 analogue standard in 1981, when this region became one of the first areas in the world to establish cellular services. Sparsely populated areas cost too much to connect by fixed wire, and this posed a further incentive for establishing cellular services. Unique to the Nordic countries were the roaming possibilities between the countries (see appendix), creating a system covering the entire Nordic area. Cellular users roam as they move from the coverage of one service provider to another. The existence of roaming agreements between service providers/operators of different areas widen the geographic coverage provided to the users. By 1994 the fruits, resulting from an early move into cellular communication along with a common standard and a coherent set of roaming agreements, had begun to show: penetration rates in this region, of up to 10 per cent, were the highest in the world. The NMT-450 and the newer NMT-900 standard had also been adopted in many other countries, such as the Netherlands, France, Belgium, Spain, Austria and Thailand, but roaming across borders was only possible within the Nordic NMT system due to the agreements existing between the governments in these countries.

Several producers of cellular telephones existed in the Nordic region. The dominant producers were Swedish L.M. Ericsson and Nokia Mobile Phones, headquartered in Finland. These were also the main providers of cellular infrastructure to the system. Other European producers of cellular telephones were Siemens, primarily focused on the German market, and Technophone Ltd, the main producer of cellular phones in the UK market. Several small, innovative companies were on the scene in the industry's infancy, like Storno and Cetelco, and major multinationals like Philips and Bosch were marketing phones under OEM agreements.

Before the implementation of the European digital standard, as described below, several analogue standards prevailed in the area. There were seven non-compatible analogue standards in Europe, led by the NMT-450 and NMT-900 standards, and the British developed TACS standard.

Most of the European telecommunications services were state-owned, resulting in monopolistic situations with the effect of slowing the growth in cellular phones and services due to the high calling fees that were demanded. In 1993, the German penetration rate was as low as 2.47 per cent due also to a poorly integrated cross-country coverage.

In the United States, commercial cellular telecommunications began in 1983, with the implementation of the AMPS (American Mobile Phone System) standard. The Federal Communications Commission (FCC) sets the rules for competition on the cellular communication scene in the United States, and has given licences to several regional operators.

The American structure was based upon regionally competing companies/operators which have made the overall network differentiated and incoherent. Roaming possibilities were technically possible, but agreements between the operators uncommon. Furthermore the US antitrust laws complicated the rise of nationwide agreements between competing entities. The penetration rate in 1993 was approximately 6 per cent, and the American manufacturer Motorola Inc. dominated this market. At this point, the innovator of the technology, AT&T, had only just started to manufacture cellular phones themselves.

Japan was the first country to licence cellular service in 1981, but the development of a nationwide service was not achieved until 1984. This service was offered by the Nippon Telegraph and Telephone Corporation, who had a monopoly position on the Japanese market. After 1985, NTT was to be privatised over a five-year period and other private companies got access to providing cellular services. The structure was controlled by the government in such a way that NTT provided national services, and the competitors had their own regional area, in which NTT was the only other competitor. The structure caused a slow growth in subscribers because of the high connection prices, and a low level of geographical coverage. This manifested itself with a base of only 1.7 million subscribers in 1993.

The Asian–Pacific countries, except for Japan, had adopted diverse standards including NMT, TACS and AMPS, and the Latin American countries had chosen the AMPS. Growth within the standards in these markets was relatively low compared to the other regions, with a subscriber base accounting only for approximately 10 per cent of the world-wide number of both analogue and digital subscribers in 1993.

In the middle of 1993, there were an estimated 27.3 million analogue subscribers world-wide, where the United States accounted for 48 per cent, Europe 25 per cent, and Asia–Pacific (including Japan) 15 per cent.

Change in technology

By 1991, the limitations of the analogue standards were becoming critical due to the high growth in subscribers, prompting the emergence of the digital technologies. The analogue standards had less capacity within a given frequency band and were also affected by wave interference, thereby easily absorbing noise.

The first standards employing digital technology were the pan-European GSM and the American TDMA. The new systems were based on digital transmission of signals (bits), eliminating noise in the transmission. Digital signals take up less bandwidth in the radio spectrum, allowing a given allotted channel range to carry more information – and as a result allowing more users on a system than the analogue technology. The digital standards also made it possible to transmit facsimile and computer files at far higher speeds and higher quality which opened up the prospects for these functions. The digital standards were, over a period of time, likely to replace the analogue standards, but as has been the case with the analogue technology, several different standards already existed within the digital technology. As a result, the global market was divided up into smaller segments according to which standards (both analogue and digital) prevailed in the regional markets.

Some drastic changes occurred in the industry along with the technological shift. In the initial stage of the digital era, development costs rose sharply, as the knowledge required to develop a handset in a digital standard was far greater than the same effort in the analogue field. Developing an analogue handset took roughly 10 man-years of engineering, while, initially, a model in the new digital standards required 150 man-years, or 15 times the amount of work, posing far larger requirements for the size of the development team. The development of software was becoming an activity of importance, as much of the functionality of handsets and networks would now depend on this component.

A notable difference between the digital and analogue technologies was an overall shift in the production process. While the analogue standards were relatively low in knowledge content, they were harder to mass produce. The digital standards required a lot of development, increasing fixed costs, but were better suited for mass production due to lower marginal costs. Moreover, the pace of development grew and the number of standards on the global market, as a whole, rose. As with the analogue standards, having developed models in one of the digital standards increased a company's knowledge base for entering the next generation of standards, creating a springboard effect. Another factor necessitating scale was the constant shortening of the model life spans. The PLC curve (Figure 1) can be viewed as an aggregate of the sales of all the cellular phone models on the market at a point in time. It is made up of the lifespan curves of the different models introduced over time.

The average market life of the various top models used to be over a year. In early 1994, a premium model marketed six months earlier was already moving into the discount segment, having been replaced by a more sophisticated version.

Many of the small national producers were hit hard by this change in the structural environment. At the time when these firms had managed to develop a digital model, the three large players were already promoting their second generation of terminals. Some of the small players disappeared, while others were bought out by rivals. Meanwhile, entrants were trying to acquire the competence to participate on the scene. A fierce battle was raging.

The market implications of the technological change

The large potential for economies of scale did not, however, result in a convergence of the many standards. The establishment of the standards had not been controlled by government intervention or voluntary international standards agreement, but rather resulted from innovations taking place in the individ-

Figure 1 PLC and model life

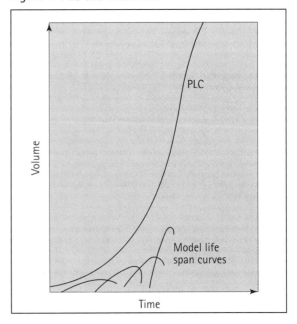

ual markets, and this was still the case as the digital standards emerged.

Europe now had two digital standards, the Group Speciale Mobile (GSM), promoted by the European Union (EU) countries, and the DCS 1800 which is explained below. The argument for implementing a pan-European digital standard was to promote the development of the European telecommunication industry and provide other industries with improved communication and information possibilities. As was the case with the NMT, the GSM was designed as an open standard in a collaborative effort between governments and industry – and could thus be adopted by any producer capable of developing the technology. The GSM was meant by the EU to replace the existing analogue standards and was supposed to reach 13 million subscribers by 1997, but the analogue systems were cash cows for the operators, so their life span was projected to reach somewhat beyond the turn of the millennium.

The GSM roaming agreements stretched across borders, allowing, for example, the use of the GSM standard to communicate to/from all EU countries, and several nations on the periphery, where a base-station was in reach. The vision of the GSM system was technical compatibility combined with roaming agreements to provide access within the system. A system could conceivably also encompass two standards, if dual standard terminals were made and roaming was agreed upon between the two subsystems. The GSM networks in other areas of the world can be said to have used the same standard, but made up separate systems of roaming. To have access to cellular communication, it was necessary to have both a handset and a service agreement. In most cellular phones, the service agreement was identified by an electronic code stored in the handset, which would identify the caller and give her access to the network. For the GSM standard, this caller ID was stored on an electronic card the size of a credit card, which was inserted in the handset in order to make it operable. Thus, the same phones could be used, but they required separate service agreements (SIM cards). GSM had already been adopted by 62 countries at the end of 1993. Another digital system, the Public Communication Network (PCN), came about due to the recognised problems of GSM capacity limitations in highly populated areas. PCNs, following the DCS-1800 standard, use a higher operating frequency than the GSM standard, and each connection takes up only half the bandwidth, thereby ensuring higher capacity. Each base station

covers an area of approximately 500 metre radius (or smaller). The capacity is greatly increased as each of the small cells is capable of carrying twice the connections of the larger one, while using only the same frequency width. Costs per connection were also expected to be much lower than for the larger radius systems, resulting over time in lower calling fees. Because of the shorter range required of the PCN terminals, battery time would increase significantly. In all, PCN was directed at the mass market, making quick reduction in unit costs possible, and thereby also lower prices. PCN systems were installed in the United Kingdom and Germany by the end of 1994.

In the United States, the FCC did not interfere in the implementation of the digital standards. The fight stood between the TDMA standard, which was largely provided by Swedish L.M. Ericsson, and the CDMA standard which was provided by Motorola. These two standards could exist side by side, but were not compatible. Implementation of digital standards in the United States was based upon a coexistence with the prevailing analogue standards (quite the opposite of the European strategy of replacing the analogue standards with the GSM system). PCN systems were also to be installed in the United States as a third digital standard.

The analogue standards were still profitable and had excess capacity, which, together with the voluntary choice of transition to digital standards, had set the pace of digital implementation to be slower than that in Europe. Critics argued that this delay would be problematic for the evolution of international standards, where some (perhaps inferior) technologies get a head start, and thereby hamper the introduction of superior technologies.

In Japan, the analogue systems were experiencing capacity overload, and implementation of a digital standard was expected in 1994. By that time, another two service providers had been licensed, but the licences given to those other than NTT were still only regional, therefore creating a poorly developed nationwide net for cellular services, with a low penetration rate as a result.

Market growth and expected changes in segments
The cellular phone market growth rates from 1991 to 1992 and 1992 to 1993 were 60 per cent and 50 per cent, respectively. The total number of subscribers amounted to 33 million by the end of 1993. Predictions on the total number of subscribers in the year 2000 range from 100 to 170 million, suggesting

high compounded annual growth rates (see Tables 1 to 3, and Figure 2).

Up to 1994, market predictions had been mostly understated. There was no doubt that the number of subscribers would rise sharply in the coming years, but the price level and thus the market size would be shaped by conditions about which there was great uncertainty. Aspects affecting growth were cost of the terminals, the pricing of air time, versatility of the product, ease of use, and coverage of the service agreements.

Nokia Mobile Phones forecast the increased importance of the consumer and mobile data market segment (Table 2). The level of product differentiation was not high, although special features were used to a certain degree, aiming to attract the higher-priced business segment.

Table 1 Number of cellular phone subscribers

	Millions of subscribers		
	End 1988	End 1992	End 1993
Europe[a]	1.5	6.0	8.3
United States	1.6	NA	15.0
Japan	0.4 [b]	0.9 [c]	1.7
Asia Pacific excluding Japan	NA	1.6	2.6
Latin America	NA	NA	1.1
Others	NA	NA	4.4
Total subscribers	4.1	22.1	33.1

[a] Including the European Economic Area and Switzerland.
[b] End 1989.
[c] Mid-1991.
Sources: *International Herald Tribune*, 27 April 1994; *Motorola Annual Report 1993*.

Figure 2 Estimates of cumulative cellular subscribers (millions)

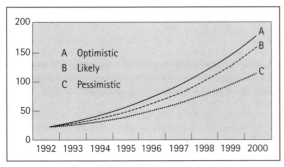

Table 2 Changes in segments (European market)

Segment	1994	1998
Consumers	15%	40%
Business	80%	45%
Mobile data	5%	15%

Source: Nokia Mobile Phones.

Table 3 Development in global unit sales of cellular handsets

Year	Unit sales
1992	8.7 million
1993	11.0 million
1997	32.3 million[a]
2001	53.0 million[a]

[a] Estimates.
Source: Nokia.

With investments made in the digital networks that had still not borne fruit, and a still low base of subscribers, operators deemed it necessary to boost sales in order to reach the degree of utilisation that would ensure returns on their investments. This was often done by subsidising the handsets when consumers signed up for service agreements. The retail promotions boosted demand from the operators to the producers. Ability to deliver was key to the operators so they pressured producers on delivery schedules rather than price.

The larger part of the sales derived from the United States and Europe, but other markets were rapidly starting to emerge. Eastern Europe and China and other Asian countries were starting to demand both infrastructure and handsets. Because of the economic growth in the regions, the demand for communications services was rising, and cellular technology was a cost-effective and speedy alternative to investing in a new fixed wire network.

NOKIA

Nokia started as a paper and pulp mill in 1865, where the first ground-wood mill was situated on the Nokia River in Finland.

In 1967, the company expanded by merging with large rubber and cable interests. Later on, through the 1970s and 1980s, Nokia added plastic, metal products, chemicals, and electronics to the group by acquisition. In 1994, Nokia consisted of five business groups: consumer electronics, telecommunications, cables

Table 4 Financial statistics of the Nokia Group: 1989–1993 (in $ millions)

Nokia Group	1993	1992	1991	1990	1989
Net sales	4,096	3,463	3,747	6,103	5,627
Costs and expenses	3,898	3,493	3,668	5,907	5,478
Earnings excluding tax, etc.	198	–30	79	196	149
Taxes/minorities, etc.	397	108	130	120	110
Net earnings	–199	–138	–51	76	39

Source: *Nokia Annual Report* 1993.

and machinery, mobile phones, and other operations (e.g. tyres), but had over a relatively short period changed its focus toward telecommunications (see Tables 4 and 5), where they ranked as the ninth largest telecommunications equipment vendor globally. Total assets of the Nokia group were $3.9 billion, with a debt to asset ratio of approximately 50 per cent.

NOKIA MOBILE PHONES

Nokia Mobile Phones represented 26 per cent of the group net sales, corresponding to $1.1 billion (see Figure 3). Research and development (R&D) expenditures were $50.3 million and $73.6 million in 1992 and 1993, respectively. The productivity within the cellular phone division increased dramatically after 1990, with an increase in sales per employee of 138 per cent.

The firm was shaped by vigorous rivalry because Finland has one of Europe's most innovative and competitive markets in telecommunications, with some 52 communications providers in 1991.

In the beginning of the 1980s, the Nokia group started producing analogue infrastructure and cellular phones for the NMT-450 standard. The small home market meant that Nokia had to export from day one in order to increase volume. Soon, the company was manufacturing to multiple standards and had thus acquired a wide base of knowledge and scale at an early stage.

The firm's main objective was to satisfy its customers, and this was used as the guiding principle on which all activities were focused. An objective was to acquire 25 per cent global market share in 1995 (see Table 6), emphasising expansion on all markets. The importance of not getting trapped producing low value-added commodity products, and remaining flexible in order to produce cellular phones to many different standards, and being able to market them, was emphasised. Priority was placed on design, consumer adaptation and user friendliness, including a focus on size and weight of the cellular phones.

The firm's strengths in fast development enabled them to be the first supplier of the GSM network in Europe and the first in the market with a commercial GSM portable phone. Furthermore, they delivered phones and network infrastructure to three of the world's four PCN systems. Nokia develops and markets all cellular infrastructure through Nokia Mobile Phones. In all, they had a broad, well-

Table 5 Nokia Group operating profit by segment, 1989–1993 (in $ millions)

Segment	1993	1992	1991	1990	1989
Telecommunications	170	81			
Mobile phones	164	83			
Consumer electronics	–129	–149			
Electronic groups total[a]	–	–	–56	144	57
Cables and machinery	45	22	24	106	100
Basic industries[b]	–	–	52	68	86
Other operations	3	18	–43	–19	–2
Nokia Group	253	55	–23	299	241

[a] 1992–1993 Nokia Tyres and Nokia Power are included in the group 'other Operations'.
[b] Nokia Data was included in electronic groups in 1989–1990.
Source: *Nokia Annual Report* 1993.

Figure 3 Sales of Nokia mobile phones (in millions of FIM)

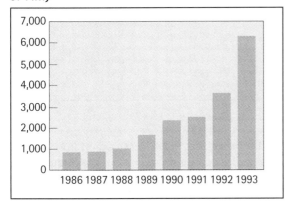

Source: *Nokia Annual Report* 1993.

Table 6 Market shares (and ranks) of incumbents of the cellular phone industry, 1988, 1992 and 1993

Market shares	May 1988	Feb 1992	End 1993
Motorola, Inc.	12.8% (2)	22.0% (1)	36.0% (1)
Nokia	13.4% (1)	13.0% (2)	20.0% (2)
L.M. Ericsson	3.9% (9)	NA	10.0% (3)
Panasonic	NA	NA	4.0% (4)

Market shares for NEC not available, but are very small.
Sources: Keinala, Severi: Finnish High-Tech Industries & European Integration, 1989; Nokia, Motorola and L.M. Ericsson.

developed knowledge base built upon the competence gained from the many offered standards. Even so, Nokia recognised the necessity of increasing the development effort to meet future challenges.

The product range included all major analogue and digital standards. They also had original equipment manufacturer (OEM) producer status for Philips, Hitachi, Swatch and AT&T. The agreement with AT&T was made in April 1994 and valued by Nokia at $170 million a year. Joint ventures with Japanese cellular companies like Mitsui and Kansai in developing digital cellular phones for the Japanese market has improved access to this market. Nokia's global market share rose when they acquired the British cellular producer Technophone Ltd in 1991.

Production facilities were situated in Finland, Germany, the United Kingdom, the United States, Hong Kong and Korea. Even though the main costs of producing a phone derived from the components and development, there were still cost advantages to assembling handsets in low-wage countries. The attractiveness of these locations was often augmented by the availability of government subsidised loans.

Nokia was not vertically integrated. Semiconductors were bought mainly from AT&T, supplying also the essential Digital Systems Processor. Components were also bought from Motorola. Nokia focused on designing the electronic components themselves, and outsourced the manufacturing to other companies. They manufactured both cellular infrastructure and handsets providing the ability to offer complete packages to operators, as well as technological spillovers.

Distribution channels to consumer markets were, however, not yet well established. Nokia, though, had a relative advantage because of their Consumer Electronics Division, which had experience promoting products to the consumer segment, and which had established access to distributions channels. Brand identification was becoming increasingly important, with the transition toward the mass market. The firm was still struggling with a low degree of recognition, but expected to intensify marketing efforts.

A study made on this subject revealed that consumers had positive opinions of Sony's cellular phone, even though it was not yet marketed – where it became clear that the major players in the cellular phone industry did not enjoy nearly the same degree of recognition among the consumers. Nokia was often thought of as a Japanese brand, which caused a problem due to still lingering negative images of Japanese producers, especially in the US market when up against an American firm. Nokia had furthermore formed numerous alliances and agreements with other firms such as Tandy Corporation in the United States in 1983, mainly to overcome some of the marketing hurdles. Nokia cellular telephones were sold under the names Nokia, Technophone, Mobira and, as mentioned, via numerous OEM deals. The terminals were sold through specialised stores, retail chains and operators. Nokia's market share in GSM phones was higher than in analogue phones. Sales in the United States increased 73 per cent in 1993, yielding a 19 per cent United States market share,[2] while European sales 'only' doubled. The growth in cellular subscribers was smaller in these two regions in 1993, meaning that Nokia gained overall market share. The number of potential users of the digital TDMA standard in the United States was increasing with positive implications for Nokia's prospects.

Nokia believed open communication to be indispensable for setting mutual targets, and each employee bore responsibility in this respect. Knowledge is a capacity only when it is shared. The development of products employed the Concurrent Engineering Process. This meant that, when designing new products, the product development, marketing, sourcing, and production departments co-operated closely as a team, making the developing process faster and more cost efficient, and cutting the product's time to market. Nokia's operations were based on decentralised structures and measured control. Fast change in the environment and technology brought opportunities which in turn provided the firm with the possibility to discover new abilities and resources within the organisation. The company consisted of young, flexible and cooperative employees, but the pressure on them was great, increasing the risk of organisational defects. They were, however, equipped with the strong fighting spirit expressed by the Finnish word Sisu.

NOKIA'S MAIN EXISTING AND POTENTIAL COMPETITORS

Motorola, Inc.

Motorola was founded in 1928 as Galvin Manufacturing Corporation and was the leading company in the cellular phone industry (see Table 6). Furthermore, it held a strong position in the field of cellular infrastructure, wireless communications, semiconductors, and advanced electronic systems and services. Of the turnover in 1993, 54 per cent was in wireless communications (including two-way radios, etc. Figures for cellular communications cannot be isolated. See Table 7). The total assets were $13.5 billion, with a debt to assets ratio of 56 per cent. They held a position as the third largest telecom equipment provider on a global scale.

Motorola focused on gaining market share, and set

a goal of obtaining more than 50 per cent of the global market for cellular terminals. Another important factor was the concept of constant renewal of technology and processes. Motorola stayed close to four closely coupled sectors including communications, components, computers, and control and constantly sought to create bridges between them. The company was characterised as a huge venture capital outfit, constantly spinning off technology and capital into new businesses. The R&D expenditures for the group were $1.5 billion in 1993. A prime example was Motorola's ambitious Iridium project, a low-orbit satellite system that was conceived with the objective of bringing wireless phone service to the world by 1998. By 1994, they had spent eight years and $100 million backing the Iridium system. However, some analysts were sceptical of Iridium's profitability, as the average connection price would be $3 per minute, and handsets would cost approximately $3,000. Motorola aimed at one million subscribers for this system by 2002, 2 per cent of the projected 200 million users of wireless telephony. The wireless connection charges in the United States were roughly one seventh of what Iridium intended to charge.

Motorola had a large home market, which was an advantage in the beginning when lag times between markets were still significant. Every time a new product was introduced, it could readily achieve higher volume in sales than companies in smaller countries. With rapid internationalisation, this advantage decreased in significance.

High competence at mass production was core to the strategy at Motorola. A quality programme called Six Sigma had been introduced and aimed at only three to four mistakes per million processes (not per million units produced). Motorola produced cellular infrastructure equipment and competed in all major analogue and digital standards and had delivered GSM infrastructure equipment to seven countries, and several US operators had ordered the Motorola-

Table 7 Key financial statistics for Motorola, 1989–1993 (in $ millions)

Motorola, Inc.	1993	1992	1991	1990	1989
Net sales	16,963	13,303	11,341	10,855	9,620
Costs and expenses	14,438	12,503	10,728	10,219	8,974
Earnings before tax	1,525	800	613	666	646
Income taxes	503	224	159	167	148
Net earnings	1,022	453	454	499	498

Source: *Motorola Annual Report* 1993.

developed CDMA digital standard infrastructure. The company also produced the digital systems processor (DSP), crucial to the digital standard terminal, in contrast to other major cellular phone producers who had to obtain this component from suppliers. Moreover, the company held fundamental patents required for the GSM standard, but was not able to deliver the complete range of infrastructure for the GSM system due to a lack of the very sophisticated switching technology needed for the roaming function.[3] The takeover of the Danish company Storno in the early 1990s was a step to gain more know-how in this area.

Motorola had a wide distribution network covering most of the world. Its phones were sold through operators, mass merchants, specialty retailers, direct sales, and as original options on cars. The marketing activities stretched over more than 80 countries either under the Motorola name or as parts of OEM agreements with companies such as Bosch and Pioneer. Motorola lacked experience in consumer marketing and focused mainly on production and market shares.

Motorola opted for a policy of decentralisation. Organisational boundaries were broken down, and cooperation between personnel and management was promoted. The result was an atmosphere of informality, where people contacted each other across the former boundaries, creating flexibility and a better flow of information. This resulted in an increase in productivity (sales per employee) of 126 per cent between 1986 and 1993.

L.M. Ericsson

L.M. Ericsson was founded in 1876 as a producer of wire-based network equipment. The company, with assets of $8.1 billion, manufactured equipment for both wired and mobile communication and also produced advanced electronic defence systems (see Table 8 for key financials). Ericsson was positioned as number five on the ranking of global telecommunications providers.

Net sales of cellular telephones was $325 million[4] in 1992, and increased 2.5 times in 1993. Within cellular communications the company controlled a leading 40 per cent of the world market for traditional analogue cellular infrastructure, and had been able to acquire 60 per cent of the surging market for digital cellular infrastructure equipment.

The objective of L.M. Ericsson was to keep its strong position in the cellular business, and to gain a part of the expected future growth in the industry, especially within infrastructure equipment, and an important factor in realising these goals was product development, a cornerstone at Ericsson. Concurrent Engineering was an important feature in achieving an effectively short cycle from a product's initial development stage to the market launch. The importance of R&D was emphasised by its budget of $1.3 billion in 1993.

The firm produced semiconductors and also had suppliers such as General Electric and Analogue Devices from which the crucial Digital Systems Processor was acquired. Ericsson focused on small production batches, having traditions in ordinary telecommunications and phones. On the cellular side, they concentrated on minor batches of advanced units.

The home market of Ericsson was rather small, necessitating exports in order to get volume in sales. This forced the company to be internationally oriented at an early stage, and it already had an integrated distribution network around the world due to sales of ordinary telecommunication equipment. Ericsson was also into several partnerships around the world, such as with Alcatel and NEC and with Nokia in China. Heavy spending on advertising in foreign markets provided the firm with a degree of brand recognition in most markets.

At Ericsson, human capabilities took on a central role. Motivation of employees through personal responsibility, and a high degree of freedom at work

Table 8 Key financial statistics for L.M. Ericsson, 1989–1993 (in $ millions)

L.M. Ericsson	1993	1992	1991	1990	1989
Net sales	7,630	6,770	8,395	7,702	6,130
Costs and expenses	7,207	6,492	8,019	6,883	5,424
Earnings before tax	423	278	376	818	576
Tax/minorities	82	210	216	NA	NA
Net earnings	341	68	160	NA	NA

Source: *Ericsson Annual Report* 1993–1994.

combined with cooperation and also a degree of independence, explained some of the success of the project-oriented organisation.

The Japanese competitors

Japan had about 20 companies selling cellular phones in 1991.[5] Some had their own production, of which Matsushita (using the brand name Panasonic) and NEC were the only ones with significant sales of cellular phones outside Japan, though they were still operating at a rather small scale compared to Motorola, Nokia and Ericsson (see Table 6). Others had signed OEM agreements with major producers outside Japan such as Motorola and Nokia. The best known in this category were Sony, Pioneer and Hitachi.

The Japanese were trying to establish themselves in the fast-growing cellular phone market. They were attracted by the high future potential in the consumer segment, especially because of the high knowledge they possessed in this area due to their consumer electronics. They were regarded as having an advantage in this area.

The Japanese home market was large, providing potential for high volume. The consumer electronics market, however, was usually characterised by being protected by import restrictions with fierce competition raging between a large number of national companies. These companies had access to low-cost capital, due to the favourable financial environment created by the culture, encompassing longer perspectives, higher savings, and high degrees of intercorporate lending. The Japanese share owners were traditionally less focused on high and immediate returns.

The Japanese generally had competence in large-scale, low-priced, high-quality production, and a comprehensive distribution network all over the world, which they coupled with strong brand names. This was particularly exhibited by their position on the consumer electronics market. However, the speed of development and the many existing cellular standards did not favour the use of reverse engineering, which was a commonly used method of development.

By 1994, Matsushita had not yet launched a globally competitive cellular terminal for the digital systems. With the industry environment current at that time, the Japanese had some difficulty entering the scene. The companies also lacked knowledge in cellular infrastructure.

FUTURE EXPECTATIONS IN THE INDUSTRY

In 1994, the industry was in turbulence, but this was expected to calm down with product standardisation. A prediction of when this would happen and which standard would become dominant was not possible due to the many possibilities of further systems' innovations.

Development could also slow down within certain standards as technologies stabilised, as was predicted to happen with the GSM not far beyond 1994. This has provided firms like the Korean company Maxon with an opportunity to enter the field. Maxon planned to produce low-price GSM phones to be marketed in Europe and other regions employing the GSM standard. In 1994, the highly innovative firms still had an edge over late entrants, in handset technology and in their ability to cover multiple standards. Two tendencies were predicted: short-term high innovation and turbulence, and medium-term maturity.

The major future objective of Nokia was to protect and expand their position. This required awareness of changes in the environment and a continuous accumulation of resources and capabilities inside the organisation in order to establish the capacity needed to cope with the expected growth in the cellular phone market.

APPENDIX:
How does cellular communication work?

An illustrative example is used to explain the functioning of the cellular technology.

Discerning between the terms system and standard is important in order to comprehend the different solutions to cellular communications offered on the market. A system, in the context of this case, is understood to be the network within which a personal service agreement and terminal can be used. This, in other words, is defined by the extent of the existing roaming (see below) agreements and whether the same terminal is compatible with the whole system. A standard defines the specific technology used for the contact to take place. In order for a terminal to be used, it must be compatible in standard and the user must have a service agreement with an operator within the system.

A person moving down the highway dials a number on a cellular handset. The handset sends a signal, with a range of 10 to 30 km, that is received by a base station (Tower), as shown by A in Figure 4. The base station has to use the same technological standard as

Figure 4 Cellular communications, illustrated

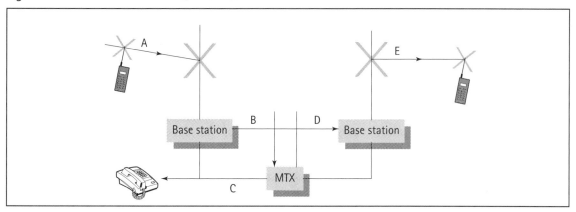

the phone does. The base station with the best contact to the cellular phone is chosen by the network and the signal passes through the public fixed wire network to the MTX (Mobile Telephone Exchange, [B]). The MTX is the brain in the system, constantly keeping track of the cellular phone on stand-by, in order to track its position. The MTX sends the signal back through the fixed public network, which, if the call is to a stationary phone, connects the call to the dialled number (C in Figure 4). If the dialled number is to another cellular telephone, the MTX locates the other terminal (the MTX tracks this, if the terminal is on standby and within range of a base station) and sends the signal to the base station – through the fixed network (D) – closest to the receiving terminal, and final contact is made (E). The second cellular phone does not have to be covered by the same service provider as the one calling. If the two service providers are different, the MTX of the first service provider will simply connect through the fixed network to the MTX of the second.

The people using cellular phones are often moving from one area (cell) to another during a conversation. The MTX ensures that seamless contact is sustained by switching the transmission from one base station to another; this is referred to as the hand-off function. The MTX will typically serve the base stations in one area. As the user moves into another area, her conversation is 'handed off' to the MTX serving that area and this capability is referred to as roaming, and provides the user with a wider area of use for her terminal.

The question of channel allocation and terminal identification also needs to be addressed. The telephone calling is registered through a signal with an access code, in order to bill the calling fee to the owner. The cellular system is closed, meaning that a terminal will not be recognised and serviced without the access code. Each operator is licensed to use a portion of the frequency band allocated for the total system/standard in a given area. This frequency portion is able to carry a certain number of simultaneous contacts. The frequency used for transmission is chosen individually for each separate call by the MTX. Each base station can utilise the whole allocated frequency band. The MTX only has to ensure that adjacent towers do not transmit two separate contacts using the same frequency, as this would cause interference between the signals.

As the systems work now, the interconnect problem, using the public fixed-wire lines, affects the prices charged by the operators. The national monopolies can use discriminatory pricing on the connections used by the external cellular operators. To overcome this problem, there are examples of operators that intend to use parabolic antennae between the base stations, in order to avoid using the fixed-wire network (at least when the contact is cellular to cellular).

Notes
1. *Motorola Annual Report*, 1993.
2. Bibliographic citation, HFD, 10 February 1992 and the *Wall Street Journal* Europe, 27 April 1994.
3. *Business Week*, 4 December 1993.
4. *Business Week*, 4 December 1993.
5. *The Economist*, 13 April 1991, pp. 62–69.

This case was prepared by Professor Steve Burgess of The School of Economic and Business Studies at the University of the Witwatersrand as the basis for class discussion rather than to illustrate either effective or ineffective handling of an administrative situation.

BASF in China: the marketing of Styropor

The news, when it came, was not a complete surprise. In early 1998 the largest customer in China for BASF's imported expanded polystyrene (EPS) packaging material decided to switch to a local producer who could deliver more quickly and cheaply. Christian Fischer, styrenics department manager of BASF China in Hong Kong, and Alice Wong, marketing manager of the department, needed urgently to overcome a fundamental problem: how to differentiate their product in what was essentially a commodity market suffering from significant oversupply. The over-supply of packaging grade (P-grade) EPS had become apparent in 1997, and would become much worse by the year 2000.

BASF itself would open an EPS production facility in Nanjing in October 1998. The imported P-grade product it had been selling so far was especially suited to high-speed vacuum moulding machines and therefore carried a premium price. BASF was the clear market leader in this segment. The problem was that most of the moulders in China transforming EPS into packaging material for consumer goods were still using manual or automatic machines, which did not need to use high performance material like BASF's. Could BASF serve this less sophisticated, but much larger, market without compromising the positioning of its EPS as a premium product?

BASF's plant in Nanjing would also supply flame retardant (F-grade) EPS for insulation use in the construction industry. The future of this product in China was equally uncertain. In 1998 the construction industry in China was only a small user of this material. The BASF product offered premium value in a market where cheaper alternatives were available. How could BASF position its EPS as the product of choice in the construction industry?

BASF IN CHINA

The BASF Group, headquartered in Ludwigshafen, Germany, had sales of DM55.8 billion (approximately US$ 31 billion) in 1997, and profits before tax of DM5.3 billion (Tables 1 and 2). Its products ranged from natural gas, oil and basic chemicals, through intermediate chemicals, to specialities, high value-added chemicals, crop protection products and pharmaceuticals. The core businesses were divided into five segments (Table 3 and Figure 1). BASF's long term strategy was based on the Verbund, or integrated petrochemical site linking production, research and logistics. The Ludwigshafen Verbund was the world's largest chemical complex; BASF had other Verbunds in Belgium, Spain and North and South America, and three more were planned or under construction in Asia (in Kuantan, Malaysia; Mangalore, India; and Nanjing, China). Existing smaller operations all over Asia plus the three new large projects made BASF one of the largest Western investors in the region. The Asian crisis which erupted in July 1997 did not seem to have a negative impact an BASF's expansion plans.

BASF net sales in the Asia Pacific region in 1997 amounted to DM5.2 billion, 9 per cent of the group's total sales. About 30 per cent of the products sold there were produced locally. BASF planned to raise that share to 70 per cent by 2010, and to double its market share. In China 1997 sales were DM1.1 billion, of which approximately 10 per cent was contributed by products from local BASF joint ventures. Sales and the share from local production in China were expected to grow rapidly as new operations came on stream. BASF's interests in China had expanded rapidly during the 1990s. As well as a Hong Kong company, which had responsibility for the marketing, sales and distribution in China of imported products produced by the company's plants around the world, by 1998 it boasted five representative offices (in Beijing, Shanghai, Guangzhou, Nanjing and Dalian), a holding company in Beijing with branch offices in Shanghai and Guangzhou, and ten joint ventures (Table 4). By far the largest capital expenditure plan, still under negotiation in 1998 and worth some DM5 billion, related to the joint construction of the Verbund in Nanjing with Yangzi Petrochemical and Sinochem. The centrepiece of this plant was a steam-cracker to provide backward integration for many of BASF's China manufacturing activities.

BASF already had a relationship with Yangzi Petrochemical, via a joint venture in Nanjing formed in 1994 called Yangzi BASF Styrenics (YBS). It was 60 per cent owned by BASF. This plant began producing ethylbenzene, styrene and polystyrene in late 1997. The EPS facility which Fischer and Wong expected to come on stream in October 1998 would be part of the YBS joint venture.

Sales of EPS handled in the BASF China office in 1997 totalled HK$280 million (about US$36 million).

STYROPOR®: BASF'S EXPANDABLE POLYSTYRENE

Expanded polystyrene foam is the familiar white, lightweight foam used for example as a shock-absorber and to hold a home appliance in place in its cardboard delivery carton. The packaging industry world-wide is one of the two major users of EPS. The other is the construction industry, which uses it as insulation material against cold and heat.

EPS was invented by BASF engineers in 1950, patented by the company, and trademarked with the name Styropor. By the 1980s the production process was no longer under patent, and EPS was produced by several, mainly European, petrochemical groups. BASF remained the world leader in EPS, and its Styropor boasted a 25 per cent global market share. BASF produces EPS, the raw material from which moulders produce in two steps EPS foam products via EPS foam beads.

To manufacture EPS styrene monomer is polymerised into polystyrene in the presence of finely dispersed pentane gas. Special grades of EPS beads for various fields of application are produced by altering formulations and adding treatment processes. An alternative low-technology process involves adding pentane gas directly to purchased polystyrene. This is the method used by countless backstreet garage operations in developing countries across the world. Moulding companies buy the EPS beads from either source and physically expand them in a two-step process (a bit like making popcorn). In a first step they expand the EPS with steam to produce prefoamed beads. In a second step the prefoamed beads are put into a confined space in a mould where they fuse together into the shapes required by the end-users. The end-users may be home appliance and computer manufacturers or construction companies.

Styropor, like other packaging and construction materials, is combustible. F-grade Styropor, therefore, is treated with a special flame retardant agent to reduce its flammability and the spread of flames. This is what distinguishes construction-use F-grade EPS from the P-grade material generally used by the packaging industry.

THE EPS MARKET IN CHINA

During the mid-1980s the market for EPS in China totalled just 20,000 metric tons (mt) per annum, for packaging use only. BASF was the market leader with a share of 60–70 per cent, the remainder being delivered by Japanese producers. BASF supplied the EPS in drums with a six-month shelf life since it took three months to ship the product from Germany to China.

In 1988 Taiwanese firms began supplying the China market. Although the Taiwanese product was of lower quality, the paper bags it came in were cheaper than the corrugated drums supplied by BASF. On the other hand EPS packed in bags had a guaranteed shelf life of one month only, compared with six months for the drums. At the end of the 1980s BASF came under pressure in Europe to demonstrate the environmental acceptability of EPS – which it did successfully. In China, EPS moulders were not prepared to pay a premium for an environmentally sound product, although their customers were quick enough to demand from BASF documentation proving the recyclability of EPS if they were exporting consumer durables from China.

By 1992 Taiwanese quality had risen sufficiently to challenge BASF's Styropor business; four years later, the Taiwanese company Honest had become the market leader in China.

In 1997 the packaging industry represented 80 per cent of total Chinese EPS demand and the construction industry 20 per cent, the reverse of demand patterns found in Europe.

Market demand from both industries for EPS that year totalled approximately 200,000 mt, after growth averaging 12 per cent per annum between 1990 and 1996. Wong and Fischer believed that demand would be significantly slower in the period 1998–2000 as the economy slowed in the wake of the Asian financial crisis suggested, and would average 7 per cent per annum between 2000 and 2005. Within this 7 per cent average, construction industry demand would grow by a faster 10 per cent as the market developed compared with 6.5 per cent for the packaging industry, which was roughly in line with GDP growth.

Industrial growth was higher than total GDP growth, but Wong's market intelligence indicated that packaging growth would not match it because of the substitution of EPS by other packaging materials, particularly for small items, and attempts by multinational firms to reduce the weight of packaging they used. One Western multinational in China, for example, expected to use 1 kg of moulded EPS to protect the new model of its product compared with the 2.5 kg required for the previous model. EPS producers were also likely to come under attack from producers of alternative packaging materials, such as paper, who would claim their material was more environmentally friendly. Fischer and Wong knew that EPS had been shown in Europe to be 100 per cent recyclable and to use fewer chemicals than paper. In China consumer education on such issues was not yet well developed.

Wong could see from the database of moulders that her team had built over the previous two years which areas of China had the strongest demand for EPS, and drawn conclusions about future patterns of demand. She estimated that there were about 350 moulders for the packaging industry and 100 for construction use, many of which were very small. Although her database did not include every moulder in the country, she was confident that she could gauge fairly accurately the entire market size. The market was transparent, so new EPS suppliers to the moulders did not remain unnoticed for long.

She could see that the major consumption areas for P-grade packaging were in Guangdong, particularly around the Pearl River delta which was the base for many export-oriented manufacturers (mostly Hong Kong and Taiwanese transplants), as well as in Jiangsu Province and Shanghai. These southern and eastern areas of China were likely to continue to drive demand for packaging materials.

In contrast, demand for the insulating properties of F-grade EPS would be greatest in northern China, followed by eastern China. Wong forecast 13 per cent growth for construction-use EPS in northern China between 2000 and 2005, but from a much lower base than P-grade.

THE PACKAGING INDUSTRY: P-GRADE EPS

Moulders in the packaging industry were segmented according to the type of machine they used to process EPS. By far the largest segment, occupying three-fifths of production capacity in 1997, was occupied by manual machines which were Chinese-made and operated at slow speeds. Labour costs in China were low and many moulders did not worry how much time it took to produce orders. Automatic machines were faster than the hand-operated machinery, and occupied 15 per cent of the market.

Vacuum machines, which occupied the remaining one-quarter of the market, were the most sophisticated. This was the segment targeted by BASF products since all European and North American moulders used these machines. Vacuum machines required high quality EPS beads to operate with maximum efficiency and at fast cycle times, thereby saving on energy and steam costs. One vacuum machine could produce 20 times the volume of EPS packaging produced by a manual machine.

Most of the vacuum moulders were Hong Kong transplants based in Guangdong. Only a few packaging plants in Eastern China used vacuum machines, although that was changing as more joint ventures between Chinese and multinational companies came on stream in the Shanghai area. In the north hardly any packaging firms used vacuum moulding machines. The Hong Kong market 15 years ago had also been heavily dependent on manual machines, but the majority of moulders there had switched to vacuum machines within five years. Fischer and Wong expected mainland Chinese moulders to upgrade their equipment too, but at a slower pace because of the rather poor financial situation of Chinese companies and a general slowdown in foreign investment in China. There was likely to be a lengthy transition phase as manual moulders graduated first to automatic machines.

BASF's Styropor was the market leader in China for this premium vacuum machine segment, with a 50 per cent share. It sold very little to the automatic and manual moulders. In the vacuum segment BASF was competing with Korean imports, as well as the Taiwanese company Honest and the Arco joint venture, Jinling, both of which produced EPS in China.

The product supplied by BASF to the packaging moulders was imported from its wholly owned Styropor facilities in Malaysia. It took up to 30 days for delivery, from the moment the letter of credit was opened. Transplant factories in Guangdong were prepared to wait because they recognised the advantages of the BASF product: superior fusion rates, pre-expansion and density; stable quality of the product; and fast cycle times leading to energy and investment cost savings. Since the Guangdong transplants were processing for the export market these moulders did not pay import duties. Non-export oriented moulders, on the other hand, had to pay import duties of 16 per cent which made the price of Styropor unattractive compared to local producers' EPS. Transportation costs from Malaysia also made it uncompetitive for Wong and her team to sell imported P-grade Styropor to moulders in North and East China.

Relatively few automatic machinery moulders were prepared to pay premium prices for BASF's product. Only those who were particularly skilful at operating their machines at fast cycle times and within narrow processing parameters could justify the higher price. It was hard to argue to state-owned companies, which in any case did not pay market prices for electricity, that BASF's product was cheaper in the long run.

'Only modern-minded Chinese moulders will believe the potential savings an energy and steam, so we have to look for these customers', explained Andy Lu, who until recently had been sales manager for China. There was no point at all in manual moulders using the BASF product. Economic conditions also had a role to play. If the moulders were not operating at full capacity, they were not interested in the fast cycle times of BASF's high performance product. Even vacuum moulders would then buy cheaper EPS beads from somewhere else and run their machines at a slower pace.

It was clear that in the packaging sector BASF's imported Styropor was confined to a limited segment: vacuum moulders based in southern China. 'We have a Ferrari product', commented Fischer, 'which makes it difficult for us to penetrate the lower segments.'

PRODUCTION CAPACITY

In October 1998 BASF was scheduled to begin producing P-grade EPS at its Yangzi-BASF Styrenics (YBS) joint venture in Nanjing, but it had become clear 18 months earlier that the China market was suffering from severe over-capacity.

Local capacity exceeded local demand of approximately 200,000 mt in 1997. However, 90,000 mt of P-grade EPS were imported into China by BASF and some Taiwanese and Korean firms. This meant that capacity utilisation at local plants was below 50 per cent. 'Importing EPS could be very difficult during the next few years', remarked Edmond Tam, division manager for plastics.

In addition to the 40,000 mt capacity of YBS, other companies were planning to start local production or expand capacity. Based on announced investment projects, Wong estimated that local production would outstrip demand by 50–70 per cent in the year 2000, no matter what the volume of imports might be. She was also keenly aware of regional over-capacities. Annual production capacity in Taiwan was over 200,000 mt, yet domestic demand was less than 40,000 mt. Korean firms were also exporting to China.

In China the largest producer of EPS beads was the Taiwanese company, Honest. It had begun local production in 1995 and by 1998 had two plants with a combined annual capacity of 100,000 mt. This made it the market leader in China. Honest's product was suitable for more or less all types of machine. Since 1997 it had begun to attack the vacuum segment. When BASF decided in 1995 to invest in an EPS plant

in China, no-one had spotted the potential threat from the Taiwanese firm. The price of Honest's locally produced EPS was 1200 RMB, or 20 per cent below that of BASF's Malaysian imports. Honest had managed to capture BASF's largest customer, which had bought additional vacuum machines, but was not using them at full capacity, reducing BASF's fast cycle advantage.

Other local producers included Xinghua (60,000 mt capacity), Pacific Ocean (30,000 mt), Mingda (another Taiwanese firm, 40,000 mt), Jiangmie (20,000 mt), and a mass of smaller facilities. All these firms were selling to the manual machine moulders. Xinghua dominated the manual segment in East China. Arco was reported to be expanding production at its Jinling joint venture by 28,000 mt in 1999. Except for Mingda and Pacific Ocean, which were in Guangdong, all other producers including BASF were located around Shanghai and Nanjing in East China. BASF justified its location in Nanjing because of the cost advantages from the plant's integration into the petrochemical complex.

There was no doubt that some of these EPS suppliers in China would not survive.

STRATEGY AT THE YBS STYROPOR FACILITY

It was obvious that due to the market situation in China the traditional products of BASF would not fit. Therefore BASF decided to design a completely new product for the Chinese market. The formerly imported Styropor from Malaysia provided good fusion and fast cycle times. The new product offered a shinier white surface after moulding, improved fusion as well as a wider and less sensitive processing window. Until now German engineers had concentrated only on the technological merits of the products.

High capacity utilisation was important to produce consistent quality. Styropor's current positioning in the China market was in the high margin vacuum segment, whose total demand was 40,000 mt in 1997. The YBS plant, though, had capacity of 40,000 mt. To obtain the necessary scale effect at YBS, BASF planned to manufacture EPS beads to different quality standards for positioning in the other market segments. They would be priced lower than YBS's premium product but above the price of competitors' EPS.

Wong and her team hoped to create a pull effect for their product by approaching the end-users of EPS packaging in China – companies like Sony and Philips – to convince them that they should specify use of

Styropor to their moulders because of its superior attributes. At the same time she had to be careful not to cannibalise the market for the Malaysian-produced imports, which would upset BASF's regional production and marketing strategy. BASF China was to continue to source some P-grade EPS from Malaysia to service certain Hong Kong transplants. Other transplants and all the local moulders would be served by the Nanjing site.

THE CONSTRUCTION INDUSTRY: F-GRADE EPS

Fischer and Wong believed that China's economy would remain export-oriented for a long time, so the construction industry in China would not dominate demand for EPS as it did in Western countries. However they did believe that prospects in China for flame-retardant EPS were positive as long as the merits of its use as insulating material were promoted in the right places: at the Ministry of Construction in Beijing, at architectural design institutes, among property developers, and among the construction companies themselves. New floor space, which according to government data was around 130 million sq. metres each year, was one way of estimating the potential demand for insulation material. Usage of EPS as insulation material in 1997 was less than 100 g per capita of urban population. In Korea, which had a similar climate to that of Beijing, per capita consumption was 3 kg. Insulation against cold was an easier concept to promote than insulation from heat, so BASF would concentrate an the northern provinces first.

The Chinese government was now paying attention to energy and investment costs and to environmental issues. A 1998 law required all new buildings in the year 2000 to achieve energy savings of 50 per cent compared with 1986 energy requirements. The construction industry was preparing building regulations determining insulation standards. China was also embarking on a new affordable residential housing policy to cope with the shift towards private house ownership. EPS boards were not the only insulating material on the market, though. Rockwool was an alternative and there were plenty of other less expensive possibilities around, including breeze blocks and simple cavity walls.

In 1997 Fischer brought experts from Germany to explain the advantages of F-grade EPS at a series of seminars for architects and government officials in cities around China. BASF China also developed and distributed a booklet explaining the various applications of EPS in floors, walls and ceilings. The EPS Association liked the booklet so much that it began copying and selling it to construction companies. BASF's efforts to transfer knowledge benefited all suppliers of F-grade EPS. A civil engineer in the Beijing representative office, Jason Guan, had the specific brief to develop F-grade EPS demand by offering solutions, not just products, to customers. As Guan pointed out, however, 'It is difficult to make customers in China realise that they should pay for this type of service.'

In 1998 BASF was the only significant importer of F-grade EPS, which it brought from a wholly owned factory in Korea. Other firms had abandoned the China market in favour of North America, where demand was more developed. It was hard for importers to compete against Chinese-made products. BASF's position had been rather comfortable until 1995, but the entry of domestic producers was beginning to erode its market share which had fallen to 21 per cent. Local F-grade producers included Huada in Shandong Province, Pacific Ocean, and Shanghai Dong Bei. Honest had launched an F-grade product in March 1998.

The F-grade EPS market was suffering from short-term over-supply, principally because demand was so under-developed. Many construction companies used packaging-grade EPS for insulation despite the risks of using non-flame retardant material, and in East China some F-grade material was used for packaging. The issue for Fischer and Wong was how to differentiate BASF's F-grade beads to the moulders and influence the construction companies to specify Styropor as the insulation material of choice.

LOCAL PRODUCTION

BASF originally intended to continue to supply F-grade Styropor from Korea, but falling prices because of local Chinese production had cut margins and market share was being lost. Traders did not want to hold stock or distribute the product in China for BASF because of price erosion between the time they placed orders and delivery in North China 35 days later.

Production at the YBS joint venture in Nanjing could be adjusted relatively easily between P-grade and F-grade EPS. The plant would begin making only P-grade Styropor and would later add F-grade. Capacity at the plant could also be ramped up easily and cheaply from the original 40,000 mt to 50–60,000 mt.

This additional production was likely to be F-grade material. What was not clear was whether, given the efforts BASF China was making to develop demand in the construction industry, this supply would be sufficient to build the BASF brand name and maintain market share. Once local production of F-grade began, imports from the Korean plant to North and East China would cease.

As with the P-grade material, BASF did not sell its F-grade Styropor directly to the end-users, in this case the construction companies, but to the intermediate users, the moulders, who moulded the beads into boards or blocks of insulation material. Very few moulders served both the construction industry and the packaging industry. Many F-grade moulders were small and situated close to their markets because of the difficulty of transporting bulky insulation boards over large distances. Wong could see some possibility of continuing a little imported F-grade business in South China, since the product was brought into ports there, but demand generally in the south was low: apart from one customer requiring 500 mt of F-grade per year, the market was too fragmented to be served other than by traders. The country's largest F-grade moulder, purchasing 2,000 mt per year, was based in Tianjin.

BASF also had to watch the producers of competing insulation materials. Owen Coming was already manufacturing rockwool at several sites in China and was building an XPS plant in Nanjing. XPS was a highly impact-resistant form of expanded polystyrene especially suitable for roofs but in general it was too expensive for walls (thus significantly reducing potential market demand). BASF no longer imported its XPS, called Styrodur©, from Germany and had also given up the idea of producing locally. The price of an XPS board was five times that of an EPS board, market potential was limited, and the most suitable place to build would have been in northern China which was too far from its source of raw materials, the BASF operations in Nanjing.

ENERSAVE

The Enersave agreement was one way for BASF to differentiate itself from other F-grade producers. Enersave was an American firm with a patented insulation system for external walls. A property developer specifying the Enersave system would require the construction company to procure and install flame retardant EPS boards on site, which Enersave engineers would then spray with a special coating material. Enersave guaranteed the system only if approved quality EPS boards – the one crucial part of the insulation it did not make – were used by the construction company.

Enersave had formed a joint venture in China to manufacture and apply the coating but, owing to concerns over the quality of locally-produced F-grade EPS, it appointed BASF as its exclusive supplier in China. BASF China would select and approve a certain number of F-grade moulders to make the boards using Styropor, and would provide a testing service an the output to guard against counterfeiting. The Enersave and BASF names would be printed by the moulder on the boards, allowing easy on-site visual verification by engineers prior to the application of the coating material. BASF also added an invisible chemical tracer to the EPS beads to allow laboratory analysis of the material supplied to the construction company.

Enersave expected to be named in the construction industry's regulations as an approved supplier of insulation systems. In 1998, the first year of operation, its systems were forecast to demand 800 mt of F-grade EPS, rising to perhaps 2000 mt in the year 2000. Enersave and BASF were together successful in convincing the Ministry of Construction to approve this system in China and promote it by their own magazines for architects and construction companies. BASF needed to appoint approved moulders in all the large cities, especially in North China. In the interests of competition and to create sufficient capacity, Fischer decided to select two moulders in each locality. He also expected to make similar exclusive supplier arrangements with other multinationals in the construction insulation business, as this appeared to be a promising method of expanding the market as well as raising BASF's share.

For the moulders, the Enersave-related business could be an interesting opportunity. A typical Enersave site might require 50 mt of EPS board, equivalent to perhaps half the moulder's normal annual production. Margins on the Enersave board would also be slightly better than for regular F-grade board. BASF hoped to expand the volume of EPS beads it supplied to each appointed moulder above the amount required for the Enersave business. Fischer was considering how else he could tie in the moulders to BASF's F-grade business.

DISTRIBUTION

For both P-grade and F-grade Styropor, distribution was an issue BASF needed to resolve in the short term.

BASF China could bring imported materials only as far as the border, since the law required a Chinese import company to bring the product into the country and distribute it or pass it on to a trader or distributor. When YBS production began in October 1998 the joint venture would be able to handle sales of its output directly, eliminating the need for import company relationships. This in turn meant that BASF China would have greater direct contact with the moulders, and eventually their customers.

In 1997 BASF China had eight key accounts for EPS which represented around 70 per cent of sales. These accounts had to be defended and new ones developed, especially in East China where so far it had only target accounts, i.e. moulders which were attractive in terms of size, value orientation and growth, and where BASF's position in terms of market share needed development. A moulder with demand for 500 mt per year was a medium-sized account for BASF China. Fischer and Wong wanted their staff to service such accounts directly, although in some instances a distributor would continue to handle the business. There could be a longstanding relationship between the moulder and the distributor, for example, or the financial standing of the moulder was doubtful so it was better for BASF China to share the risk with the distributor.

Local production would allow BASF to keep distribution points at key locations in North and South China well supplied, and although traders would be involved in the physical handling of the product BASF China staff could promote the product from the distribution points. There could even be a case for establishing distribution points next to major customers, to permit just-in-time delivery. YBS would handle distribution in East China. In North China Fischer was contemplating appointing a dedicated distributor who would set up a full distribution facility and work with regional traders to cover areas BASF China staff could not reach. Business in Beijing and Tianjin, the major areas of demand for F-grade, would be handled directly by BASF China.

This was the position in August 1998, a few weeks before local Styropor production was due to start. Over-capacity was the big threat. 'Our biggest challenge now is to get others out of business. Local producers are killing each other at the moment. We were not hurt so badly even though it was difficult to import. But as an importer we cannot influence the development of the market, so we have no choice but to produce locally. The more we sell, the more profitable we can be. We have to find ways to penetrate the market better, for P-grade and for F-grade, and we have to do it without destroying our premium position. This is our big challenge', reflected Fischer.

Table 1 BASF Group – recent sales and earnings data (in DM millions)

	1992	1993	1994	1995	1996	1997
Sales	41,933	40,568	43,674	46,229	48,776	55,780
Income from operation	1,311	1,032	2,149	4,023	4,293	5,342
Profit before taxes	1,239	1,058	2,111	4,128	4,414	5,331
Net income	613	761	1,170	2,423	2,839	3,205
Employees at year end	123,254	112,020	106,266	106,565	105,589	104,979
Net income per share (DM)*	10.8	14.9	21.5	40.5	4.54	5.22
Cash flow per share (DM)*	78	80	93	104	11.07	11.85
Return on sales before Tax & interest expense (%)	4.3	3.8	6.0	9.9	10.0	10.4
Return on assets before Tax & interest expense (%)	4.7	3.9	6.5	11.2	11.4	12.6
Return on equity After taxes (%)	4.2	5.2	7.6	14.3	14.8	14.6

*From 1996, based on shares with a nominal value of DM5
Source: Annual Reports.

Table 2 Net sales by region 1997

	Sales (DM million)	Year-on-year growth (%)
Europe	34,112	10.6
(Germany	14,380	10.9)
NAFTA	11,668	22.2
Asia, Pacific, Africa	6,722	17.8
South America	3,278	21.8

Source: *BASF Facts and Figures* – Charts 1998

Table 3 BASF core businesses

Operating areas	Products (examples)
Health and nutrition	Pharmaceuticals, fine chemicals especially vitamins, fertilisers and crop protection products
Colourants and finishing products	Dyes, pigments, finishing products, process chemicals, dispersion paints, coatings, printing systems
Chemicals	Basic chemicals, catalysts, industrial chemicals, plasticisers, solvents, glue resins, impregnating resins, intermediates, speciality chemicals, detergent raw materials, automotive chemicals and additives
Plastics and fibres	Styrenic polymers, engineering plastic polyurethanes, PVC, fibre products, polyololefins
Oil and gas	Crude oil, petroleum products such as heating oil and automotive fuels, natural gas

Figure 1 BASF core businesses

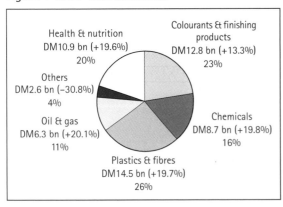

Source: *BASF Facts and Figures* – Charts 1998

Table 4 BASF joint ventures in China

Name	Partner(s)	Founded	BASF stake	Products
Shanghai Gao Qiao-BASF Latex	Shanghai Gao Qiao Petrochemical Corp	1988	50	Styrene butadiene dispersions for coating paper and carpeting
Shanghai Gao Qiao-BASF Dispersions	Shanghai Gao Qiao Petrochemical Corp	1993	50	Polymer dispersions
Shanghai BASF Colorants and Auxiliaries		1994	75	Organic pigments and cationic textile dyes
Yangzi-BASF Styrencis	Yangzi Petrochemical Corp	1994	60	Ethylbenzene, styrene polystyrene, expandable polystyrene (1998)
NEGPF-BASF (Shenyang) Vitamins	North East General Pharmaceutical Factory	1995	70	Vitamins and vitamin blends for animal feedstuffs
BASF Shanghai Coatings	Shanghai Coatings Co	1995	60	Coating products, especially for automobiles
BASF-JCIC Neopentylglycol	Jilin Chemical Industrial Corp	1995	60	Neopentylglycol
BASF Hua Yuan Nylon	China Worldbest Group Corp	1996	70	Nylon 6 for carpet fibres
Shanghai Interface Carpet	Interface Asia-Pacific, Shanghai China Textiles Internat. Science Technological Industrial City Dev't Co		5	Carpet tiles
BASF Headway Poly-Urethanes (China)	Headway Group	1997	70	Polyurethanes

This case was prepared by H. Schutte and J. Probert, Insead, Fontainbleau, as a basis for class discussion rather than to illustrate either effective or ineffective handling of an administrative situation.

PART VI

Managing the global marketing programme

CHAPTER 15

Global organisational structures

It seems incredible, and yet it has happened a hundred times, that troops have been divided and separated merely through a mysterious feeling of conventional manner, without any clear perception of the reason.

CARL VON CLAUSEWITZ (1780–1831), VOM KRIEGE (1832–1837) BOOK III, CHAPTER XI, 'ASSEMBLY OF FORCES IN SPACE'

You have no chance but to operate in a world shaped by globalisation and the information revolution. There are two options: Adapt or die ... You need to plan the way a fire department plans. It cannot anticipate fires, so it has to shape a flexible organisation that is capable of responding to unpredictable events.

ANDREW S. GROVE, INTEL CORPORATION

Chapter objectives

After reading this chapter, you will know:

- Which organisational structure is best for global companies to respond to market environment differences.
- The relationship between structure, foreign product diversification and size.
- That outsourcing becomes more and more important because corporations seek to leverage their value-chain strengths.
- The importance of core competencies within organisational networking primarily in virtual organisations.

Why is this important? Here are three situations in which you would need an understanding of the above issues:

- By means of restructuring a global company has to make decisions about a new suitable organisational structure.
- A domestic company decided to pursue international expansion therefore it has to organise its marketing function.
- In order to be competitive in a market, a global company is forced to find new forms of co-operation and identify its core competencies.

Practice link

For years Europe's managers avoided restructuring. Now many have learnt their lesson.[1] Siemens' restructuring, developed by Heinrich von Pierer, the CEO, aims to turn the German technology group into a two-tiered company. The revamp follows the company's focus on returns under its global '10-point plan', which was concluded in summer 1998 and contains measures for portfolio, management and capital. Hans-Joachim Neubürger, Siemens' finance director, is giving a clear signal to the capital markets that Siemens' restructuring is not yet complete and that there will be further changes to its portfolio. Even though Siemens' market capitalisation has doubled to €100 billion within the second half of 1999, the telecommunications take-over of Mannesmann by Vodafone AirTouch has increased the urgency with which Siemens is now seeking to raise its profitability and share price.[2] Commenting on corporate developments in Germany, Mr von Pierer said: 'With Vodafone's take-over of Mannesmann, the business world in Germany has changed forever ... There will be hunters and hunted, winners and losers. What counts in global competition is the right strategy and success.'[3]

Many analysts and investors have demanded a sharper focus on IT and industry for some time, claiming it was Siemens' only chance to compete globally. Even though Siemens managed to raise its earning before interest and tax by 82 per cent to €2.97 billion in 1999, it was still far behind General Electric, the global industry leader. Mr Neubürger stressed there could be no taboos. The 10-point programme had already broken with decades of tradition at Siemens, with the flotations of Epcos and Infineon and the sale of an entire division with €6.14 billion in turnover. 'We have clearly stated that information technology and communications, with a focus on the Internet, and industry, with a focus on process automation, are at the core of our strategy,' said Mr Neubürger.[4]

Siemens used to be typical of the European way. The German giant was an engineering powerhouse, selling everything from railway locomotives and nuclear power stations to telephone exchanges and memory chips. The company was highly centralised to capture the synergies between its remarkably broad activities. R&D was put at the heart of its operation. Sales and customer service were arranged around products, not customers. In the post-war years the system worked well. But in the 1980s time became an issue. Japanese product life-cycles in engineering were typically half the length of German ones. Moreover, it cost Japanese firms less to speed up product development. At the same time Siemens' German cost base became a burden. These days a skilled electrical worker in France or Britain costs 40–60 per cent less per hour than his German counterpart, and in Eastern Europe 80–90 per cent less. Heinrich von Pierer, the firm's boss, responded by confronting the firm's traditions; he talked of 'tearing down barriers within the company', creating a 'climate for honest open dialogue' and 'optimising entire process chains'. The company began to benchmark itself against its competitors, and has made a close study of retailers and financial-services companies to get a better grasp of logistics and customer service. Siemens also put more emphasis on profitability, creating some 250 independent business units and selling businesses such as a cardiac pacemaker firm and a high-performance printer manufacturer. Conscious that cutting was no good without growth, in 1993 Siemens introduced a company-wide innovation and growth programme for 'time-optimised processes' (TOP). But whereas in the old days everything would have been organised centrally, with TOP each business was made responsible for bringing about its own change in culture. TOP has stood Siemens on its head. Employees are now paid by results rather than by rank, and staff are expected to assess their superiors as well as being assessed by them. Senior jobs in the firm are open only to those with international experience. There are signs that the company's performance has picked up. For the moment it rules out the idea of breaking itself up, but in the longer run the logical move might be to follow AT&T and ITT down the road to demerger. Siemens scores poorly on what the management gurus call 'corporate clarity' – the degree of focus in a firm's strategy.[5]

Companies are looking to reduce bureaucracy and hierarchy to improve responsiveness and to reduce costs. As Tom Peters put it, 'You can't survive, let alone thrive, in a time-competitive world with a six- to eight-layer organisation structure. The time-obsessed organisation is flat – no barriers among functions, no borders with the outside.'[6]

Philip J. Quigley, president and chief executive officer (CEO) of Pacific Bell, sees two kinds of organisations: the large, powerful, yet cumbersome organisation that is like an elephant; and the agile, quick, but weaker, small organisation that is like a rabbit. Neither, however, is completely suited to compete in today's competitive global marketplace. Mr. Quigley's answer is a new form of organisation, the rabbiphant, which combines the strength and agility of the two present types of organisations.[7]

This chapter on organisational structures opens with a summary of conventional organisation forms and continues with new organisation designs that respond to the competitive global environment of the late 20th and the early 21st century. Organisational networking, outsourcing and the concept of core competencies make the basis for the emergence of flatter organisations. Subsequently the horizontal and the virtual organisations are discussed. Finally the chapter closes with the virtual team.

ORGANISATION

The goal in organising for global marketing is to find a structure that enables the company to respond to relevant market environment differences while ensuring the diffusion of corporate knowledge and experience from national markets throughout the entire corporate system. The pull between the value of centralised knowledge and co-ordination and the need for individualised response to the local situation creates a constant tension in the global marketing organisations. A key issue in global organisations is how to achieve balance between autonomy and integration. Subsidiaries need autonomy in order to adapt to their local environment. However, the business as a whole needs integration to implement global strategy.[8]

When management in a domestic company decides to pursue international expansion, the issue of how to organise arises immediately. Who should be responsible for this expansion? Should product divisions operate directly or should an international division be established? Should individual country subsidiaries report directly to the company president or should a special corporate officer be appointed to take full-time responsibility for international activities? Once the first decision of how to organise initial international operations has been reached, a growing company is faced with a number of reappraisal points during the development of its international business activities. Should a company abandon its international division and, if so, what alternative structure should be adopted? Should an area or regional headquarters be formed? What should be the relationship of staff executives at corporate, regional and subsidiary offices? Specifically, how should the marketing function be organised? To what extent should regional and corporate marketing executives become involved in subsidiary marketing management?

It is important to recognise that there is no single correct organisational structure for global marketing. Even within an industry, world-wide companies have developed very different strategic and organisational responses to changes in their environments.[9] Still, it is possible to make some generalisations. Leading-edge global competitors share one key organisational design characteristic: their corporate structure is simple and flat, rather than tall and complex. The message is clear: the world is complicated enough; there is no need to add to the confusion with a complex internal structuring. Simple structures increase the speed and clarity of communication and allow the concentration of organisational energy and valuable resources on learning, rather than on controlling, monitoring and reporting.[10] According to David Whitwam, CEO of Whirlpool, 'You must create an organisation whose people are adept at exchanging ideas, processes, and systems across borders, people who are absolutely free of the 'not-invented-here' syndrome, people who are constantly working together to identify the best global opportunities and the biggest global problems facing the organisation.'[11]

A geographically dispersed company cannot limit its knowledge to product, function and the home territory. Company personnel must acquire knowledge of the complex set of social, political, economic and institutional arrangements that exist within each international market. In most companies, after initial ad hoc arrangements, for example, all foreign subsidiaries reporting to a designated vice president or to the president establish an international division to manage their geographically dispersed new business. It is clear, however, that the international division in the multiproduct company is an unstable organisational arrangement. As a company grows, this initial organisational structure frequently gives way to various alternative structures.[12]

Young Akamai versus old Gillette

Gillette and Akamai are both organised as corporations, which means they are charged with the task of maximising profits and producing a return for shareholders, who are the owners. Both are overseen by a board of directors, who are supposed to look out for the interests of those shareholders and who have the ability to aggregate enormous amounts of capital.

Although Akamai and Gillette are both corporations, they are different in some important points. One operates in the New Economy and the other in the old. One employs 39,000 people and the other 400. Akamai is only one and a half year old and the other 100 years. Another difference that matters is in their approach to shareholders. Ultimately, companies that put shareholders at the centre of their concerns are more likely to succeed in the new century than those that don't. Akamai completely embraces the notion that the company exists to give shareholders a return on their investment. For George Conrades, CEO of Akamai, the interests of the company and the interests of the shareholders are in complete alignment. Gillette's Michael Hawley does not deny the essential point but is more grudging.

Akamai, one of the great Internet success stories and based in Cambridge, Mass. was founded in August 1998 by an MIT professor and his doctoral student. The company's founders were convinced they could develop a system that would radically cut the amount of time it took to download a Web page. Akamai, which is Hawaiian and means *intelligent, clever* or colloquially *cool*, helps to prevent catastrophic breakdowns during high-exposure Net events, such as NetAid in October 1999 when nearly 2.5 million Web streams were counted. One of Akamai's biggest challenges is the management of its rapid growth. By the end of 1999, Akamai's staff has grown from a few dozen employees to more than

400, among them more than 100 people in R&D, including 40 PhDs. As with any hot Internet start-up, it's hard to predict whether Akamai will ever live up to its hype. As Conrades states 'Everything moves so fast that we don't plan strategy for more than 90 days at a time'. In January 2000 the company had a market capital of €22.03 billion, despite revenues of just €1.11 million from January to September 1999 and losses of €25.71 million.

Gillette, founded in 1901, ranked 159th on Fortune 500 in 1999. It operates manufacturing plants in 25 countries. Although it has world-wide dominance of its core business, razors and toiletries, Gillette is facing its share of problems. In January 2000 Gillette announced dismal fourth-quarter results showing that the company's general malaise has spread to its core shaving and razor blade business. Until 1997 Gillette was cushioned by years of double-digit growth but then the Asia crisis caused real damage for the global company. The company's underlying weaknesses, among them a culture plagued by inertia and inefficiency, mismanaged inventories and receivables and three decades-old divisions that have consistently underperformed, were exposed. Gillette has begun to restructure. There is no doubt that investors would like to see the company leaner. A new reorganisation will shut 14 factories and 12 distribution centres world-wide, consolidate 30 offices, cut 4,700 jobs and save €171.42 million a year.

Food for thought

- Why do companies belonging to the 'New Economy' frequently achieve significantly higher market capitalisations than companies operating in the 'Old Economy'?
- Is the value of strategic planning lower in the 'New Economy' than in the 'Old Economy'?

Source: 'The corporation comes home', *Fortune*, 6 March 2000, pp. F-72–F-75; Poe, Robert 'Akamai dishes it out', *UpsideToday*, 17 January 2000, http://www.upside.com/texis/mvm/people/story?id=387e33d00; Kahn, Jeremy, 'Gillette loses face', *Fortune*, 8 November 1999, pp. 147–152.

In today's fast-changing competitive global environment, corporations are having to find new and more creative ways to organise. New forms of flexibility, efficiency and responsiveness are required to meet the market demands. The need to be cost effective, to be customer driven, to deliver the best quality, and to deliver that quality quickly are some of today's market realities.

Several authors have described new organisation designs that represent responses to the competitive environment of the late 20th century. These designs acknowledge the need to find more responsive and flexible structures, to flatten the organisation, and to employ teams. There is also the recognition of the need to develop networks, to develop stronger relationships among participants, and to exploit technology. They also reflect an evolution in approaches to organisational effectiveness. At the turn of the century, Fredrick Taylor claimed that all managers had to see the world the same way. Then came the contingency theorists who said that effective organisations design themselves to match their conditions. These two basic theories are reflected in today's popular management writings. As Henry Mintzberg has observed, 'To Michael Porter, effectiveness resides in strategy, while to Tom Peters it is the operations that count – executing any strategy with excellence.'[13] We believe that successful companies, the real global winners, must have both: good strategies and good execution.

Patterns of international organisational development

Organisations vary in terms of the size and potential of targeted global markets and local management competence in different country markets. Conflicting pressures may arise from the need for product and technical knowledge, functional expertise in marketing, finance, and operations, and area and country knowledge. Because the constellation of pressures that shape organisations is never exactly the same, no two organisations pass through organisational stages in exactly the same way, nor do they arrive at precisely the same organisational pattern. Nevertheless, some general patterns have developed.

Most companies undertake initial foreign expansion with an organisation similar to that in Figures 15.1 and 15.2. When a company is organised on this basis, foreign

Figure 15.1 Functional corporate structure, domestic corporate staff orientation, preinternational division

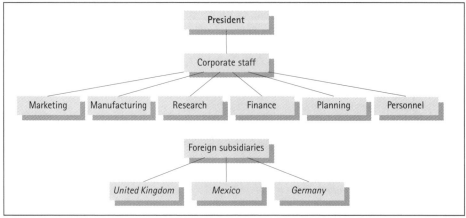

Figure 15.2 Divisional corporate structure, domestically oriented product division staff, preinternational division

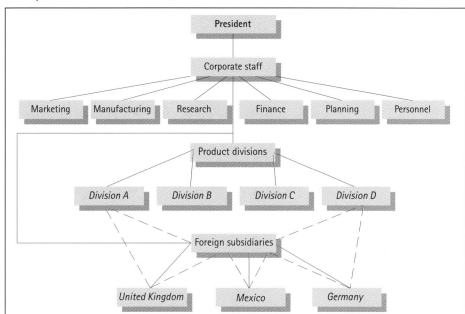

subsidiaries report directly to the company president or other designated company officer, who carries out his or her responsibilities without assistance from a head-quarters staff group. This is a typical initial arrangement for companies getting started in international marketing operations.

International division structure

As a company's international business grows, the complexity of co-ordinating and directing this activity extends beyond the scope of a single person. Pressure is created to assemble a staff group that will take responsibility for co-ordination and direction of the growing international activities of the organisation. Eventually, this pressure leads to the creation of the international division, as illustrated in Figures 15.3 and 15.4. The German Henkel group, for example, consists of more than 330 enterprises in more than 60 countries of the world. The countries of the European Union form the main emphasis of the business in Europe; overseas it is primarily the USA, Brazil, Mexico and the Asian Pacific area. Today more than 70 per cent of the world sales are obtained abroad. In 1998 the Austrian enterprise Henkel-Austria was being upgraded into the head office for eastern Europe. The Vienna-based holding company Henkel Central Eastern Europe GmbH (CEE) is to assume the responsibility for 3,500 employees in 14 countries.[14]

Four factors contribute to the establishment of an international division. First, top management's commitment to global operations has increased enough to justify an organisational unit headed by a senior manager. Second, the complexity of international operations requires a single organisational unit whose management has sufficient authority to make its own determination on important issues such as which market entry strategy to employ. Third, an international division is frequently formed when the firm has recognised the need for internal specialists to deal with the special

Figure 15.3 Functional corporate structure, domestic corporate staff orientation, international division

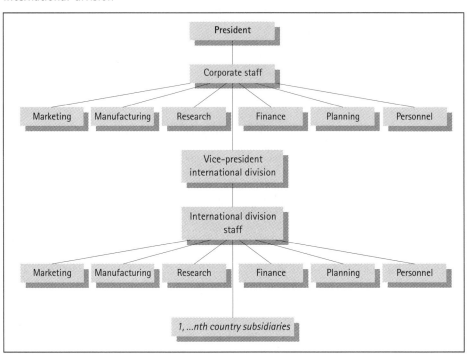

Figure 15.4 Divisional corporate structure, domestically oriented corporate staff, domestically oriented product divisions, international division

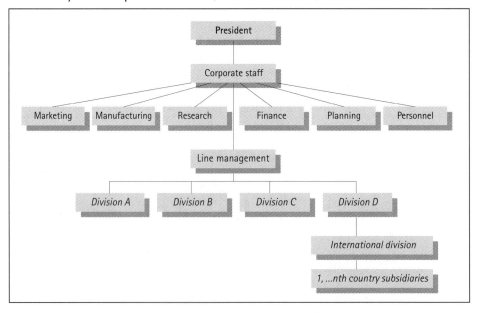

demands of global operations. A fourth contributing factor arises when management exhibits the desire to develop the ability to scan the global horizon for opportunities and competitive threats rather than simply respond to situations that are presented to the company.

Regional management centres

Another stage of organisational evolution is the emergence of an area or regional headquarters as management layer between the country organisation and the international division headquarters. This division is illustrated in Figures 15.5 and 15.6. When business is conducted in a single region that is characterised by similarities in economic, social, geographic and political conditions, there is both justification and need for a management centre. The centre co-ordinates decisions on pricing, sourcing, and other matters. Executives at the regional centre also participate in the planning and control of each country's operations with an eye toward applying company knowledge and optimal utilisation of corporate resources on a regional basis. The

Figure 15.5 Functional corporate structure, domestic corporate staff orientation, international division

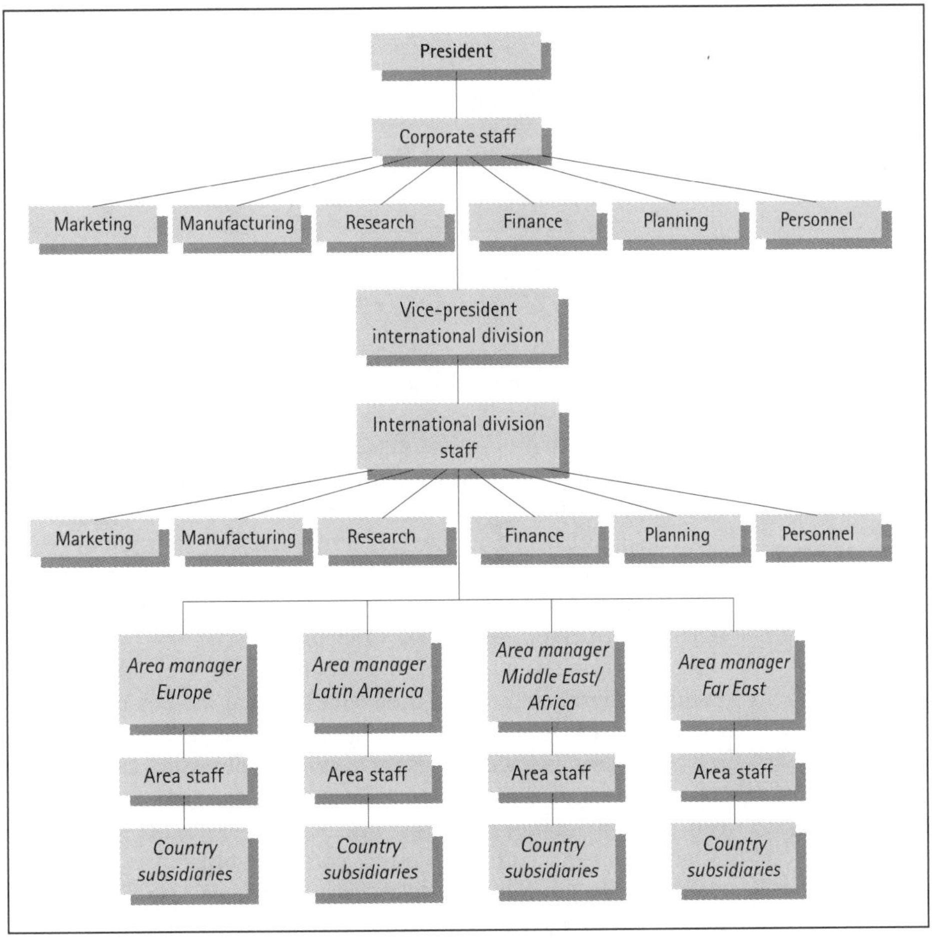

Figure 15.6 Divisional corporate structure, domestically oriented corporate staff, international division

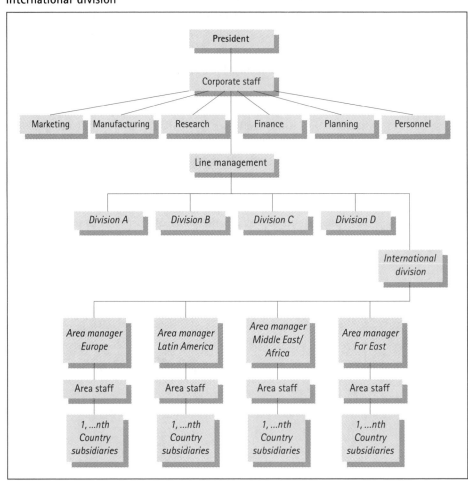

Wolford partnership, for example, is a retail concept of independence. Wolford and its partners appear world-wide under the same name. Unlike other partnerships and franchise systems Wolford doesn't stipulate any uniform appearance strictly. It takes national culture into account. The headquarters and the only production site of the Wolford group is in Bregenz, Austria. The Wolford group world-wide consists of eleven subsidiaries located in London, Paris, Milan, Madrid, Munich, St Margrethen (CH), Copenhagen, New York, s'Hertogenbosch (NL), Tokyo and Hong Kong.[15]

Regional management can offer a company several advantages. First, many regional managers agree that an on-the-scene regional management unit makes sense where there is a real need for co-ordinated, pan-regional decision making. Co-ordinated regional planning and control is becoming necessary as the national subsidiary continues to lose its relevance as an independent operating unit. Regional management can probably achieve the best balance of geographic, product and functional considerations required to implement corporate objectives effectively. By shifting operations and decision making to the region, the company is better able to maintain an insider advantage.[16]

A major disadvantage of a regional centre is its cost. Even a two-person office could cost in excess of €514,248 per year. The scale of regional management must be in line with the scale of operations in a region. A regional headquarters is premature when the size of the operations it manages is inadequate to cover the costs of the additional layer of management. Thus, the basic issue with regard to the regional headquarters is, 'Does it contribute enough to organisational effectiveness to justify its cost and the complexity of another layer of management?'

Geographic structure

The geographic structure involves the assignment of operational responsibility for geographic areas of the world to line managers. The corporate headquarters retains responsibility for world-wide planning and control, and each area of the world – including the 'home' or base market – is organisationally equal. For a company with French origins, France is simply another geographic market under this organisational arrangement. The most common appearance of this structure is in companies with closely related product lines that are sold in similar end-use markets around the world. For example, the major international oil companies utilise the geographic structure, which is illustrated in Figure 15.7. BP Amoco for example has well-established operations in Europe, North and South America, Australasia and parts of Africa.

Global product division structure

When an organisation assigns world-wide product responsibility to its product divisions, the product divisions must decide whether to rely on an international division, thereby dividing their world into domestic and foreign, or to rely on an area

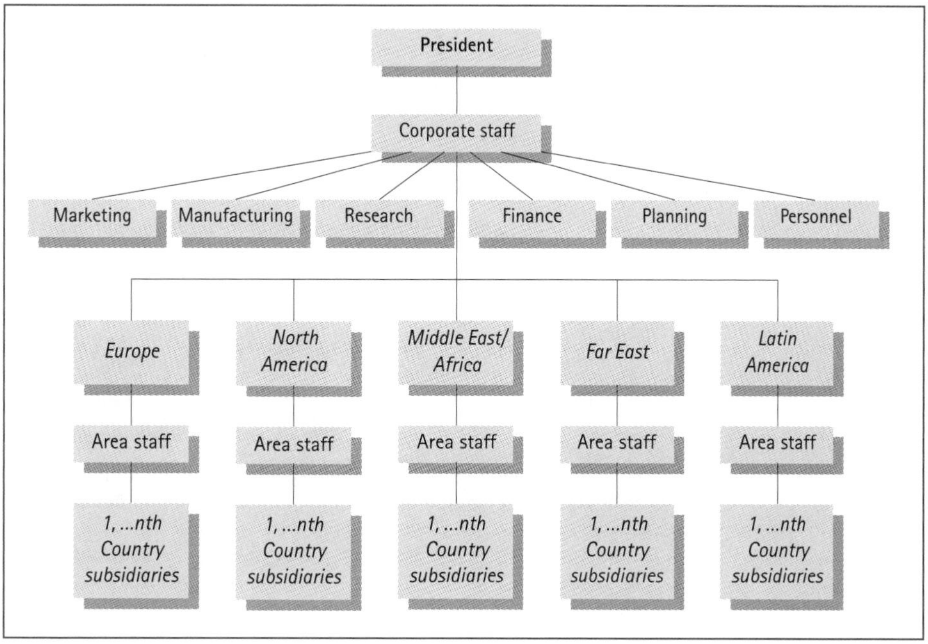

Figure 15.7 Geographic corporate structure, world corporate staff orientation, area divisions world–wide

structure with each region of the world organisationally treated on an equal basis. In most cases in which a divisional company shifts from a corporate international division to world-wide product divisions, there are two stages in the internationalisation of the product divisions. The first stage occurs when international responsibility is shifted from a corporate international division to the product division international departments. The second occurs when the product divisions themselves shift international responsibility from international departments within the divisions to the total divisional organisation. In effect, this shift is the utilisation of a geographic structure within each product division. The world-wide product division with an international department is illustrated in Figure 15.8. The product structure works best when a company's product line is widely diversified, when products go into a variety of end-use markets, and when a relatively high-technological capability is required. Goodyear, the world's largest tyre company, for example, has a presence on

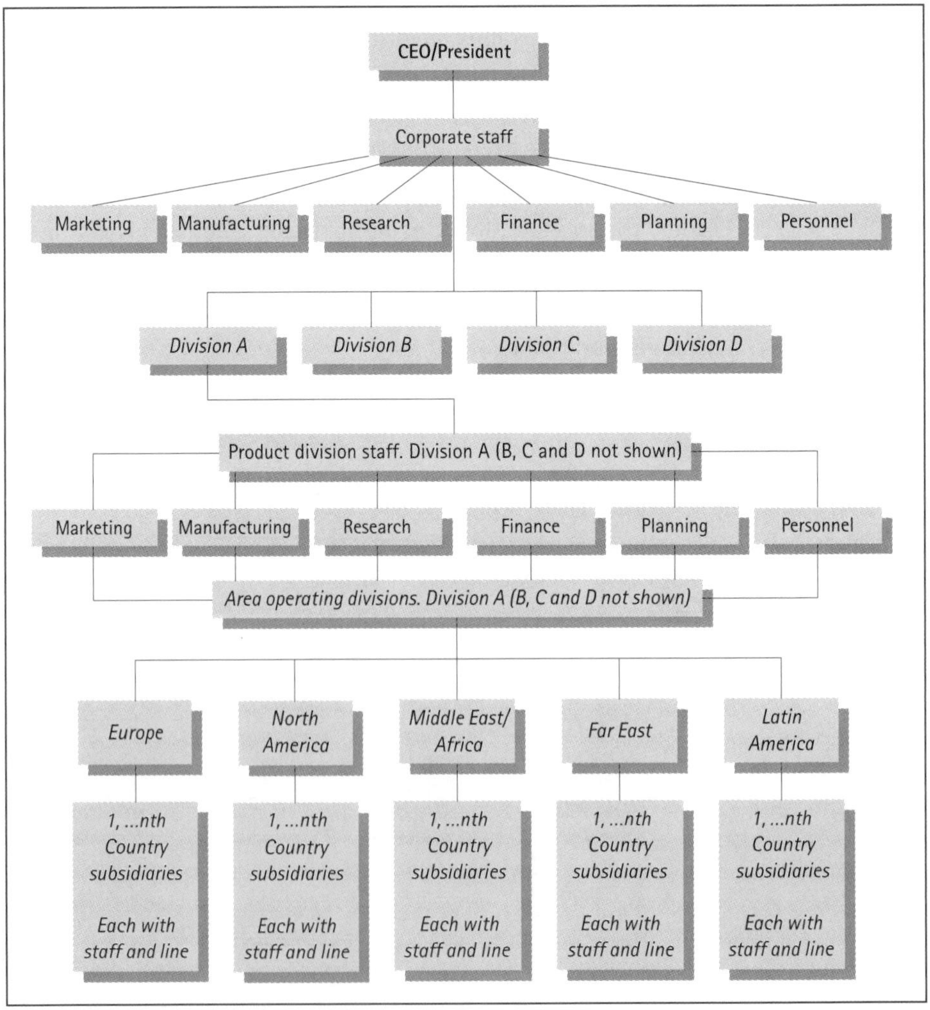

Figure 15.8 Geographic corporate structure, world corporate staff orientation, product divisions

six continents and annual sales of more than €12.86 billion. In addition to Goodyear brand tyres, it produces and sells tyres under several other well-respected brand names including Dunlop, Kelly, Fulda, Lee, Sava and Debica. Its non-tyre business units provide rubber products and polymers for a variety of automotive and industrial markets. Goodyear markets its products in 185 countries and manufactures them in 90 plants in 27 countries, with its Dunlop tyre joint ventures, and employs more than 100,000 associates.

The matrix structure

The most sophisticated organisational arrangement brings to bear four basic competencies on a world-wide basis. These competencies are as follows:

1 *Geographic knowledge.* An understanding of the basic economic, social, cultural, political, and governmental market and competitive dimensions of a country is essential. The country subsidiary is the major structural device employed today to enable the corporation to acquire geographic knowledge.

2 *Product knowledge and know-how.* Product managers with a world-wide responsibility can achieve this level of competence on a global basis. Another way of achieving global product competence is simply to duplicate product management organisations in domestic and international divisions, achieving high competence in both organisational units.

3 *Functional competence in such fields as finance, production, and especially marketing.* Corporate functional staff with world-wide responsibility contributes to the development of functional competence on a global basis. In a handful of companies, the appointment of country subsidiary functional managers is reviewed by the corporate functional manager who is responsible for the development of his or her functional activity in the organisation on a global basis.

What has emerged in a growing number of companies is a dotted-line relationship among corporate, regional and country staff. The dotted-line relationship ranges from nothing more than advice offered by corporate or regional staff to regional country staff to a much 'heavier' line relationship in which staff activities of a lower organisational level are directed and approved by higher-level staff. The relationship of staff organisations can become a source of tension and conflict in an organisation if top management does not create a climate that encourages organisational integration. Headquarters staff wants to extend its control or influence over the activities of lower-level staff.

For example, in marketing research, unless there is co-ordination of research design and activity, the international headquarters is unable to compare one market with another. If line management, instead of recognising the potential contribution of an integrated world-wide staff, wishes to operate as autonomously as possible, the influence of corporate staff is perceived as undesirable. In such a situation, the stronger party wins. This can be avoided if the level of management to which both line and staff report creates a climate and structure that expects and requires the co-operation of line and staff, and recognises that each has responsibility for important aspects of the management of international markets.

4 *A knowledge of the customer or industry and its needs.* In certain large and very sophisticated international companies, staff with a responsibility for serving industries

on a global basis exists to assist the line managers in the country organisations in their efforts to penetrate specific customer markets.

In the fully developed, large-scale international company, product, function, area and customer know-how are simultaneously focused on the organisation's world-wide marketing objectives. This type of total competence is a matrix organisation. In the matrix organisation, the task of management is to achieve an organisational balance that brings together different perspectives and skills to accomplish the organisation's objectives. Under this arrangement, instead of designating national organisations or product divisions as profit centres, both are responsible for profitability: the national organisation for country profits and the product divisions for national and world-wide product profitability. Figure 15.9 illustrates the matrix organisation. Philips, for example, has rationalised its production by the fact that eight product divisions were established (subdivided into 60 product groups). Products (and not product lines for individual markets) can be offered for global markets through this. Philips has three general types of country organisation: in 'key

Figure 15.9 **The matrix structure**

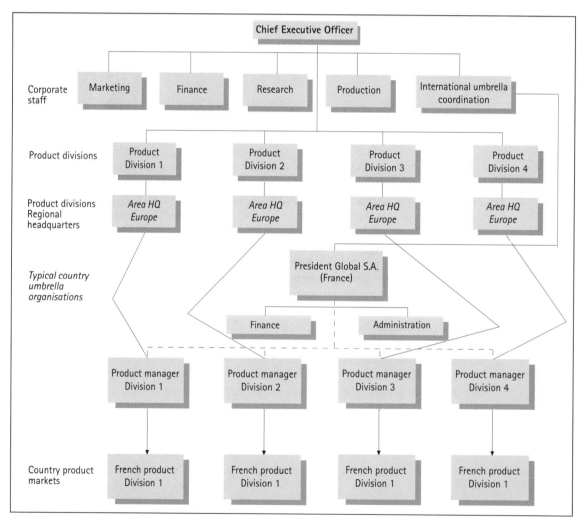

The logic of global business: the ABB group

Göran Lindahl succeeded Percy Barnevik as president and CEO of Asea Brown Boveri (ABB) on 1 January 1997. With ABB's individual businesses having been made more efficient under former CEO Barnevik, Lindahl's 'challenge' is to create and sustain synergism. The aim is to build environments in which a product in one business is linked to an idea in another business, leveraged with the resource in a third business, and the combination delivered to market as an integrated system. Trying to capitalise on the group's global presence and reputation for technological excellence, Lindahl is aggressively pursuing leadership in the business segments industrial-control systems, deep-water oil and gas exploration, intelligent electrical systems, and services. 'We shifted the balance in our management structure. We always said think global, act local. Now we say think more global and act more local', Lindahl said at the World Economic Development Congress in September 1999. Besides dramatic repositioning moves Lindahl has taken ABB out of the business of making frozen-food cabinets, arguing it wasn't even close to the company's core competencies.

ABB is an engineering-and-technology enterprise that comprises 1,000 companies operating in 100 countries. It was forged through the merger of two European companies in 1987 by Percy Barnevik, the managing director of Asea, which was created in 1883 and represented a flagship of Swedish industry. Brown Boveri was the second largest company and holding a comparable status in Switzerland since 1891. Behind the merger lay the vision of creating a new model of organisation that could cope with the competitive demands of the 21st century. In an interview the former CEO Percy Barnevik explained that ABB is an organisation with three internal contradictions: global and local, big and small, radically decentralised with centralised reporting and control. That's why the matrix as organisational structure was introduced. It offers the framework through which ABB organises its activities because it makes it possible to optimise the businesses globally and maximise performance in every country in which

ABB operates. Along one dimension, the company is a distributed global network. Executives around the world make decisions on product strategy and performance without regard for national borders. Along a second dimension ABB is a collection of traditionally organised national companies: there are 1200 local companies, each responsible for its profits and losses and each a separate legal and trading entity. The average size of employees in these units was only 200. Given these 1,200 building blocks, ABB put in place a number of different structures, roles and processes designed to interconnect the companies to ensure that their resources were most effectively used both locally and globally. In the centre of the global networking there is a small group of managers, usually five to ten who manage business areas. The 50 or so business areas are grouped into eight business segments for which different members of the executive committee, which consists of Swedes, Swiss, Germans and Americans, are responsible. The second networking hub is at the level of individual countries. The country CEOs have to look at all the resources of ABB within a particular country and to realise synergies between the business areas. In Austria, for example, ABB's national company ABB Aktiengesellschaft is managed by Robert Petsche. He plays a role comparable with those from any other Austrian company and participates fully in the Austrian apprenticeship programme. The business area structure meets the national structure at the level of ABB's member companies.

Food for thought

- What is the relationship between strategy and structure? Should a multinational company fix its strategy first and then design its structure accordingly or consider which strategy is most suitable given the organisational structure and resources?
- Is there such a thing as an 'ideal' organisational structure for a multinational enterprise? What determines which structures and processes should be chosen?

Source: McClenahen, John S., 'CEO of the year', *Industry Week*, 15 November, 1999; Hastings, Colin, *The New Organization* (Berkshire: McGraw-Hill, 1993); Taylor, Willem, 'The logic of global business: an interview with ABB's Percy Barnevik', *Harvard Business Review*, March–April 1991.

markets' like USA, France or Japan the product divisions care about marketing and production. In 'local business' areas like Nigeria or Peru the organisation is an importer for the product divisions. A hybrid form of organisation is found in 'large' markets, like Brazil, Spain or Taiwan depending on size and situation. The product divisions and the subsidiaries co-operate in a matrix form where the product divisions are responsible for global dimensions and subsidiaries are responsible for local presentation and co-ordination of general areas such as employment of new employees.

This organisation chart starts with a bottom section that represents a single-country responsibility level, moves to representing the area or international level, and finally moves to representing global responsibility from the product divisions to the corporate staff, to the chief executive at the top of the structure.

The key to successful matrix management is the extent to which managers in the organisation are able to resolve conflicts and achieve integration of organisation programmes and plans. Thus, the mere adoption of a matrix design or structure does not create a matrix organisation. The matrix organisation requires a fundamental change in management behaviour, organisational culture, and technical systems. In a matrix, influence is based on technical competence and interpersonal sensitivity, not on formal authority. In a matrix culture, managers recognise the absolute need to resolve issues and choices at the lowest possible level and do not rely on higher authority.

Relationship between structure, foreign product diversification and size

John Stopford and Louis T. Wells, Jr have hypothesised the relationship between structure, foreign product diversification (defined as sales of a firm outside its major product line expressed as a percentage of the total sales), and size. This formulation posits that when size abroad grows, the emergence of an area division develops so that whenever size abroad is 50 per cent of total size or more, several area divisions

Figure 15.10 The relationship between structure, foreign product diversification, and size abroad (as a % of total size)

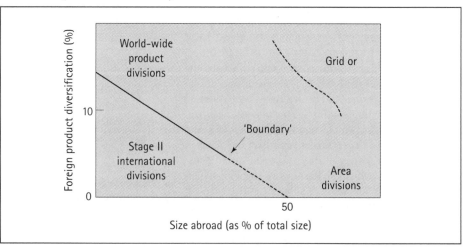

Source: Adapted from John M. Stopford and Louis T. Wells, Jr, *Managing the Multinational Enterprise* (New York: Basic Books, 1972).

will probably be adopted. On the other hand, as foreign product diversification increases, the likelihood that product divisions will operate on a world-wide basis increases. In a company in which there is both world-wide product diversity and large-scale business abroad as a percentage of total business, foreign operations will tend to move toward the matrix structure. Companies with limited foreign product diversification (under 10 per cent) and limited size as a percentage of total size will utilise the international structure. This formulation is summarised schematically in Figure 15.10.

Organisation structure and national origin

Before 1960, the American multidivisional structure was rarely found outside the United States. This structure was introduced in the United States as early as 1921 by Alfred P. Sloan at General Motors. The multidivisional structure in the United States had three distinctive characteristics. First, profit responsibility for operating decisions was assigned to general managers of self-contained business units. Second, there was a corporate headquarters that was concerned with strategic planning, appraisal and the allocation of resources among the business divisions. Third, executives at the corporate headquarters were separated from operations and were psychologically committed to the whole organisation rather than the individual businesses.[17] During the 1960s, European enterprises underwent a period of unprecedented reorganisation. Essentially, they adopted the American divisional structure. Today, at the overall level, there is little difference between European and American organisations.

The organisational structure of Japanese and other Asian companies are quite different from the US model. Japanese organisations, for example, rely on generalists as opposed to functional specialists and make greater use of project teams to design and manufacture products. They also form much closer relationships with suppliers than do American companies, and are in a different relationship to sources of capital and have a fundamentally different governance structure than US companies. The success of Japanese companies has recommended their organisational structure and design for careful evaluation, and many non-Japanese companies have successfully adopted Japanese organisational design features.

Key points

- There is no single correct organisational structure for global marketing.
- No two organisations pass through organisational stages in exactly the same way, nor do they arrive at precisely the same organisational pattern. Nevertheless, some general patterns have developed.
- The most sophisticated organisational structure is the matrix organisation, which requires a fundamental change in management behaviour, organisational culture and technical systems.

ORGANISATIONAL NETWORKING AND VIRTUAL ORGANISATIONS

Companies need to focus on core competencies, because the market environments get more and more competitive. However, business areas, which don't belong to the core competencies of a global company are being outsourced. There are a number of other pressures, i.e. risk, R&D costs, that are leading to organisational networking. Both outsourcing and organisational networking favour a flat organisational format, which ultimately leads to a virtual organisation.

Core competence

Core competence is a concept popularised by global strategy experts C.K. Prahalad and Gary Hamel. In the 1980s, many business executives were assessed on their ability to reorganise their corporations. In the 1990s, Prahalad and Hamel believed executives were judged on their ability to identify, nurture, and exploit the core competencies that make growth possible. Core competence must provide potential access to a wide variety of markets, make a significant contribution to the perceived customer benefits of the end product, and be difficult for competitors to imitate. In the 21st century core competencies become the resources and capabilities that give a company advantage over is rivals. Because of unstable conditions, caused by a range of innovations and technical changes on the market, core competencies become a basis upon which companies build their strategies. For example for Philip Morris the competencies in the general area of marketing and specific applications of special skills in advertising campaigns and the global brand are recognised as core competencies which are applied by strategic leaders to improve company performance.[18] Few companies are likely to build world leadership in more than five or six fundamental competencies.

The French computer company Bull prepares for a rougher reorganisation. Smaller participations and divisions shall be dissolved. Bull aims to become one of the leading players in the Internet and e-business markets. Thus the enterprise will concentrate on its core competencies because the development of these markets requires an organisation that encourages business area specialisation, enabling the company to respond to the demands of the customer and prospects for complete, integrated solutions. In Europe, Bull organises its sale staff in divisions specialising according to business areas. These areas are infrastructure, systems integration services, outsourcing and support services and security.[19]

In the long run, an organisation will derive its global competitiveness from its ability to bring high-quality, low-cost products to market faster than its competitors. In order to do this, an organisation must be viewed as a portfolio of competencies rather than a portfolio of businesses. Many companies have the technical resources to build competencies but key executives lack the vision to do so. According to Bartlett and Ghosal, senior management's role is not to define, control or allocate core competencies but to create an environment that ensures that competencies are developed deep within the organisation and building horizontal linkages to allow these competencies to be integrated and leveraged as broad organisational capabilities.[20] The concept of distinctive competencies and linkages challenges executives to rethink the concept of the corporation itself. It also requires redefining the task of management as building both competencies and the administrative means for assembling resources spread across multiple businesses.[21]

Outsourcing and partnership

Given the economic performance pressures, many corporations are focusing on what they do best. Outsourcing has become increasingly popular as corporations seek to leverage their value-chain strengths. If the Marriott Corporation has a competence in running company cafeterias, then why not contract with Marriott? If Pitney Bowes can run mail and copier services better, then contract with them rather than retain in-house capabilities. If IBM can manage computer installations better, then why not have IBM provide this service?

The Austrian Steyr-Daimler Puch vehicle technology, for example, has set up a central help desk for EDP problems, available to the 2,300 or so users in the Styrian sites. The helpline started in January 1999 and is available Monday to Friday from 7:00 to 17:00. Already in the first month, the team reached a solution rate of 72 per cent for problems, which has been increased to over 80 per cent since. The acceptance has been so great that the number of callers is double what was predicted.[22]

The Austrian Wienerberger brick industry AG produces roof-, wall- and blanket systems at 120 production sites in 12 countries. At present, expansion is primarily towards the east, for example Romania or Slovenia. With the growing requests of a global enterprise, however, the software solution met with its limits. 'We want to produce bricks and not struggle with EDP problems', Thomas Kleibl, member of the board, comments on the partnership with Hewlett Packard. Everybody shall do what he knows best and Wienerberger has no know-how at the communication and hardware level or with the management in the mainframe operation, he clearly states. Through partnerships the core competencies of an enterprise are granted. [23]

As more organisations outsource systems that support business processes, such as order-entry and fulfilment, their relationship with outsourcers moves from transactional to one approaching partnership. The concept of partnership is based on the assumption that the results achieved through joint actions will be greater than results achieved by transactional relationships. In a co-operative relationship, the long-term commitment to each other is seen in the processes which are used to manage the relationship. There are six determinants of partnership which partly define the context of the relationship:[24]

1 *Mutual benefits*. Entering a partnership with an outsourcer has to make sense. The risk and the investment should be shared. If an innovation is developed as a result of the partnership both parties should share it.
2 *Commitment*. A common reason for a failure of a partnership is the lack of common goals and non-existent or misaligned incentives to support them. Commitments define the effective relationship between a company and its outsource. Before signing a contract a company should be aware of future flexibility and its potential costs.
3 *Predisposition*. The approach of the outsourcer as an adversary or as a valuable team member and trust between the partners influence the ability to sustain the relationship.
4 *Shared knowledge*. The compatibility with the outsourcer's organisational culture is of particular concern to organisations externally sourcing services that require the outsourcer to associate directly with the customer, i.e. customer-service help desks. On the other hand an outsourcer that has an understanding of the company's business processes and its cultural environment can leverage the investment to its advantage.
5 *Unique resources*. The primary reason why organisations outsource is to quickly acquire skilled employees. The introduction of new technology is accelerating so rapidly that many organisations are unable to keep up. Outsourcing allows the flexibility to supplement existing staff.

6 *Linkage*. The driver for many outsourcing relationships is the exchange of information among departments, vendors and suppliers. It is a core competence of outsourcers to link internal and external departments in a seamless exchange of information. Although it is often ignored, enabling the social network is also essential to success.

According to a study conducted by the Outsourcing Institute, 80 per cent of Fortune 500 companies outsourced some or all of their information management functions in 1997. The motives behind outsourcing decisions are that it frees up resources to focus more on the core business. The partners add knowledge and give back management time. The overall quality of their outputs improve as executives stay focused on things the firm does well. Companies using outsourcing services are financially more stable. The conducted study suggests that outsourcing agreements contribute an average cost saving of 9 per cent, and a 15 per cent increase in capacity and quality. Information technology, which is the fastest growing area for outsourcing today, represents approximately 30 per cent of all outsourcing expenditures.[25]

EUROPEAN FOCUS

Management buy-out at Ericsson – there are times, when separation is beneficial to both parties ...

When in 1998 the Swedish telecommunications group Ericsson announced that it would no longer stick with its production facilities in Kindberg, Austria, this was not the end for workers in Kindberg. Rather this step marked a new era. Dovatron bought Ericsson's stake in the Kindberg operation and has been supplying the Swedish telecom giant from there ever since. Dovatron belongs to an international group, DII, which generates a turnover of more than €900 million per year. DII's strategy is clear: the company buys production facilities previously run by electronics or telecom companies, and in turn, supplies them with parts.

The benefit works both ways. Ericsson may concentrate on what it does best: designing, developing and marketing complex communications solutions, while DII can take advantage of its corporate strengths as component manufacturer by supplying to world class clients.

Similarly, Ericsson sold its manufacturing operations in the Swedish Oestersund and the French Longueness to Solectron, also an international electronic component manufacturer. The same will happen to its plant in the Swedish Katrineholm, where currently 100 people are employed. Flexotronic has put in its bid.

However, not always do outsourcing decisions bring in external companies as new owners. In January 1999, two young Austrians, formerly employed with Ericsson, entered new ground when they took over part of Ericsson's sales business in a classic management buy-out. The newly formed company, called Austrian BusinessCom Systems AG, has taken over sales and customer service to small- and medium-sized companies. Following an industry-wide trend, sales and sales support for communication systems to small- and medium-sized businesses are left to specialised sales companies. The benefit for customers from outsourcing is clear: better and more individually targeted support from a local salesperson, who devotes full attention to this customer group. Outsourcing, management buy-outs, ... you can be sure to see more of it in the future! Whenever companies find it important to return to their key strengths, they will need to identify someone who takes good care of the rest of the business!

Source: Erdmann, Heinz "Söldner des Fließbandes", *Industriemagazin Spezial*, Vol. 2, February 2000; "Management-buy out Stärkt Ericssons Vertrieb" *Die Presse*, 14 Ocober 1998.

Organisational networking

While hierarchical structure is formed from ascending and descending chains of individuals, networks are self-organised structures which are held in place by relationships of trust. Furthermore, these relationships create patterns of communication and exchange which are achieved largely through face-to-face interactions.[26]

Networking within an organisation has the goal to break down boundaries and to enable quick and open person-to-person communications. It is a general strategy which sets a style and culture for an organisation. Furthermore, specific networks of people from different departments of the organisation are built to focus activity or know-how. These internal networks are characterised and named by the topic of interest that network members share: for example, application areas for a new technological process.

Networking between organisations tends to result from the pressure to co-operate. This pressure is driven by the enormous costs of technology in areas such as health, pharmaceuticals and aircraft. Even the largest companies cannot afford to take the risks of investing in R&D alone.[27]

Horizontal organisation

The organisational structures change inevitably at the transition of a national enterprise into a multinational organisation. By doing this new strategies emerge which have to deal with different products, services, geographical markets and staff. The co-ordination needed to improve customer service, performance and competitive response is often better supported by an organisation with a flatter hierarchy. Horizontal management structures respond more quickly and flexibly to changing market conditions. In addition, the introduction of new technologies has speeded up the flattening of, for example, managing customer relationships.[28]

Frank Ostroff, consultant at A.T. Kearney, states that the vertical organisation is not always able to compete in a global environment with rapidly changing market conditions. In today's global environment, it is increasingly important to link people and units across the organisation.

Xerox, for example, was confronted in 1982 with Japanese competitors and had to undergo fundamental changes in order to maintain its hold on the market. Therefore the American company focused on changing processes. In order to grow, Xerox in 1992 determined that it had to change to a more horizontal, process-orientated company. As Paul Allaire, chairman and CEO of Xerox Corporation states, 'On the one hand, we see attractive markets, and we have superior technology. On the other hand, we won't be able to take advantage of this situation unless we can overcome cumbersome, functionally driven bureaucracy and use our quality process to become more productive.' The company, calling itself from that point *Xerox, The Document Company*, identified its objective as a promise to provide unique value by offering leading-edge products. This value proposition required that the business be reorganised into a number of horizontal, cross-functional groups organised around work flows. The new Xerox is built of four divisions, each of them reporting to an executive vice president who in turn reports to the CEO, the president and the COO.

Horizontal organisations organise around cross-functional core processes and install managers who take the responsibility for such processes in its entirety. Teams are the cornerstones of organisational design and performances and not individuals.

Another principle of the horizontal organisation is that it decreases hierarchy by eliminating non-value-added work and by giving team members the authority to make decisions directly related to their activities within the process flow. The horizontal organisation integrates customers with suppliers and empowers people by giving them the tools, skills, motivation, and authority to make decisions essential to the performance of the team. The use of information technology helps people reach performance objectives and delivers the value proposition to the customer. Multiple competencies are emphasised and people get trained to handle issues and work in cross-functional areas within the horizontal organisation, which promotes the ability to think creatively and to respond in a flexible manner to new challenges. Horizontal organisations redesign functional departments to work as 'partners in process performance' with the core process groups. Finally they build a corporate culture of openness, co-operation and collaboration that focuses on continuous performance improvement and values employee empowerment and responsibility.[29]

Virtual organisation

A virtual corporation is a temporary network or loose coalition of manufacturing and administrative services that comes together for a specific business purpose. It disassembles when the purpose has been met. The ad hoc alliances are created and dissolved quickly. Other characteristics of these alliances are short lived, focused, goal driven and powered by time-based competition. The virtual organisation does not need a central office, an organisation chart or a hierarchy. Some significant advantages of virtual corporations are, for example, low unit costs (low investments in human resources, manufacturing space, tools and development time), the focus on core competencies of each participating organisation, manufacturing flexibility (quick response to changes in the manufacturing environment which results in rapid turning out of new products), operation flexibility because partners can also be changed readily and finally the creation of best products and services since the core competencies of participating firms are integrated.

To be competitive in a market, the quality of a company's performance must be high, for example in marketing and sales, service, technology or human resource management. Demanding requirements and the need for flexibility make it virtually impossible for any company to perform all functions on its own. Therefore collaboration, which focuses on the application of core competencies, is necessary. Companies which are able to identify their core competencies are the ones that can defend their position in a partnership.[30] A virtual organisation consists of best-of-class core competencies of co-operating and legally independent companies. Each member has access to the existing resources in the whole network, therefore it is rather based on trust. A virtual organisation is not regarded as an enterprise existing beside other organisational forms, it rather is a quality which is applied to an organisation.[31]

To sum up, some significant factors contribute to the success of virtual corporations: the focus on customer needs, the right choice of partners with necessary core competencies, win–win relationships, the need for trust and open communication, up-to-date information technology, adequate measures to protect company proprietary information, a new kind of computer-literate managers and educated workers.

Because of the reliance on information technology a virtual organisation is leaner and flatter than a conventional organisation. Furthermore, information technology replaces the middle management which formerly was an information conduit. These changes lead to a flattened organisation in that managers need to have expertise in communication, for example via e-mail, and they have a broader span of control. To sum up, virtual organisations have the essence of traditional organisations without the structure and boundaries.[32]

Table 15.1 shows three important characteristics of virtual organisations and their effects on competitiveness in a global setting. For example, neither Nike nor Reebok own many production facilities, rather they outsource nearly all production to companies based in Taiwan or other Asian countries. Therefore, the goal of the virtual organisation is to extract the maximum value from its partner organisations while making minimum investment. Regarding temporal and spatial independence the virtual organisation overcomes such barriers by linking together remote resources and by allowing employees to work in a variety of locations, for example at home or in aeroplanes. Finally the virtual organisation is characterised by flexibility which is important for transnational companies because of the changing opportunities in global markets. However, flexibility means that parts of the global organisation may be formed, disbanded and reformed if necessary.

Virtual teams

A virtual organisation definitely makes use of virtual teams. Team membership in a virtual organisation is seen as dynamic and constantly changing. One's role in one team may be in a support capacity and in another it may be as a leader. A team of the same people only has a finite life span in which it can be truly productive.[33]

The practice of using self-directed work teams to respond to competitive challenges is becoming more widespread. Reports vary as to how widely teams are being used today. One study found that 47 per cent of Fortune 1,000 companies used teams with at least some of their employees. With increased usage of e-mail, team members may be located on different continents.[34, 35]

Jon Katzenbach and Douglas Smith believe 'teams will become the primary unit of performance in high-performance organisations'.[36] The implementation of self-directed work teams is another example of the need for organisational innovation to

Table 15.1 Characteristics of virtual organisations and their effects on global competitiveness

Characteristics	Effects on competitiveness
Dependence on a federation of alliances and partnerships with other organisations.	Corporate functions can be easily integrated with functions provided by allied partners to enhance and extend corporate reach worldwide.
Relative spatial and temporal independence.	Geographical boundaries can be easily transcended, providing competitive presence in global markets and improving access to natural and human resources.
Flexibility.	Resources can be easily reassigned to respond to shifting opportunities in global markets.

Source: Adapted from: Marie-Claude Boudreau, Karen D. Loch, Daniel Robey and Detmar Straud, 'Going global: using information technology to advance the competitiveness of the virtual transnational organization', *Academy of Management Executive*, 12, 4 (1998): p. 120–128.

maintain competitiveness. They represent another corporate response to the need to flatten the organisation, to reduce costs and overheads, and to be more responsive. The change from traditional teams to virtual teams mainly derives from five factors. These are, firstly the increasing prevalence of flat or horizontal organisations and, secondly, environments that require inter-organisational co-operation as well as competition, such as strategic partnerships or outsourcing. A third major factor focuses on the changes in the expectations of the employee regarding organisational participation. Finally, a shift from production to service and knowledge work environments and increasing globalisation of trade and corporate activity encourages the development of virtual teams.[37]

Eastman Kodak used virtual teams when the single-use camera was developed for the European market. Kodak wanted to adapt the appearance and features of the product so that it would be attractive to European buyers. The functional features of the camera, however, were similar to those marketed world-wide. The virtual team acted independently of time and space; it consisted of two German engineers who worked with the design team first in Rochester, New York and later from Germany through telecommunications links.[38] Another example is Intel who used virtual teams for formulating and delivering sales strategies for specific products, developing new products, and manufacturing microprocessor elements. The team-members from Ireland, Israel, England, France and Asia came together quickly, they did their work and finally disbanded. The team also regrouped with a variety of other teams.[39]

Critical factors for the success of virtual teams are:[40]

- Human resource policies
- Training and development
- Standard organisational processes
- Electronic communication and collaboration technology
- Organisational culture
- Leadership
- Competence

In the virtual organisation, the classical role of management, that is, planning, organising, directing and controlling, is changing. Table 15.2 summarises four areas of leadership behaviour which enables successful virtual teamwork.

Key points

- New organisational designs acknowledge the need to find more responsive and flexible structures, to flatten the organisation and to employ teams.
- Very demanding requirements and the need for flexibility make it virtually impossible for any company to perform all functions on its own. Therefore collaboration such as outsourcing, which focuses on the application of core competencies, is necessary.
- There is the recognition of the need to develop networks, to develop strong relationships among participants and to exploit technology.

Table 15.2 Leadership behaviours that support virtual team success

	Behaviours
Communicating	The business necessity of virtual teams
	That virtual teamwork is respected
	The value of diversity and of leveraging skills
	The benefits and results of working virtually
Establishing expectations	Definition how virtual teams work and clear procedures and goals
	High standards for virtual team performance
	Of customers and other important stakeholders
	Start-up costs and times
Allocating resources	Time and money for training for virtual team leaders and members
	Time and money for travel for team leaders for face-to-face meetings
	For technology
Modelling behaviours	Align crossfunctional and regional goals and objectives
	Work together on management team across geographic and cultural boundaries
	Solicit input from and display trust in team members
	Show flexibility

Source: Deborah L. Duarte and Nancy Tennant Snyder, *Mastering Virtual Teams: Strategies, Tools, and Techniques that Succeed* (San Francisco: Jossey-Bass, 1999), p. 22.

Summary

To respond to the opportunities and threats in the global marketing environment, a firm must have a global vision and strategy. By providing leadership and organising a global effort a firm can exploit global opportunities. In organising the global marketing effort, a structure that enables the company to respond to relevant differences in international market environments and enables the company to extend valuable corporate knowledge is the goal. A balance between autonomy and integration must be established. Within this organisation, firms must establish core competencies to be competitive. A way in which global companies can respond to these requirements is to enable organisational networking and virtual organisations.

Concepts and definitions

Matrix structure In the fully developed, large-scale international company, product, function, area, and customer know-how are simultaneously focused on the organisation's worldwide marketing objectives. In the matrix organisation, the task of management is to achieve an organisational balance that brings together different perspectives and skills to accomplish the organisation's objectives.

Core competence Core competence must provide potential access to a wide variety of markets, make a significant contribution to the perceived customer benefits of the end product, and be difficult for competitors to imitate. Core competencies become the resources and capabilities that give a company advantage over its rivals.

Network organisation Networking within an organisation has the goal to break down boundaries and to enable quick and open person-to-person communications. It is a general strategy which sets a style and culture for an organisation.

Horizontal organisation	Horizontal organisations are organised around cross-functional core processes and install managers who take the responsibility for such processes in its entirety. The co-ordination needed to improve customer service, performance and competitive response is often better supported by an organisation with a flatter hierarchy.
Virtual organisation	A virtual corporation is a temporary network or loose coalition of manufacturing and administrative services that comes together for a specific business purpose.
Virtual team	The change from traditional teams to virtual teams mainly derives from five factors. These are, firstly the increasing prevalence of flat or horizontal organisations and, secondly, environments that require inter-organisational co-operation as well as competition, such as strategic partnerships or outsourcing. A third major factor focuses on the changes in the expectations of the employee regarding organisational participation. Finally, a shift from production to service and knowledge work environments and increasing globalisation of trade and corporate activity encourages the development of virtual teams.

Discussion questions

1 Why do organisations differ in their organisational structures?

2 What are the benefits gained in adopting a matrix approach in terms of organisational structure?

3 How does a firm's size abroad influence the organisational structure?

4 What is the concept of core competencies and what role does it play in virtual organisations?

5 What are the effects of virtual organisations on global competitiveness?

6 What are virtual teams?

Webmistress's hotspots

The Outsourcing Institute

The Outsourcing Institute is a global network providing information, advice and networking opportunities to professionals engaged in all types of outsourcing services.

http://www.outsourcing.com/

Virtual Team Assistant

Teamworks is a website developed to provide support for group communication processes.

http://www.vta.spcomm.uiuc.edu/

Working By Wire

Virtual Teaming and Virtual Work solutions help individuals, managers, and whole virtual teams achieve high performance and personal satisfaction in this new way of working.

http://www.knowab.co.uk/wbw2c.html

Suggested readings

Bartlett, Christopher A. and Sumantra Ghoshal, *Managing across Borders: The Transnational Solution*. Boston: Harvard Business School Press, 1989.

Bennis, Warren, *Organising Genius: The Secrets of Creative Collaboration*. Reading, MA: Addison-Wesley, 1997.

Cho, Namshin, 'How Samsung organised for innovation', *Long Range Planning*, 29, 6 (1996): pp. 783–796.

Cohen, Susan G., 'Designing effective self-managing work teams', *CEO* Publication – University of Southern California (1993): pp. G93–99.

Davidow, William H. and Michael S. Malone, *The Virtual Corporation*. New York: HarperBusiness, 1993.

Egelhoff, W.G., 'Exploring the Limits of Transnationalism', Fordham University, Report 90-6-2 (September 1990).

Florida, Richard, 'The new industrial revolution', *Futures* (July/August 1991).

Gerlach, Michael L., *Alliance Capitalism: The Social Organisation of Japanese Business*. Berkeley and Los Angeles: University of California Press, 1992.

Ghoshal, Sumantra and Christopher A. Bartlett, *The Individualized Corporation*. New York: HarperBusiness, 1997.

Hammer, Michael and James Champy, *Reengineering the Corporation*. New York: HarperCollins, 1993.

Hax, Arnoldo C., 'Building the firm of the future', *Sloan Management Review*, 30, 3 (Spring 1989): pp. 75–82.

Johansson, Johny K. and Ikujiro Nonaka, *Relentless, The Japanese Way of Marketing*. New York: HarperBusiness, 1997.

Kashani, Kamran, 'Beware the pitfalls of global marketing', *Harvard Business Review*, 67, 5 (September/October 1989): pp. 91–98.

Katzenbach, Jon R. and Douglas K. Smith, 'The discipline of teams', *Harvard Business Review* (March/April 1993).

Katzenbach, Jon R. and Douglas K. Smith, *The Wisdom of Teams: Creating the High Performance Organisation*. Boston: Harvard Business School Press, 1993.

Kogut, Bruce and Udo Zander, 'What forms DD? Coordination, identity and learning', *Organisation Science*, 7 (September–October 1996): pp. 502–518.

Krugman, Paul, 'Competitiveness: a dangerous obsession', *Foreign Affairs*, 73, 2 (March/April 1994): pp. 28–44.

Kuniyasu, Sakai, 'The feudal world of Japanese manufacturing', *Harvard Business Review* (November/December 1990): pp. 38–49.

Maruca, Regina Fazio, 'The right way to go global: an interview with Whirlpool CEO David Whitwam', *Harvard Business Review*, 72, 2 (March–April 1994): pp. 134–145.

McDonald, Malcolm and Warren J. Keegan, *Marketing Plans that Work: How to Prepare Them, How to Use Them*. Newton, MA: Butterworth Heinemann, 1997.

Mintzberg, Henry, 'The effective organisation: forces and forms', *Sloan Management Review* (Winter 1991).

Moore, James F., *The Death of Competition: Leadership & Strategy in the Age of Business Ecosystems*. New York: HarperBusiness, 1996.

Morrison, Allen J., David A. Ricks and Kendall Roth, 'Globalization versus regionalization: which way for the multinational?', *Organisational Dynamics* (Winter 1991).

Nakatani, Iwao, *The Japanese Firm in Transition*. Tokyo, Japan: Asian Productivity Organisation, 1988.

O'Reilly, Anthony J.F., 'Leading a global strategic charge', *Journal of Business Strategy*, 12, 4 (July/August 1991): pp. 10–13.

Peters, Tom, 'Time obsessed competition', *Management Review* (September 1990).

Prahalad, C.K. and Gary Hamel, 'The core competence of the corporation', *Harvard Business Review*, 68 (May–June 1990): pp. 79–93.

Quelch, J., 'Marketing responsibilities of country managers in multinational corporations in the 1990s', Marketing Science Institute Report, 1992.

Thurow, Lester, 'Who owns the twenty-first century?' *Sloan Management Review*, 33, 3 (Spring 1992): pp. 5–17.

Tuller, Lawrence W., *Going Global: New Opportunities for Growing Companies to Compete in World Markets*. Homewood, IL: Business One Irwin, 1991.

Webster, Frederick E. Jr, 'The changing role of marketing in the corporation', *Journal of Marketing*, 56, 4 (1992): pp. 1–17.

Notes

1. Carr Edward, 'A survey of business in Europe: present pupils – a fortress against change', *The Economist*, 23 November 1996.
2. Rüdiger Köhn, 'Siemens prepares for shake-up', 21 February 2000: http://news.ft.com/ft/gx.cgi/ftc?page name=View&c=Article&cid=FT4OV3T2X4C&live= true&useoverridetemplate=IXLZHNNP94C
3. Bertrand Benoit, 'Siemens on acquisition hunt', 25 February 2000: http://news.ft.com/ft/gx.cgi/ftc?pagename=View&c=Article&cid=FT40GZET25C&live=true&useoverridetemplate=IXLZHNNP94C
4. Rüdiger Köhn, 'Siemens prepares for shake-up', 21 February 2000: http://news.ft.com/ft/gx.cgi/ftc?page

name=View&c=Article&cid=FT4OV3T2X4C&live=
true&useoverridetemplate=IXLZHNNP94C

5. Edward Carr, 'A survey of business in Europe: wake up or die – new ways to manage old companies', *The Economist,* 23 November 1996.

6. Tom Peters, 'Time obsessed competition', *Management Review,* September (1990): p. 18.

7. Philip J. Quigley, 'The coming of the rabbiphant: towards decentralized corporations'. In *Vital Speeches,* 535, 1990.

8. George S. Yip, *Total Global Strategy* (Upper Saddle River, NJ: Prentice Hall, 1992).

9. Christopher A. Bartlett and Sumantra Ghoshal, *The Transnational Solution* (Boston: Harvard Business School Press, 1989).

10. Vladimir Pucik, 'Globalization and human resource management'. In *Globalizing Management: Creating and Leading the Competitive Organization,* ed. V. Pucik, N. Tichy and C. Barnett, New York: Wiley, 1992, p. 70.

11. Regina Fazio Maruca, 'The right way to go global: an interview with Whirlpool CEO David Whitwam', *Harvard Business Review,* 3 January 1994, pp. 136–137.

12. John M. Stopford and Louis T. Wells, *Managing the Multinational Enterprise* (New York: Basic Books, 1972).

13. Henry Mintzberg, 'The effective organization: forces and forms', *Sloan Management Review,* Winter 1991, Vol. 32, No. 2, pp. 54–55.

14. 'Henkel legt im Osten stark zu und bündel Aktivitäten in Wien', *Die Presse,* 24 September 1998.

15. http://www.wolford.com/

16. Allen J. Morrison, David A. Ricks and Kendall Roth, 'Globalization versus regionalization: Which way for the multinational?', *Organizational Dynamics,* Winter (1991): p. 25.

17. Lawrence G. Franko, 'The move toward a multinational structure in European organizations', *Administrative Science Quarterly,* 19, 4 (December 1974): pp. 493–506.

18. Duane R. Ireland and Michael A. Hitt, 'Achieving and maintaining strategic competitiveness in the 21st century: the role of strategic leadership', *Academy of Management Executive,* 13, 1 (1999): pp. 43–57.

19. 'Bull strukturiert um', *Der Standard,* 24 February 2000.

20. Sumantra Ghosal and Christopher A. Bartlett, *The Individualized Corporation* (New York: HarperBusiness, 1997).

21. C.K. Prahalad and Gary Hamel, 'The core competence of the corporation', *Harvard Business Review,* 1990, pp. 79–86.

22. 'Tech in Use: Wie Unternehmen neue Produkte in der Praxis einsetzen', *Das Österreichische Industrie Magazin Spezial,* 2, February 2000, p. 24.

23. 'Stein für Stein', *Output,* 1 (2000): pp. 44–45.

24. Marianne Kosits, 'Outsourcing in the spirit of partnership', 18 February 2000: http://www-1.ibm.com/ibm/palisades/abi/html/wpoutsourcing–nn.html

25. The Outsourcing Institute, *The Outsourcing Index,* 1997, http://www.outsourcing.com.

26. Karen Stephenson and Stephan Haeckel, 'Making a virtual organization work', http://www.1.ibm.com/ibm/palisades/abi/html/wpvorg.html

27. Coling Hastings, *The New Organization* (London: McGraw-Hill, 1993).

28. Jeff Watkins, *Information Technology, Organisations and People* (London: Routledge, 1998).

29. Frank Ostroff, *The Horizontal Organization* (New York: Oxford University Press, 1999).

30. Bo Hedberg, Göran Dahlgren, Jörgen Hansson and Nils-Göran Olve, *Virtual Organizations and Beyond* (Chichester: Wiley, 1998).

31. Frank-O. Zimmermann, 'Structural and managerial aspects of virtual enterprises'. Paper presented at the European Conference on Virtual Enterprises and Networked Solutions – New Perspectives on Management, Communication and Information Technology, Paderborn, Germany 1997.

32. P. Maria Joseph Christie and Reuven R. Levary, 'Virtual corporations: recipe for success', *Industrial Management,* July–August (1998): pp. 7–11.

33. Richard Hale and Peter Whitlam, *Towards the Virtual Organization* (London: McGraw-Hill, 1998).

34. Susan G. Cohen, 'Designing effective self-managing work teams', 3 (University of Southern California, 1993).

35. K. Nancy Austin, 'Workers unite!', *Incentive,* February (1993): p. 15.

36. John R. Katzenbach and Douglas K. Smith, 'The discipline of teams', *Harvard Business Reviews,* March/April 1993, p. 119.

37. Anthony M. Townsend, Samuel M. DeMarie and Anthony R. Hendrickson, 'Virtual teams: technology and the workplace of the future', *Academy of Management Executive,* 12, 3 (1998): pp. 17–29.

38. Marie-Claude Boudreau, Karen D. Loch, Daniel Robey and Detmar Straud, 'Going global: using information technology to advance the competitiveness of the virtual transnational organization', *Academy of Management Executive,* 12, 4 (1998): pp. 120–128.

39. Marie-Claude Boudreau, Karen D. Loch, Daniel Robey and Detmar Straud, 'Going global: using information technology to advance the competitiveness of the virtual transnational organization', *Academy of Management Executive,* 12, 4 (1998): pp. 120–128.

40. Deborah L. Duarte and Tennant Nancy Snyder, *Mastering Virtual Teams: Strategies, Tools and Techniques that Succeed* (San Francisco: Jossey-Bass, 1999).

CHAPTER 16

Global marketing management audit and control

It is easier to exclude harmful passions than to rule them, and to deny them admittance than to control them after they have been admitted.
SENECA

Watch out for the fellow who talks about putting things in order! Putting things in order always means getting other people under your control.
DENIS DIDEROT, SUPPLEMENT TO BOUGAINVILLE'S 'VOYAGE', 1796

Who controls the past controls the future. Who controls the present controls the past.
GEORGE ORWELL

Chapter objectives

After reading this chapter, you will know:

- The differences between the various types of control.
- The factors supporting or inhibiting a global control system.
- The key elements of a global marketing audit.

Why is this important? Here are three situations in which you would need an understanding of the above issues:

- You need to measure and evaluate performance of global management.
- You need to establish a global marketing control system in your company.
- You need to organise a global marketing audit.

Practice link

Global marketing presents formidable problems to managers responsible for marketing control. Each national market is different from every other market. Distance and differences in language, custom and practices create communication problems. In larger companies, the size of operations and number of country subsidiaries often result in the creation of intermediate headquarters. This adds an organisational level to the control system.

PepsiCo, the US soft drink and snacks group announced in early 1997 that it was to sell off its fast-food business and concentrate on its soft drink business. The restaurant division comprises the Pizza Hut, Taco Bell and KFC – formerly Kentucky Fried Chicken – chains. With about 29,000 restaurants, it has more outlets than any fast-food company in the world.

The reason for the move, after 19 years of involvement in fast food, was a setback that the company had experienced in its competition with Coca-Cola and poor performance by the quick-food outlets of Pizza Hut, Taco Bell and KFC. Mr Roger Enrico, PepsiCo's chairman and chief executive, said the spin-off was intended to sharpen PepsiCo's focus: 'Given the distinctly different dynamics of restaurants and packaged goods, we believe all our business can better flourish with two separate and distinct managements and corporate structures'.

The PepsiCo example shows that planning and control often requires unusual or innovative responses to the challenging marketplace. In many reviews of control or bad performance, it is often implicit that the marketing objectives and strategy assume that the company will stay as it is, which is often counter-productive to the marketer, as limitation of both money and resources may often be the result of belonging to a conglomerate.

This chapter compares different types of control mechanisms and illustrates the various variables affecting control. Then, it identifies the major factors that influence the design of a global control system and reviews the global marketing audit. Finally, the balanced scorecard is described.

TYPES OF CONTROLS

In the managerial literature, control is defined as the process by which managers ensure that resources are used effectively and efficiently in the accomplishment of organisational objectives. Control activities are directed toward marketing programmes and other programmes and projects initiated by the planning process. Data measures and evaluations generated by the control process in the form of a global audit are also a major input to the planning process.

In order to institute either measures of output (i.e. balance sheets, sales and production data, product line growth, etc.) or of behaviour, two types of control may be used in regulating subsidiaries: first, bureaucratic, which is used extensively in Western organisations, and second cultural, which is prevalent in Japanese organisations. The level of delegation must be considered separately, and is frequently dependent upon a subsidiary's position and importance in the organisation. Table 16.1 displays a comparison of the two types of controls and their objectives.

Bureaucratic or formalised control includes budgets as more short-term elements in areas such as investment, cash, personnel and long-range programmes or plans.[1] Besides budgets, policy manuals, which direct functional performance, are also a bureaucratic type of control. In countries in which formal control mechanisms are less important, values and culture are objects of control. To gain control, it is evaluated to which extent an employee 'fits in'. Shared norms or shared philosophy are obtained by socialisation processes within the corporation and intensive personal and informal interactions.

Another useful distinction can be made between formal and informal control. In general, formal marketing control systems include performance standards, evaluation of actual performance and corrective action to remedy shortfalls. Self-control, group control and cultural control through the value system of a corporation can be summarised as informal control process.[2] The most common informal control tools are corporate culture and human resource development. It is assumed that in global companies, shared values are more appropriate to link the subsidiaries than formal control methods. To shape a shared vision, cultural values should include properties such as clarity, continuity and consistency. Two complementary culture-based processes are possible. First, the clan-based culture embodies a long socialisation process with strong norms and a defined set of internalised controls. In global companies in which integration is of high significance, a clan-based culture is instrumental in creating a shared vision. Second, the market-based culture is characterised by a limited socialisation process and loose norms. The control system in market-based cultures rests on performance measures. Another major informal control tool are the management development programmes. Training programmes aim at helping managers world-wide to understand the mission and the vision of their company. The programmes can also ensure the transfer of new values and provide a platform for managers to share their best practices and success stories.[3]

Table 16.1 Comparison of bureaucratic and cultural control mechanisms

| | Type of control | |
Object of control	Pure bureaucratic/formalised control	Pure cultural control
Output	Formal performance reports	Shared norms of performance
Behaviour	Company policies, manuals	Shared philosophy of management

Source: Michael R. Czinkota and Ilkka A. Ronkainen, *Global Marketing* (Fort Worth: The Dryden Press), p. 285.

Another classification of the marketing control process makes a clear distinction between two complementary processes: strategic control and operations control. Strategic control refers to an organisation's implicit and explicit goals, objectives, strategies, and capacity to perform. These variables influence the direction of the organisation, thus, strategic control ensures that they are performed well, which means 'doing the right things'. Finally, strategic control aims at defining on the one hand the fit between the capabilities and objectives of an organisation and on the other hand its environmental threats and opportunities. The second process, operations control, is concerned with the task of how well the organisation performs its marketing activities regarding its planned outcomes, or in other words, 'doing things right'. While strategic control considers primarily the direction of the organisation, operations control assumes that the direction is correct and puts the main emphasis

 EUROPEAN FOCUS

Diageo started with a clean sheet of paper

Many companies have decided that conventional budgeting is no longer worthwhile. Brian Lever, principal consultant at PwC in London, states that they want to go ahead and abandon budgeting but the staff have become so used to the budget as a means of control that they feel unsure without it. Robin Fraser is the director of the forum 'Beyond Budgeting Round Table', which is an initiative by about 20 companies in Europe. He says it is well known that budgets result in distortions. If an estimate of the likely outcome is realistic, it cannot be a testing target; the budget becomes a floor as well as a ceiling. Another effect is the constriction on managers' freedom to respond to customer demands in a fast-changing market.

Diageo is one of the world's leading consumer goods companies. Formed in 1997 through the merger of GrandMet and Guinness, Diageo has an outstanding portfolio of world-famous food and drinks brands including Smirnoff, Johnnie Walker, J&B, Gordon's, Pillsbury, Häagen-Dazs, Guinness and Burger King. Because of the merger, Diageo had to restructure radically. In the new focus on value, rationalising the planning and budgetary processes for the brands was an immediate priority. Pavi Binning, the group financial controller of Diageo, sees the finance function as an agent and not as an opponent of change. Diageo needed to focus on consumers, on people, on its brands and on per-

formance. In the spirits business, as Binning explains, 'a painstaking economic profit analysis was carried out and the markets and brands with the highest value potential selected. Then specific "value levers" likely to improve profit were identified – it could be volume, price, cost, marketing expenditure, or some other factor.' In the next step, strategies and action plans were devised to work on the 'levers', and indicators agreed to track progress against targets, while keeping a check on factors such as brand awareness and market penetration. This by now forms the control mechanism at Diageo. At group level, Diageo now focus on year-on-year performance and on whether the operating unit is delivering against the trajectory agreed in its strategic plan.

Removing the budget, however, is only possible once people are ready to accept the responsibility. Organisational support is needed to change behaviour and build capabilities.

Food for thought

- Why does Robin Fraser state that budgets can result in distortions? What are the disadvantages of budgeting?
- Do you think Diageo will succeed in their attempt to abandon budgeting? What do you think about the idea?

Source: http://www.diageo.com/, Lester, Tom, 'Cutting the ties that bind', *Financial Times*, 9 May 2000, p. 16.

on the improvement of the organisation's ability to perform specific tasks. The results of the two processes differ in an important manner. Undesirable results such as declining sales, eroding market share or sinking profits can result within both marketing control systems. But the difference between strategic control and operational control lies in the remedies. Strategic control orientation influences the effectiveness, which addresses the question of whether the organisation is achieving its intended goals of seeking opportunities and reducing threats in an organisation's environment. Operations control orientation is characterised by efforts in increasing the marketing effort or in finding ways to improve the efficiency, which relates to productivity.[4]

VARIABLES AFFECTING CONTROL

A marketing management control system is affected by many aspects. Of particular importance are the communication system, the adequacy of data and the diversity of environments.

Communication systems

An important aspect of communication is the distance between the head office and the overseas divisions. The greater the distance, the more likely it is that time, expense and errors will increase. This even holds despite the use of electronic communication systems that operate in real time. In contrast, the closer the subsidiary is to its headquarters, the less control is lost. Besides the distance, the location plays an important role in communication: the more advanced the telecommunications of a country, the easier the communication process.

As already described earlier in this book, information technology (IT) has an enormous impact on communication systems. In the last 20 years, technology has improved greatly. Global voice mail, facsimile transmissions and telephone communications, for example, improve reporting. Finally, the Internet enables global networks by linking computer users who have unlimited access to databases. IT reduces a lot of geographical constraints.[5]

Data

Economic, industrial and consumer information is a necessary part of control. In countries where this data is readily available and dependable, marketing planning and control can work on the basis of accurate external data. Where such data are not readily available, as is the case in many developing countries and markets, there are problems. In 1996, for example, Russian economic data showed that the country's GDP had fallen by 6 per cent. At the same time, the *Financial Times* was including Russian firms in its '500 index' of the world's leading companies and the prospects for the economy were thought to be improving.[6] The interpretation of the data by economists revealed that it had underestimated GDP output figures by not accounting for the service sector. Some companies had also reported lower output to avoid taxation.

Diversity of environment

The diversity of environment will influence the development of the marketing plan and its implementation. This is because the successful development and control of a marketing programme depends on variables such as currency values, legal structures, political systems, advertising options and cultural factors. The needs of the local situation might therefore differ from corporate goals, and this has to be taken into account. It is no surprise that the diversity of environments can lead to conflicts between the needs of the local situation and overall corporate goals.

ESTABLISHING A CONTROL SYSTEM

A good control system consists of three basic elements:

● the establishment of standards
● the measurement of performance
● the analysis of deviations.

Each of these elements is simple to understand and conceptualise, but their use in practice creates tensions and problems. A variety of problems arise, for example, when overdue reliance on each of the elements creates the illusion of control. Besides this, corporate strategy can be harmed by ineffective or defective control systems.

Establishment of standards

For purposes of control, standards are a necessary part of the control system. In general, the corporate headquarters' personnel together with the local marketing organisation set the standards through a joint process. Efforts of managers are directed through the standards which they should clearly define and accept. The corporate goals, which direct the process of setting standards, are achieved through effective and efficient implementation of a marketing strategy. Due to their extreme importance, standards should be strongly connected to the strategy of the corporation and to the sources of long-term competitive advantage.

Control standards rest on the desired behaviour of the people. The behaviour should reflect the actions to be taken to implement the strategy. Statements about what is to be accomplished serve as performance standards which can be defined as an expected level of performance against which actual performance can be compared.

Evaluating performance

The second basic element consists of processes which monitor performance. Measurement of performance against standards can occur at various levels in the organisation.

Three financial measures are used most to evaluate international performance. These are return on investment, budget analysis and historical comparison. In a survey, 95 per cent of corporate officers stated that they use the same evaluation technique for foreign and domestic operations. The rate of return was mentioned as the single most important measure. Because of aspects such as foreign currencies, different rates of inflation or different tax law the return on investment can cause problems when applied to international operations. Both the net income figure and the investment base may be seriously distorted.

Using standards is not without problems. One obvious difficulty is knowing which standards to use. Global managers may judge themselves successful in their cost performance but find that the product is rejected in the marketplace. Implied in the problem of standards is the issue of compatibility. As with corporate objectives, tension can exist between standards that can cause problems for the organisation. Driving down costs can often be achieved by reducing labour costs and increasing workloads. This can increase pressure and raise absenteeism, which in turn hits productivity. Seeing the connections between performance standards is a necessary part in appraising corporate performance.

In this context, it has been argued that the control and reward systems should differ between global and multidomestic MNCs. While the multidomestic MNC should use loose controls with its foreign units, the global MNC needs tight controls over its many units. The multidomestic MNC's management of each geographic unit should be given considerable operational latitude but be expected to meet some performance target. Its top management should also emphasise budgets and non-financial measures of performance, such as market share, productivity, public image, employee morale and relations with the host country government, because profit and return on investment are unreliable measures in international operations. In order to differentiate between subsidiary worth and management performance, multiple measures should be used. The global MNC spreads the manufacturing and marketing operations of a few uniform products around the world in order to reduce costs and gain competitive advantage. From there, the strategic operational decisions must be centralised.[7]

Analysis of deviations

When the actual performance falls short of the expected standard, management is forced to initiate actions. In order to achieve the corporate goals and to reduce discrepancies between established standards and actual performance, several options exist. Either the actual performance is improved, the performance standard is changed, or both options are applied. In an international setting this can be rather difficult because of geographical and cultural differences.

Key points

- Formal and informal control are two types of control. While the former includes performance standards, evaluation of actual performance and corrective action to remedy the shortfalls, informal control consists of self-control, group and cultural control.

- Formalised and cultural control are used to regulate subsidiaries. Depending on the type of control, output and behaviour are different.

- The management control system can be influenced by the communication system of the corporation, the available data and the diversity of the environment.

- A control system includes three basic elements, which are (1) the establishment of standards, (2) the measurement of performance and (3) the analysis of deviations.

THE GLOBAL MARKETING AUDIT

A global marketing audit can be defined as a comprehensive, systematic and periodic examination of a company's or business unit's marketing environment, objectives, strategies, programmes, policies and activities, which is conducted with the objective of identifying existing and potential problems and opportunities and recommending a plan of action to improve a company's marketing performance.

The global marketing audit is a tool for evaluating and improving a company's global marketing operations. The audit is an effort to assess effectiveness and efficiency of marketing strategies, practices, policies and procedures vis-à-vis the firm's opportunities, objectives and resources.

A full marketing audit has two basic characteristics. The first is that it is formal and systematic. Asking questions at random as they occur to the questioner may bring about useful insights, but this is not a marketing audit. The effectiveness of an audit normally increases to the extent that it involves a sequence of orderly diagnostic steps, as is the case in the conduct of a public accounting audit.

The second characteristic of a marketing audit is that it is conducted periodically. Most companies in trouble are well on their way to disaster before the trouble is fully apparent. It is therefore important that the audit be conducted periodically and that this even includes periods when there are apparent problems or difficulties inherent in the company's operations.

The audit may be broad or it may be a narrowly focused assessment. A full marketing audit is comprehensive. It reviews the company's marketing environment, competition, objectives, strategies, organisation, systems, procedures and practices in every area of the marketing mix, including product, pricing, distribution, communications, customer service, and research strategy and policy.

There are two types of audit: independent and internal. An independent marketing audit is conducted by someone who is free from influence of the organisation being audited. The independent audit may or may not be objective: it is quite possible to influence a consultant or professional firm that you are paying. The company that wants a truly independent audit should discuss with the independent auditor the importance of objectivity. A potential limitation of an independent marketing audit is the lack of understanding of the industry by the auditor. In many industries, there is no substitute for experience, because if auditors do not have it, they are simply not going to see the subtle clues that any pro would easily recognise. On the other hand, the independent auditor may see obvious indications that the experienced pro may be unable to see.

An internal or self-audit may be quite valuable because it is conducted by marketers who understand the industry. However, it may lack the objectivity of an independent audit. Because of the strengths and limitations of the two types of audit, we recommend that both be conducted periodically for the same scope and time period, and that the results be compared. The comparison may lead to insights on how to strengthen the performance of the marketing team.

Setting objectives and scope of the audit

The first step of an audit is a meeting between company executives and the auditor to agree on objectives, coverage, depth, data sources, report format, and time period for the audit.

Gathering data

One of the major tasks in conducting an audit is data collection. A detailed plan of interviews, secondary research, review of internal documents, and so forth is required. This effort usually involves an auditing team.

A basic rule in data collection is not to rely solely on the opinion of people being audited for data. In auditing a sales organisation, it is absolutely essential to talk to field sales personnel as well as sales management; and, of course, no audit is complete without direct contact with customers and suppliers.

Creative auditing techniques should be encouraged and explored by the auditing team. For example, if an organisation has developed an elaborate marketing incentive programme that is purported to generate results with customers, an audit should involve customer contact to find out if indeed the programme is actually having any impact.

Preparing and presenting the report

After data collection and analysis, the next step is the preparation and presentation of the audit report. This presentation should restate the objectives and scope of the audit, present the main findings, and present major recommendations and conclusions as well as major headings for further study and investigation.

Components of the marketing audit

The six major components of a full global marketing audit are marketing environment audit, marketing strategy audit, marketing organisation audit, marketing systems audit, marketing productivity audit and marketing function audit (see Table 16.2).

Problems, pitfalls, and potential of the global marketing audit

The marketing audit presents a number of problems and pitfalls. Setting objectives can be a pitfall, if indeed the objectives are blind to a major problem. It is important for the auditor to be open to expanding or shifting objectives and priorities while conducting the audit.

Similarly, new data sources may appear during the course of an audit, and the auditor should be open to such sources. Thus, the approach of the auditor should simultaneously be systematic, following a predetermined outline, and perceptive and open to new directions and sources that appear in the course of the audit investigation.

Report presentation

One of the biggest problems in marketing auditing is that the executive who commissions the audit may have higher expectations about what the audit will do for the company than the actual results seem to offer. An audit is valuable even if it does not offer major new directions or panaceas. It is important for all concerned to recognise that improvements at the margin are what truly make a difference between success and mediocrity. Marketers understand this fact and recognise it in the audit. Do not look for dramatic revolutionary findings or panaceas. Accept and recognise that improvement at the margin is the winner's game in global marketing.

Global marketers, even more than their domestic counterparts, need marketing audits to assess far-flung efforts in highly diverse environments. The global marketing audit should be at the top of the list of programmes for strategic excellence and implementation excellence for the winning global company. The relationship among strategic planning, operational planning and control is illustrated in Figure 16.1.

Table 16.2 The six major components of a full global marketing audit

Components	Auditing variables
1. Marketing environment audit	
– Macro-environment	Demographic
	Economic
	Ecological
	Technological
	Political
	Cultural
– Task environment	Markets
	Customers
	Competitors
	Distribution and dealers
	Suppliers
	Facilitators and marketing firms
	Publics
2. Marketing strategy audit	Business mission
	Marketing objectives and goals
	Strategy
3. Marketing organisation audit	Formal structure
	Functional efficiency
	Interface efficiency
4. Marketing systems audit	Marketing information system
	Marketing planning system
	Marketing control system
	New product development system
5. Marketing productivity audit	Profitability analysis
	Cost effectiveness analysis
6. Marketing function audit	Products
	Price
	Distribution
	Advertising, sales, promotion and publicity
	Salesforce

Source: Philip Kotler, *Marketing Management. Analysis, Planning, Implementation, and Control* (London: Prentice-Hall, 1991).

For companies with global operations, marketing control presents additional challenges. The rate of environmental change in a global company is a dimension of each of the national markets in which it operates. At the beginning of this book, we examined these environments; each is changing at a different rate, and each exhibits unique characteristics. The multiplicity of national environments challenges the global marketing control system with much greater environmental heterogeneity and, therefore, greater complexity in its control. Finally, global marketing can create special communications problems associated with the great distance between markets and headquarters and differences among managers in languages, customs and practices.

When company management decides that it wants to develop a global strategy, it is essential that control of the subsidiary operations of the company shifts from the subsidiary to the headquarters. The subsidiary will continue to make vital inputs into the strategic planning process, but the control of the strategy must shift from subsidiary to headquarters. This involves a shift in the balance of power in the organisation and may result in strong resistance to change. In many companies, a tradition of subsidiary autonomy and self-sufficiency limits the influence of headquarters. Three types

Figure 16.1 Relationship of strategic control and planning

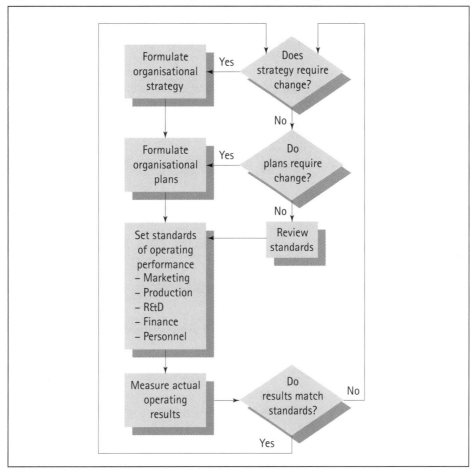

of mechanisms are available to help headquarters acquire control: (1) data management mechanisms, (2) managers' management mechanisms that shift the perception of self-interest from subsidiary autonomy to global business performance, and (3) conflict resolution mechanisms that resolve conflicts triggered by necessary tradeoffs.

Key points

- The global marketing audit is a tool for evaluating and improving a company's global marketing operations. It involves comprehensive, systematic and periodic examination of a company's marketing environment, objectives, strategies and activities.

- Two types of marketing audit exist. The independent marketing audit is conducted by an external auditor in order to restrict the influence of the audited organisation. The self-audit is carried out by a company's internal management.

- A full marketing audit comprises six major components, namely marketing environment audit, marketing strategy audit, marketing organisation audit, marketing systems audit, marketing productivity audit and marketing function audit.

GLOBAL PERSPECTIVE

KPMG's new approach to auditing

KPMG, Peat Marwick, one of the former 'Big Six' accounting firms, decided to reengineer its audit methodology in 1994. Industry pressures and competition led the 100-year-old firm to change its audit approach to allow it to add more value to the audit process for its clients. The new approach, the Business Measurement Process (BMP), delivers an audit by focusing on the client's business processes and risks instead of traditional transaction-based auditing. The audit goes beyond the numbers to provide the client with insight about its business and industry.

Once the firm developed the new approach, the challenge was to implement it world-wide. Because the new approach represented a comprehensive change, simply issuing a new manual for the staff to read was inadequate. Behavioural and cultural changes were at issue as well.

What is BMP? The Business Measurement Process (BMP) adds another dimension to the audit process by evaluating business processes and risks. Five interrelated principles define the BMP approach: strategic analysis of the client's operations, business process analysis, risk assessment, business performance measurement, and continuous improvement to improve the client's performance.

1 *Strategic analysis.* During the initial stage, the KPMG team works with the client to identify and understand critical elements of the business and the environment – including the competition, technology, economic conditions, legislation, industry issues, the client's objectives and strategies, and the key risks that threaten achievement of the objectives.

2 *Business process analysis.* In this stage, the team studies the client's business processes that most closely relate to achieving the business objectives. Information gathered during this stage is used in preparing the business model profile.

3 *Risk assessment.* The KPMG team, in conjunction

with management, identifies processes in place to address and control risks and considers how they are being addressed and controlled. Information gathered during this stage is used in preparing the business risk profile.

4 *Business measurement.* Driven by the risk assessment of the previous stage, the audit is completed during the business measurement stage. The team focuses on processes and variables that have the greatest impact on financial results. Comparisons of these measurements, along with financial results, benchmark data, or other appropriate measures are obtained to develop a 'gap analysis'.

5 *Continuous improvement.* The gap analysis allows the team to identify a client's performance improvement opportunities. In this stage, the team focuses on both the financial and non-financial measures most likely to generate the improvement the client seeks.

According to Leslie A. Coolidge, partner in charge, Centre for Leadership Development, KPMG's clients are very positive about the new approach, particularly with the client service team's level of understanding of clients' business. KPMG client, Margaret Cass, associate vice-president for finance and administration, Rocher Institute of Technology says: 'BMP isn't just a once-a-year-audit – it's a year round relationship. It is much more valuable than the type of audit we had in the past.'

Food for thought

● From the point of view of an executive of an internationally operating company, what might be the key advantages of KPMG's change towards business process and risk based auditing?

● Which additional skills do KPMG auditors need to develop in order to carry out valuable and effective business process and risk auditing?

Source: Adapted from Kristine Mayer Brands, 'KPMG Peat Marwick's Business Measurement Process – Implementing Change', *Managing Accounting*, January 1998, p. 72.

THE BALANCED SCORECARD

Many companies, such as the Swedish furniture group IKEA, the bearing-maker SKF, the oil services company Schlumberger or the Danish petrochemicals group Borealis, recognise that the traditional command-and-control budgeting systems are perhaps the greatest barriers to change. The tools of product profitability, departmental costs, unit sales or capital efficiency ratios were used for decades to plan, control and evaluate performance. But in modern business they are increasingly seen unsuitable because they ignore, for example, knowledge or intellectual capital, factors which are expected to improve shareholder value. Moreover, the company's budgets and forecasts give the illusion of control and make it harder for managers to react quickly to business opportunities. In order to address these problems, Borealis sets targets by the balanced scorecard process and emphasises management performance rather than the business cycle: fixed costs are controlled through trend reporting, activity-based management and cost targets. Higher level financial and tax planning relies on rolling financial forecasts. Bjarte Bogsnes, vice-president for corporate control, simply says, 'The new system is not just simpler – it gives us far more information and far more control than the traditional budget ever did.'[8]

The term 'balanced scorecard' was coined in 1992 by Robert S. Kaplan and David Norton.[9] The concept offers a way for a corporation to achieve a wider perspective on its strategic decisions rather than looking at financial measures alone in assessing organisational performance. It represents a methodology which turns a business's strategic objectives into specific measures in four key dimensions: finance, customer, internal processes and innovation and learning for employees. Figure 16.2 shows how the scorecard lets managers introduce the four management processes which contribute to linking long-term strategic objectives with short-term actions.

The balanced scorecard can be seen as a concept which is based on the assumption that for every action, there is an equal and opposite reaction. Thus, it helps companies to determine what impact a potential change will have on the rest of the organisation. The benefits and its popularity are due to its simplicity, with clear cause and effect relationships.[10]

By now, the balanced scorecard has become very popular and it is expected that its popularity will increase in future. The Gardner Group, for example, predicts that by the end of 2000 at least 40 per cent of Fortune 1,000 companies will be using the balanced scorecard.[11] Another survey, conducted in the last two years by the IMA's Cost Management Group shows that 40 per cent of the companies are in the process of changing their performance measurement systems. The interviewed managers say that the balanced scorecard provides a better understanding of non-financial areas, such as on-time delivery and defect rates, which ultimately impact the financials.

Using the balanced scorecard, managers can see cause-and-effect relationships. Figure 16.3 displays how every objective measurement managers select is part of the chain of events that leads to the corporate goal. Companies typically develop their objectives and measures for the internal-business-process perspective after formulating objectives and measures for the financial and customer perspective. The most critical processes for achieving customer and shareholder value are identified.

Linked to the strategic themes displayed in Figure 16.3, measures are the quality of market share (profitability by segment), per cent of revenue from new products, channel transactions mix, internal customer satisfaction, cross-sell ratio, selling contacts per salesperson and new revenue per salesperson.

Figure 16.2 Translating vision and strategy

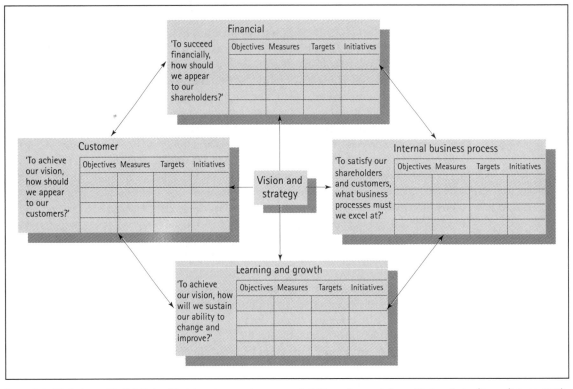

Source: Robert S. Kaplan and David P. Norton, 'The balanced scorecard – measures that drive performance', *Harvard Business Review* (January/February 1992).

Figure 16.3 The generic value chain model

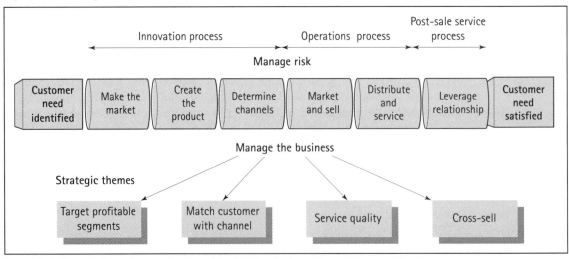

Source: Adapted from: 'The balanced scorecard: not just another fad', *Executive Journal* (January/February 2000): p. 13.

EUROPEAN FOCUS

Balanced Scorecard in the Royal Bank of Scotland Group

The Royal Bank of Scotland Group, headquartered in Edinburgh, provides high quality banking, insurance and related financial services. Its core market is the United Kingdom, but the Royal Bank is also active in Europe to serve and develop the UK banking customer base, and in the north-east USA to diversify earnings. In striving towards the aim to be recognised as the best performing financial services group in the United Kingdom, the Royal Bank of Scotland is mindful of the responsibilities to shareholders, customers, employees and the communities in which it operates. The primary challenge is achieving the aim while successfully balancing these responsibilities.

In common with many organisations, the Royal Bank of Scotland used to use financial numbers to manage the business. It also rewarded performance on current results rather than a balance of current and future value. This resulted in problems with the translation and the communication of strategic plans. To address this problem, a cross-functional team, including internal consultants, Finance and HR, was set up. This team introduced a classic four-quadrant balanced scorecard. Scott Fairburn,

member of the bank's internal consultancy arm, describes the benefits of the reporting for each Business Unit Head as follows: 'The main benefits have been to encourage senior management to focus on measures in all the four quadrants when considering operational and strategic development and plans.' Certainly, some difficulties in implementing the balanced scorecard occurred. First, the team was confronted with the reluctance to change existing management information and reporting. Then, balancing bottom-up/top-down objectives was another issue. It was observed that the setting of targets can be difficult when linked to rewards. And finally, where does the scorecard stop and individual performance management start?

Food for thought:

- What are the potential advantages and problems of a balanced scorecard approach to performance measurement?
- Are balanced scorecards equally useful in different industries and countries? What are the limitations to using balanced scorecards?

Source: http://www.royalbankscot.co.uk/; Michael Tuck and Ruki Clark, 'World productivity congress', *Management Services*, January 2000.

Essentially, there are six basic questions a balanced scorecard seeks to address:

1 How well are you meeting customer expectations (customer perspective)?
2 How well are you developing your human resources (HR) (HR perspective)?
3 How well are you meeting financial expectations (financial perspective)?
4 How productively are you operating (operating systems perspective)?
5 How effectively are you operating (learning or change perspective)?
6 How well are you dealing with environmental or regulatory forces that may alter the organisational playing field (environmental perspective)?[12]

Key points

- The balanced scorecard offers a way for a corporation to achieve a wider perspective on its strategic decisions than would be possible by looking at financial measures alone.
- Using the balanced scorecard, managers can see cause-and-effect relationships.
- Balanced scorecards focus on four key areas, namely finance, customer, internal processes and innovation and learning for employees.

Summary

By establishing control procedures, a firm can exploit global opportunities. For global marketing control practices to be effective, differences from purely domestic control must be recognised and implemented in planning and control practices. The marketing audit, which includes several components, serves as a tool for evaluating and improving a company's global marketing operations. As many companies recognise that the traditional command-and-control budgeting systems do not fit into a changing environment, they decrease the emphasis on formal budgeting and implement the balanced scorecard. This new approach is expected to become more popular, since it represents a methodology which turns a business's strategic objectives into specific measures in the areas of finance, customer, internal processes and innovation and learning for employees.

Concepts and definitions

Control

Control is defined as the process by which managers ensure that resources are used effectively and efficiently in the accomplishment of organisational objectives. Control activities are directed toward marketing programmes and other programmes and projects initiated by the planning process.

Control system

A good control system consists of the establishments of standards, the measurement of performance and the analysis of deviations. In practice, their use creates tensions and problems. A variety of problems arise for example when overdue reliance on each of the elements creates the illusion of control. Besides this, corporate strategy can be harmed by ineffective or defective control systems.

Global marketing audit

A global marketing audit can be defined as a comprehensive, systematic and periodic examination of a company's or business unit's marketing environment, objectives, strategies and activities, which is conducted with the objective of identifying existing and potential problems and opportunities and recommending a plan of action to improve a company's marketing performance.

Balanced scorecard

A balanced scorecard represents a methodology which turns a business's strategic objectives into specific measures in four key dimensions: finance, customer, internal processes and innovation and learning for employees. The balanced scorecard can be seen as a concept which is based on the assumption that for every action, there is an equal and opposite reaction. Thus, it helps companies to determine what impact a potential change will have on the rest of the organisation.

Discussion questions

1 Describe the various types of control.

2 What are the major variables influencing control in a global company?

3 What are the key elements of a good control system?

4 What is a global marketing audit and what are its main components?

5 Discuss the possible advantages/disadvantages of an independent and an internal or self-audit.

6 Why should the balanced scorecard be used in a global company?

Webmistress's hotspots

Beyond Budgeting Round Table
The BBRT was formed in 1998 to investigate companies that have replaced budgeting with new performance management processes. Join it to receive past deliverables and benefit from the current work.
http://www.cam-i.org/bb

KPMG
KPMG is the global professional advisory firm whose aim is to turn knowledge into value for the benefit of its clients, its people and its communities. With more than 100,000 people collaborating world-wide, the firm provides consulting, tax and legal, financial advisory and assurance services in more than 820 cities in 159 countries.
http://www.kpmg.com/

The Marketing Audit
The Marketing Audit, which was founded in December 1984 by Jonathan R. Lax as an industrial market research firm, is committed to improving strategic decision making when companies are faced with specific business challenges.
http://www.marketingaudit.com/

Balanced Scorecard (BSC) home page
The BSC is a conceptual framework for translating an organisation's vision into a set of performance indicators distributed among four perspectives: Financial, Customer, Internal Business Processes, and Learning and Growth.
http://www.pr.doe.gov/bsc001.htm

Balanced Scorecard Board
The board is to be used by members of the Leading Edge Forum for discussions of the Balanced Scorecard.
http://webteach.ubalt.edu/Scorecard/index.html

Jokes on accountants
http://www.home.cybrnet.net/~bfinlay/account.htm
http://www.yonkers.org/engineersplace/Humor/TrainTickets.htm
http://www.execpc.com/~thorsten/FUNGUYS.HTML

Suggested readings

Epstein, M.J. and J.F. Manzoni, *The Balanced Scorecard and Tableau De Bord: A Global Perspective on Translating Strategy into Action*. Fontainebleau: INSEAD, The European Institute of Business Administration, 1997.

Halal, William E., 'Global strategic management in a new world order', *Business Horizons* (November/December 1993).

Kaplan, Robert S. and David P. Norton, *The Balanced Scorecard: Translating Strategy into Action*. Boston: Harvard Business School Press, 1996.

Schill, Ronald L. and David N. McArthur, 'Redefining the strategic competitive unit: towards a new global marketing paradigm?', *International Marketing Review*, 9, 3 (1992): pp. 5–24.

Stevenson, Howard H. and Jeffrey L. Cruikshank, *Do Lunch or Be Lunch: The Power of Predictability in Creating Your Future*. Boston: Harvard Business School Press, 1997.

Womack, James P. and Daniel T. Jones, *Lean Thinking:* *Banish Waste and Create Wealth in Your Corporation*. New York: Simon & Schuster, 1996.

Yip, George S., *Total Global Strategy*. Upper Saddle River, NJ: Prentice Hall, 1992.

Notes

1. Michael R. Czinkota and Ilkka A. Ronkainen, *Global Marketing* (Fort Worth: The Dryden Press, 1996), p. 285.

2. Sally Dibb, Lyndon Simkin, William M. Pride and O.C. Ferrell. *Marketing*. European Edition (Boston: Houghton Mifflin Company, 1991).

3. Masaaki Kotabe and Kristiaan Helsen, *Global Marketing Management* (New York: John Wiley, 1998).

4. Roger A. Kerin and Robert A. Peterson, *Strategic Marketing Problems*. 6th edn (Boston: Allyn and Bacon, 1993).

5. Jean-Pierre Jeannet and H. David Hennessey, *Global Marketing Strategies* (Boston: Houghton Mifflin Company, 1998).

6. 'FT 500', *Financial Times*, 24 January 1997.

7. Thomas L. Wheelen and David J. Hunger, *Strategic Management and Business Policy*. 5th edn (Reading, Massachusetts: Addison-Wesley, 1995).

8. Jeremy Hope and Robin Fraser, 'Technology and management: Counting on a new measure of success', *Financial Times*, 25 May 1999.

9. Robert S. Kaplan and David P. Norton, 'The balanced scorecard – measures that drive performance', *Harvard Business Review* (Jan/Feb 1992).

10. Robin Robinson, 'Balanced scorecard', *Computerworld*, 24 January 2000, p. 52; Cheenu Srinivasan, 'From "vicious" to "virtuous" scorecards', *Australian CPA*, October (1999): pp. 48–50.

11. Mark L. Frigo and Kip R. Krumwiede, 'The balanced scorecard', *Strategic Finance* (January 2000): pp. 50–54.

12. 'The balanced scorecard: not just another fad', *Executive Journal* (January/February 2000): pp. 12–16.

CHAPTER 17

The future of global marketing

The only way to predict the future is to have the power to shape the future.
ERIC HOFFER, THE PASSIONATE STATE OF MIND (1954)

I never think about the future, it comes early enough.
ALBERT EINSTEIN

Chapter objectives

After reading this chapter, you will know:

● Some of the major forces shaping the future of global marketing.
● The demands that increasing business complexity will place on global business leaders.
● The different opportunities open to you, if you intend to pursue a career in global marketing.

Why is this important? Here are three situations in which you would need an understanding of the above issues:

● You have been asked to work on a long-term plan for a global trading company, in which you need to develop different scenarios for future development opportunities.

● The human resources department of your company has asked for your advice in drafting an ideal profile for new appointments into an international marketing function.

● A friend has asked you which opportunities are open to someone interested in pursuing a career in global marketing.

Practice link

Providing a business example for something that will happen in the future is as impossible as nailing jelly onto the wall. Consequently, we decided to simply share with you two contrasting scenarios of how life for an international marketing executive *might* look like in future. You will be the judge of which scenario is more realistic:

First, meet John Steiner, who was originally born in Vienna but now lives in Toronto.[1] He is 38, likes eating sushi, and is Executive Vice President for a Canadian consulting firm with offices in Toronto, Vancouver, Beijing, Frankfurt and Singapore. Although he lives in Toronto, he spends two thirds of his time consulting throughout China. In addition, he has some clients elsewhere in Asia and North America. Sitting beside an attractive female British executive on the plane, he tries out his new opening line as a conversation starter (in this respect, we do not expect any changes):

'Where is the plane landing?' John asks. Seventeen flights in two weeks have left him genuinely confused. Still, his approach seems to work, she gives him a smile and he proceeds to tell her about this one horrid week, in which he left Singapore with the flu, arrived home in Toronto to discover that a frozen pipe had burst and had to leave immediately to board a plane to Chicago for a two-day client workshop. On to Detroit, he was still battling jet lag and battling the flu. Eventually, he came back to Toronto to take a brief look at his flooded house. Deciding that he could not do anything about this right now, he returned to the airport to board another plane to China.

'And what, if anything, is the upside of your lifestyle?' she asks.

'You get to know how the world really turns,' replies John. 'And the benefit of having an eclectic soap collection should not be underestimated.' By now, his fellow passenger was mildly amused and willing to continue the conversation.

'But surely there are downsides of being an international marketing executive?' she inquires.

'Sure, subtract all the years I have been living in Nanjing, Nairobi and New York, and you find that I have the social development of a 16-year-old. You become a nomad, who is economically and spiritually detached from home – wherever this might be.'

Should I invite her over to Toronto to show her my international soap collection, he wonders ...

Leaving our vision of John, the nomadic road warrior, behind us, let's meet Helen Kowatschek. After completing her distance learning PhD with CNN.Com, she joined e-tea, a company specialising in trading Asian herbal teas. Having an affinity with Scotland, she decided to live in Edinburgh. Currently, Helen is just preparing for a meeting with a Chinese supplier. His life-size hologram will appear in her office in a few minutes.[2] She floats her chair to the meeting space of her office, asks her digital assistant, embedded in her chair, to enable noise cancellation and to adjust the virtual dividers of her office space. For some years now, ubiquitous technology is accomplishing the tedium work in Helen's job, so that she can focus nearly entirely on relationship building.

The hologram appears; a good-looking chap in his late 20s, about her own age. He smiles in a friendly way and sits down opposite her. But what is going on, why does she not understand him? Well the automatic language detection and translation function seems faulty. The Chinese hologram speaks Italian – well even in 2050, technology is still not perfect ...

Will the life of a future international marketing executive resemble John's existence, a hectic nomad who looks for a restaurant that serves breakfast at midnight because his body clock has not yet adjusted to his current location? Or will it be the quiet and serene life of Helen, who enjoys the advances in teleconferencing facilities that have largely eliminated the need for long-distance travel and who is surrounded by unobtrusive machines that take care of everyday chores?

While, in this final chapter, although it is fun to speculate, we clearly do not know the answer. However, what we already know today is that certain key trends exist which permit a glimpse into the future of international marketing. Below, we shall identify some of these trends, look at possible managerial responses and discuss the likely leadership challenges. The chapter ends with a brief look at career opportunities in international marketing.

FORCES SHAPING THE FUTURE OF GLOBAL MARKETING

International marketing scholars generally agree that in future the pace of change will accelerate further. This acceleration will not only happen in terms of technological development, but also in terms of political and socio-cultural trends.[3] But even focusing on information technology alone, a further acceleration in the speed of change is difficult to comprehend. Already, observers are struggling for expressions that adequately describe the pace of changes. Phrases like 'revolution' and 'paradigm shift' have been coined and comparisons to the industrial revolution, the discovery of electricity or even the invention of the wheel are commonplace. And another revolution, voice recognition technology, is just round the corner; rendering keyboards largely superfluous and thus finally fulfilling the science-fiction notion of commanding a machine through the human voice, this technology will dramatically accelerate the use of computers and drive information and communication technology into completely new applications.[4]

It is expected that the 'technological shock' will fundamentally reshape the way marketing is done.[5] In such an environment, experience, products and processes are becoming obsolete at a breathtaking pace. Add the accelerated speed, intensity and diversity of competition and we can observe a paradox: never before has the time for aggressive market entries been as good as today. And never before has the value of incumbency been as low as today.

Below, we have singled out some of the forces likely to shape the future of global marketing. As you will see, the future can be expected to be full of contradictions, paradoxes and complexities.

Growth and prosperity versus poverty and despair

An encouraging development we can observe is that *most* of the world's poor countries are getting richer. The emergence of newly rich countries from among the ranks of the former less developed group breaks the long monopoly of Western Europe, the United States and Canada, and in this century Japan, on the rich nation status. These countries prove that it is not necessary to be European, North American or Japanese to be rich. Countries like Singapore and Hong Kong are already high-income countries; East Asia in particular is home to many countries that have been growing at annual rates of 7 per cent or higher. A 7 per cent real growth rate will double real income in a decade. The emerging rich countries include smaller countries like South Korea as well as the largest countries in the world, China and India, which have begun to develop a middle class. Even in Africa south of the Sahara, many countries are for the first time in decades experiencing a growth in real income that is greater than the growth in population. For the first time in the history of the world, there is the very real likelihood of a much broader global prosperity. For the international marketer, these developments translate into dramatic growth opportunities. For example, some 65 per cent of the world's population have never received a phone call and some 75 per cent have never taken a photo.[6]

There is, however, also a darker side to globalisation: the gap between the rich and the poor is increasing. 'Globalisation and the growth in international trade have driven down the wages of the unskilled and increased mobility at the top has driven up executive pay.'[7] In the UK, for example, the gap between the rich and poor rose to a level greater than at any time since records began 100 years ago.[8] In addition to the gap between rich and poor, there is also the danger that some countries or entire regions are bypassed by the benefits of globalisation and are marginalised. Today, many African children still lack the resources to learn reading and writing, while their contemporaries in the developed world use satellites and telephones and computers and e-mail.[9] The Norwegian Prime Minister commented: 'Globalisation will – unless it takes place within a democratic system of political checks and balances – increase inequalities within nations and between nations. It creates wealth among those who have the ability to profit from the new opportunities. But it also punishes those who do not have access to the resources necessary to become competitive. It would be dishonest to blame all social ills on globalisation. But there is a strong body of evidence that globalisation may deepen some of negative sides of modern society.'[10]

Free markets or growing protectionism

After almost a century of debate in the world about the merits of markets and marketing versus a state-controlled system of allocating resources and controlling production, the capitalist/marketing model has clearly won. Markets are king the world around, with the exception of Cuba and North Korea. The big issue today is whether economic democracy (the market allocation of resources, one Euro, dollar, yen, or rupiah/one vote) must be combined with political democracy. This debate will continue. What is no longer debated is the global emergence of the acceptance of markets and marketing.

Despite the nearly universal acceptance of free market principles, protectionism appears to be on the rise. 'Around the world,' observed *The Economist*, 'support for free trade is weak at best.'[11] The WTO has become the focal point for resistance to globalisation. Many poorer countries, such as India, argue that the WTO-led trade negotiations have been unbalanced: while the developing countries gave ground in areas such as intellectual property and investor protection, they are still unable to reap the benefits of agriculture or textile trade liberalisation. The EU remains highly protectionist with respect to its agricultural policy, Japan does not want to liberalise fish and forestry products and the United States has slowed down its textile liberalisation. Add the desire of Europe, the US and Japan to link trade issues with a discussion of labour rights (to make sure that trade liberalisation does not lead to job losses or lower wages) and the vehement opposition of the developing countries against linking these issues (because it is seen as a pretext for rich-country protectionism), further trade liberalisation is far from obvious.

Population growth and population shortage

Over the last 40 years, world population doubled from three to six billion; in the last century it has more than trebled. And growth patterns have varied substantially (see Figure 17.1). In the past 100 years, for example, Europe's population has risen by 80 per cent. Over the same time, the population has nearly quadrupled in Asia, has multiplied 5.5 times in Africa and has grown sevenfold in Latin America. Now, the growth is predicted to slow down and is expected to reach 8.9 billion by the year 2050. Is this slowing population growth signalling an end to the widely feared population explosion that threatens to overwhelm the earth's resources? Will this be the end to food crises and famine? Does it open the door to better living standards? Possibly, but the new demographic development will also give rise to new problems, notably of an ageing population, even in the poor world. Thus, according to *The Economist*, '...whereas population growth may not be a global problem, it could often be a nasty local one, causing conflict over local resources, especially water, and privation when politics (frequently) or natural disaster (occasionally) cause local scarcity or epidemic disease even within a wider world of abundance and improving health.'[12]

In the developed world, the slowdown in population growth may bring problems of another nature, since it begins at the same time that retirees are staying alive longer. In most of Western Europe and Japan, the average woman has fewer than 1.5 children in her lifetime. In the US an average fertility rate of 2.0 is seen as roughly the number needed to maintain long-term population stability.[13] The hope is that the fewer children can compensate for their smaller numbers with high productivity. Only if 'quality' in the form of higher education will be able to make up for the lack in 'quantity' will the working-age population be able to support the growing number of retirees.

And what are the implications for international marketers? Hermann Simon predicts that the combination of decreasing birth rates and increasing life expectation are by far the most important societal challenges of the future: the desire to grow old while remaining healthy could lead to radical changes in the behaviour of the young and middle-aged generation. This affects all dimensions of life: consumption, work, leisure time and retirement planning. Consequently, nearly all industries are

GLOBAL PERSPECTIVE

Should Kurdistan be a nation? Scotland? How about New York City?

In 1950, there were 58 nations in the UN. Today, there are 185. If that rate of proliferation continues for another century, the UN or its successor will have nearly 2,000 members. Imagine some of the new governments, replete with flags, anthems, national birds, and Olympic bobsledders: Scotland, Quebec, Palestine, Kosovo, Tibet, Kashmir, South Ossetia, Kurdistan, Timor, Biafra and New York City.

Countries are fractured into new nations by two global forces that were supposed to pull everyone together: the Internet and the global economy. The Net, often seen as a force for universalism, actually makes nationalism easier to express and share. Basque or Quebecker Web pages abound, concentrating the power of breakaway elements. At the same time, the globalisation of the economy enables small fry to go it alone. With open trade, countries with something to sell can break away from bigger neighbours and support themselves. They do not even need their own money supplies. Even old-time powers like France and Germany are dropping their national currencies. And with regional security umbrellas, small countries need not bother with their own armed forces.

However, too often the birth of nations will be violent. The same welling up of nationalism that gives rise to new countries also produces a reaction from mother countries that do not want to give up parts of themselves. China refuses to cede Taiwan. Israel hangs on to the West Bank, Indonesia to East Timor. Imagine the horror of Yugoslavia's break-up repeating over and over again.

All this talk of blood and soil seems irrelevant to globetrotting multinationals, whose world revolves around conference tables, laptop computers, frequent-flier miles and stock options. These globalists speak the cool, rational language of money. But such people are in the minority. Nationalists speak of ancient loyalties and grievances, and theirs is the language that stirs the blood among people whose allegiances are local and tribal.

It may be possible to accommodate nationalistic fervour in a relatively civilised fashion. Great Britain, for instance, has granted a form of home rule to the Scots and Welsh without undue trauma. But even in Britain, there are fears that one effect of the semisplit will be to isolate Scotland and Wales from the world economy. For other regions, this risk is even bigger. As advanced information societies such as the US and Western Europe form transnational confederations, regions left out of the confederations will go in the opposite direction. They may become even more nationalistic, more torn by violence and eventually break up into thousands of pieces.

Food for thought

- Is the growing number of nations also indicating a growing importance of nation-states? Why? Why not?
- Compare the relative power of small and medium-sized nations with the power of large multinational companies. What are the important differences? Which conclusions can you draw?

Source: Adapted from Stephen Baker, '21 ideas for the 21st century', *Business Week*, 30 August 1999, pp. 42–44.

involved: consumer goods, health care, financial services and leisure. The fight against ageing and its consequences is set to become one of the biggest markets of the 21st century.[14]

Rule of global institutions and resurgence of nation–states

In the political arena, we saw, in a relatively short time period, the demise of communism, the break-up of the former Soviet Union and the reunification of Germany. We observed the opening of China and the problems of Japan. Currently, we are also witnessing the decreasing influence of nation-states. More and more, political and economic power appears to be transferred to regional and global institutions. Think about the power of EU institutions, such as the European Court of Justice, consider the influence of the Organisation of Petrol Exporting Countries (OPEC) in setting oil prices or bear in mind the importance of transnational institutions like the World Trade Organisation (WTO) or the International Monetary Fund (IMF).

Simultaneously, there is a contradictory trend, namely a flurry of nationalism and a sprouting of new countries everywhere. Old established nations are breaking up into new countries. It appears that increasing globalisation is fostering an emotional desire for allegiances and a new desire for national identity.

CONVERGENCE AND FRAGMENTATION OF CONSUMER TASTE

Turning to consumers, future international marketers will be faced with increasingly complex trends. On the one hand, there appears to be a convergence of tastes and consumer habits around the globe. Nearly everywhere in the world, one can buy Coca-Cola or Perrier water, eat a McDonald's hamburger, watch CNN, buy a Sony Walkman, rent a Toyota or listen to Madonna – not that one really always wants to listen to Madonna. Today, more than ever before, there are global segment opportunities. In category after category, global efforts succeed. For example, the soft drink industry was first successful in reaching a global cola segment and has now moved to address the fast-growing fruit-and-flavour segment. There are global segments for luxury cars, wine and spirits, every type of medical and industrial product, teenagers, senior citizens, and enthusiasts of every stripe and type, from scuba divers to snowboarders.

The rapidly growing diffusion of Internet access combined with the rapidly expanding bandwidth and capacity of the global Internet itself will play a major role in supporting the growth of global markets and global marketing. Amazon.com, the pioneering Internet bookstore, can reach customers in Taiwan and Tokyo just as easily as it can reach customers in London, Frankfurt or Vienna. Customers anywhere in the world are only a click away from the book of their choice. With express mail service, customers are only two days away from delivery wherever they live, and with credit cards they can pay for goods and services in any currency.

Parallel to the convergence of consumer taste around the world, there also appears to be a seemingly contradictory trend towards a fragmentation of tastes and consumption habits. Consumers around the world are not displaying clear cut and easily interpretable taste preferences and consumer habits any more. Instead, one and the same consumer is ready to wear a Gucci suit for work, have Italian for lunch, Chinese for dinner and wear Levi's in the evening while attending a Japanese exhibition. What is emerging is the simultaneous presence of different and essentially incompatible patterns and modes of life represented by a variety of products, lifestyles and experiences that do not fit each other but represent different cultural identities and histories.[15] One of the authors has coined the phrase *fragvergence* to describe this phenomenon.[16]

The oxymoronic coexistence of convergence and fragmentation has been made possible through the globalisation of information. Indeed, the globalisation of information has not only broken down country and cultural barriers, but contributed to the creation of new ones. Barriers which do not follow traditional ethnic or religious affiliations, but are based on sub-cultures such as 'techies' versus 'greens'. Arguably, barriers within country boundaries will become more important than differences between countries.

Fragvergence of cultural differences will have profound implications for the definition of international marketing. When target groups are routinely scattered throughout different countries around the globe, the majority of all marketing activities will have to be international. Marketing managers, therefore, need to develop a deep understanding of the idiosyncrasies of global marketing. But companies can no longer rely on geographical markets to be dominated by a singular culture (e.g. the Spanish culture). Ethnically based cultural differences (e.g. food consumption habits) are widely experienced outside their original context. Culture itself is becoming a commodity represented through its tradable artifacts. Thus, marketing managers will need to revisit the meaning of cultural differences in an environment, where information is global and cultural and social proximity – feelings of 'closeness' and 'familiarity' – are created through media.

Industry concentration and blurring industry boundaries

The future is likely to be dominated by mega-acquisitions. Until recently, large multinationals appeared to be safe, but now even they are fair game. In the US, Bankers Trust, ranked 53 in Forbes' top 100 international companies only a year earlier, was recently acquired by Germany's Deutsche Bank. Amoco, placed 28 in the same Forbes list, is now part of the United Kingdom's BP Amoco. And Chrysler, which was ranked 23 with $7.7 billion in revenues from outside the US, was bought by Germany's Daimler-Benz.[17] In fact, the world's top 50 companies, measured by a composite ranking of sales, net income, assets and market value, employ 7.3 million of the world's population. Table 17.1 provides a list of the world's top 20 public companies[18] and Table 17.2 separately list the top companies in Europe.[19]

And while companies are likely to grow even bigger in future, the answer to the proverbial question – what business are we in – is getting more and more complex. Chemical companies are increasingly relying on electronics to manage production processes and large retailers have to be good at database management to administer the flow of their products. Of course, we are long used to the fact that car companies sell financial services (e.g. GM), petrol stations transformed themselves into supermarkets (e.g. BP) and software companies edge into the consulting business (e.g. SAP). Now, cable companies are offering access to the Internet through Web-TV and computer companies are selling gateway servers that make it easy to phone via the Net. Similarly, computer modelling techniques have reduced the requirement for 'wet' chemistry in the design of new drugs. The application of computer technology to biological research, 'bioinformatics', is rapidly becoming a key component of pharma-

Table 17.1 The world's top 20 companies

Rank	Company	Business	Country	Revenue (€ mil)	Market value (€ mil)	Employees (thousand)
1	General Electric	Elec & electron	US	85,227	282,188	284.5
2	Citigroup	Insurance	US	64,836	126,605	173.7
3	Bank of America	Banking	US	43,074	95,750	176.1
4	HSBC Group	Banking	UK	36,739	79,669	136.4
5	DaimlerChrysler	Automobiles	D	124,252	73,987	433.9
6	Ford Motor	Automobiles	US	121,023	55,239	345.2
7	Exxon	Energy	US	85,421	164,510	79.5
8	Nippon Tel & Tel	Telecomm	Japan	64,468	135,505	216.8
9	International Business Machines	Computer systems	US	69,278	178,584	280.2
10	American International Group	Insurance	US	28,244	120,133	40.0
10	ING Group	Financial svcs	Neth.	48,549	43,540	82.8
12	General Motors	Automobiles	US	112,684	42,889	397.0
13	AT&T	Telecomm	US	45,149	149,814	119.3
14	Fannie Mae	Financial svcs	US	26,720	160,911	3.7
14	Toyota Motor	Automobiles	Japan	84,473	90,009	183.9
16	BP Amoco	Energy	UK	57,429	148,494	99.0
16	Wal-Mart Stores	Retailing	US	116,754		867.5
18	Allianz Worldwide	Insurance	D	55,019	52,442	105.7
19	Chase Manhattan	Banking	US	27,467	51,895	70.9
20	Philip Morris Cos	Bev & tobacco	US	49,042	78,928	148.0

Source: Eric S. Hardy, 'Almost perfect world', *Forbes Magazine*, 26 July 1999 (http://www.forbes.com/forbes/99/0726/6402160a.htm).

Table 17.2 Europe's largest companies (billion Euro)

Rank	Company	Country	Market value
1	Vodafone Airtouch	GBR	247.6
2	Nokia	FIN	204.6
3	Deutsche Telekom	GER	169.4
4	Royal Dutch/Shell	NED/GBR	166.0
5	BP Amoco	GBR	162.1
6	Ericsson	SWE	140.3
7	France Telekom	FRA	134.8
8	British Telecom	GBR	96.8
9	Glaxo Wellcome	GBR	95.6
10	Total Fina Elf	FRA	88.9
11	Novartis	SUI	86.0
12	HSBC Holding	GBR	81.3
13	Roche	SUI	80.0
14	Allianz	GER	78.8
15	Siemens	GER	72.0

Source: 'Größte Unternehmen Europas', *Kurier*, 5 May 2000, p. 22.

ceutical research.[20] In medicine, too, new technologies are blurring industry boundaries. The need to make diagnostic services available in remote locations – telemedicine – will require a redefinition of the skills required by medical personnel.

Blurring of industry boundaries will go hand-in-hand with increased uncertainty. The implications for future international marketing managers will be twofold. First, managers will need to develop an ability to gain a quick but firm grounding in the scope offered by new and unfamiliar technologies. Second, in an attempt to reduce uncertainty, marketing managers will have to find new avenues to support their strategic decision making. To this end, the application of sophisticated modelling techniques to forecast consumer acceptance of emerging business concepts and the use of the web for product testing and development is likely to increase.

Virtual enterprises and electronic markets

Virtual enterprises and electronic markets most clearly represent the transformation of the traditional economy to the electronic-economy or e-economy for short. Specifically, they demonstrate the development of the Internet from an entertainment / infotainment medium to a marketplace. To enable a smooth running of such virtual enterprises or inter-firm cooperations, the use and optimal configuration of so-called enterprise-resource planning (ERP) applications is required. For international marketing, which has traditionally focused on managing the relationships between a single company and its customers and – to a lesser extent – to its suppliers, this situation radically alters their role definition. No longer will information technology be used to automate well-defined tasks within an organisation which can be left to information technology specialists, but information technology is the framework and key instrument for designing and managing company external relationships. Consequently, the driving force for the success of virtual enterprises will be the ability of international marketing managers to develop a sound understanding of the technological capabilities on offer and their ability to coordinate with information technology specialists in their own and other network companies.

Since the new information and communication technology environment largely feeds on ideas and knowledge rather than being dependent on fixed assets, companies are likely to appear from nowhere to take advantage, and often lead, new business opportunities opened through technological advances. One indication of the developments to come is Yahoo Inc., which provides the largest search engine on the Internet. Only a few years ago, Yahoo's co-founder David Filo was a relatively poor ex-student. Today, his online service leads the field in both traffic and advertising revenues.[21] We coined such companies *mushroom companies*, since they grow virtually overnight but sometimes also disappear rather quickly. However, Yahoo might well survive. It has three times the market share of any of its competitors and has the advantage of being the first kid on the block.

Mushroom companies represent one of the most disturbing and difficult challenges to future international marketing managers, namely the rapidly diminishing value of incumbency versus the increasing importance of speed and time-to-market. Seemingly strong market positions can erode overnight and new empires emerge with breathtaking speed. For international marketers, an efficient and quick promotion of ideas, business concepts and services has become the key to success. To achieve this, the emphasis of communication policy is shifting from traditional media towards the Internet. But while the interactive nature of the Internet offers a wide array of communicative possibilities, such as the integration of text, video and sound, most marketers still need to acquire the necessary experience and knowledge to utilise all facets of the new medium.

In the race to be noticed, branding has also acquired a new dimension. An important way to differentiate against competitors is to offer a unique www-address (a so-called 'URL', i.e. unique resource locator) which is easy to remember and intimately resembles the company's name. Although it may be useful to provide certain 'local' Internet pages according to the country of origin of the surfing individual, many commercial product vendors register with the '.com' rather than the local country domain (for example: '.uk' for Britain, '.de' for Germany or '.at' for Austria) since this supposedly signals a stronger emphasis on global presence and provides a 'global branding'.

Key points

- The future business environment will be characterised by an increased complexity and a number of seemingly contradictory developments.

- Over the last 40 years, world population has doubled to six billion. Now, it is expected to grow with decreasing speed to reach 8.9 billion by the year 2050.

- From 1950 to now, the number of nation-states has increased more than threefold. At the same time, more and more political and economic power has been transferred to regional and global institutions.

- Future international marketing managers will have to cope with the rapidly diminishing value of incumbency versus the increasing importance of time-to-market.

LEADERSHIP CHALLENGES

Trying to identify future trends in international marketing would be incomplete without reference to the human resource dimension. Given the complexities and contradictions to be expected, it is paramount to reflect on the requirements placed on managerial talents. In fact, in a knowledge based society, competition to attract the best managers will be fierce. As *The Wall Street Journal* puts it: '... global corporations are at war for 21st century executive talent. Attracting world-class is getting more and more difficult. Firms big and small need to provide talented people with a compelling reason to join and stay with a company.'[22] Below, we briefly review the demands placed on future global leaders.

Demands on global leadership

Global marketing demands exceptional leadership. As we have said throughout this book, the hallmark of a global company is the capacity to formulate and implement global strategies that leverage world-wide learning, respond fully to local needs and wants, and draw on all of the talent and energy of every member of the organisation. This is a heroic task requiring global vision and a sensitivity to local needs. Members of each operating unit must address their immediate responsibilities and at the same time cooperate with functional, product and country experts in different locations. Furthermore, top managers are expected to understand that the uncertainty created by the global economy affects people at the top as well as the members in the organisation.

C.K. Prahalad identifies four forces which will generate enhanced demand for leaders and which 'force leaders to confront an extraordinary range of ambiguities and uncertainties'.[23] The role of leadership within a competitive environment is firstly determined by a new pressure for global efficiency. A second force derives from the change in business models which creates a different demand on managing. For example in telecommunications, managers have to move from one applicable market to markets with restricted or no competition to one that can function in open and global markets. Resulting activities are mergers and acquisitions. A third force Prahalad mentions is competitive demands which derive from the convergence of computing, communications, consumer electronics and entertainment. Finally the Internet creates new modes of economic transactions which result in new opportunities.[24]

Figure 17.1 summarises some differences between effective strategic leadership practices in the 20th and global leadership in the 21st century. 'A person's ability to anticipate, envision, maintain flexibility, think strategically, and work with others to initiate changes that will create a viable future for the organisation' defines strategic leadership.[25] According to a survey conducted by Andersen Consulting, the ideal leader creates a shared vision, ensures customer satisfaction, lives the values, builds teamwork and partnerships and thinks globally. It can be concluded that the need for shared or team-based leadership will continue to grow.[26] Another survey done by Personnel Decisions International (PDI) showed that 37.3 per cent of respondents agreed about the importance of leaders' skills in communication and interpersonal relationships.[27]

The world's most respected business leaders

Leadership consists of the principles, skills and attitudes that harness and integrate the triad knowledge, trust and power.[28] Leaders like Jürgen Schrempp at Daimler-

Figure 17.1 Leadership practices

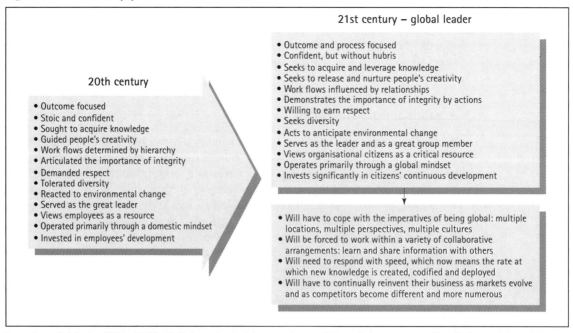

Source: Duane R. Ireland and Michael A. Hitt, 'Achieving and maintaining strategic competitiveness in the 21st century: The role of strategic leadership', *Academy of Management Executive*, 13, 1 (1999): p. 54; C.K. Prahalad, 'Emerging leaders', *Executive Excellence*, November (1999): pp. 3–4.

Chrysler, Jorma Ollila at Nokia, Richard Branson at Virgin Atlantic or Fred Newman at Omnibank are characterised by wisdom, integrity and courage, which foster and synthesise knowledge, trust and power. But they are also transformational leaders, capable of managing massive turnaround. It has been argued that where radical transformation is the goal, an entirely new definition of the business is needed, led by a figure with a new and inspiring vision of the future of the company.[29] Transformational leadership is about change, innovation and entrepreneurship which means a behavioural process capable of being learned and managed. It is a leadership process that is systematic, consisting of purposeful and organised search for changes, systematic analysis, and the capacity to move resources from areas of lesser to greater productivity.[30]

Even if leadership is only one of several variables affecting the performance of a firm, leaders of multinational firms have the ability to consistently engender performance at levels well above similar firms in their industry. Successful leadership in multinational operations includes besides marketing orientation the ability to instigate product innovation and a strong feeling for tracking the inherent capabilities of all members in an organisation. Multinational leaders during the 1990s cared about customers as Paolo Cantarella, head of the Italian car maker Fiat did, who pushed to develop a 'world car' for emerging markets. Michael Dell, CEO of Dell Computers, cared secondly about product or process innovation. He consistently employed the latest products and process refinements to capture an impressive share of the worldwide market. Finally multinational leaders have committed people and maintain the organisational flexibility that these people need. These three keys to the success for the multinationals constituted a new paradigm of management.[31] Table 17.3 shows 10 of the world's most respected business leaders.

Table 17.3 World's 10 most respected business leaders in 1999

Rank 1999	Rank 1998	Name	Company
1	(1)	Jack Welch	General Electric
2	(2)	Bill Gates	Microsoft
3	(4)	Lou Gerstner	IBM
4	(3)	Jürgen Schrempp	DaimlerChrysler
5		Michael Dell	Dell
6	(8)	Warren Buffet	Berkshire Hathaway
7	(15)	Hiroshi Okuda	Toyota
8	(7)	Nobuyuki Idei	Sony
9	(10)	John Browne	BP Amoco
10	(6)	Percy Barnevik	Investor

Source: 'World's most respected business leaders', http://www.ft.com/specials/sp41d2.htm.

CAREERS IN GLOBAL MARKETING

There has never been a better time to prepare for a career in global marketing. Now that you are completing this book, the authors would like to offer a few suggestions on how to jump-start your global marketing career.

First and foremost, global experience counts. Only the truly lost do not recognise that we are in a global market with global competition, and those with global experience have a definite advantage. Consequently, you should aim to gain such experience as early as possible. If you missed out and did not spend time abroad when you attended school, you should definitely try to arrange one or two semesters abroad during your university career. Most European universities participate in exchange schemes that make it possible to study abroad and reintegrate in your home university without lengthening the overall time before graduating. The better universities

EUROPEAN FOCUS

Skills without frontiers

Unemployment may remain serious in Germany, where nearly 10 per cent of the workforce does not have a job, but the German government is now offering term-limited employment opportunities for as many as 30,000 people recruited from outside the European Union. The hope is to attract workers with high-technology skills from areas such as Bangalore, southern India's 'Silicon Valley'.

A similar approach is being taken by the Canadian, Australian and Swedish governments. Even in the UK, the government is looking for incentives that would attract key personnel for short periods to fill vacancies arising from the lack of home-grown talent. What is becoming painfully clear is that there are simply not enough knowledge workers in the world to meet business demand.

At the executive level, the competition for top skills has already intensified. Non-British business leaders are increasingly dashing the ambitions of UK executives by beating them to the nation's top jobs. The number of non-UK nationals heading Britain's leading companies has more than doubled from 11 per cent in 1990 to 23 per cent at the end of the decade.

'UK nationals should not be complacent that length of tenure will stand them in good stead for winning the CEO job against the rising tide of experts from continental Europe and the US,' said Andrew Simpson, UK managing partner of TMP Worldwide Executive Search.

This has been partly due to cross-border mergers and acquisitions. Dutchman Bart Beecht, for example, is head of the recently merged Reckitt Benckiser, the household cleaners group. In addition, several leading companies have more than one chief executive, of different nationalities. The UK's John Bryant and Fokko van Duyne of the Netherlands jointly run Corus, the group formed from the merger of British Steel and Hoogovens. South African chief executives have multiplied, as companies such as Billiton, the diversified mining group, have moved to a London listing to improve their access to capital markets.

Non-UK chief executives feature particularly highly in the financial sector. Irish-Canadian Matthew Barrett came in as chief executive of Barclays, the UK bank, while Bob Mendelsohn of the US heads Royal & Sun Alliance, the insurance group.

US representation has grown most, from 2.5 per cent in 1990 to 8 per cent at the beginning of 2000. European Union nationals account for 6 per cent of the non-UK total, compared with 1 per cent a decade ago.

Food for thought

- Should the European labour market be more heavily regulated to preserve jobs for European citizens? What would be the advantages and disadvantages of more regulations?
- What is the impact of increasing cross-border mergers and acquisitions on the European market for (1) middle-managers, (2) unskilled and semi-skilled workers and (3) chief executives?

Source: Adapted from: Robert Taylor, 'Skills without "frontiers" '*Financial Times*, 28 April 2000, p. 13 and Alison Maitland, 'US and Europe muscle in on British CEO jobs', *Financial Times*, 30 March 2000, p. 9.

are also offering placements in China, Thailand or Eastern Europe. If you are studying in the UK, think carefully whether your semester abroad has to be spent in a Western European destination or the US. And if you are studying in Western Europe, do consider other destinations than the UK and the US. Sometimes, the choice of a more unusual destination will be a more enriching experience.

If you are lucky enough to find yourself in a university belonging to the Community of European Management Schools (CEMS), an association of top business schools in Europe, you may want to consider pursuing a CEMS-Degree in parallel to your regular studies. CEMS students spend at least one semester at one of the CEMS partner universities and complete an internship with one of the corporate partners. Furthermore, every CEMS graduate speaks three languages fluently.

An option already worth pursuing during your studies are traineeships. The student-run organisation International Association of Students of Economics and Commercial Sciences (AIESEC) provides a good starting point. It is the world's largest student organisation consisting of a global network of 50,000 members across more than 87 countries and territories at more than 741 universities world-wide. This excellent organisation facilitates international exchange of thousands of students and recent graduates each year. It provides both paid traineeship and volunteers for non-profit organisations.

In particular for those who are not studying business or economics but, for example, have completed a degree in engineering, MBA programmes offer a route to an international management career. Ideally taken after gathering a few years of practical work experience, the completion of most leading MBA programmes will improve your job prospects considerably. Some business schools offer programmes that have earned a particularly good reputation for focusing on international business. Thunderbird's Master of International Management (MIM) programme and the International MBA offered jointly by the University of South Carolina and Vienna University of Economics and Business Administration are currently the top ranked programmes in this area (see Table 17.4).

Regardless of how you prepare yourself for a career in international marketing, one aspect is certain: the competition for the best jobs will increasingly ignore national boundaries. Top executives in international marketing are likely to be individuals who not only have the technical knowledge needed as a manager, but also have the language skills, flexibility and cross-cultural competence to work in different locations around the globe.

Table 17.4 Top ranked international business programmes

1.	Thunderbird Graduate School (AZ)
2.	University of South Carolina (Moore)
3.	University of Pennsylvania (Wharton)
4.	Columbia University (NY)
5.	Harvard University (MA)
6.	New York University (Stern)
7.	University of Michigan–Ann Arbor
8.	Stanford University (CA)
9.	University of California–Los Angeles (Anderson)
10.	University of California–Berkeley (Haas)

Source: 'America's Best Graduate Schools 2000', *US News & World Report*, p. 24 or http://www.usnews.com/usnews/edu/beyond/grad-rank/gbmbasp5.htm.

Key points

- Global marketing demands exceptional leadership. According to Andersen Consulting, the ideal leader creates a shared vision, ensures customer satisfaction, lives the values, builds teamwork and partnerships and thinks globally.

- Global experience counts. You should aim to gain such experience as early as possible by gaining some of your university education abroad, by pursuing internships or by taking part in MBA programmes with an international orientation.

- Competition for the best jobs will increasingly ignore national boundaries.

Summary

The future of global marketing will be characterised by increased environmental complexity and seemingly contradictory trends. Among the most noteworthy developments are a drastically accelerated change, in particular in technological development, but also in terms of political and social trends. Following almost a century of debate about the merits of free markets versus state-controlled systems of allocating resources, the future promises a nearly universal acceptance of free market principles. Despite a further growth in world population, there is a very real likelihood today of a much broader global prosperity as *most* of the world's poor countries are getting richer. For global marketers, this will translate into dramatic growth opportunities.

However, globalisation also has a darker side. We are witnessing a flurry of nationalism and a sprouting of new countries. In some countries, the gap between the rich and the poor is widening and, fuelled by the desire to curb job losses and lower wages caused by globalisation, protectionism remains a danger to further trade liberalisation.

Whatever the future will hold, increased complexities and contradictory trends will place exceptional demands on the leadership skills of global marketing managers. The competition for the best managerial talents will be fierce and will increasingly ignore national boundaries. The value of global experience for managers world-wide is set to grow. Continue to learn more about global marketing and start to gather international experience now and you will be able to look forward to a career in global marketing that is challenging, rewarding and fun.

Concepts and definitions

Paradigm shift	A fundamental and dramatic change in established patterns. In the context of the discussion on the impact of information technology on business, the term is used to refer to a dramatic shift in the way business is conducted.
World population	Over the last 40 years, world population has doubled. It now stands at six billion and, with a decreasing speed of growth, is predicted to reach 8.9 billion by the year 2050.
Nation–states	From 1950 to now, the number of nation-states has increased more than threefold. At the same time, more and more political and economic power has been transferred to regional and global institutions.
Fragvergence	The oxymoronic coexistence of a converging consumer taste and a fragmentation of lifestyles and consumption habits that represent different cultural identities and histories which appear to be incompatible.
Blurring industry	The blurring of industry boundaries will require a constant questioning of core competencies and will go hand in hand with increased uncertainty.
Mushroom companies	Companies that grow virtually overnight but sometimes also disappear rather quickly have been termed mushroom companies. They reflect one of the most difficult challenges to future marketing managers, namely the rapidly diminishing value of incumbency versus the increasing importance of time-to-market.
Global leadership	Global marketing demands exceptional leadership. According to Andersen Consulting, the ideal leader creates a shared vision, ensures customer satisfaction, lives the values, builds teamwork and partnerships and thinks globally.

Discussion questions

1 Do you believe that economic democracy (free markets) will inevitably lead to political democracy? Why? Why not?

2 Will the proliferation of nation states lead to an increase in protectionism? What, in this context, is the role of transnational institutions like the World Trade Organisation?

3 How would you characterise the changes in the demands placed on business leaders due to increasing globalisation of the economy?

Webmistress's hotspots

Homepage of AIESEC
This is the online centre for the world's largest student organisation. AIESEC is a global network of 50,000 members across more than 87 countries and territories at more than 741 universities world-wide.
http://www.aiesec.org/

List of business schools
If you want to select a business school, find out which ones are rated best and get access to background articles on MBA programmes, this is the site for you.
http://www.usnews.com/usnews/edu/beyond/bcbiz.htm

Homepage of Global Careers in Commerce
There are many sites on the Web that allow you to post your resumé and to search for global career opportunities. Global Careers in Commerce exemplifies this genre of websites.

http://www.globalcareers.com/commerce/index.html

Homepage of the *Journal of International Marketing* (JIM),
The website to the *Journal of International Marketing* (JIM), the pre-eminent publication in the field of international marketing. The journal's mission is to contribute to the advancement of international marketing practice and theory. JIM brings to the readership a selection of original articles, executive insights, and reviews.

http://www.wu-wien.ac.at/imm/jim/

Suggested readings

Albers, S. and K. Peters, 'Die Wertschöpfungskette des Handels im Zeitalter des Electronic Commerce', *Marketing ZFP*, Heft 2, 2. Quartal (1997): pp. 69–79.

Baker, Stephen, '21 ideas for the 21st century', *Business Week*, 30 August 1999, pp. 42–44.

Darling, John R. and Thomas M. Box, 'Keys for success in the leadership of multinational corporations, 1990 through 1997', *S.A.M. Advanced Management Journal*, Autumn (1999): pp. 16–24.

Deighton, John, 'Commentary on exploring the implications of the Internet for consumer marketing', *Journal of the Academy of Marketing Science*, 25, 4 (1997): pp. 347–351.

Doyle, Peter, 'Marketing in the new millennium', *European Journal of Marketing*, 29, 13 (1995): pp. 23–41.

Firat, Fuat, 'Globalization of fragmentation – a framework for understanding contemporary global markets', *Journal of International Marketing*, 5, 2 (1997): pp. 77–86.

Handy, Charles, *The Age of Unreason*. Boston, Harvard Business School Press, 1989.

Hoffman, Donna L. and Thomas P. Novak, 'Marketing in hypermedia-computer-mediated environments: conceptual foundations', *Journal of Marketing*, 60 (July 1996): pp. 50–68.

Ireland, Duane R. and Michael A. Hitt, 'Achieving and maintaining strategic competitiveness in the 21st century: the role of strategic leadership,' *Academy of Management Executive*, 13, 1 (1999): p. 43.

McKenna, R., *Real Time: Preparing for the Age of the Never Satisfied Customer*. Boston: Harvard Business School Press, 1997.

Peterson, R.A., S. Balasubramanian and B.J. Bronnenberg, 'Exploring the implications of the Internet for consumer marketing', *Journal of the Academy of Marketing Science*, 25, 4 (1997): pp. 329–346.

Prahalad, C.K. 'Emerging leaders', *Executive Excellence*, November (1999): pp. 3–4.

Schlegelmilch, Bodo B. and Rudolf Sinkovics, 'Marketing in the information age: can we plan for an unpredictable future?', *International Marketing Review*, 15, 3 (1998): pp. 162–170.

Simon, Hermann, *Trends und Herausforderungen für das 21, Jahrhundert*. Wien: Simon Kucher & Partners, September 1999.

'Survey 20th Century', *The Economist*, 11 September 1999, p. 6.

Watkins, Jeff, *Information Technology, Organisations and People*. London: Routledge, 1998.

Notes

1. This example has been adapted from 'The Nomads shall inherit the airport lounge', *Business Week*, 30 August 1999, pp. 80–81.
2. Adapted from 'Office fantasies of the future', *Fortune*, 6 March 2000, pp. F-44–F-48.
3. Susan P. Douglas and Samuel G. Craig, *Global Marketing Strategy* (New York: McGraw-Hill, Inc. 1995), pp. 372–373.
4. 'Special report: let's talk', *Business Week*, 23 February 1998, pp. 44–56; 'Smitten with the written word', *Financial Times*, 12 February 1998, p. 21.
5. John Deighton, 'Commentary on exploring the implications of the Internet for consumer marketing', *Journal of the Academy of Marketing Science*, 25, 4 (1997): pp. 347–351.
6. Hermann Simon, *Trends und Herausforderungen für das 21 Jahrhundert* (Wien: Simon Kucher & Partners, September 1999), p. 5.

7. Julian Le Grand, 'Social exclusion: problems that just won't go away', *Financial Times – The Millennium 21*, 6 December 1999, p. 21.

8. Julian Le Grand, 'Social exclusion: problems that just won't go away', *Financial Times – The Millennium 21*, 6 December 1999, p. 21.

9. Michael Holman, 'Hope springs from marginalisation', *Financial Times – The Millennium 21*, 6 December 1999, p. 12.

10. Prime Minister of Norway, Mr. Kjell Magne Bondevik, 'The social side of globalisation', speech at World Economic Forum, Davos, 31 January 1999 (http://odin.dep.no/smk/taler/1999/990131.html).

11. 'Storm over globalisation', *The Economist*, 27 November 1999, p. 13.

12. 'Survey 20th century', *The Economist*, 11 September 1999, p. 6.

13. Peter Coy, 'The little emperors can save the world's aging population', *Business Week*, 30 August 1999, p. 72.

14. Hermann Simon, *Trends und Herausforderungen für das 21 Jahrhundert* (Wien: Simon Kucher & Partners, September 1999), p. 28.

15. Fuat Firat, 'Globalization of fragmentation – a framework for understanding contemporary global markets', *Journal of International Marketing*, 5, 2 (1997): pp. 77–86.

16. Bodo B. Schlegelmilch and Rudolf Sinkovics, 'Marketing in the Information Age: Can we plan for an unpredictable future?', *International Marketing Review*, 15, 3 (1998): pp. 162–170.

17. Brian Zajac, 'Spanning the world', *Forbes Magazine*, 26 July 1999 (http://forbes.com/Forbes/99/0726/6402202a.htm).

18. Eric S. Hardy, 'Almost perfect world', *Forbes Magazine*, 26 July 1999 (http://www.forbes.com/forbes/99/0726/6402160a.htm).

19. 'Telekom führt EU-Firmen-Hitliste', *Kurier*, 9 May 2000.

20. *Financial Times*, 'Smitten with the written word', 12 February 1998, p. 21.

21. Konr@d, 'Monitor: Blick in die digitale Welt.' January (1998) 11. http://www.pathfinder.com/money/hoovers/corpdirectory/y/yahoo.html, 2 April 1998.

22. 'World-Class Talent', *The Wall Street Journal*, 23 February 1999.

23. C.K. Prahalad, 'Emerging leaders', *Executive Excellence*, November (1999): pp. 3–4.

24. C.K. Prahalad, 'Emerging leaders', *Executive Excellence*, November (1999): pp. 3–4.

25. Duane R. Ireland and Michael A. Hitt, 'Achieving and maintaining strategic competitiveness in the 21st century: The role of strategic leadership', *Academy of Management Executive*, 13, 1 (1999): p. 43.

26. 'Global leader of the future', *Management Review*, October (1999): p. 9.

27. 'What makes a good boss?', *HRFocus*, March (1999): pp. 10–11.

28. Dale E. Zand, *The Leadership Triad* (New York: Oxford University Press, 1997), p. 4.

29. Jeff Watkins, *Information Technology, Organisations and People* (London: Routledge, 1998).

30. Noel M. Tichy and Mary Anne Devanna, *The Transformational Leader* (New York: John Wiley & Sons, 1990), p. xii.

31. John R. Darling and Thomas M. Box, 'Keys for success in the leadership of multinational corporations, 1990 through 1997', *S.A.M. Advanced Management Journal*, Autumn (1999): pp. 16–24.

Benetton Group SpA: raising consciousness and controversy with global advertising

Benetton Group SpA, the Italy-based global clothing retailer, seems to have fallen on hard times. Until recently, financial results were excellent: world-wide sales of Benetton's brightly coloured knitwear and contemporary clothing doubled between 1988 and 1993 to 2.75 trillion lire ($1.63 billion). In 1993 alone, sales were up about 10 per cent, and net income increased by 13 per cent. The strong showing in 1993 was due in part to the devaluation of the Italian lire, which enabled Benetton to cut prices for its clothing around the world.

By contrast, 1994 results were discouraging. Sales were flat at $1.69 billion, operating profits fell 5 per cent, to $245 million, and margins narrowed to 13.9 per cent down from 14.7 per cent during the three-year period 1991–1993. The sales slump was surprising in view of the fact that Benetton had opened stores in China, Eastern Europe and India, and extended the brand into new categories such as footwear and cosmetics. Some industry observers believed that Benetton's wounds were self-inflicted. According to this view, 1994's results represented the backlash from Benetton's highly controversial global advertising campaigns, now several years old, keyed to the theme 'The United Colors of Benetton'.

Various executions of the ads, in magazines and on posters and billboards, featured provocative, even shocking photos designed to focus public attention on social and political issues such as the environment, terrorism, racial issues and sexually transmitted diseases. The creative concept of the ads reflected the views of Oliviero Toscani, creative director and chief photographer for Benetton. 'I have found out that advertising is the richest and most powerful medium existing today. Therefore, I feel responsible to do more than say, "Our sweater is pretty",' he told *The New York Times*. Noted Vittorio Rava, world-wide advertising manager, 'We believe our advertising needs to shock, otherwise people will not remember it.'

One of the first ads to stir controversy depicted a white hand and a black hand joined by handcuffs; another showed an angelic white child embracing a

black child whose hair was unmistakably styled to resemble the horns of a devil. An ad with a picture of a black woman nursing a white baby appeared in 77 countries; while not used in the United States and the United Kingdom, the ad won awards in France and Italy. In the fall of 1991, several US magazine publishers refused to carry some of the ads; one depicted a nun kissing a priest. A picture of a newborn baby covered with bloody placenta was also rejected. According to Benetton's Ravo, 'We didn't envision a political idea when we started this "Colors" strategy five years ago, but now, with racist problems becoming more important in every country, it has become political on its own.'

With its next series of ads, Benetton began using images associated with sexuality. As Peter Fressola, director of communications, explained the message strategy, 'We're saying there are two important issues to be addressed, and they are overpopulation and sexually transmitted diseases such as AIDS. I think it is time to take the gloves off and put on the rubbers and address these issues.' In an interview with *Advertising Age*, Mr Toscani explained, 'Everybody uses emotion to sell a product. We want to show, in this case, human realities that we are aware of.' The ads broke new ground for the images they presented: A man dying of AIDS surrounded by his family; a montage of multicoloured condoms; a group of people with the initials 'HIV' stamped on their arms; test tubes filled with blood labelled with the names of world leaders.

In France, the HIV ad caused a great deal of controversy. One man who was dying of AIDS ran an ad with a picture of his own face above a tagline that read 'during the agony, the sales continue'. In the United States, where the number of Benetton stores had been slowly dwindling, the ads were poorly received by many customers and Benetton retailers. The manager of a Benetton store in Biloxi, Mississippi, received telephone calls from people who said they refused to shop at stores selling products from a 'sick' company. In Florida, one franchisee closed a dozen Benetton locations, noting, 'It is not our function as retailers to raise the consciousness of people. I've had long, hard fights with Italy over the advertising.' In an effort to help mollify its American licensees, Benetton began providing them with local ads featuring clothing instead of social issues. At the national level, however, Benetton continued the controversial ads. When asked about the possible negative impact of customer boycotts, Luciano Benetton, president of the company's US division, said, 'It's silly to change direction because someone in the market thinks it's not right. We are sincere, and we are consistent in pursuing it this way.'

In the spring of 1994, it appeared that Benetton had finally gone too far. A new $15 million ad campaign that ran in 25 countries featured a picture of the bloody uniform of a Croatian soldier who had died in the Bosnian civil war. While Benetton executives had come to expect criticism, they were unprepared for the latest reaction. The company was accused of exploiting the war for the sake of profit. In France, many of the offending posters were pulled down or covered with grafitti reading 'Boycott Benetton' and 'This is blood for money.' The French minister for humanitarian affairs even made a public announcement discouraging people from buying Benetton sweaters; he called for his fellow citizens to 'pull [the sweaters] off people who are going to wear them.' In some parts of Germany and Switzerland, the company's products were banned. Some media reports in Europe questioned the authenticity of the uniform, alleging it did not belong to the fallen soldier named in the ad. The Vatican newspaper charged Benetton with 'advertising terrorism'.

Mr Benetton acknowledged that 'this is not what a corporate communications campaign should do. It should create interest'. Still, he vowed the company would continue 'to search for new facts and new emotions' to include in its ads. Indeed, when the Sarajevo daily newspaper *Oslo bodhenie* ('Liberation') requested posters of the ad to put up around the city, Benetton supplied 10,000 copies. In France, however, a court ordered the company to pay $32,000 to French HIV victims; a German court banned several of the most controversial ads.

Discussion questions

1 What is your personal reaction to the controversial Benetton ads?

2 Do you believe Benetton is 'sincere' in its campaign, or is the company just exploiting human misery?

3 There is a saying in the marketing world that 'there is no such thing as bad publicity'. Does that apply in the Benetton case?

4 From a marketing (as opposed to personal) point of view, advise Benetton on its campaign. Should the company continue, expand, change, or terminate the campaign?

Source: John Rossant, 'The faded colors of Benetton', *Business Week*, 10 April 1995, pp. 87, 90; Peter Gumbel, 'Benetton is stung by backlash over ad', *The Wall Street Journal*, 4 March 1994, p. A8; Gary Levin, 'Benetton ad lays bare the bloody toll of war', *Advertising Age*, 21 February 1994; Judith Graham, 'Benetton "colors" the race issue', *Advertising Age*, 11 September 1989: p. 3; Kim Foltz, 'Campaign on harmony backfires for Benetton', *The New York Times*, 20 November 1989, p. 32; Dennis Rodkin, 'How colorful can ads get?', *Mother Jones* (January 1990): p. 52; Stuart Elliott, 'Benetton stirs more controversy', *The New York Times*, 23 July 1991, p. 19; Gary Levin, 'Benetton brouhaha', *Advertising Age*, 17 February 1992, p. 62; Teri Agins, 'Shrinkage of stores and customers in US causes Italy's Benetton to alter its tactics', *The Wall Street Journal*, 24 June 1992, pp. B1, B10.

Sicom GmbH and CD piracy

'As far as I am concerned, it is not an issue we need to worry about', said Josef Radler in April 1997. Radler was the chief executive of the German firm Sicom GmbH (Sicom). Sicom, the leading firm in the compact disc (CD) equipment industry, produced CD replicators. CD replicators were used to produce copies of CDs from master versions.

> We are the world's leading manufacturer of CD replicators. When you are the biggest player, you have the biggest chance of supplying people who infringe on other people's rights. I am not going to stop selling replicators in Asia. How can I control who uses our product? What about the manufacturers of photocopiers? They must know that some of their machines are used to illegally copy books and other printed materials and even money. Should these companies be held responsible for illegal photocopying?

Radler had recently discussed the issue of CD piracy in China with Sicom's managing director for Asia, John Thomson. Thomson, based in Hong Kong, was adamant that CD piracy was not Sicom's concern. According to Thomson:

> I am not here to enforce the law. My job is to sell products. If I sell you a car, do I ask if you have a valid driver's licence? No. It is not our responsibility to determine if our Chinese customers have licences to import CD replicators. Sometimes we ask them and sometimes we don't. When we ask them, they just say they applied and expect to get one soon. What more are we supposed to do?

SICOM GMBH

CD replicators were used to reproduce CDs from master copies. A decade ago, producing CDs required large clean rooms that sealed out dust and other substances that could damage disc quality. The equipment used in these clean rooms was very expensive, required great technical expertise to operate, and cost about $30 million. In 1987, Josef Radler developed technology that greatly simplified CD manufacturing. This technology resulted in glass-enclosed units that were much smaller than the clean rooms and could be used as self-contained assembly lines. Radler's machines were easy to use, portable, and most important, were priced at about $2.5 million. Based

on the new technology, Radler had built a successful business based in Rosenheim, a small town near Munich. Sicom became the world's largest producer of CD replicators, sales in 1996 were $120 million, 45 per cent in Asia. Sicom had a reputation for high quality and timely delivery and was recognised as the industry technology leader.

Most of Sicom's replicators destined for the Asian market were air-freighted to a Hong Kong agent for shipment to final destinations. Because Hong Kong was a free port, there were no import or export restrictions on replicators. When CD replicators arrived at a customer's premises in China, Sicom engineers were called in to set up the equipment. Sicom engineers did not attempt to determine if the CD production line was a legal or illegal line.

CD PIRACY

According to one estimate, nearly 200 million pirate CDs were produced annually, with 60 per cent coming from China. The International Federation of the Phonographic Industry (IFPI) claimed losses of $2.2 billion due to CD piracy. The largest market for pirate CDs was Russia, mainly imported from China and Bulgaria. Despite new intellectual property laws introduced on 1 January 1997, piracy in movies, computer software and CDs was rampant in Russia. In Western Europe, Italy was considered the largest market for pirate CDs. Significant declines in the sale of pirate CDs had occurred in a number of countries, including the United Kingdom, South Korea and Thailand.

As a measure to reduce piracy, a coding system was introduced in 1992 as a joint initiative by Philips Consumer Electronics, which issued licences to use its CD manufacturing technology, and the IFPI, which oversaw the code-monitoring system. The coding system involved two code numbers applied to the silver inner part of the disc. One number identified the plant that manufactured the master CD and another number identified the plant where the disc was replicated. The latest IFPI figures estimated that 68 per cent of all CD production plants worldwide were using the codes. In China, the coding system became mandatory for all CD production in August 1994, following pressure from the US Trade Representative.

CD PIRACY IN CHINA

Despite the efforts of the Chinese government to crack down on piracy by closing CD plants and destroying illegal CDs, piracy continued to flourish. It was estimated that about 90 per cent of the CDs purchased in China were counterfeit. Many of the illegal factories reportedly were joint ventures with Taiwanese businesses, which helped finance the equipment used to produce counterfeit CD products. The majority of pirate CD plants were believed to be located in the South China province of Guangdong, often operating with the cooperation and support of provincial officials. Until the development of replicators like those produced by Sicom, China-based pirate CD manufacturers struggled to deal with the environment and, in particular, the high humidity prevalent in South China. Pressing digital discs of any quality required sterile, temperature- and humidity-controlled conditions that were difficult to create. The new replication equipment overcame this problem with self-contained manufacturing systems that could be operated virtually anywhere. One report suggested that with a reliable, portable power supply, pirates could produce CDs from the back of container trucks in the near future, perpetually and untraceably roving the countryside like truck-mounted Cold War Soviet missiles.

Many of the pirate CDs produced in China were shipped around the world through Hong Kong. Given the huge volume of goods that passed through Hong Kong, there was little customs inspectors could do to stem the flow of illegal goods. Each day, more than 15,000 trucks and 300 container ships moved from the Chinese border to Hong Kong. Random checks were carried out only on goods destined for the Hong Kong market and on those that had to be off-loaded and stored in Hong Kong for more than 24 hours.

One of the complaints of the music industry was that Chinese restrictions against the importing of legitimate CDs contributed to the growth of the pirate industry. The situation with respect to imported music seemed to be changing. According to the IFPI, the number of titles approved for import to China had grown from 150 in 1992 to 300 in 1995 and about 450–600 in 1996. Nevertheless, although official import quotas for recordings had been abolished, significant hurdles remained for the music companies trying to develop the Chinese market. The many steps involved in getting a licence for the sale of a music recording included: identifying a Chinese record company as a business partner, showing proof of copyright ownership of the recording to be licensed, discussing trade terms, signing a letter of intent, providing a sample of the recording and translation of the lyrics for censorship review, signing a contract and registering the deal with the national copyright-administration officials, and providing a master recording once approval was obtained. Compounding the difficulties of licensing was a royalty rate as low as 10 cents per cassette or $1 per CD, long waiting periods for payment, the lack of promotion and marketing for releases, the restricted sale of products through only a single company; and the virtual impossibility of verifying sales figures.

A further issue associated with the sale of legitimate CDs in China was that only about 10 per cent of the population had enough disposable income to spend on consumer products such as audio recordings. Nevertheless, 10 per cent of the population represented a potential market of 120 million, predominantly in the country's major cities. With the growth of satellite television, Chinese consumers were becoming more aware of different forms of entertainment.

THE POLITICS OF PIRACY

The issue of piracy had become a contentious political issue. In 1996, the US government threatened to impose trade sanctions on China if the Chinese government did not clamp down on the illegal production of US films, music and computer properties. Under an intellectual property rights agreement negotiated between the United States and China in June 1996, China agreed that imports of CD replicators would require a licence. The Chinese government promised that no new licences would be issued. The government also agreed to the prosecution or investigation of about 70 individuals involved in the pirate trade and committed to 'special enforcement' periods in which actions would be taken on illegal products already in the marketplace.

In 1997, according to Chinese government officials, no new licences for the importation of replicators had been issued. Since signing the intellectual property rights agreement, the Chinese government had closed dozens of illegal CD operations and destroyed hundreds of thousands of pirate CDs. In December 1996, 20 illegal production lines were closed and the Chinese government indicated that new pirate plants would be shut down as they were discovered. However, the US State Department estimated that at least 27 production lines with the capacity to produce

150 million CDs annually were set up in China in the second half of 1996. It appeared that as the Chinese government clamped down in one region, the illegal and very portable factories moved to other parts of China. Within China, it was suspected that there was a market for used CD replicators. Equipment was also being moved out of China to Macau and Hong Kong.

Officials from the United States were putting pressure on their European counterparts to deal with the piracy problem at the source, which meant going after the manufacturers of CD replication equipment. Most of these firms were in Germany, Holland, and Sweden. EU officials insisted that the problem was in China and must be solved by the industry and by China. In reaction, US Trade Representative Charlene Barshefsky publicly stated:

> The focus is to do whatever we can to help ensure that CD presses do not go into China. So far, in spite of our repeated efforts, the EU and member states take a 'see-no-evil' attitude.

SICOM'S SITUATION

Josef Radler recognised that his company could get caught in the middle of a battle between US and EU government officials. Publicly, his position was that Sicom should not be held accountable for the actions of others.

> If CDs are being made illegally with Sicom equipment, it is up to the various countries to enforce their laws. In a free market, Sicom should be able to sell to any customer that wants the product and has the money to pay for it. We are a small company with limited resources in a highly competitive industry. If I refuse sales because I am concerned about possible illegal use of the equipment, I can assure you there are other CD equipment firms who would gladly take the orders. I have to keep my costs down and improve my technology. I cannot afford to cut my sales back. If I do, I might as well shut my business down. How am I supposed to explain that to my employees? I have worked hard to build this business and support my community. My equipment is the best in the industry. Why should I stop selling to certain customers just because of rumours that my customers are not using the equipment properly?

This case was written by Andrew Inkpen from Thunderbird, the American Graduate School of International Management, Arizona.

Index of company names

Subject index